C000186989

HISTORICAL ATLAS OF NORTH YORKSHIRE

HISTORICAL ATLAS
OF
NORTH YORKSHIRE

EDITOR: ROBIN A BUTLIN

Professor of Historical Geography,
University of Leeds

CARTOGRAPHER: NICK STALEY
North York Moors National Park Authority

WESTBURY

Westbury Publishing
Ilkley Road
Otley
West Yorkshire
LS21 3JP

Westbury Publishing is an imprint of
Smith Settle Printing & Bookbinding Ltd

ISBN Hardback 1 84103 020 1
Paperback 1 84103 023 6

Text © the contributors 2003

Illustrations © the copyright holders 2003

First printing October 2003
Second printing December 2003
Reprinted with corrections February 2004

All rights reserved. No part of this book may be reproduced,
stored or introduced into a retrieval system, or transmitted
in any form or by any means (electronic, mechanical,
photocopying, recording or otherwise) without the
prior permission of Smith Settle Ltd.

The rights of the contributors to be identified
as the authors of this work have been asserted
by them in accordance with the Copyright,
Designs and Patents Act 1988.

Where indicated, mapping reproduced from
Ordnance Survey mapping on behalf of
The Controller of Her Majesty's Stationery Office
© Crown Copyright. Licence Number MC 100038389

Set in Monotype Bembo

Designed, printed and bound by
SMITH SETTLE PRINTING & BOOKBINDING LTD
Ilkley Road, Otley, West Yorkshire LS21 3JP

CONTENTS

LIST OF MAPS AND GRAPHS

Acknowledgements

The editor is grateful for the permissions for reproduction and use of maps and illustrations given by the Ordnance Survey, English Heritage, North Yorkshire County Record Office, North York Moors National Park Authority, Yorkshire Dales National Park Authority, the British Library, Yorkshire Gardens Trust, Leeds University Library, Ryedale Folk Museum, the *Yorkshire Archaeological Journal*, the *Dalesman*, Marie Hartley, Ripon Museum Trust Workhouse Museum of the Yorkshire Poor Law, York St John College, and a large number of individuals who have kindly provided illustrative material. I am particularly grateful to Robert White, Graham Lee and David MacLeod for their help in identifying a range of illustrations for use in the *Atlas*. Specific acknowledgement of sources and permissions is given in text sections, and map and illustration captions. Copyright and reproduction permission from the Ordnance Survey (maps) and English Heritage (photographs) is given below, and on individual maps and photographs.

Crown copyright: figures 3.8, 4.5, 8.8 and 9.2 are reproduced from Ordnance Survey material with the permission of Ordnance Survey on behalf of the Controller of Her Majesty's Stationery Office © Crown copyright. With the exception of Figures 2.8, 3.2, 3.3, 4.3, 6.20, 8.2, 8.5, 10.2, 10.3, 10.9, 11.7, 11.8, 12.1-12.5 and 13.11, the remaining maps are reproduced from Ordnance Survey material on behalf of the Controller of Her Majesty's Stationery Office © Crown copyright MC100038389.

English Heritage: Crown copyright material is reproduced by permission of English Heritage acting under licence from the Controller of Her Majesty's Stationery Office.

Editorial Board:

Professor Robin A. Butlin, School of Geography, University of Leeds.
Dr Margaret Atherden, director, PLACE Research Centre, York St John College.
Professor Richard Lawton, emeritus professor of geography, University of Liverpool.
Graham Lee, North York Moors National Park Authority.
Dr Adam Menuge, English Heritage.
Dr Noël James Menuge, Development Officer, East of England, Heritage Lottery Fund.
Dr William J Sheils, School of History, University of York.
Professor Ian Simmons, Department of Geography, University of Durham.
Professor John Stillwell, School of Geography, University of Leeds.
Robert White, Yorkshire Dales National Park Authority.
Dr Peter Wilson, English Heritage.
Blaise Vyner, archaeological consultant.
Dr Alan Young, independent scholar; formerly York St John College.

Section Editors:

1: Professor Robin A Butlin, School of Geography, University of Leeds.
2: Dr Margaret Atherden, director, PLACE Research Centre, York St John College.
3: Professor Ian Simmons, Department of Geography, University of Durham; Blaise Vyner, archaeological consultant.
4: Dr Peter Wilson, English Heritage.
5: Dr Peter Wilson, English Heritage
6: Dr Noël James Menuge, Heritage Lottery Fund; Dr Alan Young, independent scholar, formerly York St John College.
7: Professor Richard Lawton, emeritus professor of geography, University of Liverpool; Dr William J Sheils, School of History, University of York.
8: Professor Robin A Butlin, School of Geography, University of Leeds.
9: Graham Lee, North York Moors National Park Authority; Robert White, Yorkshire Dales National Park Authority.
10: Dr Adam Menuge, English Heritage.
11: Dr Adam Menuge, English Heritage; Dr Noël James Menuge, Heritage Lottery Fund.
12: Professor Robin A Butlin, School of Geography, University of Leeds.
13: Professor John Stillwell, School of Geography, University of Leeds.
14: Professor Robin A Butlin, School of Geography, University of Leeds.

Contributors

The late Dr John Addy, formerly archivist, College of Ripon and York St John, and honorary archivist, diocese of Wakefield
Alison C Armstrong, natural sciences curator, Bradford Museums Service
Dr Margaret Atherden, principal lecturer in geography and director of research & scholarship, York St John College
Dr Ken Atkinson, senior lecturer in geography, University of Leeds
Rosalin Barker, honorary research fellow, University of Hull
Dr Heather M Beaumont, WEA (North Yorkshire district)
Professor Richard Britnell, professor of history, University of Durham
Dr Janet E Burton, reader in history, University of Wales, Lampeter
Professor Robin A Butlin, professor of historical geography, University of Leeds
Dr John Chapman, senior lecturer in geography, University of Portsmouth
Dr Richard Chiverrell, lecturer in geography, University of Liverpool
Carol B Cook, local historian, Swainby, Darlington
Dr David J F Crouch, research associate, Centre for Medieval Studies, University of York
Matthew Cutler, independent scholar
Christopher Daniell, research associate, Centre for Medieval Studies, University of York
Dr Ian Dormor, research associate, PLACE Research Centre, York St John College
Tom Gledhill, independent scholar, Rookhope, Bishop Auckland
Dr Jeremy Goldberg, senior lecturer in history, University of York
Dr Richard A Hall, York Archaeological Trust
Professor Anthony F Harding, Department of Archaeology, University of Durham
John K Harrison, industrial archaeologist, Guisborough, Teesside
Dr Paul Hastings, independent scholar, Bramerton, Norwich
Albert Henderson, School of Biology, University of Leeds
Valerie Hepworth, Yorkshire Gardens Trust
Dr Michael F Hopkinson, principal lecturer in geography, York St John College
Peter D Horne, English Heritage Aerial Survey, York
Dr Andy J Howard, research fellow, School of Geography, University of Newcastle-upon-Tyne
Richard Lawton, emeritus professor of geography, University of Liverpool
Graham Lee, archaeological conservation officer, North York Moors National Park Authority, Helmsley
Dr Mark Lee, Department of Marine Sciences and Coastal Management, University of Newcastle-upon-Tyne
Professor Christine Leigh, professor of geography, University of Leeds
John Mackenzie, Rockliffe, Dalbeattie; formerly of the Forestry Commission
Professor Mark G Macklin, professor of geography, Institute of Geography and Earth Sciences, University of Wales, Aberystwyth
T G Manby, archaeological consultant
Dr James R Mathieu, Department of Anthropology, University of Pennsylvania Museum, Philadelphia, USA
Dr Gerry McDonnell, senior lecturer in archaeological sciences, Ancient Metallurgy Research Group, University of Bradford
Dr Isabel Anne McLean, local historian, Normanby, Sinnington
Dr Adam Menuge, senior investigator, English Heritage, Cambridge
Dr Noël James Menuge, Development Officer, East of England, Heritage Lottery Fund
Paddie Morrison, cartographer and map librarian, York St John College
Dr Richard Muir, independent scholar, Harrogate
Dr Patrick Ottaway, York Archaeological Trust
Professor John Pethick, Department of Marine Sciences and Coastal Management, University of Newcastle-upon-Tyne
Dominic Powlesland, Landscape Research Centre, Yedingham, North Yorkshire
David Pybus, local historian, archaeologist and industrial chemist, Sandsend, Whitby
Professor Edward Royle, professor of history, University of York
Dr William J Sheils, senior lecturer in history, University of York
Professor Ian G Simmons, professor of geography, University of Durham
Dr Peter Smithson, senior lecturer in geography, University of Sheffield
Derek Statham, Thirsk, North Yorkshire; formerly National Park officer, North York Moors National Park Authority
Nick Staley, cartographer, North York Moors National Park Authority, Helmsley
Professor John Stillwell, professor of geography, University of Leeds
David Taylor, geologist
Dr Deborah Turnbull, Yorkshire Gardens Trust
Blaise Vyner, archaeological consultant, heritage and arts
Edward Waterson, partner, Carter Jonas; past chairman of the Georgian Society for East Yorkshire
Robert F White, archaeological conservation officer, Yorkshire Dales National Park Authority, Leyburn
Dr Peter R Wilson, English Heritage Centre for Archaeology, Portsmouth
Dr Roger Wolfe, assistant archivist, York St John College
Dr Alan Young, independent scholar; formerly principal lecturer in history, York St John College
Mike Younge, director, Local Studies Research Centre, Ripon

Fig. 1.1

NORTH YORKSHIRE AND YORK

—— COUNTY BOUNDARY

Unitary Authority

District Boundaries

Durham

North Sea

DURHAM

Middlesbrough

DARLINGTON

STOCKTON ON TEES

MIDDLESBROUGH

REDCAR & CLEVELAND

Whitby

Stokesley

Scarborough

RICHMOND

North York Moors

Richmondshire

Catterick

NORTHALLERTON

CUMBRIA

Hawes

Yorkshire Dales

Leyburn

Hambleton

Bedale

Helmsley

Pickering

SCARBOROUGH

Thirsk

Ryedale

Filey

Ingleton

NORTH YORKSHIRE

Craven

Pateley Bridge

Ripon

Easingwold

MALTON

Settle

Grassington

Boroughbridge

Vale of York

Harrogate

Knaresborough

Yorkshire Wolds

Forest of Bowland

SKIPTON

HARROGATE

City of York

YORK

LANCASTRE

Tadcaster

EAST RIDING OF YORKSHIRE

Selby

Leeds

WEST YORKSHIRE

SELBY

Hull

R. Humber

SOUTH YORKSHIRE

NORTH LINCOLNSHIRE

Pennines

Pennines

Scotland

North Sea

Irish Sea

NORTH YORKSHIRE

England

Wales

>1000 ft (> 305 mtrs)
600-1000 ft (183-305 mtrs)
200-600 ft (61-183 mtrs)
<200 ft (<61 mtrs)

Kms 0   5   10
Miles 0   5   10

N

Reproduced from Ordnance Survey material on behalf of The Controller of Her Majesty's Stationery Office
© Crown copyright MC100038389 2003

I

INTRODUCTION

The idea of an historical atlas of North Yorkshire was conceived in York about six years ago, its intention being to engage the expertise of a group of scholars and scientists in the production of an authentic and innovative illustration of the environmental and human history of the large and attractive county of North Yorkshire, and to give some pointers to its future development.

An attempt has been made to link together a wide range of new and existing information and ideas, and we have been extremely fortunate to have obtained the contributions of such an impressive range of contributors to this pioneer volume. We have also attempted, wherever appropriate, to point to gaps in our knowledge of various aspects of the distant and more recent history of North Yorkshire, and view this, the first edition of the *Atlas*, as the beginning of perhaps a longer period of review and revision, with a view to the incorporation into future editions of new knowledge as it arises.

Nonetheless we are very happy that the contents of this first edition represent an accurate picture of much of what we currently know of North Yorkshire and its history. Inevitably there are gaps: some on account of the relevant experts not being able to contribute, others because there are areas of knowledge and information that remain incomplete.

One aspect of the *Atlas* which has posed a clear challenge has been the choice of the basic geographical unit. The editorial decision was to base the *Atlas* on the modern county of North Yorkshire, plus the York Unitary Authority.

As two contributors on administrative change and local government 1580-1792 (chapter 7) and on the twentieth century (chapter 13) show, there have been major changes through time in the administrative geography of North Yorkshire. The county of Yorkshire was created before the Norman Conquest, and the North Riding is one of the three Ridings into which it had been divided since at least the Anglo-Scandinavian period (and possibly before that, in terms of territorial grouping, though not in title). The administrative history of the North Riding is complex, while the city of York maintained a separate administrative existence for much of historical time.

Major changes were effected with the creation of the county of North Yorkshire in 1974, and a new geographical entity emerged which included much of the old North Riding, but with a stronger southern component (**Maps 1.1, 7.7,** and **13.2**). While the areas north of the Cleveland Hills and the watershed south of the Stainmore Pass became part of Cleveland and Durham, and parts of the north-west and west of the North Riding were transferred to Lancashire and Cumbria, parts of the former East and West Ridings were added to the remnant of the old North Riding. Thereafter, in 1996, the larger York Unitary Authority (YUA) was created for the area in and around York. The resulting area of the North Riding plus the YUA is 3,212 square miles (8,321km²), and is the largest county in England.

Swaledale near Thwaite. © R Muir.

Rievaulx Abbey. © R A Butlin.

The boundaries of the modern county of North Yorkshire, together with York UA, have been adopted for the *Atlas*: they are the functional units within which public services and administrative systems now operate, and with which most people are familiar. The use of the present county as the basic unit of mapping and description gives consistency in comparisons across time. It also provides an important point of reference against which to measure and even to influence future decisions and developments: a tool for understanding the future as well as the past.

Use of modern boundaries inevitably posed interesting but not insuperable challenges to authors working on data assembled for the former North Riding, and for other and earlier secular and ecclesiastical units of administration. We have accepted that historical necessity would require some cross-referencing to the former North Riding, and that some of the maps and the text would have to stray, for purposes of completeness of the historical record, from current boundaries.

One of the important features that emerges from the text and maps of the *Atlas* is the immense amount of change experienced by North Yorkshire in the immediate and more distant past, including the major effects in landscape of glaciation, sea-level and vegetational changes, and the complex interactions with human occupation from prehistoric times onwards. An area that for much of prehistoric time had very low population densities now experiences a much wider regional range of habitation, from the larger cities to attractive, thinly populated areas such as the North York Moors and parts of the Pennines. Through time, the area has offered a varied set of resources and opportunities that have been used and modified by changing resource appraisals and technologies.

A major and still prominent feature of the landscape has been the impact of religious activity, witnessed in the major cathedrals, medieval churches and relics of major monastic buildings. In contrast, the impact of modern industrialisation has been relatively limited, though the history of the industries of the region nonetheless offers a fascinating story.

Agriculture, long the backbone of the regional economy, is at present faced with major problems. The rural record, as in other parts of England, is of early subsistence systems being partially overtaken through modern times by more market-related systems of production. The related changes in infrastructure and ownership of land have been partly the result of parliamentary enclosures and of changes in communications, notably the coming of the railway. Many parts of North Yorkshire have nonetheless witnessed a remarkable persistence of complex and tightly knit community life in villages, hamlets and small towns, and in regional and local affiliations of political and cultural activity.

The urban presence has not been massive, at least in the sense of modern conurbations, but North Yorkshire possesses a rich urban heritage which reaches back deep into the past and which is important in the regional economy. The city of York is one of Britain's major historic cities, with both an impressive heritage and a range of planning problems for modern conservation and development.

The varied and attractive landscapes of North Yorkshire pose interesting and challenging questions of the rich historical past of North Yorkshire that we have tried to capture in this *Atlas*, a richness deriving from the complexities of human habitation and culture, and adaptation

The beach at Scarborough, looking south. © R A Butlin.

to change. The first element of presentation is the map, and the large number of original maps produced for the *Atlas* offer some very interesting distributions, enhanced by the accompanying textual narrative which assists with their interpretation.

We have tried to present maps and text in a digestible fashion, with opportunities for further reading. In addition, detailed references to specialist sources of published information have been provided, where required by authors, in the form of endnotes consolidated at the end of the *Atlas*.

The production of the *Atlas* has been a long and very complex process. A great debt of gratitude is owed to Dr Margaret Atherden of the PLACE Research Centre at York St John College, who enthusiastically supported the idea when I first proposed it, who has given a great deal of her time and energy to the project, including scientific and editorial expertise, and whose PLACE funds supported the cartographic and some of the secretarial work. Sheridan Stead and Andrew Milner from PLACE provided invaluable secretarial and cartographic support, with additional cartographic support being provided by Paddie Morrison.

The *Atlas* could not have been produced without the invaluable expertise and gifted abilities of Nick Staley, the cartographer, who has given much time and shown much patience in turning the not-infrequently 'basic' first drafts by authors into sophisticated and very interesting maps: to him, equally, we owe an enormous debt of gratitude. His flair for the appropriate layout and design of maps, including the use of colour, and his early insistence on the use of a common map basis and format wherever possible, have been vital ingredients in the composition of the *Atlas* and in the determination of its character. The agreement of the North York Moors National Park Authority that Nick could use the cartographic facilities at their Helmsley headquarters, where he is cartographer, is much appreciated.

The members of the editorial board, listed separately, provided encouragement and support when it was badly needed, and a significant, effective and knowledgeable link with the contributors. Much of the initial groundwork in compiling lists of potential contributors was undertaken by the section editors, who have also managed the flow of information to the general editor.

To the contributors themselves, my thanks for their valuable work, and for patiently and effectively responding to seemingly never-ending streams of editorial enquiries and requests. I am deeply indebted to those section editors and authors who, at quite short notice, agreed to take responsibility for the writing of sections of the *Atlas* for which contributions had not been forthcoming as anticipated.

I am grateful also to the School of Geography at the University of Leeds for support facilities and materials, and for the encouragement and participation in the project of a number of colleagues. The publishers Smith Settle took on the project and have expertly seen it through to final product, and we thank them for their interest, support and professional expertise.

We hope that the *Atlas* will be an inspirational guide to all who are interested in North Yorkshire's fascinating history and landscape heritage, and that it will raise many questions for discussion and opportunities for further investigation.

Robin Butlin
School of Geography,
University of Leeds
December 2002

2

PHYSICAL GEOGRAPHY

2.1 INTRODUCTION   MARGARET ATHERDEN

North Yorkshire is one of the most beautiful and scenically varied parts of Britain. The largest of the English counties, it spans a maximum distance of ninety-three miles (150km) east–west, from the coast at Filey to the Pennines near Ingleton, and fifty-nine miles (95km) north–south, from the Cleveland plain to the Aire Valley (**fig 2.1**). Within its 3,165 square miles (8,200km²) is to be found a great variety of geology, topography, climate, soils and vegetation, which has set the physical parameters for human settlement and land-use throughout the post-glacial period.

In the west of the county lies part of the Pennine chain, based on rocks of Carboniferous age, with over 6.5 square miles (17km²) above 1,000 feet (300m) in altitude. Notable peaks include Whernside (2,414 feet/736m), Ingleborough (2,373 feet/723m), Great Whernside (2,310 feet/704m) and Pen-y-Ghent (2,273 feet/694m). In the north-east of the county, the Jurassic upland of the North York Moors is of lower altitude, reaching a maximum height of 1,489 feet (453m) on Urra Moor. The northern part of the Yorkshire Wolds is also included, its chalk escarpment

Sheep grazing in a dry chalk valley on the Yorkshire Wolds near Great Givendale.
© M A Atherden.

View of Yorkshire Wolds, near Burdale. Arable land on the floor of a chalk dry valley with rough pasture on the steep hillsides.
© M A Atherden.

Coastal scenery of the North York Moors near Port Mulgrave.
© North York Moors National Park Authority, NYM SC0279.

The Pennines: unimproved limestone grassland near Conistone, Wharfedale.
© M A Atherden.

View over the Vale of York from the top of Sutton Bank, looking towards the Pennines in the distance.
© North York Moors National Park Authority, NYM SV0054.

Heather moorland on Live Moor in the North York Moors National Park.
© North York Moors National Park Authority, NYM 0315.

Enclosed farmland in Danby Dale, North York Moors, nestling among the heather moorland.
© North York Moors National Park Authority, NYM SD0290.

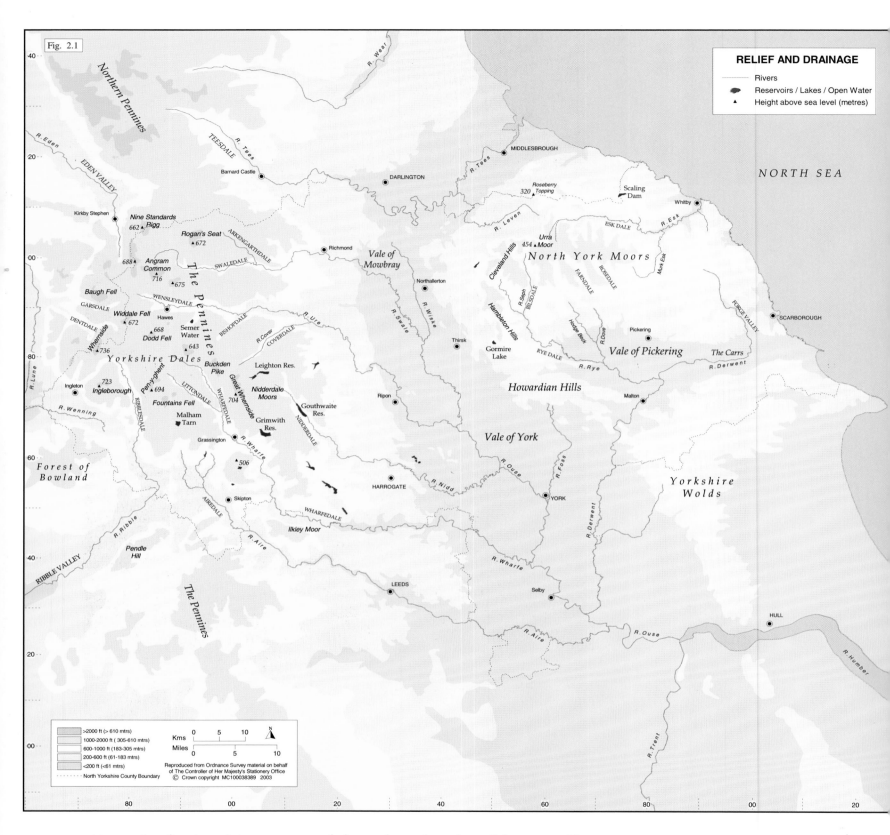

Fig. 2.1

RELIEF AND DRAINAGE

—— Rivers
Reservoirs / Lakes / Open Water
▲ Height above sea level (metres)

NORTH SEA

Northern Pennines

R. Wear

R. Eden

TEESDALE

R. Tees

EDEN VALLEY

Barnard Castle

MIDDLESBROUGH

DARLINGTON

R. Tees

Roseberry Topping 320 ▲

Scaling Dam

Whitby

Kirkby Stephen

Nine Standards Rigg 662 ▲

R. Leven

ESK DALE

R. Esk

Rogan's Seat ▲ 672

ARKENGARTHDALE

Richmond

Vale of Mowbray

Urra 454 ▲ Moor

North York Moors

Mur Esk

688 ▲ Angram Common 716 ▲ ▲ 675

SWALEDALE

Cleveland Hills

ROSEDALE

FARNDALE

Baugh Fell

The Pennines

WENSLEYDALE

Northallerton

R. Seph

BILSDALE

Hodge Beck

FORGE VALLEY

GARSDALE

Widdale Fell ▲ 672

Hawes

BISHOPDALE

R. Cover

R. Ure

R. Wiske

R. Swale

Hambleton Hills

R. Dove

SCARBOROUGH

DENTDALE

Whernside ▲ 736

668 ▲ Dodd Fell

Semer Water ▲ 643

COVERDALE

Thirsk

Gormire Lake

RYE DALE

Pickering

Pickering

R. Lune

Yorkshire Dales

Buckden Pike

Leighton Res.

R. Rye

Vale of Pickering

The Carrs

Ingleton

723 ▲ Ingleborough

Pen-y-ghent ▲ 694

LITTONDALE

Nidderdale Moors

R. Derwent

R. Wenning

Fountains Fell

WHARFEDALE

Great Whernside ▲ 704

Gouthwaite Res.

Ripon

Howardian Hills

Malton

Malham Tarn

NIDDERDALE

Grimwith Res.

RIBBLESDALE

Grassington

▲ 506

R. Wharfe

Vale of York

Yorkshire Wolds

HARROGATE

R. Nidd

R. Ouse

YORK

R. Foss

Forest of Bowland

AIREDALE

Skipton

WHARFEDALE

Ilkley Moor

R. Ribble

Pendle Hill

RIBBLE VALLEY

R. Aire

R. Wharfe

R. Derwent

HULL

The Pennines

LEEDS

Selby

R. Aire

R. Ouse

R. Humber

R. Trent

>2000 ft (> 610 mtrs)
1000-2000 ft (305-610 mtrs)
600-1000 ft (183-305 mtrs)
200-600 ft (61-183 mtrs)
<200 ft (<61 mtrs)
North Yorkshire County Boundary

Kms 0 5 10
Miles 0 5 10

N

Reproduced from Ordnance Survey material on behalf
of The Controller of Her Majesty's Stationery Office
© Crown copyright MC100038389 2003

rising to 800 feet (245m) in an arc around the south-east boundary of the county. The Howardian Hills form a bridge between the North York Moors and the Wolds, and isolate the low-lying Vale of Pickering to the east. Running through the central part of North Yorkshire is a vast lowland area, from the Tees Valley in the north through the Vale of Mowbray into the Vale of York in the south. The majority of the county's rivers feed into this lowland area, including the major east-flowing rivers of the Yorkshire Dales, and the Derwent and its tributaries from the North York Moors.

This first section of the *Atlas* will show how the underlying geology determines the major structural features of North Yorkshire and gives rise to many of the characteristic landscapes of the county. Glaciation has also played a major part in eroding valleys, altering the courses

The Pennines: aerial view of limestone scars and glaciated valley, Conistone, upper Wharfedale.
NMR 12972/17 © *Crown Copyright. NMR.*

Rosedale, North York Moors.
© M A Atherden.

of many rivers and depositing glacial debris in the lowland areas. Changes in sea-level since the last glacial period have altered the coastline beyond all recognition, and part of the original county has eroded into the sea. The climate of North Yorkshire varies from the high, wet, windswept Pennine peaks to the relatively dry, sheltered Vale of York, and has had a major influence on human activities. During the post-glacial period, soil and vegetation cover have also changed, partly as a result of climate change and partly as a result of human impact. Recent research has shown that this impact is of much greater antiquity and extent than was formerly realised, extending right back to the first hunter-gatherers who colonised North Yorkshire nearly 10,000 years ago. Not only have humans felled woodland, cultivated soils and drained marshlands, but their impact has extended to coastal erosion and modific-ations to the flow and courses of rivers. The landscape of North Yorkshire has undergone continual change during the entire post-glacial period, and is the product of an intricate and fascinating interaction between people and their environment, as will be demonstrated on the following pages.

It is not surprising that such a large county as North Yorkshire should exhibit a great variety of scenery, and much of this variety, both physical and human, is a product of the underlying solid geology (**fig 2.2**). In the geological time-scale, this almost exclusively sedimentary framework extends from small inliers of ancient Ordovician and Silurian rocks in the west to the Cretaceous Chalk of the northern part of the Yorkshire Wolds, with a Tertiary volcanic dyke making a minor contribution.

The majority of the Yorkshire Dales National Park lies within the county. This largely Carboniferous area, sculptured by rivers and ice, is rightly protected for its outstanding landscape, but especially for the extent and beauty of the limestone scenery ('karst'), which is unsurpassed in England. Swaledale, Wensleydale, Nidderdale, Wharfedale and Airedale, as well as the upper reaches of Ribblesdale, each have similar but distinctive features resulting from the incision of their steep-sided valleys into the Great Scar Limestone, Yoredale rocks, Millstone Grit or a combination of all three.[1]

The Yoredales, a cyclic succession of limestones, shales and sandstones, are well displayed in the stepped flanks and tributaries of the two northern dales, Swaledale and Wensleydale, where the more resistant beds of limestone and sandstone, lying almost horizontally, result in

The Mid-Craven Fault at Attermire, near Settle, where uplift of the Askrigg Block has raised the Carboniferous Limestone in the background. The rounded hills in the middle distance are fossilised coral reefs, known as 'reef knolls'.
© R White 3010.

View across Robin Hood's Bay, exposing the dome structure of the Lower Lias rocks of the wave-cut platform. The cliffs behind are formed of Middle and Upper Lias rocks.
© North York Moors National Park Authority, NYM SC0298.

Upper Jurassic Limestone exposed in Caulkland Quarry in the southern part of the North York Moors..
© North York Moors National Park Authority. NYM NO0113.

structural terraces ('scars'), separated by the softer shales. The moorland between the dales, the interfluves, is underlain by the less dramatic coarse sandstone and thin shales of the Millstone Grit, as is most of neighbouring Nidderdale, with darker grit outcrops contrasting with the almost white limestone scars of the Yoredales.[2]

Upper Wharfedale, Airedale and Ribblesdale display a range of the Carboniferous succession from the Great Scar Limestone at the base through the Yoredales to the Millstone Grit. The Great Scar Limestone, more than 800 feet (250m) thick, is well seen at Kilnsey Crag in Wharfedale, Malham Cove amphitheatre in Airedale and in Raven Scar west of Ingleborough. Here, limestone pavement is seen, devoid of any surface drainage, the run-off from the Yoredales above having disappeared into the cave systems of the enlarged joints and bedding planes in the limestone, to reappear at the junction with the impermeable Ordovician and Silurian rocks beneath. These ancient beds are to be seen in the valley bottoms in Ribblesdale, Crummackdale and Chapel le Dale immediately north of the North Craven Fault. The Yoredales, lying above the thick limestone, again show the relatively thin beds of limestone and sandstone with shales, leading up to the capping of Millstone Grit on the highest peaks such as Whernside, Ingleborough and Pen-y-Ghent. Mineral veins and 'flats' in some limestones resulted in mining, particularly for galena in Swaledale, near Grassington and at Greenhow.[3]

The Millstone Grit disappears beneath the low ridge of Permian Magnesian Limestone, which itself dips east below the soft Triassic sandstone, mudstone and siltstone in the Vales of Mowbray and York. Most of this solid rock is masked by thick glacial till and lacustrine deposits. To the east the impressive escarpment of the North York Moors overlooks the vales between the Tees Lowlands and the Howardian Hills. The solid geology of the moors is almost entirely Jurassic, dominated by an eroded anticline, reaching over 1,300 feet (400m), drained eastward by the River Esk and to the south by tributaries of the River Derwent. The lowest Jurassic beds, the Lias, are mainly mudstones, with the resistant Staithes Formation sandstone forming a terrace feature in the north-facing scarp. Above this level, seams in the Cleveland Ironstone Formation have been extensively mined in the north, as have the jet shales. The overlying Ravenscar Group is mainly sandstone which has been eroded to expose inliers of the Liassic beds, such as in Westerdale and Fryupdale draining to the Esk and Rosedale and Farndale to the south. All of these Lower and Middle Jurassic beds are well exposed along the cliffed coastline.[4]

The basaltic Cleveland dyke, of Tertiary age, is intruded into these beds in Levendale and Eskdale. Reaching a maximum width of eighty feet (25m), the intrusion results in a conspicuous ridge in the Great Ayton area. Towards the south of the moors, the Tabular Hills form a pronounced north-facing escarpment of Corallian Limestone and grit, dissected by streams flowing south from the higher moors to link with the River Rye. The succeeding Jurassic beds are soft Kimmeridge Clay beneath the glacio-lacustrine and alluvial deposits of the Vale of Pickering. The River Derwent makes its devious way from east to west through the Vale, then through the Howardian Hills via the Kirkham Abbey 'gorge', before joining the River Ouse.

The Cretaceous rocks of the county form the northern extremity of the Yorkshire Wolds. The north-facing chalk escarpment overlooking the Vale of Pickering is almost

Limestone pavement near Ingleborough.
© M A Atherden

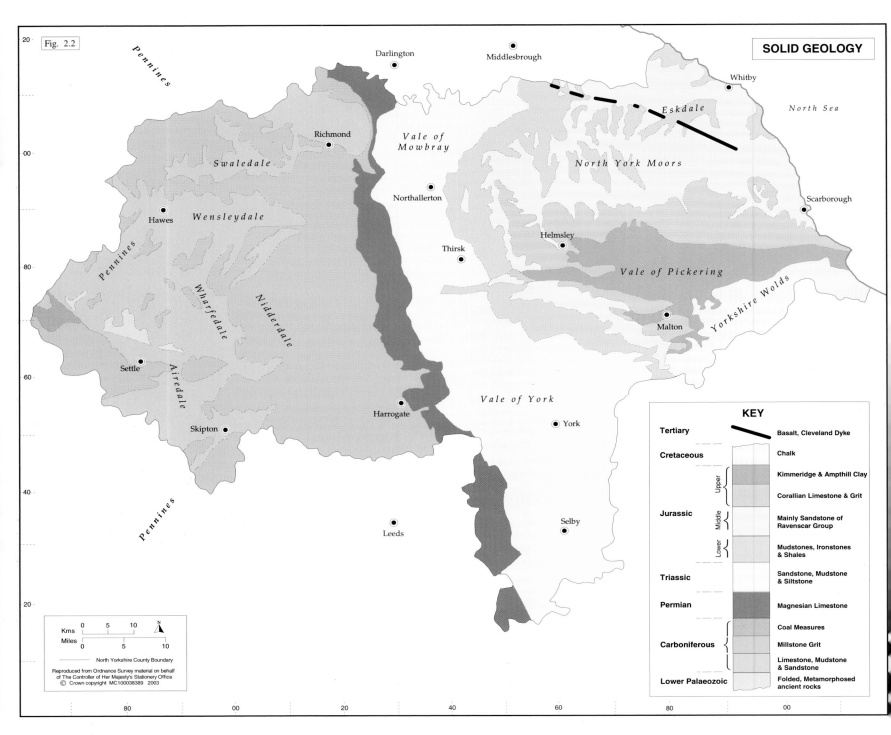

Fig. 2.2

SOLID GEOLOGY

Pennines

Darlington

Middlesbrough

Whitby

Richmond

Swaledale

Vale of
Mowbray

North York Moors

Eskdale

North Sea

Scarborough

Pennines

Hawes

Wensleydale

Northallerton

Helmsley

Thirsk

Vale of Pickering

Pennines

Wharfedale

Nidderdale

Yorkshire Wolds

Settle

Malton

Airedale

Vale of York

Harrogate

York

Skipton

Pennines

Selby

Leeds

KEY

Tertiary		Basalt, Cleveland Dyke
Cretaceous		Chalk
	Upper	Kimmeridge & Ampthill Clay
		Corallian Limestone & Grit
Jurassic	Middle	Mainly Sandstone of Ravenscar Group
	Lower	Mudstones, Ironstones & Shales
Triassic		Sandstone, Mudstone & Siltstone
Permian		Magnesian Limestone
		Coal Measures
Carboniferous		Millstone Grit
		Limestone, Mudstone & Sandstone
Lower Palaeozoic		Folded, Metamorphosed ancient rocks

Kms 0 5 10

Miles 0 5 10

North Yorkshire County Boundary

Reproduced from Ordnance Survey material on behalf
of The Controller of Her Majesty's Stationery Office
© Crown copyright MC100038389 2003

uninterrupted, while the dip slope is characterised by branching dry valleys. Extensive superficial glacial and glaciofluvial deposits from the most recent of the Pleistocene glacial periods, the Devensian, are found throughout the county, as will be described in the next section (**fig 2.3**).

2.3 GLACIAL HISTORY KENNETH ATKINSON

Ice-sheets occupied the area on several occasions during the Pleistocene Period (**fig 2.4**), but the last glaciation (or Dimlington Stadial)[1] during late Devensian times (c26,000–10,000 years ago) was so intensive that it destroyed most of the evidence of earlier Pleistocene events and their deposits.[2]

However, there is some evidence of the last (Ipswichian) interglacial, from the deposition of river sands and gravels, and organic silts at Austerfield near Bawtry (South Yorkshire), from Langham and from Westfield Farm.[3] Also dating from this interglacial are the cave deposits in Raygill Fissure, near Skipton, and the famous mammalian faunas found in Victoria Cave near Settle and in Kirkdale Cave near Kirkbymoorside.

Geology — Further Reading:

D H Rayner and J E Hemingway (eds), *The Geology and Mineral Resources of Yorkshire* (Leeds: Yorkshire Geological Society, 1974).

T Waltham, *Yorkshire Dales National Park* (Exeter: Webb and Bower, 1987).

I Carstairs, *The North York Moors National Park* (Exeter: Webb and Bower, 1987).

A Staniforth, *Geology of the North York Moors* (Helmsley: North York Moors National Park Information Service, 1990).

A Wilson, *Geology of the Yorkshire Dales National Park* (Grassington: Yorkshire Dales National Park Committee, 1992).

S R Eyre and J Palmer, *The Face of North East Yorkshire* (Clapham: Dalesman, 1973).

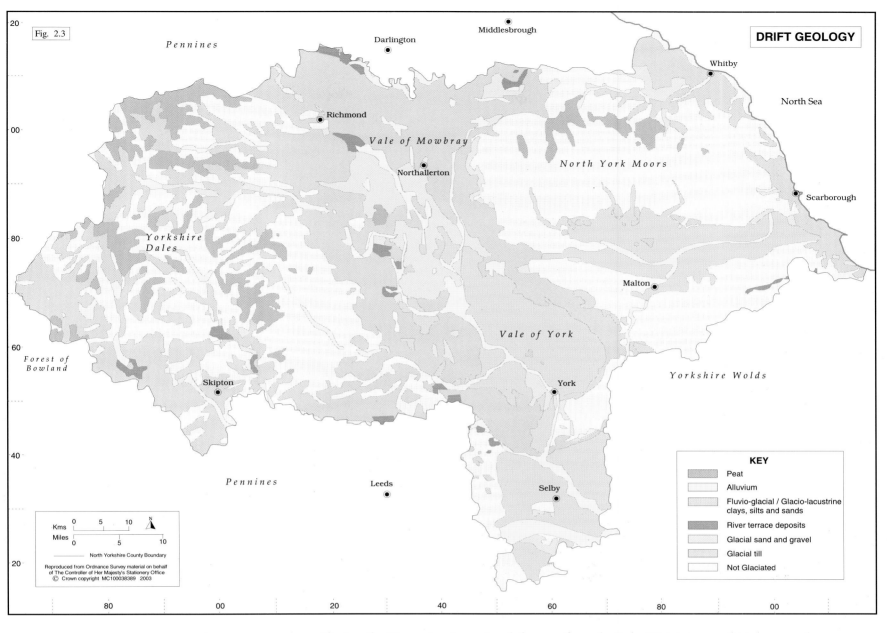

Fig. 2.3

DRIFT GEOLOGY

Pennines

North Sea

Middlesbrough

Darlington

Whitby

Richmond

Vale of Mowbray

North York Moors

Northallerton

Scarborough

*Yorkshire
Dales*

Malton

Vale of York

*Forest of
Bowland*

Yorkshire Wolds

Skipton

York

Pennines

Leeds

Selby

KEY

	Peat
	Alluvium
	Fluvio-glacial / Glacio-lacustrine clays, silts and sands
	River terrace deposits
	Glacial sand and gravel
	Glacial till
	Not Glaciated

Kms 0   5   10   N

Miles 0   5   10

North Yorkshire County Boundary

Reproduced from Ordnance Survey material on behalf
of The Controller of Her Majesty's Stationery Office
© Crown copyright MC100038389 2003

Dating Systems:
Archaeological chronologies often use the BC/AD
calendar system for timelines. Environmental
scientists, because of scientific dating systems such as
radiocarbon dating, use the concept of years before
present, written as BP. The present, for standardiza-
tion and fixed base-line purposes, is fixed as
AD 1950. Conversion from BC to BP is made,
therefore, by adding 1,950, so that 1500 BC
becomes 3450 BP. Conversion from BP to BC
involves a subtraction of 1,950.

During the Devensian, ice entered the area from the Lake District across Stainmore and
Teesdale, and joined with Cheviot ice moving southwards through north-east England.[4] In
the Tees lowland the ice built up to a thickness of 2,600 feet (800m), and one ice-stream
swung south through the Vale of Mowbray and into the Vale of York, whilst another
continued in a southerly direction along the North Sea coast. This North Sea ice made
incursions inland into low-lying areas such as the Esk Valley, Robin Hood's Bay, the Vale of
Pickering and the lowland of Holderness. The highest parts of the Yorkshire Pennines also
acted as areas of ice accumulation, as at Great Shunner Fell, Baugh Fell, Mallerstang and
Langstrothdale Chase.

From these ice-fields were generated glaciers which flowed down Swaledale, Wensleydale,
Nidderdale and Wharfedale to join the Vale of York glacier.[5] The Airedale glacier flowed
south-east but did not join up with the Vale of York glacier, and the Ribblesdale glacier
flowed southwards towards the Vale of Eden.

The maximum extent of the ice is marked in many dales by barriers of glacial moraine, and
other moraines mark stages in the retreat of the glaciers. Along the coast the ice reached its
maximum extent at Dimlington (East Yorkshire) *c*18,000 years ago.[6] In the Vale of York the
short-lived maximum of 18,000 BP* reached Wroot.[7] After retreating, the Vale of York glacier
readvanced to form the York and Escrick terminal moraines by 13,000 BP. The Cleveland
Hills, North York Moors, Howardian Hills and the Yorkshire Wolds protruded above the ice-
surface as nunataks, but the upper limits of the ice-margins in the Pennine Dales are more
uncertain, though it is probable that high interfluves away from the source areas were
exposed as nunataks.

Glacial till (boulder clay) covers much of the lower ground and can reach thicknesses of 200 feet (60m). The upper limit of the till approximates to the margin of the ice-sheet against the flanks of the Pennines, the Wolds and the North York Moors. Drumlins ('whale-back' mounds of till, typically 65 feet (20m) high, 1,600 feet (500m) long and 650 feet (200m) wide) form a swarm in the Craven Lowlands between Settle and Hellifield. Lower densities of drumlins are found in the Vales of Mowbray and York, and in upper Wensleydale.

The till-sheet gives an undulating topography, with prominent ridges of till, gravel and boulders marking still-stand phases in the retreat of the ice, as in the Thirsk district, and in the moraines at York and Escrick. Meltwaters from the glaciers produced sandy terraces, and wind action blew the fine sands into dunes (coversands) south-east of York and as far north as Thirsk. Also landforms of eskers and kames were formed, eg in the Vale of York near Raskelf, Angram Hall and Carlton Husthwaite, as deglaciation exposed deposits which had been laid down both within and upon the surface of the glaciers.

Terminal moraines indicating ice-retreat are found in the valley bottoms of the rivers Swale, Ure, Nidd, Wharfe and Aire, where they blocked streams and resulted in lake-flats in the Dales, eg in Airedale.[8] These lake-flats were later to be important habitats for early post-glacial human occupation. In late-glacial times, westerly winds picked up the silts from glacial deposits and deposited them as loess (windblown silt) on the Hambleton Hills (the western part of the North York Moors), the Howardian Hills and the Yorkshire Wolds.

Today the River Wharfe forms a misfit stream in the vast glacial trough of Wharfedale.
© R White/Yorkshire Dales National Park Authority, ANY 332/36.

Lake Gormire in snow. Lake Gormire occupies a former ice-marginal channel on the eastern edge of the Vale of York near Thirsk.
© R White/Yorkshire Dales National Park Authority, NYM NS0033.

Aerial view of drumlin field at Ribblehead, upper Ribblesdale.
© R White/Yorkshire Dales National Park Authority, ANY 211/21.

Glacial History — Further Reading:

M D Bateman, P C Buckland, C D Frederick and
    N J Whitehouse (eds), *The Quaternary of East
    Yorkshire and North Lincolnshire* (London:
    Quaternary Research Association, 2001).
D R Bridgland, B P Horton and J B Innes (eds),
    The Quaternary of North-East England: Field Guide
    (London: Quaternary Research Association, 1999).
J Ehlers, P L Gibbard and J Rose (eds), *Glacial
    deposits in Great Britain and Ireland.* (Rotterdam:
    Balkema, 1991).
A .J Howard and M G Macklin (eds), *The Quaternary
    of the Eastern Yorkshire Dales* (London: Quaternary
    Research Association, 1998).
D H Rayner and J E Hemingway (eds), *The Geology
    and Mineral Resources of Yorkshire* (Leeds: Yorkshire
    Geological Society, 1974).

* Land levels measured with references to Ordnance
    Datum — OD — which is the average sea-level at
    Newlyn, Cornwall.

The erosive effects of ice are seen in many Pennine valleys, eg upper Wharfedale, Littondale, Bishopdale and upper Swaledale. The valleys display straightened, trough-like shapes while the considerably deepened valley bottoms have an infill of till, glaciofluvial sands and gravels, and lake deposits (**fig 2.3**). In upper Wharfedale, the famous rockface of Kilnsey Crag is a truncated spur of Great Scar Limestone.

Around Ingleborough and Malham, North Yorkshire contains some of the best-known limestone pavements (glacio-karst) in the British Isles. Ice removed surface soil to leave scars and pavement consisting of flat-topped 'clints' separated by widened joints called 'grykes'. These massive pavements are formed by ice cutting deeply into the limestone surface to expose fresh beds of limestone.[9]

Evidence from the glacial period may also be found below ground, in the many caves and subterranean passages in the limestone Pennines. Uranium-series dating of stalactites and stalagmites provides a chronology for some of the Pleistocene stages.[10]

Beyond the ice-limits, pro-glacial lakes were formed in the late Devensian when the seaward exits of rivers were dammed by ice and/or glacial moraines. Glacial Lake Humber was created by ice blocking the Humber Estuary. An early high-level phase is marked by sands and gravels on its shoreline at 108 feet (33m) OD* as at Brayton Barff, Holme-on-Spalding Moor and Pocklington. This was followed by a low-level phase, with a shoreline at 26 feet (8m) above current sea-level, as indicated by deposits at Brayton Barff and on the Escrick moraine. Glacial Lake Humber lasted until 11,000 BP. Glacio-lacustrine clays up to a thickness of sixty-five feet (20m) were deposited up to the 26 foot (8m) shoreline, as the lake gradually silted up.[11]

In the Vale of Pickering, a temporary lake was formed between ice from the Vale of York and ice from the North Sea, although its precise extent is a matter for conjecture.[12] Glacial drainage channels carried water from the North York Moors, the most spectacular example being Newton Dale, a pre-glacial valley which breached the main watershed and flowed south into Glacial Lake Pickering.[13] Lake Pickering itself drained into the Vale of York via the Kirkham Abbey gorge. Numerous other such channels may be seen on the North York Moors, which originated as subglacial, ice-marginal or meltwater channels. Often they bear little relationship with the present-day drainage and many of them contain several metres of post-glacial peat deposits. There is palaeobotanical evidence for the late-glacial period from the North York Moors, Vale of Pickering and Vale of York, as well as from sites just outside the county boundary, eg Bingley Bog (West Yorkshire).[14]

The glaciation of North Yorkshire is not just of academic interest, as it continues to affect the economic activity of the region. Glacial deposits greatly influence the nature of the soils, their natural fertility for farming, and also the distribution of settlement. Constructional materials of clay, sand and gravel are equally important results of Devensian events. Finally, the scenery, so attractive for tourism and educational visits, owes much to over-deepened valleys, to glacial drainage channels and to glacio-karst.

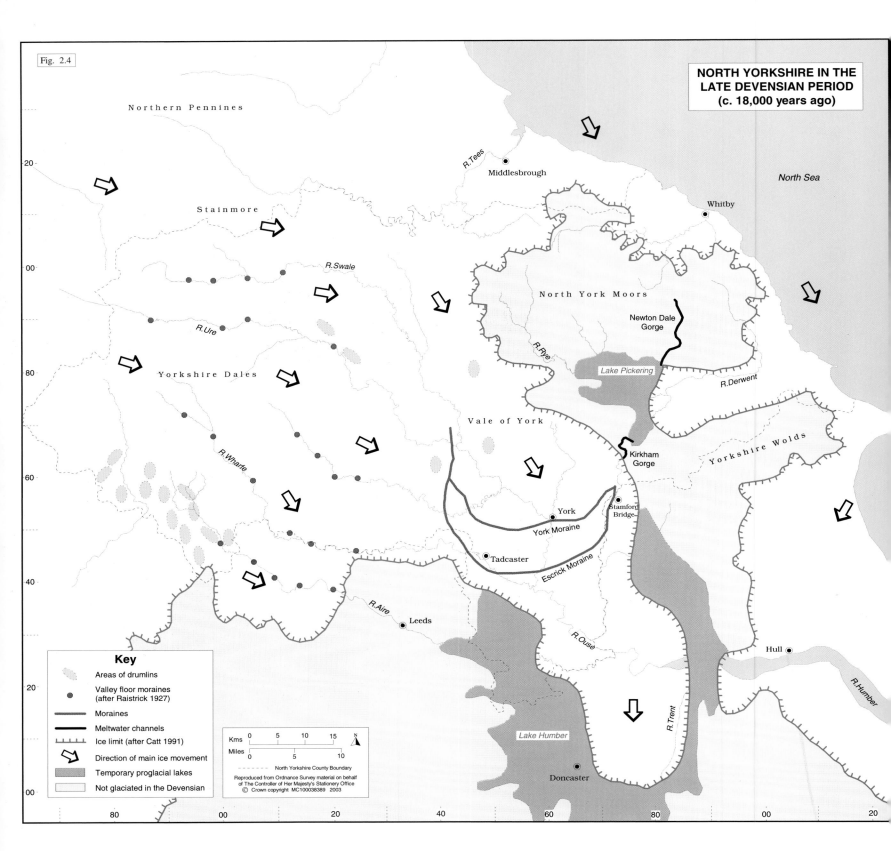

Fig. 2.4

**NORTH YORKSHIRE IN THE
LATE DEVENSIAN PERIOD
(c. 18,000 years ago)**

Northern Pennines

North Sea

R.Tees

Middlesbrough

Whitby

Stainmore

R.Swale

North York Moors

Newton Dale
Gorge

R.Ure

R.Rye

Yorkshire Dales

Lake Pickering

R.Derwent

Vale of York

Yorkshire Wolds

R.Wharfe

Kirkham
Gorge

York

Stamford
Bridge

York Moraine

Tadcaster

Escrick Moraine

R.Aire

Leeds

R.Ouse

Hull

R.Humber

R.Trent

Lake Humber

Doncaster

Key

- Areas of drumlins
- Valley floor moraines
  (after Raistrick 1927)
- Moraines
- Meltwater channels
- Ice limit (after Catt 1991)
- Direction of main ice movement
- Temporary proglacial lakes
- Not glaciated in the Devensian

Kms 0   5   10   15   N
Miles 0   5   10

North Yorkshire County Boundary

Reproduced from Ordnance Survey material on behalf
of The Controller of Her Majesty's Stationery Office
© Crown copyright MC100038389 2003

2.4   THE RIVERS   ANDY J HOWARD AND MARK G MACKLIN

Rivers are an important feature of the North Yorkshire landscape and, in part, define the
contemporary administrative boundaries of the county at its northern (the Tees), southern (the
Wharfe) and eastern (the Derwent) margins. Eight major rivers flow through the county fed by
numerous smaller rivers, streams and becks (**fig 2.1**). The rivers Swale, Ure, Nidd, Wharfe and
Aire all rise on the Carboniferous uplands of the central and eastern Yorkshire Dales, and flow
south and south-east through glacially modified valleys into the Permo-Triassic lowlands of the
Vale of York. In the Vale, these rivers progressively meet up to form the River (Yorkshire) Ouse,

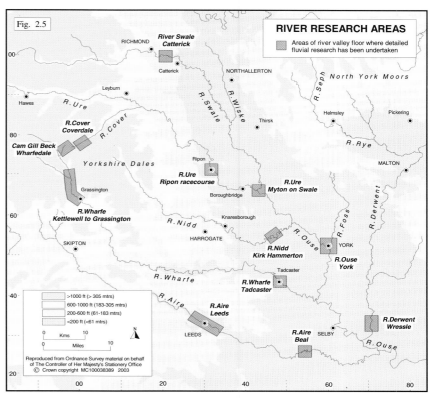

Fig. 2.5

RIVER RESEARCH AREAS

Areas of river valley floor where detailed fluvial research has been undertaken

RICHMOND

River Swale Catterick

Catterick

NORTHALLERTON

North York Moors

R. Seph

Leyburn

Hawes

R. Ure

R. Swale

R. Wiske

Thirsk

Helmsley

Pickering

R.Cover Coverdale

R.Cover

Ripon

R. Rye

MALTON

Cam Gill Beck Wharfedale

Yorkshire Dales

R.Ure Ripon racecourse

Boroughbridge

R.Ure Myton on Swale

R. Derwent

Grassington

R.Wharfe Kettlewell to Grassington

R. Nidd

Knaresborough

R. Foss

R. Ouse

SKIPTON

HARROGATE

R.Nidd Kirk Hammerton

YORK

R.Ouse York

Tadcaster

R.Wharfe Tadcaster

R. Wharfe

R. Aire

R.Aire Leeds

R.Derwent Wressle

LEEDS

R.Aire Beal

SELBY

R. Ouse

>1000 ft (> 305 mtrs)
600-1000 ft (183-305 mtrs)
200-600 ft (61-183 mtrs)
<200 ft (<61 mtrs)

0   Kms   10
0   Miles   10

N

Reproduced from Ordnance Survey material on behalf of The Controller of Her Majesty's Stationery Office
© Crown copyright MC100038389 2003

00   20   40   60   80

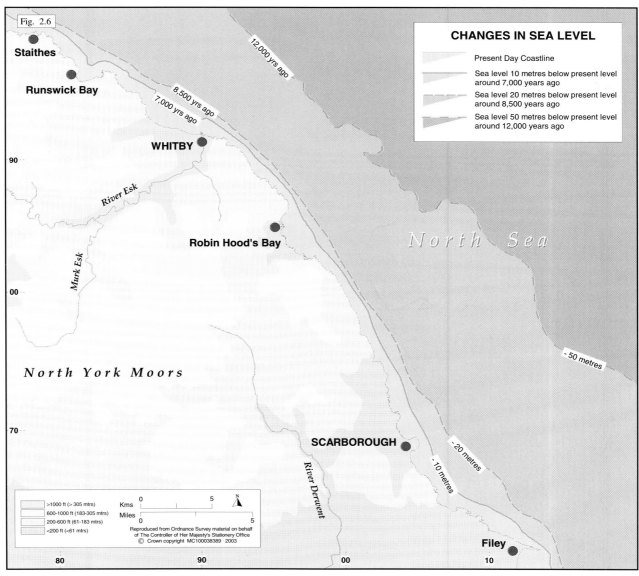

Fig. 2.6

CHANGES IN SEA LEVEL

Present Day Coastline

Sea level 10 metres below present level around 7,000 years ago

Sea level 20 metres below present level around 8,500 years ago

Sea level 50 metres below present level around 12,000 years ago

Staithes

Runswick Bay

12,000 yrs ago

8,500 yrs ago

7,000 yrs ago

WHITBY

90

River Esk

Robin Hood's Bay

North Sea

00

Murk Esk

- 50 metres

North York Moors

70

SCARBOROUGH

- 20 metres

River Derwent

- 10 metres

>1000 ft (> 305 mtrs)
600-1000 ft (183-305 mtrs)
200-600 ft (61-183 mtrs)
<200 ft (<61 mtrs)

0   Kms   5
0   Miles   5

N

Reproduced from Ordnance Survey material on behalf of The Controller of Her Majesty's Stationery Office
© Crown copyright MC100038389 2003

Filey

80   90   00   10

and are joined by the River Derwent flowing south from the Jurassic plateau of the North York Moors, before the Ouse enters the Humber Estuary. Overall, this river network which forms the Yorkshire Ouse basin, drains the majority of North Yorkshire (c3,000 square miles/ 8,000km^2), though the extreme west of the county is drained by the River Ribble, while in the north-east the River Esk drains the northern North York Moors, entering the North Sea at Whitby.

During the 1990s, the geomorphology, geochemistry and hydrology of the rivers of the Yorkshire Ouse basin, particularly those draining from the Pennine uplands, were intensively studied as part of the Natural Environment Research Council's (NERC) Land Ocean Interaction Study,[1] and through a number of other projects funded by NERC and the Engineering & Physical Sciences Research Council (**fig 2.5**). The fluvial data-sets generated were correlated with proxy climate records elucidated from peatbogs in the region. Combined with continued investigations,[2] Holocene (post-glacial) river evolution and landscape history of the Yorkshire Ouse basin is one of the most comprehensively researched in the UK.

By the early Holocene (c9,000 years ago), river systems in the North Yorkshire uplands and foothills were progressively incising their valley floors in response to declining sediment supply and ice-sheet unloading (isostatic rebound), leaving a series of river terraces above the contemporary channel.[3] The vertical and lateral instability of rivers within the uplands and at the upland margin contrasts with that of the lowland and perimarine river landscape, where low gradient multi-channelled ('anastomosed') systems were characterised by low rates of lateral movement and relatively high rates of fine-grained sedimentation.[4] Documentary and cartographic evidence indicates that many of these anastomosed rivers survived in the southern part of the county until large-scale drainage and land reclamation in the early seventeenth century AD.

Radiocarbon (^{14}C) dating of organic materials including wood, bone and charcoal recovered from alluvial units has shown that Holocene river activity can be correlated with periods of climate change and, particularly in the last 1,000 years, with human impact.[5] In upland and piedmont (foothill) regions, river incision took place between 1850-900 BC, AD 775-1015, AD 1205-1450 and at *circa* AD 1800. All of these incision phases coincide with periods of wetter and probably colder climate. Alluviation is recorded in many parts of the Ouse basin in 3700-3380 BC, 2320-1850 BC, 900-430 BC, AD 645-775, AD 1015-1290, AD 1420-1645 and AD 1750-1800.[6] Variation in flood frequency and magnitude associated with climate change appears to be the principal underlying mechanism influencing river processes, though human activity has become increasingly important. Since c1850 BC, progressive deforestation, associated with pastoral and arable farming, has probably enhanced both run-off and the supply of fine-grained sediments to river-valley floors. This process accelerated in the eleventh century AD, although the impact of changing land-use practices on river behaviour is rather difficult to quantify because they are spatially diffuse and poorly constrained in terms of their timing and distribution.

The River Swale near Muker.
© M A Atherden

Flooding in the Aire Valley just south of Skipton on the 29th March 1987.
© R White/Yorkshire Dales National Park Authority, ANY 314/19.

The Rivers — Further Reading:

J Lewin (ed.), *British Rivers* (London: George Allen and Unwin, 1981).

D Knighton (ed.), *Fluvial forms and processes. A new perspective* (London: Arnold, 1998).

A G Brown, *Alluvial Geoarchaeology. Floodplain archaeology and environmental change. Cambridge Manuals in Archaeology* (Cambridge: Cambridge University Press, 1997).

Since the eleventh century AD and during the last 250 years, the base-metal mining industry of the Yorkshire Dales has been a major source of fine-grained sediments for rivers of the Ouse basin.[7] Introduced into upland river channels through the erosion of mine spoil heaps or by ore processing and extraction, metal-contaminated sediments have been transported and deposited on floodplains throughout the Ouse basin.[8] Whilst metal contaminants provide useful geochemical time-markers in affected floodplains, the long-term environmental management of these sediments remains problematical.

Both documentary and geomorphological evidence indicate that the first half of the twentieth century was a period of relatively low flood frequency and magnitude in the Yorkshire Ouse basin.[9] However, since c 1940 the number and severity of floods has increased. Whilst climate change is still considered the primary driving mechanism of this change, the run-off to rivers has also been affected by moorland drainage (gripping) and changing land-use practices, particularly over-grazing of pasture and increased arable production.[10]

2.5   THE COAST   MARK LEE AND JOHN PETHICK

Despite the impression that may be gained during a storm, the shape of the North Yorkshire coastline owes less to present-day processes than to the legacy from past periods of climatic and sea-level change. At the beginning of the Holocene period, global sea-levels were nearly 330 feet (100m) lower than the present day, with large volumes of water still locked up within the decaying ice-sheets of the Devensian glaciation (**fig 2.6**). The retreating ice exposed a broad, gently sloping coastal plain covered by glacial till. An almost continuous scarp slope would have marked the western margin of the coastal plain. This scarp was a long-abandoned sea-cliff cut in Jurassic sedimentary rocks during the previous (Ipswichian) period of higher sea-levels, around 130,000 years ago. Scree slopes and solifluction sheets (the product of the various cold-climate slope processes that operated throughout the Devensian glaciation), would have fronted the cliffline. Glacial till mantled the scarp face and crest.

The period between 10,000 and 6,000 years ago was marked by rapidly rising sea-level. Large amounts of sand and gravel were moved onshore, forming beaches that may have extended along the whole coastline. Sea-cliffs would have been cut in the glacial till forming the coastal plain. During these early years of the Holocene, the North Yorkshire coast might have looked like the rapidly eroding Holderness coast to the south, beyond Flamborough Head.

The process of removing the glacial till deposits forming the coastal plain continues today on parts of the coast (eg the high cliffs developed in glacial till at Whitby West Cliff, Robin Hood's Bay and Filey Bay). Elsewhere, the sea has reached the abandoned cliffline of the last (Ipswichian) interglacial and now erodes the *in situ* Jurassic rocks and overlying glacial tills.

Cliff recession rates have probably been relatively slow. Comparisons of cliff-top positions on various Ordnance Survey map editions since 1892 indicate that the rock cliffs have retreated at an average rate of less than four inches (0.1m) per year, whereas the glacial till cliffs have retreated at around ten inches (0.25m) per year.[1] However, the long-term effect of differential erosion of the more resistant rocky headlands, and the softer rocks and tills in the intervening bays, has gradually created the present-day sequence of bays with isolated pocket beaches.

A remarkable feature of the cliff retreat has been the regular occurrence of dramatic landslide events. The most recent example was in June 1993 on the South Bay cliffs, Scarborough, where a major landslide occurred on the 230 feet (70m) high coastal cliffs in front of the Holbeck Hall Hotel.[2] Over 195 feet (60m) of the cliff (developed in Jurassic Scalby Formation sandstones, mudstones and siltstones, and mantled by up to 100 feet (30m) of glacial till) was lost overnight, leaving the hotel in a very dangerous position. A further 115 feet (35m) of cliff collapsed over the next three days, undermining the hotel, which gradually toppled over the cliff edge. Eye-witness accounts suggest that the landslide developed rapidly from an initial small failure above the seawall. This was followed by a series of progressively larger rotational failures which resulted in debris extending over 330 feet (100m) across the rocky shore platform (**fig 2.7**). The landslide involved an estimated one million tonnes of material, and measured approximately 800 feet (250m) from crest to toe and 330 feet (100m) wide.

In contrast with most eroding clifflines, the Holbeck cliff was protected by a seawall built in the 1890s and, hence, the landslide was unexpected by the local community. However, it was not the first major landslide to occur on the South Bay cliffs. The town's first spa was demolished in 1737-8 as an acre (0.4ha) of cliff-top land sank around fifty feet (15m), complete with cattle grazing on it.[3] Other major landslides have occurred in South Bay, at the South Bay

Pool and South Cliff Gardens landslides (**fig 2.8**), although it is not known when. In North Bay, the 'Great Landslip' of 1890 involved the failure of around 1000 square feet (100m²) of the cliff top at the extreme north-west corner of Castle Hill, triggered by heavy rain. The rockfall/rockslide was a sudden and dramatic event, involving an estimated 5.3 million cubic feet (1,500,000m³) of material and accompanied by considerable noise and dust.[4]

Elsewhere, many of the coastal settlements have experienced the effects of major landslides. Runswick was almost destroyed in 1682, when 'The whole village, except a single house, sunk down in one night, the ground on which it stood…having suddenly gave way'.[5] The upper section of King's Street and two rows of cottages in Robin Hood's Bay were destroyed by a landslide in 1780: 'A grotesque appearance, the houses being strangely scattered over the steep cliff and some of them hanging in an awful manner on the projecting ledges of the precipice'.[6] On Christmas Eve 1787 a large landslide at the Haggerlythe, Whitby, resulted in the loss of at least five houses and led to 196 families being made destitute: 'Buildings parted from their adjoining ones, forming chasms from their roofs to the foundations several feet wide'.[7] In 1829, the entire village of Kettleness slid into the sea and fortunately the inhabitants were rescued by ships lying offshore, waiting to take on cargoes of alum.[8]

Upper Jurassic strata eroded into structural benches, Filey Brigg.
© North York Moors National Park Authority, SC0076.

Caves eroded by wave action in the chalk cliffs at Flamborough with glacial drift on the cliff top.
© North York Moors National Park Authority, SC0119.

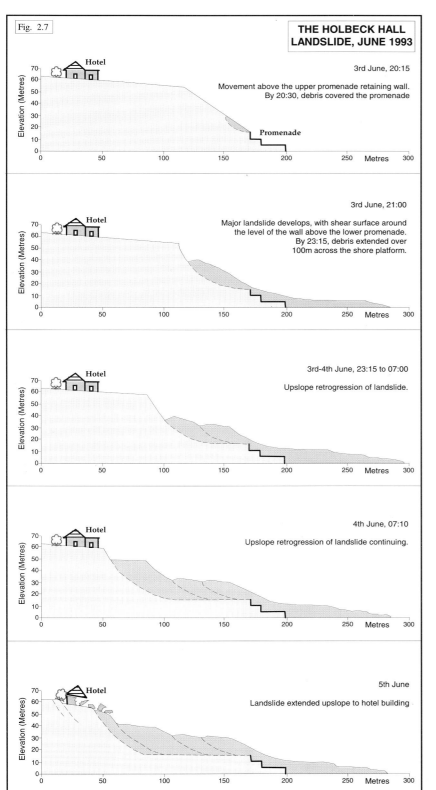

Fig. 2.7

THE HOLBECK HALL LANDSLIDE, JUNE 1993

3rd June, 20:15

Movement above the upper promenade retaining wall. By 20:30, debris covered the promenade

3rd June, 21:00

Major landslide develops, with shear surface around the level of the wall above the lower promenade. By 23:15, debris extended over 100m across the shore platform.

3rd-4th June, 23:15 to 07:00

Upslope retrogression of landslide.

4th June, 07:10

Upslope retrogression of landslide continuing.

5th June

Landslide extended upslope to hotel building

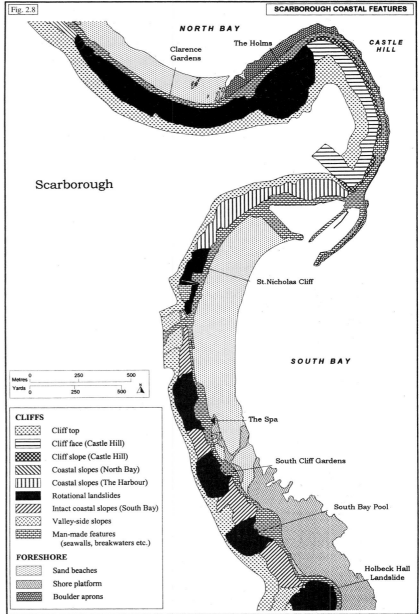

Fig. 2.8

SCARBOROUGH COASTAL FEATURES

NORTH BAY

Clarence Gardens

The Holms

CASTLE HILL

Scarborough

St. Nicholas Cliff

SOUTH BAY

The Spa

South Cliff Gardens

South Bay Pool

Holbeck Hall Landslide

CLIFFS

- Cliff top
- Cliff face (Castle Hill)
- Cliff slope (Castle Hill)
- Coastal slopes (North Bay)
- Coastal slopes (The Harbour)
- Rotational landslides
- Intact coastal slopes (South Bay)
- Valley-side slopes
- Man-made features (seawalls, breakwaters etc.)

FORESHORE

- Sand beaches
- Shore platform
- Boulder aprons

The Coast — Further Reading:

P W French, *Coastal and Estuarine Management* (London: Routledge, 1997).

J Pethick, *An Introduction to Coastal Geomorphology* (London: Arnold, 1984).

R W G Carter, *Coastal Environments: an introduction to the physical, ecological and cultural systems of coastlines* (London: Academic Press, 1989).

The threat of coastal erosion has led to the construction of various sea-walls and harbour breakwaters along the coast, along with drainage and regrading works to stabilise the cliffs. Although these defences have provided protection, they have also caused local coastal changes, notably falling beach levels due to scour in front of the sea-walls, and the reduced inputs of sand and gravel from cliff erosion. Most of the material that makes up the beaches was 'bulldozed' in from the sea-bed as the Holocene sea-levels rose, and is therefore a finite resource with only small additions from modern cliff erosion. The gradual movement of this sand and gravel back to the sea driven by natural processes is an inevitable progression of the present interglacial period. The modern obsession for stabilising the coast, so preventing any new inputs to these diminishing beaches, merely hastens the inexorable trend of exhumation of a coastline inherited from the past.

The climate of an area is determined by a variety of geographical factors. Its latitudinal position will determine the amount of solar energy received and the wind regime, its location relative to oceans will influence seasonality, and its location relative to topography will control precipitation distributions. Superimposed on this pattern will be the factor of altitude, as climate changes quite rapidly with height above sea-level. This means that whilst North Yorkshire at sea-level has a climate determined by its geographical setting between the Pennine summits and the East Coast, there is considerable variety brought about by the differences in altitude and proximity to the sea.

Average temperature values at sea-level do not vary greatly across the region (**fig 2.9**). Mean daily maximum temperatures in July reach about 20°C in the Vale of York but only about 19°C along the coast, where sea-breezes can lead to cooling.[1] Lowest monthly temperatures usually occur in January, with mean minimum values of 1.5°C on the coast and about 0.0°C inland. The temperature range from day to night, and from winter to summer, is usually lower in coastal areas because of the effect of the sea, which only warms and cools relatively slowly. Extremes of temperature are also more likely to occur inland, with Driffield and Harrogate having recorded -18.9°C, and for maximum temperature Cawood has reached 33.9°C. At higher altitudes the temperatures decline on average by about 0.6°C per 330 feet (100m) of ascent, but the precise value is affected by sunshine, mean temperature, degree of vertical mixing and atmospheric humidity. With warm temperatures and moist air, the decrease of temperature with height slows down, whilst it steepens with more sunlight. At night, windy conditions increase the rate of decline.[2] As a result, the mean annual temperature on Fountains Fell (2,165ft/660m) near Malham Tarn is 4.8°C, at Malham Tarn (1,295ft/395m) 7.0°C, and at Silpho Moor (665ft/203m) north-west of Scarborough 8.0°C, compared to 9.0°C at York.[3] Manley estimated the average lapse rate between Fountains Fell and lowland Lancashire as 0.68°C per 330 feet (100m).[4]

Rainfall distribution closely relates to altitude[5] (**fig 2.9**). Highest mean annual totals are found in the west with about seventy-eight inches (2,000mm) per year on the watersheds of upper Swaledale and Wensleydale. About sixty per cent of this falls between October and March. Totals decline rapidly on the leeward side of the Pennines. Lowest totals are found in the southern Vale of York, where Selby has twenty-one inches (536mm) per year but only forty-eight per cent falls in the winter period. The higher ground of the North York Moors and Wolds reverses the rainfall gradient. The highest summits of the Moors receive more than thirty-nine inches (1,000mm) per year on average, and the Wolds up to about thirty-one inches (800 mm), with about fifty-five per cent falling in the winter six months.

Annual totals may give information about the average patterns of precipitation but they mask individual events which may be significant. Extreme events may produce floods or droughts, and North Yorkshire does not escape. Flooding may occur as a result of several days of steady rainfall from low-pressure systems. In July 1930, Eskdale experienced flooding when a slow-moving low-pressure system centred over Lincolnshire gave four days of heavy rain and a total of over twelve inches (300mm) at Castleton. As the winds are blowing from

Snow covers the higher ground of Urra Moor, North York Moors, in the winter.
© North York Moors National Park Authority, NS0162.

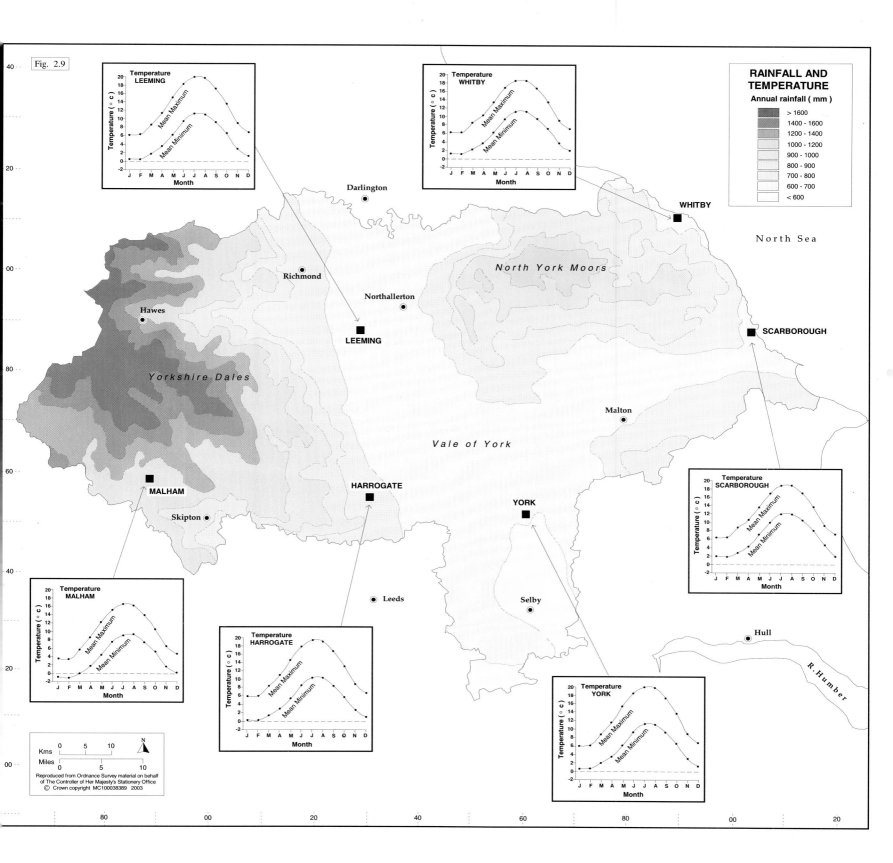

Fig. 2.9

RAINFALL AND TEMPERATURE

Annual rainfall (mm)

> 1600
1400 - 1600
1200 - 1400
1000 - 1200
900 - 1000
800 - 900
700 - 800
600 - 700
< 600

the North Sea under these conditions, it is often the eastern parts of the region that are worst affected. Floods may also occur as a result of localised thunderstorms, such as four inches (100mm) near Leyburn in August 1990, but their effects are usually less widespread. Droughts are normally associated with prolonged spells of anticyclones though, in the east, the rain-shadow effect of prolonged westerlies can give low totals. It is the drier regions that experience a greater impact. In 1989, only 16.8 inches (427mm) rainfall was received at Whitby, sixty-eight per cent of the average.

The patterns of cloud produce variations in sunshine totals between 1,200 and 1,400 hours per year. The cloudiest areas are over the Pennines, where uplift of moist westerly air can lead to extensive and persistent cloud (eg Malham, 1,176 hours). Coastal areas are usually clearest, as daytime convection cloud is less prevalent in summer near the cool North Sea, but the differences are not large (eg Whitby, 1,478 hours). This effect is counterbalanced by coastal fogs with some easterly winds. Warm air from the Continent is cooled to saturation point to produce the notorious sea-frets or 'haars'. Normally this cloud evaporates inland, though with strong winds it may stretch across the Vale of York to the Pennines.

Snowfall is normally confined to the November to May period when air temperatures fall below about 4°C.[6] The frequency of falls increases with altitude and latitude. Its occurrence is very variable from year to year, so that average figures are not very useful. The highest values would be on the Pennines, where Malham Tarn has an average of about forty days per year with snow falling, and the lowest values in the Vale of York, with Askham Bryan recording sixty days per year. The North York Moors and Wolds, and the coastal zone receive more snow than might be expected from their altitude, as they are exposed to winds from the north and east, which are responsible for much snowfall. At lower sites much of this snowfall soon melts, but at higher locations the lower temperatures mean that there are more days with snow lying on the ground than days with snowfall — the reverse of the situation at low levels.

Predictions of climate change resulting from greenhouse warming should not be applied to a specific region, as the models used are intended for the global scale. Temperature predictions suggest increases over north-west Europe of about 2°C by 2100. If this were true, temperatures throughout the North Yorkshire region would increase, with more hot days, and less frost and snow. For higher altitudes, research suggests that lapse rates should become less steep for the warmer, moister atmosphere of the 'greenhouse' world.[7] This does not necessarily mean that trees would suddenly start growing on Pennine hilltops, as factors such as soils also affect the natural vegetation. Predictions about precipitation are much less certain. In a warmer world, it is believed that more rain could fall with a greater proportion in winter and less in summer in these latitudes. However, the warmer environment would produce more evaporation that could easily counteract the higher rainfall. Unfortunately, the computer models are insufficiently consistent to state what rainfall trends there will be on a global scale and so cannot be used at a regional scale.

The Climate — Further Reading:
Meteorological Office, *Climatological Memorandum No. 128. The Climate of Great Britain: Pennines and Lake District* (Bracknell: Meteorological Office, 1985).
Meteorological Office, *Climatological Memorandum No. 129. The Climate of Great Britain: East Yorkshire and Humberside* (Bracknell: Meteorological Office, 1985).
D Wheeler, North-east England and Yorkshire, in D Wheeler and J Mayes (eds), *Regional Climates of the British Isles* (London: Routledge, 1997), 158–80.

2.7 CLIMATE CHANGE
RICHARD C CHIVERRELL AND NOËL JAMES MENUGE

The climate of North Yorkshire has varied considerably since the end of the Devensian period, with evidence for climate change recorded in sediment sequences, tree rings, historical documents and long instrumental measurement records. Peat bogs provide important evidence of climatic change, because flora, fauna and bog-development are controlled by wetness of the environment, which in turn is affected by regional climate. Peat sequences from across the region have yielded information about mire surface wetness, particularly from peat bogs on the North York Moors,[1] the Humberhead Levels[2] and the Pennines. These climate records are not as complete as those yielded by peat sequences from western Britain,[3] probably owing to the lower rainfall rendering eastern Britain marginal for peat accumulation. Nevertheless, climate changes can be inferred from fluctuations in mire surface wetness recorded within the peat stratigraphy. Early Holocene peat deposits (9,500–7,000 years ago) on the Pennines and the North York Moors are very dark, well humified and often contain tree stumps.[4] These sediments were originally regarded as reflecting a drier climate, although peat sequences elsewhere in the country show climate fluctuated markedly during this period.[5] Good examples of these early Holocene well-humified peat deposits exist at Harwood Dale Bog[6] on the North York Moors and at Malham Moss[7] and upper Teesdale[8] in the Pennines.

Detailed palaeoecological analyses targeting plant macrofossil, testate amoebae and humification stratigraphies of peat sequences across the North York Moors and in the Humberhead Levels have revealed a complex climate history, as summarised in the table opposite. Testate amoebae fossils in particular allow semi-quantitative reconstruction of water table fluctuations, for example the sequence from May Moss on the North York Moors.[9] Testate amoebae are unicellular protozoa whose occurrence on peat bogs is controlled by surface wetness, and so the fossil record can be used to identify changing water-tables. When testate amoebae analysis is applied to peat bogs that receive water solely as rainfall, the water-table depths reconstructed from the fossil record approximate to a climate history in that they reflect

Period (A.D.)	Quality and quantity of climatic information	Crop failure / Famine	Severe winter	Cold winter	Great storm	Heavy snow	Wet weather	Flooding	Pestilence	Drought	Murrain	Hot summer	Good crop yield
458							458						
500	7 entries containing generalised information not specific to the region and only 3 references to climate.				515								540
600	11 entries with no reference to climate. The plague in AD 664 or 682, in response to crop failure and famine, could have been triggered by either an extremely wet or dry summer.												
700	11 entries with 4 references to climate. Incidents of drought and dysentery, a disease more commonly associated with warmer climes, in AD 721, 737, 741 and 759-761.								759	737 741		721	
800	3 entries containing no reference to climatic conditions												
900	5 entries identifying a famine in AD 976 and disease amongst cattle in AD 986. The winter of AD 991 was unusually severe, wet and cold.	976	991	991	991						986		
1000	17 references to climate - some specific to the region. The data identifies a country blighted by cold and wet weather, which produced famine and poor crop yields.	1005 1070 1086 1087 1088 1093 1095	1047	1047	1047 1086		1092 1094 1096 1097		1086 1087				
1100	122 entries mostly specific to the region, but concentrating upon the landscape with only 14 references to climate.	1103 1104 1111 1123	1111	1111 1115	1120 1121		1115 1117	1124			1111 1131		
1200	42 entries mostly specific to the region, which identify a climate fluctuating between wet winters and dry summers.	1238 1241 1252 1257 1258 1271		1246 1258	1251		1236 1237 1257	1237 1253 1257 1271	1254	1238 1240 1241 1242 1252 1253		1236 1248 1262 1265 1266 1270 1272 1273	1239 1240 1244 1245 1247 1251 1254 1248 1255 1272 1273
1300	21 entries concentrating upon the landscape and plagues, with only 5 references to the climate.	1315			1395	1395	1315 1325			1325			
1400	8 entries containing information about land-use, with no reference to climate.												
1500	13 entries containing information about livestock and the landscape, but with no reference to climate.												
1600	18 entries containing information about livestock and the landscape, but only 3 references to climate.	1621-1623			1619 1621-1623 1641 1642	1641 1642							
1700	7 entries, with specific references to climate and the earliest meteorological records - AD 1788-1792.		1782 1783	1788-1792									
1800	43 entries, with specific references to climate and the early meteorological records from Whitby.			1800-1802			1841-1843 1867-1895	1857		1842			
1900	Good regional coverage and continuous meteorological records. Alternating wet and dry weather throughout the century, but with a concentration of wet and cold events AD 1900-1940.			1900-1940			1900-1940						
1996													

Summary of the climatic information pertaining to the North York Moors collated from documentary sources.

© N James Menuge.

climatic wetness. Plants also leave a fossil record within peat sequences, and relating the occurrence of certain species to their environmental tolerances allows reconstruction of changes in mire surface wetness. Furthermore, the decay of peat is controlled by wetness of the bog surface, and so changes in the degree to which peat is humified reflect changing moisture conditions. This group of techniques allows the hydrological history of peat bogs to be reconstructed with some clarity. Changes to a wetter climate have been recorded in peat sequences from across Yorkshire at 3000-2500 BC, 1000-400 BC, AD 400-600, AD 800-900, AD 1400-1500 and AD 1700-1800. Warmer or drier periods are evidenced circa 1500-1000 BC, AD 0-400, AD 700-800, AD 1150-1350 and AD 1600-1700.

Documentary evidence must be used cautiously to determine broad shifts in climate change. A volume of material was collated for the North York Moors Climate Database (1997 unpublished)[10] and is used in conjunction with the palaeoenvironmental research.[11] Documentary evidence for climate change is problematic, and is difficult to map. References specific to the palaeoecological sites are rare in historical documents, and many sources can only be interpreted in a regional context. Most of the references to climate do not become area-specific to the North York Moors until the twelfth century. With the exception of the *Domesday Book* (1086), most references point vaguely to the North of England: to York in some cases, and in others to Whitby and Lastingham. Furthermore, area-specific references are not always weather-specific, but offer instead descriptions of landscape and astronomical phenomena, both of which tend to lean towards spiritual symbolism rather than concrete evidence of surroundings. Nevertheless, through careful interpretation constrained by the limitations of the data and, most importantly, with interdisciplinary use of more accurate forms of climate determination, these early documentary sources provide useful information. Later documentary sources provide more reliable evidence, some of which is site-specific and most of which is both area- and climate-specific. Bearing these points in mind, a brief (and sometimes sparse) climate picture of the North York Moors between AD 450 and the present day is summarised in the table on page 23, and is discussed in comparison with the palaeoecological data.[12]

Between AD 450 and 799 the information and location is generalised, but there are references to cold winters, outbreaks of plague and famine between AD 450 and 599. Plague and famine can reflect either cold and wet weather or drought and murrain (an infectious disease in cattle). There are no weather references between AD 600 and 699, but there is evidence for plague and 'a bloody rain' in which 'milk and butter were turned into blood' is mentioned and which might signify a sirocco. Between AD 700 and 799 there is evidence for hot summers, drought, infertile land and plague, but these references are not specific to Yorkshire. The period AD 800-899 yields little climatic information in the documentary sources. Between AD 900 and 999 there are some references to famine, cattle murrain and widespread crop failures due to intense winters and frost in northern England, leading to further famine and pestilence. Information pertaining to AD 1000-1099 is still generalised but does contain evidence specific to the North Riding. The north of England at this time was afflicted by severe famine, widespread crop failures, severe winters, hard frosts, pestilence among livestock, recurring wet weather and heavy rainfalls, which encouraged a high mortality among both humans and livestock.

Climatic references in the documentary record become more specific between AD 1100 and 1199, identifying crop failures, severe murrain and hard winters, with heavy rainfall in the first half of the century resulting in famine and pestilence. Between AD 1200 and 1299 documentary information becomes increasingly local, identifying heavy rains and floods in the winters, alongside drought and very hot summers. The weather encouraged good crop growth, which usually failed by the harvest, with famine ensuing. During the last quarter of the thirteenth century crop yields improved, but famines still occurred. Heavy rains and crop failures afflicted the first half of the century AD 1300-99, and sheep and deer murrain took its toll upon the livestock. Furthermore, the first outbreaks of the Black Death decimated the population, and caused agriculture to come to a virtual standstill. Between AD 1400 and 1499 there is little reference to climate, but incidents of murrain specific to the North York Moors imply wetter conditions. Documentary sources pertaining to AD 1500-99 concentrate upon agriculture and vegetation rather than climate. Between AD 1600 and 1699 there is reference to wet weather and cooler winters in the first half of the century resulting in poor harvests and demographic crises arising from famine and pestilence. Documentary sources for the period AD 1700-99 contain few references to climate concentrating upon improved agricultural methods. The second half of the century AD 1800-99 was generally cold, wet and frosty, although there were some hot summers towards the mid-half of the century. Meteorological evidence for AD 1900-2000 is abundant owing to continuous measurement records from meteorological stations.

Comparison of the historical data with the palaeoecology record reveals a broad agreement between the two approaches. The most significant wet shifts in the peat climate history occurred *circa* AD 400-600, 800-900 and 1400-1500, and these are all supported to some extent by the documentary evidence. AD 700-800 encompasses one of driest phases recorded in the peat stratigraphies on the North York Moors, when there is supporting historical evidence for droughts and hot summers. There is no unambiguous dry phase synonymous with the Medieval Warm Period,[13] with the peat stratigraphy displaying fluctuating water-tables and the documentary evidence indicating a changeable climate. The

Climate Change — Further Reading:

M A Atherden, The Vegetation History of Yorkshire: A Bog-Trotter's Guide to God's Own County, *Naturalist*, 124 (1999), 137-56.

R S Bradley, & P D Jones (eds), *Climate since AD 1500* (London: Routledge, 1992).

D R Bridgland, B P Horton and J B Innes (eds), *Quaternary of Northeast England: Field Guide* (Quaternary Research Association, 1999).

R C Chiverrell, A proxy record of late Holocene climate change from May Moss, Northeast England, *Journal of Quaternary Science* 16 (2001), 9-29.

J Grove, *The Little Ice Age* (London: Routledge, 1988).

H H Lamb, *Climate, Past, Present and Future*, 2 vols (London: Methuen, 1972, 1977).

H H Lamb, *Climate History and the Modern World*, second edition (London: Routledge, 1995).

N J Menuge, *Climate Change on the North York Moors* (York: PLACE Research Centre Occasional Paper No. 1, 1997).

D A Spratt (ed.), *Prehistoric and Roman Archaeology of North-East Yorkshire*. CBA Research Report 87, revised edition (London: Council for British Archaeology, 1993).

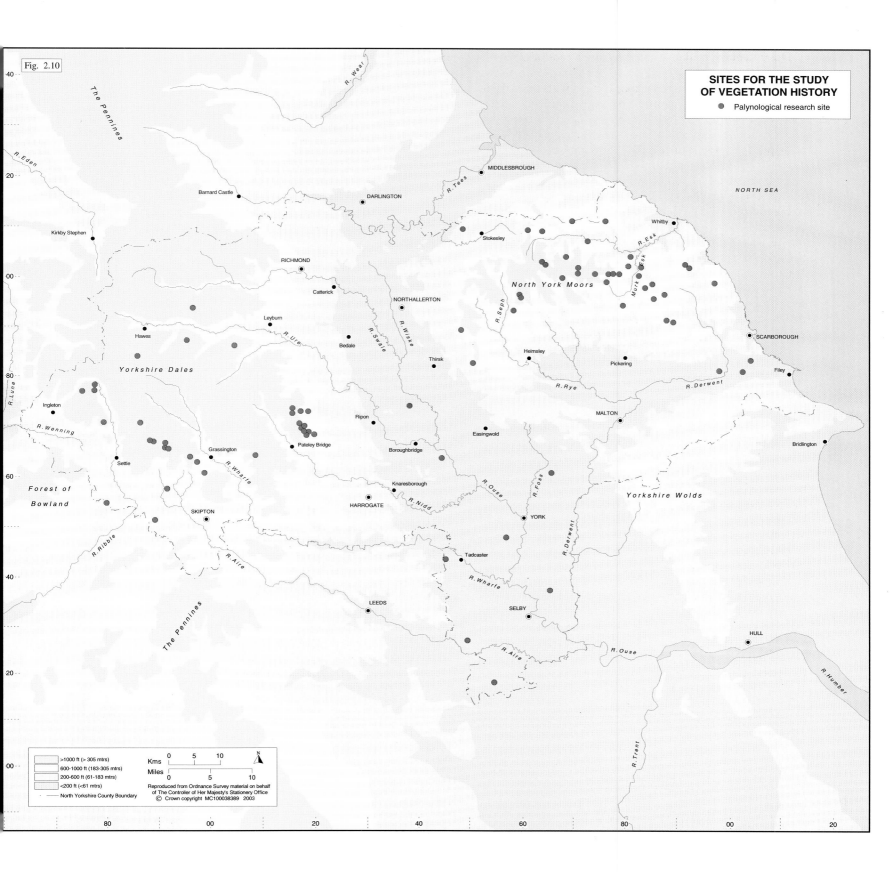

Fig. 2.10

**SITES FOR THE STUDY
OF VEGETATION HISTORY**

● Palynological research site

NORTH SEA

The Pennines

R. Eden

R. Wear

MIDDLESBROUGH

DARLINGTON

R. Tees

Whitby

Barnard Castle

Kirkby Stephen

Stokesley

R. Esk

Murk Esk

RICHMOND

North York Moors

Catterick

NORTHALLERTON

R. Seph

SCARBOROUGH

Leyburn

R. Swale

R. Wiske

Helmsley

Hawes

Bedale

Pickering

Yorkshire Dales

R. Ure

Thirsk

Filey

Ingleton

R. Rye

R. Derwent

R. Lune

R. Wenning

Ripon

MALTON

Settle

Grassington

Pateley Bridge

Easingwold

Bridlington

Forest of
Bowland

R. Wharfe

Boroughbridge

Yorkshire Wolds

R. Ribble

Knaresborough

R. Ouse

R. Foss

SKIPTON

HARROGATE

R. Nidd

YORK

R. Derwent

R. Aire

Tadcaster

R. Wharfe

LEEDS

SELBY

HULL

The Pennines

R. Aire

R. Ouse

R. Humber

R. Trent

>1000 ft (> 305 mtrs)
600-1000 ft (183-305 mtrs)
200-600 ft (61-183 mtrs)
<200 ft (<61 mtrs)
North Yorkshire County Boundary

Kms 0   5   10
Miles 0   5   10

N

Reproduced from Ordnance Survey material on behalf
of The Controller of Her Majesty's Stationery Office
© Crown copyright MC100038389 2003

80   00   20   40   60   80   00   20

onset of the Little Ice Age is clearly identified within the peat stratigraphies across Yorkshire, although the finer palaeoecological detail suggests this was no uniform cool and wet period and that it contained warmer/drier periods.[14] The historical data for AD 1400 onwards records poor harvests and cooler/wetter conditions, but with incidents of hotter summers. In summary, integrating historical and palaeoecological data, whilst not without problems and limitations, appears capable of resolving a climate history for North Yorkshire, which cumulatively covers most of the last 10,000 years.

North Yorkshire's vegetation history has been studied by many researchers over the past seventy years.[1] The county offers abundant peat deposits, a few lakes and various archaeological sites which preserve wood remains, fruits, seeds, pollen grains and fern/moss spores. All these may be used to reconstruct the past vegetation cover, but the microscopic pollen grains and spores are the most abundant and useful sources of evidence. Pollen diagrams have been published from about eighty sites, the distribution of which is shown on **fig 2.10**. Particular clusters of sites are found on the North York Moors and Millstone Grit areas of the Pennines, but coverage is poorer in the lowlands and calcareous uplands, owing to the scarcity of surviving peat deposits. Radiocarbon dating provides a chronology for most of the pollen diagrams and others may be dated approximately by comparison with them.

Some pollen diagrams, such as those from the Vale of York and the Cleveland plain, provide a picture of the vegetation at the end of the last glaciation. The North Yorkshire landscape then resembled the tundra, with dwarf trees and shrubs only in sheltered spots. About 10,000 years ago, a rapid amelioration of climate led to colonisation by a succession of forest trees, starting with the pioneer species of birch, willow and hazel, followed by pine and later by elm, oak, lime and alder. Research in many parts of the county has shown that by about 7,000 years ago most of North Yorkshire was covered in closed forest, dominated by oak, alder and hazel, and the climate was 1–2°C warmer than it is today. The only gaps in this canopy would have been natural clearings in the wood or areas of high ground where the trees thinned out, eg on the summits of the Pennines.[2]

Prehistoric people had an impact on the vegetation cover from the beginning of the Holocene. Birch trees were used to construct a platform at the early Mesolithic site of Star Carr in the Vale of Pickering, and reed-swamps were burned around the edge of a large shallow lake ('Lake Flixton'). In the later Mesolithic, fire was used in association with hunting activities on both the North York Moors and Pennines, resulting in clearance of the undergrowth and inhibition of tree regeneration.[3] The opening up of the tree canopy facilitated leaching of the upland soils and initiated the spread of a heathland ground flora. Thus, even before the advent of agriculture, the vegetation of North Yorkshire could not be described as entirely natural, although the greatest impact seems to have been on the uplands, with relatively little effect being felt in the denser, wetter lowland forests.

The first arable farmers were attracted to the lighter, calcareous soils of the limestone Pennines, the southern North York Moors (the Tabular Hills) and the northern escarpment of the Wolds. Other upland areas were used mainly for grazing, which prevented tree regeneration and led to the gradual replacement of the forest cover by heathland and grassland. On the Pennines, pollen diagrams from Nidderdale and Wensleydale record a major impact on vegetation in the Bronze Age. Parts of the North York Moors were also

Peat coring at May Moss on the North York Moors.
© R Chiverrell.

Peat core from blanket peat on May Moss, North York Moors, showing darker, more humified peat (right of photograph) giving way to lighter coloured, less humified peat (left) that accumulated in a wetter climatic phase.
© R Chiverrell.

Vegetation History —Further Reading:

M A Atherden, The Vegetation History of Yorkshire: a bog-trotter's guide to God's own county, *Naturalist* 124 (1999), 137-56.

O Rackham, *The History of the Countryside* (London: Dent, 1986).

I G Simmons, M A Atherden, E W Cloutman, P R Cundill, J B Innes and R L Jones, 'Prehistoric Environments', in D A Spratt (ed.), *Prehistoric and Roman Archaeology of North-East Yorkshire* (London: Council for British Archaeology Research Report no. 87, revised edition, 1993), 15-50.

losing their tree cover and undergoing acidification of soils, as demonstrated by the work of Dimbleby on soils buried under archaeological earthworks.[4] A much more widespread and sustained impact on the vegetation cover was seen in the Iron Age and Romano-British periods, with pollen diagrams from all over the county recording a major clearance of woodland, and expansion of grassland and other open communities. A climatic deterioration in the first millennium BC had led to a shift in population towards the lower ground but the uplands continued to be exploited for grazing and wood production. Factors which contributed to this major impact on the vegetation cover included the systematic coppicing of woodland to produce charcoal for iron smelting; the use of the iron-shod plough, which could tackle the heavier lowland soils; and the cumulative effect of centuries of grazing by domestic animals. By the time the Romans left in the early fifth century AD, the outlines of North Yorkshire's major vegetation communities were more or less established along their modern lines.[5]

A regeneration of trees and shrubs in the Dark Ages is recorded on many pollen diagrams, especially from the uplands, but there is another major clearance phase in the Medieval period, corresponding with a slightly warmer climate. Monastic houses, such as Fountains, Bolton Abbey and Rievaulx, were important landowners and exploited both the dales for arable agriculture and the uplands for sheepwalks. Pollen diagrams record species characteristic of arable and pastoral farming, including grasses, cereals and a range of weed species. Further changes occurred in the following centuries. In the lowlands, such as the vales of York and Pickering, intensification of farming led to clearance of most of the remaining woodlands and drainage of the soils. On the uplands, moorland management by regular burning from the mid-nineteenth century onwards has led to a decrease in species diversity and an almost total dominance of heather in areas overlying acid soils. Grasslands continued to dominate the landscape on the calcareous soils of the Craven Pennines and the Tabular Hills, interspersed with arable land. Forestry plantations were established in the twentieth century on many upland areas, dominated by exotic conifers, such as sitka spruce and lodgepole pine. Remnants of the original deciduous forest cover only survive today in scattered localities, and management for timber and wood over the centuries has led to many changes in their species composition and structure.

Thus, enormous changes have taken place in the vegetation cover of North Yorkshire over the past ten millennia but they will not be the last. Global warming, the fluctuating economics of farming and public attitudes towards blood sports may all cause major changes in the North Yorkshire landscape over the next few centuries.

Soil is the basis for the growth of all crops, forests and natural vegetation, and its characteristics depend mainly on climate and geology. The considerable range of climates within the county, and the great variety in the solid and drift geology ensure a diversity of soil groups. The time a soil has had to develop is also important, and as most soils have formed in the short period since the Pleistocene glaciers retreated, the influence of geology remains strong. In upland areas, relief and elevation influence precipitation, temperature and soil drainage, and produce soil-slope sequences or soil catenas. These have poorly drained soils (peats and gleys) on flat hill-tops and gentle slopes, with better-drained soils (brown earths and podzols) on moderate and steep slopes, and poorly drained soils again in valley bottoms. In lowland areas, soil properties depend mainly on micro-topography and the texture or particle size of the soil parent material. Textures vary from pure sand, silt or clay to various mixtures of these, of which loam is the most important. Glacial tills are clayey or loamy, glaciofluvial deposits sandy or loamy, glacio-lacustrine deposits clayey or silty, and aeolian deposits sandy or silty.

It is convenient to describe the soils (**fig 2.11**) on the basis of soil-landscape areas.[1] On the Pennine foothills, most of the Carboniferous rocks are masked by till, glaciofluvial deposits and alluvium, giving large areas of surface-water gleys (stagnogleys) and peaty gleys (stagnohumic gleys). These soils are slowly permeable and are waterlogged for long periods. They have a short growing season, and are acid and poor in nutrients. Plant yields are low, and therefore they form rough grazing land which is expensive to reclaim. Carboniferous limestone has two types of soil. The first is a shallow ranker soil of loamy texture, a slightly acid reaction and a dark humus-rich topsoil. The second is a brown earth on silty aeolian drift amidst bare limestone pavements. The soils are permeable, well drained and support good

Podzol showing a layer of raw, acid humus over a bleached and leached layer from which iron has been removed to the reddish-brown layer below.
© K Atkinson.

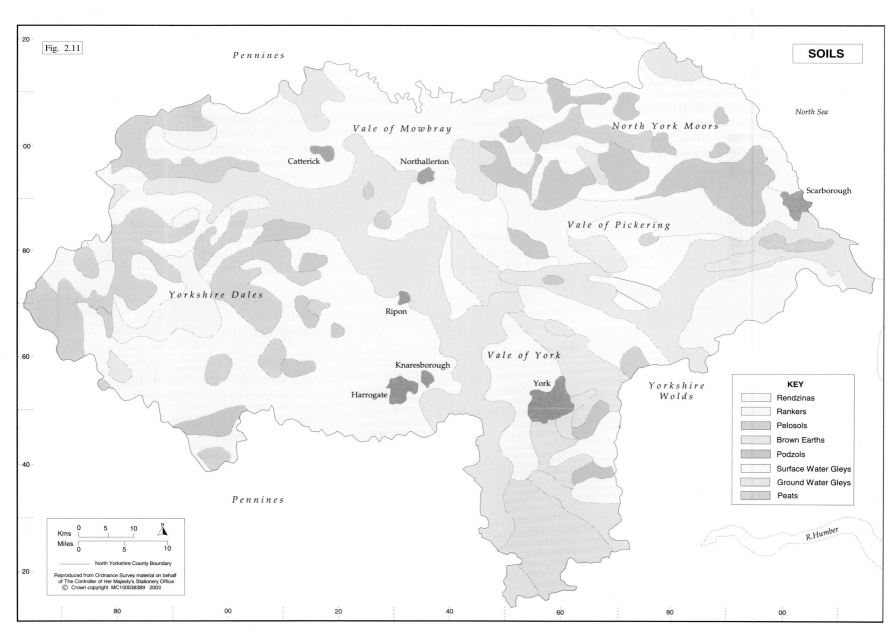

Fig. 2.11

SOILS

Pennines

Vale of Mowbray

North York Moors

North Sea

Catterick

Northallerton

Scarborough

Vale of Pickering

Yorkshire Dales

Ripon

Vale of York

Knaresborough

York

Yorkshire Wolds

Harrogate

Pennines

R. Humber

KEY

	Rendzinas
	Rankers
	Pelosols
	Brown Earths
	Podzols
	Surface Water Gleys
	Ground Water Gleys
	Peats

Kms 0 5 10
Miles 0 5 10

N

North Yorkshire County Boundary

Reproduced from Ordnance Survey material on behalf of The Controller of Her Majesty's Stationery Office
© Crown copyright MC100038389 2003

right Warp soil showing a layer of estuary silts above the black former humus layer, typical of the lower reaches of the rivers Humber and Ouse.
© K Atkinson.

The Carboniferous Limestone of the Pennines weathered to form a brown earth soil with a dark, humus-rich surface overlying a thin, greyish silt-loam subsoil.
© K Atkinson.

Alluvial gley soil, typical in river valleys throughout the region.
© K Atkinson.

Soils — Further Reading:

D M Carroll and V C Bendelow, *Soils of the North York Moors: Soil Survey Special Survey No. 13* (Harpenden: Soil Survey of England and Wales, 1981).

R A Jarvis, J W Alison, V C Bendelow, R I Bradley, D M Carroll, R R Furness, I N L Kilgour, S J King and B Matthews, *Soils of England and Wales, Sheet 1: Northern England* (Harpenden: Soil Survey of England and Wales, 1983).

R A Jarvis, J W Alison, V C Bendelow, R I Bradley, D M Carroll, R R Furness, I N L Kilgour and S J King, *Soils and their use in Northern England* (Harpenden: Soil Survey of England and Wales, 1984).

grassland. Millstone Grit produces acid brown earths, acid rankers and stagnopodzols, whilst deep blanket peat covers the higher parts of the Pennine moors, irrespective of underlying rock. The farming potential of the peat is low, giving only poor grazing land for sheep, though there has been some afforestation.

The Magnesian Limestone belt in the western Vale of York has calcareous brown earths of twenty inches (50cm) thickness with shallow and stony rendzinas locally. The soils are well drained, easy to work and warm up rapidly. They have large magnesium and potassium contents but are deficient in phosphorus. The vales of York and Mowbray have soils developed on a variety of glacial materials. Till and glaciofluvial deposits give well drained loamy brown earths of high fertility. Reddish clay soils of the pelosol group are found on till from Permo-Triassic mudstones and shales. They have poor drainage in winter, but desiccation cracking in summer can promote rapid soil drainage, giving droughts. Clayey tills and glacio-lacustrine clays give surface-water gleys in contrast to adjoining light-textured sandy gleys (ground-water gleys) in aeolian sands, which are prone to wind erosion. The soils are fertile after drainage, but they require careful management to avoid damage to soil structure. Acid gley-podzols with an ironpan below the plough layer are found in sandy areas with deep water-tables. These soils are very difficult to manage as normal cultivations do not remove the pan. Along tidal parts of the River Ouse, natural soils have been masked by recent alluvial warp, a fifteen inch (40cm) layer of marine silts of high fertility, formed by the deliberate flooding of low-lying areas to allow the river-borne sediments to settle out.

On the chalk of the Wolds, the typical soil is a brown silty rendzina of fifteen inches (40cm) thickness, with variable stone and flint content. Thinner grey rendzinas occur on steeper slopes where cultivation and erosion have removed much of the topsoil. Calcareous brown earths of about thirty inches (80cm) thickness are found on lower slopes where colluvium has accumulated, and in alluvial valley bottoms. These soils also occur on flat hilltops where aeolian silts were deposited as loess during Pleistocene times. Where the soils are thick, they are well drained, easily worked, warm up rapidly in spring and contain sufficient water for crops.

As drift is mostly absent from the North York Moors, the lithology of the Jurassic rocks is crucial for soil characteristics and properties. Mudstones, shales and clays support peaty gleys (stagnohumic gleys). Sandstones give rise to peaty gley podzols on the higher ground or well-drained coarse loamy brown earths at lower elevations on moderate slopes. Upper Jurassic rocks contain important calcareous strata, which have silty and stony brown rendzina soils, with brown earths in colluvial deposits on lower slopes. Brown alluvial soils are found in valley bottoms. The Vale of Pickering is underlain by Kimmeridge Clay, but is everywhere covered by Quaternary deposits. At the eastern end the 'carrs' have organic soils of amorphous peat, marking the extent of the post-glacial 'Lake Flixton', whilst the glacio-lacustrine clays at the western end of the Vale support ground-water gleys (pelo-alluvial gleys), and the glaciofluvial and colluvial deposits which surround the Vale produce brown earths.

3
PREHISTORY

3.1   INTRODUCTION   BLAISE VYNER

These short essays hardly do justice to the varied and intensive evidence for over 10,000 years of human settlement in an area so large as North Yorkshire. Yet, for all its interest and extent, the prehistory of Yorkshire remains poorly known by comparison with that for parts of southern England, or indeed, Scotland. North Yorkshire, well known as a predominantly rural and thinly populated county, has also traditionally harboured relatively few archaeological fieldworkers. In recent years the county has experienced a comparable dearth of development, with commensurate absence of fieldwork inspired by impending destruction. Thus the very full record of prehistoric sites known through earthworks and cropmarks is remarkable for extent rather than detail.

Although the detail of particular sites may be gained through fieldwork or excavation, the range of prehistoric archaeology is matched in North Yorkshire by the variety of landscapes in which it can be found, so that generalisations are hard to seek and it is, perhaps, no surprise that no overview has replaced that presented before the middle of the last century, evidenced by Frank Elgee and Harriet Elgee in their book *The Archaeology of Yorkshire*, published in 1933. Even taking into account variations in land use and topography, and the accidents of discovery, it appears that contrasting locations have been favoured at various times in the past. Mesolithic activity appears most clearly in locations which are marginal today — the low-lying lands of the Vale of Pickering, or the upland spine of the Pennines. The situation of earlier Neolithic mortuary monuments on the uplands of eastern Yorkshire contrasts with the lowland riverine locations favoured later in the period, while Bronze Age activity seems once again to have been concentrated in eastern Yorkshire. The pre-Roman Iron Age saw a developing intensity of settlement across the lowlands, increasingly revealed by air photography and the construction of roads and pipelines.

Close examination repeatedly reveals the careful selection of specific locations — bounded by rivers or streams, marked out by hill slopes, marshes or wooded areas — chosen for settlement or ritual activity. This informed interest in the character of the landscape, and its potential for assisting in the definition of special places, appears to have extended throughout prehistory and beyond. Thus linear boundaries augment defining rivers, small burial mounds remain nearly invisible from some viewpoints yet are prominent from others, while prehistoric farmsteads often occupy the overseeing location chosen by farmers of any period. Such subtleties of location can never become apparent through the pages of a small-scale atlas, but they are there to be recognised by the fieldworker whose curiosity may have been aroused by the very broad-brush picture necessarily painted here.

3.2   THE UPPER PALAEOLITHIC AND THE EARLIER MESOLITHIC   BLAISE VYNER

Evidence for late glacial, or perhaps more likely, interglacial human activity in North Yorkshire is very limited, as it is in most areas of Britain beyond those with caves in which archaeological deposits have survived the destructive effects of the ice. In the north-west part of our area the presence of caves has preserved limited evidence for the glacial and interglacial period from at least 100,000 years BC, but this for the most part shows animal rather than human presence. An antler harpoon point from Victoria Cave, Settle, has produced a date in the ninth millennium BC — roughly contemporary with the use of caves in Derbyshire. The object does not demonstrate human occupation in the cave, since it could have arrived with an injured animal or as an adjunct of ritual activity. In North Yorkshire, as elsewhere, human activity during the continuing very cold period of the Upper Palaeolithic may have been restricted to occasional and seasonal hunting expeditions by small groups who may have been based a considerable distance — perhaps hundreds of miles — to the south. The presence of a small quantity of flints at Flixton Carr, at the eastern end of the Vale of Pickering, tends to support the hypothesis that hunting forays could on occasion extend far into inhospitable territory.[1]

TIMELINE FOR PREHISTORIC AND MAIN HISTORICAL PERIODS

	2000	Modern
	1750	Early Modern
	1550	Medieval
A.D	1066	
		Early Medieval
	410	Roman
	70	Later Iron Age
	100	Middle Iron Age
	400	Early Iron Age
B.C	600	Later Bronze Age
	1000	Middle Bronze Age
	1500	
		Early Bronze Age
	2500	
		Late Neolithic
	3000	
		Early Neolithic
	4000	
		Late Mesolithic
	6600	
		Early Mesolithic
	8000	
		Late Upper Palaeolithic
	11500	

Dating Systems: archaeological chronologies often use the B.C./A.D. calendar system for timelines. Environmental scientists, because of scientific dating systems such as radiocarbon dating, use the concept of years before present, written as B.P.

The Present, for standardisation and fixed base-line purposes, is fixed as A.D 1950. Conversion from B.C to B.P. is made therefore, by adding 1950, so that 1500 B.C becomes 3450 B.P. Conversion from B.P to B.C involves a subtraction of 1950.

above   The entrance to the Palaeolithic site at Victoria Cave. This was enlarged by excavation in the 1870s.
© R White/Yorkshire Dales National Park Authority, 3314.

above right   The location of a Palaeolithic site, Victoria Cave, in the Carboniferous Limestone near Settle.
NMR 17033/06 © Crown copyright. NMR.

right   The early Mesolithic site at Star Carr was located on the edge of former Lake Flixton, seen here in the lighter soil in the left of the photograph. The darker peat on the right covers the former area of water.
© M A Atherden, 14200.

The final retreat of the ice, around 10,000 years ago, resulted in a warming climate which led to the establishment of widely variable environments — large expanses of water and marsh which shrank in size through time, and mixed forest which became increasingly dominated by deciduous trees. The limited range of resources which restricted human activity in the early post-glacial period became much richer as the climate ameliorated, so that by 8,000 BP North Yorkshire contained a range of environments which were attractive to a wide variety of plant, fish, and animal species. It was attractive, also, to a human population with a hunter-gatherer life which is still labelled Mesolithic. Around this time, rising seas isolated Britain from the Continental landmass, isolating a widespread population which, to judge by variations in lithic and bone tools, comprised a number of social groups which cleaved to their own territories.[2]

In North Yorkshire, early Mesolithic activity (**fig 3.1**) is widely evidenced by scatters of flint artefacts and waste, especially in upland areas which were at the time heavily forested. Star Carr, near Scarborough (**fig 3.2**), is particularly important as it remains one of the few excavated Mesolithic sites where wood and bone objects have been preserved by water-logging, although it is known to be just one of a number of sites of this period around the former Lake Flixton, where Seamer Carr has been the subject of more recent investigation. Excavated in 1950, the Star Carr site comprised a birch-wood platform set on clayey silts and

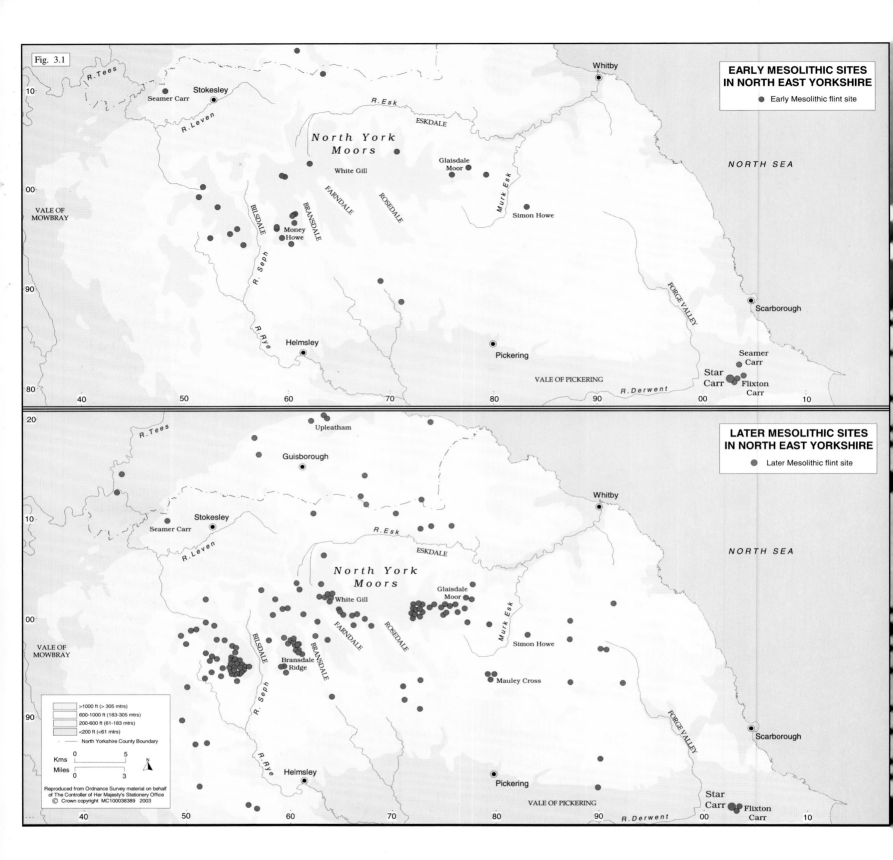

Fig. 3.1

EARLY MESOLITHIC SITES
IN NORTH EAST YORKSHIRE

● Early Mesolithic flint site

R.Tees

Whitby

Seamer Carr

Stokesley

R.Leven

R.Esk

ESKDALE

NORTH YORK
Moors

White Gill

Glaisdale
Moor

NORTH SEA

VALE OF
MOWBRAY

BILSDALE

BRANSDALE

FARNDALE

ROSEDALE

R. Seph

Money
Howe

Murk Esk

Simon Howe

R. Rye

Helmsley

Pickering

FORGE VALLEY

Scarborough

Seamer
Carr

Star
Carr

Flixton
Carr

VALE OF PICKERING

R. Derwent

LATER MESOLITHIC SITES
IN NORTH EAST YORKSHIRE

● Later Mesolithic flint site

R.Tees

Upleatham

Guisborough

Whitby

Seamer Carr

Stokesley

R.Leven

R.Esk

ESKDALE

North York
Moors

White Gill

Glaisdale
Moor

NORTH SEA

VALE OF
MOWBRAY

BILSDALE

Bransdale
Ridge

BRANSDALE

FARNDALE

ROSEDALE

R. Seph

Murk Esk

Simon Howe

Mauley Cross

FORGE VALLEY

Scarborough

>1000 ft (> 305 mtrs)
600-1000 ft (183-305 mtrs)
200-600 ft (61-183 mtrs)
<200 ft (<61 mtrs)
North Yorkshire County Boundary

Kms   0   5
Miles 0   3

N

Reproduced from Ordnance Survey material on behalf
of The Controller of Her Majesty's Stationery Office
© Crown copyright MC100038389 2003

R. Rye

Helmsley

Pickering

Star
Carr

Flixton
Carr

VALE OF PICKERING

R. Derwent

later engulfed in peat. Lithic material included flint cores, microliths and scrapers which are thought to have been used in preparing carcases and skins. Objects of bone and antler included pins and spears, while elk antlers may have been used as mattocks. Several wooden items of uncertain purpose were preserved, while stone items included shale and amber beads, and iron pyrites for setting fires. A number of stag antler frontlets may have been used as a hunting disguise, or, perhaps more likely, used in ritual activity. The faunal evidence included the bones of red deer, roe deer, elk, ox, pig and wildfowl, as well as bones from domesticated dogs. Radiocarbon dates place Star Carr around the mid-eighth millennium BC, but the duration of activity is unclear, as is the full extent of the site.[3]

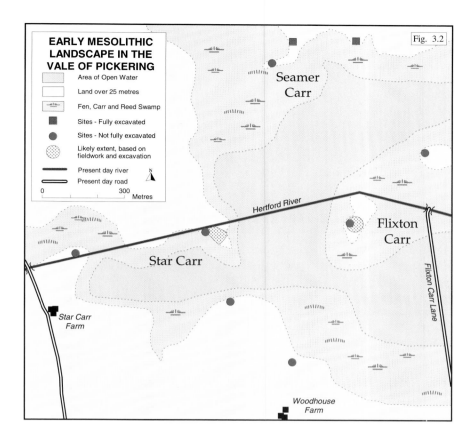

EARLY MESOLITHIC
LANDSCAPE IN THE
VALE OF PICKERING

Area of Open Water

Land over 25 metres

Fen, Carr and Reed Swamp

Sites - Fully excavated

Sites - Not fully excavated

Likely extent, based on
fieldwork and excavation

Present day river

Present day road

0   300
                    Metres

Fig. 3.2

Seamer
Carr

Hertford River

Flixton
Carr

Flixton Carr Lane

Star Carr

Star Carr
Farm

Woodhouse
Farm

The excavator favoured an interpretation of Star Carr as a seasonal hunting camp which was used in the winter and spring, and dependent to a great extent on the migratory habits of deer. Subsequent re-interpretations have suggested a late spring and summer use which may have taken place in conjunction with semi-permanent occupation at various locations around the lake margins. More recent investigation at Seamer Carr and elsewhere around Lake Flixton has identified a series of activity locations on what were islands around the shallow lake. These may not all be contemporary, but their close spacing suggests that may have been used by the same group for varying purposes and at various times of the year.[4]

Elsewhere in North Yorkshire, concentrations of flint implements and waste around Malham Tarn, and to a much lesser extent Seamer Carr (Stokesley), underline the importance of the animal and wildfowl resources associated with watery locations. Beyond the watery focuses of Lake Flixton, Malham Tarn and Seamer Carr (Stokesley), the evidence for early Mesolithic activity is limited to scatters of flint which are difficult to interpret. Revised interpretations based on the evidence from other parts of Britain now call into question some long-standing interpretations of the North Yorkshire evidence. Differences between 'broad blade' and 'narrow blade' flint implements have in the past been interpreted as chronological differences, but they may reflect differences in subsistence strategies. Similarly, flint scatters on the high moors of the Pennines and North Yorkshire Moors, formerly seen as the sign of wide-ranging hunting groups, may instead be the scant remains of semi-sedentary settlement.[5]

In North Yorkshire, pollen and other evidence for the environment during the early Mesolithic is as important as the archaeological evidence. Pollen analysis of cores from peat bogs presents the picture of widespread birch woodland succeeded by pine-hazel forest and eventually oak-rich forest. Topographic variation also resulted in expanses of water, marshland, open grass and heathland. Temperatures during much of the Mesolithic are thought to have equalled or bettered those obtaining today, so there may have been little need for animals to travel any great distances for winter shelter in North Yorkshire. The range of resources available year-round may well have enabled human groups to occupy selected locations for much of the year, with both fast and slow food fairly readily available. Although hunting camps would have been established in response to particular animal or fish availability, increased — but still low — population levels probably ensured that these were not greatly distant from base settlements.

The notion of a population which may have been semi-sedentary even in the seventh millennium BC finds increasing support from the pollen evidence. This combines with

Palaeolithic / Mesolithic — Further Reading:

I G Simmons, The history of the early human environment, in B E Vyner (ed.), *Moorland Monuments: studies in the archaeology of north-east Yorkshire, in honour of Raymond Hayes and Don Spratt* (York: CBA Research Report, 1995), 101, 7-10.

J Hunter and I Ralston (eds), *The Archaeology of Britain* (London and New York: Routledge, 1999).

J G D Clark, *Excavations at Star Carr: an early Mesolithic site at Seamer near Scarborough, Yorkshire* (Cambridge: Cambridge University Press, 1954).

P Mellars, *Star Carr in Context: new archaeological and palaeoecological investigations at the early Mesolithic site of Star Carr, North Yorkshire* (Cambridge: McDonald Institute for Archaeological Research, 1998).

C Smith, *Late Stone Age Hunters of the British Isles* (London and New York: Routledge, 1992).

R White, *Yorkshire Dales: Landscapes Through Time* (London: Batsford/English Heritage, 1997).

charcoal traces to suggest that tree cover was being deliberately reduced by fire from fairly early in the Mesolithic onwards at a number of locations on the North York Moors. Most of these disturbances are recorded from the higher, watershed, locations, but there is also some evidence for the reduction of tree cover on the margins of Seamer Carr (Stokesley). At North Gill, on Glaisdale Moor, forest disturbance by fire took place intermittently from the mid-seventh millennium BC onwards, later becoming more extensive. Such activities would have increased the range of habitats, and thus the available range of animals and birds, making more extensive hunting expeditions less necessary. While longer-distance travel in would have taken place, it may often have been as much a response to social or religious requirements as to those of subsistence.

3.3   THE LATER MESOLITHIC   IAN G SIMMONS

Here we account for the last of the hunter-gatherer-fisher economies of the region that preceded the adoption of agriculture, with the development of the culture known as the Neolithic after about 3500 BC. Our direct knowledge of the later Mesolithic period between c6600 and 3500 BC is confined to small spreads of flint and charcoal with occasional patterns of stones that could have been hearths or the foundations of windbreaks. This meagre evidence is complemented by a great deal of palaeoecological data, much of which comes from the uplands. Since the flint-charcoal material is also largely an upland phenomenon, there has been the temptation to regard the later Mesolithic as an occupation of the higher ground in Yorkshire. Yet as the work from the early Mesolithic in the Vale of Pickering shows, intensive fieldwalking and excavation in lower areas produces later Mesolithic flints. So it seems likely that the whole area was subject to some kind of human presence, but since the population density was no doubt low, and since the way of life may well have involved seasonal movement, the impress at anyone place may have been light and quite possibly transient.

Such inconspicuous levels of visible presence have not precluded an active interest in the Mesolithic of the region. On the North York Moors, for example, Frank Elgee took a strong interest in the relation between prehistoric remains and their environment;[1] Raymond Hayes[2] was assiduous in collecting and recording sites of all kinds; and Geoffrey Dimbleby produced some of the first-ever soil-pollen diagrams from the slopes near White Gill.[3] In particular, he was concerned to suggest that Elgee's hypothesis that the heather moorlands were relics of the Ice Age was probably incorrect and that open vegetation had been produced at human hands during prehistoric times, let alone by nineteenth-century grouse moor management. Both Dimbleby and Hayes were sure that distribution maps of flint and charcoal finds were problematic, for they knew that the plots depended a great deal on what had been revealed by fire and erosion, and then what has been discovered by flint collectors. Hence, regional maps of finds of the kinds constructed for later periods are only a tenuous guide to human occupancy of the land. In the uplands we can differentiate between sites with a variety of flint tools and covering a relatively large area, and the smaller spreads with usually only one or two types of microliths; the former are usually interpreted as general-purpose sites where a band of hunter-gatherer people have carried out diverse activities, and the latter as 'hunting camps' where a small group of (probably) men have prepared weapons (especially arrows) ready for culling mammals such as red and roe deer, and possibly the aurochs. A 1970s map of flint sites on the North York Moors[4] shows a distribution which is far from random: they tend to be on slopes below the crests, and not far from spring-lines (**fig 3.1**). In the case of Yorkshire, coastal sites of the type found in, for example, Co Durham, seem to have been lost in the course of coastal retreat since the mid-Holocene, but it is likely that coastal food resources were important to any food-collecting economy. But the location of the coastline in 9000 BP (before present) is not far off the present position, and further retreat south of Flamborough Head by 8000 BP makes the difference virtually insignificant except in so far as there was no Humber estuary until after 8000 BP.

Given the small size of the tools which dominate Mesolithic finds in North Yorkshire, it would be easy to conclude that it was only a hunting culture; we cannot, however, exclude the possibility that shafted flints were useful for gathering and processing plant material as well. No investigators, however, have seriously proposed that the human populations of the later Mesolithic were sedentary so long as they hunted animals and gathered plant material: once domesticated plants and animals other than the dog became available, this settlement pattern is likely to have changed radically.

Of considerable interest, therefore, is the notion of a subsistence model which integrates the archaeological information and the palaeoecological data, and its application to a region such as North Yorkshire. A very generalised model is shown in **fig 3.3** where an upland is transected by a river valley which debouches to the coast via an estuary. (This is not totally unlike North Yorkshire but it must not be assumed that it can be 'mapped' onto that region.) It is assumed that a hunter-gatherer band had access to the coast and its resources, and that they manipulated the vegetation of the uplands in order to increase the probability of hunting kills and to help certain plant resources flourish. The sites whose vegetation was manipulated may well not have been the 'camp' sites where hunters prepared their weapons, and where spreads of charcoal and flint debitage and tools are found today. So maps like **fig 3.1** are inadequate in yet another way.

The general model needs to be adapted for the North Yorkshire region. Questions that need to be asked include a discussion not only of how far off the present shoreline the coast was found but also what sort of coast it was. Open straight shorelines, for example, present fewer resources than inlets of all kinds, but especially they contrast with estuaries, which have high silt loads and enhanced biological productivity. Its tidal range would also have affected biological productivity. It would also be interesting to know how significant was the lack of a major estuary south of the Tees until the disappearance of land as the North Sea pushed southwards.[5] Would Mesolithic populations wanting access to productive coasts have had access to estuaries like those of the Tees and 'Doggerland', or would they have been in the territories of other groups? Can we imagine social arrangements that allowed use of their resources in, for example, late winter when other foods were scarce? Indeed, is it likely that groups whose summer territory was the central uplands of the Pennines also ranged as far as the coast? It is not difficult to imagine groups from the North York Moors incorporating the coast (and the Vale of Pickering or the Tees estuary) into their seasonal round, but from upper Swaledale to Scarborough seems a long way: not on the grounds of sheer distance, but because of the intervening territories of other groups.

There are currently no reliable answers to these questions: access to resources via trade or kinship is one general possibility but there is no material evidence in this region for such possibilities. Nevertheless we can suggest that, in the later Mesolithic of North Yorkshire, the land was occupied fully by food-collecting groups who probably spent much of the year in bands of around twenty-five people, coming together with other such groups at one or more times of year. The overall population density was probably of the order of 0.04 persons per square mile (0.1/km^2), giving a total of around 830 for North Yorkshire, though this is a very hazardous estimate. We might want to reiterate that one of the principal food sources is likely to have been the sea, and access to it at times of low supply from the land (such as late winter–early spring) might have been a key element in the seasonal supply of foodstuffs. The negotiation of social mechanisms enabling access to the resources of the shore and offshore zone for those who had no obvious propinquity to the coast could have been a vital element in survival. Though not necessarily a crucial element in diet, meat was nevertheless sought, and it was deemed worthwhile to keep open small clearings in the uplands where the grassy ground flora and surrounding shrubby vegetation, together with open water where possible, attracted grazing and browsing species. Deer are the obvious prey but wild pig and wild cattle (aurochs) are other likely game. The level of the tree-line may also have been manipulated for the same purpose and the removal of trees on areas of low slope at high altitudes facilitated the growth of blanket peat.[6]

The ability of human groups to manage their environments to some extent, and the consequent growth of peat in wet uplands (especially on the interfluves above the Dales), make it possible to acknowledge that some key elements of the upland landscapes of Yorkshire, such the openness above 1,000 feet (300m) and the presence of blanket bogs, owe their inception to the human populations of later Mesolithic times.[7]

Later Mesolithic — Further Reading:

S Mithen, Hunter-gatherers of the Mesolithic, in J Hunter and I Ralston (eds), *The Archaeology of Britain* (London and New York: Routledge, 1999), 35-57.

I G Simmons, *The Environmental Impact of Later Mesolithic Cultures* (Edinburgh: Edinburgh University Press, 1996).

I G Simmons and J B Innes, The archaeology of an episode of prehistoric cereal cultivation on the North York Moors, England, *Journal of Archaeological Science,* 23 (1996), 613-18.

C Smith, *Late Stone Age Hunters of the British Isles* (London and New York: Routledge, 1992).

D A Spratt and I G Simmons, Prehistoric activity and environment on the North York Moors, *Journal of Archaeological Science,* 3 (1976), 193-210.

R Young (ed.), *Mesolithic Lifeways. Current Research from Britain and Ireland* (Leicester: Leicester Archaeology Monographs No. 7, 2000).

3 . 4   THE NEOLITHIC   ANTHONY HARDING

Little can be said about the earliest stages of Neolithic settlement (**fig 3.4**) in Yorkshire from archaeological evidence alone. The presumed effects of human interference with the forest cover — deforestation in order to facilitate crop cultivation — can be seen in a number of pollen diagrams, notably those in which a reduction in elm pollen (the 'elm decline') is discernible, for this phenomenon is commonly considered to have stemmed at least in part from human action, even if elm disease was also to blame. Upland sites, such as Glaisdale

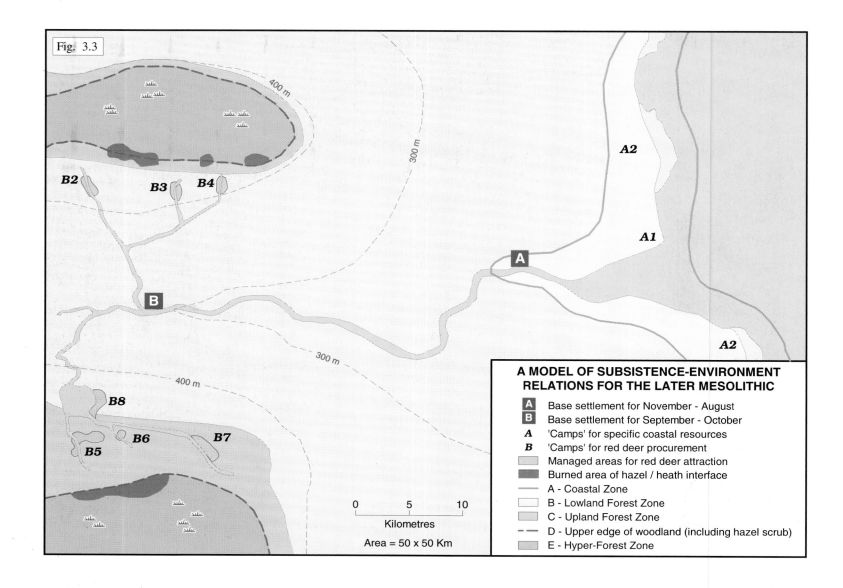

Fig. 3.3

A MODEL OF SUBSISTENCE-ENVIRONMENT RELATIONS FOR THE LATER MESOLITHIC

A	Base settlement for November - August
B	Base settlement for September - October
A	'Camps' for specific coastal resources
B	'Camps' for red deer procurement
	Managed areas for red deer attraction
	Burned area of hazel / heath interface
	A - Coastal Zone
	B - Lowland Forest Zone
	C - Upland Forest Zone
	D - Upper edge of woodland (including hazel scrub)
	E - Hyper-Forest Zone

0   5   10
Kilometres
Area = 50 x 50 Km

Moor on the North York Moors, and lowland ones, such as Seamer Carr near Stokesley, show this effect, which from its dating on other sites is likely to have fallen around 4700 BP (3650-3370 BC). Other pollen diagrams show fluctuating values of tree pollen, indicating the appearance and disappearance of clearings in the forest, presumably for agricultural purposes and thus indicating the presence of Neolithic farmers even where no characteristic artefacts are present.[1]

It is indeed striking that in Yorkshire there is very little evidence of settlement sites of Neolithic date. Part of a rectangular structure with central post line was found beneath a round barrow at Kemp Knowe, Cowlam, on the Wolds, but the site was excavated in 1878 and the dating evidence is poor. A possible settlement was noted at Mill Street, Driffield, in 1989; while an oval post-built structure with hearth from Beacon Hill, Flamborough, probably belongs to a late part of the Neolithic or the Beaker period. Pits containing both earlier and later Neolithic pottery (Grooved Ware) have turned up at various sites on the Wolds, and lines of pits containing Grooved Ware have been found on the Wolds at Hayton and in the Vale of York at Marton-le-Moor, Nosterfield, and Boroughbridge, though these latter may not in fact be domestic but of ritual character. Pottery of the various Neolithic styles is in fact well represented in Yorkshire, which suggests that the absence of settlement sites may be more apparent than real.[2]

Neolithic burial sites in Yorkshire are relatively few in number but of great importance. Long barrows, such as those at Hanging Grimston, Kilham, or Willerby Wold, have been known for many years, and their internal structures dissected and discussed (though most were initially excavated in the nineteenth century and re-excavated more recently).[3] An exception to this is the remarkable site at Street House, near Loftus on the northern edge of the Cleveland Hills, which was intact when discovered, and offered an unrivalled insight into the construction, appearance and use of such northern barrow sites. A small mortuary

opposite top   Aerial view of the circular ditches and ramparts (bottom left quadrant) of Hutton Moor Henge.
NMR 12139/12 © Crown copyright. NMR.

opposite bottom   Great Ayton Moor Square Enclosure (centre) of the Iron Age.
© B E Vyner.

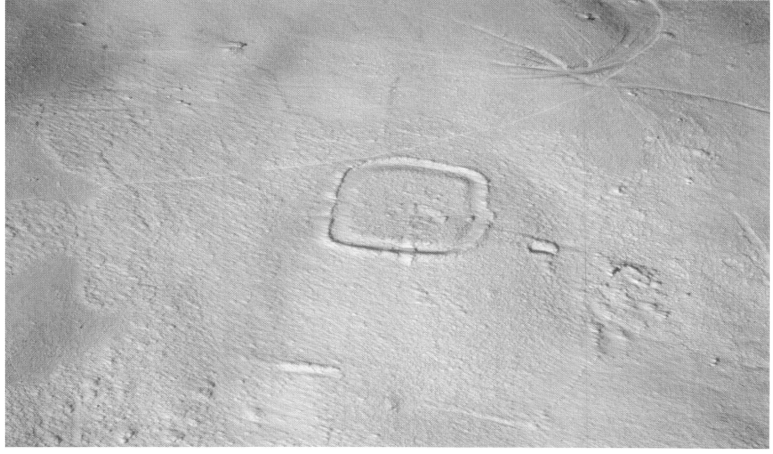

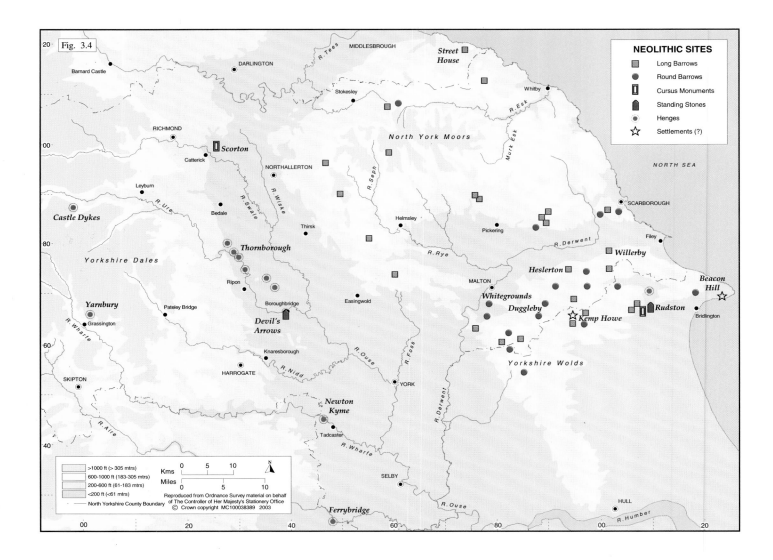

Reproduced from Ordnance Survey material on behalf of The Controller of Her Majesty's Stationery Office © Crown copyright MC100038389 2003

construction, built over three large axial pits, was supported by massive end posts; charcoal and calcined bone were scattered through this area, while to the rear was a kerbed enclosure that may have served for the initial exposure of bodies. The eventual destruction of the façade and mortuary structure by fire was followed by the erection of a low rectangular stone cairn. These details may apply in part to other Yorkshire sites, though each has its own peculiarities; destruction by fire was, however, the norm, whether or not this is to be associated with the cremation of bodies.

As well as the long barrows, some Neolithic people were buried in barrows that were circular: Duggleby Howe is perhaps the most notable example, a massive mound surrounded at a distance of 590 feet (180m) by an irregular and incomplete ditch circuit.[4] Grave goods found with burials of the second and third phases of use included a flint adze, an antler mace-head, a flint knife, several flint arrowheads, bone pins, and a series of boars'-tusk objects. Another site which shows the increasing concern with the individual is Whitegrounds, where a multiple deposit of jumbled bones was succeeded by a single inhumation with a fine flint axe with concave sides, jet belt-slider, amber pendant and other objects. These objects are unusual and indicate special status in their owners.

The final and most spectacular element of the Yorkshire Neolithic consists of the sites that can be called ritual: henge monuments, standing stones, and cursus monuments. Henges, roughly circular enclosures with internal ditch and external bank broken by one or two entrances, are known principally from the Vale of York, especially in the Ripon area, but others occur at Newton Kyme on the Wharfe, Ferrybridge on the Aire, and at Rudston on the Wolds. Possible examples are to be found at Castle Dykes near Aysgarth in Wensleydale and at Yarnbury above Grassington in Wharfedale. Of these, the most spectacular in their surviving form, and the only sites to have been partially excavated, are the Thornborough Circles on the gravels of the River Ure between Ripon and Boroughbridge. The three circles have multiple ditches and banks, and lie equally spaced along the same axis. Little is known

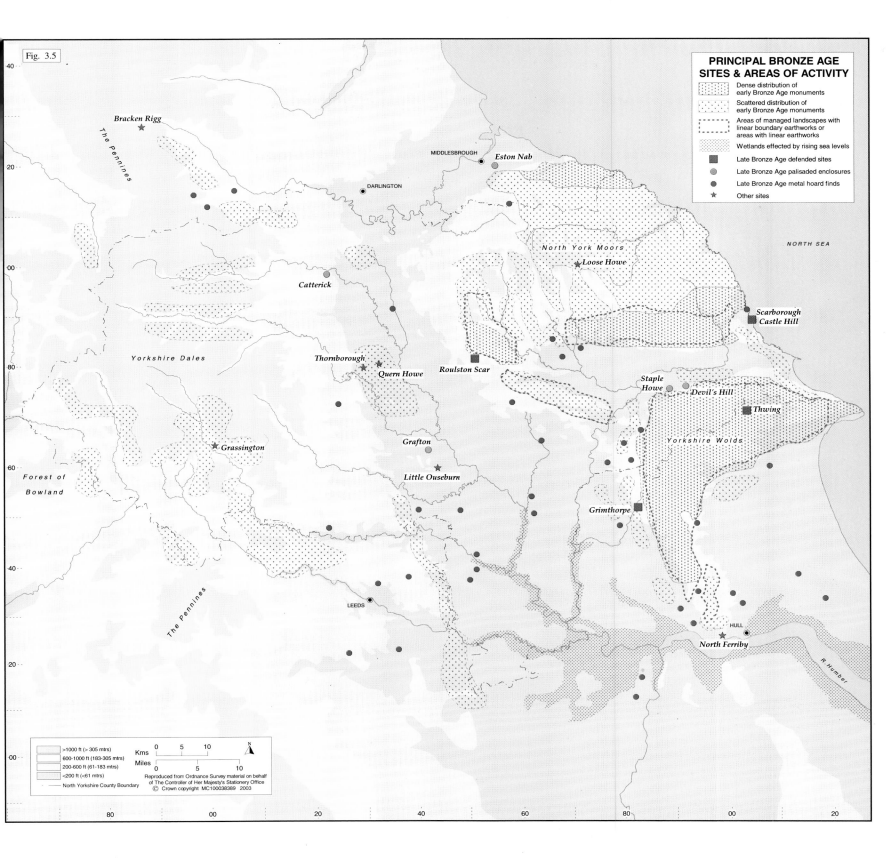

Fig. 3.5

**PRINCIPAL BRONZE AGE
SITES & AREAS OF ACTIVITY**

Dense distribution of early Bronze Age monuments

Scattered distribution of early Bronze Age monuments

Areas of managed landscapes with linear boundary earthworks or areas with linear earthworks

Wetlands effected by rising sea levels

Late Bronze Age defended sites

Late Bronze Age palisaded enclosures

Late Bronze Age metal hoard finds

Other sites

Bracken Rigg

The Pennines

MIDDLESBROUGH Eston Nab

DARLINGTON

NORTH SEA

North York Moors

Loose Howe

Scarborough
Castle Hill

Catterick

Yorkshire Dales

Thornborough
Quern Howe   Roulston Scar

Staple Howe   Devil's Hill

Thwing

Grassington

Yorkshire Wolds

Forest of
Bowland

Grafton

Little Ouseburn

Grimthorpe

The Pennines

LEEDS

HULL

North Ferriby

R. Humber

>1000 ft (> 305 mtrs)
600-1000 ft (183-305 mtrs)
200-600 ft (61-183 mtrs)
<200 ft (<61 mtrs)
North Yorkshire County Boundary

Kms 0   5   10
Miles 0   5   10

Reproduced from Ordnance Survey material on behalf
of The Controller of Her Majesty's Stationery Office
© Crown copyright MC100038389 2003

N

about the north circle; excavation in the central circle produced little information, but the site overlies a cursus. Most interest centres on the south circle, currently the focus of excavation work; outside the henge lies a curious double pit alignment. These massive sites were clearly the centre of major ceremonial interest; appearance, manpower requirements and situation all indicate their importance to those who built them.[5]

Not far away to the south, near the Ure, lie the Devil's Arrows at Boroughbridge, a line of three massive standing stones. Little can be said about their date and associations, but a late Neolithic or early Bronze Age date is likely by analogy with other sites. Even more impressive is the huge monolith in Rudston churchyard, twenty-five feet (7.7m) high and thus the largest standing stone in Britain. Smaller standing stones are occasionally present on the North York Moors and the Pennine Dales, though their date is unknown.[6]

The Rudston monolith lies at the centre of what appears to be an extraordinary concatenation of linear double-ditched alignments, or cursus monuments. At least four such features are present at Rudston, and all appear to line up with the monolith. Popularly assumed to be ceremonial ways, other examples are to be found at Scorton near Catterick and possibly at other sites on the Wolds.[7]

The Neolithic in Yorkshire was evidently a period of major change and development in social and economic terms. Though domestic evidence is still scanty, the existence of major monuments shows that, as in central southern England, this was a time when human groupings were becoming both larger and more complex than in previous periods of the human past.

The Neolithic — Further Reading:

I G Simmons, M Atherden, E W Cloutman, P R Cundill, J B Innes and R L Jones, Prehistoric environments, in D A Spratt (ed.), *Prehistoric and Roman Archaeology of North-East Yorkshire* (London: CBA Research Report 87, 1993), 15-50.

T Darvill, Neolithic houses in England, Wales and the Isle of Man, in T Darvill and J Thomas (eds), *Neolithic Houses in North-west Europe and beyond* (Oxford: Oxbow, 1996), 77-111.

T G Manby, Neolithic occupation sites on the Yorkshire Wolds, *Yorks Arch Jnl* 27 (1975), 23-60.

T G Manby, The Neolithic in eastern Yorkshire, in T G Manby (ed.), *Archaeology in Eastern Yorkshire. Essays in Honour of T C M Brewster FSA* (Sheffield: Department of Archaeology and Prehistory, University of Sheffield, 1988), 35-88;

A F Harding, with G E Lee, *Henge Monuments and Related Sites of Great Britain. Air Photographic Evidence and Catalogue* (Oxford: British Archaeological Reports 175, 1987).

3 . 5   THE BRONZE AGE   T G MANBY

Metal, copper and gold came into use around 2500 BC in a society that continued the late Neolithic way of life and subsistence economy. Flint and hard stones continued to be used for another thousand years for common tools such as scrapers, knives, and arrowheads. By 2000 BC the supply of metal goods into Yorkshire increased from sources on the Continent, Scotland and Ireland in the shape of axes, knives, and ornaments; these were status objects that accompanied a small number of the burials interred in the round barrows.

The extent of early Bronze Age (*c*2500-1500 BC) land use is shown by the distribution of burial monuments and stone circles; and by the casual discoveries of flint, stone and metal artefacts often brought to the surface by modern soil disturbance (**fig 3.5**). The circular burial mounds — barrows, or cairns if built of stones — are the most widespread early Bronze Age monument. Barrows were constructed in clusters and groups across the traditional community territories; many mounds were used as a family cemetery over several generations. The Wolds and the Tabular Hills have barrows constructed in grassland areas long cleared of their original forest. But on the watershed of the North York Moors, and the Cleveland Hills, the wide distribution of individual mounds, or mounds in adjacent twos or threes, had been constructed in clearings within extensive woodlands. Some, like Loose Howe, are prominently sited on ridges and summits which now dominate an extensive landscape. During the Middle Ages, many large barrows on the Wolds and North York Moors were given 'Howe' names (*haugr* is the Old Norse for burial mound), particularly when they served to define the boundaries of land holdings and parishes.[1]

Burial mounds survive today on agriculturally marginal moorlands of north-east Yorkshire and the Pennines. In the fertile soil areas cultivated during the Middle Ages, and down to the twentieth century, the sites of mounds are now being recorded by air photography as cropmarks caused by the infilled encircling ditches. Other early Bronze Age monuments are ring cairns and circles of standing stones which survive on the moorlands of the Pennines and the North York Moors. Early Bronze Age activities in the Pennines and North York Moors above the 1,000 foot (300m) contour benefitted from the shelter provided by natural woodland and a warmer climate, compared with the present, which enabled water chestnut to grow in the contemporary wetlands of east Yorkshire.[2]

Living sites did not have substantial structures. They are marked by scatters of flint-working waste, fragmentary pottery and burnt stones turned up by modern ploughing. Naked and hulled barley were the common cereals grown during the early Bronze Age, but stock-rearing was the more important subsistence activity. Woodlands and wetlands were also a significant economic resource, and large numbers of flint arrowhead finds show that hunting was a major activity. Bronze, an alloy of copper and tin, was used for axe blades and spearheads. Some regionally characteristic types were certainly produced in Yorkshire, but others derived from production centres in eastern Scotland and southern England.

Around the middle of the second millennium BC came great social and economic changes. The construction of burial mounds ceased and unmarked cremation cemeteries came into use. The subsistence basis changed to settled agriculture with small embanked fields laid out for cereal growing and separated from livestock pasturage. It has still to be established if the initial development of small rectilinear field systems, like those in Eskdale or in Craven at Grassington, that continued in cultivation for many centuries, had their origin in this period.[3]

Bronze Age round barrow, Robin Hood's Butts, north end of Danby to Waupley Moor road, North York Moors.
© North York Moors National Park Authority, NYM, GEL 05416.

Bronze Age round barrow at Copt Hewick in the Vale of York.
© M A Atherden.

Pit alignments on Danby Moor, North York Moors.
© B E Vyner.

To control the upland pastures, linear boundaries defined by pits or a bank and ditch came into use on the Wolds. In the Pennines, cattle-rearing on the high-level pastures must be the purpose of some walled curvilinear enclosures with round houses. The best example has two joined ovoid enclosures with a circular stone walled house at Bracken Rigg at 1,250 feet (381m) in upper Teesdale: at such a high altitude, a seasonal occupation is likely. Characteristic of the middle Bronze Age are 'burnt mounds', composed of fire-cracked stones, the by-product of dropping fire-heated stones into a trough of water. Their purpose has been variously interpreted for cooking meat or felting wool, or for a steam bath. Many burnt mounds have been recognised in Wensleydale, Swaledale and upper Teesdale, sited beside springs along the upper edge of these Pennine dales. The mounds would have been in contemporary woodlands, where firewood was readily available. Finds of middle Bronze Age bronze axes, spearheads and rapiers indicate there was much activity in the Vale of Pickering, the Vale of Mowbray, along the eastern and western side of the Vale of York, and in lowland Craven. The distinctive character of many axes indicates they were produced in the region.[4]

Late in the second millennium BC the climate became cooler, with increased rainfall causing blanket bog to spread on the summits of the North York Moors and the Pennines above 1,150 feet (350m). The wetter climate contributed to the spread of lowland wetlands, especially in the southern Vale of York, where estuarine conditions were spreading inland throughout the Bronze Age along the rivers of the Humber system during periods of rising sea-level. These provided waterways across the central lowlands to the Pennines, and by the River Trent southwards into the Midlands. Large boats, constructed of planks sewn together by withies, found beached on the Humber shore at North Ferriby, were suitable for river, estuary and coastal transportation.[5]

The changing climate caused economic and social changes reflected by innovations in metal-working and agricultural activity. The Wolds and the Hambleton and Tabular Hills became managed landscapes divided up by linear boundary earthworks separating pasture with water sources, from woodland and hunting areas. The use of these boundary systems continued into later periods, but west of the Wolds and north of the Tabular Hills comparable boundary systems are unknown and the older subsistence economies continued in the Vale of York and the Pennines. Animal husbandry was equally based on cattle-rearing on the better pastures, sheep on drier uplands, and pigs, either domestic or wild, provided a substantial meat diet. However, wheat was cultivated on the better soils, especially Spelt, which was adaptable to a wetter climate.

Fortified sites were strategically sited: Grimthorpe on the western escarpment,[6] and Thwing overlooking the Great Wold Valley, were circular fortified enclosures with a timber-framed rampart fronted by a defensive ditch. The ring-fort at Thwing and the naturally defensive Scarborough Castle Hill were economic centres for bronze-working and craft activities utilising raw materials from distant sources. The areas of managed landscape and the fortified sites may indicate increased pressures on resources, leading to a more aggressive and ranked society. Bronze was widely used for swords and spearheads, many of the latter are of large size and likely to have been prestige pieces. These were amongst a wide range of weapons, tools and ornaments produced by bronze smiths in Yorkshire: accumulations of scrap were buried for security; hoards of metal never recovered for re-use are found in lowland areas, especially along the margins of the Vale of York.

Individual farmsteads of high-status families were on the palisaded enclosed hilltops like Staple Howe[7] and Devils Hill, West Heslerton, on the northern edge of the Wolds; and at Grafton and Catterick on the western side of the vales of York and Mowbray. That they were occupied for two or more generations can be seen in the phasing of the houses and changes in the palisade defences. During the occupational life of Staple Howe and Scarborough Castle Hill, a new functional metal — iron — came into use and sometime after 700 BC replaced bronze for all weapons and tools.

Bronze Age — Further Reading:

T C M Brewster, *The Excavation of Staple Howe* (Scarborough, 1963).

T G Manby, Bronze Age Settlement in Eastern Yorkshire, in J Barrett & R Bradley (eds), *Settlement and Society in the British Later Bronze Age* (Oxford: British Arch Rep 83, 1980), 307-70.

T G Manby, The Bronze Age in Western Yorkshire, in T G Manby & P Turnbull (eds), *Archaeology in the Pennines: Studies in Honour of Arthur Raistrick*, British Arch Rep 158 (Oxbow: Oxford, 1986), 55-126; Manby, 1980, *op cit.*

T G Manby, A King, and B E Vyner, The Neolithic and Bronze Ages: a time of early agriculture, in P Ottaway, T G Manby, and S Moorhouse (eds), *The Archaeology of Yorkshire: an Assessment at the end of the Twentieth Century* (forthcoming).

R van de Noor and S Ellis, *Wetland Heritage of the vale of York: an Archaeological Survey* (Hull: University of Hull, 1999); E V Wright, *The Ferriby Boats: Seacraft of the Bronze Age* (London, 1990).

J Radley, The prehistory of the Vale of York, *Yorks Arch Jnl* 46 (1974), 10-22.

D A Spratt (ed.), *Prehistoric and Roman Archaeology of North-East Yorkshire* (London: CBA Research Report 87, 1993).

I M Stead, An Iron Age hill-fort at Grimthorpe, Yorkshire, *Proc Prehist Soc* 34 (1968), 148-90.

C Stoertz, *Ancient Landscapes of the Yorkshire Wolds* (London: RCHM England, 1997).

3.6   THE IRON AGE   BLAISE VYNER

The Iron Age is heralded by the transition of some late Bronze Age semi-defensive hilltop palisaded sites into defensive hillforts, although North Yorkshire is not dominated by hillforts in the way that some other areas of the country appear to be. Here hillforts are generally small in area and limited in the complexity of their defences, with a preference for scarp edge sites (**fig 3.6**). There is only limited excavated evidence: Staple Howe, set on a knoll overlooking

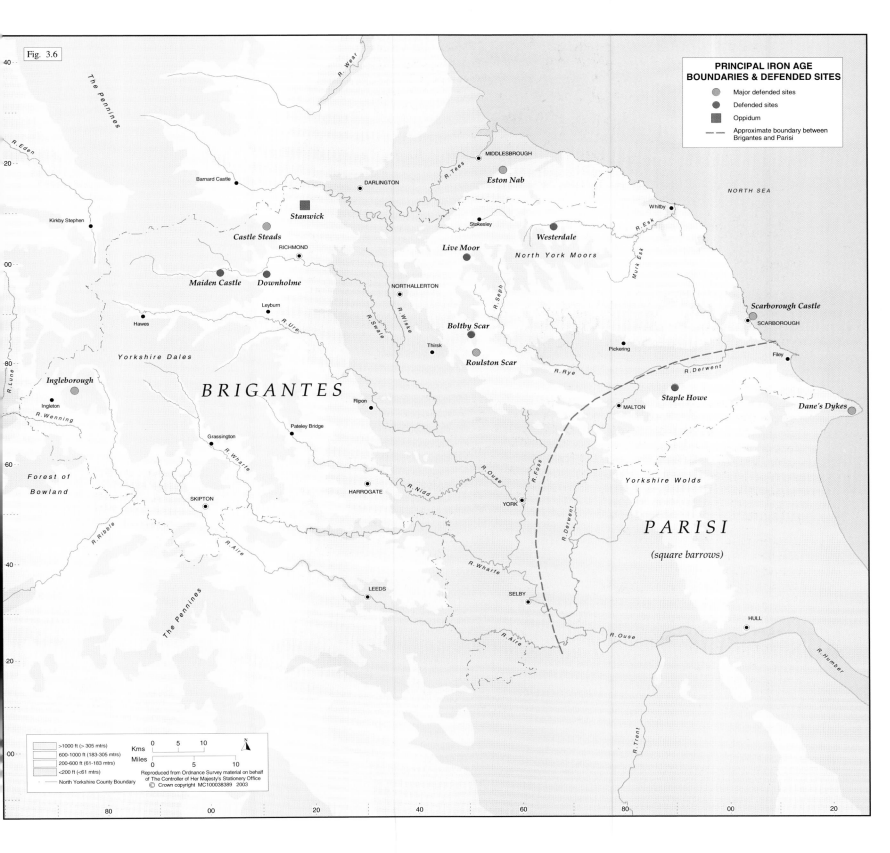

Fig. 3.6

PRINCIPAL IRON AGE
BOUNDARIES & DEFENDED SITES

⬤ Major defended sites
● Defended sites
▪ Oppidum
– – – Approximate boundary between
Brigantes and Parisi

The Pennines

R. Wear

R. Eden

MIDDLESBROUGH

NORTH SEA

Kirkby Stephen

Barnard Castle

DARLINGTON

R. Tees

Eston Nab

Stanwick

Stokesley

Whitby

R. Esk

Castle Steads

RICHMOND

Westerdale

North York Moors

Murk Esk

Live Moor

Maiden Castle   *Downholme*

NORTHALLERTON

R. Swale

R. Wiske

R. Seph

Leyburn

Hawes

R. Ure

Boltby Scar

Scarborough Castle

SCARBOROUGH

R. Lune

Yorkshire Dales

Thirsk

Roulston Scar

Pickering

Filey

R. Rye

R. Derwent

Ingleborough

BRIGANTES

Ingleton

R. Wenning

Ripon

Ripon

Staple Howe

MALTON

Dane's Dykes

Grassington

Pateley Bridge

R. Wharfe

Yorkshire Wolds

Forest of
Bowland

R. Nidd

R. Ouse

R. Foss

R. Derwent

R. Ribble

SKIPTON

HARROGATE

YORK

PARISI

(*square barrows*)

R. Aire

R. Wharfe

LEEDS

SELBY

HULL

The Pennines

R. Aire

R. Ouse

R. Humber

R. Trent

>1000 ft (> 305 mtrs)
600-1000 ft (183-305 mtrs)
200-600 ft (61-183 mtrs)
<200 ft (<61 mtrs)
North Yorkshire County Boundary

Kms   0   5   10
Miles 0   5   10

N

Reproduced from Ordnance Survey material on behalf
of The Controller of Her Majesty's Stationery Office
© Crown copyright MC100038389 2003

the Vale of Pickering, was established as a palisaded enclosure in the late Bronze Age; Eston
Nab, situated on a scarp edge overlooking the Tees estuary, also started off as a palisaded
enclosure, probably in the sixth century BC, but was later enlarged and defended by a massive
boulder wall, before the wall itself was covered in the upcast from a massive defensive ditch
in the mid-fifth century BC. Pottery and structural evidence suggest that the palisaded
enclosure here may have been permanently occupied, but thereafter the site was instead
used only when defensive action was necessary, or simply was a place where gatherings took
place — perhaps a rougher equivalent of the fair of more recent times. Among the very few
large hillforts, Ingleborough occupies a bleak summit; the stone foundations of at least twenty

The recently identified Iron Age hillfort at Roulston Scar (Sutton Bank), on the western edge of the North York Moors, occupies a large area of the flat plateau top. In the foreground is the famous White Horse at Kilburn.
NMR 12954/20 © Crown copyright. NMR.

Aerial view of the Iron Age hillfort on the top of Ingleborough, with hut circles within the enclosure.
NMR 12601/32 © Crown copyright. NMR.

hut circles enclosed by a single rampart wall. Pollen diagrams from the North York Moors show that tree clearance, begun well before the Iron Age, was consolidated during this period, while the extent of settlement evidence from the lowlands of the major river valleys shows that this must have been the case in these areas as well.[1]

Iron Age settlement sites, enclosed and unenclosed, are widespread. Enclosed sites survive as earthworks in upland areas where later agriculture has not destroyed them, and are found as cropmark sites in lowland areas. The settlement record is dominated by sub-rectangular banked and ditched enclosures containing one or more round houses. Where detailed excavation has taken place, these often turn out to have been preceded by less substantially enclosed activity, and succeeded by more extensive settlement over a larger area. Unenclosed settlement, present as earthwork foundations of round houses on the uplands, is less readily revealed through cropmark generation, but pipelines and other linear ground disturbances are now revealing unenclosed settlement in lowland areas. The earthwork sites on the uplands, exemplified by unenclosed hut circles on Percy Rigg, or the enclosure on Levisham Moor, now turn out to be much more thinly distributed than sites on better lowland soils, excavated examples of which include an enclosure at Catterick and unenclosed settlement at

Roxby (North York Moors), Iron Age farmstead enclosure (centre).
© B E Vyner.

West Rounton. On gravel soils in the middle Tees Valley south of Piercebridge, the distribution of Iron Age settlement enclosures has been compared with that of eighteenth-century farms, while limestone-based soils on the western fringe of the Vale of York also reveal extensive settlement of Iron Age type. The cropmark sites show that by the Iron Age the focus of agricultural activity had moved — perhaps driven by a combination of climate change and social factors — onto the lowland areas, where arable agriculture may have predominated, with pastoral farming perhaps concentrated on the higher ground fringing the Pennines and North York Moors. Pottery, querns and metal items are found on the settlement sites, but the extent to which they were used appears to have been dependent on social and cultural preferences, with a marked fall-off in material culture items west of the Vale of York.[2]

With the recognition of formerly unsuspected densities of settlement comes the question of the extent to which the landscape was enclosed during the Iron Age. Querns and carbonised grain found in settlements suggest that crop-growing was an increasingly intensive activity, while bones testify to pastoral agriculture. In some areas, the cropmarks of settlement enclosures are juxtaposed with those of field systems — especially on soils over limestone, but it is difficult to demonstrate a direct relationship which can be attributed to the Iron Age rather than the Romano-British period. Of the many sub-rectangular enclosures distributed across the lower Tees Valley and north-eastern Yorkshire north of the Vale of Pickering, few are directly associated with field systems. At Scorton near Catterick, area excavation has revealed an enclosed settlement of Iron Age date which appears to have been abandoned by the time of the establishment of a near-contiguous system, the ditches of which contained debris from third- and fourth-century AD Romano-British settlement which must have existed nearby. The cumulative evidence now suggests that, although patches of enclosed fields were established in the Iron Age, the settlement enclosures were more widely associated with ditched paths or tracks, a good example of which exists at Manfield, on the south bank of the Tees to the east of Piercebridge, where a sub-rectangular farmstead enclosure of Iron Age type, later to become a Romanised farm, is set against the cropmarks of two parallel ditches which can be traced over a distance of 0.6 miles (1km).[3]

Ditched trackways may well also have served as local boundaries, but there are areas of Yorkshire which are notable for the presence of more substantial boundaries which can be attributed to the Iron Age. On the Tabular Hills (**fig 3.8**) along the northern side of the Vale of Pickering, extensive systems of earthwork banks and ditches, in places preceded by pit alignments, interact with the natural contours of scarp edges and stream valleys to create small territories which can be closely compared in area and boundaries with the later townships. These may have developed from still-earlier territorial arrangements, chronological depth being suggested by the relationship of some of these linear features to earlier Bronze Age burial mounds. A close chronology for these boundary systems has yet to be established, since there has been little detailed investigation of them, while associated

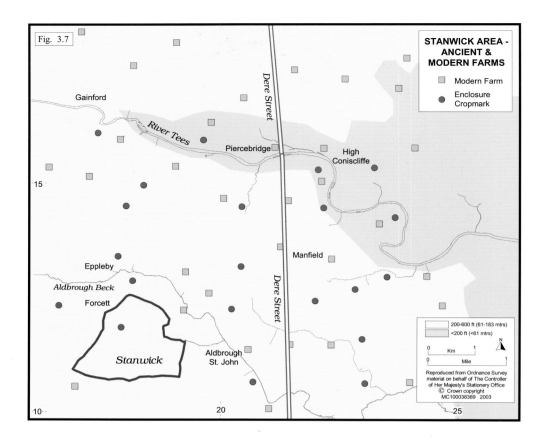

Fig. 3.7

STANWICK AREA - ANCIENT & MODERN FARMS

□ Modern Farm
● Enclosure Cropmark

Gainford

River Tees

Piercebridge

High Coniscliffe

Dere Street

15

Manfield

Eppleby

Aldbrough Beck

Forcett

Dere Street

Stanwick

Aldbrough St. John

□ 200-600 ft (61-183 mtrs)
■ <200 ft (<61 mtrs)

0 — Km — 1
0 — Mile — 1

N

Reproduced from Ordnance Survey
material on behalf of The Controller
of Her Majesty's Stationery Office
© Crown copyright
MC100038389 2003

10

20

25

Stanwick: a northern 'oppidum' of the late Iron Age, constructed north of the Dales and near the Stainmore trans-Pennine route as a fortress of the Brigantes in the first century AD.
© B E Vyner.

settlement sites have yet to be identified. However, the relationship of Cleave Dyke with Boltby Scar hillfort suggests that these two sites were at least partly contemporary, and probably in use from the early Iron Age.[4]

The boundary systems may well relate to the areas of farms occupied by extended families; the boundaries of the larger tribal areas are harder to establish. By the time of contact with the Romans, almost the whole of Yorkshire was part of the territory of the Brigantes, a confederacy of tribes who occupied the area between the Humber and the Scottish border. Eastern Yorkshire was occupied by the Parisi, whose tradition of constructing square barrows for the dead — including, occasionally, the chariots of the aristocracy — enables their tribal

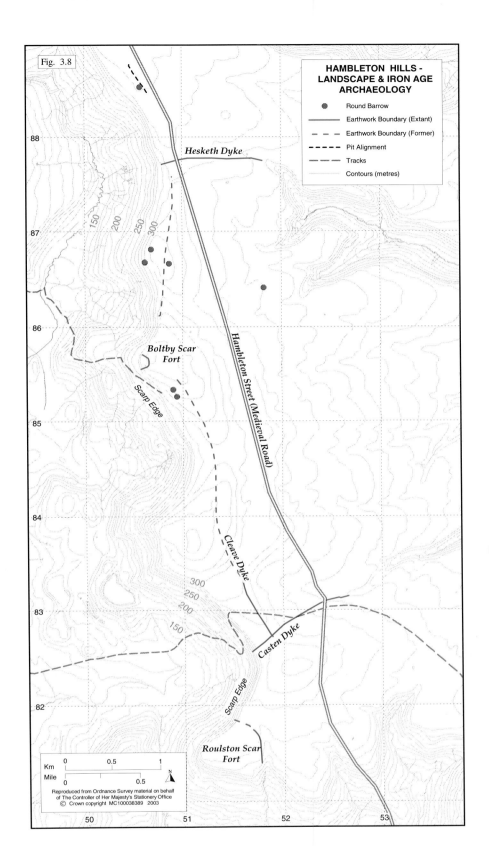

Fig. 3.8

HAMBLETON HILLS -
LANDSCAPE & IRON AGE
ARCHAEOLOGY

● Round Barrow
Earthwork Boundary (Extant)
Earthwork Boundary (Former)
Pit Alignment
Tracks
Contours (metres)

Hesketh Dyke

Boltby Scar
Fort

Scarp Edge

Hambleton Street (Medieval Road)

Cleave Dyke

Casten Dyke

Scarp Edge

Roulston Scar
Fort

Km   0   0.5   1
Mile 0   0.5

Reproduced from Ordnance Survey material on behalf
of The Controller of Her Majesty's Stationery Office
© Crown copyright MC100038389 2003

The Iron Age — Further Reading:

T C M Brewster, *The Excavation of Staple Howe*
(Scarborough, 1963).

B Hartley and L Fitts, *The Brigantes* (Gloucester:
Sutton, 1988).

C Haselgrove, The later pre-Roman Iron Age
between the Humber and the Tyne, in P R
Wilson, R F J Jones and D M Evans (eds),
Settlement and Society in the Roman North
(Bradford, 1984), 9-25.

D A Spratt, *Linear Earthworks of the Tabular Hills*
(Sheffield, 1989).

D A Spratt (ed.), *Prehistoric and Roman Archaeology of
North East Yorkshire* (London: CBA Research
Report 87, 1993), 142-44.

H G Ramm, *The Parisi* (London: Duckworth, 1978).

G J Wainwright and I H Longworth, The excavation
of a group of round barrows on Ampleforth Moor,
Yorkshire, *Yorks Arch Jnl* 42 (1968), 283-94.

area to be identified as the area bounded by the River Derwent to the west and extending into North Yorkshire perhaps only so far as the Derwent in the Vale of Pickering, although a few square barrows do occur further north. Death and ritual are barely visible in the territory of the Brigantes, being restricted to a few cremations beneath mounds on Ampleforth Moor. The extensive enclosing earthworks at Stanwick (**fig 3.7**) may be interpreted not so much as a defence against the Roman military, but a northern equivalent to the *oppida* or proto-towns which developed more fully in areas with closer contacts with the Roman world in the late Iron Age, and as such marks the final development of Iron Age society.[5]

4

THE ROMAN PERIOD

4.1 THE FIRST AND SECOND CENTURIES   PETER WILSON

The Roman period over most of North Yorkshire conventionally starts in circa AD 71 with the military advance to York from the territory of the Parisi, the tribe that occupied East Yorkshire possibly as far north-west as the Derwent. This advance led to the establishment of the legionary fortress at York (see case study 1 on pages 55–57). However, the impact of Rome is seen earlier. From soon after the Claudian invasion of Southern England in AD 43 the Brigantes, the pre-Roman tribal grouping whose territory incorporated most of North Yorkshire appear to have allied themselves with Rome (**fig 4.1**). This was certainly the case by AD 47 when the Roman province had reached their borders. By AD 48 the Roman army was in Brigantia assisting Queen Cartimandua in suppressing rebels. In AD 52 Caratacus, the leader of British resistance to Rome, fled to Cartimandua, who handed him over to his enemies. In the mid-AD 50s, Cartimandua's rule needed bolstering against an anti-Roman faction led by her husband Venutius. By this time Roman forts existed as far north as Rossington Bridge near Doncaster. In AD 69, while the Roman Empire was wracked by civil war, Cartimandua and Venutius again fell out. Cartimandua divorced Venutius, and the resulting military struggle left Venutius in control of Brigantia and Cartimandua having to be rescued by Roman troops, who were thereafter at war with the Brigantes.

This early relationship with Rome is best seen at Stanwick, where the Brigantian aristocracy imported Romanised goods and masonry buildings were constructed. The latter were circular in plan and therefore native in inspiration, but formal masonry construction was a Roman innovation and may have been undertaken as a favour to a pro-Roman leader. Stanwick is a 740 acre (300ha) *oppidum*, or proto-town, enclosed by earthworks[1] that appears to have been the base of one of the key players in the events leading up to the invasion of Brigantia in AD 71. Other potential locations for major sites of this period have been suggested at Barwick in Elmet, or near York and/or Aldborough, but to date none has produced evidence comparable with that from Stanwick.

The extent of the pre-AD 71 incursions into Brigantia is not known, although some of the camps known in the county probably belong to this period. Camps are difficult to date, as their temporary nature tends to preclude the discovery of substantial assemblages of finds. However, the recognition of Roman occupation dating to AD 72–3 in Carlisle[2] suggests that Roman forces had ventured deep into Brigantia at a time when it has traditionally been believed that they had only just established themselves in York. Although there is increasing evidence that the advance to Carlisle included troops operating west of the Pennines by the early AD 70s,[3] the route across Stainmore also appears to have been used, and some of the sites there, and in North Yorkshire, may have their origins as part of that campaign.

AD 71–2 sees a change in the character of Roman sites in the county with the establishment of permanent Roman military installations. The earliest include the fortress at York, the newly discovered fort at Roecliffe[4] and probably Malton fort. During the governorship of Agricola, *c*AD 77–83, further forts were established at Catterick, Cawthorn Camps, Lease Rigg, possibly at Roall, Healam Bridge, Wensley and perhaps Stamford Bridge. However, the situation was not static and the fort at Roecliffe was abandoned in the AD 80s. Despite its short occupation it attracted a civilian extra-mural settlement, as did many other forts. Roecliffe may have been succeeded by a fort on the site of the later Roman town of Aldborough, where military finds are known but certain structural evidence for a fort is lacking. A similar shift may be seen at Bainbridge. There the fort, which survives as a prominent earthwork (see photo on page 49), was established in *c*AD 90–105, possibly as a successor to a smaller fort near Wensley that is only known from air photographs. Another fort of possible Agricolan date is known at Newton Kyme and a further early fort has been suggested on Carkin Moor, but the identification of the latter as a fort has been questioned.

Intimately associated with the military occupation of the county is the system of Roman roads.[5] First and foremost they represent military infrastructure — they were built to aid the movement of troops both through and within the area. Dere Street (M8b), which runs up the west side of the Vale of York, is the most significant road, linking York and the south with the northern frontier. Dere Street itself runs north to Corbridge and the east end of Hadrian's

TIMELINE FOR THE HISTORICAL PERIOD

A.D
2000 | 1996 Designation of City of York as a Unitary Authority
1974 Local Government Re-organisation
1973 Britain joined the European Economic Community
1970 Opening of M62 Motorway
1963 Opening of the University of York
1954 Designation of Yorkshire Dales National Park
1952 Designation of North York Moors National Park
1949 National Parks and Access to the Countryside Act
1939-1945 The Second World War
1928 Representation of the People Act
1919 Establishment of the Forestry Commission
1914-1918 The First World War
1900 | 1895 Foundation of National Trust
1887 Opening of newly-built railway station at York
1875 Opening of Settle - Carlisle Railway
1872 Public Health Act
1854 Establishment of Great North Eastern Railway Co.
1851 Religious Census
1841 York - Newcastle Railway
1835 Municipal Corporation Act
1834 The Poor Law Amendment Act: the New Poor Law
1832 The Reform Act
1825 Opening of the Stockton and Darlington Railway
1817-1818 Christopher Greenwood's Map
1811 National Society for the Education of the Poor founded
1800 | 1801 First Census of Population
1794 Tuke's General Survey of agriculture in N.Yorkshire
1784 Power spinning of cotton introduced at Skipton
1777 Thomas Jeffery's Map
1752 York-Scarborough Turnpike Road
1747-1768 Construction of water races, North York Moors
1741 Turnpiking of Great North Road
1739 Foundation of Methodism by John & Charles Wesley
1727 Act for Improvement of River Ouse
1719 Founding of York Courant newspaper
1701-1724 Navigation work on the River Derwent
1700 | 1700-1737 Building of Castle Howard
1697-1698 Celia Fiennes travels in Yorkshire
1689 Toleration Act
1660 Restoration of the Monarchy
1653-1659 The Protectorate
1650s Development of Quakerism
1649-1653 The Commonwealth
1648 Second Civil War
1644 Battle of Marston Moor
1642-1646 The Civil War
1611 John Speed's map
1600 |
c.1570 - 1646 Rise and development of Puritanism
1577 Christopher Saxton's Map
1547,1572,1597,1601 Poor Law Acts
1536-1539 Dissolution of Monasteries
1536-1537 Pilgrimage of Grace
1514-1530 Cardinal Wolsey Archbishop of York
1500 | 1485 Battle of Bosworth Field
1455-1485 Wars of the Roses
1400 | 1377,1379,1380-81 Poll Taxes
1361,1369,1375 Further Plague Outbreaks
1349-1351 Black Death (Bubonic Plague)
1300 | 1300-1399 Defence against the Scots
1215 Magna Carta
1200 |
1132 Cistercian Monastery established at Rievaulx
1130-1190 peak of development of religious houses
1100 | 1086 Domesday Book
c.1080-1342 Building and Rebuilding of York Minster
1069 Benedictine Monastery established at Selby
1066-1216 The Consolidation of the North
1066 Norman Conquest: Battle of Stamford Bridge
1000 |
900 | 866 Capture of York by Viking army
c.851-1066 Anglo-Scandinavian & later Anglo-Saxon period
800 |
700 |
657 Founding of Whitby Abbey
600 | 627 Foundation of church at York by Edwin
500 |
410 End of Roman Occupation
400 | 400- c.850 Early-Middle Anglo-Saxon period
c.400 Roman army withdrawal from York
300 | 306 Constantine proclaimed Roman Emperor at York
200 | c.211 York the largest town in Britain
100 |
71 Roman Military advance to York
0 | 43 Roman Invasion

The Roman fort at Bainbridge with traces of the annexe in the foreground. The outline of the defences can be clearly seen with multiple ditches on the west (top of photograph), along with the gates on each side. Within the fort the *via principalis* linking the north and south gates and traces of military buildings can be seen. The buildings are partially obscured by spoil heaps from excavations.
NMR 12971/25 © Crown copyright. NMR.

Wall, with a link to Carlisle across Stainmore (M82). Dere Street is studded with forts, but curiously none are known along the other main north–south route through the county on the eastern side of the Vale of York (M80). The reasons for the difference are not known, but it possible that the eastern route was later and had less military significance. York itself is pivotal in the road system and in the eastern part of the county, Malton, by virtue of its position at a key river crossing, also acts as a major route focus. A further piece of military infrastructure has been suggested at Catterick, where rescue excavations uncovered what was claimed as an amphitheatre or *ludus* for military training.[6] Air photographs have clearly demonstrated that it is a Neolithic henge which must have been reduced in height substantially by the Roman period when Dere Street was built over it.[7]

One of the Romans objectives in conquering Brigantia was to gain access to its natural resources, the best attested of which is the lead of the Pennines. In North Yorkshire, Roman lead pigs stamped with the emperor's name are known from Heyshaw Moor (Domitian, AD 81–96) and Greenhow Hill (Trajan, 98–117), both near Grassington. A further lead pig is reported from Hurst in Swaledale, apparently stamped Adrian (? = Hadrian, 117–38).[8] How long this exploitation extended is not known, but the demand for lead would have been there throughout the Roman period. It is probable that direct imperial control would fairly rapidly have been replaced by private leasees, and stamped and dateable pigs would no longer have been produced.

Away from York, most if not all the forts were abandoned from the time of Hadrian, with some being reoccupied in around AD 161–3 when the death of Antoninus Pius led to the abandonment of Scotland. At that date, forts at Catterick, Bainbridge and Malton were re-established, with the latter two at least being occupied until the end of the Roman period, and probably into the fifth century.

Civilian settlement during the first two centuries appears in a number of forms. The extra-mural settlements around forts contained official buildings such as the *mansio*, inn or posting-house for officials using the *cursus publicus* (imperial post), known at Catterick. In addition they incorporated shops serving the needs of the soldiery not covered by the military supply system, and the homes of craftsmen and the unofficial families of the soldiers. Such settlements, normally termed *vici*, are known at Catterick, Bainbridge, Malton and Newton Kyme, and one probably formed the nucleus for the development of Aldborough. In the second century, probably under Hadrian, Aldborough became the centre of the Brigantian *civitas* or civilian administrative area that took in the whole of North Yorkshire and probably most of northern England, although how military and civilian government interrelated in the North is not clear.

In addition to York (*Eboracum*), the Latin names of a number of sites are known: Aldborough (*Isurium Brigantum*), Catterick (*Cataractonium*) and Bainbridge (*Virosidum*).[9] Traditionally Malton has been identified as *Derventio*; however, it has been persuasively argued that it ought to be equated with *Delgovica*, and *Derventio* identified as the little-known site at Stamford Bridge.[10] Those names that we know derive from Ptolemy's *Geography*,

Cawthorn camps, on the North York Moors, near Pickering. Early Roman military complex.
NMR 12381/27 © Crown copyright. NMR.

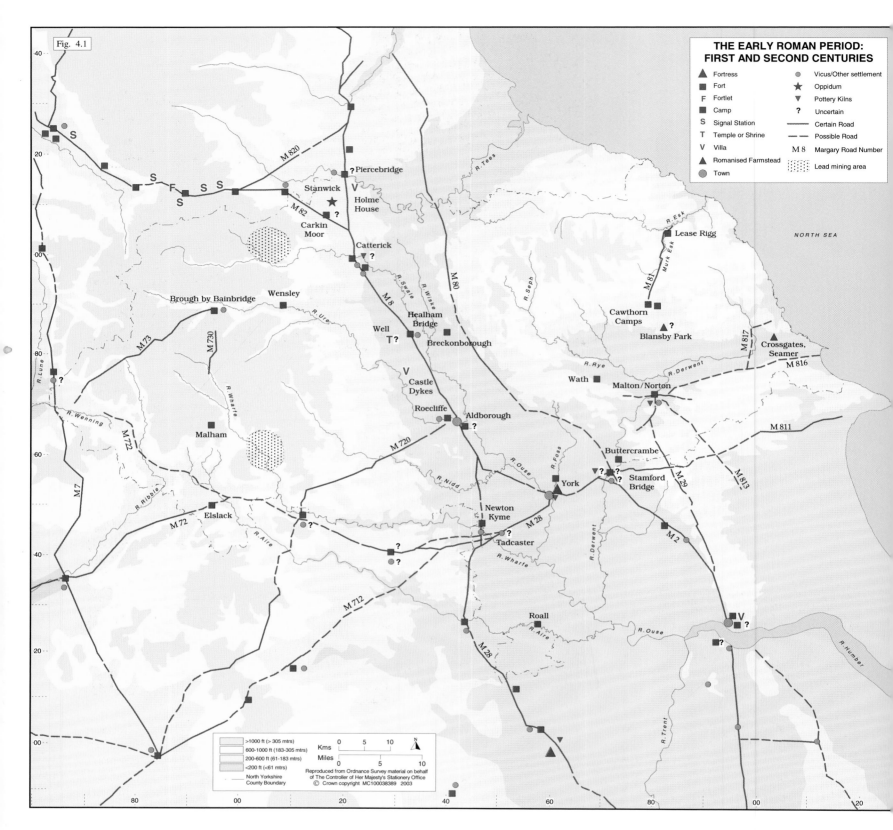

Fig. 4.1

**THE EARLY ROMAN PERIOD:
FIRST AND SECOND CENTURIES**

▲ Fortress   ● Vicus/Other settlement
■ Fort   ★ Oppidum
F Fortlet   ▼ Pottery Kilns
■ Camp   ? Uncertain
S Signal Station   —— Certain Road
T Temple or Shrine   - - - Possible Road
V Villa   M 8 Margary Road Number
▲ Romanised Farmstead   ⬚ Lead mining area
● Town

>1000 ft (> 305 mtrs)
600-1000 ft (183-305 mtrs)
200-600 ft (61-183 mtrs)
<200 ft (<61 mtrs)
North Yorkshire County Boundary

Reproduced from Ordnance Survey material on behalf
of The Controller of Her Majesty's Stationery Office
© Crown copyright MC100038389 2003

Roman road books (the *Antonine Itinerary* and *Ravenna Cosmography* — albeit in post-Roman copies) and the *Notitia Dignatatum*, a late Roman army list.

Other settlements develop, such as that astride Dere Street at Bainesse three miles (2km) south of *Cataractonium*. Here from *c*AD 80, rectilinear buildings line Dere Street, the settlement eventually extending for three-quarters of a mile (1.25km). Another roadside settlements is suspected at Thornton-le-Street; Tadcaster (?*Calcaria*) has long been suggested as a Roman settlement, although little physical evidence has been found; and ribbon development is known south of the Tees at Piercebridge, where the main settlement and fort site lie on the north bank.

In the early Roman period, most of the native population will have carried on much as before (see case study 2 on pages 58-61) living in a variety of isolated farmsteads, small

Line of Roman Road (left of photograph), from Copmanthorpe to Tadcaster, Vale of York.
NMR 12148/31 © *Crown copyright. NMR.*

Second- and third-century buildings at Bainesse Roman roadside settlement near Catterick.
© English Heritage.

villages and elongated settlements focused on trackways. The immediate impact of Rome is often negligible, the first centuries of Roman rule often only being betrayed by a few sherds of hard-fired Romanised pottery, and in the uplands there is sometimes not even that. During the first and second centuries some changes are seen. A minority of morphologically native sites, such as Staxton[11], acquire elements of Roman material culture; at least one villa develops, at Holme House near Piercebridge;[12] and a limited number of sites display Roman attributes such as rectilinear masonry structures, for example Crab Lane,[13] Crossgates. However, we are woefully ignorant of the origins of most of the villas: in many cases only the latest (third- and fourth-century) levels have been investigated, and consequently they are largely seen as third- and fourth-century phenomena. One exception is the Whin Fields site at Langton, where some second-century stone buildings are known and appear to represent a development from a first-century farmstead within a ditched enclosure.[14] Both Holme House and Crab Lane are abandoned by the end of the second century, a time when there are changes in the rural landscape which are far from being understood.

Beyond the obvious changes represented by forts, *vici* and those Romanised buildings that appear in the countryside, the Roman period brought other developments. The late pre-Roman Iron Age pottery tradition had been conservative with little evidence of innovation,[15] but the arrival of the Roman army brought new types of hard-fired ceramics and a vast increase in the import of fine pottery, such as samian from Gaul, as well as luxury goods represented by amphorae. Pottery was manufactured under military control at York, Malton and possibly Catterick, where pottery production from at least the second century is known. Although freestone had been used in constructing roundhouses in the Iron Age, a massive expansion of quarrying was required to cater for the construction of buildings in stone once the initial timber phases of forts and other sites were renewed. Vast quantities of tile were required for roofing and use in hypocausts (heating systems). Although Iron Age Brigantia had a rich tradition of decorative art,[16] new artforms were introduced, notably sculpture and stone-carving, along with major changes in existing art forms such as jewellery.[17] Crafts and industries known in the Iron Age continued to be practised. The quarrying of stone for querns continued, and although the Iron Age beehive type remained to be used until at least AD 200,[18] the flat rotary quern was introduced, local products being supplemented by examples in lava imported from Germany. Both beehive and flat rotary querns are known from quarries on the North York Moors and are common site-finds. Iron-working continued in the Iron Age tradition on 'native' sites, such as Roxby[19] and Levisham Moor;[20] however, on Romanised sites the scale of use expanded considerably. Similarly, leather must have been utilised in the Iron Age but we have little direct evidence. In contrast a massive midden associated with the Flavian fort at Catterick demonstrates the scale of leather use in the Roman period, including considerable evidence for recycling of unworn parts of artefacts.

Changes in agriculture are more difficult to recognise. However, the reorganisation of landholdings can be seen; in part these may arise from the establishment of forts, but also possibly as a result of the increased demand that the army and the new civilian settlements represented. Regular land divisions in the Tadcaster area have been argued as representing part of the territorium of the York fortress.[21] The most obvious impact was in animal husbandry, where by the end of the second century the appearance of 'unimproved' 'Celtic shorthorn' cattle in bone assemblages from York is unusual.[22]

One half of a Roman flat rotary quern. Now in the Ryedale Folk Museum.
© P Wilson.

4.2 THE THIRD, FOURTH AND FIFTH CENTURIES
PETER WILSON

North Yorkshire occupies what can be seen as the interface between 'civilian' southern and eastern Britain, and the 'military' north and west. Despite this, the number of forts occupied in the later Roman period was limited (**fig 4.2**). Until recently it was believed that military occupation at Catterick ended around AD 200. However, the discovery of a third fort on the site suggests its military history may have been similar to that of Bainbridge and Malton, and extended into the fourth if not fifth century;[23] and at Newton Kyme a new fort was established in the late third century after a period of abandonment. In the last decades of the fourth century, possibly as late as the AD 380s, a series of 'signal stations' was established on the coast. Four are known for certain: Filey, Scarborough (see illustration on page 54), Goldsborough and outside the county at Huntcliff, whilst a fifth is suspected at Ravenscar on the basis of an inscription. Traditionally they are seen as a system designed to combat the threat of coastal raiding, either signalling to a fleet, or to troops stationed at Malton via intermediate stations. This view has been challenged due to the incompleteness of the system, the lack of evidence for a late Roman fleet on the Yorkshire coast, the difficulty of signalling given the prevalence of sea-frets and the time it would take for troops from Malton to respond.[24]

Through the third century, Romanisation may be seen to increase. At Catterick and Malton, stone buildings become the norm in the civil settlements, and Catterick at least can reasonably be termed a town. Similar structural change can be suggested for Aldborough, but the site is so poorly known that little can be said with certainty. However, it is likely that the changes there started in the second century following its elevation to *civitas* capital, a time when it is known that the town was defended with an earthen rampart and ditch. Stone defences were constructed at Aldborough around AD 200, during the third century at Malton and around the end of the third century at Catterick. Aldborough is a conventional Roman town with a street grid that presumably originated in the second century, and Catterick has regular elements in its planning, whereas Malton appears to represent organic growth focused on the roads leading to the fort. At Norton, across the Derwent from Malton, a substantial suburb existed from the mid-second century, if not before, but as with many aspects of the Roman archaeology of North Yorkshire, the third and fourth centuries

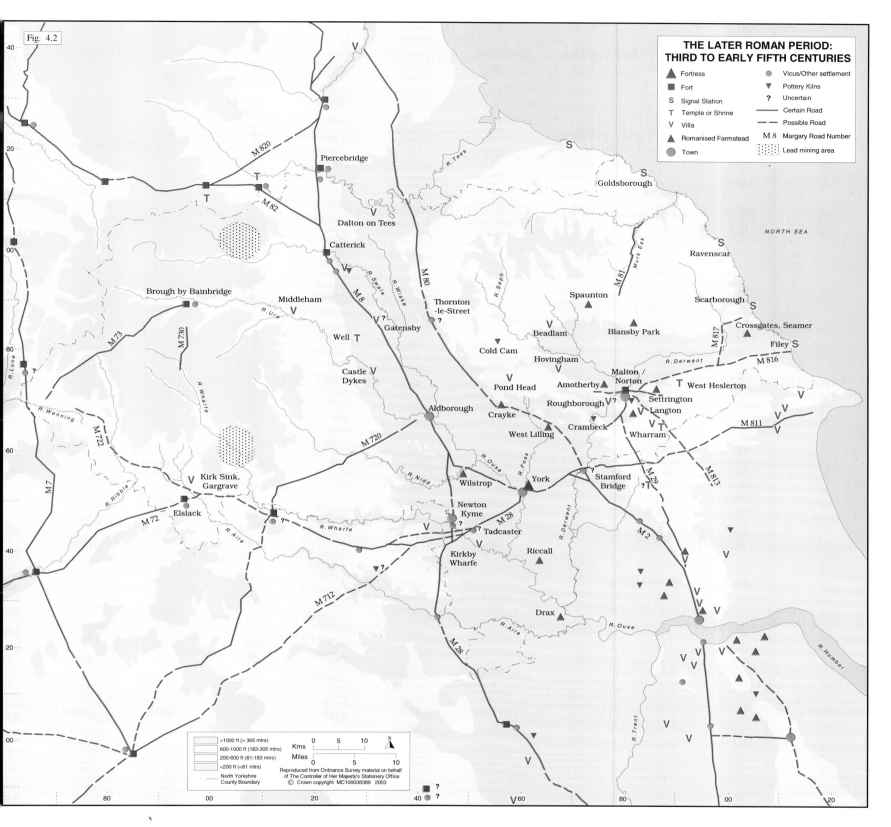

Fig. 4.2

**THE LATER ROMAN PERIOD:
THIRD TO EARLY FIFTH CENTURIES**

	Fortress		Vicus/Other settlement
■	Fort	▼	Pottery Kilns
S	Signal Station	?	Uncertain
T	Temple or Shrine		Certain Road
V	Villa		Possible Road
▲	Romanised Farmstead	M 8	Margary Road Number
●	Town		Lead mining area

NORTH SEA

Piercebridge
Goldsborough
Dalton on Tees
Catterick
Ravenscar
Brough by Bainbridge
Middleham
Spaunton
Scarborough
Thornton-le-Street
Crossgates, Seamer
Gatensby
Beadlam
Blansby Park
Filey
Well
Cold Cam
Castle Dykes
Hovingham
Malton / Norton
West Heslerton
Pond Head
Amotherby
Aldborough
Crayke
Roughborough
Settrington
Langton
West Lilling
Crambeck
Wharram
Kirk Sink, Gargrave
Wilstrop
York
Stamford Bridge
Elslack
Newton Kyme
Tadcaster
Kirkby Wharfe
Riccall
Drax

>1000 ft (> 305 mtrs)
600-1000 ft (183-305 mtrs)
200-600 ft (61-183 mtrs)
<200 ft (<61 mtrs)
North Yorkshire County Boundary

Kms 0 5 10
Miles 0 5 10

Reproduced from Ordnance Survey material on behalf
of The Controller of Her Majesty's Stationery Office
© Crown copyright MC100038389 2003

are better known. Roman Norton appears to have had a large 'industrial' component, with a major pottery industry in the third century.

In the countryside there was an expansion of villas, villas being Romanised farms rather than simply country houses. However, as noted above, we do not really have the evidence to generalise on their development and it is possible that the model of gradual development proposed for Whin Fields, Langton, may be the norm. Langton also demonstrates another important aspect of the countryside, that there was a continuing process of change. There is evidence for two villas and a farmstead in the Langton area, and it seems that over a period of time the Whin Fields villa absorbed both the other sites into its 'estate',[25] although, as only the Whin Fields site has been excavated, the chronology of these changes is uncertain. It is possible that Whin Fields and other villas did control a centralised estate, but again our knowledge of the tenurial position is uncertain. Villas such as Beadlam, which has three major ranges and subsidiary buildings,[26] were clearly complex entities, but was the village known at Wharram Percy village dependent on the putative villa?[27] Did the villas have control of a range of land types, including upland grazing away from their core? Does the development of the probable villa at RAF Catterick[28] represent the cause or consequence of the decline of the roadside settlement at Bainesse some 1,600 feet (500m) to the west?

Uncertainty surrounds the identification of some sites generally regarded as villas, particularly those partially excavated sites associated with water sources, such as Wharram le Street[29] and Well,[30] which may represent shrines. The recent discovery of a late Roman shrine site at West Heslerton,[31] apparently constructed when Christianity was meant to be in the ascendancy, suggests that the population of the North Yorkshire countryside may have been socially conservative. Although a possible temple site is known at Catterick, away from York our information on Roman period religion is limited. There is no physical evidence of Christianity, other than two putative *chi-rho* symbols from Catterick, both of which are probably misidentifications. However, we know that a bishop from York attended the Council of Arles in AD 314.

The north range of Beadlam villa with a mosaic in situ towards the top of the photograph. The mosaic had been damaged through collapse of the underlying hypocaust.
© R H Hayes.

The Roman signal station at Scarborough surrounded by the medieval castle. The defensive ditch, outer wall and the central tower of the signal station can be seen overlain by the remains of the chapel of Our Lady and associated medieval domestic buildings.
NMR 12618/04 © Crown copyright. NMR.

Catterick Roman town. Dere Street, part of the Roman street grid and some of the buildings within the town can be seen to the right of the modern road; traces of the fort are visible in front and to the left of the farm.
NMR 12743/31 © Crown copyright. NMR.

Mosaic from the Roman site at Well. Now displayed in Well Church.
© P Wilson.

The Malton area developed as a major pottery-producing centre in the third and fourth centuries, with production at Norton (noted above), (East) Knapton and in particular Crambeck. Pottery from the latter site dominated the pottery supply of northern England throughout the fourth century. Third- and fourth-century pottery production is also known at other sites including Catterick and Cold Cam, the latter example possibly being a single isolated kiln.

Other crafts and industries that are known in North Yorkshire or the wider region include the manufacture of pewter, mosaic manufacture, wall-painting, iron-working, and coal mining. Inscriptions become less common, but quarrying presumably continues given the evidence of new buildings, although the dating of quarries is difficult. Similarly, the extraction of iron ore and lead must have continued. However, much probably went on that is almost invisible to archaeology except under the most favourable circumstances, such as the coppicing of woodland for fuel and the manufacture of wooden and leather artefacts.

The end of the Roman period has been seen as a time of decline, typified by 'squatter occupation', people continuing to occupy sites, but not in their previous style. Beadlam and the Malton 'Town House' both providing evidence of poor-quality repairs to mosaic floors, and at Catterick the unfinished fourth-century bath-house was used for accommodation.

Although the existence of fifth-century occupation on a number of sites has been known for some time, the end of the Roman period is only now beginning to be understood and models being developed for the period post-AD 400. A recent suggestion that we may be able to distinguish fifth-century finds assemblages from those of the late fourth century may offer a way forward.[32] The occupation in towns appears to fade away, or fade imperceptibly into less intensive Anglian occupation. 'Town life', where it continued, may have become 'life in towns', and the use of a number of Roman sites for sixth-century burials[33] suggests occupation continued on some sites, albeit in restricted areas, or was located close to the Roman occupation areas. We cannot see an end to Roman North Yorkshire, only that Anglian material culture became dominant, presumably in many cases used by the descendants of Romano-Britons. That there was conflict is dramatically demonstrated by the evidence of violence at Goldsborough signal station,[34] but the loss of late levels on many sites to agriculture, and the unsophisticated techniques of earlier excavators, biases our data-sets. We might anticipate some considerable Anglian settlement amongst the existing population and a British 'kingdom' may have survived for some time in the Craven Dales.[35] The latter would have existed alongside the better known post-Roman British Kingdom of Elmet and the, presumably British, *regio* of Loidis mentioned by Bede, both of which extended into the southern part of the county.

THE FUTURE

Although there are many areas where additional data would be welcome, we might highlight the following as particular problems requiring urgent attention: the lack of large well-excavated cemeteries away from York; the need for extensive excavation of the early levels underlying a villa complex; the limited excavated evidence from non-villa rural sites, and a general lack of good-quality environmental evidence away from York. On a broader scale, to address the transition from the Roman to Anglian periods we need further large-scale exploration of sites using modern techniques that target the later Roman and later levels to redress the imbalances in our evidence.

Mosaic from Roman Malton. Found in the fourth-century 'Town House' excavated in 1949-52.
© R H Hayes.

4.3 CASE STUDY I: ROMAN YORK (*EBORACUM*)
PATRICK OTTAWAY

INTRODUCTION

The Roman Ninth Legion arrived in York in *circa* AD 71 and built a fortress on the north-east bank of the River Ouse (**fig 4.3**). In addition to its strategic value as a base for the conquest of northern Britain, the site had a number of natural advantages. Firstly, it lay close to a glacial moraine which had provided a raised land route running east-west across the low-lying Vale of York throughout prehistory. Secondly, York lay at the junction of the moraine with the Ouse at a point where the river could be easily crossed. Thirdly, the River Foss, approaching from the north, meets the Ouse at York and together the rivers provided a natural defence for two sides of the fortress. Finally, the Ouse provided a navigable route, via the Humber Estuary, to the East Coast and North Sea some thirty-seven miles (60km) distant.

In Roman times the Ouse at York was probably a little wider than it is today, but its level was, on average, about ten feet (3m) lower than today. The course of the Foss has changed

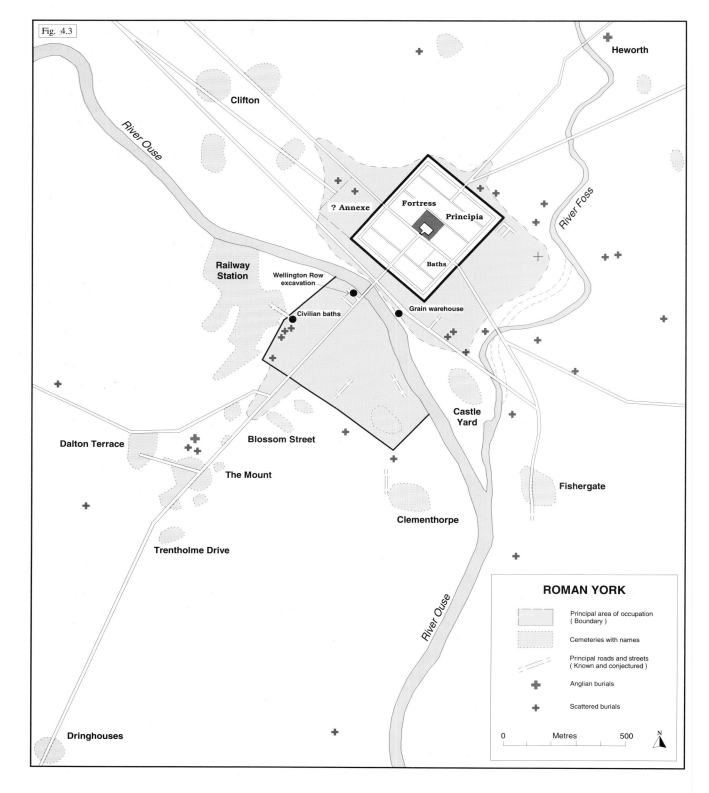

Fig. 4.3

Heworth

Clifton

River Ouse

? Annexe

Fortress

Principia

River Foss

Railway
Station

Wellington Row
excavation

Civilian baths

Baths

Grain warehouse

Castle
Yard

Dalton Terrace

Blossom Street

The Mount

Fishergate

Clementhorpe

Trentholme Drive

River Ouse

ROMAN YORK

Principal area of occupation
(Boundary)

Cemeteries with names

Principal roads and streets
(Known and conjectured)

Anglian burials

Scattered burials

Dringhouses

0   Metres   500

N

considerably due to the creation of the King's Fishpool in the Norman period and to canalisation in more recent times.

THE ROMAN FORTRESS

The legionary fortress, base of the Ninth Legion until *c*AD 120 and then of the Sixth, occupied a playing card-shaped site of around sixty-five acres (*c*26ha).[36] Its corners were close to the cardinal points and it faced south-west towards the Ouse. The line of the two principal streets, the *via praetoria*, running north-east/south-west, and *via principalis*, running north-west/south-east, are closely followed today by Stonegate and Petergate respectively.

Fortress buildings which can be securely located include the headquarters (*principia*), of which the main hall was examined in excavations at York Minster.[37] The bath house lay in the south quadrant, and barracks stood both north-west of the headquarters and on the north-east and south-west sides of the fortress. The headquarters and baths may have been built of stone without timber precursors, but other buildings were initially timber before being replaced in stone in the mid-second century.[38]

The fortress defences initially consisted of a ditch, a rampart, and timber gates and towers.[39] Reconstruction in stone took place largely in the late second and early third centuries. This involved great architectural splendour on the south-west side of the site with a polygonal projecting tower at both the south and west corners (the latter surviving today as the Multangular Tower), and between them six projecting interval towers.

In the late first to early second century, army supply facilities were located immediately outside the fortress. Excavations have located a grain warehouse on the banks of the Ouse,[40] and evidence for pottery and tile manufacture between the east corner of the fortress and the Foss. The main Roman roads radiating from the fortress probably belong to the early years of occupation,[41] although only the road to the south-west has been dated to this period archaeologically.

THE CIVILIAN SETTLEMENTS

Civilian settlement of urban character both north-east and south-west of the Ouse began in earnest in the mid- to late second century.[42] By the time of the Emperor Septimius Severus, who died in York in AD 211, *Eboracum* was the largest town in northern Britain. In the reign of Caracalla (211-217), York became the capital of the province of lower Britain (*Britannia Inferior*). The town was promoted to *colonia* status at about the same time. In first-century Britain a *colonia* had been a settlement of legionary veterans, but by the third century the title was largely honorary.

North-east of the Ouse, evidence for urbanisation comes largely from areas south-east and south-west of the fortress. A new riverside street was laid out, and temples dedicated to Hercules and to the Imperial cult,[43] the existence of which are suggested by inscriptions, may have been more or less contemporary.

South-west of the Ouse, the dominant influence on the settlement plan was the main road from the south-west. Excavations at Wellington Row showed the road level was raised in the mid-second century in such a way as to create a causeway probably related to the construction of a bridge over the Ouse. Other streets south-west of the Ouse appear to originate in the mid-late second century. The town's public buildings are not well known, although parts of one and possibly two public bath houses have been found.[44] The presence of a number of temples is implied by inscriptions. In the south-eastern part of the settlement, evidence has been found for substantial terraces which supported stone buildings, probably large houses.[45]

It is likely that the settlement south-west of the Ouse was walled along a line followed by the surviving medieval defences, although archaeological evidence for this is slight.[46] Outside the fortress and principal urban areas, scattered evidence for Roman settlement, largely in the form of ditched enclosures and refuse deposits, has been found up to a distance of some two miles (3km). In addition, peripheral areas were occupied by the extensive cemeteries which appear to have been focused on the main approach roads.

YORK IN THE FOURTH CENTURY

On the death of his father Constantius I in York in AD 306, Constantine the Great was acclaimed emperor here. The extent to which the fortress was garrisoned in the fourth century is unclear, although it may have been the base of an officer known as the *Dux Britanniarum*.[47] There is little evidence for new military buildings, although there was some reorganisation of the headquarters and adjacent barracks. The latest resurfacing of the principal streets dates to the mid-fourth century. The so-called 'Anglian Tower', some 250 feet (75m) north-east of the Multangular Tower, is probably a late Roman addition to the defences.[48] The *colonia* retained its status as a provincial capital after Diocletian's further subdivision of Britain and also became the seat of a bishop. Evidence for new buildings is, however, limited to a small number of houses with mosaic pavements.[49]

In the second half of the fourth century, minor streets were abandoned and some buildings were deliberately demolished, although others survived and refuse deposits continued to accumulate. There is no suggestion of wholesale abandonment until the collapse of the political and economic system on which Roman York depended in the early fifth century. The continuing importance of the city as a central place is suggested by the presence of two late-fifth or early-sixth century cremation cemeteries, one at Heworth and the other on the Mount, both adjacent to Roman roads.[50]

INTRODUCTION

The historical evidence, even when combined with that from archaeological excavations, provides only a very limited picture of what North Yorkshire was like in Roman times. A scattering of forts and small towns, the city of York and a handful of villas provide tangible remains of the most Romanised parts of society, but what of the rest of the countryside and the major part of the population? Over the last fifty years our understanding of the extent of settlement in the Roman and preceding periods has been changed by the use of aerial photography.

Much of North Yorkshire responds well to aerial reconnaissance and each year continues to provide many, sometimes hundreds, of new discoveries.[51] When the sun is low in the sky, slight earthworks, almost invisible at ground level can be recorded from the air by the shadows they cast. Flying over areas with free-draining soils, especially where the geology is limestone, chalk or sands and gravels, and particularly in dry summers, buried remains can be identified by the differential growth of plants. Because of this, aerial survey remains the single most effective tool for archaeological prospection for much of the area.

Careful study of photographs taken for archaeological and non-archaeological purposes can reveal not only the whereabouts and form of past settlements, but also the extent and some of the character of the contemporary field systems that covered much (even most) of the landscape. However, aerial photography cannot normally be used to identify the date of a site with certainty or precision, but what it does provide is the basis for a general overview that can then be tested by selective excavation. By 2000 about half of North Yorkshire's archaeology had been mapped from the air by English Heritage's National Mapping Programme (NMP) and this has generally doubled the number of known sites of any given period. **Fig 4.4** shows the distribution of sites with a possible Roman date on the databases of the National Monuments Record (NMR) and outlines show the area mapped by the NMP projects.[52]

THE RURAL LANDSCAPE

The wide variety of natural landscapes in the county of North Yorkshire have resulted in a similar wide variety of rural settlements and economies, and the evidence suggests that in the Roman period there was equal variety. The Ordnance Survey map of Roman Britain shows remarkably few sites in North Yorkshire (**figs 4.1** and **4.2** are based on this), but whilst the upland areas of the high moors and Pennine Dales may have always been relatively sparsely settled, the whole of the landscape probably saw a degree of exploitation in the Roman period.

The evidence suggests that the major part of the landscape of Roman North Yorkshire was parcelled up and farmed at a local level, perhaps sometimes maintaining field systems that were already well established. Only a few Roman roads striding across the countryside and a few earlier boundaries suggest any larger-scale land division.[53] Between the forts and the towns lay a network of fields, farms and small settlements which, although able to supply the

Roman site at Lilling Green showing internal structures and part of the surrounding field system.
NMR 4429/35. © Crown copyright. NMR.

new bigger market of the towns and army, were probably operated at a local level. At this local level there is often a considerable degree of coherency in the plan of the field systems, sometimes covering an area not dissimilar to those of a modern civil parish.

Many field systems surviving as earthworks or revealed by cropmarks have a layout based on evenly spaced parallel field boundaries lying along one predominant axis and often up to about 0.6 mile (1km) long, known as a coaxial system. As the few selected areas in **fig 4.5** show, there are considerable variations — in the spacing of the boundaries, whether they include trackways and on the regularity of internal cross-divisions. Evidence is very limited, but these coaxial field systems appear to have first been laid out in North Yorkshire in the Iron Age and Roman periods. In South Yorkshire, an extensive area of coaxial fields has been shown by excavation to have been in use in the later Roman period, but there is some evidence from Swaledale of coaxial systems in an upland area originating in the Iron Age.[54]

RURAL SETTLEMENT

The rural settlements found both in conjunction with the field systems and in apparent isolation show a wide variety of forms. Foundations of individual buildings are relatively rare in the record from aerial photography and so the evidence tends to be biased towards the enclosure surrounding the buildings; it is hard to estimate how many may have enclosed quite Romanised, but small, villa buildings as at Whin Fields, Langton.[55] Simple enclosures containing a single large hut circle are a recurring feature in the evidence from cropmarks in the Vale of York. A group associated with fields (**fig 4.5**) has been excavated near Naburn, and appears to have been in use in the early Roman period but may have been built earlier.[56] Sometimes strings of enclosures are strung out along trackways, suggesting an elongated village.[57]

More elaborate sites showing a higher degree of planning are also known, usually consisting of a large regular enclosure surrounded by a single or double ditch and subdivided internally. These are sometimes referred to as villa-type enclosures, because field-walking and excavation evidence has shown that some at least contained buildings with tiled roofs, mosaics and wall plaster. Examples at Wharram Grange, Settrington and Lilling Green have a fairly regular system of internal pens and may be indicative of stock-rearing.[58] The system of small pens and enclosures would have provided ideal conditions for sorting/trading and breeding stock from a farm surrounded by fields for grazing, but equally they may have been paddocks for use with animals used for draught and transport. At Burythorpe a similar site shows several phases of development which may reflect the gradual growth in wealth of a farm or villa.[59]

LOCAL LANDSCAPES

Where the evidence from aerial photographs has been pulled together by mapping, it is possible to make a few generalised statements about regional variations in the form of the Roman landscape.

On the Yorkshire Wolds[60] there is evidence that practically the whole landscape was subdivided long before the Roman conquest and that a large part of this structure remained throughout the Roman period. As well as the major boundaries, numerous trackways can be seen, often running for several miles and frequently with settlements strung out along them. Sometimes secondary boundaries run parallel to the settlements and, in between, the landscape is divided up with roughly perpendicular field boundaries suggesting a local parcelling up for farming purposes. Known patterns of coaxial field system are very limited in their extent and do not appear to have been a major feature of this landscape.

In the Pennine Dales of North Yorkshire,[61] all the major valleys show evidence of fairly intensive agricultural use which appears to predate the medieval landscape — although this is often most apparent on the higher ground that saw less intensive use in later periods. Dating evidence is very limited, but suggests intensification of use from the later Iron Age and continuing into the Roman period.[62] The best-known early field systems are those near Grassington showing a coaxial pattern, but other similar landscapes appear throughout Wharfedale, and undated examples like that in the valley bottom north of Kettlewell (**fig 4.5**) may also have Roman or even prehistoric origins. Similar systems are known in Wensleydale and its side valleys, Swaledale and Ribblesdale. Work in Littondale, where coaxial field systems are again prevalent, has started to reveal a pattern of Roman farms and fields in use in the third century AD,[63] but it is not clear whether the fields originated at an earlier period.

In the Vale of York,[64] air-photo evidence shows that on the free-draining soils there were extensive field systems defined by ditches. The pattern of these fields sometimes suggest that they continued onto the lower lying ground, into areas more prone to waterlogging where the ditches could have helped to drain the ground, however, air-photo evidence is less forthcoming in such areas. The commonest plan for the field systems is a coaxial one with enclosures containing hut circles generally dispersed amongst the fields.

Further Reading

M K Clark, *A gazetteer of Roman remains in East Yorkshire* (Leeds: Roman Malton and District Report 5, 1935).

S S Frere, *Britannia: A history of Roman Britain,* 3rd edition (London: Guild Publishing, 1987).

B R Hartley and R L Fitts, *The Brigantes* (Gloucester: Sutton, 1988).

B Jones and D Mattingley, *An Atlas of Roman Britain* (Oxford: Blackwell, 1990).

P Ottaway, *Roman York* (London: Batsford/English Heritage, 1993).

H Ramm, *The Parisi* (London: Duckworth, 1978).

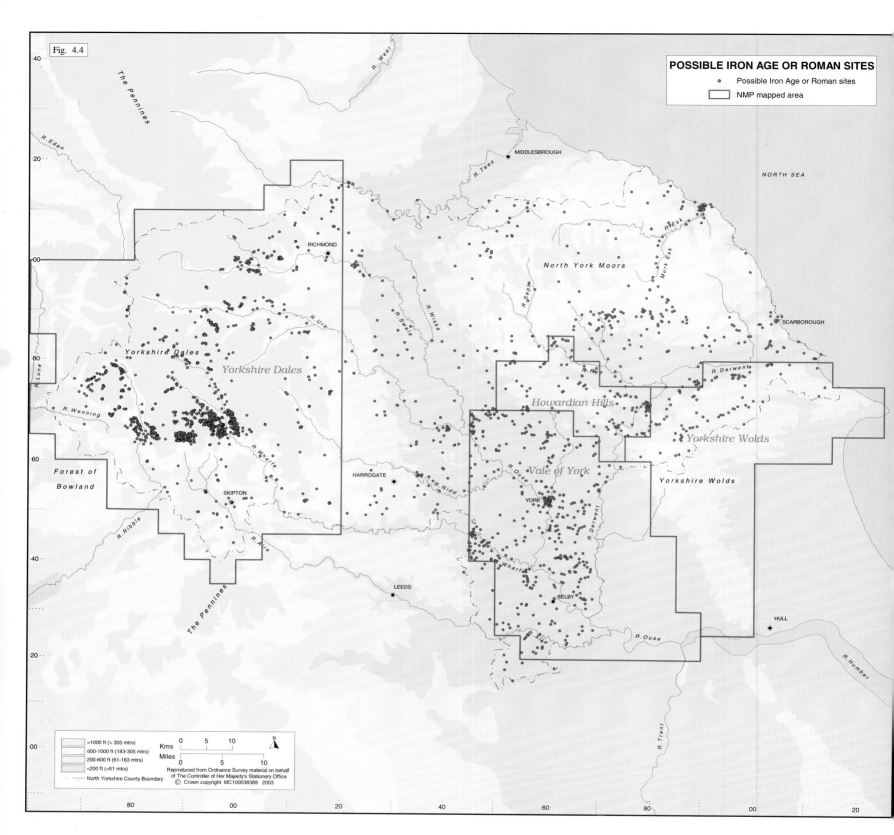

Fig. 4.4

POSSIBLE IRON AGE OR ROMAN SITES

· Possible Iron Age or Roman sites

▢ NMP mapped area

>1000 ft (> 305 mtrs)
600-1000 ft (183-305 mtrs)
200-600 ft (61-183 mtrs)
<200 ft (<61 mtrs)
- - - North Yorkshire County Boundary

Kms 0 5 10
Miles 0 5 10

Reproduced from Ordnance Survey material on behalf
of The Controller of Her Majesty's Stationery Office
© Crown copyright MC100038389 2003

CONCLUSION

Where the conditions are good for aerial archaeological survey (earthworks under short vegetation mainly in the Pennine Dales, or cropmarks on the free-draining soils under arable elsewhere), the landscape appears to have been as intensively used in the Roman period as today, but perhaps with fewer nucleated settlements. The basic pattern of field systems over quite extensive areas of Roman North Yorkshire is now beginning to be appreciated but the careful analysis, which can lead to a more detailed understanding of the nature of farming, remains to be done.

For example, droveways are common in the evidence from aerial photos and are often used as an indicator of a mixed farming economy, keeping stock from arable fields,

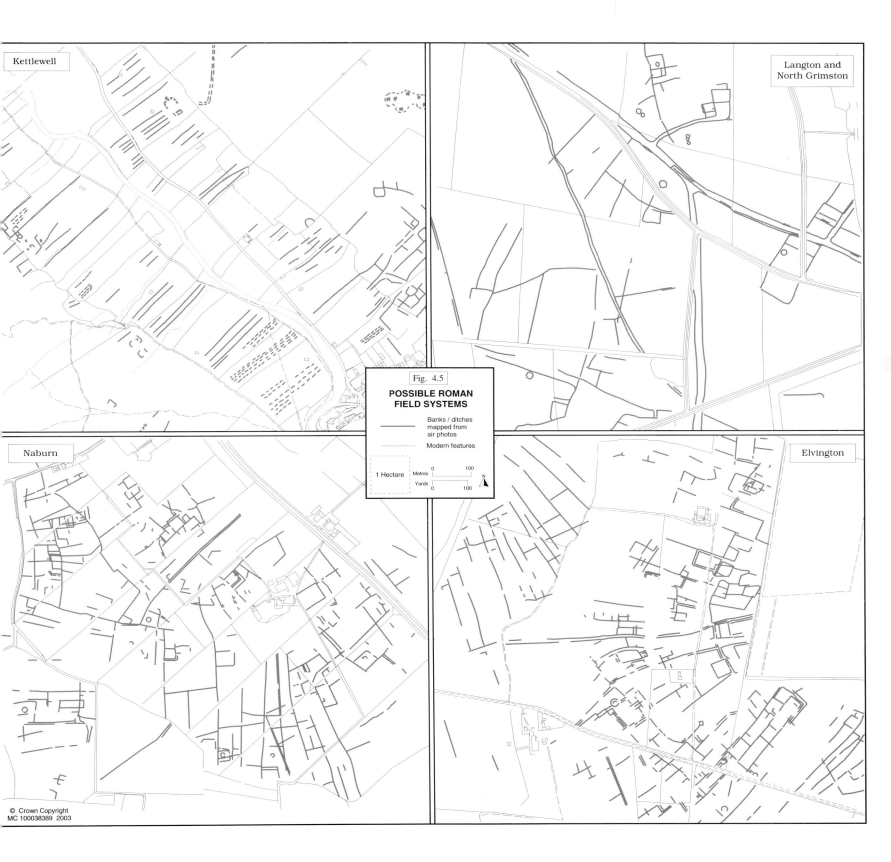

Fig. 4.5

POSSIBLE ROMAN FIELD SYSTEMS

— Banks / ditches mapped from air photos

— Modern features

1 Hectare

Metres 0 — 100

Yards 0 — 100

N

Kettlewell

Langton and North Grimston

Naburn

Elvington

© Crown Copyright
MC 100038389 2003

but they can equally be used to keep animals from other animals. Similarly identifying which animals were farmed on specific farms is problematic — excavation evidence tends to reveal only what animals were eaten on-site. Currently our best guess might come from looking in detail at the plans of fields and related enclosures, considering the requirements for handling different stock, and so trying to understand what they were likely to be used for. [65]

The aerial perspective is allowing us to see the bones of the Roman landscape, sometimes in considerable detail, but this evidence now needs to be taken forward and used in detailed landscape survey, supported by excavation, to flesh out the story of the Roman landscape.

5

THE EARLY MEDIEVAL PERIOD

5.1 THE EARLY–MIDDLE ANGLO–SAXON PERIOD (AD 400–AD 850) DOMINIC POWLESLAND

Work, principally in West Heslerton in the former East Riding (now in North Yorkshire), during the last twenty years has produced a wealth of new evidence[1] which prompts a radical reinterpretation of the Early Anglo-Saxon period, and its relationship to the end of Roman Britain (**fig 5.1**). The interpretation of Early and Middle Saxon England has in the past been driven by a series of concepts that require reassessment in the face of the new archaeological evidence. The term, for instance, 'Dark Ages' owes much to a view of the past in which Roman Britain was perceived as highly civilised and, in the later years, Christian; a social and cultural high-point followed by a period in which un-civilised pagans took over either by invasion or migration. The lack of contemporary documentary evidence and the desire to see 'history' confirmed by drawing upon much later documents such as the *Anglo-Saxon Chronicle* has likewise provided an unsound framework for the interpretation of the Early Anglo-Saxon past.

Another vehicle used for interpreting this period has been the study of place-names which, once again, are rarely documented until the eighth century at the very earliest, a time by which many of the early settlements are being deserted in favour of new locations. Even the archaeological evidence has been so biased in favour of burial evidence that it has, in reality, been impossible to establish a balanced view of the period. The relative invisibility of Early Anglo-Saxon settlement sites in the countryside, and the limited number of excavated examples nationwide, has meant that research over the last century has been focussed on such questions as the relationship between Briton and Saxon, or the phases of migration/invasion which, in neither case, can be satisfactorily answered on the basis of material culture evidence alone. The fact is that it was not until the 1960s that post-hole buildings were first accepted as components in Early Anglo-Saxon settlements, which had previously been seen to comprise simply *Grubenhäuser* (buildings that incorporate a pit within the body of the building) — see the diagram opposite. The then established view of our Anglo-Saxon origins was that the inhabitants of the *Grubenhäuser* lived in squalor 'amid a filthy litter of broken bones, of food and shattered pottery'.[2] To use a legal analogy, the Early Anglo-Saxons have been deemed guilty until proven innocent, occupying a primitive and unsophisticated past that is quite at odds with, for instance, the sophisticated material culture evidence so often discovered in their burials. Scholarship has been handicapped by outmoded views of 'pagan' culture, and by very limited and often misinterpreted evidence from settlements; a situation not improved by the recovery in recent years of metalwork dug up by treasure hunters, systematically turning over whole cemeteries, in the hunt for items of treasure.

About fifty Early Anglo-Saxon, or Anglian, cemeteries have been identified in North Yorkshire, mostly in and around the margins of the vale of Pickering, with others on the periphery of the North York Moors and a scatter on the margins of the Vale of York. The density of these sites is low, and, if we exclude those on the southern side of the Vale of Pickering, which belong to a relatively dense distribution associated with the Yorkshire Wolds, then the reflected density of Early Anglo-Saxon settlement in North Yorkshire may seem slight. Despite the low density of known sites, the discovery of burials of an early date at Catterick[3] (see photo on page 73) and nearby Scorton,[4] at York[5] and Malton/Norton[6] indicate that Early Anglo-Saxon burial practices were being applied by the middle of the fifth century around the declining settlements and institutions of Roman Britain. The evidence for burial does offer some important and general insights into the Early Anglo-Saxon population. Early Anglo-Saxon graves in the North of England are generally well furnished, and although weapons frequently accompany burials (and it now appears of either sex), there is virtually no evidence of fractures that might have come from warfare. The weapon burials that have led people to support the invasion theories of the past would appear to contain weapons that represent symbols of power. The population on average probably lived into their forties and were relatively healthy.

New evidence now emerging from DNA analysis in progress on the burials from West Heslerton indicates that not only were a number of female burials accompanied by weapons,

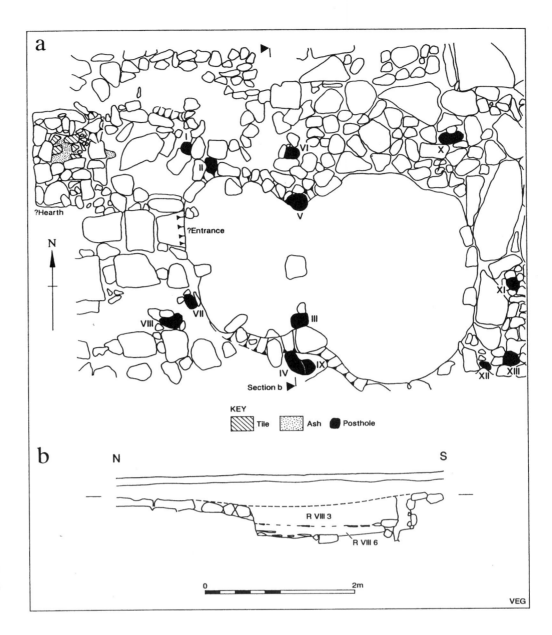

a

?Hearth

?Entrance

N

KEY
/// Tile   :::: Ash   ● Posthole

b   N   S

R VIII 3

R VIII 6

0   2m

VEG

Plan (a) and (b) of sixth-century *Grubenhaus* from
north of the River Swale at Catterick.

P R Wilson, P Cardwell, R J Cramp, J Evans, R H Taylor-Wilson, A Thompson
and J S Wacher, Early Anglian Catterick and Catreath, *Medieval Archaeology*,
40, figure 7. Figure courtesy of English Heritage, drawn by V E Griffin, English
Heritage Centre for Archaeology Graphics Studio.

but also that a number of males were accompanied by extensive assemblages of brooches and beads, and other items in the past interpreted as female indicators.[7] There is obviously a need to extend this type of research given the light that it may throw on Early Anglo-Saxon society. Besides being frequently well furnished, the burials do not seem to reflect a great range in individual status, if this is at all reflected in the grave goods; rather one is tempted to see a rather egalitarian society.

We can identify an Early Anglo-Saxon, or Anglian, presence in large areas of eastern North Yorkshire with cemeteries distributed around the Vale of Pickering and the Vale of York. In addition there are also cemeteries associated with the remains of the once-flourishing military and urban centres of York, Malton and Catterick. However, there is still very limited evidence of settlement and this makes the production of any broad regional assessment difficult.

The very extensive excavation of the Early Anglo-Saxon cemetery at West Heslerton, with the total exposure and sample excavation of the West Heslerton Anglian settlement, have provided a wealth of new evidence which allows us to re-examine the four centuries which comprise the formative years of Anglo-Saxon England.[8] There is insufficient evidence to determine whether the settlement at West Heslerton is in anyway unusual, beyond the fact that it is the only fully excavated example in the North of England. There is, on balance, nothing to indicate that this site was particularly rich or poor — if anything, the major distinctive feature is the association of the settlement with what appears to have been an earlier ritual site that flourished in the closing years of the fourth century.

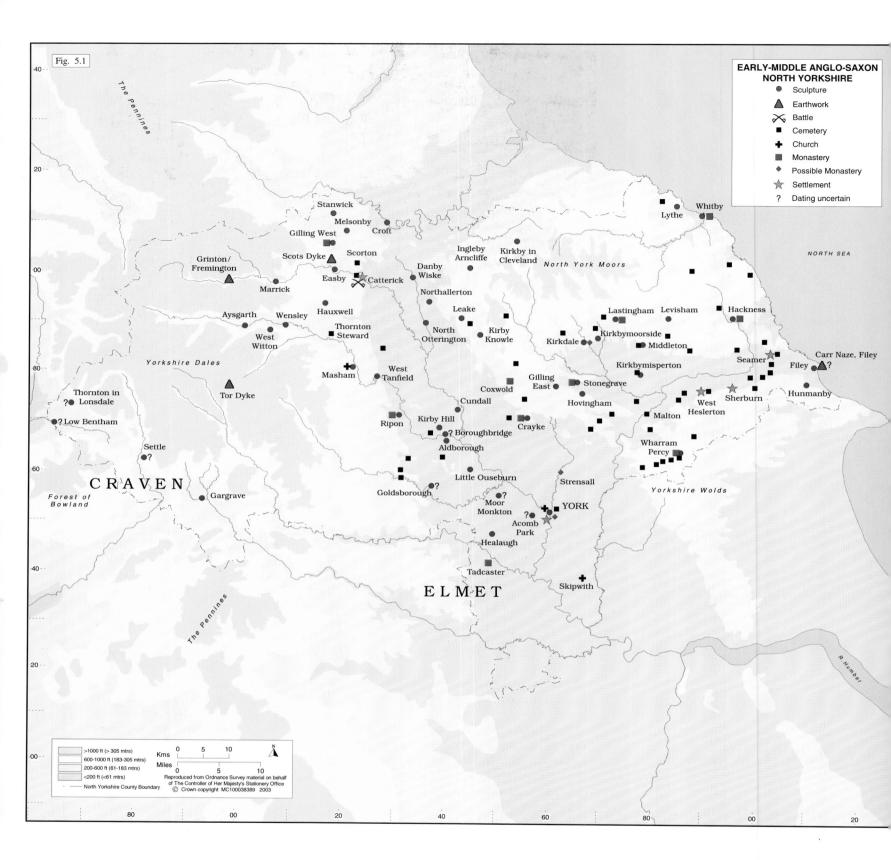

Reproduced from Ordnance Survey material on behalf
of The Controller of Her Majesty's Stationery Office
© Crown copyright MC100038389 2003

The traditional view of a Roman Britain that flourished in all its urban magnificence until the beginning of the fifth century has long been discarded by most scholars; but we cannot undertake any assessment of Early Anglo-Saxon England without attempting to set the scene at the end of Roman Britain. It is the pre-existing situation which made possible the rapid and apparently willing adoption of Anglo-Saxon material culture, settlement and building styles which are so at odds with what went before. Although we tend to perceive that we have a reasonably detailed understanding of Roman Britain, this is hardly the case in eastern North Yorkshire; the lion's share of our understanding of Roman Britain comes out of the large urban rescue excavations undertaken in York and elsewhere during the 1960s and 1970s.

Reconstructed early Anglo-Saxon house at West Stow, Suffolk.
© P Wilson.

Add this body of evidence to that gained earlier in the twentieth century, when much energy was directed towards military aspects of Roman Britain, and we find that the record is biased and unbalanced. The archaeology of rural areas has gone largely unnoticed despite the pivotal role that the countryside played in supporting the towns. Limited investigations on a number of Roman villas, which have a very low density but widespread distribution in eastern Yorkshire (see section 4 of this atlas), makes the picture of Roman Britain, particularly in the fourth century, very patchy.

Air photography, multi-spectral image scanning and geophysical survey have revealed, in eastern Yorkshire and elsewhere, large settlement complexes following trackways termed 'ladder settlements' which appear to have formed the basis of most rural settlement in the region from the middle of the Iron Age to the end of the Roman period.[9] These appear as ribbon developments stretching for many miles along, for instance, the margins of the Vale of Pickering (see also case study 2 on pages 58-61). These settlements, positioned on the edge of the extensive fenland that then occupied the Vale of Pickering, were located to benefit from access to a wide range of environmental conditions and soils including the chalk downland of the Yorkshire Wolds, the sandy light and easily tilled soils from the foot of the Wolds to the fen edge, and the fenland itself which provided a suitable environment for water-meadows, hunting, fishing and for gathering building materials such as reeds for thatch.

Archaeological and palaeobotanical evidence from a number of sites indicates a climatic decline during the fourth century that is accompanied by an increase in rainfall and consequently ground-water levels. Limited sample excavation on a ladder settlement in Sherburn, Vale of Pickering,[10] reveals that one part of this site at least was suffering from increasing ground-water levels and general wetness during the fourth century, and by the beginning of the fifth century this settlement complex was abandoned. The excavation of two *Grubenhäuser* within this settlement complex indicates that an Anglo-Saxon presence was already established by the time this move took place. One of the most problematic issues with regard to Early Anglo-Saxon settlement in England is why so many settlements appear on *de novo* sites, indicating a complete shift in the settlement distribution. It is possible that we have been addressing this question from the wrong direction, trying to find a reason why there was a settlement shift in the Early Anglo-Saxon period, rather than wondering why there had not been a settlement shift during the fourth century, when the Heslerton ladder settlement at least was showing serious signs of problems relating to rising ground-water. It is possible that the reason that the new Anglo-Saxon settlements developed where they did is simply because a collapse in the Roman economy and the land tenure arrangements meant that areas which previously were controlled now became available. In this context, it is of the greatest importance that *Grubenhäuser* have been discovered on a number of essentially Roman sites in the Vale of Pickering, at Sherburn[11] and at Seamer[12] in particular.

Although full analysis of the radiocarbon dating programme for West Heslerton is not yet complete, a preliminary assessment reveals that the earliest Anglo-Saxon buildings had been built by AD 400. The Dark Ages have finally disappeared, leaving us in an interesting but difficult position that calls for a careful examination of at least one fourth-century rural Roman settlement complex.

Regardless of the date range of the Anglian settlement at West Heslerton, which is currently seen as between AD 380-AD 850, the site reveals much that contrasts with the established view of Early Anglo-Saxon settlement.[13] The settlement was well organised or even planned, with different zones within the whole settlement performing different functions. The picture of shifting farmsteads that has so often been presented for settlements of this period is not supported by the evidence. It would appear that the whole site was actively in use for most of its life; certainly buildings were re-built and replaced but, rather than produce a settlement shifting in a linear pattern, the settlement framework remained intact and very extensive, building replacements being made within the un-defined property boundaries.

The buildings include both *Grubenhäuser*, the most distinctive feature of Early Anglo-Saxon settlements, and post-hole buildings. The *Grubenhäuser* which served as granaries, storage and general-purpose buildings appear to have had walls of turf; all had suspended floors. The post-hole buildings, which include both 'halls' (for which we prefer the term house) and other ancillary buildings which in the later period seem to have replaced the *Grubenhäuser*, once again all appear to have had suspended floors. The larger houses, which measured up to thirty feet by fifteen (10 x 4.5m) in ground-plan, employed sophisticated construction methods and imply highly developed carpentry skills. It is likely that the exteriors of these buildings were heavily embellished.

An important feature of the Early Anglo-Saxon settlements in England is the remarkable uniformity of building tradition that is displayed, in which post-hole building from sites from Hampshire to Northumberland show such remarkable similarities as to be considered effectively as from the same plan. This, and the fact that these buildings reflect entirely different building traditions to the bulk of the examples from the Continental homelands, indicate much greater social interaction and cohesion than we might at first suspect when considering Britain in the fifth century AD. Whilst we may debate the form of the superstructure to which these post-holes relate (for example the illustration on page 65), the similarity in ground plan provides compelling reasons to suggest that the structural form was instantly recognisable, and demonstrably Anglo-Saxon.[14]

The identification of a number of examples of buildings of 'Anglo-Saxon' ground plans on the Continent may be used to argue that this structural form originated on the Continent; however, it is just as possible that this structural form was exported back to the Continent from England. The limited structural evidence that does survive indicates that the Early Anglo-Saxons possessed sophisticated carpentry techniques that were used in a limited range of building styles. By the end of the seventh century, perhaps the time of greatest change in Anglo-Saxon England, changes in building construction techniques emerged. However, the ground plans continued to follow similar forms to the earlier examples; for example, the use of double-plank post arrangements identified in early post-hole buildings continues to develop, with the posts set into construction trenches rather than individual post-holes.

The lack of property boundaries in settlements of this period is one of the distinctions between Germanic settlements on the Continent with those in England. Although the cemetery contained many well-furnished graves, the settlement does not seem to encompass any obvious hierarchy and we are inclined to interpret the social structure as having only a limited range of social stratification. The settlement appears to be neither rich nor poor. The evidence emerging from the excavation analysis programme may indicate that West Heslerton was part of a settlement hierarchy that includes both well maintained and large settlements like Heslerton, and also higher-status sites to which places like Heslerton paid tribute in the form of cattle. This is inferred from the lack of market-age cattle in the huge animal bone assemblage; either they were being traded or used as tribute, most likely both factors were working together.[15]

Recently, examination of air-photographic evidence, coupled with geophysical survey and limited surface collection, has led to the discovery of a new Early Anglo-Saxon settlement of similar size to West Heslerton only one and a half miles (2.5km) from the excavated settlement. If this pattern is repeated around the Vale of Pickering, then we should anticipate the existence of as many as fifteen to twenty settlements in the area, representing a sizeable population of say 2,000 people. Even if the level of settlement drops off in western parts of the county, what is clear is that areas with extensive rural populations seem, not surprisingly, to have maintained similar levels in the Early Anglo-Saxon period as they had done in the Iron Age and Roman periods before.

Taking the example of Heslerton as a standard reference, Early Anglo-Saxon eastern North Yorkshire supported a well-developed agricultural regime of mixed farming, which produced a wide range of crops including foodstuffs and raw materials for the manufacture of textiles, flocks of sheep and goats kept mostly for their wool and milk, and cattle for traction; and the frequency of pigs or more likely managed wild boar is relatively high. A broad range of both wild and domesticated fowl supplemented the meat diet; both hunting dogs and birds of prey are a feature of the animal bone assemblage. Palaeobotanical evidence indicates that wild and domesticated fruits and berries were also collected. None of these facts is particularly surprising. What is important, however, is that, now, we are able to look towards the reconstruction of the agrarian economy, and aspects of diet and lifestyle with precision. The picture that is emerging is of a sophisticated society continuing to manage and work the Roman landscape, living in large settlements with high-quality housing, supported by domestic industry and trading in goods that came from as far apart as the Red Sea to Scandinavia.

By the middle of the seventh century, the nature of the settlement at West Heslerton began to change. Fenced enclosures were built, presumably for stock management purposes, new ceramic forms were introduced and a new cemetery was established at an as yet unidentified location. We are beginning to think that this was the significant period of change, rather than the Early Anglo-Saxon period; the context for this change is most likely to be attributable to the re-introduction of Christianity. North Yorkshire, with sites like Whitby and Kirkdale Church, had an important role in the re-emergence of Christianity.

By AD 850, sites like West Heslerton were deserted in favour of new sites which, in the case of Heslerton, provided greater defensive potential in the face of Viking activities. By this time Anglo-Saxon England had become a reality, one in which urban settlements with far-flung trading connections but supported by the countryside around them re-emerged.

Whilst the eastern part of the county, despite the very limited amount of excavation conducted as a whole, gives us an increasingly clear picture of the processes through which Anglo-Saxon England evolved, the picture to the west is quite different. The lack of evidence in the west should not be seen as a simple indication of an unpopulated landscape. The difficulty here is in identifying that population and their archaeology, an archaeology which may look little different to that of the Iron Age. Certainly there is almost no evidence of Early Anglo-Saxon activity; however, the presence of churches and ecclesiastical foundations in the ninth century may be used to infer a larger population than we might otherwise identify.

5.2 CONTACT, CO-EXISTENCE AND CONFLICT: ADDITIONAL ASPECTS OF THE EARLY-MIDDLE ANGLO-SAXON PERIOD   PETER WILSON

As indicated above, the arrival of the early Anglo-Saxon population has been traditionally associated with a period of conflict, but this view is now being challenged. One of the few possible historical references to North Yorkshire in the Early Anglo-Saxon period does suggest that conflict was part of the picture. Y Gododdin, an early British poem,[16] records a battle at 'Catraeth' around AD 590-600 when the men of the British kingdom of Rheged, centred west of the Pennines, marched against, and were defeated by, Anglo-Saxons who apparently controlled the area of Catraeth at the time. Catraeth is usually associated with Catterick.[17] Bede, writing early in the eighth century, tells of Paulinus, in circa AD 627, baptising many, presumably Anglo-Saxon, converts in the River Swale at Catterick, which he states was within the Anglo-Saxon kingdom of Deira.[18]

The British kingdom in Craven probably disappeared in the sixth century,[19] while Elmet appears to have survived into the early seventh century as an independent kingdom.[20] Some evidence for conflict, or at least possible attempts to establish boundaries, is provided by a series of earthworks. The Grinton/Fremington dykes which serve to partially block Swaledale represent one such system and, like Scots Dyke which lies east of Richmond, faces east. Both dyke systems appear as attempts by, probably British, groups in the Dales to prevent westward expansion, possibly by Anglo-Saxon controlled Deira. However, Tor Dyke, between Coverdale and Wharfedale, faces south-west, and, if our understanding of the areas of Anglo-Saxon and British political control is correct, could indicate that Anglo-Saxon areas in Wensleydale and the Vale of Mowbray may have been subject to pressure from British Craven. A further post-Roman earthwork of early, but uncertain, date has been recognised on Carr Naze, Filey. It serves to cut off the headland, to create either a military strongpoint or a fortified dwelling that incorporated the site of the late Roman signal station.[21]

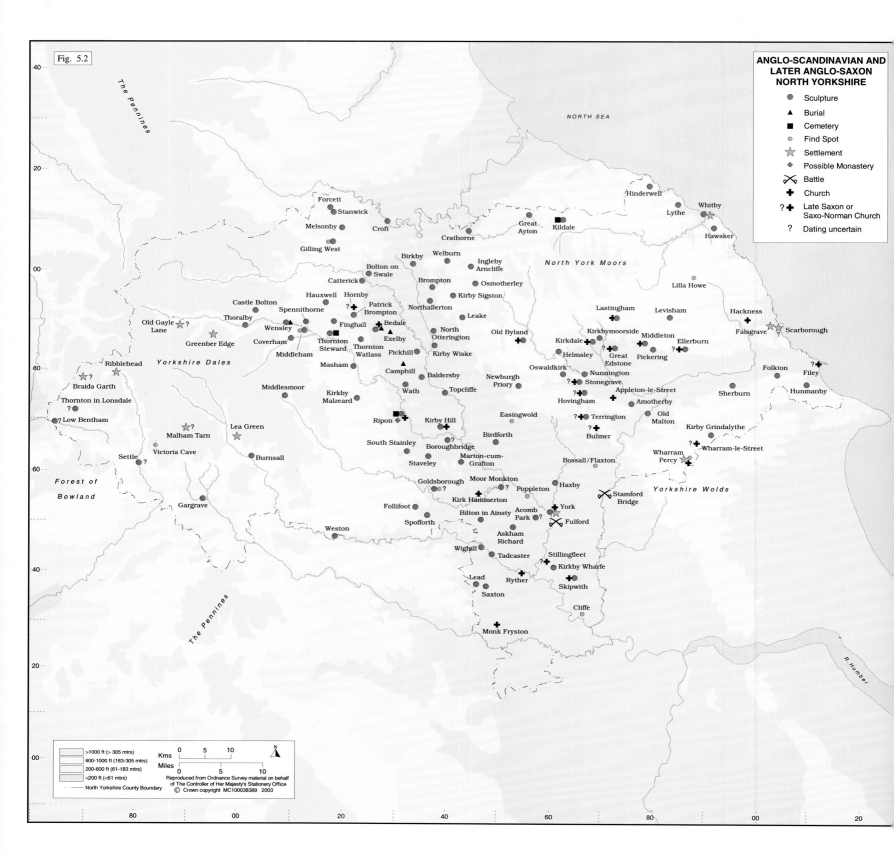

Fig. 5.2

ANGLO-SCANDINAVIAN AND LATER ANGLO-SAXON NORTH YORKSHIRE

- ● Sculpture
- ▲ Burial
- ■ Cemetery
- ● Find Spot
- ★ Settlement
- ◆ Possible Monastery
- ✕ Battle
- ✚ Church
- ?✚ Late Saxon or Saxo-Norman Church
- ? Dating uncertain

5.3 ANGLO-SAXON AND LATER ANGLO-SAXON NORTH YORKSHIRE (AD 850–1066)[22] PETER WILSON

Although Scandinavian raids in southern England are recorded from the late eighth century,[23] it is with the capture of York by the Danish army in AD 866 that the Anglo-Scandinavian period in North Yorkshire can be said to begin. Halfdan took control of Northumbria in 875 and in the following year he '... shared out the lands of Northumbria [amongst his followers], and they were engaged in ploughing and in making a living for themselves'.[24]

St Gregory's Minster, Kirkdale.
© North York Moors National Park Authority, HC0049.

The Scandinavians who settled Yorkshire (**fig 5.2**) largely came from two areas, Denmark and Norway. In general, the Danes came from the east starting in the ninth century, and the Norwegians from the west *via* Scotland, Ireland and the north-west of England from the early tenth century and are often referred to as Hiberno-Norse. However, the various war-bands and groups of settlers would probably each have had mixed origins.[25] The ethnic origins of the incomers are as difficult to disentangle as the Anglo-Scandinavians are from the pre-existing Anglo-Saxon population. Similar complexities can be seen in the historical record, where Anglo-Saxon *eorls* are found supporting Anglo-Scandinavian kings, and Anglo-Scandinavian earls, Anglo-Saxon kings.[26]

Away from York, the one certain town (see case study which follows), physical evidence of the Scandinavian presence is hard to find. The majority of places where clear evidence of the ninth-eleventh centuries can be recognised are those where monasteries are known or believed to exist, or where pre-Norman churches are known, or where sculpture is recorded. However, occupation material of ninth to eleventh century date has recently been discovered at Whitby.[27]

A number of graves containing Anglo-Scandinavian objects are known from the county. Single burials are recorded at Wensley, Camphill, and at and near Bedale[28] with a group from Kildale.[29] Those at Wensley and Kildale were in the churchyard and under the church respectively; however, they were pagan in form and probably ninth century in date, and may point to the Scandinavian incomers using existing cemeteries, rather than demonstrating the early adoption of Christianity. In Ripon, excavated burials in the St Marygate area suggest continuous burial activity from the eighth to tenth centuries.[30] Recent work at Thornton Steward has located seventeen burials without diagnostic grave goods dated to the Middle and Later Saxon periods (AD 660-1029) by radiocarbon dating.[31] Whether the later burials in the Thornton Steward group represent the descendants of people of Anglo-Saxon, Anglo-Scandinavian or mixed ancestry is not clear.

In addition to material from excavations, artefacts that are clearly Anglo-Scandinavian in style are known from a number of finds spots, including: hoards from Bossall/Flaxton[32] and Goldsborough,[33] a harness bow from Cliffe,[34] a silver ingot from near Easingwold,[35] strap-ends from Poppleton, and a rune stone from Victoria Cave, Settle, which has also produced a comb of Late Anglo-Saxon or Anglo-Scandinavian date.[36] Four strap-ends and two gold discs are all that now survive from a more extensive find from Lilla Howe on the North York Moors; the strap-ends are Anglo-Saxon, probably belonging to the ninth century, while the gold discs are likely to have been imported from Scandinavia.[37] The latter two finds, along with the Anglo-Saxon swords that were found in the (possibly) Anglo-Scandinavian graves from Wensley Churchyard[38] and Camphill[39], point to the difficulty of assigning ethnic origins on the basis of artefactual finds.[40] Objects could be traded, stolen or otherwise acquired, and may not reflect the ancestry of the deceased. Equally, mixed marriages must have been common and although artefacts may have been seen as a form of cultural expression, if the descendants favoured one ancestry over the other, they could also simply reflect what was available or the personal taste of the individual. A further late Anglo-Saxon sword is known from Gilling West,[41] but the limited number of finds spots recorded here points to the relative invisibility of many aspects of the Late Anglo-Saxon and Anglo-Scandinavian period. Indeed, away from York, coin finds are few, although a hoard is known from Middleham.[42]

A later ninth-century pastoral settlement has been excavated near Ribblehead,[43] and a number of other *possible* Anglo-Scandinavian rural sites are known in the Dales at Braida Garth in Kingsdale, Greenber Edge in Wensleydale, Lea Green above Grassington, and perhaps above Malham Tarn and at Old Gayle Lane, Hawes.[44] In the eastern part of the county there is very limited structural evidence from the Anglo-Scandinavian period at Wharram Percy, although a Borre-style strap-end and belt-slide from the site suggest occupation in the late ninth and tenth centuries, as do elements of the church.[45] Despite the limited evidence, it has been suggested that the site was laid out in the tenth century.[46] That having been said, there is evidence for metal-working from the site dating to the late ninth or tenth century, a period when metal-working is more usually found in towns.[47]

Occupation through the Later Anglo-Saxon/Anglo-Scandinavian period into the Later Medieval period as suggested at Wharram is one model for settlement in the county. A possible alternative is provided by Cottam in the East Riding, where an eighth-ninth century farmstead (Cottam A) was relocated to be replaced by an apparently higher-status site about 0.6 mile (1km) away. After a generation or so Cottam B was abandoned, possibly in favour of the site of one of the medieval villages of Cowlam or Cottam itself,[48] suggesting the period also saw considerable change in the settlement pattern.

King Harald's Saga claims a 'town' at Scarborough which it is said was captured and burnt by the Norse prior to the Battle of Stamford Bridge in 1066, but the thirteenth-century source is untrustworthy.[49] Indeed, in the Later Anglo-Saxon period, Scarborough lay within the extensive royal manor of Falsgrave. A similar possible pairing of inland sites with subordinate coastal settlements can be recognised along the length of the North Yorkshire coast.[50]

The largest body of evidence for Anglo-Scandinavian settlement comes in the form of place-name evidence, with a number of readily recognisable forms being known, such as those ending in '-by' (from the Old Norse *-by* meaning 'village'),[51] as in Whitby; those incorporating the element Old Norse element *– þorp*,[52] such as Mowthorpe; and hybrids, where a Scandinavian or Scandinavianised first element is combined with the Old English *-tun* meaning 'farmstead or village'.[53] A further group of place-names are those that derive from the Norwegian, or Hiberno-Norse settlement from the west, such as Melmerby and Carperby, which incorporate Norwegian/Irish personal names.

Although recognising place-names with Old Norse elements is relatively easy, understanding their significance is rather more complex. It is certain that not all of the settlements are new creations, and it is perhaps increasingly clear that many of them represent the renaming of settlements already in existence at the start of the Scandinavian invasions and that Danes sometimes settled in English villages without changing their names.[54] Equally, *-tun* hybrids are likely to have been coined by English speakers, even when they incorporated a Scandinavian first element.[55] Although names of Norwegian origin are recognisable in the Dales, for example the river name Bain, many are also recorded in the eastern part of the county.[56] Does this represent the results of Hiberno–Norse settlement, or of political control?

This leads to another area of debate with regard to the scale of the Scandinavian settlement. Do the large numbers of names equate with extensive settlement, or do they relate more to changes in ownership and control of villages and land?[57] The balance of opinion appears to favour relatively small Viking armies, numbered in hundreds, who paved the way for extensive settlement.[58] A further complication is provided by the continued use of Old Norse elements in place-name formation long after the Norman Conquest, and therefore names that suggest Scandinavian settlement activity, such as clearing land (incorporating the element *-thveit*, for example Inglethwaite), may only appear in the twelfth or thirteenth century and may relate to land newly assarted then.[59]

In the face of the gradual reconquest of the Danelaw and its amalgamation into the West Saxon kingdom, the Dublin Norse gained control of York and established the Hiberno-Norse kingdom of York, linked with Dublin. The Anglo-Saxon reconquest of Yorkshire was completed under Athelstan in 927 and Wessex ruled North Yorkshire until Athelstan's death in 939. At that time Óláfr II Gothfrithsson, king of Dublin, recovered Northumbria and in 940 the Danelaw, and heralded a very turbulent phase in the history of the region. In 944, Edmund of Wessex drove Óláfr Cuarán, successor to Óláfr II Gothfrithsson, out of York. Three years later, Archbishop Wulfsan of York and the Northumbrian Witan submitted to Eadred, Edmund's successor, but shortly afterwards accepted the Norwegian Eiríkr Bloodaxe as king. The following year had Eadred ravaging Ripon and forcing York to reject Eiríkr. In

949 Óláfr Cuarán returned to York, only to be expelled and replaced by Eiríkr again in 952. Eiríkr reigned until 954, when he too was expelled by the Northumbrians and killed on Stainmore,[60] thereby ending Anglo-Scandinavian rule.

A further period of raiding and warfare started in 980 with attacks on various parts of England. North Yorkshire was largely spared direct involvement, but came under Knut through the Peace of Alney and the subsequent death of Edmond Ironside in 1016. The final military actions in Late Anglo-Saxon North Yorkshire, or on its borders, were the battles of Fulford and Stamford Bridge in 1066, following the invasion of Harald of Norway supported by Earl Tostig. Fulford ended in a defeat for northern earls Edwin and Morcar at the hands of the Norwegians, and Stamford Bridge a victory for the English King Harold.

As tumultuous as these events must have been, they are largely invisible, at least away from York. Some Hiberno-Norse or Norwegian place-names may derive from the period of the kingdom of York. However, the place-names are not chronologically sensitive and, in general, archaeological material cannot be associated with either phase of events.

During the initial conquest and settlements the Scandinavians were pagan, but appear to have gradually accepted Christianity, and the largest surviving bodies of physical evidence for the period are represented by the churches and sculpture — much if not all of the latter Christian in context, if not necessarily content.[61]

CHURCHES AND SCULPTURE

In the Middle Saxon period, York is well authenticated as the seat of the archbishop and it is known that a number of monasteries were established in North Yorkshire including Coxwold, Crayke, Hackness, Lastingham, Ripon, Stonegrave, Tadcaster, Gilling West, Whitby, and possibly Kirkdale and Wharram Percy.[62] It is highly likely that others existed, including one at Strensall, which may plausibly be argued to be the location of Bede's *Streanæshalch* and therefore the location of the 'Synod of Whitby' held in 664, when the supremacy of the Roman over the Celtic Church was confirmed. The link between Whitby and *Streanæshalch/* Strensall may be explained in a number of ways. Strensall may have formed a twin monastery with Whitby, like Monkwearmouth–Jarrow; it may have been given to Whitby when the latter was founded; or Whitby may itself have started as a daughter house of Strensall.[63] The monastic system collapsed during the Scandinavian settlements, and by around the middle of the tenth century there appear to have been few, if any, monasteries surviving in Northern England.[64]

The church at Ripon was built in stone in the AD 670s and, despite the impact of the Anglo-Scandinavian invasions at Ripon, we appear to be seeing religious continuity over some considerable time, perhaps representing an exception to the general absence of monasteries. Elsewhere in the county, parts of St Mary Bishophill Senior (York) and excavated structures at Whitby have been assigned a pre-800 date, although parts of St Mary's, Masham, and St Helen's, Skipwith, could also be that early[65] (**fig 5.2**). The Anglo-Saxon churches on **fig 5.2** are later and probably only represent a proportion of those that once existed, as is hinted at by the survival of pre-Norman conquest sundials re-used in the fabric of later churches at Kirkbymoorside and Sinnington.[66] The parish structure was probably in place by the Late Anglo-Saxon period and the existence of at least one church in each parish can be expected, with the possibility of field churches in larger parishes.[67] It is also likely that a large proportion of these churches were constructed in stone, indeed the *Domesday Book* entry for Old Byland records the existence of a wooden church as if it were something unusual and worthy of note.[68] The existence of a wooden church at Old Byland points to another problem, the longevity of Anglo-Saxon architectural motifs. The present church at Old Byland incorporates an Anglo-Saxon sundial which, along with other early features, is clearly not *in situ*, but on the evidence of Domesday must originate as part of a church constructed after 1086.[69] Other churches such as Ellerburn,[70] Great Edstone[71] and Stillingfleet[72] contain work that is Norman or earlier, and could belong to the Late Anglo-Saxon period.

Pre-Viking free-standing crosses have been shown to relate to monastic sites, while later Anglo-Scandinavian ones that post-date the decline of the monasteries necessarily relate to lay patronage.[73] Other earlier Anglo-Saxon sculptural forms include grave-markers or *stelae* (found only in York), grave-covers (for example from Wensley and Kirkdale), and architectural fittings and furnishings (for example: panel from a shrine from Hovingham; a plaque from Middleton; door jambs and parts of a stone chair from Lastingham).[74] In the Scandinavian period, grave-markers and grave covers are known, along with hogbacks — house-shaped monuments that appear to have originated in the region around Brompton.[75] Although some hogbacks have similarities to house-shrines that are known in metalwork, it has been argued that they are a secular response to saints' shrines that were common in Western Europe. Ripon, and possibly Sherburn-in-Elmet, appear to have continued to have a particular status after the disappearance of the monasteries by virtue of acting as administrative centres for the archbishop of York's estates.[76]

HISTORICAL EVIDENCE

There is only limited contemporary documentary evidence relating to North Yorkshire and, as mentioned above, very little for the Early-Middle Anglo-Saxon period. Some seven charters are known for the period AD 959-1066 which refer to places in North Yorkshire.[77] The information they offer is variable, including the bounds of Drax,[78] and confirmations of grants of lands, for example at Sherburn-in-Elmet (*Sireburnan*) to Æslac wherein a list of dependencies includes seven places in North Yorkshire.[79] The best documentary evidence for the latter part of the period comes from the *Domesday Book*. Although it was compiled after the Norman Conquest, most if not all of the information it gives on features such as mills and fisheries can be projected back into the Late Anglo-Saxon period, as Domesday was intended to reflect the position '*tempus Rex Edwardus*' (in the time of King Edward). Areas where Domesday is silent may also help with the Later Anglo-Saxon period: halls are only mentioned when they are absent and this suggests that a hall might be expected for every manor.[80]

ADMINISTRATIVE LEGACY

A number of administrative arrangements that were introduced during the Anglo-Scandinavian period in Yorkshire survived into the later medieval period. The best known of these are the Ridings which remained the administrative units for the county until 1974. The customs enshrined in Anglo-Scandinavian law survived the re-conquest of Yorkshire by the Anglo-Saxon kings, and the region's commitment to Scandinavian law was a factor in the Northumbrian revolt of 1065.[81] Scandinavian influence is seen in the survival of wapentakes as sub-divisions of the West and North Ridings, the use of carucates as the standard land unit rather than hides, and by the use of the duodecimal system for counting land units — twelve carucate units being used as opposed to the five-hide unit used in Wessex and western Mercia.[82] Many of the vills/townships may also be delineated in the Early Medieval period, although when is far from clear.

5.4 CASE STUDY: ANGLIAN AND ANGLO-SCANDINAVIAN YORK
RICHARD A HALL

The Roman army's withdrawal from York *c*AD 400 brought the first phase of the city's existence to an end. An economic lifeline disappeared, and things were bound to change. What actually happened in the city and to the city over the next few centuries is, however, a matter largely for conjecture — this period still remains a mysterious 'Dark-Age' bereft of contemporary documentation and a challenge to the archaeologist.

The archaeological interface — if there was one — between sub-Roman Britons and incoming Anglo-Saxons has yet to be clearly identified. There may have been some occupation in the early fifth century at least, most probably by local aristocrats and dignitaries continuing to exercise ceremonial and customary roles. Evidence from below York Minster can be taken to support this contention.[83] Probably, however, deserted Roman buildings were demolished, or decayed and collapsed over the next few hundred years, allowing the creation of routeways between adjacent Roman gateways in the fortress, cutting diagonally across the Roman street grid. Within 0.6-1.2 miles (1-2km) of the Roman walls, cremation cemeteries, represented by Anglo-Saxon style urns, were in use from the later fifth century onwards, but no traces of where these communities lived have yet been found.

Whatever the city's overall condition, it was here that the Roman missionary Paulinus baptised Edwin, the Anglo-Saxon king of Northumbria, in 627.[84] His cathedral church (**fig 10.3** p197), dedicated to St Peter, is the direct predecessor of York Minster, but where precisely it stood is unproven; perhaps to the north of the minster, in Deans Park.[85] The church was given a large part — perhaps as much as one third — of the former Roman fortress. Another important focus of ecclesiastical life may have existed in the Bishophill area of the old *colonia*, where the churches of Holy Trinity, St Mary Bishophill Junior, St Mary Bishophill Senior (demolished 1963) and St Gregory (demolished *c*1549) hint at a monastic enclave.[86] The legacy of this era is not, however, in buildings but in the international reputation which York won in the eighth century as a centre of learning.

Sixth-century burial from Bainesse, Catterick with two annual brooches. The grave also produced an iron buckle, iron knife, iron hobnail and three beads (one each of glass, amber and faience).

(P R Wilson, P Cardwell, R J Cramp, J Evans, R H Taylor-Wilson, A Thompson and J S Wacher, Early Anglian Catterick and *Catreath, Medieval Archaeology*, 40, 40-41, figure 21). Photograph courtesy of English Heritage.

A combination of academic reputation and missionary zeal forged links with north-west Europe as well as the papacy. These links then acted as a spur to the development of trading contacts, and a group of Frisian merchants was present in York in the late eighth century. German lava quern-stones and Rhenish pottery associated with the wine trade, found at sites along the River Ouse and River Foss, suggest that these were where traders did business in *Eoforwic*.[87] The only site where seventh- to ninth-century structures have yet been found is just beyond the rivers' confluence, at Fishergate. Three buildings excavated there are not densely packed as in the contemporary *wics* of Southampton or Ipswich; exploring, defining and explaining the pre-Viking settlement pattern remains a top priority for archaeologists in York.[88]

Seaborne Viking raiders never penetrated up the Ouse to York, but in 866 Viking invaders captured the city, and snuffed out the line of independent Northumbrian Anglo-Saxon kings. The archbishopric survived, however; the new Viking rulers and established churchmen both recognised the political and economic benefits of collaboration; not least, they shared a desire to remain independent of the kings of Wessex, the only surviving Anglo-Saxon royal dynasty, who gradually took over all the other Viking conquests in England. Irish Vikings targeted York in the early tenth century, and Viking kings of Dublin ruled briefly in the city before Athelstan, Alfred the Great's grandson, imposed his authority on York in 927, and incorporated Northumbria into the new state of England. After his death in 939, control of York and the Northumbrian throne was keenly contested by Hiberno-Norse dynasts, Southern English kings and the exiled Norwegian prince Erik Bloodaxe until, after Erik's final expulsion, *Jorvik* was brought back finally into England. It was again in Scandinavian hands only when Cnut and his sons ruled England (1016-42), and for a week in 1066 between the Norwegian King Harald Hardrada's victory at the Battle of Fulford (just outside York), and his defeat and death at the Battle of Stamford Bridge.

In the middle years of the ninth century, approximately when the Vikings arrived, areas of York which had apparently been deserted for centuries were re-occupied; by the early tenth century York was a boom town, with new streets densely packed with typical urban tenement plots. *Jorvik*'s economy was fuelled in part by the importation of exotic luxury items channelled to the city from Scandinavian merchants' enterprises in Europe and Asia. Increasingly, however, York functioned as a manufacturing centre, supplying basic necessities and minor luxuries. In houses-cum-workshops built in the post-and-wattle technique at the street frontages, craftsmen worked on an industrial basis, mass-producing items for sale. As the only town north of the Humber, York's market served not only the increasing urban population, but the wide hinterland which supplied it with raw materials and foodstuffs.[89]

By 1066 it seems that the Roman walls on two sides of the fortress no longer served as a defensive barrier — extensions to the other, refurbished, walls ran down to the rivers, forming a larger enclosure. Across the Ouse, the Roman's *colonia's* walls defended an area which was also re-shaped internally. A new crossing point on the Ouse was established where

Jorvik's townscape: the plank-lined basement of a late tenth-century building excavated by York Archaeological Trust at 16-22 Coppergate, York. © YAT.

Ouse Bridge now stands, replacing the old Roman bridge around 800 feet (c250m) upstream. A new southern approach to the bridge was required, and thus the sweeping curve of Micklegate was created. Along its line several churches were founded, and others in the area — St Mary Bishophill Junior, St Mary Bishophill Senior and Holy Trinity — were rebuilt. Although not much else is known archaeologically about tenth/eleventh century development in the former *colonia*, it has been suggested that a deliberately planned grid of streets was laid out in the Bishophill area, and that this was an important merchants' quarter.[90]

There is also growing evidence for occupation along Walmgate, east of the River Foss, while beyond the city's western edge, at *Earlsburgh*, was a residence of the earls of Northumbria. By 1066 York was the second-largest and second-most prosperous city in England, with approximately 2,000 properties; topographically it was recognisable as the medieval and modern city.[91]

THE FUTURE

Given our paucity of knowledge for the period prior to AD 850 in the west of the county, research thereon must be a priority, including examination of the character of settlement; the nature of burial/funerary practices; and the lack of visibility of the British population.

For the whole county there is a need for: excavation of rural sites that might test the validity of the 'Heslerton model'; an understanding of what happened on the sites of Roman towns and *vici*, including York, in the fifth and sixth centuries; and of the origins of towns not thought to have Roman antecedents; and excavation of a monastic site, building on the important work at Kirkdale. The location and excavation of the post-AD 650 West Heslerton cemetery can provide a basis for comparison with the earlier excavated cemetery and other contemporary settlement evidence. For the period after AD 850, further work is needed: in York, to test the 'Coppergate model'; on the location and character of rural settlement; on recognition and excavation of rural sites across the county; and excavation of a large post-AD 850 cemetery.

Of particular importance to all of these questions would be further work designed to elucidate the environmental conditions and economies of the early medieval period.

Further Reading:

R N Bailey, *Viking Age Sculpture in Northern England* (London: Collins, 1980).

R A Hall, *Viking Age York* (London: English Heritage/ Batsford, 1994).

C Haughton and D Powlesland, *West Heslerton: The Anglian Cemetery* (Yedingham: Landscape Research Centre, 1999).

D W Rollason, *Sources for York History to AD1100* (York: Council for British Archaeology, Archaeology of York 1).

H M Taylor and J Taylor, *Anglo-Saxon Architecture* vols I and II (Cambridge: Cambridge University Press, 1980), and vol III (Cambridge: Cambridge University Press, 1978).

D Tweddle, J Moulden and E Logan, *Anglian York: a Survey of the Evidence (*York: Council for British Archaeology, Archaeology of York: Anglian York 7/2, 1999).

D M Wilson (ed.), *The Archaeology of Anglo-Saxon England* (Cambridge: Cambridge University Press, 1976).

P R Wilson, P Cardwell, R J Cramp, J Evans, R H Taylor-Wilson, A Thompson, and J S Wacher, Early Anglian Catterick and *Catraeth, Medieval Archaeology* 40, 1-61.

6

MEDIEVAL NORTH YORKSHIRE

6.1 INTRODUCTION
NOËL JAMES MENUGE AND ALAN YOUNG

In the eleventh century, North Yorkshire was a frontier zone to a kingdom neither defined or united. This is well attested by the involvement of Scandinavians (Norwegians and Danes), Anglo-Saxons and Normans in military conflict there. In the twelfth century and the late thirteenth/early fourteenth centuries, Scottish military threats maintained North Yorkshire's role as a frontier zone. The need to consolidate royal authority in the region in the twelfth century obviously led to the establishment of castles as prominent features on the landscape.

Yet this was only one of several long-lasting influences on the North Yorkshire landscape deriving from significant developments within the medieval period. Frontier zones were also lands of opportunity and this is borne out by developments, many interrelated, in the religious and economic spheres. Over fifty religious houses were established in the area in the medieval period, with the peak of this development occurring in the 1130s to 1180s. Religious houses, as well as castles, should be seen as symbols of a new governing aristocracy who required religious as well as secular bases in the region. This group could also take advantage of the widespread deer parks and forests rich in game for their leisure pursuits.

As well as adding buildings of permanent architectural interest to the landscape, the distinctive Cistercian order revolutionised economic and agricultural practices in the region from over eighty grange sites. These sites, in turn, contributed to communication routes stimulated by economic activity during the medieval period; these helped to form the basis of a long-lasting pattern of common route-ways in the region.

The twelfth century saw a remarkable development of boroughs, markets and fairs and this, like the development of religious houses, should be seen as part of the political consolidation of the region. The development of markets and boroughs was often associated with the castles of major Yorkshire baronial families.

While the twelfth century was a key period for many significant and long-lasting influences on the North Yorkshire landscape, developments did not end there. The Scottish raids of the early fourteenth century and the usurpation of the throne by Henry IV in 1399 meant that royal presence had to be again re-emphasised through castle development and acquisition. On the economic scene, opportunities for new ventures still existed in the fourteenth century.

6.2 MEDIEVAL WOODLAND   TOM GLEDHILL

WOODLAND DISTRIBUTION

It is not an easy task to judge how wooded or otherwise North Yorkshire was in the Middle Ages. Evidence can be difficult to interpret, and is not always as complete as one would wish. The aim here is to make a critical study of the information available from documentary sources to provide an overview of medieval woodland distribution and management in North Yorkshire. Thus, this is as much a study of the nature of the evidence as of the woodland itself.

A number of different sources of information are useful in establishing the distribution of medieval woodland. Place-names often reflect the landscape settled by the Anglo-Saxons and Scandinavians in the late first millenium AD. The *Domesday Book* provides a record of woodland in 1086. A wide variety of other medieval documentary evidence, including charters, fines and inquisitions, also record woodland.

Element	Meaning	Modern Equivalent
Leah	ley, ly, laugh	clearing or wood
thwait	thwait, waite	clearing
weald	wold, wald	woodland
scaga	shaw, saw	wood
scogr	scoe, skew, sque	wood
vithr	with	wood
lundr	lund, lunt	wood
fridd	frith	wood

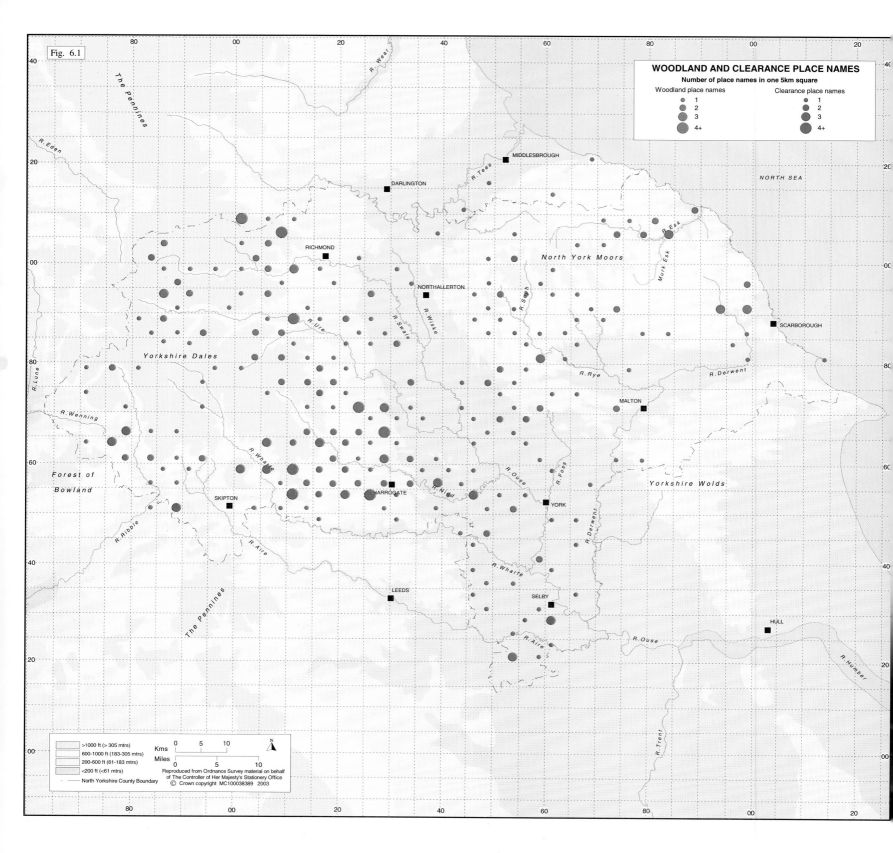

Fig. 6.1

WOODLAND AND CLEARANCE PLACE NAMES
Number of place names in one 5km square

Woodland place names		Clearance place names	
•	1	•	1
•	2	•	2
•	3	•	3
●	4+	●	4+

Some place-names record the presence of woodland, or of clearings within woodland. A list of the most common place-name elements of these types is given on the previous page.

In general, areas with many clearing names are considered to be well wooded, those with many wood names slightly less so, and the areas with few names of either type are the least wooded (**fig 6.1**). Unfortunately the frequency of these types of place-names also appears to have been influenced by topography, with the result that place-names tend to record the woods which were most visible in the landscape.[1]

Domesday Book has some fairly obvious shortcomings as a record of woodland (**fig 6.2**). Woodland for the area of Craven is not recorded at all. Elsewhere, woodland is recorded at

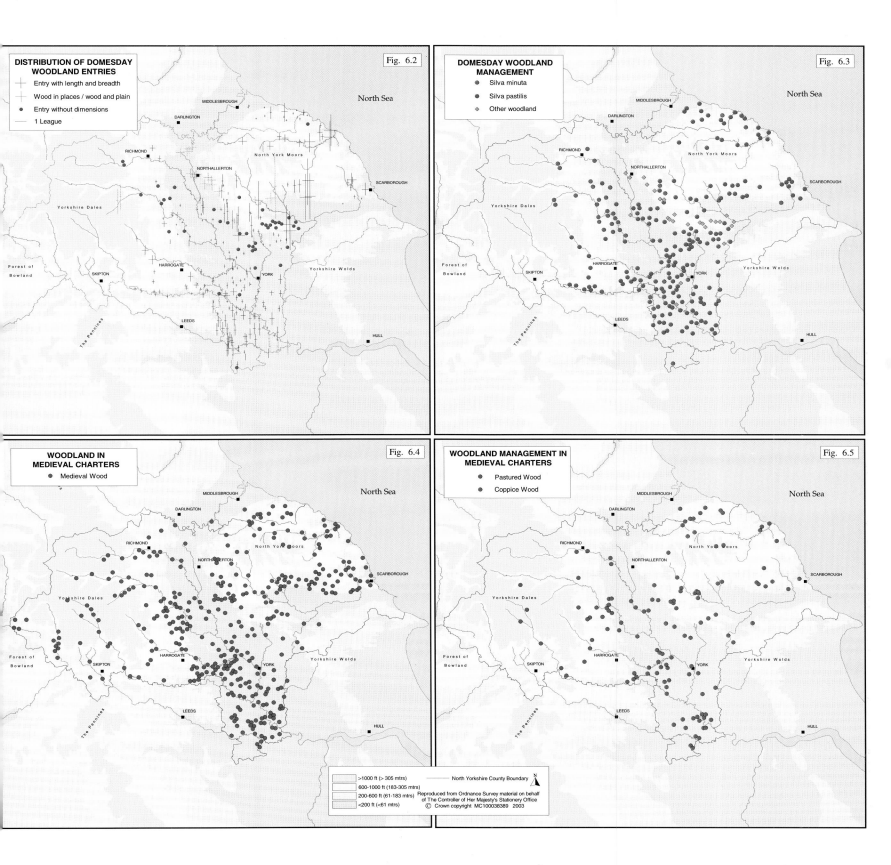

DISTRIBUTION OF DOMESDAY WOODLAND ENTRIES — Fig. 6.2
- Entry with length and breadth
- Wood in places / wood and plain
- Entry without dimensions
- 1 League

DOMESDAY WOODLAND MANAGEMENT — Fig. 6.3
- Silva minuta
- Silva pastilis
- Other woodland

WOODLAND IN MEDIEVAL CHARTERS — Fig. 6.4
- Medieval Wood

WOODLAND MANAGEMENT IN MEDIEVAL CHARTERS — Fig. 6.5
- Pastured Wood
- Coppice Wood

>1000 ft (> 305 mtrs)
600-1000 ft (183-305 mtrs)
200-600 ft (61-183 mtrs)
<200 ft (<61 mtrs)
North Yorkshire County Boundary

Reproduced from Ordnance Survey material on behalf of The Controller of Her Majesty's Stationery Office © Crown copyright MC100038389 2003

best by vill (aproximately equivalent to a modern civil parish), and in some cases the woodland of several vills are grouped together as one entry. In general, woodland which was difficult to exploit appears to have been under-recorded. One consequence of this appears to be that woodland in the Pennine Dales is under-represented in the Domesday record, possibly because Norman control had not yet been fully established in this area by 1086.[2]

The medieval charters and inquisitions seldom give the size of the woods. The distribution of references may also to some extent reflect the distribution of monastic holdings, as much of the evidence derives from monastic chartularies. Although, of the three sources of evidence, the charters and inquisitions probably provide the most reliable impression of medieval woodland distribution, it is by putting the evidence from these sources together that we get the best picture.

It is clear that the tree cover varied considerably across the county (**fig 6.3**). Some areas such as the Wolds, the Vale of Pickering, the Vale of Mowbray and the Cleveland Plain appear to have had very little woodland at any time during the medieval period. In contrast, extensive areas of woodland were attached to most vills in the Vale of York. In the eastern fringe of the Pennines, most vills had some woodland; but many of these woods may have been relatively small. In the Pennine Dales the woodland was probably mainly confined to the steep valley sides, but may have been widespread in these locations. Craven probably had rather less woodland than the Dales, but it may have been in similar locations. A similar pattern might be proposed for Eskdale, and the upper portions of other moorland dales where they broaden out north of the Tabular Hills. The western scarp of the North York Moors was well wooded, as was the northern side of the Howardian Hills. Along the northern edge of the Vale of Pickering, woodland may have been mainly confined to steep-sided gorges and to the southern scarp of the Tabular Hills.

MEDIEVAL WOODLAND MANAGEMENT

Two main traditions of woodland management were current during the medieval period. Coppicing takes advantage of the tendency for deciduous trees to re-grow from the stump after felling. Woods were felled on a rotation to produce a regular crop of poles. Coppicing extends the life of the stump or stool indefinitely, provided coppicing continues. Coppice woods were enclosed against stock to prevent damage to the young growth.

Wood-pasture is the practice of grazing a woodland. Trees in wood-pasture were often pollarded, producing a regular crop of poles at a height, out of reach of grazing animals. Coppice compartments sometimes also existed in wood-pastures. These would be enclosed for a few years after cutting to allow the new growth to get beyond the reach of grazing animals. Many wood-pastures were commons and, in addition to grazing rights, villagers often had rights to wood for burning, for mending tools and carts, and repairing houses.

Domesday Book records two main types of woodland. These are *silva pastilis*, or wood-pasture; and *silva minuta*, which probably represents coppice. Analysis of the later medieval documents is a little more complicated. Coppicing can be inferred from references to woodland enclosure, from characteristic coppice names such as 'hagg', 'fall' and 'spring', and, much more rarely, from detailed descriptions. References which record grazing in woodland are interpreted as wood-pasture. **Figs 6.4** and **6.5** show that wood-pasture was both more common and more widespread than coppice in medieval North Yorkshire. Only along the east fringe of the Pennines are references to coppice a frequent occurrence.

Analysis of the documentary evidence shows that the emphasis on different methods of exploiting woods changed in the course of the medieval period. Up to about 1200, the charge made for allowing pigs into the woods to fatten on acorns in autumn appears to have been a major source of income (this charge is called pannage). This indicates a large number of mature oak trees, and few pollards or coppices. From 1200 this practice became less important. Between 1200 and about 1320, pasture is the most frequently recorded woodland use, probably reflecting an increasing need to manage and control woodland pasture. When a series of surveys of woods belonging to former monasteries was undertaken, coppice was the most common type of woodland. The degree of change is best illustrated by the number of woods with coppice wood names of 'hagg', 'fall', or 'spring'. In the sixteenth-century evidence, 70 coppice names occur in approximately 350 references (ie 20%), compared to just 17 in the pre-1400 literature out of a total of *circa* 900 references (0.02%).

The intensity of this change varied from place to place. Its causes were complex. It may have been linked to the expansion and localisation of industry, changes in the rural economy, and a less vigorous defence of common rights after the Black Death. The legacy of the coppice expansion is represented by a large number of woods which still retain their coppice names (**fig 6.6**), the survival of old coppice stools, and of archaeological remains such as the platforms used to make charcoal for the iron industry.

Medieval Woodland — Further Reading:
T D Gledhill, Medieval Woodland in North Yorkshire, in M A Atherden and R A Butlin (eds), *Woodland in the Landscape: Past and Future Perspectives* (Leeds: Leeds University Press, 1997), 103-19.
W E Wightman, The significance of waste in Yorkshire Domesday, *Northern History* 5 (1970), 55-71.

6.3   MEDIEVAL FORESTS AND PARKS   IAN DORMOR

One of the principal impacts of the Norman Conquest upon the rural population of North Yorkshire was the declaration of extensive tracts of land as royal hunting forests (**fig 6.7**). In this

Deer were important features of the medieval economy and landscape.
© North York Moors National Park Authority, NC0053.

context, the term 'forest' described a tract of land where the protection of the king's deer (and also wild boar) was enforced by the rule of law, rather than a stand of woodland in modern parlance.

There were nine royal forests in the North Riding of Yorkshire. Nearest to York was the Forest of Galtres, which extended twenty miles (32km) north-west of York to Aldborough and fifteen miles (24km) north to the summit of Crayke Hill. A perambulation of 1316 shows that it comprised about sixty townships and 100,000 acres (40,000ha). To the west of York lay the Forest of Knaresborough, twenty miles (32km) long by eight miles (13km) wide. On the southern flank of the North York Moors, extending westwards towards the Vale of York, were the forests of Spaunton and Pickering, the latter being sixteen miles (26km) long by four miles (6.5km) wide. To the south of York, between the rivers Ouse and Derwent, there was yet another. The Pennine moorlands hosted vast areas for the hunting of deer, and here were located the royal forests of Wensleydale, covering an area eighteen miles (29km) by six miles (9.5km) and centred on Middleham, Bishopdale, Coverdale, Langstrothdale (in Wharfedale), and Craven at the headwaters of the River Aire on the eastern flank of the Pennines.

Woodland would have formed a significant component of all the North Yorkshire royal forests, but of these only the Forest of Pickering is thought to have had a density of woodland cover that would have matched today's connotation of the term 'forest'.

Stringent penalties were handed down by forest courts for offences committed against the king's game. These ranged from stealing wild animals to placing obstacles such as hedges around crops that had the effect of denying free access to the deer. The rights to growing and fallen timber were also strictly controlled. The enforcement of forest law was dependent upon the presence of wardens and foresters, and a complicated system of administration.

In addition to their function as hunting reserves, the forests were a source of meat for the royal table and of raw materials. They held supplies of timber for buildings and ships, and of underwood for charcoal and wood fuel. Some forests also incorporated industrial sites connected with mining and smelting. The royal forests grew to their largest extent under Henry II (1154-89), and by the thirteenth century they covered about one fifth of the entire country. But after this time their popularity began to wane, and by the middle of the fourteenth century they had entered a period of decline. By the fifteenth century they had largely fallen out of use, with land being sold off.

Another common feature of the medieval landscape of North Yorkshire was the deer park. These tended to be located in the areas away from the royal forests, because of the legal restraints which prevented emparking in forests. A deer park differed from a royal hunting forest in terms of its size — normally between 100 and 200 acres (40-80ha) — and the presence of enclosure boundaries, whose purpose was the secure containment of deer. Park boundaries characteristically consisted of an earthwork bank, upon which was set a fence or pale made of wooden stakes. In some cases the bank was topped by a hedge, a palisade or a

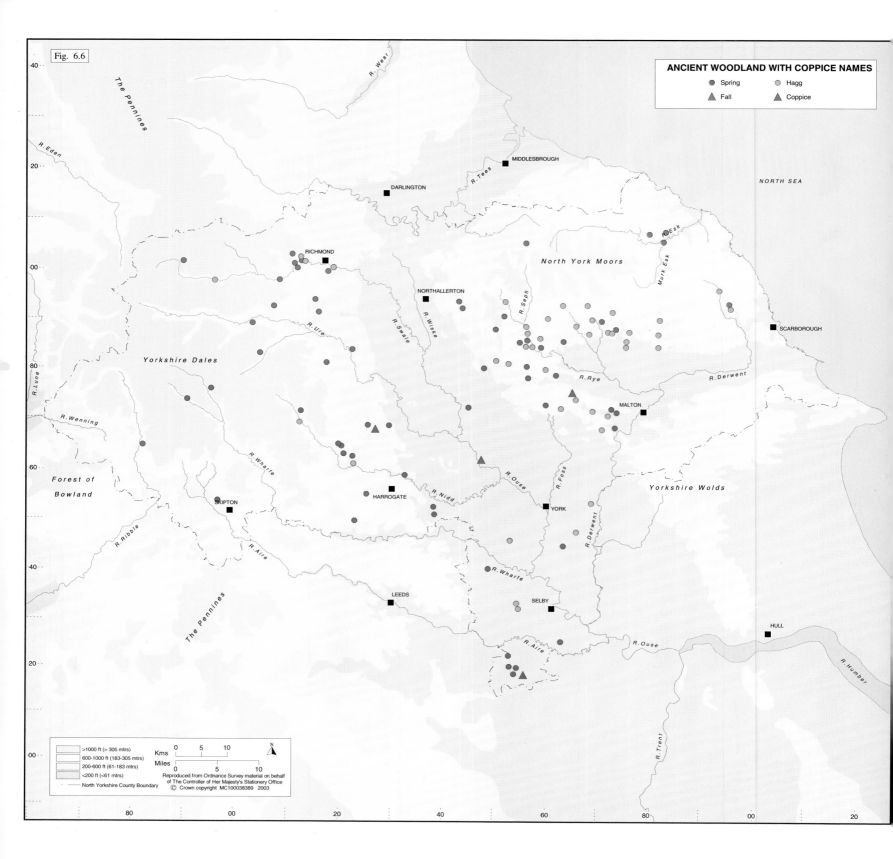

Fig. 6.6

ANCIENT WOODLAND WITH COPPICE NAMES

● Spring   ● Hagg

▲ Fall   ▲ Coppice

>1000 ft (> 305 mtrs)
600-1000 ft (183-305 mtrs)
200-600 ft (61-183 mtrs)
<200 ft (<61 mtrs)
— North Yorkshire County Boundary

Kms   0   5   10
Miles   0   5   10

Reproduced from Ordnance Survey material on behalf of The Controller of Her Majesty's Stationery Office © Crown copyright MC100038389 2003

stone wall. The bank enclosed an inner ditch, and these structures, in combination, effectively contained the deer. Some park boundaries incorporated a deer leap — an ingenious feature that enabled other people's, or wild, deer to gain access to the park, but prevented their escape.

Parks were extremely widespread in Yorkshire; there were sixty-seven in the North Riding and seventy-three in the West Riding. They were created and owned by the Crown, manorial lords, religious houses, wealthy bishops or merchants. Normally part of the demesne land (the land that the lord of the manor worked or had exploited for him), parks were usually laid out on unimproved pasture and woodland. In some instances, the creation of parks gave protection to

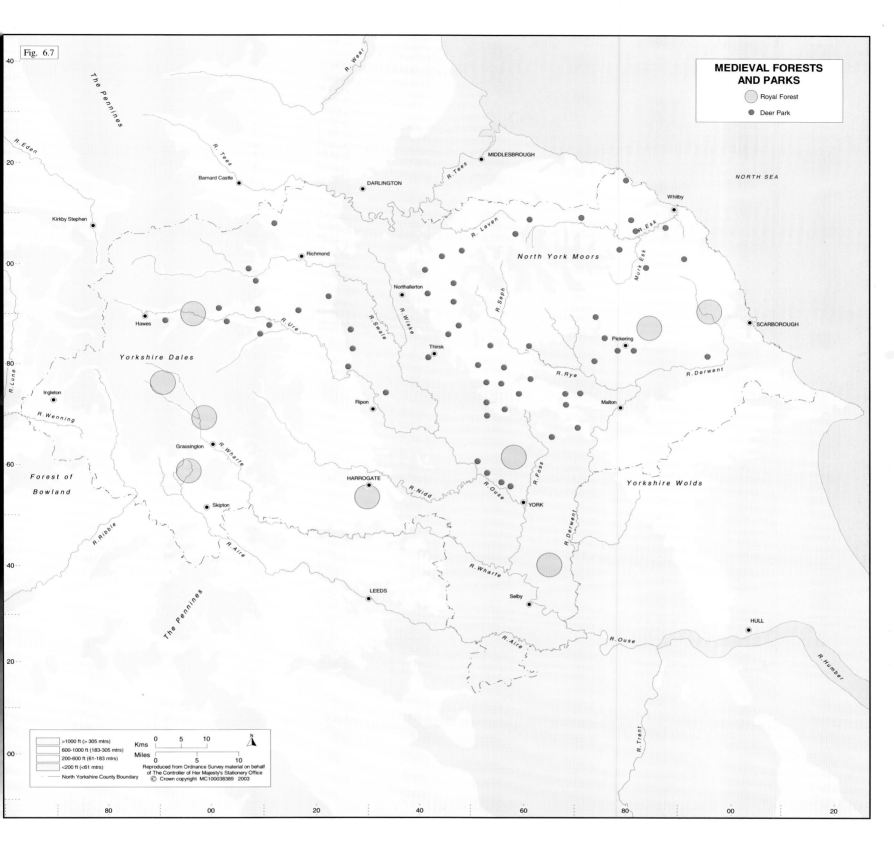

Fig. 6.7

MEDIEVAL FORESTS AND PARKS
- Royal Forest
- Deer Park

woodland that would otherwise have been exposed to assarting (the clearing of forest or 'waste' for agricultural use) by the rapidly growing and land-hungry rural population.

The park was in all respects a status symbol — a reflection of the wealth and social position of its owner. But apart from this, it had a wider function — that of a self-contained economic unit. While many parks were created by enclosing woodland for the purposes of hunting, the principal function of most parks would have been the provision of grazing and shelter for horses, and the location of dog kennels. Commonly, parks incorporated large areas of meadow from which vital hay crops were taken. In addition to this, parks were a source of holly — grown and harvested as an important supplemental winter feed for livestock, especially deer. Livestock farms formed a common feature of many parks, and useful income could be generated from the letting of stinted grazing and pannage for pigs in the woodland. Parks also provided locations for fishponds and warrens where fish and rabbits could be bred and taken within the secure environment provided by the park boundary.

The lodge was a feature of many parks. It usually occupied the highest point within the enclosed landscape, and many remain today either as earthworks, farm buildings or, in some cases, houses.

Emparking of land had reached its peak by the mid-fourteenth century, and with the onset of the Black Death and the resulting labour shortage, the demise of the park was assured. Following an acceleration in disparking between 1500 and the end of the English Civil War, many parks all but disappeared. Today their outlines remain etched in the landscape as hedge-lines, boundary ditches or fragmentary walls. They represent an era of ostentation, the elements of which were perpetuated in the designed landscapes of later centuries.

Medieval Forests and Parks — Further Reading:

L M Cantor (ed.), *The English Medieval Landscape* (London: Croom Helm, 1982).

L M Cantor and J Hatherly, The Medieval Parks of England, *Geography* 64 (2) (1979), 71-85.

A Raistrick, Forests of the Dales, in D Joy (ed.), *Arthur Raistrick's Yorkshire Dales* (Lancaster: Dalesman Books, 1991).

P Stamper, Woods and Parks, in G Astill and A Grant (eds), *The Countryside of Medieval England* (Oxford, 1988).

6.4 MEDIEVAL ROYAL BUILDINGS   JAMES R MATHIEU

From the Norman Conquest and the introduction of the castle to Britain, some of the most prominent landscape features of North Yorkshire were the castles and houses owned and used by the Crown to fulfil its residential and military needs.[1] Significant examples can be found substantially intact throughout the county's more lowland regions, particularly near the rivers which flow into the Humber Estuary, eg Knaresborough, Richmond, and York (see **fig 6.8**). In general, the history of these royal buildings can be best appreciated by focusing on the trends noted during four periods of time.

THE CONSOLIDATION OF THE NORTH (1066-1216)

Throughout the Norman and Angevin periods, the Crown pursued a strategy of military consolidation in Yorkshire. Initially, this focused on controlling the Anglo-Saxon population, and relied upon the maintenance and garrisoning of baronial castles and a few royal ones (eg York's two motte and bailey castles).[2] However, as time went by, royal authority was increasingly challenged by the Anglo-Norman barons themselves (as well as by the Scottish kings). To counteract this, the Crown made its presence more pervasive throughout Yorkshire's lowlands by acquiring major castles in Knaresborough (*c*1080, a ringwork), Pickering (*c*1100, a motte and bailey), Scarborough (1154, a keep with the huge promontory over the sea as its ward) and Richmond (1171, a keep with a triangular ward), while at the same time suppressing baronial rebellions by capturing, destroying or confiscating baronial castles.[3] **Fig 6.8** shows these castles, clearly emphasising the pervasiveness of royal authority. In particular, note that most of lowland North Yorkshire was within a day trip (nine miles/15km) of either a royal castle or a captured baronial one at some point during this period.

PATRONAGE AND BUILDING ALIENATION (1216-1300)

Beginning with Henry III's regency (1216-27), the royal presence in Yorkshire began to dissipate as minor castles (eg Aldborough and Helmsley) were returned to their rightful owners to resolve baronial grievances held against the late King John. More importantly, however, the mature Henry III (1227-72) introduced to Yorkshire the practice of granting important royal buildings to royal favourites and family members, particularly the king's brothers and younger sons (meaning they would not normally return to royal possession in the future). The first of these was Knaresborough Castle, granted initially to Hubert de Burgh (1229), and then after Hubert's fall from power (1234) to Henry III's brother Richard, the Earl of Cornwall (1235).[4] This was followed by the alienation of Richmond Castle (*c*1240), Pickering Castle (1267, by now rebuilt in stone) and the royal house at Easingwold, with the latter two granted to Henry's second son Edmund, the new Earl of Lancaster.[5] **Fig 6.9** shows the results of this patronage, with the royal presence in North Yorkshire by Edward I's reign (1272-1307) limited to the major castles at York (by now rebuilt in stone) and Scarborough. This suggests that Yorkshire was successfully consolidated by this date and no longer required several royal castles to maintain royal authority in the region.

DEFENCE AGAINST THE SCOTS AND PATRONAGE (1300-1399)

This general pattern persisted throughout the next century, with the only significant change resulting from Edward II's (1307-27) defeat at Bannockburn (1314) and the need to defend

The Great Keep at Hemsley Castle. The castle was constructed in the late twelfth and the early thirteenth century.
© North York Moors National Park Authority, HD006

Bolton Castle. A baronial example of a fourteenth century quadrangular castle
© Marie Hartley, 1930s.

York Castle was built on a defensible site near the junction of the Rivers Ouse (left of picture) and Foss (right of picture). The core was the motte, constructed in the eleventh century, on top of which sits the thirteenth century Clifford's Tower.

NMR 17552/06 © English Heritage. NMR.

Maiden's Bower, Topcliffe, vale of York. A baronial example of a Norman period motte and bailey castle.

NMR 17031/32 © Crown copyright. NMR.

Yorkshire against Scottish raids. To achieve this, relatively minor earth and timber fortifications were erected at Northallerton (1314) and around the new royal house at Haverah Park (built c1300 and defended in 1316).[6]

At the same time, two formerly alienated castles escheated to the Crown when their owners died without issue or an adult heir ('escheat' is the reversion of land or property to a lord of the manor or the Crown when there are no heirs at the death of the owner). Knaresborough escheated with the Earl of Cornwall's death (1300) and was soon granted by

Richmond Castle and Town. Richmond Castle, built by the Norman Alan 'the Red' in the late eleventh century, clearly forms a triangular defensive site above the River Swale (foreground). The keep was constructed in the twelfth century, and King Henry II had control of the castle from 1171.
NMR 17674/01 © English Heritage. NMR.

Edward II to his favourite, Piers Gaveston (1307). However, with the latter's execution (1312), it once again became a royal possession.[7] Similarly, Pickering Castle escheated with the Earl of Lancaster's execution (1322), but was soon returned to Lancaster's brother, now the Duke of Lancaster (1326).[8]

Under Edward III the granting of Yorkshire buildings continued, with Knaresborough being granted to Isabella the Queen Mother while she served as regent (1327-30). However, when Edward assumed power he confiscated it and instead granted it to his own Queen Philippa (1331). When it returned to the Crown upon her death (1369), Edward once again granted it, along with the royal house at Haverah Park, to his younger son, John of Gaunt (1372), thus permanently alienating it to the Duchy of Lancaster.[9] **Fig 6.10** shows these minor changes, with York and Scarborough representing the major royal presence in the county, while Pickering and eventually Knaresborough represent the growing importance of the duchy of Lancaster.

SUCCESSION AND THE COUNCIL OF THE NORTH (1399-1539)

When Henry Bolingbroke, the Duke of Lancaster, usurped the throne as Henry IV (1399-1413), North Yorkshire's complexion changed significantly. Specifically, the royal presence within the county was increased by the addition of the Duchy's major castles at Knaresborough and Pickering.[10] Furthermore, Henry initiated a new trend, reversing previous emphasis upon patronage and building alienation, causing the first major building acquisitions in Yorkshire since the Angevin period.

Though occasional building grants were still made (eg Knaresborough to the Queen Mother (1422-37) and Scarborough to Edward IV's brother Richard (1472-83)),[11] the overwhelming pattern during the fifteenth century was the succession of new monarchs who brought new buildings to the Crown.

The castles at Scarborough, Middleham (a huge keep with a concentric ward) and Sheriff Hutton (a large courtyard castle) were acquired with Richard III's succession (1483-85), while Henry VII's succession (1485-1509) made Richmond Castle a royal building

Medieval Royal Buildings — Further Reading:
R A Brown, *Castles from the Air* (Cambridge: Cambridge University Press, 1989).
R A Brown, Castles: I Medieval, in J Turner (ed.), *The Dictionary of Art* (London: Macmillan, 1996), 6:49-58.
H M Colvin (ed.), with R A Brown and A J Taylor, *The History of the King's Works, Vols I & II: The Middle Ages* (London: HMSO, 1963).
H M Colvin (ed.), with D R Ransome and J Summerson, *The History of the King's Works, Vol III: 1485-1660 (Part 1)* (London: HMSO, 1975).
N J G Pounds, *The Medieval Castle in England and Wales: A Social and Political History* (Cambridge: Cambridge University Press, 1990).

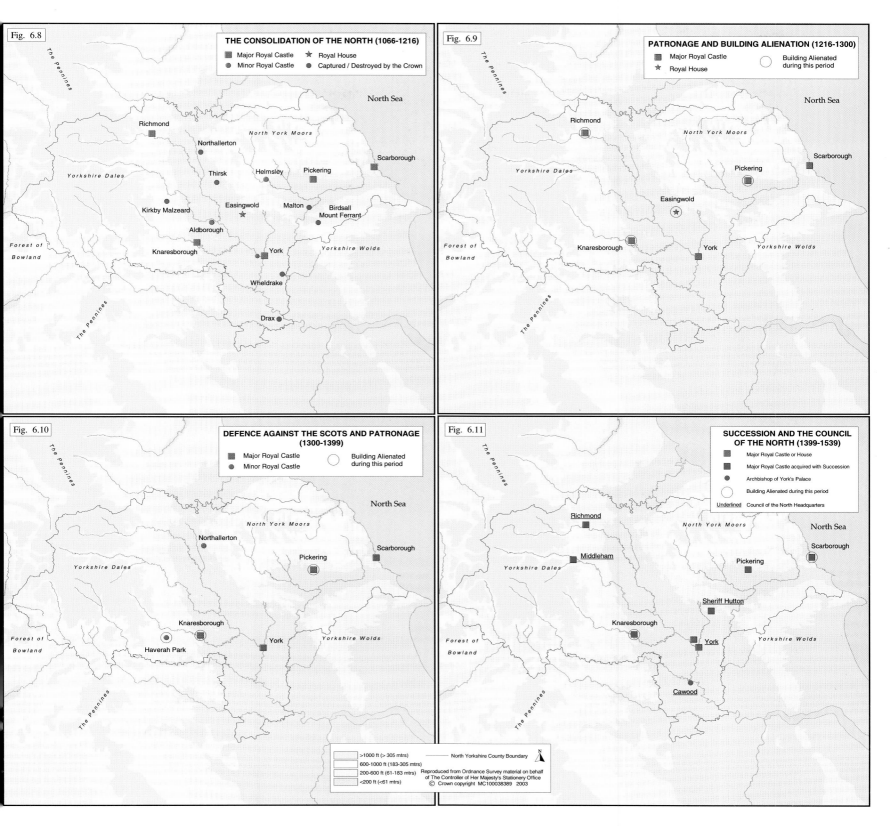

Fig. 6.8

THE CONSOLIDATION OF THE NORTH (1066-1216)

- ■ Major Royal Castle
- ● Minor Royal Castle
- ★ Royal House
- ● Captured / Destroyed by the Crown

The Pennines

North Sea

Richmond
Northallerton
North York Moors
Thirsk
Helmsley
Pickering
Scarborough
Yorkshire Dales
Kirkby Malzeard
Easingwold
Malton
Birdsall
Mount Ferrant
Aldborough
Forest of Bowland
Knaresborough
York
Yorkshire Wolds
Wheldrake
The Pennines
Drax

Fig. 6.9

PATRONAGE AND BUILDING ALIENATION (1216-1300)

- ■ Major Royal Castle
- ★ Royal House
- ○ Building Alienated during this period

The Pennines

North Sea

Richmond
North York Moors
Scarborough
Yorkshire Dales
Pickering
Easingwold
Forest of Bowland
Knaresborough
York
Yorkshire Wolds
The Pennines

Fig. 6.10

DEFENCE AGAINST THE SCOTS AND PATRONAGE (1300-1399)

- ■ Major Royal Castle
- ● Minor Royal Castle
- ○ Building Alienated during this period

The Pennines

North York Moors
North Sea
Northallerton
Pickering
Scarborough
Yorkshire Dales
Forest of Bowland
Knaresborough
York
Yorkshire Wolds
Haverah Park
The Pennines

Fig. 6.11

SUCCESSION AND THE COUNCIL OF THE NORTH (1399-1539)

- ■ Major Royal Castle or House
- ■ Major Royal Castle acquired with Succession
- ● Archbishop of York's Palace
- ○ Building Alienated during this period
- <u>Underlined</u> Council of the North Headquarters

The Pennines

Richmond
North York Moors
North Sea
Middleham
Scarborough
Yorkshire Dales
Pickering
Sheriff Hutton
Knaresborough
York
Yorkshire Wolds
Forest of Bowland
Cawood
The Pennines

>1000 ft (> 305 mtrs)
600-1000 ft (183-305 mtrs)
200-600 ft (61-183 mtrs)
<200 ft (<61 mtrs)

—— North Yorkshire County Boundary

Reproduced from Ordnance Survey material on behalf of The Controller of Her Majesty's Stationery Office © Crown copyright MC100038389 2003

for the first time since the thirteenth century.[12] **Fig 6.11** shows the result of these acquisitions, particularly the renewed pervasiveness of royal authority in the North Yorkshire lowlands (though also note the highland presence suggested by Richmond, Middleham, and Pickering).

Finally, royal authority in northern England was further extended with the establishment of the Council of the North (1484) to oversee regional matters in the six counties south of the Scottish Border. North Yorkshire witnessed the most visible manifestation of this new administrative body, as many of the major royal buildings depicted on the map served as council headquarters before this was more or less permanently established at York's St Mary's Abbey, the renamed King's Manor, after the Dissolution of the Monasteries (1538).[13]

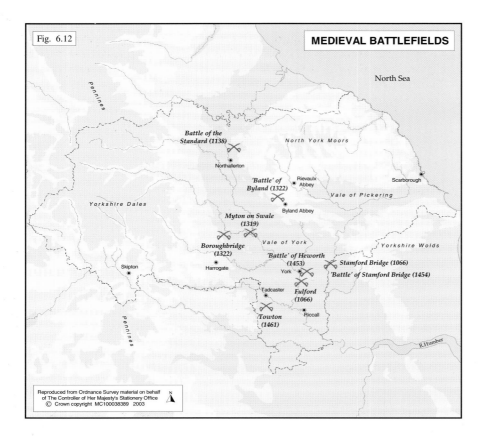

Reproduced from Ordnance Survey material on behalf of The Controller of Her Majesty's Stationery Office © Crown copyright MC100038389 2003

6.5 MEDIEVAL BATTLES 1066-1485 ALAN YOUNG

Study of battles in North Yorkshire for the period 1066-1485 (**fig 6.12**) reflects a number of important themes in the political development of England, and shows North Yorkshire's significance in this development. They highlight, for example, the lack of definition of the English kingdom in the North in 1066 and, indeed, during the century afterwards; they mark the importance of Scotland to the history of North Yorkshire for much of the medieval period; and they reveal the vulnerability of northern England, including North Yorkshire, to political crises of an English government based in the south, and with interests and ambitions south of the Channel.

THE BATTLES OF FULFORD (20TH SEPTEMBER 1066), STAMFORD BRIDGE (25TH SEPTEMBER 1066) AND THE STANDARD (22ND AUGUST 1138)

Set alongside the documentary evidence of the Domesday Survey (1086), and the physical evidence of castle- and monastery- building in the area (**figs 6.8, 6.14, 6.15**), these battles reflect the reality that North Yorkshire was the frontier zone to a kingdom neither fully defined or united. The hard-fought battles of Fulford (an English defeat) and Stamford Bridge (an English victory) were practical expressions of the military threat posed by the Norwegian king, Harald Hardrada (assisted by Tostig, the rebellious brother of Harold, king of England). Scandinavian threats continued after Hardrada's death at Stamford Bridge. York and its two Norman castles were taken, albeit briefly, in 1069 by a force led by Swein, king of Denmark. The Domesday Survey of 1086, itself a response to a further Danish threat in 1085, clearly revealed that the administrative system of the English kingdom only ran to the Tees in the east.

Another political crisis, the civil war of Stephen's reign (1135-54), provided the background to the battle of the Standard, three miles (5km) north of Northallerton, in 1138. The battle marks a time when North Yorkshire was still only lightly settled by Norman/French, York was an isolated outpost of the English king's influence,[1] and David I, king of Scots (1124-53), had the confidence to attempt to stretch Scottish control as far as York. In this period, the archbishopric of York claimed ecclesiastical jurisdiction over the Scottish Church. In 1138, the secular leadership of Thurstan, archbishop of York (1114-40), was vital. According to Richard of Hexham, the northern nobility would actually have abandoned the defence of themselves and the country, had not their archbishop Thurstan animated them by his counsel and exhortation.[2] Defeat at the battle of the Standard did not prevent David I from plotting in 1149 with Henry of Anjou (the future Henry II), Ranulf of Chester and the new (disputed by King Stephen) Archbishop of York, Henry Murdac, to capture York and make it a political and ecclesiastical capital within a Scoto-Northumbrian state.[3] Fulford, Stamford Bridge and the Standard reflect the fact that York could have been a capital of a kingdom under either Scandinavian or Scottish control.

THE BATTLES OF MYTON-ON-SWALE (12TH SEPTEMBER 1319), BOROUGHBRIDGE (16TH MARCH 1322) AND 'BYLAND' (c12TH OCTOBER 1322)

In another period of English internal political weakness under Edward II (1307-27), the Scots once more posed a real threat to North Yorkshire, especially after they captured the last English-garrisoned castle in Scotland — Berwick — in 1318. In 1319, in the absence of the York militia which was at Berwick, Archbishop Melton of York was forced to muster a citizens' army to fight a Scottish force encamped at Myton-on-Swale near Boroughbridge. On 12th September 1319, the English force, 'unskilled in war … they marched all scattered through the fields and in no kind of array',[4] was defeated at 'the Chapter at Myton', as the battle became known due to the large number of clergy present.

Scottish control over northern England was recognised by the wealthiest northern baron, Thomas of Lancaster, who was also leader of the opposition to Edward II. Lancaster's negotiations with the Scots lost him much support in England. Attempting to return to the safety of his new castle at Dunstanburgh (Northumberland), Lancaster's forces were intercepted by Andrew Harclay and his Cumberland levies (mustered troops) at Boroughbridge on 16th March 1322 as Lancaster attempted to cross the Ure. Boroughbridge was a significant royal victory against political opposition — Lancaster was captured, sentenced and executed.

In October 1322, however, Edward II, camped at Rievaulx Abbey, was almost captured by a pincer movement of two Scottish forces, one approaching from Northallerton, the other positioned at Malton.[5] John of Brittany, sent from Rievaulx to reconnoitre the approaching Scottish force 'from a certain height between Byland abbey and Rievaulx abbey',[6] was ambushed at the battle of 'Byland'. The Scottish policy of trying to capture key English personnel almost succeeded.[7]

THE BATTLES OF HEWORTH (24TH AUGUST 1453), STAMFORD BRIDGE (31ST OCTOBER OR 1ST NOVEMBER 1454) AND TOWTON (29TH MARCH 1461)

The Wars of the Roses were more than just a dynastic struggle between the houses of York and Lancaster. The issues were complicated by family feuds and vendettas, such as the one which escalated into private war between the Percy and Neville families in the 1450s.

Percy resentment of the Nevilles' landholding success led to an unsuccessful attack on the wedding party of Thomas Neville and his new bride, Maude Stanhope, niece and co-heiress of the wealthy Ralph, Lord Cromwell, at Heworth Moor. A second skirmish occurred at Stamford Bridge in 1454 where Lord Egremont, second son of Henry Percy, Earl of Northumberland, was captured and heavily fined.

The battle of Towton had more profound consequences as one of the most decisive battles of the Wars of the Roses. The Yorkists gained a complete victory which confirmed Edward, Duke of York, as Edward IV in a region where the Lancastrians had their greatest strength. After the battle, Edward spent three weeks in York while Henry VI and Queen Margaret escaped to Scotland.

Medieval Battles — Further Reading:

J C Appleby and P Dalton, *Government, Religion and Society in Northern England* (Stroud: Sutton Publishing, 1997).

P Dalton, *Conquest, Anarchy and Lordship: Yorkshire 1066-1154* (Cambridge: Cambridge University Press, 1994).

J Gillingham, *The Wars of the Roses* (London: Weidenfeld and Nicolson, 1990).

F Musgrove, *The North of England: a History from Roman Times to the Present* (Oxford: Basil Blackwell, 1990).

W Seymour, *Battles in Britain Vol I, 1066-1547* (London: Sidgwick and Jackson, 1975), for details of Fulford, Stamford Bridge and Towton.

A Young and M J Stead, *In the Footsteps of Robert Bruce* (Stroud: Sutton Publishing, 1999).

6.6   NORTH YORKSHIRE AND THE ANGLO-SCOTTISH WARS, 1318-27   MATTHEW CUTLER

The aim of **fig 6.13** is to illustrate the impact of the Anglo-Scottish wars on North Yorkshire in the early thirteenth century. An important turning point in these wars came in June 1314, when the Scots under Robert Bruce routed an English army led by Edward II at the Battle of Bannockburn.

Following this English defeat, Robert Bruce, who in a remarkable *coup d'état* had seized the Scottish kingship in 1306, was able to adopt a far more aggressive policy towards England than had previously been possible. In Scotland his authority was all but unchallenged, his kingship justified by his military success, while across the border the north of England was left virtually undefended as Edward II, humiliated by defeat, fled south. For the next fourteen years until an Anglo-Scottish peace was finally negotiated in 1328,[1] the military initiative remained for the most part with the Scots; Scottish raids across the border became virtually an annual occurrence, while the English attempts to reverse this situation remained largely ineffectual.

Inevitably, it was the most northerly counties of England that suffered the most at the hands of the Scots. However, in the six years that followed Bannockburn, a number of raids came as far south as North Yorkshire. Of these, the most damaging and widespread took place in May 1318, September 1319 and October 1322. Both in 1318 and 1319, the Scots took similar routes through Yorkshire, advancing down through the Vale of York as far as Pontefract and Castleford, before returning to Scotland via Airedale and Wharfedale and up through the Skipton Gap.[2] Similarly, in 1322, the main Scottish army again invaded Yorkshire via the Vale of York, although this time the raiders then spread out to occupy much of eastern Yorkshire including the Vale of Pickering.

Only on two occasions did the raiders meet with any real resistance. The first of these occasions was at Myton-on-Swale near Boroughbridge in 1319, when the Scots defeated an English army hastily assembled by the archbishop of York,[3] while in 1322, near Old Byland on the edge of the North Yorkshire Moors, the Scots defeated another hastily assembled force, this time led by the Earl of Richmond.[4]

Chronicle accounts paint a fairly graphic picture of the devastation caused by the Scots as they passed through North Yorkshire. According to the *Gesta Edwardi*, for example, in 1318 the Scots 'destroyed the town of Northallerton, burnt the church and adjacent countryside and then wasted and plundered on all sides as far as the abbey of Bolton'.[5] In 1319, according to the same source, the Scots 'entered England with an army, spoiling and burning the country on all sides as far as York';[6] and in 1322, the Meaux chronicle states that the raiders invaded Yorkshire 'bearing no deference to churches or monasteries…they consumed many towns with fire'.[7]

In order to avoid such devastation, many North Yorkshire communities resorted to buying truces with the Scots. The best-known example of this occurred at Ripon in 1318, when the frightened inhabitants, huddled in the cathedral, promised to pay the raiders 1,000 marks.[8] Similarly, in the same year, Fountains Abbey was 'redeemed by paying a fine',[9] while in 1322 the men of the Vale of Pickering ransomed their district for 300 marks.[10] For others, however, the only recourse when faced with the arrival of the Scots was simply to flee, seeking refuge either in the countryside or if possible in one of the nearby castles.[11]

In addition to the chronicle accounts, the best evidence we have for the impact of the Scottish raids on North Yorkshire is a series of ecclesiastical revaluations and taxation exemptions dating from 1318, 1319 and 1327, and it is evidence from these financial documents that has been plotted on the map. Firstly, we have the revaluation of the *Novo Taxatio* of 1318, by which, ostensibly on account of the damage caused by the Scots, the taxation value of many benefices in the north of England was severely reduced;[12] secondly, there are two taxation exemption lists surviving from 1319, which list over 100 Yorkshire villages exempted from the payment of lay subsidies, again apparently because of the depredations caused by the Scots;[13] and thirdly, we have the ecclesiastical revaluation of 1327 covering the archdeaconries of Cleveland and the East Riding, two areas largely unaffected by the Scots when the revaluation of the *Novo Taxatio* was made in 1318.[14] When plotted, these revaluations and taxation exemptions provide us with a clear impression of the areas of North Yorkshire most severely affected by the Scottish raids and the extent of the damage they caused.[15]

Having said this, however, whether these ecclesiastical revaluations and taxation exemption lists are reliable indicators of the extent of the damage caused by the Scottish raids is open to question. For one thing, as Ian Kershaw has pointed in his study of the economy of Bolton Priory, the revaluation of the *Novo Taxatio* of 1318 appears to have reflected little of the real economic worth of the northern benefices.[16] Moreover, with regard to both the benefices seeking reassessment and the villages seeking exemption, there was clearly a financial incentive to exaggerate the devastation caused by the raids.[17] Finally, it seems unlikely that the two taxation exemption lists of 1319 record all the villages severely affected by the Scots, and those villages that are listed probably owed their exemption to the influence of important patrons.[18]

Moreover, it would be wrong to attribute all of North Yorkshire's economic problems in the early thirteenth century to the Scots. When the Scots arrived in Yorkshire in 1318, they found a countryside already wracked by civil unrest and economic depression. Since 1315, for example, much of England had been suffering from famine and an agrarian crisis brought on in part by the poor harvests of 1308-10 and 1315, and this clearly intensified the economic

Anglo-Scottish Wars — Further Reading:

I Kershaw, A Note on the Scots in the West Riding, 1318-19, *Northern History* XVII (1981), 231-9.

C McNamee, *The Wars of the Bruces: Scotland, England and Ireland, 1306-1328* (East Linton: Tuckwell Press, 1997).

J Scammell, Robert I and the North of England, *English Historical Review* LXXIII (1958), 385-403.

J F Willard, The Scotch Raids and the Fourteenth Century Taxation of Northern England, *University of Colorado Studies* V (1907-8), 237-42.

A Young and M Stead, *In the Footsteps of Robert Bruce* (Stroud: Sutton, 1999).

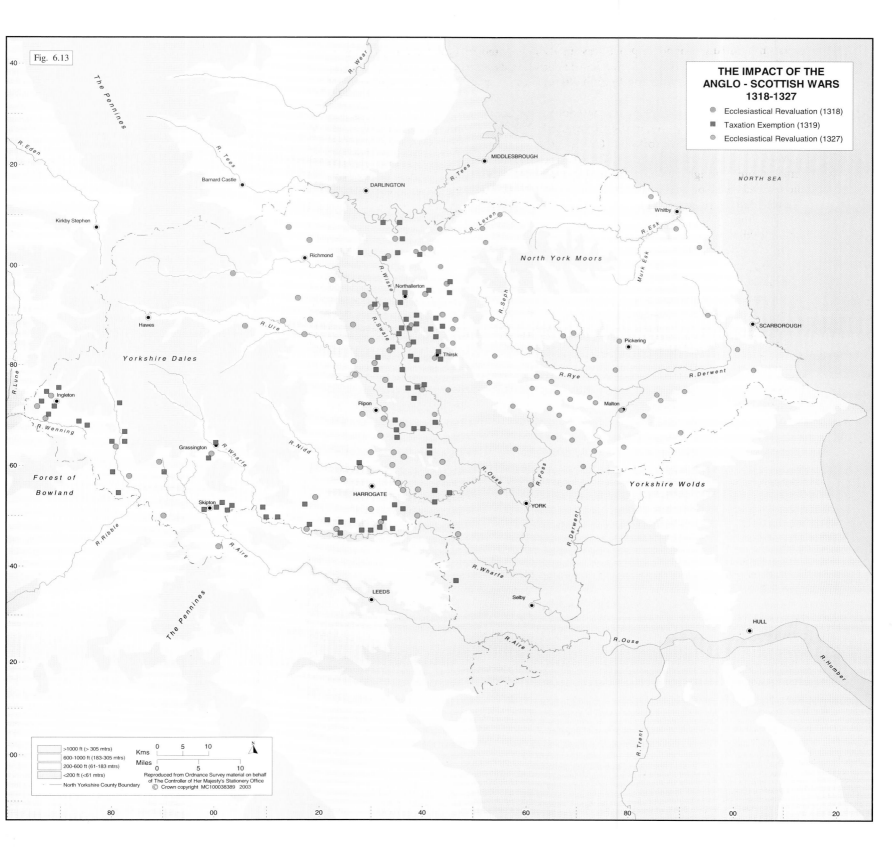

Fig. 6.13

THE IMPACT OF THE
ANGLO - SCOTTISH WARS
1318-1327

- Ecclesiastical Revaluation (1318)
- Taxation Exemption (1319)
- Ecclesiastical Revaluation (1327)

>1000 ft (> 305 mtrs)
600-1000 ft (183-305 mtrs)
200-600 ft (61-183 mtrs)
<200 ft (<61 mtrs)
North Yorkshire County Boundary

Kms 0   5   10
Miles 0   5   10

Reproduced from Ordnance Survey material on behalf
of The Controller of Her Majesty's Stationery Office
© Crown copyright MC100038389 2003

problems of the north.[19] Furthermore, as a result of York's importance as a war capital in the years after 1298, Yorkshire was constantly called upon throughout the early thirteenth century to help resource both the Edwardian government and the English war-machinery campaigning in Scotland.[20] Lastly, for those North Yorkshire communities lying either side of the main supply routes, the transportation of these resources as well as the general trafficking of military personnel to and from Scotland provided for further economic disruption.[21] Arguably, therefore, with regard to North Yorkshire's economic decline in the early thirteenth century, the arrival of the Scots was merely 'the straw that broke the camel's back'.

MEDIEVAL NORTH YORKSHIRE   89

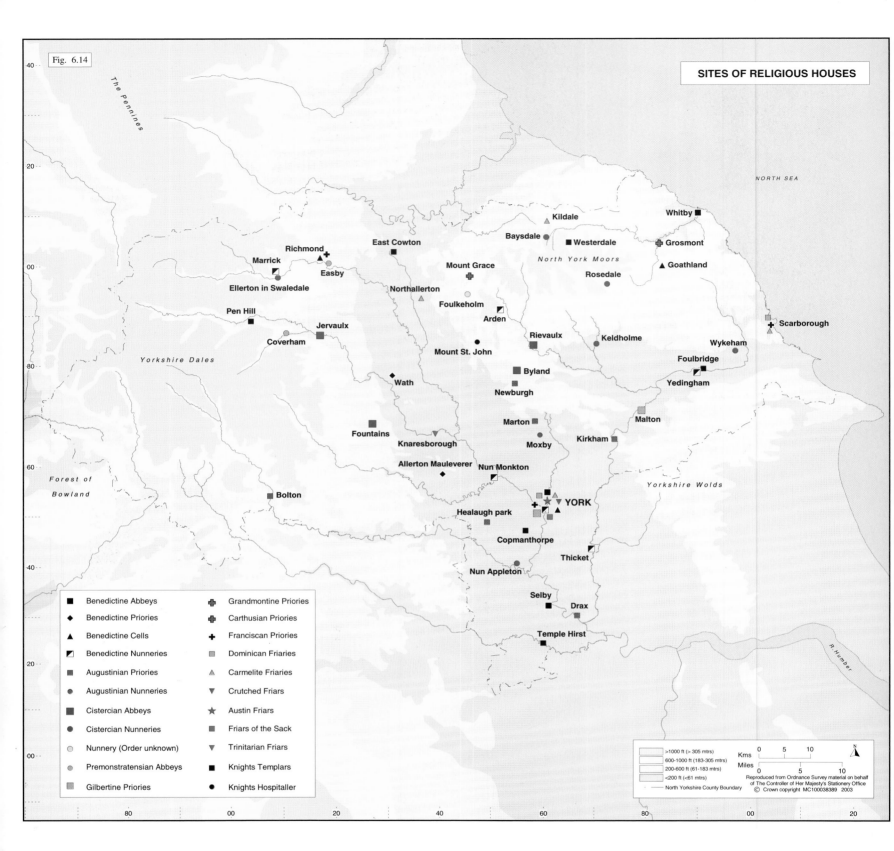

Fig. 6.14

SITES OF RELIGIOUS HOUSES

The Pennines

40

20

00

NORTH SEA

Kildale ▲

Whitby ■

Baysdale ●

■ Westerdale

✠ Grosmont

East Cowton ■

North York Moors

Richmond ▲ ✠

Marrick ◪

Easby

Mount Grace ✠

▲ Goathland

Ellerton in Swaledale

Northallerton

Rosedale ●

Pen Hill ■

Foulkeholm ●

Jervaulx

Arden ◪

■ Scarborough ✠
▲

Coverham ●

Rievaulx ■

Keldholme ●

Wykeham ●

Yorkshire Dales

Mount St. John ●

Byland ■

Foulbridge

Wath ◆

Newburgh ■

Yedingham

Marton ■

Malton ◪

Fountains ■

Knaresborough ▼

Moxby ●

Kirkham ◪

Yorkshire Wolds

Forest of Bowland

Allerton Mauleverer ◆

Nun Monkton ◪

▲
★ ▼ **YORK**
▲

Bolton ■

Healaugh park ●

✠ ◼

Copmanthorpe ■

Thicket ◪

Nun Appleton ●

Selby ■

Drax ●

Temple Hirst ■

R. Humber

■	Benedictine Abbeys	✠	Grandmontine Priories
◆	Benedictine Priories	✠	Carthusian Priories
▲	Benedictine Cells	✚	Franciscan Priories
◪	Benedictine Nunneries	■	Dominican Friaries
■	Augustinian Priories	▲	Carmelite Friaries
●	Augustinian Nunneries	▼	Crutched Friars
■	Cistercian Abbeys	★	Austin Friars
●	Cistercian Nunneries	■	Friars of the Sack
○	Nunnery (Order unknown)	▼	Trinitarian Friars
●	Premonstratensian Abbeys	■	Knights Templars
■	Gilbertine Priories	●	Knights Hospitaller

>1000 ft (> 305 mtrs)
600-1000 ft (183-305 mtrs)
200-600 ft (61-183 mtrs)
<200 ft (<61 mtrs)
North Yorkshire County Boundary

Kms 0 5 10
Miles 0 5 10

Reproduced from Ordnance Survey material on behalf of The Controller of Her Majesty's Stationery Office © Crown copyright MC100038389 2003

80   00   20   40   60   80   00   20

6.7 RELIGIOUS HOUSES   JANET BURTON

In the Middle Ages, North Yorkshire boasted over fifty religious houses of various sizes, orders and observances (**fig 6.14**). This was the result of sustained activity which began in 1069 and reached a peak in the 1130s to 1150s, with the coming of the Cistercians and the spread of houses for women. Although the momentum of foundation declined after the middle of the twelfth century, North Yorkshire experienced new religious trends: the coming of the friars in the thirteenth century, and the Carthusians in the fourteenth.

above Rievaulx Abbey, near Helmsley, North York Moors. This Cistercian abbey was founded in 1132.
© R White 3328.

top right Aerial view of Mount Grace Priory, on the edge of the North York Moors near Osmotherley. This Carthusian monastery was founded in 1398, and was terminated in 1539, at the time of the general dissolution of the monasteries in England. The main Church and cloister are clearly visible.
NMR 12052/05 © *Crown copyright. NMR.*

bottom right Fountains Abbey, founded by the Cistercians in 1132.
© N Butlin.

Rejuvenated monasticism came to North Yorkshire along with the Normans, when the vocation of the hermit-monks, Benedict of Auxerre and Reinfrid of Evesham/Jarrow, combined with the religious sentiments and political acumen of the Norman conquerors to plant Benedictine monasteries on the banks of the Ouse at Selby (1069) and on the dramatic cliff-top site of the former Anglo-Saxon monastery at Whitby (*c* 1078). Within a few years, part of the Whitby community moved, first to Lastingham, and then to the urban centre of York, where the abbey of St Mary's became a potent symbol of the might of the Norman kings who were regarded as founders of the abbey. The link between monasticism and conquest was also manifest in the foundation of dependencies of foreign houses, such as Holy Trinity, York (Marmoutier), and the smaller cell of Wath (Mont St Michel).

Benedictine monasteries such as Selby, Whitby and York had at the heart of their existence the strict liturgical routine laid down in the Rule of St Benedict. They were maintained in their lifestyle by landed estates granted by those who desired to benefit from their prayers.

From the early years of the twelfth century, the nobility of North Yorkshire found other targets for their religious patronage, and houses of regular canons began to appear. The canons followed a similar daily routine to monks, as laid down by the Rule of St Augustine; many were also priests. Houses of Augustinian canons had begun to be founded in England in the late eleventh century, and this was a trend in which North Yorkshire participated, with six such houses. It has been suggested that founders were attracted to the regular canons

above Whitby Abbey, founded as a priory by Benedictine monks in the late eleventh century, it became an abbey by 1109.
© North York Moors National Park Authority, HA0089.

left Jervaulx Abbey (founded 1147) and Garden earthworks.
NMR 17523/23 © English Heritage. NMR.

because their houses were inexpensive to establish, requiring less outlay than a Benedictine monastery, but the founders of a number of North Yorkshire houses, notably Bolton and Kirkham, were not ungenerous in their endowments.

In many ways, however, North Yorkshire was dominated by the Cistercians or White Monks, who belonged to the order of Cîteaux (Côte-d'Or). Although Rievaulx (1132) was not the first Cistercian house to be founded in England, it was one of the most important. Established by a group of monks sent from Clairvaux (Aube) by one of the most influential of all Cistercians — St Bernard — Rievaulx became the mother house of a family of monasteries which spread north into Scotland and south into Lincolnshire.

Its impact on northern monasticism began even before the monks had settled in the valley of the River Rye. As they passed through York they fanned the flames of a reform movement in the abbey of St Mary's, resulting in the secession of a group of monks and — although this was not planned at the time — the foundation of a second Cistercian monastery, Fountains Abbey.

Rievaulx and Fountains were to become major landowners, and influential in the development of wool production and export. Membership of an international order brought them, and the monks of Byland and Jervaulx, into regular contact with overseas trends and developments.

The Cistercians are always associated with the foundation of monasteries 'in the desert', in locations which lay — in the words of their own regulations — 'far from the concourse of men'. From the map, however, it is clear that they did not have a monopoly of such sites, and women's houses, too, could occupy liminal positions. Nunneries tended to be smaller and less well endowed with lands than male houses. Some were established in parish churches, which they shared with the local community. Others, such as Arden, Baysdale, Thicket and Rosedale, lay in remote and inhospitable moorland.[1] The North Yorkshire nunneries provided the opportunity for women to follow a life of prayer, contemplation and poverty.

If the Cistercians, and the other eremitical (hermit or reclusive) orders of the Grandmontines (Grosmont, 1204) and Carthusians (Mount Grace, 1398), were largely rural, the last great religious expansion of the Middle Ages, that of the friars, was quite the opposite. The major orders were dominated by two principles: poverty, to such a degree that they depended on begging to survive; and preaching. For both they needed an urban environment. Within years of their arrival in Britain the friars came to North Yorkshire. In York, houses of Dominican, Franciscan, Carmelite, Austin and Crutched Friars, as well as the Friars of the Sack, joined the Benedictine monks and nuns, and Gilbertine canons, who had already settled in the city. Friars settled too at Knaresborough, Northallerton, Richmond and Scarborough.

The richness and diversity of the religious orders had a profound effect on the physical, ecclesiastical and cultural landscape of North Yorkshire, on its economy and its architecture. Although the expansion was a phenomenon largely associated with the twelfth century, and although from the thirteenth century the monastic order faced a challenge from new forms of expressing religious devotion, monasteries, nunneries and friaries remained an integral and respected part of the fabric of society.

Religious Houses — Further Reading:
Janet Burton, *The Monastic Order in Yorkshire, 1069–1215*, Cambridge Studies in Medieval Life and Thought, fourth series, 40 (Cambridge: Cambridge University Press, 1999).
Janet Burton, *The Yorkshire Nunneries in the Twelfth and Thirteenth Centuries*, Borthwick Paper 56 (York: University of York, 1979).
Glyn Coppack, *Fountains Abbey* (London: English Heritage and Batsford, 1993).
Bernard Jennings, *Yorkshire Monasteries. Cloister, land and people* (Otley: Smith Settle, 1999).
Ian Kershaw, *Bolton Priory. The economy of a northern monastery* (Oxford: Clarendon Press, 1973).
Michael Robson, *The Franciscans in the Medieval Custody of York*, Borthwick Paper 93 (York: University of York, 1997).

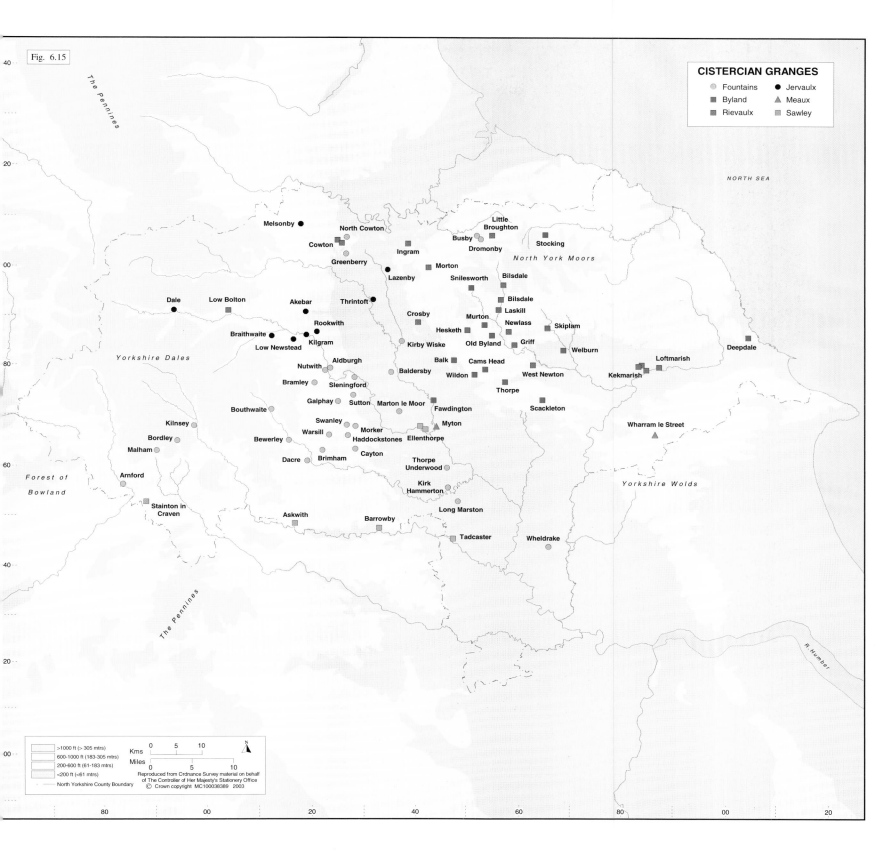

Fig. 6.15

Despite the power and wealth of the religious orders, there is no evidence for hostility towards them.[2] When in the 1530s they were faced with the seemingly irresistible force of a king in need of their resources, they did not go without a struggle. Indeed it was in the North that the leaders of the Pilgrimage of Grace emerged. One of them, Robert Aske, maintained to the end that religious houses performed a valuable function in society, in the provision of education, care for the sick and hospitality. Some Yorkshire monks, canons and friars suffered death for treason for their opposition to the king, among them Adam Sedbar, Abbot of Jervaulx, and William Thirsk, former Abbot of Fountains. Resistance was short lived, and in January 1540 the last religious house in North Yorkshire was suppressed.

Grange site: the home grange of Rievaulx Abbey at Griff.
© R White/Yorkshire Dales National Park Authority, ANY 17904.

6.8 CISTERCIAN GRANGES   JANET BURTON

The monastic orders revolutionised economic and agricultural practices in North Yorkshire. In the forefront of change was the Cistercian order, an international congregation which spread rapidly during the twelfth century.

Through their legislative body, the annual general chapter, the Cistercians developed stringent economic practices. Theirs was intended to be a land-based economy, with consolidated estates managed in isolation from the manorial structure from farms known as granges. These were to be staffed by *conversi* (lay brothers) and worked using hired labour, to be situated within a day's journey from the abbey, and at least two leagues (about six miles/4km) from granges of other houses.

In recent years, scholars have debated the chronology of the development of a distinctive Cistercian economy, in particular the policy of rejecting revenues (such as tithes) derived from the work of others. However, it is clear that, from within a decade of the coming of the Cistercians to North Yorkshire, they developed consolidated grange estates through grant, exchange and lease which enabled them to emerge as highly successful farmers, industrialists and traders.

Fig 6.15 locates over eighty grange sites controlled by the North Yorkshire abbeys of Rievaulx, Fountains, Byland and Jervaulx, with the minor presence of Meaux (East Yorkshire) and Sawley (Lancashire). Two words of warning should be given. In some cases where full documentary and archaeological evidence is lacking, the precise location of a grange may not be known. Moreover, not all these sites may have functioned as 'classic' granges throughout their existence. It is not certain, for example, if Cams Head (Byland) was a small grange or a lodge.[1]

The spread of Cistercian granges was rapid. Fountains had established Cayton and Aldburgh by 1138, and Warsill, Cowton, Dacre and Sutton by 1146. Byland created its first grange at Wildon in 1142.

The Cistercian ideal was isolation, and the establishment of some granges, such as Old Byland (Byland) and Thorpe Underwood and Baldersby (Fountains) involved depopulation. The creation of the 'home grange' of Rievaulx Abbey at Griff may also have involved the relocation of the rural population.

In contrast, some granges were created or extended by assarting — the clearance of unprofitable land — and there is a high correlation between areas which are recorded as waste or partially waste in *Domesday Book* (1086) and Cistercian granges.[2] Although the degree of recovery of such lands by the mid-twelfth century is a matter for debate, it seems that in North Yorkshire the reputation of the Cistercians as pioneers in the extension of cultivable lands is deserved. Rievaulx's Pickering granges contained over 1,000 acres (400ha) of land which had lain waste in 1086.

The Cistercian granges formed a strategic chain of farms managing extensive estates, and allowed movement of goods and personnel from the abbey to its outlying estates. Dale Grange controlled Jervaulx's pastures in Wensleydale. Of the granges of Fountains,

Sleningford managed lands in lower Wensleydale, and Aldburgh and Nutwith those in upper Wensleydale; Dacre and Bouthwaite controlled Nidderdale; and Kilnsey, Wharfedale.[3]

The activity of each grange was determined by location and terrain. Some, like the moorland granges of Rievaulx (Griff, Newlass and Skiplam) and Fountains (Dacre, Bouthwaite), were at the centre of extensive sheep-pastures. Jervaulx kept cattle on its Nidderdale estates. There were fisheries at Malham (Fountains) and Cams Head (Byland). Elsewhere there is evidence of industrial activities: tile manufacture at Old Byland; pottery production at Sutton (Fountains); and forges at Aldburgh (Fountains).

Such activities would have influenced the nature of the grange buildings, some of which have been excavated or can be traced through earthworks. Cowton Grange is known through excavation; and there are surviving buildings at Bewerley and Thrintoft.[4] There are traces of peasant settlements adjoining twelve granges.

From the early thirteenth century the Cistercian general chapter allowed abbeys to break from the pattern of direct exploitation and in some cases to lease lands to tenants. However, it was not until the fourteenth century, when unsettled political conditions and war with Scotland wrought severe damage on Cistercian estates in North Yorkshire, that changes in grange management can be seen.[5]

In 1336 Fountains applied to lease three of its granges. By the mid-fourteenth century, four granges of Jervaulx had been converted to vills (settlements); and in 1363 Fountains was allowed to lease to tenants its granges of Aldburgh, Sleningford, Sutton, Cowton, Cayton, Bramley, Kilnsey and Thorpe Underwood. Dissolution accounts, however, reveal that many Cistercian granges were still held in demesne (owned by the lord and not occupied by tenants), and that the grange remained an enduring feature of the economic activity of the White Monks, activity whose impact on the North Yorkshire countryside was so great.

6.9 POPULATION AND SETTLEMENT IN THE LATER MIDDLE AGES   JEREMY GOLDBERG

The distribution of the county's population only a generation after the Black Death can be seen from the numbers of taxpayers for each vill (settlement) in the first Poll (or head) tax of 1377.[1] These totals exclude youngsters below the age of fourteen and the indigent. Others may have evaded the tax, though the problem was much less acute than for the subsequent Poll Taxes of 1379 and 1380-1. For York we have (incomplete) nominal listings, that is actual names of tax payers (other than servants). These only strengthen confidence in the quality of the evidence. The clergy were taxed separately. On balance, the totals of taxpayers recorded provide a good comparative indicator of population levels and distribution, though we need to be somewhat cautious about absolute numbers (**fig 6.16**). The same is true of attempts to convert taxpayers into actual population totals, though here a multiplier of 1.65 has been used.

Cistercian Granges — Further Reading:

J Burton, The Estates and Economy of Rievaulx Abbey in Yorkshire, *Cîteaux: Commentarii Cistercienses* 49 (1998), 29–93.

Glyn Coppack, *Fountains Abbey* (London: English Heritage and Batsford, 1993).

R A Donkin, *The Cistercians. Studies in the geography of medieval England and Wales*, Pontifical Institute of Medieval Studies 38 (Toronto: Pontifical Institute, 1978).

R A Donkin, The Cistercian Grange in England in the 12th and 13th Centuries, with Special Reference to Yorkshire, *Studia Monastica* 6 (1964), 95–144.

James S Donnelly, Changes in the Grange Economy of English and Welsh Cistercian Abbeys, 1399-1540, *Traditio* 10 (1954), 399-458.

Colin Platt, *The Monastic Grange in Medieval England* (London: Macmillan, 1969).

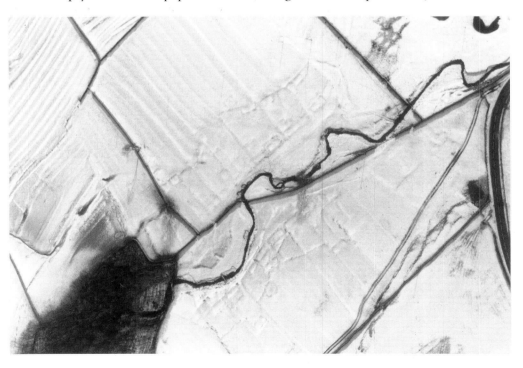

Walburn deserted medieval village, north of Leyburn. The aerial view, taken when snow covered the ground, shows the outline of village houses and tofts, together with the fossilized ridges and furrows of the former open fields.

NMR 12348/17 © Crown copyright NMR.

The only place of any size within the modern county boundary was York with a population of some 12,000 persons. Together with the towns of Beverley and Hull to the south-east and Pontefract to the south-west, York drew people away from elsewhere within the region. This is demonstrated by the toponymic bynames (surnames) among York residents contained in the Poll Tax returns and the city's Register of Freemen. The only other centre of population was Scarborough with some 2,400 persons. No other settlement in the county had a population in four figures and, even allowing for the high mortality in the Black Death, it is unlikely that the picture would have differed before 1349.

The remaining communities that had populations in excess of 500 persons and may indeed have demonstrated other urban characteristics, whether boroughs or otherwise, were mostly associated either with religious houses or great aristocratic residences. Whitby and Selby, associated with Benedictine monasteries, had tax populations of 640 and 586 respectively. The Gilbertine Priory at Old Malton (and associated hospital at New Malton) help explain a tax population for the two communities of 434 (mostly in New Malton). Ripon (tax population in 1379 of 482) was partly dependent on its minster. Pickering (tax population 420) and Richmond (568) were both associated with castles, though the recorded taxation populations of the other settlements with important castles at Helmsley (282), Skipton (176) and Middleham (145) were more modest. The population of Middleham probably grew when it became the seat of the Duke of Gloucester (later Richard III) in the later fifteenth century. Cawood (tax population 316) was the location of one of the Archbishop of York's palaces. Only Kirkbymoorside (tax population 511) and Northallerton (312) do not fit the model. The nascent urban identity of the latter is reflected in the foundation there of the Carmelite friary in 1356-7, but it also possessed a hospital founded c1200.

Aside from these larger settlements, population tended to be concentrated along river valleys, along the coast and within the Vale of York. Upland areas, particularly the Pennine dales, were generally sparsely populated. The increasing dependence of the great Cistercian houses of Fountains, Rievaulx, Jervaulx and Byland, together with the Premonstratensian houses of Coverham and Easby, on contracted lay employees rather than lay brothers, and the general expansion of demand for textiles, probably served to sustain population levels even in these least populous regions. Certainly the nominative Poll Tax listings for the West Riding wapentakes of Ainsty, Claro and Staincliffe (corresponding in part to the western part of the modern county) show evidence for textile manufacture. Four weavers were listed, for example, at Bishop Monkton (near Ripon).

It is difficult to assess patterns of population movement over the course of the later Middle Ages. York, with its high demand for labour, was a magnet for rural migrants into the fifteenth century. In particular we can detect demand for adolescents and young adults of both sexes: the demand for live-in servants was very high — some third of households employed servants — and the sex ratio of the tax population in 1377 favoured women. By the middle of the century, York was probably both less attractive a centre and less successful in attracting migrants; the population slowly declined, and may have fallen below 10,000 by the early sixteenth century.

Despite the high level of depopulation consequent upon the advent of plague, some rural areas continued to attract migrants, notably where land relatively unencumbered by customary obligations was available. This was true, for example, of Bilsdale: it was here that John Helmslay (alias Skryvener), a serf of Meaux Abbey's grange at Wharram, fled around 1390. He presented himself as a freeman, married a local woman of good family, but was recaptured a number of years later.[2] Analysis of the 1379 Howdenshire nominative Poll Tax listings suggests a movement of persons, especially young women, from settlements along the lower Derwent Valley and (outside the modern county) from the lower reaches of the Ouse around Howden itself, to Barmby, Hemingbrough and Cliffe, the two last being within the modern county.

Population movements in Howdenshire may have something to do with growing employment opportunities in textile manufacture; they may also be related to patterns of flooding associated with rising water-levels and gradual shifts in river courses. The Derwent suffered from flooding early in 1436, for one John Cundall, chaplain, was drowned in the river. A witness in a church court case recalled a 'memorable [famosa] flood in the north parts of England' in 1433, referring to a drowning near Kexby bridge. Around the same time, substantial bequests were made by York merchants for local bridges: Margaret, the widow of Nicholas Blackburn senior, left sums of £100 in 1434 towards Catterick and Kexby bridges.[3] A run of wet summers between 1438 and 1440, however, precipitated a regional 'agrarian crisis'. The rivers Tees and Ure both flooded; other regional rivers probably also overflowed their banks.[4]

More significant in shaping population movements were shifts in the agrarian economy consequent upon falling demand for grain, following the advent of plague. Some areas previously devoted to grain production, which ceased to be economically viable as labour

Appleton-le-Moors. A medieval planned village, probably of Norman origin, on the North York Moors.

© North York Moors National Park Authority, NYM 107.

Population & Settlement — Further Reading:

M W Beresford, The Lost Villages of Yorkshire, *Yorks Arch Jnl* XXXVII 474–91; XXXVIII 44–70, 215–40, 280–309 (1954–5).

P J P Goldberg, *Women, Work, and Life Cycle in a Medieval Economy: Women in York and Yorkshire c1300–1520* (Oxford: Oxford University Press, 1992).

P J P Goldberg, Mortality and Economic Change in the Diocese of York 1390–1514, *Northern History* XXIV (1988) 38–55.

P McClure, Patterns of Migration in the Late Middle Ages: The Evidence of English Place-Name Surnames, *Economic History Review*, 2nd series, XXXII (1979), 167–82.

costs rose and prices fell, probably shed labour even at a time more broadly characterised by labour shortage. This is true of the Wolds, where several settlements came to be deserted, and of the Vale of York. For example, we glimpse migrants from the subsequently deserted village of Stockeld (near Wetherby) in a church court case of 1418.[5] In addition to the localities already noticed, there was a concentration of desertion in the central part of the county, some of which may be attributed to Scottish raids in the earlier fourteenth century.

To the above evidence for population distribution and movement, we can add patterns of mortality. A fuller picture also requires information about fertility. This last hardly exists, but there is room for speculation. The region was severely hit by the twin catastrophes of the agrarian crisis and Scottish raiding (and virtual civil war) during the second and third decades of the fourteenth century. The impact on population levels (as opposed to distribution) is unknown, though it may not have been particularly profound. Much more significant was the advent of plague in the summer of 1349. The current consensus is that nearly half the population perished, though there was considerable local variation. Clerical mortality for the diocese and the reported mortality of monks at the East Riding monastery of Meaux suggest that this region did not escape lightly, indeed the aetiology of plague indicates particular virulence during the late summer season.

The advent of plague in 1349 heralded an era of epidemic followed by endemic disease. The Meaux Chronicle and the Anonimalle Chronicle, associated with St Mary's Abbey, York, both record (in derivative terms) the epidemics of 1361 and 1369. The latter records a further (or fourth) epidemic 'in the north country' in 1375, distinguishing this from the fourth epidemic in York three years later. The years 1361, 1369 and (uncommented on by the chroniclers) 1384 all appear as years of high mortality from the pattern of wills registered by the dean and chapter of York, although many of these fall outside the bounds of the modern county. The chroniclers record a 1391 epidemic focused on York, which appears also in the Exchequer court probate series (from 1389).[6]

Poor harvests in 1398 and 1400–1 are mirrored in higher levels of mortality in the Exchequer court series. There are further indications of regional epidemic in 1421 (outside the Exchequer series) and high rates of mortality also show in 1429 and 1436. The regional crisis of 1438 probably had the most profound impact since, perhaps, the second pestilence of 1361. Heavy rains led to harvest failure; dysentery and similar diseases were likely rife. Further high mortality appears in the exchequer series for 1459, 1467, 1471, 1474 and 1483.

It is unclear if any were due specifically to plague; none compared with 1438. The background level of endemic plague was, however, probably quite high until about this time. High levels of mortality recurred through the first decade of the sixteenth century, reaching a peak in 1505–6. 'Sweating sickness' has been blamed, though a Ripon source refers enigmatically to the 'plague of pestilence'. Further years of increased mortality are noted in York in 1522 and 1538. The highest levels were reached in 1550–2 and 1558–9. These last were not confined to York, though their precise regional impact has yet to be explored.[7]

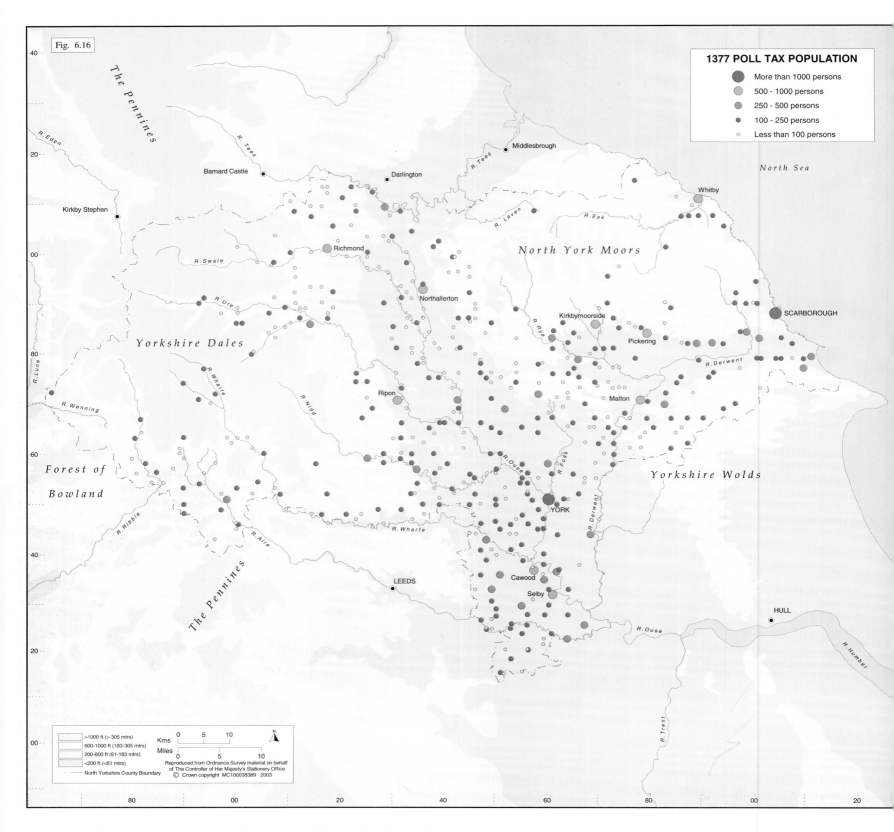

Fig. 6.16

1377 POLL TAX POPULATION

- More than 1000 persons
- 500 - 1000 persons
- 250 - 500 persons
- 100 - 250 persons
- Less than 100 persons

The Pennines

R. Eden

R. Tees

Barnard Castle

Kirkby Stephen

Middlesbrough

R. Tees

Darlington

R. Leven

R. Esk

Whitby

North Sea

R. Swale

Richmond

North York Moors

R. Ure

Yorkshire Dales

Northallerton

R. Rye

Kirkbymoorside

Pickering

SCARBOROUGH

R. Derwent

Malton

R. Lune

R. Wenning

R. Wharfe

R. Nidd

Ripon

Forest of

Bowland

Yorkshire Wolds

R. Ribble

R. Aire

R. Ouse

R. Foss

YORK

R. Derwent

The Pennines

LEEDS

R. Wharfe

Cawood

Selby

HULL

R. Ouse

R. Humber

R. Trent

>1000 ft (> 305 mtrs)
600-1000 ft (183-305 mtrs)
200-600 ft (61-183 mtrs)
<200 ft (<61 mtrs)
North Yorkshire County Boundary

Kms 0   5   10
Miles 0   5   10

Reproduced from Ordnance Survey material on behalf
of The Controller of Her Majesty's Stationery Office
© Crown copyright MC100038389 2003

The county's population was presumably much reduced through the second half of the fourteenth century by the impact of epidemic plague. Decline probably continued into the fifteenth century due as much to endemic as epidemic disease. The crisis of 1438 perhaps coincided with a regional nadir in population levels. Mortality was again high in the 1470s, the 1500s and the 1550s, but the national perspective is that population was beginning to recover through this period and growing fast by the start of parish registration in 1538. This implies that underlying levels of fertility rose as more women married and at earlier ages. It may be possible to relate this to changes in the structure of the labour market and to demand for female employment in particular. We know that the economy of York contracted from about the middle of the fifteenth century. It may also be that the crisis of 1438 had a debilitating effect on regional agriculture and hence jobs.

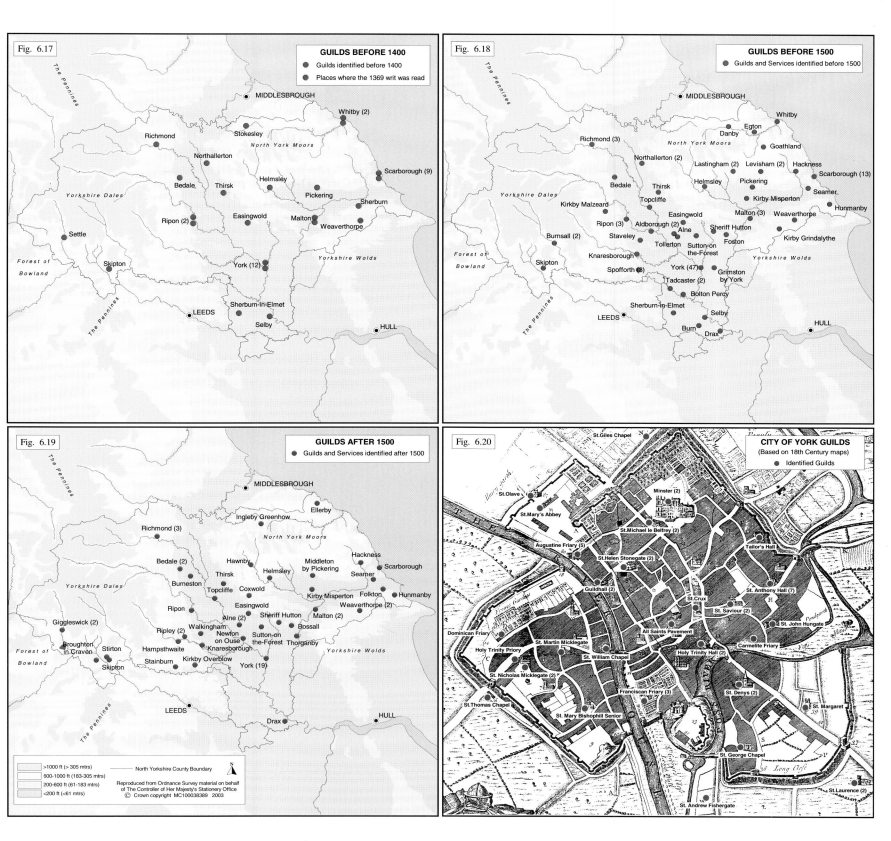

Fig. 6.17

GUILDS BEFORE 1400
- Guilds identified before 1400
- Places where the 1369 writ was read

The Pennines

MIDDLESBROUGH

Whitby (2)

Richmond   Stokesley

Northallerton   *North York Moors*

Bedale   Thirsk   Helmsley   Scarborough (9)

Pickering

Sherburn

Ripon (2)   Easingwold   Malton   Weaverthorpe

Settle   *Yorkshire Dales*

York (12)   *Yorkshire Wolds*

Skipton

The Pennines

Sherburn-in-Elmet

LEEDS   Selby   HULL

Forest of Bowland

Fig. 6.18

GUILDS BEFORE 1500
- Guilds and Services identified before 1500

The Pennines

MIDDLESBROUGH

Whitby

Egton   Danby   Goathland

Richmond (3)   Lastingham (2)   Levisham (2)   Hackness

Northallerton (2)   Helmsley   Pickering   Scarborough (13)

Bedale   Thirsk   Topcliffe   Kirby Misperton   Seamer

Kirkby Malzeard   Malton (3)   Weaverthorpe   Hunmanby

Ripon (3)   Easingwold   Alne   Sheriff Hutton   Kirby Grindalythe

Burnsall (2)   Aldborough (2)   Staveley   Foston

Knaresborough   Tollerton   Sutton-on-the-Forest   *Yorkshire Wolds*

Skipton   Spofforth (3)   York (47)   Grimston by York

Tadcaster (2)   Bolton Percy

Sherburn-in-Elmet   Selby

LEEDS   Burn   Drax   HULL

Forest of Bowland

The Pennines

Fig. 6.19

GUILDS AFTER 1500
- Guilds and Services identified after 1500

The Pennines

MIDDLESBROUGH

Ellerby

Ingleby Greenhow

Richmond (3)   *North York Moors*   Hackness

Hawnby   Middleton by Pickering   Scarborough

Bedale (2)   Helmsley   Seamer

Burneston   Thirsk   Kirby Misperton   Hunmanby

Topcliffe   Coxwold   Folkton

Gigleswick (2)   Ripon   Easingwold   Weaverthorpe (2)

Alne (2)   Sheriff Hutton   Malton (2)

Ripley (2)   Walkingham   Bossall

Broughton in Craven   Stirton   Newton on Ouse   Sutton-on-the-Forest   Thorganby

Hampsthwaite   Knaresborough   *Yorkshire Wolds*

Stainburn   Kirkby Overblow

Skipton   York (19)

Forest of Bowland

LEEDS   Drax   HULL

The Pennines

>1000 ft (> 305 mtrs)	North Yorkshire County Boundary
600-1000 ft (183-305 mtrs)	N
200-600 ft (61-183 mtrs)	Reproduced from Ordnance Survey material on behalf of The Controller of Her Majesty's Stationery Office © Crown copyright MC100038389 2003
<200 ft (<61 mtrs)	

Fig. 6.20

CITY OF YORK GUILDS
(Based on 18th Century maps)
- Identified Guilds

St.Giles Chapel

St.Olave

St.Mary's Abbey   Minster (2)

St.Michael le Belfrey (2)

Augustine Friary (5)   Tailor's Hall

St.Helen Stonegate (2)

Guildhall (2)   St.Anthony Hall (7)

St.Crux   St.Saviour (2)

Dominican Friary   St.John Hungate

All Saints Pavement

St.Martin Micklegate   Carmelite Friary

Holy Trinity Priory   St.William Chapel   Holy Trinity Hall

St.Nicholas Micklegate (2)   St.Denys (2)

Franciscan Friary (3)   St.Margaret

St.Thomas Chapel   St.Mary Bishophill Senior

St.George Chapel   St.Laurence (2)

St.Andrew Fishergate

6.10 RELIGIOUS GUILDS IN LATE MEDIEVAL NORTH YORKSHIRE (1389–1547) DAVID J F CROUCH

Although religious guilds were basically pious institutions, their influence permeated the social, economic and political lives of medieval people in cities, towns and villages throughout the country. It seems likely that there were guilds in most parishes. They varied in size from the mighty Corpus Christi Guild of York, with a country-wide membership, to parish guilds in small villages such as Burnsall, Foston and Levisham. Some were founded for special purposes: for example, the Paternoster Guild of York performed an annual play, and the St Mary, St Wilfrid and All Saints Guild of Ripon maintained an ancient chapel and paid for daily mass to be said there. Some urban guilds became associated with particular occupations, although, in York, crafts or misteries remained distinct from any guilds that they might support throughout this period.

Despite variations, all guilds shared common characteristics. The most basic of these was the special veneration of the saint, saints or cult to which the guild was dedicated. This was displayed publicly by holding a procession on the appropriate day. It often involved the wearing of livery, and might include the carrying of a shrine and other cult objects and the observation of special rituals, culminating in a mass and prayers for the dead. Wealthy fraternities employed full-time guild chaplains.

In order to fulfill such functions, guilds had to be economically successful. Many of them were major landlords of urban or agricultural real estate. The administration of such assets inevitably brought guilds into close contact with local government: with the lord of the manor or the town, or city corporation. These relationships were formalised by the act of 1436, which empowered all such local authorities to supervise and license guilds. Records, such as those of York, show that office-holders in government were members of not only one but often several guilds, thus creating webs of political, social and economic influence.

Members joined on payment of an entrance fee and some guilds also imposed special restrictions, especially with regard to the good character of entrants. Induction often involved the swearing of an oath of loyalty. The benefits of membership lay in the concept of fraternity. This was symbolised by the guild feast. It was usually held on the same day as the annual procession, and might also be combined with a meeting where accounts were presented and next year's officers chosen. Guilds usually supported brothers and sisters who had fallen on hard times and provided official funerals. Membership continued beyond death and the prayers of the fraternity were intended to smooth the passage of the soul of a dead brother or sister through the pains of purgatory.

In North Yorkshire there are no surviving guild records outside York itself, nor are there any extant parish records. The major source establishing the existence of guilds within the boundaries of the modern county is testamentary. Study, based largely on a sample of one third of all wills recorded in the probate registers of the archbishops, of the Dean and Chapter of York Minster and in the archbishops' own registers, has established the presence of 159 religious guilds and fraternities during the late medieval period, up to 1547, in North Yorkshire. Of these, fifty-nine were found in York and its immediate suburbs. Testamentary evidence yields somewhat random results. Wills were made only by rich people, and bequests to guilds were rare. It is, however, likely that the most successful guilds in the most prosperous places are those that can be identified in this way.

In 1398, Richard II's government ordered the county sheriffs to carry out a survey of all religious and occupational guilds. Although only five returns from North Yorkshire have survived (for three places, Bedale, Ripon and York), the seventeen places where the king's writ was proclaimed are known. It seems likely that guilds were present in those locations, even if they might not have been prominent enough to have figured in local wills or be otherwise recorded. **Figs 6.17**, **6.18** and **6.19** show that guilds flourished in towns and villages that were on or near established roads or navigable water, and that were associated with markets and fairs, suggesting local prosperity. Exceptions to this are small villages connected with the castles of the crown or the nobility. Spofforth, for example, had three recorded guilds and was dominated by a castle owned by the Percies. No guilds were found in the sparsely populated areas of the North York Moors and the high Dales.

In the rest of Yorkshire there was a marked proliferation of identified guilds after 1500, especially in the south-western Dales, where the textile trade was flourishing, and in Holderness, where there seems to have been an upturn in agriculture. The maps indicate that this increase in guild activity did not occur in North Yorkshire, suggesting that the early sixteenth century was, perhaps, not a period of great affluence here. This is underlined by a sharp fall in references to guilds in Scarborough that coincides with a decline in its fishing industry. Local shifts in bequests to guilds between the two periods may have purely local explanations but are probably related to the random nature of the evidence.

York itself (**fig 6.20**) supported a large number of guilds. The three large civic guilds of Corpus Christi, St Christopher and St Anthony attracted members from the city élite and from the county at large. The York map shows that many other guilds were based in the city's religious houses and parish churches. The decline in the numbers of guilds recorded here after 1500 is largely the result of larger guilds absorbing smaller ones throughout the fifteenth century. Bequests to York guilds diminished as a response to the early phases of the Henrican reformation and especially following the failure of the Pilgrimage of Grace in 1536. Occupationally based guilds survived the dissolution of the guilds in 1546-8 as secular

Seal of Corpus Christi Guild, York.
From Surtees Society, R H Skaife (ed.), *The Register of the Guild of Corpus Christi in the City of York*, 1871-1 (1872), frontispiece.

Religious Guilds — Further Reading:
D J F Crouch, *Piety, Fraternity and Power: Religious Guilds in Late Medieval Yorkshire* (Woodbridge: Boydell & Brewer, 2000).
D J F Crouch, Gazetteer of the Religious Guilds and Services of Late Medieval Yorkshire, http://www.york.ac.uk/inst/cms.
G Rosser, Going to the Fraternity Feast: Commensiality and Social Relations in Late Medieval England, *Journal of British Studies* 33 (4), (October 1994), 430-46.
Skaife, R H (ed.), *The Register of the Guild of Corpus Christi in the City of York*, Surtees Society 57 (1872).
Westlake, H F, *The Parish Guilds of Mediæval England* (London, 1919).
White, E, *The St Christopher and St George Guild of York*, Borthwick Paper 72 (York: Borthwick Institute of Historical Research, St Anthony's Press, 1987).

institutions. Most of the rest, throughout the whole county, disappeared and it is certain that most of them anticipated their fate by destroying their records, closing themselves down and concealing, from the king's commissioners, much of their considerable wealth by absorbing it into local communities.

6.11   COMMUNICATIONS   CHRISTOPHER DANIELL

The road network in medieval North Yorkshire (**fig 6.21**) criss-crossed the countryside and interconnected with the river systems. The rivers flowed to the North Sea coast or Humber Estuary, where ports allowed for coastal and foreign trade. The more enterprising merchants formed guilds, such as the Merchant Adventurer's Guild in York, to trade nationwide and overseas. The majority of trade, however, was local, with regular markets being held in market towns or villages dotted across the countryside. Each settlement had its own system of roads and trackways out into the hinterland, with major roads leading to other settlements .

THE RIVER SYSTEM

The Humber Estuary was the gateway into the heart of Yorkshire, and the rivers feeding into the estuary were important routes for communications and trade. In the fourteenth century the citizens of York described the River Ouse as being a 'highway' for trade. Many rivers were accessible for ships and light craft far upstream: for example, vessels could reach Doncaster on the Don, Stamford Bridge on the Derwent, Tadcaster on the Wharfe and north of York on the Ouse.

For centuries, river traffic was the cheapest way to transport material. An account of 1365, describing the carriage of lead, gave the sum of £7 4s for carrying it overland twenty leagues in North Yorkshire, compared with the cost of £2 14s for carriage sixteen leagues by land and water.[1]

However, there were two main problems with river transport: the tide and the man-made fish garths. The tidal range along the rivers meant that at certain times of the year — if the sequence of tides and moon combined — ships at York could be stranded for up to two weeks. While this was exceptional, all ship owners had to take careful account of the tides in their calculations. The second problem was the numerous fish garths built out from the banks to catch fish. These were made of wooden stakes and netting, but they extended into the shipping lanes and were a constant hazard. Even substantial vessels could be sunk or holed: in 1376, John York of Swinefleet lost his ship and cargo valued at £80 because of the fish garths, while two Austin friars drowned when the fish garths caused their boat to be capsized.[2]

At trading points were the quays, or staithes, at which ships docked. The larger staithes could have have cranes and warehouses. At York the city council owned the crane situated on Skeldergate. Sometimes institutions would have their landing places (such as St Leonard's Hospital, also in York) and the archbishop had his own staith at his palace at Cawood.

The difficulties of navigating far upstream meant that Hull quickly grew from its origins in the twelfth century to be the premiere port in Yorkshire, eclipsing the North Yorkshire ports of York, Scarborough and Whitby. Ships from Hull travelled as far afield as Spain, Gdansk and Iceland. Scarborough and Whitby were of regional importance, while the other small ports along the coast, such as Filey and Bridlington, were mainly small fishing ports. Items traded at Scarborough included: cloth and wool, skins of lambs, rabbits and hares, a tun of woad, and various types of fish, including herring, lampreys, salmon (fresh and salted) and stockfish.[3]

ROADS

Travel by road was often difficult and dangerous. The roads were frequently in terrible disrepair, with pot-holes and deep mud. Journeys were slow and expensive in comparison with river costs. The terrain and landscape could also be unforgiving, with the high and steep Pennines and North York Moors, and then many smaller ranges of hills, such as the Howardian Hills and the Yorkshire Wolds. It is therefore no surprise that the main roads ran through the remarkably flat Vale of York, but difficulties here included the wetness of the ground and the Forest of Galtres, which lay directly to the north of York. Wolves were a documented source of worry as late as the seventeenth century and so were probably a potential source of danger to medieval travellers. The building and upkeep of bridges was also a constant source of concern. In York, the bridge masters collected rents for upkeep of Ouse Bridge and Foss Bridge, and it was a common act of piety to leave money in a will for the repair of bridges or roads.

A 'trod' (old medieval pannier way). Lealholm Rigg, North York Moors.
© North York Moors National Park Authority, HM0013.

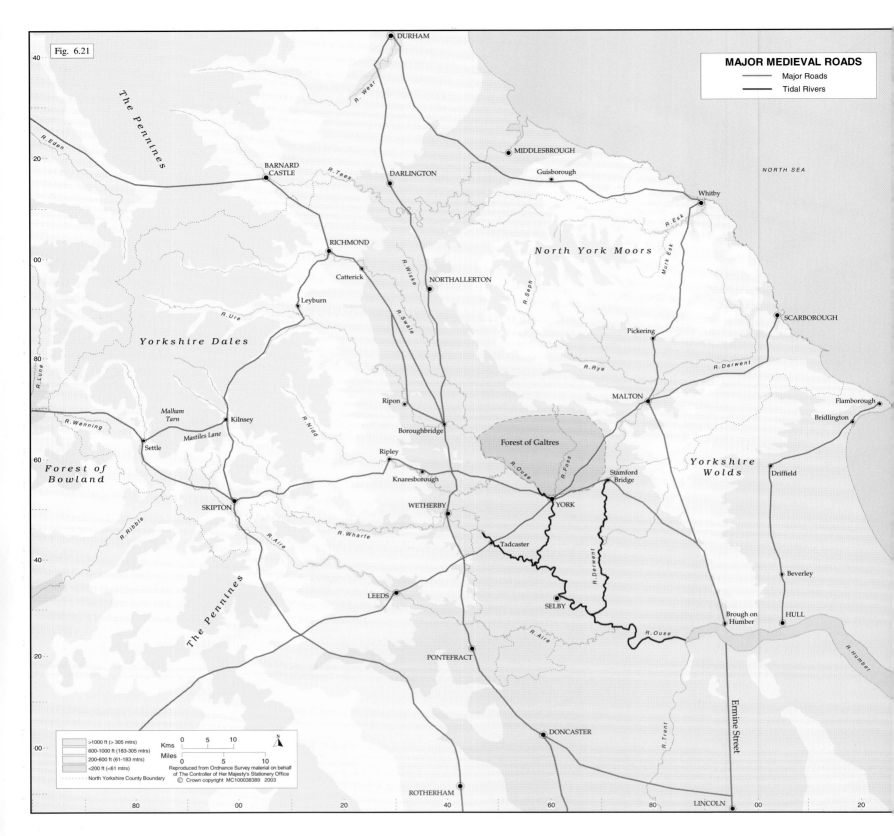

Fig. 6.21

MAJOR MEDIEVAL ROADS
— Major Roads
— Tidal Rivers

The foundation, literally, of many of the great medieval roads was the previous system of Roman roads. Well built and direct, they were re-used through the centuries following the departure of the Romans. A section of original Roman road can still be seen on the North York Moors. The Great North Road, which often followed the line of the Roman Ermine Street, ran from London northwards, but during its course the road divided frequently, with the result that today several routes north can be called the Great North Road. One section of this road ran through Barnsdale, which in medieval times was notorious for robbers and thieves. Today Barnsdale is famous as the place of origin of many of the Robin Hood tales. The road divided after Barnsdale at Ferrybridge, with one part running north through Wetherby, and another part going to Tadcaster and York.

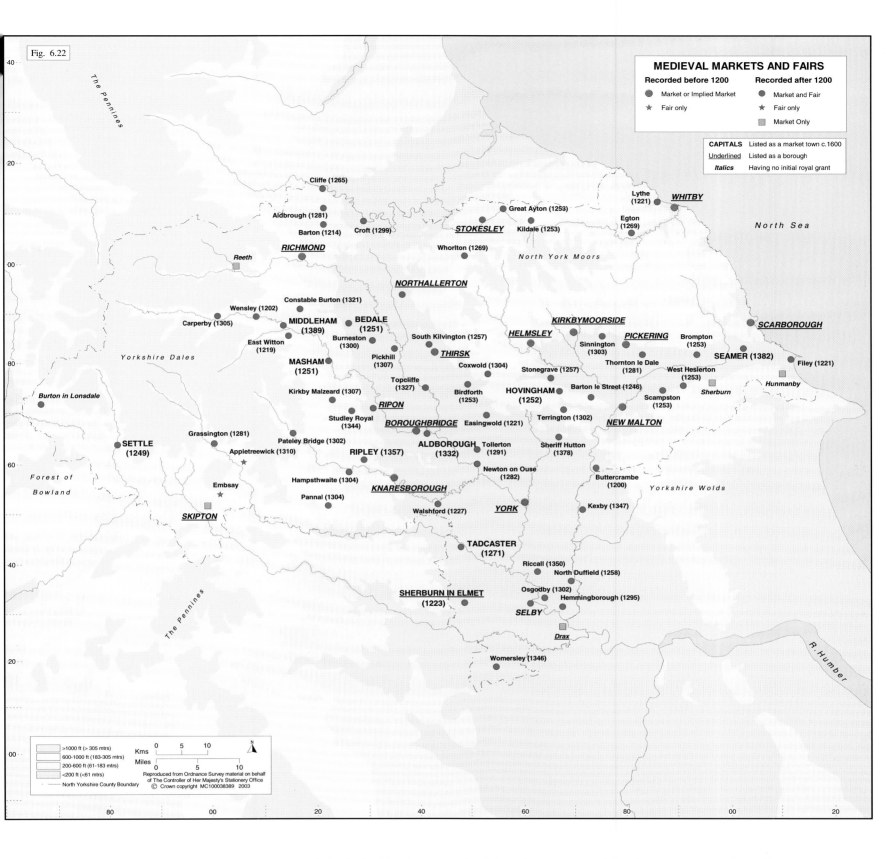

Fig. 6.22

MEDIEVAL MARKETS AND FAIRS

Recorded before 1200	Recorded after 1200
● Market or Implied Market	● Market and Fair
★ Fair only	★ Fair only
	▪ Market Only

CAPITALS	Listed as a market town c.1600
Underlined	Listed as a borough
Italics	Having no initial royal grant

The Pennines

North Sea

Cliffe (1265)

Lythe (1221)   *WHITBY*

Aldbrough (1281)

Great Ayton (1253)

Egton (1269)

Barton (1214)   Croft (1299)

STOKESLEY   Kildale (1253)

RICHMOND   Whorlton (1269)

Reeth   North York Moors

NORTHALLERTON

Constable Burton (1321)

Wensley (1202)   *KIRKBYMOORSIDE*   *SCARBOROUGH*

Carperby (1305)   MIDDLEHAM (1389)   BEDALE (1251)   *HELMSLEY*   *PICKERING*   Brompton (1253)

East Witton (1219)   Burneston (1300)   South Kilvington (1257)   Sinnington (1303)   SEAMER (1382)

Yorkshire Dales   Pickhill (1307)   *THIRSK*   Thornton le Dale (1281)   West Heslerton (1253)   Filey (1221)

MASHAM (1251)   Coxwold (1304)   Stonegrave (1257)   *Sherburn*   *Hunmanby*

Topcliffe (1327)   Birdforth (1253)   Barton le Street (1246)

Kirkby Malzeard (1307)   HOVINGHAM (1252)   Scampston (1253)

Burton in Lonsdale   *RIPON*   Terrington (1302)   *NEW MALTON*

Studley Royal (1344)   Easingwold (1221)

Grassington (1281)   *BOROUGHBRIDGE*   *Yorkshire Wolds*

SETTLE (1249)   Pateley Bridge (1302)   Tollerton (1291)   Sheriff Hutton (1378)

Appletreewick (1310)   RIPLEY (1357)   ALDBOROUGH (1332)

Forest of Bowland   Hampsthwaite (1304)   Newton on Ouse (1282)   Buttercrambe (1200)

Embsay   *KNARESBOROUGH*   Kexby (1347)

Pannal (1304)   *YORK*

SKIPTON   Walshford (1227)

The Pennines   TADCASTER (1271)

Riccall (1350)   North Duffield (1258)

SHERBURN IN ELMET (1223)   Osgodby (1302)   Hemmingborough (1295)

SELBY

Drax

Womersley (1346)

R. Humber

	>1000 ft (> 305 mtrs)
	600-1000 ft (183-305 mtrs)
	200-600 ft (61-183 mtrs)
	<200 ft (<61 mtrs)
	North Yorkshire County Boundary

Kms 0 5 10
Miles 0 5 10

Reproduced from Ordnance Survey material on behalf of The Controller of Her Majesty's Stationery Office © Crown copyright MC100038389 2003

The difficulties, however, should not be exaggerated for there were many long-distance journeys. King John was a noted traveller even in his own time, and there was only one month during his reign in which he made no journeys, and that was while he was besieging Rochester Castle in 1215. Even though road transport was slow and cumbersome, the roads must have been in reasonable condition for most of the time and acceptably safe.

As well as re-using the surviving Roman roads, new medieval road and track networks were created. The importance of sheep in the local economy meant that routes were created to connect the granges of the monasteries with the sheep pastures. The most famous monastic trackway, Mastiles Lane, links the Malham Moor estates of Fountains Abbey with the important monastic grange at Kilnsey. Such trackways in the Dales formed an extensive communication system for the movement of sheep and goods, and every monastery in the region, such as Rievaulx, Byland and Jervaulx, had networks of roads and tracks connecting the abbeys, granges and lands. Across the bleaker North York Moors, many routeways were signposted, or parish boundaries marked, by the use of moorland crosses. There are over thirty named crosses such as Ralph Cross, the earliest of which, Lilla Cross, is reputedly of seventh-century origin.

Through the following centuries the communication network evolved into an ever-more elaborate system, but the pattern that is visible today is based on the system formed in the Middle Ages.

Communications — Further Reading:
J J Jusserand, *English Wayfaring Life in the Middle Ages* (London: T Fisher Unwin, 1884).
Paul Hindle, Medieval Roads and Tracks (Princes Risborough: Shire Publications, 1998).
Ivan Margary, *Roman Roads in Britain* (London: John Barker, 1973).
Christopher Taylor, *Roads and Tracks of Britain* (London: J M Dent and Sons Ltd, 1979).

6.12 BOROUGHS, MARKETS AND FAIRS   RICHARD BRITNELL

The vigour of urban growth in Anglo-Saxon York is not a reliable guide to the growth of towns and organised trade elsewhere in North Yorkshire. There are no traces before the Norman Conquest of anything comparable to the urban expansion of southern England and the Midlands. The twelfth century, however, was a remarkable period of development when marketing institutions of enduring significance for local trade were newly created. Places recorded as trading centres before 1200 have been singled out on **fig 6.22** with red symbols to demonstrate this point.

In most cases these places are first mentioned in charters as boroughs — Boroughbridge in 1165, Helmsley sometime between 1186 and 1210, Kirkbymoorside between 1154 and 1179, Knaresborough in 1168-9, Malton between 1154 and 1179, Pickering in 1201 (but with the clear implication that the market was much older), Richmond between 1136 and 1145, Scarborough in 1155, Thirsk in 1145 and Whitby in 1122. Some other boroughs of the region are likely to be early, since it would be difficult otherwise to explain the absence of licences for their markets and fairs. In this category come the castle markets of Skipton and Stokesley, and the ecclesiastical boroughs of Northallerton, Ripon and Selby.[1] The designation 'market only' does not necessarily mean that there was no fair in reality; it signifies only that no fair is recorded.

A distinctive feature of the earliest boroughs was their frequent association with the castles of major Yorkshire baronial families. Another characteristic, demonstrable from the map, was their impressive permanence. Once launched, with the assistance of investment and supervision by their landlords, they became firmly entrenched in the North Yorkshire landscape, and were still regarded as principal market towns in the region in the late sixteenth century. This characteristic gives another reason for supposing that the markets at Skipton, Stokesley, Northallerton, Ripon and Selby were comparatively early. Most of the twelfth-century marketing centres were either on the coast (Whitby, Scarborough) or on the principal rivers (Boroughbridge on the Ure, Helmsley on the Rye, Knaresborough on the Nidd, Malton on the Derwent, Richmond on the Swale); they were probably also located by reference to regular overland routes.

The thirteenth and early fourteenth centuries in North Yorkshire — as elsewhere — saw the proliferation of new weekly markets and annual fairs, licensed by the Crown, some of which were of lasting significance. In most cases, royal charters granted both a market (specifying the day) and a fair (specifying the days of the year), so that the green circle representing 'Market and Fair' is the most prominent on the map. The trading centres of this period that established themselves well enough to survive as market towns around 1600, all indicated on the map in capital letters, were Sherburn in Elmet (1223), Settle (1249), Bedale (1251), Masham (1251), Hovingham (1252), Tadcaster (1271), Aldbrough (1332), Ripley (1357), Seamer (1382) and Middleham (1389).[2]

If these dates are reliable for the first foundation of these markets, the evidence implies a surge of new development in the mid-thirteenth century, but also (and more unusually) the continuing availability of new investment opportunities well into the fourteenth century. The late creations at Seamer and Middleham were the work of the great Neville and Percy families respectively, and their success is doubtless to be explained partly in terms of the power and wealth of their respective patrons. Many of these exceptionally successful new ventures owed their vigour to the fact that they were serving regions not previously supplied with marketing facilities, some of them higher up the dales (Settle, Masham, Ripley, Middleham), or on cultivable and relatively populous land in between (Bedale, Hovingham). They facilitated the development of an exchange economy in the outlying parts of Yorkshire by enabling local inhabitants to reduce the cost of their marketing transactions, so that by the

Pickering Castle and town. The castle, dating from the eleventh and twelfth centuries, is based on an earlier motte and bailey structure. Pickering received its charter as a borough in 1201, but it functioned as a market centre from an earlier time.
NMR 17001/19 © Crown copyright. NMR.

Helmsley Castle and town. Helmsley received its borough charter sometime between 1186 and 1210. It remains an important market town and has in modern times become a popular tourist centre.

NMR 17602/04 © English Heritage. NMR.

Boroughs, Markets & Fairs — Further Reading:

M W Beresford, *New Towns of the Middle Ages: Town Plantation in England, Wales, and Gascony* (London: Lutterworth Press, 1967).

R H Britnell, Boroughs, Markets and Trade in Northern England 1000-1216, in R H Britnell and J Hatcher (eds), *Progress and Problems in Medieval England: Essays in Honour of Edward Miller* (Cambridge: Cambridge University Press, 1996), 46-67.

A Everitt, The Marketing of Agricultural Produce, in J Thirsk (ed.), *The Agrarian History of England and Wales IV: 1500-1640* (Cambridge: Cambridge University Press, 1987), 466-592.

K L McCutcheon, *Yorkshire Fairs and Markets to the End of the Eighteenth Century* (Leeds: Thoresby Society, 1940).

C M Newman, *Late Medieval Northallerton: A Small Market Town and its Hinterland, c1470-1540* (Stamford: Shaun Tyas, 1999).

mid-fourteenth century only the thinly inhabited uplands of the Pennines and the Yorkshire Moors were without convenient local trading centres.

The map is littered with the many minor markets licensed in the period before 1350 about which little is known. Some of them should probably not be shown at all, since not all royal grants of markets and fairs resulted in working institutions. The market and fair authorised at Walshford in 1227 cannot have been much of a success, since in 1240 the Knights Templar were allowed to establish a new market and fair at Wetherby in lieu of them.[3] Since all we know of many markets and fairs is the royal charter that authorised them, it is impossible to be precise about their standing or longevity, or even to be certain that they were ever set up. Some new markets lapsed, and were then restarted, implying that they either failed or took a long time to become an established component of the local marketing network. The Thursday market at Hovingham granted in 1252, although marked on the map as surviving to 1600, took some time to get going, since in 1293 it was not being held. The township, it was said, was 'in waste country' (*'in vasta patria'*); an unauthorised Monday market was held there when the people around wanted to come — by implication intermittently.[4] The market and fair at North Duffield licensed in 1253 were granted to a new lord of the manor in 1294 by Edward I, but apparently they were not held between that date and 1363, when King Edward III granted them again.[5]

Some other minor markets acquired a recognised if ephemeral role in the economy of the thirteenth and fourteenth centuries before being squeezed out by changing commercial pressures or legal challenges. The Friday market at Filey, chartered 1221, whose day was subsequently changed to Sunday sometime after 1227 and back to Friday in 1240, was sufficiently successful to attract the antagonism of both the lord of Hunmanby (in 1241-2) and the burgesses of Scarborough (in 1256), and was still operating in 1293.[6] In the many instances where nothing is heard of any market or fair after a grant was made (such as Aldbrough, Barton le Street, Birdforth, Hemingborough, Kexby, Osgodby, Riccall and Sheriff Hutton),[7] it is not safe to assume that these grants had no implications for the settlements in question, but it is unlikely that they resulted in any movement of local trade away from older centres or offered much competition to other new ones.[8]

7

NORTH YORKSHIRE *c*1500-1900

7.1   INTRODUCTION   RICHARD LAWTON

North Yorkshire was, historically and physically, marginal between lowland and upland Britain. Although its vales and wolds were to provide productive and varied arable farming areas by the mid-nineteenth century, there were extensive wastes of carr, moor and wold in the early sixteenth century (see section 8). Moreover, with the defeat of the Yorkist cause at Bosworth Field (1485) the county was politically marginalised. Nevertheless York, long the historic and ecclesiastical capital of northern England and with its guild structure still intact, was among the country's top five provincial towns with a population of some 10,000 in the mid-sixteenth century.

Despite a long-standing tradition of both urban-centred and rural craft industry, North Yorkshire was peripheral to the major centres of textile innovation of the late eighteenth century. Nevertheless a wide range of natural resources — lead and iron ores, alum, jet, building stone and brick clays — supported a diverse rural economy of particular importance to small communities in the Pennine dales and the North Yorkshire Moors that is reflected in the relative surge in population in the late eighteenth and early nineteenth centuries.

Despite its marginality, natural corridors along the east coast route to Scotland, significant since Roman times, through the Aire Gap to Lancashire and via the east coast seaway to London and the Continent ensured that North Yorkshire was not isolated. The Ouse and its tributaries gave good inland water communication with York, Selby and the port of Hull. Key bridge-points along its many rivers, and contact lines between upland and lowland, were marked by market centres, many with Norman castles, that gave strong internal cohesiveness.

The historical interaction of Romano-British, Anglian, Scandinavian and Norman is reflected in both the settlement pattern and administrative structure of the former North Riding, including the ancient wapentakes which persisted into the nineteenth century.

Other than York (a Whig stronghold), North Yorkshire's nine pre-reform parliamentary boroughs largely reflected the political affiliation of controlling landed gentry. Both were to change after parliamentary reform (1832) and the sequence of changes in local government and the poor law from 1834. The advance of the Liberal cause in both rural and urban seats, though not sustained into the late nineteenth century, was not surprising in an area of below-average rural poverty where Nonconformity was more widely supported than the Established Church in large towns and many rural parishes.

Despite its early rural craft and mining industries, North Yorkshire remained peripheral to the industrial revolution, and the loss of handicraft and extractive industry underlined rural population decline from the 1830s.

It was the railway age that gave new impetus to York, both as a major centre of communications and in railway-related and consumer industry, and promoted the rise of seaside and inland resorts which sustained growth up to 1900, presaging the dual attractions of a richly diverse landscape and heritage for an increasingly mobile modern society.

7.2   THE DISSOLUTION OF THE MONASTERIES
WILLIAM SHEILS

A contemporary observer, writing soon after the dissolution of the religious houses, noted with some justification that Yorkshire had 'the greatest shire of ... late religious houses within the realm';[1] within that shire the present North Yorkshire contained the greatest concentration in numbers, wealth and personnel.

When the visitors appointed by Henry VIII came to the area early in 1536, it contained forty-six religious houses, including fifteen convents of nuns, and all the main religious orders were represented, as well as lesser-known ones such as the Grandmontines at Grosmont, and two houses of the native order of Gilbertines at Malton and in York. These houses were spread throughout the area in both town and country and they recruited locally from among the reasonably prosperous farming and craftsman families (**fig 7.1**). Thus at Rievaulx the monks resident at the dissolution came originally from the towns of Helmsley, Malton,

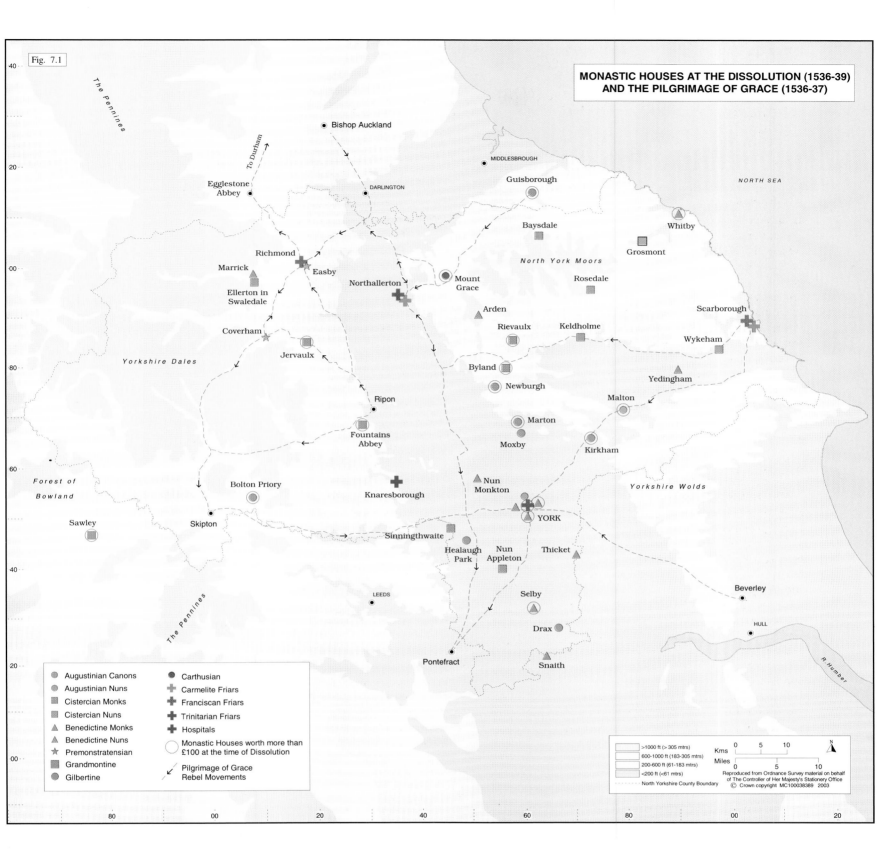

Fig. 7.1

MONASTIC HOUSES AT THE DISSOLUTION (1536-39)
AND THE PILGRIMAGE OF GRACE (1536-37)

The Pennines

To Durham

Bishop Auckland

MIDDLESBROUGH

20

NORTH SEA

Egglestone
Abbey

DARLINGTON

Guisborough

Baysdale

Whitby

Grosmont

Richmond

Marrick

Easby

00

Northallerton

Mount
Grace

North York Moors

Rosedale

Ellerton in
Swaledale

Arden

Rievaulx

Keldholme

Scarborough

Wykeham

Coverham

Jervaulx

Yorkshire Dales

80

Byland

Newburgh

Yedingham

Ripon

Malton

Marton

Moxby

Kirkham

Fountains
Abbey

60

Forest of
Bowland

Bolton Priory

Knaresborough

Nun
Monkton

Yorkshire Wolds

Sawley

Skipton

YORK

Sinningthwaite

40

Healaugh
Park

Nun
Appleton

Thicket

Beverley

LEEDS

Selby

The Pennines

Drax

HULL

20

Pontefract

Snaith

R. Humber

Legend:

- Augustinian Canons
- Augustinian Nuns
- Cistercian Monks
- Cistercian Nuns
- Benedictine Monks
- Benedictine Nuns
- Premonstratensian
- Grandmontine
- Gilbertine
- Carthusian
- Carmelite Friars
- Franciscan Friars
- Trinitarian Friars
- Hospitals
- Monastic Houses worth more than £100 at the time of Dissolution
- Pilgrimage of Grace Rebel Movements

>1000 ft (> 305 mtrs)
600-1000 ft (183-305 mtrs)
200-600 ft (61-183 mtrs)
<200 ft (<61 mtrs)
North Yorkshire County Boundary

Kms 0 5 10
Miles 0 5 10

Reproduced from Ordnance Survey material on behalf of The Controller of Her Majesty's Stationery Office © Crown copyright MC100038389 2003

Pickering, Bedale, Thirsk, Scarborough, Whitby, Guisborough, Yarm, Richmond, North–
allerton and Ripon, and from nearby villages like Gilling, Ampleforth, Yearsley, Farlington
and Broughton.

This was a community well integrated into local society, and the records tend to suggest
that in the early 1500s, despite occasional abuses noted at visitation, the religious orders made
a valuable contribution to the community, which was recognised by their neighbours.
The monasteries themselves varied hugely in size and wealth, from the extraordinarily rich
abbey of St Mary's in York, with its fifty monks and properties valued at £1,650, to the
small community at Grosmont, valued at £12 2s 8d and housing five monks. On the eve of

dissolution the combined value of the monastic estates, which covered large areas of the Dales and the northern Vale of York, were assessed at £7,243. In circumstances when the monastic ideal had come in for criticism from humanist scholars, and a newly declared national church and central government were concerned about the international connections of the great religious orders (which saw the abbots of the great Cistercian houses of Jervaulx, Rievaulx and Fountains in regular contact with their peers abroad), this wealth made them vulnerable.

Thus the arrival of royal visitors and the suppression of the smaller religious houses combined with other grievances in 1536 to produce the largest mass rising against the Tudor state. Known as the Pilgrimage of Grace, and coinciding, and sometimes linking, with other risings in east Yorkshire, Lincolnshire, Durham and the Lake Counties, the rebellion attracted support from a wide section of the Dales tenantry and peasantry, and had the support of local magnates like Sir Thomas Percy, as well as from leading ecclesiatics like the Abbot of Jervaulx.

In North Yorkshire the centre of the revolt was based around Richmondshire, Mashamshire and Nidderdale, which rose in rebellion in early October 1536. Some of the rebels marched north-east to meet with Durham contingents and those from near Guisborough, while others moved south towards Ripon before marching west towards Skipton, which held out against them. Thereupon this contingent turned east and marched on the castle at Pontefract, where it joined with the Durham rebels and those from the East Riding and near Malton, capturing the castle on the 21st October.

By this time the rebels numbered 30,000, including gentry, priests and people, and the Crown decided to negotiate, using the respected Duke of Norfolk, victor of Flodden, as spokesman. A truce was arranged on the 27th October, and further negotiations took place at York and Pontefract until the 6th December, when peace terms were agreed. These terms included a promise to restore the abbeys provided they surrendered to the king, whereupon the pilgrims began to disperse. The Crown ignored its promise, and early in 1537 a new rising in east Yorkshire — by gentry who felt they had been betrayed — gave Henry VIII the excuse to suppress the traditional leadership of the region, executing 200 of the rebels, including Lord Darcy, Sir Thomas Percy, and Adam Sedber, Abbot of Jervaulx, whose monastery passed to the Crown.

The pilgrimage was a response to the dissolution of the smaller religious houses (sixteen in North Yorkshire) but the great landowning houses continued to exist, some of them receiving displaced monks and nuns from dissolved houses, as did some lesser communities like Marrick Priory in Swaledale with its thirteen nuns. These remaining houses were dissolved in 1538 and 1539, and their lands and assets handed to the Crown, with pensions being offered to the priests and nuns to assist their compliance.

Thus in five years between 1535 and 1540, a way of life which, at the time, still had over 700 men and women, mostly from the region, living in community, and which occupied several hundred more as tenants, servants, provisioners and agents, passed away in the face of a determined central authority, leaving today's majestic ruins as at Rievaulx, small isolated ruins with trees appearing from the cracked stonework as at Ellerton on Swale, or a few bumps in the ground as at Moxby near Brandsby. Beside some former monastic precincts, like that at Fountains, there rose great country houses from the monastic stone, and at others like Newburgh the house incorporated the old monastic buildings themselves, as lay owners purchased these estates from the Crown or received them in return for service.

The dissolution thus led to a great transfer of land within the county as the Crown sold off or gave away its new wealth, and many families, including some of those who had risen in defence of the monasteries in 1536, were to find themselves as owners of ex-monastic land in the late sixteenth and early seventeenth centuries. Not all beneficiaries were laymen, however, and among the most substantial grantees was the Established Church, as successive archbishops were required to exchange some more desirable lands (from the Crown's point of view) in return for monastic estates. Thus the archbishopric became owner of an extensive estate in Ryedale made up of former granges of the monasteries of Newburgh, Rievaulx, Byland and Mount Grace. Just as some land remained in ecclesiastical use, so some buildings retained their religious purpose, as Bolton, Selby, Drax and Holy Trinity, York, continued to be used as parish churches.

For the monks and nuns themselves, the example of the Abbot of Jervaulx made public opposition unwise and fruitless, and the great majority moved back into secular life or joined the ranks of the secular clergy, like Edmund Skelton, a former monk of Grosmont who served as curate of nearby Egton where he was instrumental in keeping traditional religious values alive. Among others, a more enduring commitment to the community life from which they had been uprooted can be discerned. Six Carthusians from Mount Grace joined the

Dissolution — Further Reading:

Claire Cross and Noreen Vickers, *Monks, Friars and Nuns in Sixteenth-Century Yorkshire* (Yorkshire Archaeological Society Record Series, 150, 1995), contains an extensive list of sources.

M L Bush, *The Pilgrimage of Grace, a Study of the rebel armies* (Manchester: Manchester University Press, 1997).

B Jennings, *Yorkshire Monasteries* (Otley: Smith Settle, 2000).

J Caley and J Hunter (eds), *Valor Ecclesiasticus* (6 vols, 1810–34), vol 5.

G W O Woodward, *The Dissolution of the Monasteries* (London: P Blandford, 1966), uses much Yorkshire material.

revived house at Sheen in the reign of the Catholic Mary, and two moved across the channel to the Bruges charterhouse in Elizabeth's reign, where they were joined by a former novice. At Wykeham it is clear that the community kept in touch after dissolution — Katherine Nandike, the former prioress, mentioning all her fellow nuns in her will of 1541; and in 1554 George Richmond, a former monk of Bolton Priory, left his chalice and two vestments 'to the monastery of Bolton whensoever it shall please God that it shall be restored'. That hope was not to be fulfilled, of course, and these institutions were no longer to influence the character of the rural landscape of the county.

7.3 ROMAN CATHOLIC RECUSANCY 1580–1792
WILLIAM SHEILS

The history of post-Reformation Catholicism in North Yorkshire cannot be entirely separated from that of the late medieval church. We have already discussed the support for the region's monastic houses, and suggested that former monks may have contributed to the survival of traditional religious practices in the years between 1540 and 1570, and enough was still in evidence to shock the Protestant Archbishop Grindal when he arrived in York as archbishop in the latter year. Grindal's arrival came in the wake of another rising against the Tudor regime organised by the earls of Northumberland and Cumberland in 1569, and involving many of their tenants in the western uplands and dales. The ostensible reason was support for Catholicism and for Mary Queen of Scots, and many of the townships involved in the events of 1535 were involved once again.

It is against this background of conservative loyalties that the history of recusancy, as Roman Catholicism came to be defined, has to be constructed. If one was to construct a map recording every occurrence of Roman Catholicism in the county, there would hardly be a place unlisted either for the years before 1660 or thereafter — Catholicism cropped up everywhere. In this context, some choices have to be made in order to bring out the important trends, and shifts in emphasis and growth within the community. The map (**fig 7.2**) has therefore been devised to show both change over time and also to concentrate on those places where sizeable Catholic congregations (of at least twenty persons) have been recorded in at least two decades within each time-band. The division of the period at 1660 acknowledges both a change in the relations between Catholic gentry and the Stuart regime in the years after the Civil Wars, when a number of landowning families returned to Anglicanism, and also approximates to the setting up of the administrative clerical machinery under the vicars apostolic from 1685, which gave added coherence and clerical leadership to the Catholic mission.

The earlier period owed a great deal to gentry leadership and, as can be seen, there were very few places where a sizeable Catholic congregation can be traced over more than one decade where there was not also a strong gentry presence to support it. This was certainly the case at Brandsby, where junior branches of the Cholmley and Fairfax families sustained a congregation of between twenty and forty-five in the first half of the seventeenth century, but it was not only the more substantial gentry families who acted in this way. Nearby at Hovingham the community, which numbered between thirty and forty in these decades, was sustained by the presence of a number of modest, or parochial, gentry families — the Holtbys, Bullocks, Crathornes and Nendykes — none of whom ever played any role at county level. These families, two of which also provided priests for the mission, were more typical of the gentry support for Catholics in the county than those great landowning patrons, such as the Throckmortons or Stonors, who dominate the history of recusancy in southern England. Nor did those major gentry households which provided bases for priests necessarily produce Catholic congregations in their parishes: this did not happen at South Kilvington where the Constables kept a priest; nor did it happen at Naburn, where the Palmes family kept an 'old Scots priest disguised as a gardener' in 1582, and where other gentry families, the Babthorpes and Thwengs, shared their religion later.

The failure to build local congregations in the parishes was not a failure in itself, however, for these households provided mass centres for communities spread across several parishes, and a safe base from which the priests could go out on missions. The county, with its extensive coastline, was a favoured landing place for clergy returning from the Continental seminaries, and many returned through Whitby, moving inland to safe houses such as that at Ugthorpe, on land once owned by the former Prior of Guisborough, Robert Pursglove, before going on to York or other important centres throughout the North. York itself remained a centre of recusancy with a sizeable Catholic community throughout the period

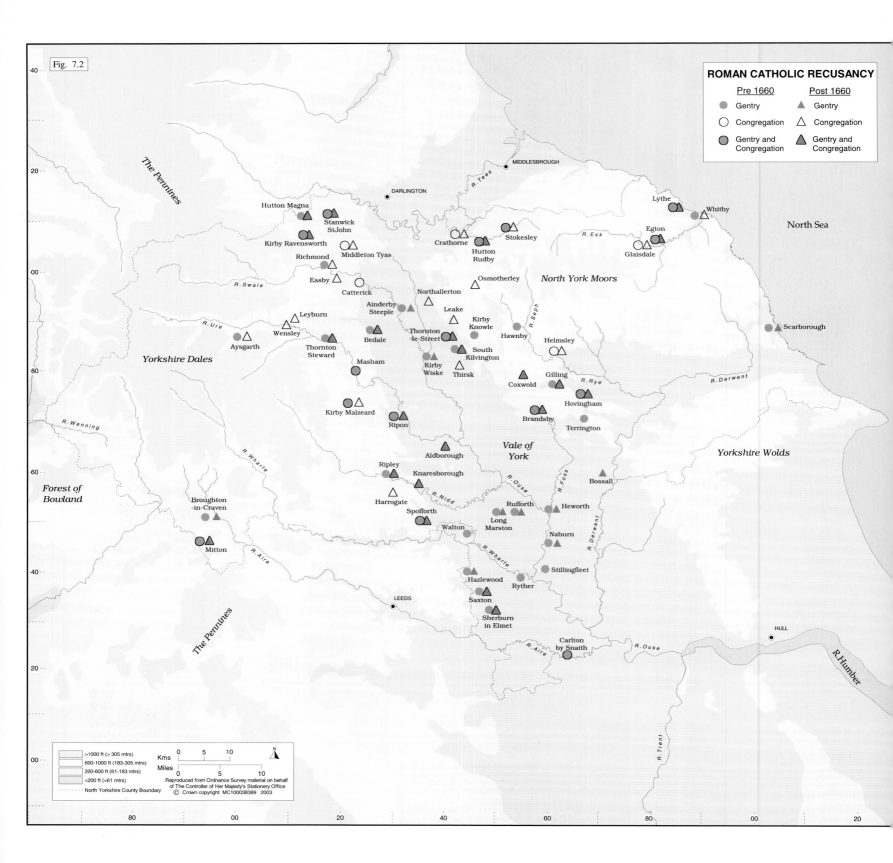

Fig. 7.2

ROMAN CATHOLIC RECUSANCY

Pre 1660   Post 1660

● Gentry   ▲ Gentry

○ Congregation   △ Congregation

◉ Gentry and Congregation   ▲ Gentry and Congregation

MIDDLESBROUGH

DARLINGTON

The Pennines

North Sea

Lythe   Whitby

Hutton Magna

Stanwick St.John

Kirby Ravensworth

Richmond   Middleton Tyas

Crathorne   Stokesley

Hutton Rudby

Egton

Glaisdale

R. Esk

Easby

R. Swale

Catterick

Ainderby Steeple

Northallerton

Osmotherley

North York Moors

Leyburn

Wensley

R. Ure

Aysgarth

Leake

Kirby Knowle

Hawnby

Helmsley

R. Seph

Yorkshire Dales

Bedale

Thornton Steward

Masham

Thornton-le-Street

Kirby Wiske

South Kilvington

Thirsk

Coxwold

Gilling

R. Rye

R. Derwent

Scarborough

Kirby Malzeard

Ripon

Hovingham

Brandsby

Terrington

Aldborough

Vale of York

Yorkshire Wolds

Ripley

Knaresborough

R. Nidd

R. Ouse

R. Foss

Bossall

Forest of Bowland

Broughton-in-Craven

Harrogate

Spofforth

Walton

Long Marston

Rufforth

Heworth

Naburn

R. Derwent

R. Wharfe

Stillingfleet

Mitton

R. Aire

Hazlewood

Ryther

LEEDS

Saxton

Sherburn in Elmet

HULL

Carlton by Snaith

R. Aire

R. Ouse

R. Humber

The Pennines

R. Trent

>1000 ft (> 305 mtrs)
600-1000 ft (183-305 mtrs)
200-600 ft (61-183 mtrs)
<200 ft (<61 mtrs)
North Yorkshire County Boundary

Kms   0   5   10

Miles   0   5   10

Reproduced from Ordnance Survey material on behalf of The Controller of Her Majesty's Stationery Office © Crown copyright MC100038389 2003

and a strong clerical presence, both in the city and its prison, where many Catholics found themselves in the years before 1685. Indeed the prison was viewed as a pastoral opportunity by those priests incarcerated there. Outside its walls, however, gentry support, of both priests and people, was crucial to the spread and maintenance of recusancy up to 1640, with especially important clusters in Ryedale to the north of York, in the parishes bordering the Ouse in the southern Vale of York, and on the northern edge of the North York Moors.

The pattern of distribution set in the years before 1640 did not undergo dramatic shifts in the century and a half following 1660, but the character of the communities changed considerably. As can be seen from the map, far more congregations were operating independently of gentry households, although these did remain important, and families like the Meynells at South Kilvington and the Fairfaxes at Gilling continued to exert considerable influence on the character of the county's Catholicism. Increasingly, however, the missions were being run, not from gentry households, but from towns like Helmsley, Thirsk and Richmond, where there was no gentry presence and from where priests could reach a wide catchment within a particular market area.

What the map reveals, under an overall impression of continuity, is a shift within the community from a seignorial sect to an essentially urban denomination in which the clergy increasingly assumed leadership, supported by substantial tradesmen and farmers. In this respect, the experience of North Yorkshire fits closely the general view of the changing social basis of the Catholic community that emerges from John Bossy's book *The English Catholic Community 1570-1850*.

That change can be illustrated best by the career of Nicholas Postgate. Born into a moorland farming family in the 1590s, he studied for the priesthood at Douai and returned to Yorkshire in 1630, serving in gentry households at Saxton, Halsham and North Kilvington until 1659. From these bases he exercised a ministry which, he claimed, reached over 2,000 people throughout the region, but from 1660 he left his gentry patrons and returned to the moors. From a base at Egton near his original home he pursued a successful mission among the farming community of the moors, until his arrest and execution at York in 1679 during the Popish Plot. In this career which straddled the period of the Civil Wars, we can see the move from a household based to a more independent mission. Postgate's ministry was to be the pattern that emerged in the market towns of the county in the century following his death, until a new pattern emerged in the nineteenth century under the influence of both Catholic emancipation and increasing urbanisation.

7.4 POLITICAL LOYALTIES AND THE CIVIL WARS
WILLIAM SHEILS

In writing his *History of the Civil War*, the Earl of Clarendon noted of Yorkshire in 1642 that 'the greatest part of the gentry of that populous country... did behave themselves with signal fidelity and courage to the king's service',[1] and within the county this was most pronounced in the northern regions: in the North Riding, Royalists outnumbered Parliamentarians by almost two to one; and in Richmondshire, where continuing attachment to Catholicism was strong among the gentry, the ratio was even higher. Indeed there was a close relationship between religious affiliation and politics in the 1640s, with over half the Catholic gentry of Yorkshire as a whole siding with the king and only 6.4 per cent with Parliament. The strong presence of Catholics in the king's army in the North was seized on by the Parliamentarians as a sign of Charles's untrustworthiness, and was even a matter of some concern to Anglican Royalist supporters.

Roman Catholic Recusancy — Further Reading:
The history of Roman Catholicism in the county has been covered by J C H (earlier Hugh) Aveling in the following studies:
Northern Catholics, the Catholic recusants of the North Riding 1558-1790 (1966).
Post-Reformation Catholicism in East Yorkshire 1558-1790 (East Yorkshire Local History Society, 11, 1960).
The Catholic recusants of the West Riding of Yorkshire, 1558-1790, *Proceedings of the Leeds Philosophical and Literary Society*, 10, part 6 (1963); *Catholic Recusancy in the City of York, 1558-1790* (Catholic Record Society, 1970).
For a study to provide a general overview see J Bossy, *The English Catholic Community 1570-1850* (London: Darton, Longman and Todd, 1975).

Friars Head, Winterburn, an imposing gentry house built in c1590.
© R White.

What these figures reveal also, however, is the large number of gentry families — thirty-nine per cent of those in the old North Riding — who tried to keep out of the conflict and remained neutral, as did George Wandesford of Kirklington who, on his return from the Continent in 1643, 'saw that it was in vaine to strive . . . and involve himselfe in utter ruine wilfully, when noe good could possibly be don by his service to the king'.[2] Within families themselves, generations could be split: Sir Thomas Mauleverer of Allerton Mauleverer raised two regiments of horse and one of foot for Parliament, whilst his son fought for the king and was imprisoned for his pains. Under the course of events, individuals also changed allegiance. Most notable of those in the county was Sir Hugh Cholmley of Whitby, who defected from Parliament following the landing of Queen Henrietta Maria at Bridlington in February 1643.

Within these shifting patterns, however, it can be said that the northern and western upland regions of the county were predominantly Royalist, a characteristic which they shared with their neighbouring counties, whilst the main strength of Parliament lay in the vale to the south and west of York close to the clothing districts of West Yorkshire, from where the Fairfax family recruited the main northern support for Parliament. It is no surprise, therefore, that, once hostilities broke out, the main theatre of action in the county took place around York itself, and in those areas which provided the boundaries between the two opposing forces.

Having withdrawn from London in March 1642, Charles I established his headquarters at York during the summer months, where the Court attracted supporters from around the country (**fig 7.3**). From there Charles attempted unsuccessfully to capture the magazine at Hull before withdrawing to Nottingham, where he raised his standard on the 11th August. Charles had left a royalist garrison at York which was soon re-inforced by the Earl of Newcastle's northern forces. On the 3rd December 1642 this army met the Parliamentarians at Tadcaster, capturing the town and forcing their opponents to retreat to Selby. Newcastle's forces then moved to the south and occupied Sherburn-in-Elmet and Pontefract, effectively cutting the communications between the Parliamentarian armies in the West Riding and those around Selby and Hull.

These successes were followed up in April 1643 when the army of Ferdinando, Lord Fairfax, was forced to withdraw from Selby towards Leeds, and by victories at Bramham and Seacroft near Leeds, but the populous regions of the West Riding were proving impervious to Royalist attack, and a major defeat at Wakefield in May 1643 resulted in 1,400 royalist soldiers being taken prisoner. During the summer months of 1643, Newcastle's army successfully took Bradford, but its achievement there was matched by the capture of Ripon for Parliament by Sir Thomas Mauleverer, thereby cutting off one of the main routes linking the Royalist strongholds in the Dales to the city of York. The entry of the Scots into the war on the side of Parliament early in 1644 altered the balance of power in the North, and Newcastle took his army north to counter act this intervention. The capture of Selby by the Fairfaxes on the 11th April, involving the heavy defeat of the remaining Royalist forces stationed at York and over 2,000 dead, forced Newcastle to march south again to secure the city, arriving there on the 16th April. He was followed down by the Scots army, which met up with the army of the Fairfaxes at Wetherby on the 18th April.

The next three months proved to be the decisive phase in the Civil War in the North. The joint Scots and Parliamentary armies, about 20,000 strong, moved east and laid siege to the west and south of the city of York on the 23rd April. For ten weeks York became the centre of the conflict, and the Prince Rupert moved north to the Royalist stronghold at Knaresborough, from where it marched north-east, crossing the Swale at Thornton Bridge and approaching York from the less well-defended north. On the 30th June the army had reached Skip Bridge, four miles (6.5km) west of the city, whereupon the Parliamentarians lifted the siege, Manchester's army crossing the Ouse at Clifton Ings on a bridge of boats and Fairfax's doing likewise to the south at Fulford. Rupert's army cut north and used the boats at Clifton Ings to cross the river and enter York late on the 1st July, from where he set out to meet the enemy the next day. In late afternoon on the 2nd July 1644 the armies had massed at Marston Moor, and at 7pm a surprise attack by the Parliamentarians began one of the decisive battles of the Civil Wars. The Royalists were comprehensively defeated, with over 4,000 dead and 1,500 taken prisoner; two days later the city of York surrendered to Parliament, whose armies now controlled the North.

During the following year and a half the remaining Royalist strongholds in the county fell to the Parliamentary army one by one: Helmsley Castle was besieged in the autumn of 1644 and eventually surrendered on the 21st November following the defeat of a Royalist relieving force at Hambleton; Knaresborough Castle was taken by Colonel Lilburne on the

Civil War — Further Reading:
R T Cliffe, *The Yorkshire Gentry from the Reformation to the Civil War* (London: Athlone Press, 1969).

W Grainge, *Battles and Battlefields of Yorkshire from the earliest time to the end of the great civil war* (1858).

L P Wenham, *The great and close siege of York, 1644* (Kineton Roundwood, 1970).

R Newman, *Marston Moor, 2 July 1644: the sources and the site* (York: Borthwick Papers 53, 1978).

T J Hopper, '*The Readiness of the People': The formation and emergence of the army of the Fairfaxes* (Borthwick Papers 92, 1997), 642–3.

T J Hopper, *The Popish Army of the North: anti-Catholicism and Parliamentary Allegiance in Civil War North Yorkshire, Recusant History* 25 (2000).

20th December after a siege lasting three weeks; Scarborough Castle proved more difficult to capture — the town succumbed in February 1645, but it took a further five months and the assistance of a naval blockade and battery before the castle finally fell on the 22nd July 1645; Bolton Castle, held by the Scropes in the Royalist stronghold of Wensleydale, capitulated on the 5th December 1645; and, finally, Skipton Castle, which had been the scene of intermittent siege for almost three years, surrendered on the 22nd December. This was the end of serious Royalist resistance during the first Civil War and, although Scarborough Castle returned to Royalist hands during the second Civil War following the escape of the king, it was secured for Parliament once again in December 1648.

7.5 HEARTH TAX RETURNS   WILLIAM SHEILS

To historians concerned with wealth distribution and housing in early modern society, the hearth tax returns of the 1660s and 1670s deposited in the Public Record Office are an essential source for the study of regional variations. The tax, which was on the numbers of hearths in houses, was introduced in 1662 and revised in the following years before its administration was set out to farm (empowerment of individuals to collect and take the income from a tax or payment of a fixed sum) in 1666. The difficulties and fraud which followed under these arrangements, by which exemptions could be made for individuals 'by reason of poverty' and to others who could get a certificate signed by the local incumbent and a parochial officer, countersigned by two JPs, led to a tightening of procedures and the appointment of receivers in 1670. It is from this period of administration that the information discussed below mostly derives, but after 1674 the tax was again farmed out, and by the time of the repeal of the tax in 1689 it was said to be making £200,000 a year profit to the tax farmers, some of whom were accused of fraud and malpractice.

The returns survive in varying states of completeness, and those used here are from a variety of dates: that for York and the Ainsty comes from 1665, which is the only year with complete records surviving for those areas; that for the old North Riding comes from Michaelmas 1670; and those for parishes in the old East and West Ridings from 1672.

Taken together, the returns can be used to indicate both social structure and housing within the different administrative units of the county, but variations in local practice need to be recorded. Most importantly the collectors in the old West Riding took a much stricter line on exemptions for poverty than any other collectors: only about 10 per cent of the houses were granted exemptions in that county, whereas elsewhere the figure for exemptions varied between 18.6 per cent in Ouse and Derwent wapentake to the south of York, and 31.6 per cent in Gilling East wapentake in Richmondshire. For this reason, comparisons are not easy to make and, although almost all exempt houses would have been one or two hearth dwellings, it has been decided that only the percentages for hearths in houses considered chargeable should be used in discussing the distribution of house sizes.

What the figures reveal is that the countryside was populated with small dwellings of one or two hearths, and that within that pattern the western uplands of Staincliffe and Hang West, and the moorland parishes in Langbarugh and Pickering Lythe wapentakes, contained the highest proportions of modest cottages. It was only in the urban centre at York that larger houses predominated, with over half of the chargeable houses having more than three hearths and 235 with more than seven; but in those wapentakes with sizeable market towns like Whitby, Scarborough and Northallerton, the presence of these centres kept the number of small cottages below eighty per cent. This was due to the emergence of urban rentier and professional classes who were identified by name in the returns, and numbered twenty-one in Scarborough and thirty-one in Richmond. The only area to have such a low percentage of cottages without the presence of a large market town was the wapentake of Barkston Ash to the south and west of York in the old West Riding, the most prosperous and populous part of the county, where even small villages like Wistow with 101 houses in total had 14 of them occupied by members of the gentry or professional classes.

The tax returns can thus be used not only to give a broad picture of housing conditions in the county but also to indicate its social configuration (**fig 7.4**). The moorland wapentake of Pickering Lythe was clearly an area with inhabitants in very modest circumstances. Ninety four per cent of the chargeable houses were of two hearths or less, and as there were only nine houses among the 2,284 listed with more than seven hearths, the gentry presence in this region was very sparse. Conversely, in Bulmer wapentake to the north of York, a high density of modest dwellings (89.4 per cent) co-existed with a substantial number of larger houses

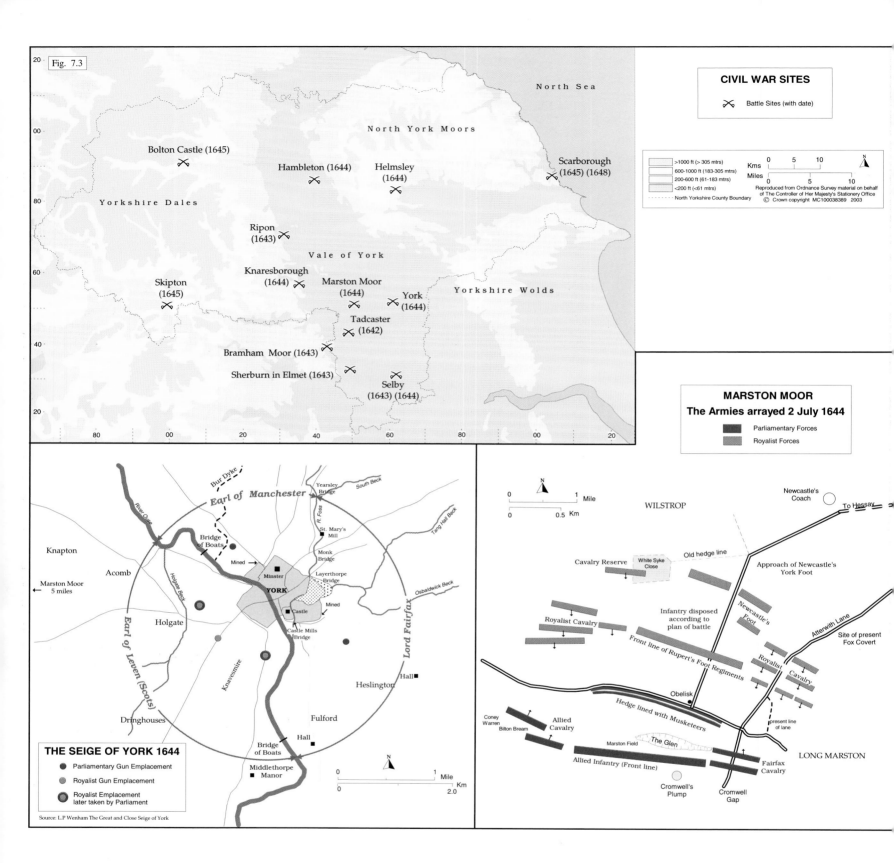

Source: L.P Wenham The Great and Close Seige of York

(fifty-one), representing the residences of a number of gentry families scattered throughout the area and an increasing presence of professionals in parishes like Sutton-on-the-Forest and Stillington which were connected by good routes to York, as well as in suburban townships like Heworth and Clifton.

Within these broad patterns, wide local variations existed, as can be demonstrated from the return for Ryedale wapentake, which included moorland parishes as well as a number of more fielden (arable) townships on the lower slopes of the Howardian Hills. Of the forty-eight townships listed in the return, ten were comprised entirely of one or two hearth households, and one, Pockley in the parish of Helmsley, did not contain a single house of over one hearth

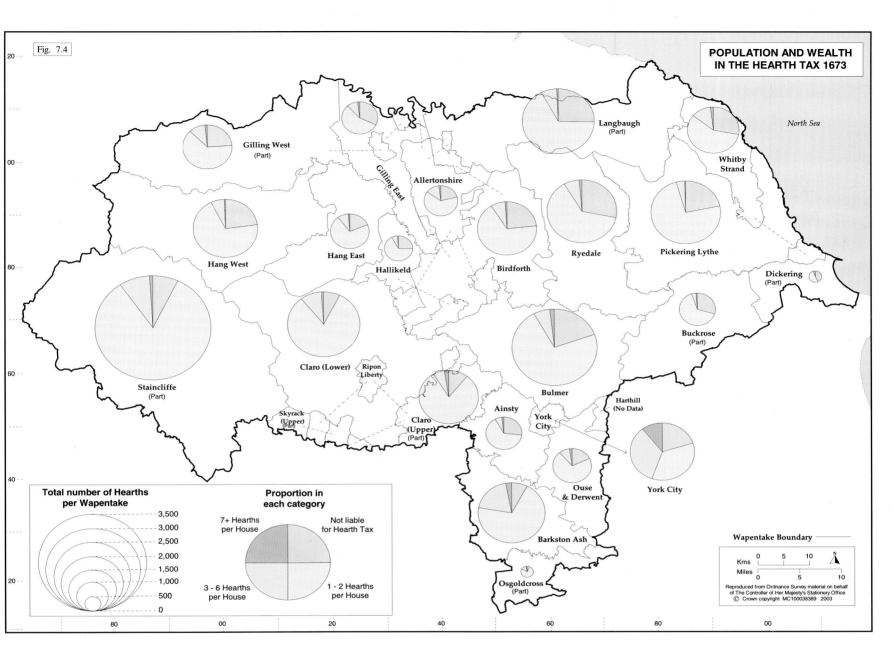

Fig. 7.4

**POPULATION AND WEALTH
IN THE HEARTH TAX 1673**

North Sea

Gilling West
(Part)

Gilling East

Langbaugh
(Part)

Whitby
Strand

Allertonshire

Hang West

Hang East

Hallikeld

Birdforth

Ryedale

Pickering Lythe

Dickering
(Part)

Claro (Lower)

Ripon
Liberty

Staincliffe
(Part)

Skyrack
(Part)

Claro
(Upper)
(Part)

Bulmer

Buckrose
(Part)

Ainsty

York
City

Harthill
(No Data)

York City

Ouse
& Derwent

Barkston Ash

Osgoldcross
(Part)

**Total number of Hearths
per Wapentake**

3,500
3,000
2,500
2,000
1,500
1,000
500
0

**Proportion in
each category**

7+ Hearths
per House

Not liable
for Hearth Tax

3 - 6 Hearths
per House

1 - 2 Hearths
per House

Wapentake Boundary

Kms 0 5 10

Miles 0 5 10

Reproduced from Ordnance Survey material on behalf
of The Controller of Her Majesty's Stationery Office
© Crown copyright MC100038389 2003

among the twenty-four recorded there. The wapentake also contained four market towns — New Malton and its smaller neighbour Old Malton on the River Derwent, and Helmsley and Kirkbymoorside in the moorland region. Larger houses could be found in all these towns: in New Malton, almost one third of the 201 chargeable houses had three hearths or more, but in its poorer neighbour of Old Malton this proportion went down to ten per cent; at Kirkbymoorside the larger houses comprised 25 per cent of those chargeable; and at Helmsley the proportion went down to 13 per cent. This reflected the rural/urban split noted earlier, but there were also villages which contained a significant proportion of larger houses. At Hovingham the seven larger houses were indicative of the increasing prosperity of the farming community there, as the only gentleman or professional noted was Thomas Worsley; but at Oswaldkirk nearby, the larger houses were almost entirely occupied by professionals or self-styled gentry. In their contrasting ways, these two rural townships were sharing in the increasing prosperity of the nation in the same way as the villages to the south and west of York were doing more generally.

The returns demonstrate the variation in both wealth and population density between the upland regions and the parishes and townships of the Vale of York, and also show the growing disparity between urban and rural housing conditions as even the smaller market towns began to attract prosperous tradesmen and professionals to their amenities; but within these overall patterns there were still exceptions to be found whose distinctiveness was often rooted in local peculiarities of land tenure, agrarian practice or social composition.

Hearth Tax Returns — Further Reading:

D J Purdy, *The Yorkshire Hearth Tax Returns* (Hull: Hull University Press, 1991), analyses the returns for 1672 and 1674, and provides an excellent introduction to the source.

M Alldridge (ed.), *The Hearth Tax, problems and possibilities* (Hull: Hull University Press, 1983), contains essays on using this source.

P M Tillott (ed.), *Victoria County History of the City of York* (London: Oxford University Press for the Institute of Historical Research, 1964), deals with the York city returns in the chapter on the seventeenth century.

Ripon Historical Society have published the returns for Lady Day 1672 covering the whole county in a series of pamphlets, *Hearth Tax Returns* (1990–1994).

The Reformation came slowly to North Yorkshire and, outside of the city of York and one or two other localised cases, Puritanism made little headway in the years before the Civil War. The boundary between conformity and Nonconformity in the years between 1560 and the Civil War was a constantly shifting one, in which Puritan clergy could find themselves in trouble with the authorities one year and not the next.

Nevertheless there were a few localities in which a Puritan tradition emerged which later translated into dissent after the break which took place with the enforcement of Subscription to the Thirty Nine Articles in 1662: to the west and south of York, there were a number of parishes with Puritan clergy before 1640 which had sizeable dissenting congregations recorded in 1676, most notably at Tadcaster and Hampsthwaite, but smaller groups were spread throughout the neighbourhood; and in York itself, a noted Puritan centre during the Civil Wars, Nonconformity had made substantial inroads with just under five per cent of the families in 1676 being recorded as dissenters of some sort, with particularly strong representation in the central parishes of All Saints', Pavement and St Michael's, Spurriergate.

In all these cases the continuity between pre- and post-Civil War Nonconformity testifies to the extent to which it had permeated important sectors of the community. This was also true in the south-eastern borders of the county as well, at Hackness and Langton, where the local gentry were sympathetic.

Elsewhere in the county, however, the strength of post-Restoration dissent owed as much to the new denominations which emerged during the Civil War as to any earlier Puritan tradition. Most notable among these were the Quakers, who attracted sizeable support in York and Thirsk from the 1650s and '60s, as well as in the Dales near Settle. The Quakers were also particularly successful in the upland regions of the North York Moors and Ryedale, areas which had been largely untouched by early seventeenth-century century Puritanism. Thus the Quakers can be said to have redrawn the religious map of the county during the later part of the century.

The distribution of dissent in the 1670s, drawn chiefly from the details of the Compton census of 1676 and from diocesan records for those areas (particularly parishes in the diocese of Chester) not covered in the census, therefore attests to the vigour of the new dissenting sects rather than to continuities, and records the disposition of groups of lay adherents rather than gathered churches round a particular minister, though these are also included (**fig 7.5**).

A century later, the pattern of dissent had once again been transformed. By the 1760s the 'old dissent' congregations, represented chiefly by the Presbyterians but also including some Baptists, had retreated to the major market towns of the county and had even disappeared from some, such as Tadcaster where dissent had been so strongly represented in the 1670s, whilst in others like New Malton the chapel continued but the congregation met only rarely.

Wesleyan Methodist Chapel, Reeth. Originally built in the eighteenth century, but modified in 1822, 1840 and 1907.
© R White/Yorkshire Dales National Park Authority, NCC 47.

Against this pattern of decline, one can contrast the experience of the Quakers who, not dependent on a formal ministry, were able to exist in small meetings and groupings attached to their monthly meetings located in the market towns. Thus in 1764 the visitation returns revealed small groups of worshipping Quakers in many of the towns and villages where they had been recorded ninety years earlier (**fig 7.6**). The impression is that, while numbers had not grown, the society proved to have an enduring place in the religious configuration of the county, which probably owed much to its democratic and locally managed organisation.

In addition to the Quakers, two new sects — the Moravians and the Sandemanians — were recorded as having meeting houses in York at this date, but the real change to the religious geography of the county in the 1760s is explained by the growth of Methodism, with groups of adherents being recorded in very many parishes in the county and places of worship being mentioned in thirty-six parishes, one of which, Northallerton, included three chapels. Even within these figures the overall figure for the county is likely to be an underestimate, for although many Anglican clergy were unsympathetic to the Methodists and clearly counted them as dissenters, there were others, like Richard Conyers at Helmsley, who shared many of their values and did not see them as Nonconformists, a view which the Methodists had of themselves at this time also, for they had not yet formally split off from the Established Church.

It must be said, therefore, that the attempt to map the distribution of Methodism in the 1760s shares something of the limitations of any attempt to show the distribution of Puritanism in the 1620s, in that its categorisation as dissent owed as much to local custom and practice as to ecclesiological definitions. Despite this problem, one which is common to religious geography in most periods and places, the pattern which emerges from the map provides a pointer to the subsequent history of Nonconformity in the county and reveals some points of interest: Methodism made more progress in the lowland rural parishes than Quakerism; and several parishes immediately to the north and east of York, as well as some to the south, were noted centres at this date. Although there were congregations in the upland areas, such as Fylingdales and Lastingham, its strength was in the farming villages of the vale, such as Alne on the banks of the Ouse and Stockton-on-the-Forest to the east of York.

What the map reveals, therefore, is that the religious character of the county underwent considerable adjustment between 1660 and 1800 under the influence of two quite distinct movements, Quakerism and Wesleyan Methodism, to each of which the Established Church responded with varying degrees of success. The effectiveness of the Anglican response often depended on the energy of the local incumbent and, therefore, varied from place to place. It was no doubt influential in curbing the growth of dissent in particular localities, but general patterns of Nonconformity emerged. Though the market towns were to play an increasing role in both communities, as indeed was also the case with Roman Catholicism, the map reveals that Quakerism from the 1650s and Methodism from the 1750s drew a significant proportion of their adherents from rural communities located in differing economic and agrarian contexts.

Nonconformity & Dissent — Further Reading:

Anne Whiteman (ed.), *The Compton Census of 1676* (London: British Academy, Records of Social and Economic History 10, 1986).

C Annesley and P Hoskin (eds), *Archbishop Drummond's Visitation Returns, 1764*, 3 vols (York: Borthwick Texts and Calendars, 1997, 1998, 2001).

B Dale, *Yorkshire Puritanism and Nonconformity* (Bradford: privately printed, 1909).

J Jago, *Aspects of the Georgian Church: visitation records of the diocese of York 1761-1776* (Madison, N J: Fairleigh Dickinson University Press, 1997).

W P Thistlethwaite, *The Quaker Meeting Houses of Yorkshire 1647-1900: a gazetteer* (privately printed, 1983).

7.7 ADMINISTRATIVE CHANGES AND LOCAL GOVERNMENT, 1600-1900 EDWARD ROYLE

The county of North Yorkshire, formed in 1974, is based on the historical North Riding but includes parts from all three Ridings of Yorkshire. The former North Riding had its northern boundary along the River Tees, westwards as far as the heights of Mickle Fell, but the areas to the north of the Cleveland Hills and the watershed south of the Stainmore Pass were transferred to Cleveland and Durham respectively in 1974 (**fig 7.7**). The former southern boundary was extended southwards from the River Ure to the Wharfe, westwards to the Great North Road and southwards to include the district around Selby, all formerly in the West Riding; in the east, the west bank of the Derwent and the north Wolds to near Flamborough Head were included from the former East Riding. Within these boundaries the city of York was part of North Yorkshire between 1974 and 1996 when it again became administratively separate.

North Yorkshire, therefore, had no historical administrative unity or county coherence before 1974 and included parts of the separate county jurisdictions of all three Ridings as well as the county as a whole, being administered in parts at different times and for different purposes from York, Beverley, Wakefield and Northallerton, the latter becoming the county town for North Yorkshire in 1974.

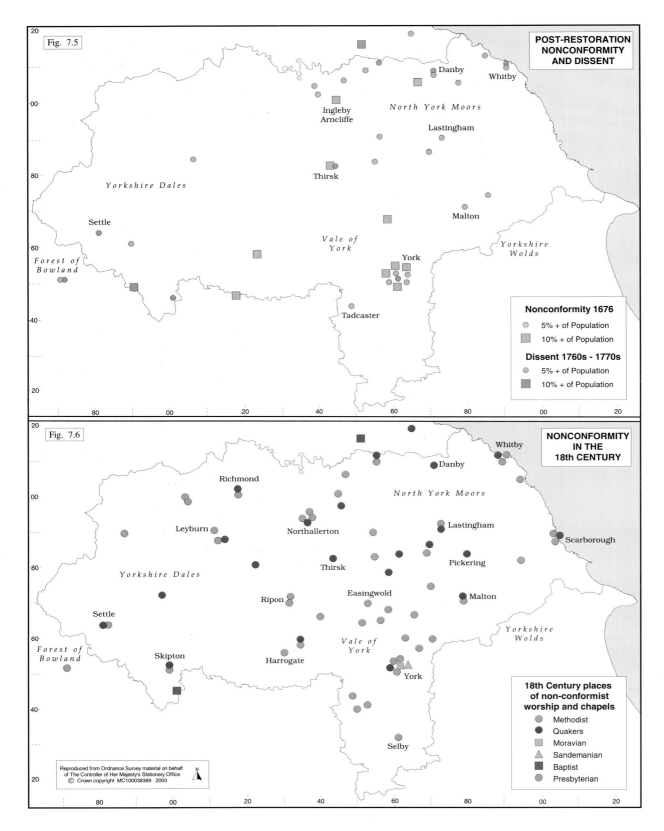

Fig. 7.5

POST-RESTORATION NONCONFORMITY AND DISSENT

Danby
Whitby
North York Moors
Ingleby Arncliffe
Lastingham
Yorkshire Dales
Thirsk
Malton
Settle
Vale of York
Yorkshire Wolds
York
Forest of Bowland
Tadcaster

Nonconformity 1676
○ 5% + of Population
■ 10% + of Population

Dissent 1760s - 1770s
● 5% + of Population
■ 10% + of Population

Fig. 7.6

NONCONFORMITY IN THE 18th CENTURY

Whitby
Danby
Richmond
North York Moors
Leyburn
Lastingham
Northallerton
Scarborough
Yorkshire Dales
Thirsk
Pickering
Ripon
Easingwold
Malton
Settle
Yorkshire Wolds
Forest of Bowland
Skipton
Vale of York
Harrogate
York
Selby

Reproduced from Ordnance Survey material on behalf of The Controller of Her Majesty's Stationery Office © Crown copyright MC100038389 2003

18th Century places of non-conformist worship and chapels
● Methodist
● Quakers
▪ Moravian
▲ Sandemanian
■ Baptist
● Presbyterian

The county administration in the Ridings before 1888 consisted of the justices meeting in the quarter sessions. Though cast in judicial language, their work extended far wider and included the enforcement of social legislation which gave the sessions a central role in local government. This was slowly whittled away during the course of the nineteenth century with the establishment of other agencies, most significantly the poor law guardians in Poor Law Unions under the 1834 Poor Law Amendment Act (see Hastings, section 7.11). These also formed the new registration districts of 1836, a unit used for a variety of purposes including the collection of census data, which together formed the 'registration county' of Yorkshire. The northern, eastern and southern borders of North Yorkshire still follow closely the boundaries of registration districts.

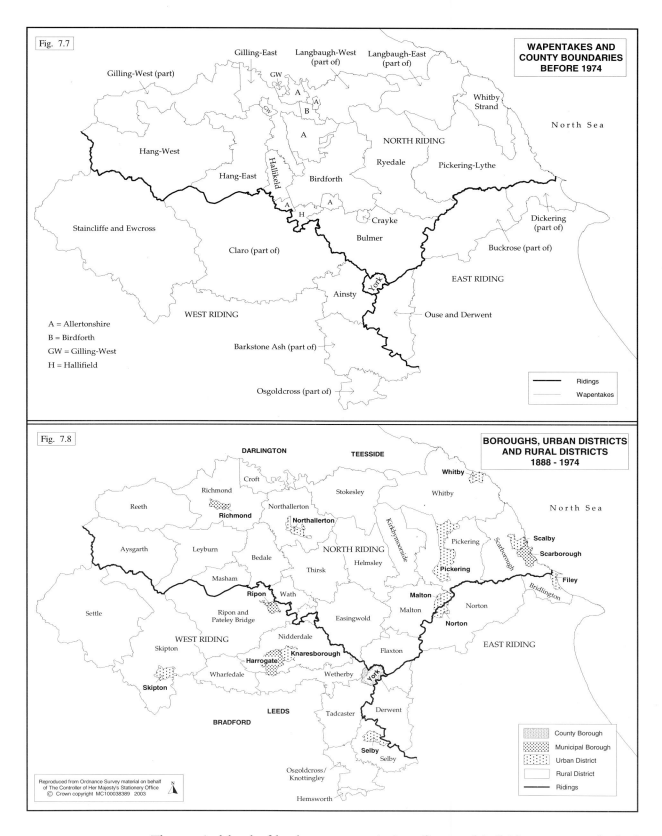

Fig. 7.7

WAPENTAKES AND COUNTY BOUNDARIES BEFORE 1974

Gilling-West (part)

Gilling-East   Langbaugh-West (part of)   Langbaugh-East (part of)

GW

A

A

B

A

Hang-West

Whitby Strand

North Sea

NORTH RIDING

Hang-East

Hallikeld

Birdforth

Ryedale

Pickering-Lythe

A

A

H

A

Crayke

Dickering (part of)

Staincliffe and Ewcross

Bulmer

Buckrose (part of)

Claro (part of)

York

EAST RIDING

Ainsty

WEST RIDING

Ouse and Derwent

A = Allertonshire
B = Birdforth
GW = Gilling-West
H = Hallifield

Barkstone Ash (part of)

Osgoldcross (part of)

—— Ridings
—— Wapentakes

Fig. 7.8

BOROUGHS, URBAN DISTRICTS AND RURAL DISTRICTS 1888 - 1974

DARLINGTON   TEESSIDE

Croft

Whitby

Richmond

Stokesley

Whitby

Reeth

Northallerton

North Sea

Richmond

Northallerton

Aysgarth

Leyburn

Bedale

NORTH RIDING

Kirkbymoorside

Pickering

Scalby

Scarborough

Helmsley

Masham

Thirsk

Pickering

Ripon

Wath

Settle

Ripon and Pateley Bridge

Easingwold

Malton

Malton

Norton

Filey

Bridlington

WEST RIDING

Nidderdale

Norton

EAST RIDING

Skipton

Knaresborough

Flaxton

Harrogate

Skipton

Wharfedale

Wetherby

York

LEEDS

Tadcaster

Derwent

BRADFORD

Selby

Selby

Osgoldcross/ Knottingley

Hemsworth

Reproduced from Ordnance Survey material on behalf of The Controller of Her Majesty's Stationery Office
© Crown copyright MC100038389 2003

County Borough
Municipal Borough
Urban District
Rural District
—— Ridings

The nominal head of local government, in its military and judicial aspects, was the lord lieutenant, one for each Riding after 1660. For some purposes under the lieutenancy, the ancient wapentakes were still used as county subdivisions: ten (Gilling East, Hang West, Hang East, Hallikeld, Allerton, Birdforth, Whitby Strand, Pickering Lythe, Ryedale and Bulmer) from the North Riding fell wholly within North Yorkshire, and three (Gilling West, Langbaurgh East and Langbaurgh West) fell partly in the county; together with most of Claro, Staincliffe and Ewcross, and Barkstone Ash, parts of Osgoldcross as well as the Ainsty from the West Riding; and Ouse and Derwent, and parts of Buckrose and Dickering from the East Riding. These wapentakes formed the basis of the petty sessional divisions referred to in the Parliamentary Redistribution Act of 1885, though for most purposes by the nineteenth century they were no longer significant.

The lowest levels of administration in the county were the manorial court leet and the parish vestry. By the nineteenth century the former was concerned with little more than the transfer of copyhold land. Some large parishes were divided into townships which operated as parishes. Vestries continued to play an important role in local administration, doubling as sanitary authorities in some areas after 1848 and assuming powers as highway authorities. However, in 1872 the Public Health Act confirmed the subdivision of the entire county into sanitary districts, which in turn were the basis for new parish councils under the Local Government Act of 1894.

The boroughs — urban administrative areas between the parish and the county — were few: of fourteen which may have been considered boroughs at some time, only York and three others (Richmond, Ripon and Scarborough) were corporate boroughs and became municipal boroughs under the Municipal Corporations Act of 1835. Harrogate was added in 1884, while other nineteenth-century towns in the North Riding passed to Cleveland in 1974.

There were three administrative anomalies in the former North Riding: Crayke, near Easingwold, was in County Durham until 1844; the county gaol at York Castle, within the city of York, was in the jurisdiction of all three Ridings until 1974; and the Ainsty, between the Nidd and the Wharfe to the west of York, which had been annexed to York from the West Riding in 1449, was returned to the West Riding in 1836, before becoming part of North Yorkshire in 1974. The city of York itself, although part of North Yorkshire only between 1974 and 1996, can be considered within this survey, being the largest corporate borough before 1835, the largest municipal borough from 1835 and the only county borough in the area from 1888.

A major change in local administrative boundaries came under the Local Government Acts of 1888 and 1894. In 1888 most of the administrative powers of the quarter sessions were transferred to the elected councillors of the new administrative county councils which comprised the three Ridings with their county towns — Beverley (ER), Northallerton (NR) and Wakefield (WR) — shorn of their major urban areas which became county boroughs (**fig 7. 8**). The county (and county borough) had responsibility for such matters as policing, licensing, reformatory and industrial schools (but not elementary schooling before 1902), public health, bridges and roads, and pauper lunatic asylums (but not the Poor Law until 1929).

Within the county structure, a new level of local government was created in 1894 with urban and rural districts and, in the latter, parish councils which replaced the vestries. By the end of the nineteenth century North Yorkshire had, in addition to the county borough of York and the four municipal boroughs of Harrogate, Richmond, Ripon and Scarborough, ten urban district councils (Filey, Knaresborough, Malton, Northallerton, Norton, Pickering, Scalby, Selby, Skipton and Whitby) and thirty rural district councils.

Administrative Changes — Further Reading:
William Page (ed), *The Victoria History of the Counties of England. A History of Yorkshire North Riding*, vol 1 (London: Constable, 1914), map facing page 1.
Royal Commission on Local Government in England 1966-1969, chaired by Lord Redcliffe-Maud, Cmnd 4040 (London: HMSO, 1969), vol 1, map 1.
Royal Commission on Local Government Boundary Commission for England, Report No 1 (November 1972), Cmnd 5148 (London: HMSO, 1972), map 2.
Statutes of the Realm, 51 & 52 Victoriae, cap 41 (1888), county and county borough councils.
Statutes of the Realm, 56 & 57 Victoriae, cap 73 (1894), parish councils, and rural and urban districts.
Frederic A Youngs Jnr, *Guide to Local Administrative Units of England, vol. 3: Northern England* (London: Royal Historical Society, 1991).

7.8 ELECTORAL POLITICS BEFORE AND AFTER THE REFORM ACT
EDWARD ROYLE

At the beginning of the nineteenth century Yorkshire elected two county MPs, but in 1821 two further seats were added. There were also within the area of North Yorkshire nine boroughs, each with two MPs — Richmond, Northallerton, Thirsk, Malton and Scarborough in the North Riding; Ripon, Boroughbridge, Aldborough and Knaresborough in the West Riding; and the city of York. Freeholders from the Ainsty (although part of York until 1836) were confirmed as Yorkshire county voters in 1735 and West Riding voters in 1832. Crayke, near Easingwold, although a detached part of County Durham, was included within the North Riding constituency from 1832.

The 1832 Reform Act gave two seats to each of the Ridings but reduced the borough representation outside the industrialised West Riding. Boroughbridge and Aldborough lost their seats, and Northallerton and Thirsk each lost one. Whitby was created a parliamentary borough with one seat. At the next major redistribution of seats in 1867, Knaresborough, Malton, Richmond and Ripon each lost one member, having populations of under 10,000, and no new seats were created.

A further Redistribution Act in 1885 removed the distinction between the borough and county franchises (**fig 7.9**). Of the ancient parliamentary boroughs, York kept both its members and Scarborough one. The others were incorporated within county divisions, each with one MP: Thirsk and Malton (which included the Ainsty), Richmond, Whitby and

Cleveland in the North Riding; and Ripon, Skipton and Otley in the West Riding. To these should be added part of Barkstone Ash and a fragment of Osgoldcross in the West Riding; and parts of Howden and Buckrose in the East Riding. So in 1900 the area of North Yorkshire had at most fourteen MPs compared with twenty-two in 1800.

Before 1832, party politics meant little compared with family tradition and influence, even when these carried a party label. In the county of Yorkshire between 1802 and 1831, with an electorate of over 20,000 freeholders, there were nine general elections but only three contests — in 1807, 1830 and 1831. In 1802 two Tories (William Wilberforce and Henry Lascelles) held both seats in an uncontested election, and in 1831 Whigs took all four seats in the contested election of that year. Otherwise the seats were divided equally between the two parties. In the next-largest constituency, York, with about 2,345 freeholder electors, the Whigs held both seats in 1802-7 and 1820-6: otherwise they were shared. In nine elections there were four contests — in 1807, 1818, 1820 and 1830.

Politics before 1832 were quite different in the other nine boroughs. Aldborough, a scot and lot borough (where all ratepayers could vote) with sixty electors, and Borough-bridge, a burgage borough (where entitlement to vote came from specified types of property) with sixty-four electors, were both in the pocket of the Duke of Newcastle and returned uncontested Tory MPs, except in 1802 when an independent Whig bought his seat from Newcastle and 1818 when an anti-Newcastle candidate headed the only poll held in these years. Malton, with about 500 scot and lot voters, was similarly controlled by Earl Fitzwilliam in the Whig interest, except when a minor rebellion let a Tory in for a year in 1807.

Elsewhere, matters ran even more smoothly. The Duke of Devonshire secured two Whigs for Knaresborough (96 burgage voters), the Dundas family did the same for Richmond (270 burgage voters), as did Sir Thomas Frankland for Thirsk (50 burgage voters). On the other side, Miss Elizabeth Lawrence chose Tories for Ripon (146 burgage voters) on every occasion except 1831 when the sitting Tory members were returned as Whigs. In Northallerton the 200 burgesses chose a representative of each of the leading families without a contest: an independent Whig and a Tory until 1824, and then two Tories. Similarly in Scarborough, where the forty-four members of the corporation chose the MPs, the patronage was shared between Lord Mulgrave and the Duke of Rutland in the Tory interest, except in 1818-20 when Mulgrave's son was elected and then supported the Whigs. In the election of 1830, the last before the Reform Bill crisis broke, North Yorkshire returned 13 Tories and 11 Whigs.

The Reform Act made little immediate difference in most places, beyond abolishing Newcastle's two Tory boroughs of Aldborough and Boroughbridge. The county always returned one Liberal and one Tory in the five contested and seven uncontested elections between 1832 and 1884. In six of the boroughs, elections frequently were uncontested before 1868. Malton and Richmond continued to return Liberals, though in Thirsk the Whig/Liberal tradition was broken in 1847 when the sitting member switched to the Protectionist side and the seat thereafter was Conservative. Northallerton, initially Liberal, became Conservative in 1865. The new seat of Whitby went the other way: initially Conservative, the Liberals took it in a by-election in 1859, lost it in 1865 but thereafter the seat was Conservative. In Ripon, the complexion of the seat reflected the changing politics of the patron (the earls de Grey), following the Peelites from Conservative to Liberal: a Conservative constituency until 1857, it was thereafter solidly Liberal.

By contrast there were keenly fought elections in Knaresborough, Scarborough and York. In Knaresborough, where every election between 1832 and 1880 was contested, party fortunes fluctuated throughout, with the Conservatives gradually coming to predominate. Scarborough was similarly contested (except in 1847) but here a previously Tory borough passed to the Liberals. York, with the largest borough electorate, was also contested on every occasion but here honours were usually even. In total, North Yorkshire Liberals held 67 per cent of borough seats in the four general elections between 1832 and 1841; and 64 per cent in the next five elections to 1865; but in the three elections of 1868-1880 their share rose to 70 per cent.

Comparisons before and after the 1885 Redistribution Act are difficult. In York, Conservative strength increased with the usual division of seats being upset at a by-election in 1898 and the general election in 1900 when the Conservatives held both seats (**fig 7.10**). Scarborough remained consistently Liberal from 1895. In the principal county divisions the Conservatives were dominant, winning in each of the eight general elections (not all contested) between 1885 and December 1910 in Thirsk and Malton, Whitby, Barkstone Ash, and Howden; and losing in Ripon and Richmond only in 1885 and 1906. The Liberal

Electoral Politics — Further Reading:

F W S Craig (ed.), *Boundaries of Parliamentary Constituencies, 1885-1972* (Chichester: Political Reference Publications, 1972).

F W S Craig, *British Parliamentary Election Results, 1832-1885* (Dartmouth: Parliamentary Research Services, 1989).

F W S Craig, *British Parliamentary Election Results, 1885-1918* (London: Macmillan, 1974).

Charles R Dod, *Electoral Facts from 1832 to 1853 Impartially Stated*, (ed.) H J Hanham (Brighton: Harvester, 1972).

Philbin, J Holladay, *Parliamentary Representation, 1832. England and Wales* (New Haven: Connecticut, 1965).

W E Tate, and F B Singleton, *A History of Yorkshire* (Beaconsfield: Darwen Finlayson, 1960).

Henry Stooks Smith, *The Parliaments of England from 1715 to 1847* (1844-50), 2nd ed. by F W S Craig (Chichester, Political Reference Publications, 1973).

Statutes of the Realm, 48 & 49 Victoriae, cap 23 (1885), Parliamentary Redistribution Act.

R G Thorne, *The History of Parliament. The House of Commons, 1790-1820*, 5 vols (London: History of Parliament Trust, 1986).

J Vincent and M Stenton, *McCalmont's Parliamentary Poll Book. British Election Results 1832-1918*, eighth edition with new introduction and additional material (Brighton: Harvester, 1971).

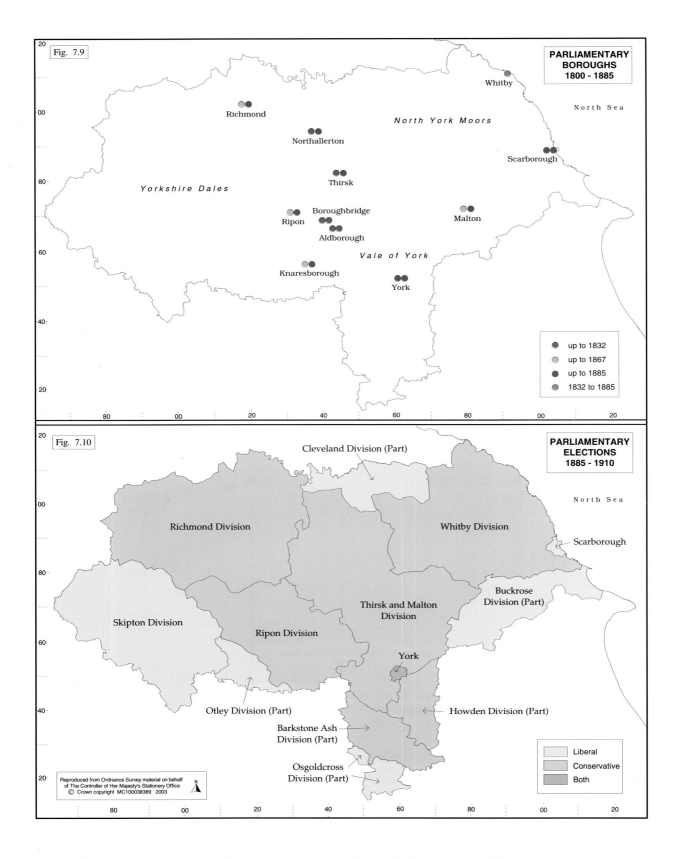

Fig. 7.9

PARLIAMENTARY BOROUGHS 1800 - 1885

Whitby

North Sea

Richmond

North York Moors

Northallerton

Scarborough

Yorkshire Dales

Thirsk

Boroughbridge

Ripon

Malton

Aldborough

Vale of York

Knaresborough

York

- up to 1832
- up to 1867
- up to 1885
- 1832 to 1885

Fig. 7.10

PARLIAMENTARY ELECTIONS 1885 - 1910

Cleveland Division (Part)

North Sea

Richmond Division

Whitby Division

Scarborough

Buckrose Division (Part)

Skipton Division

Thirsk and Malton Division

Ripon Division

York

Otley Division (Part)

Howden Division (Part)

Barkstone Ash Division (Part)

Osgoldcross Division (Part)

Reproduced from Ordnance Survey material on behalf of The Controller of Her Majesty's Stationery Office © Crown copyright MC100038389 2003

N

Liberal
Conservative
Both

strongholds were at the margins: Skipton, lost only in 1886 and 1895 (to a local Liberal Unionist); Otley, lost only in 1895; Buckrose, held by the Liberals from 1892; and Cleveland and Osgoldcross, solidly Liberal thanks to urban areas outside the later North Yorkshire. The merging of the small borough seats into the counties in 1885 confirmed the decline of the Liberals. Between 1885 and 1910, the North Yorkshire area was represented by 57 Conservatives and Unionists, and 55 Liberals, 31 of whom were in the two boroughs and the marginal districts of Osgoldcross and Cleveland.

The effect of the 1832 Reform Act had been to strengthen the Liberal interest and weaken the Conservative; by the end of the century the position was reversed.

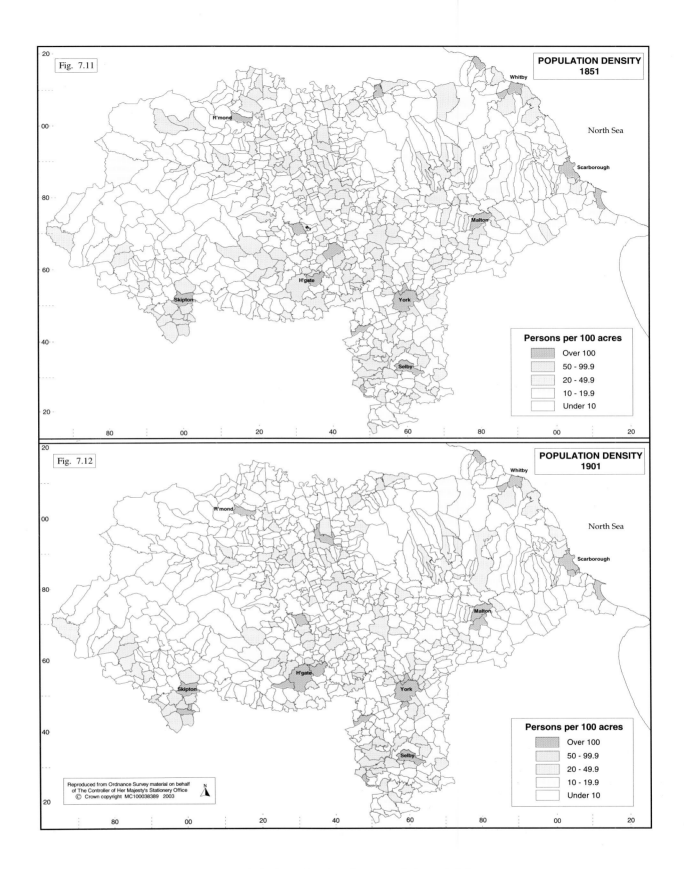

7.9 POPULATION CHANGE, 1700–1900
RICHARD LAWTON

North Yorkshire is mainly closely settled but relatively sparsely populated. Back projections from the first census of 1801, using estimates of natural change from parish registers of births and deaths, suggest a population of nearly 120,000 in 1700 for North Riding, but increased mortality led to a fall to under 110,000 by 1750.

The impact of enclosure and intensification of agriculture, especially in the lowland areas, accompanied by a considerable expansion of textile and other rural craft industries in the

Pennine Dales, saw rapid growth to 163,275 in 1801 when the estimated population of the present county was 275,000. Estimates from parish birth and burial registers suggest net annual natural growth of 1.2 per cent, partly due to increased birthrate, partly to a falling deathrate. But, with 40 per cent (36,000) of its natural increase lost to net out-migration, North Riding's 48 per cent growth between 1750 and 1801 was one fifth lower than national growth.

Urban development lagged, especially in the early eighteenth century. York, the substantial regional capital, grew relatively slowly to some 17,000 by 1801, well below the rate of the emerging ports and industrial towns of northern England. Of North Yorkshire's coastal towns, Whitby flourished on its East Coast trade, whaling and shipbuilding, but it was Scarborough, benefiting from the late eighteenth-century craze for sea-bathing, that jumped rapidly to some 7,000 by 1801. Harrogate's emerging spa was still 'a quiet genteel retreat'. In their substantial Georgian heritage, most of the market towns reflect the growing prosperity of the countryside, and an increasing range of handicraft and service industries.

Although substantial increases in total population between the censuses of 1801 and 1821 reflect expansion of farming — not least on uplands enclosed during the Napoleonic Wars — and continuing competitiveness of lead mining and textiles (both handicraft weaving and knitting, and in the water-powered cotton and worsted mills of Craven), out-migration continued.

Agricultural recession from the 1820s and the decline of handicraft industry led to steady losses, and in some districts (eg Pateley Bridge, Reeth and Helmsley) numbers fell in the 1820s. Indeed, almost all parts of the county except York experienced a sharp downturn in population increase. Of the estimated 67,000 natural growth in the North Riding between 1801 and 1831, over half (35,000) left the area.

Fig 7.11 shows North Yorkshire around the peak of its rural population, though, in parts of the Pennine Dales, numbers had already begun to fall.

Three major features stand out: first, the higher densities in parishes of the Vale of York and in and around the Vale of Pickering; secondly, the relative emptiness of the upland west and the North Yorkshire Moors; thirdly, urban growth.

In the latter, York (36,303) and the coastal towns — especially Scarborough (12,915) and Whitby (10,899) — were prominent, while the rapidly growing Harrogate had 3,434 inhabitants. Smaller market towns under 2,000 people and sub-regional centres such as Richmond, Ripon, Skipton, Northallerton and Malton (ranging from 3-7,000) had grown steadily between 1801 and 1851 (**fig 7.13**). Most arable districts also experienced growth but, in many townships in the pastoral uplands, population fell below that in 1801 by mid-century, though, where textiles and other handicraft industry provided a more broadly based rural economy, growth continued.

Between 1851 and 1901, rural depopulation became county-wide (**fig 7.14**). It was severe in upland areas except where, as in parts of Wharfedale, textile factories were still important. The collapse of lead prices (undermined by imported ores) was severely felt in Wensleydale and Swaledale. The decline of rural hinterlands and competition from bigger towns reduced the range of crafts and services in market towns, all of which experienced a fall in population. Except where there was substantial industry — eg Skipton (11,986 in 1901) or Selby (7,424) — even sub-regional 'capitals' such as Ripon and Northallerton experienced little growth or, as with Malton (4,758) and Richmond (3,837), decreased.

Growth in the larger towns was the major factor in North Yorkshire's increase of 90,000 (26 per cent) between 1851 and 1901: York and its suburbs, Scarborough and Harrogate together accounted for four-fifths (71,000) of that growth. Whilst the impact of the sharp contrast between trends in the early and late nineteenth century on the map of population density (**fig 7.12**) is less marked, the larger urban centres stand out more clearly from a declining countryside, while higher rural densities were largely confined to the Vale of York, Airedale and the coastal area.

The demographic basis of change from mid-century can be assessed from civil registration of births and deaths established in 1837. Growth was continuous over the area approximating to the present county, except for a fall of 408 between 1881 and 1891, but few registration districts retained even a small proportion of their natural increase (**fig 7.15**).

Settle, Selby, Stokesley, Pickering and Whitby districts grew by under 10 per cent in 1851-1901: only in Skipton (40 per cent), York (57.1), Scarborough (79.6), and Knaresborough including Harrogate (109.7) was there consistent and substantial increase, and only in York, Scarborough and Knaresborough districts was there positive inward migration, which in the latter exceeded its natural growth.

The rural districts lost heavily through migration at net rates of 1 to 1.6 per cent per annum which exceeded natural growth: Reeth, decimated by the collapse of lead mining,

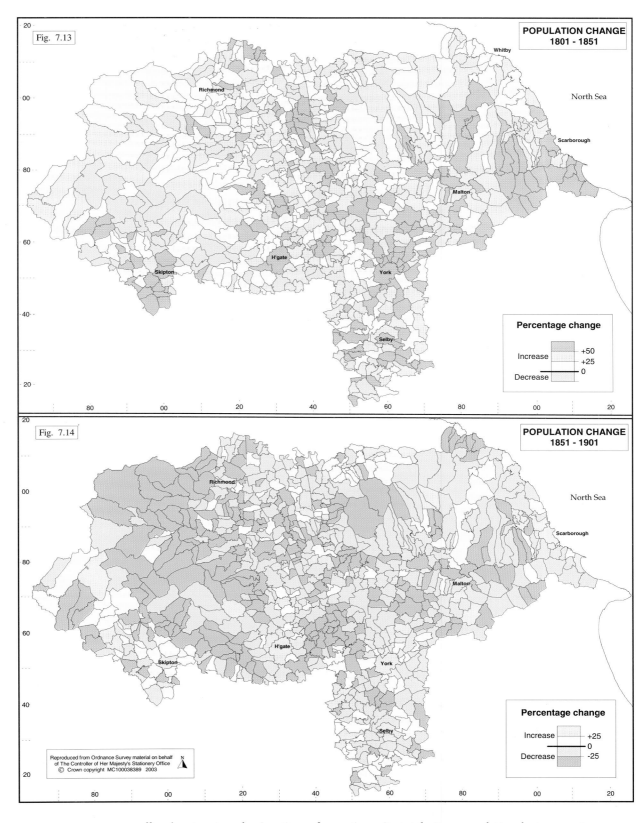

Fig. 7.13

**POPULATION CHANGE
1801 - 1851**

Whitby

North Sea

Richmond

Scarborough

Malton

H'gate

Skipton

York

Selby

Percentage change

Increase +50
          +25
          0
Decrease

Fig. 7.14

**POPULATION CHANGE
1851 - 1901**

Richmond

North Sea

Scarborough

Malton

H'gate

Skipton

York

Selby

Reproduced from Ordnance Survey material on behalf
of The Controller of Her Majesty's Stationery Office
© Crown copyright MC100038389 2003

N

Percentage change

Increase +25
          0
Decrease -25

Population Changes — Further Reading:

The maps and analysis are based on the censuses of
Great Britain 1851, and of England and Wales 1861-1901.

C Hallas, *Rural Responses to Industrialisation. The North
Yorkshire Pennines 1790-1914* (Bern: Peter Lang AG,
1999).

suffered net outward migration of 1.33 times its total 1851 population between 1851-1901. Village after village was depleted as young people left the farms. Handicraft textile workers went to mills in West Yorkshire and east Lancashire.

The negative migrational balance and the low proportion of the county's population born outside Yorkshire (in most districts under 10 per cent) reflect limited in-movement, though specific labour demand — as at Hellifield in the building (from the 1860s) and operating of the Midland Railway to Carlisle (completed 1876) — and the rapid growth of York, Scarborough and Harrogate drew in some long-distance migrants. However, North Yorkshire's population growth was largely self-sustaining in the nineteenth as in the eighteenth century.

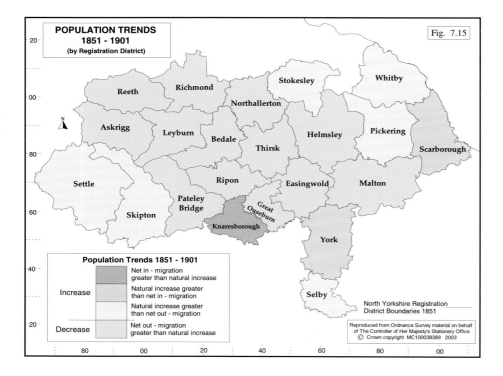

POPULATION TRENDS 1851 - 1901
(by Registration District)

Fig. 7.15

Reeth • Richmond • Stokesley • Whitby • Northallerton • Askrigg • Leyburn • Bedale • Thirsk • Helmsley • Pickering • Scarborough • Settle • Ripon • Easingwold • Malton • Pateley Bridge • Great Ouseburn • Knaresborough • Skipton • York • Selby

Population Trends 1851 - 1901

Increase	Net in - migration greater than natural increase
	Natural increase greater than net in - migration
	Natural increase greater than net out - migration
Decrease	Net out - migration greater than natural increase

North Yorkshire Registration District Boundaries 1851

Reproduced from Ordnance Survey material on behalf of The Controller of Her Majesty's Stationery Office © Crown copyright MC100038389 2003

7.10 COMMUNICATIONS WILLIAM SHEILS

With the seat of royal government in the North located at York, the county occupied a strategic position within government communications which went back to the Roman occupation. With the main route between London and Edinburgh passing through the county to the west of York, relations with Scotland, or Scottish armies, resulted in the city being at the hub of government business on several occasions between the Anglo-Scottish war of 1514 and the Jacobite rising of 1745. Added to this strategic role, economic relations with the North were sustained by means of the drovers' road which came down through the Vale of Mowbray and the Hambleton Hills to the York market.

The main thrust of economic activity, however, was not north-south but west-east, bringing the wool and cloth reared and finished in the Dales, and the lead mined in the

above Duck Bridge, Eskdale: a packhorse bridge connecting with a pannier way. The height of the bridge accommodated extreme flooding.
© North York Moors National Park Authority, HF0036.

left Westerdale Bridge, Eskdale, North York Moors.
© North York Moors National Park Authority, HF0005.

northern Dales, to the ports of York and Hull. From these ports, goods were exported to the Continent and to London, and through them other goods arrived for distribution throughout the north of England: timber from the Baltic, finished cloth from Flanders, wine from Gascony and, later, the spices and other products of the New World which were shipped north from London via the coastal trade. This was a trade in which smaller ports, such as Whitby and Scarborough, were also engaged in supplying the capital's needs.

In this movement of goods, the river system played a crucial role and, as technology improved and the Ouse ceased to be navigable for larger craft, York gave way to Hull as the chief port for overseas trade, though it retained its importance as a distribution centre for consumer goods, its merchants supplying retailers throughout the northern counties in the eighteenth century. The river system feeding the Ouse was a natural resource for the county but by the eighteenth century the need to improve parts of it in order to assist the flow of goods and provide access to markets for the products of some inland towns was recognised.

RIVERS AND CANALS (fig 7.16)

Attempts had been made on several occasions during the seventeenth century (consistently opposed by York merchants who saw the plans as a threat to their livelihoods) to improve communication between the cloth-producing areas of Leeds and Wakefield and the port of Hull, via the rivers Aire and Calder. Eventually in 1699 an Act of Parliament established the Aire and Calder Navigation, beyond the southern and western boundaries of the county, in order to improve the river route with channels and locks, joining the Humber at Goole.

This posed a threat to York's trade, a threat which was increased by the act of 1701 designed to make the River Derwent, to the east of York, navigable from where it met the Humber at Barmby-on-the-Marsh as far as Scarborough mills, and to provide a towpath. Serious work did not begin until 1720, but by 1724 the river was navigable as far as Malton, being used chiefly for coal and corn. By this date York merchants were determined to improve the Ouse and regain some of the river trade lost, and an act was secured to improve the Ouse in 1727. Though work was undertaken, little improvement was made in water levels, and in 1757 money was raised and shares issued for the construction of a lock at Naburn, just south of the city.

Following this, further attempts were made to improve the Ouse to the north of the city at Newton-on-Ouse, opening up efficient access to the Ure and the Swale by construction of a lock at Linton in 1767. The Ure scheme was successful, with a cut through Boroughbridge linking with Ripon by means of a canal for the last two miles (3km), and from 1773 there was a regular service to York, extending to Hull in 1777, for coal, timber, lime and stone. The Swale scheme was abortive, as were a number of other small schemes, including one to link the Ouse with Easingwold and another to join the linen town of Knaresborough to the Ouse system, as well as an ambitious plan to link the Ouse and the Tees.

The only other York-based scheme to take effect was the Foss Navigation, which was established by act of parliament in 1793 to provide access for the agricultural region to the

above Milestone on the former turnpike road from Grassington to Skipton.
© R White/Yorkshire Dales National Park Authority, RS 54.

right Dandry Mire viaduct on the Settle-Carlisle railway; the former Wensleydale branch of the railway is in the background.
© R White/Yorkshire Dales National Park Authority, ANY 229/30.

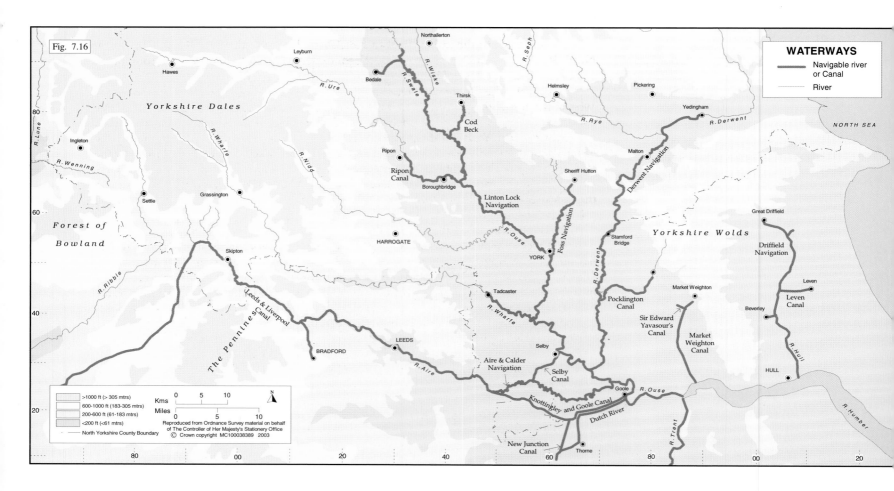

WATERWAYS

━━━ Navigable river
        or Canal

──── River

Fig. 7.16

Reproduced from Ordnance Survey material on behalf
of The Controller of Her Majesty's Stationery Office
© Crown copyright MC100038389 2003

>1000 ft (> 305 mtrs)
600-1000 ft (183-305 mtrs)
200-600 ft (61-183 mtrs)
<200 ft (<61 mtrs)
North Yorkshire County Boundary

north of York, down the river to York and beyond. Eventually the river was made navigable as far as Sheriff Hutton Bridge and opened in 1804, meeting with modest success. This completed the Ouse schemes, but further work had taken place on the Aire and Calder in 1774 with the cutting of a canal from Haddlesey lock on the Aire to Selby on the Ouse. The canal was opened in 1778, making Selby a shipbuilding town and a key transhipment port for most goods from the West Riding in the first decades of the nineteenth century.

The greatest single enterprise passing through the county, however, looked not to the East Coast but westwards, with the extension of the Aire and Calder Navigation into the Leeds-Liverpool canal from 1770, opening the west Yorkshire industrial towns to the Atlantic trade by a route through Skipton, and this extensive and successful project survives today as an important recreational facility.

All these schemes were eventually to face competition from the railway, but before considering that, the work of road improvement, for the transport of post and people rather than goods, needs discussion.

Rivers & Canals — Further Reading:

C Hadfield, *The Canals of Yorkshire and North-East England*, 2 vols (Newton Abbot: David and Charles, 1972-3).

B F Duckham, *The Yorkshire Ouse: the history of a river navigation* (1967).

ROADS (fig 7.17)

The strategic importance of roads in the county has already been mentioned, with the Great North Road, passing through Wetherby and Boroughbridge, being the main post route to Berwick and Scotland. From 1603, following the accession of James I, York itself was placed directly on the post route with the making of a side route through Ferrybridge and Tadcaster.

Although of national importance, the responsibility for maintaining the road networks was placed in the hands of parish officers in 1555, a system which was ill-equipped to deal with the increasing movement of goods and people consequent on commercial expansion after 1660, and the movement of heavy goods by road was often impossible, packhorses still plying the ancient routes across the Peninnes as late as 1760.

By that date new measures, whereby trusts set up under act of parliament, called turnpike trusts, could improve and maintain roads in return for tolls charged on goods and persons, had begun to assist in the improvement of existing roads and the development of regional networks. These trusts were largely the result of local initiative, developing in the metropolitan area and the Home Counties in the early eighteenth century, but it was national needs which brought the earliest trust to North Yorkshire with the turnpiking of the Great North Road between Doncaster and Boroughbridge in 1741, followed by the section north of Boroughbridge as far as Piercebridge in Co. Durham in 1745.

By that date the important commercial route between Leeds and Selby, linking the West Yorkshire clothing districts to Hull had also been turnpiked, and it was economic considerations which were to dominate the emergence of the network in the county thereafter.

A trust between York and the post town of Tadcaster was established in 1745, joining the easterly spur from the Great North Road, and the city was linked directly to that route by the York–Boroughbridge turnpike in 1750. Further links to the road, and also to York, were established in the early 1750s by the Knaresborough–Green Hammerton trust in 1752 and the Tadcaster–Otley trust the following year, both of them linking important manufacturing towns to the main north–south route.

At the northern end of the county, a trust linking Catterick with Stockton and Durham provided access for produce from the northern Dales to important local markets, as well as having some strategic importance following the 1745 rebellion, and an important trans-Pennine route between Richmond and Lancaster, linking the northern Dales and turnpiked in 1751, also served that dual purpose. In 1755 a more southerly trans-Pennine route between Leeds and Preston, passing through Skipton, improved communications between the developing manufacturing areas of both counties.

The next twenty years saw a number of smaller trusts linking up to both the north–south and east–west arterial routes, from towns like Harrogate and Grassington.

It was not only manufacturing towns which were able to raise the capital to set up trusts, however. The market towns of Thirsk and Nothallerton were linked to York by a trust in 1753, providing an alternative northerly route from the city, and this road subsequently fostered spurs into the agricultural hinterlands around Masham (1755) and Yarm (1803), whilst the turnpike between York and Oswaldkirk (1768) linked the farming area of Ryedale and the Vale to its most important market.

Leisure, too, could stimulate development, and the increasing use of sea bathing for that and for health was a factor in the York–Scarborough trust established in 1752.

By 1780 the main routes had been established, though some important routes were never turnpiked, such as that between York and Selby, nor were some of the lesser routes through the Dales or to the East Coast. There were few new turnpikes in the county after 1800, the last being set up in 1836 to run from Reeth to Richmond, thus linking the agricultural and mineral products of Swaledale with the main land routes of the county.

The overall impact of these trusts on economic development in the county remains hard to measure: they no doubt extended the market areas for agricultural products and greatly improved the personal mobility of those who could afford coaches and put up with the discomforts inevitable on long journeys. By 1796 there were three daily coaches travelling between York and London, two between York and Leeds, and one between York and Liverpool, whilst the city was also connected to Newcastle and Edinburgh by regular

Roads — Further Reading:

W Albert, *The Turnpike Road System in England, 1663-1840* (Cambridge: Cambridge University Press, 1972).

M Hartley *et al* (eds), *James Fothergill and the Richmond to Lancaster Turnpike* (1985).

W B Taylor, *All Roads leading to York: a comparative study of turnpike development 1745-1830* (unpublished M Phil dissertation, University of York 1992).

Toll House on the former Richmond to Reeth turnpike road at Haggs Gill, near Ellerton Abbey.
© R White, 661/5.

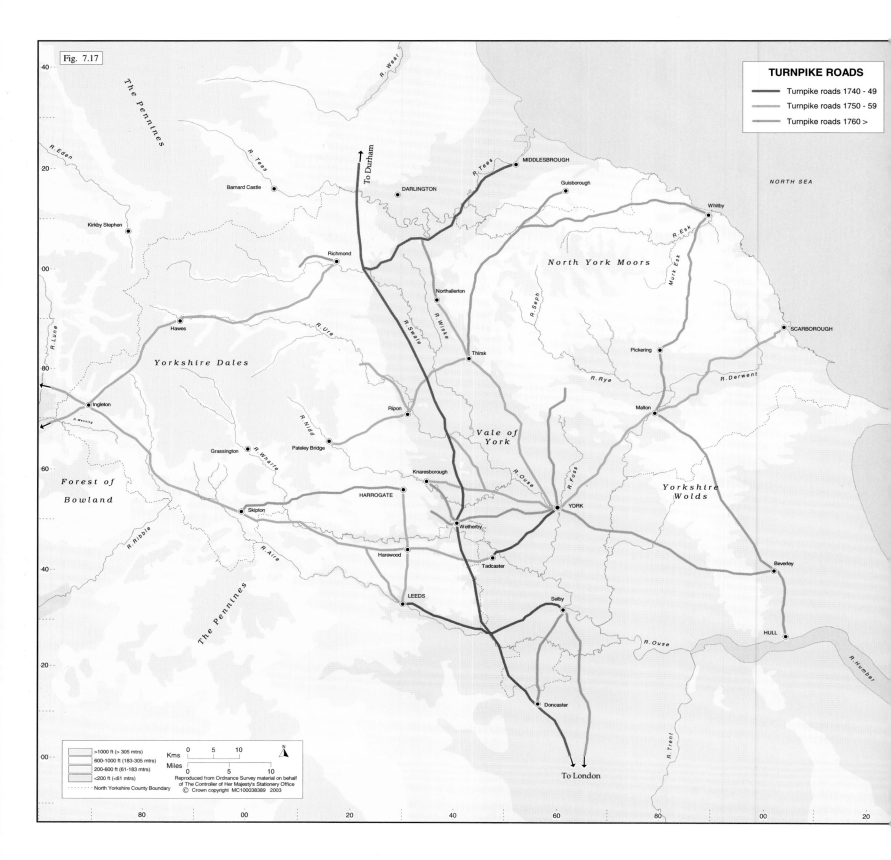

Fig. 7.17

TURNPIKE ROADS

— Turnpike roads 1740 - 49
— Turnpike roads 1750 - 59
— Turnpike roads 1760 >

>1000 ft (> 305 mtrs)
600-1000 ft (183-305 mtrs)
200-600 ft (61-183 mtrs)
<200 ft (<61 mtrs)
---- North Yorkshire County Boundary

Kms 0   5   10

Miles 0   5   10

Reproduced from Ordnance Survey material on behalf
of The Controller of Her Majesty's Stationery Office
© Crown copyright MC100038389 2003

services, and at the peak of the coaching period there were thirty-two coaches a day plying
their way along the York–Tadcaster road.

For heavier goods, however, water continued to be the more effective means of transport,
and it is likely that the rivers and canals played a greater part than the roads in the economic
growth of the region between 1660 and 1830. That was soon to change.

RAILWAYS (**fig 7.18**)

As with river and road improvement, the first route to attract entrepreneurs developing the
railways was that between Leeds and Selby, giving access to the port at Hull. Plans were

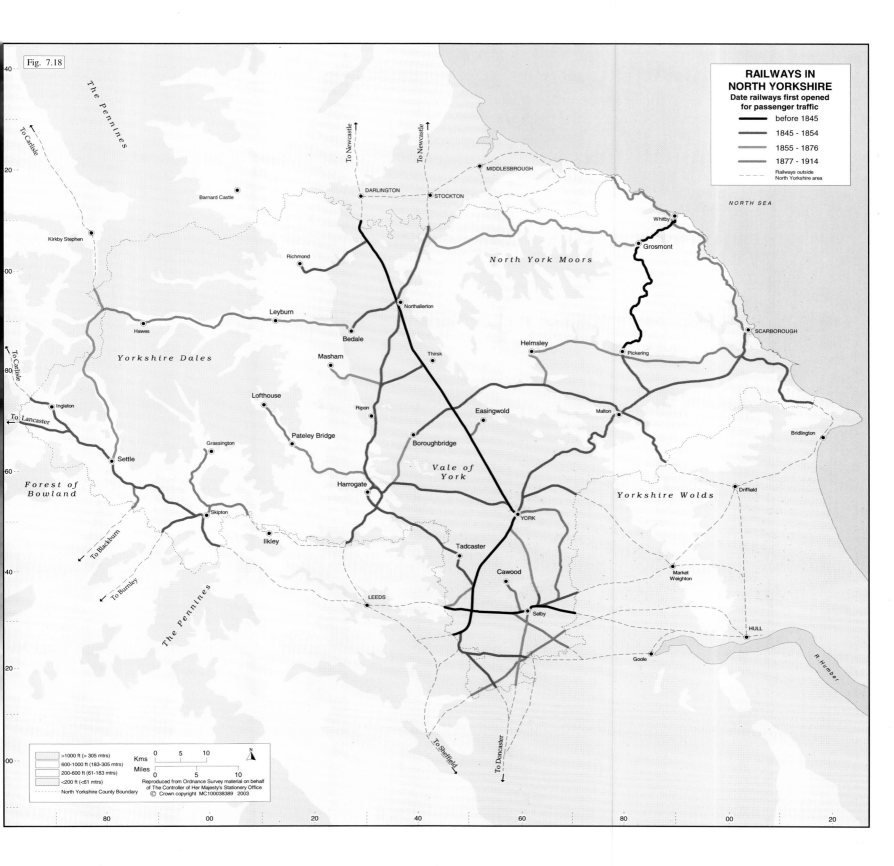

Fig. 7.18

RAILWAYS IN
NORTH YORKSHIRE
Date railways first opened
for passenger traffic

— before 1845
— 1845 - 1854
— 1855 - 1876
— 1877 - 1914
--- Railways outside
North Yorkshire area

NORTH SEA

The Pennines

To Carlisle

Barnard Castle

Kirkby Stephen

MIDDLESBROUGH

DARLINGTON   STOCKTON

Whitby

Richmond

Grosmont

North York Moors

Leyburn

Hawes

Bedale

Masham

Northallerton

Yorkshire Dales

Thirsk

Helmsley

Pickering

SCARBOROUGH

To Carlisle

Lofthouse

Ripon

Easingwold

Malton

To Lancaster

Ingleton

Pateley Bridge

Boroughbridge

Bridlington

Grassington

Settle

Vale of
York

Yorkshire Wolds

Driffield

Forest of
Bowland

Harrogate

Skipton

YORK

Ilkley

To Blackburn

Tadcaster

Cawood

Market
Weighton

To Burnley

LEEDS

Selby

HULL

The Pennines

Goole

R. Humber

To Sheffield

To Doncaster

To Newcastle   To Newcastle

>1000 ft (> 305 mtrs)
600-1000 ft (183-305 mtrs)
200-600 ft (61-183 mtrs)
<200 ft (<61 mtrs)
North Yorkshire County Boundary

Kms   0   5   10
Miles   0   5   10

N

Reproduced from Ordnance Survey material on behalf
of The Controller of Her Majesty's Stationery Office
© Crown copyright MC100038389 2003

discussed in 1830, and a line was built between the two in 1834, linking to the steam–packet
service down river from Selby to Hull. The other line mooted in 1830 was one between
Pickering and Whitby, but this was for a horse-drawn and cable service to carry lime and
stone quarried on the moors to the port at Whitby, from where it could be taken by sea up
the coast to the rapidly expanding industrial centres on the Tees. This line was opened in
1836, and locomotives introduced after further engineering works in 1847. In 1833 a line
between York and Leeds was proposed and in 1839 a line was built linking with the Leeds-
Selby line at Milford, continuing from there to Castleford from where it linked with the
Midland Railway to connect with London via Derby.

The entrepreneurial energy of George Hudson and his Great Northern Railway was a key factor in the development of the new technology, and in 1841 a line north of York to Newcastle was opened, but in these early years the railways did not have everything their own way. There were still five coaches a day travelling between York and Leeds in the mid-1840s due to the unreliability of the rail link, and the steam-packet services which had developed in the early 1800s continued to attract river trade on the Selby to Hull route to 1860, with many passengers preferring the coastal sea route from there to the capital over the new railway routes. A more direct route to London, established by the Great Northern Railway in 1850, made the new mode of transport more attractive, providing ready access to the rapidly expanding markets in the capital for the goods and produce of the region.

Goods still needed to reach the main line, however, but the competitive dash for profits from this revolutionary mode of transport meant that, in the next few years, links to the main route were established from Boroughbridge, Harrogate, Wetherby, Tadcaster, Richmond, Malton, Pickering and Scarborough, and a route from Leeds to Middlesbrough through Northallerton was developed by the Leeds Northern company to try to break Hudson's hold on the main north-south route.

In 1854, however, an amalgamation of the companies providing these routes created the North Eastern Railway, in effect a monopoly on the eastern routes within the county, with over 700 miles (1,100km) of track under its control and its headquarters at York. Meanwhile westerly routes had been constructed to link Leeds with Manchester and Liverpool, and also with Lancaster, from where the main line could be picked up to Glasgow. By the mid-1850s, with the exception of places like Leyburn in the Pennines, all the larger towns in the county had links to the main line, and thus to the rapidly growing industrial heartlands of the nation.

The period between 1855 and 1875 saw further expansion of the railways into the rural areas of the county, prompted by the need for agricultural products and mineral resources to reach the rapidly expanding urban centres throughout the country. A new line linking Whitby with Middlesbrough along the northern edge of the moors replaced the old rail and sea route through Whitby, and the quarries and products of the western Dales were opened up by lines to Leyburn and Masham.

The largest and most famous of the lines built in this period, however, did not involve the extension of an already co-ordinated system, but was due to the Midland Railway's determination to compete with its competitors on the main north-western route to Scotland. Excluded from this line, the Midland undertook to open a route via Settle and Carlisle, which involved extensive engineering works in tunnelling and building viaducts, of which that at Ribblehead remains the most famous. After eight years' work, the line was opened to goods in 1875 and to passengers the following year. The East Coast line was also improved about this time, by shortening the existing route between York and Doncaster and by building a new railway station at York, opened fully in 1877, which greatly eased the flow of traffic.

By that date most of the main features of the rail provision in the county were settled, both in terms of routes and organisational structure. As urbanisation increased and real wages improved in the last quarter of the century, the railways began to attract an increasing leisure market as the more prosperous workers and their families sought to escape the dirt of the industrial towns at the weekends. The line to Leyburn was extended the length of Wensleydale to Hawes, linking with the Settle-Carlisle route at Garsdale, and a coastal route was opened north of Scarborough through Whitby to the new resorts at Redcar and Saltburn.

These routes, of course, were also prompted by the need to get agricultural produce to the larger markets, and to bring in coal to provide energy for the homes and industries in the countryside, and a small spur was built from the main line to Easingwold in 1891, too late to arrest the decline of that former coaching town which had failed to capitalise on early railway development. Marketing of rural produce stimulated the last line to be built in the region during this period when, in 1913, the Derwent Valley Light Railway linked the rural hinterland to the east of York with the city's market by way of a station situated at Layerthorpe beside the market area just beyond the city walls.

By 1914 the railways of the county provided access to national markets for the agricultural and mineral resources of the county, brought coal in from the adjacent Yorkshire and Durham fields to provide energy for industry and heat for homes. They carried the businessmen and leaders of the region to other major centres of industry and to the capital, and conveyed their products to the ports from where they reached international markets, provided a cheap and reliable mode of transport to those wishing to relax in the countryside and by the sea, and enabled the better-off professionals and clerks to escape the worst aspects of urban living by residing in the commuter villages, like Poppleton and Strensall near York, which were beginning to spring up around railway stations. In order to achieve this, and to maintain the network, the railway had become one of the largest employers in the region, and York a major railway town with a carriageworks and the headquarters of the North Eastern Railway located there.

CONCLUSION

The increasing importance of effective communications in an expanding economy meant that, between 1660 and 1900, the highly localised nature of responsibility in these matters developed under the Tudor state was no longer effective and new structures were needed, both to develop and maintain the system, and to provide the capital required to take advantage of technological advances. In all areas of transport — water, road and rail — this was provided through a combination of state regulation and private finance which, in the period under review, transformed the traditional pattern of mobility for both goods and people.

The experience of North Yorkshire reflected significant changes at international, national and regional levels: internationally, the shift towards an Atlantic economy meant that communications between the county and the western ports in Lancashire and Cumbria became progressively more important as time went on; nationally, the rise in real wages experienced by large sectors of the population in the latter half of the nineteenth century created a market in transport for leisure (a concept unfamiliar, even inconceivable to the traveller of an earlier period); and regionally, industrialisation had led to a massive growth in population on Teesside, just beyond the northern boundary of the county, which required infrastructure and services.

Within these changes, however, continuities can also be identified: firstly, the importance of good communications between the West Riding clothing districts and their national and international markets meant that efficient links between Leeds and Hull remained essential, and that route was the first to be considered and funded by entrepreneurs, whether they were interested in water transport in the seventeenth century, roads in the eighteenth or railways in the nineteenth. Secondly, York, which was at the centre of communications at the start of the period because of its administrative and political importance, retained its key position within the network by redefining itself as a major railway town in the later nineteenth century, when its administrative pre-eminence had long gone, and it had been surpassed in economic importance by the industrial centres of the West Riding and Teesside.

Communications are both a source of and a response to economic and political change and, throughout the period under discussion, increasing numbers of men and women travelled beyond their immediate home in search of fame and fortune, especially in a county which did not exhibit much industrial development itself and was not well placed to take advantage of the Atlantic trade. Although in 1900 many people still lived within a world bounded physically by home, work and local market town, most were familiar with worlds far away from their own neighbourhood, either by direct experience of periods of time spent working in different parts of the country or through schooling, newspapers and letters home from the increasing numbers of North Yorkshire men and women who had emigrated to or served in far-away countries, or gone to the growing industrial cities to earn a living.

Railways — Further Reading:
Railway history is an industry in itself and most of the lines in Yorkshire have their own historians. For background and overview see:
J Simmons, *The Railway in England and Wales, the system and its working 1830-1914* (Leicester: Leicester University Press, 1978).
J Simmons and G Biddle, *The Oxford Companion to Railway History* (Oxford: Oxford University Press, 1997).
D Joy, *A Regional History of the Railways of Great Britain* vols 4 and 8 (Newton Abbot: David and Charles, 1960-).

7.11   THE OLD AND NEW POOR LAW   PAUL HASTINGS

The sixteenth-century increase in poverty led to a system of poor relief evolving from acts of parliament of 1597 and 1601 and lasting, with modification, until 1834. The acts established a poor rate and overseers to care for the 'settled' impotent poor of every parish. The able bodied were to be set to work. In their homes the poor received 'out-relief' in cash, food, clothing, fuel, rent and medical aid. Since poverty was caused by unemployment, parishes were empowered 'to set the poor on work' in 'Abiding and Working Houses'. In 1662 poor law responsibility passed from the large North Riding parishes to their smaller townships, creating 546 relieving authorities.

Workhouses increased after Knatchbull's Act of 1722 permitted parishes or groups of parishes to build or rent them to 'receive the labour' of their inmates. Refusal to enter meant ineligibility for relief. By 1776, the basic pattern of a North Riding workhouse system had emerged (**fig 7.19**). There were at least thirty-five workhouses capable of housing 964 inmates. The largest, at Bedale and Whitby, held eighty and seventy paupers respectively. Each market town had one and some lesser townships too, although these were often short-lived. Thirteen, with thirty-six per cent of the county's total capacity, were in the western leadmining districts.

Rising poor rates and Gilbert's Act of 1782, authorising unions of parishes to establish common workhouses controlled by guardians for 'the aged, infirm and impotent poor',

Guisborough Union Workhouse, founded in 1838.
© Ripon Museum Trust, Workhouse Museum.

Stokesley Union Workhouse, founded in 1848.
© Ripon Museum Trust, Workhouse Museum.

produced further workhouse building. By 1802-3, seventy-three townships kept all or part of their poor in workhouses, where 506 indoor paupers were maintained at a cost of £5,410. The 13,309 outdoor poor (96.3 per cent of all paupers) cost £43,156. Although seventy-three townships had indoor poor, there were fewer workhouses, since sharing of workhouse accommodation was common. In 1775, eighteen linen-making townships in Cleveland had paupers in Stokesley workhouse. Fylingdales, Whitby, Easingwold, Kirkbymoorside and other parishes also charged subscriptions to neighbouring townships.

Between 1812 and 1825 Gilbert legislation was belatedly adopted by the Bainbridge, Leyburn and Hinderwell-Lythe incorporations, and some individual townships of the eastern moorlands. Thirteen townships in the southern Vale of York joined the West Riding Great Ouseburn Union. By 1813-15, eighty-five townships kept 644 persons (9.3 per cent of their permanent poor) in workhouses. Only six English counties had fewer indoor paupers, not unexpected in a 'high wage' county without serious poor law problems whose surplus labour was largely absorbed by migration overseas and neighbouring industrial districts.

Consequently, North Riding workhouses largely housed the impotent poor: of fifty-seven inmates at Scarborough in 1833, only four were able-bodied. With the exceptions of Whitby (100), Scarborough (150-200) and Malton (120-150), the workhouses were small and inadequate; Guisborough's was 'an old tumbledown cottage'. Only Whitby and Richmond tried unsuccessfully to use their workhouses as a deterrent: deliberate cruelty was unusual; workhouse rules, although harsh, were rarely enforced; and diet was adequate. Workhouses were characterised by slackness and squalor rather than severity. Without endemic low wages

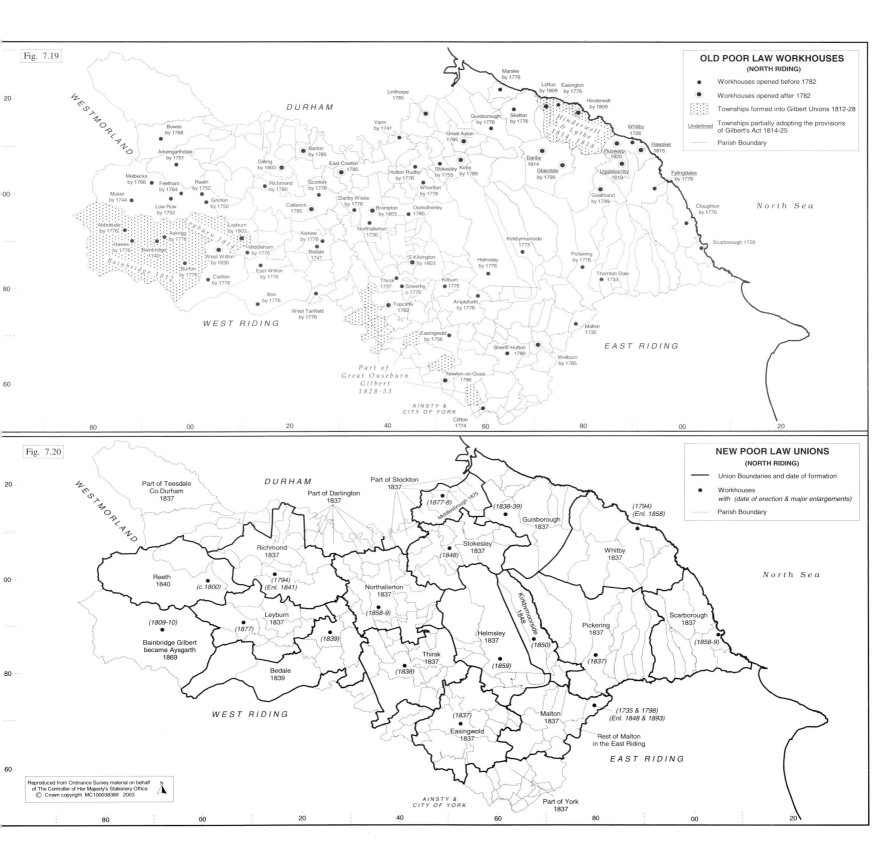

Fig. 7.19

OLD POOR LAW WORKHOUSES
(NORTH RIDING)

- ● Workhouses opened before 1782
- ⦿ Workhouses opened after 1782
- ▦ Townships formed into Gilbert Unions 1812-28
- <u>Underlined</u> Townships partially adopting the provisions of Gilbert's Act 1814-25
- —— Parish Boundary

WESTMORLAND
DURHAM

Marske by 1776
Loftus by 1809
Easington by 1776
Hinderwell by 1809
Linthorpe 1785
Guisborough 1776
Skelton 1776
Hinderwell & Lythe 1814 & 1818
Whitby 1726
Hawsker 1815
Bowes by 1768
Arkengarthdale by 1751
Barton by 1785
Yarm by 1741
Great Ayton 1785
Ruswarp 1820
Gilling by 1803
East Cowton 1785
Stokesley by 1755
Kirby by 1789
Danby 1814
Glaisdale by 1799
Ugglebarnby 1819
Melbecks by 1766
Feetham by 1764
Reeth by 1752
Richmond by 1780
Scorton 1776
Hutton Rudby by 1776
Whorlton by 1776
Fylingdales by 1776
Muker by 1744
Low Row by 1752
Grinton by 1752
Catterick 1785
Danby Wiske by 1776
Goathland by 1799
North Sea
Abbotside by 1776
Leyburn by 1803
Brompton by 1803
Osmotherley 1780
Cloughton by 1776
Askrigg by 1776
Aiskew by 1776
Northallerton 1730
Scarborough 1728
Hawes by 1776
Bainbridge 1740
Middleham by 1776
Bedale 1747
S. Kilvington by 1803
Kirkbymoorside 1773
Bainbridge 1812
Burton by 1776
West Witton by 1830
Helmsley by 1776
Pickering 1776
Carlton by 1776
East Witton by 1776
Thornton Dale 1733
Thirsk 1737
Sowerby c.1778
Kilburn 1778
Ilton by 1776
Ampleforth by 1776
West Tanfield by 1776
Topcliffe 1782
Malton 1735
WEST RIDING
Easingwold by 1756
Sheriff Hutton 1780
Welburn by 1785
EAST RIDING
Part of Great Ouseburn Gilbert 1828-53
Newton-on-Ouse 1796
AINSTY & CITY OF YORK
Clifton 1774

Fig. 7.20

NEW POOR LAW UNIONS
(NORTH RIDING)

- —— Union Boundaries and date of formation
- ● Workhouses with (date of erection & major enlargements)
- —— Parish Boundary

WESTMORLAND
Part of Teesdale Co.Durham 1837
DURHAM
Part of Stockton 1837
Part of Darlington 1837
Part of Stockton 1837
(1877-8) Middlesbrough 1875
(1838-39)
(1794) (Enl. 1858)
Richmond 1837
Guisborough 1837
Reeth 1840
(c.1800)
(1794) (Enl. 1841)
Stokesley 1837
(1848)
Whitby 1837
Northallerton 1837
North Sea
(1809-10)
Leyburn 1837
(1877)
(1858-9)
Bainbridge Gilbert became Aysgarth 1869
(1839)
Kirkbymoorside 1848
Scarborough 1837
Helmsley 1837
Pickering 1837
(1850)
(1858-9)
Bedale 1839
Thirsk 1837
(1859)
(1837)
WEST RIDING
(1838)
(1837)
(1735 & 1798) (Enl. 1848 & 1893)
Malton 1837
Easingwold 1837
Rest of Malton in the East Riding
EAST RIDING
Reproduced from Ordnance Survey material on behalf of The Controller of Her Majesty's Stationery Office © Crown copyright MC100038389 2003
AINSTY & CITY OF YORK
Part of York 1837

or high unemployment, except during depression, outdoor relief was similarly dispensed. The poor were largely: the elderly; the sick; the widowed; one-parent families; and dependent children. The able-bodied were less in evidence.

The notorious 'Speenhamland System', in which overseers gave outdoor relief to able-bodied men in work, was only common in the lead dales. Child allowances to labourers in work, with families they could not support, were more widespread. The Roundsman system, whereby the unemployed were sent round the farmers for a wage subsidised from the poor rate, was not intensively used.

In summary, many criticisms made by the 1832 commissioners did not apply. Nevertheless poor rates were rising after the Napoleonic Wars and the burden upon the ratepayers was

Leyburn Union Workhouse, founded in 1877.
© Ripon Museum Trust, Workhouse Museum.

increasing. Consequently the new uniform system introduced by the 1834 act with a view to economy met no violent opposition, although assistant commissioner John Revans found many landowners and ratepayers 'strongly opposed to any change'.

The commissioners dealt first with the low-wage rural south of England. In October 1836 Revans arrived in the North Riding and by March 1837 had created eleven wholly North Riding unions (**fig 7.20**). Another five peripheral unions crossed county boundaries: twenty-six Malton Union townships lay in the North Riding and forty-three in the East Riding; twelve North Riding townships, including Yarm and Middlesbrough, were placed initially in Stockton Union, Co Durham, while another dozen joined Darlington Union. Twenty-one north-western townships entered Teesdale union, while nineteen southern townships were pressed into York Union.

Unions were formed: firstly, to ease the travel of guardians, paupers and commissioners in a county with large tracts of barren moorland impassable in snow; secondly, where existing workhouse buildings could be re-used; and, thirdly, where they were approved by local landowners. Where these criteria were not met, Revans' scheme was quickly modified: a separate Bedale Union was formed from Northallerton Union in 1839; distance and inaccessibility required a new Reeth Union (out of Richmond Union) in 1840; while Kirkbymoorside split from Helmsley in 1848. The Gilbert unions were easily dissolved, except the Bainbridge Incorporation which became Aysgarth Union only in 1869. In 1875, burgeoning industrial Middlesbrough united with eleven other North Riding townships in Stockton Union to create the Middlesbrough Union.

Both popular and Tory resistance to the 'Whig' Poor Law were weak. Much depended upon dominant proprietors. At Thirsk, Easingwold, Guisborough, Pickering and Bedale, new workhouses were built quickly. In the other Whig strongholds of Malton, Leyburn, Richmond, Reeth and at Scarborough, alterations were made, often less successfully, to existing workhouses. The 'Tory' workhouses of Whitby, Northallerton and Helmsley, where the Fevershams blocked any 'effective workhouse system', underwent little change until later. The New Poor Law before mid-century was oppressive through insensitivity rather than sadistic cruelty. The worst workhouse conditions were in unions controlled by its opponents.

The centralised, uniform system which the commissioners sought had progressed little by 1850. The workhouse test and the relief principles of 1834 were not really implemented. Supervision by the assistant commissioners was hampered by overwork, distance and terrain. Child allowances, rent payments and relief in kind eventually vanished, though some able-bodied outdoor relief continued. Private rates, evading expensive workhouse entry, illegal loans and roundsmen (subsidised farm workers) persisted. Only eight per cent of North Riding paupers were receiving indoor relief by 1840-41 as against the national average of fifteen per cent. The saving made was less than claimed, while comparative prosperity and continuity with the old system prevented serious resistance. But, from the 1870s, demands upon the Poor Law increased as prolonged agricultural depression combined with the effects of strikes and depressions in the Teesside mining and iron industries.

Poor Law — Sources and Further Reading:

R P Hastings, *Poverty and the Treatment of Poverty in the North Riding of Yorkshire c1780-1847*, 2 vols (D Phil thesis, University of York, 1977).

R P Hastings, *Essays in North Riding History 1780-1850* (Northallerton: North Yorkshire County Record Office, 1981).

R P Hastings, *Poverty and the Poor Law in the North Riding of Yorkshire c1780-1837*, Borthwick Paper no 61 (York: University of York Borthwick Institute of Historical Research, 1982).

R P Hastings, *More Essays in North Riding History* (Northallerton: North Yorkshire Record Office, 1984), 19-90.

Paul Hastings, *The New Poor Law in the North Riding: The First Ten Years 1837-1847* in *The New Poor Law* (Middlesbrough: Middlesbrough Centre Occasional Paper no l, 1985), 54-79.

Kathryn Morrison, *The Workhouse; A Study of Poor Law Buildings in England* (London: English Heritage, 1999).

Ripon Workhouse Museum of the Yorkshire Poor Law, Sharow View, Allhallowgate, Ripon.

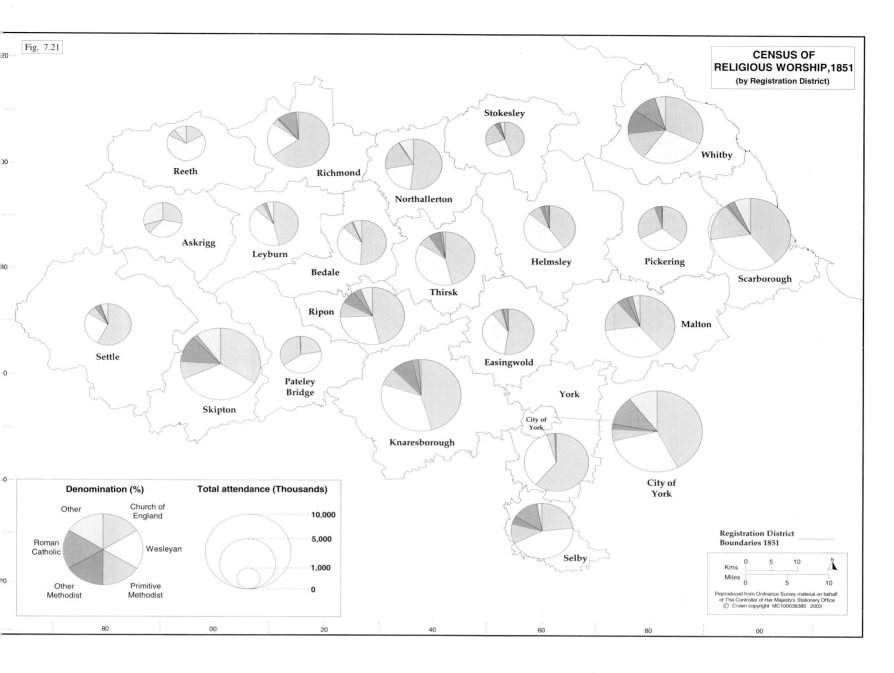

Fig. 7.21

CENSUS OF RELIGIOUS WORSHIP, 1851
(by Registration District)

Reeth
Richmond
Stokesley
Whitby
Askrigg
Leyburn
Bedale
Northallerton
Helmsley
Pickering
Scarborough
Settle
Thirsk
Ripon
Pateley Bridge
Skipton
Easingwold
Malton
Knaresborough
York
City of York
City of York
Selby

Denomination (%)

Other
Church of England
Roman Catholic
Wesleyan
Other Methodist
Primitive Methodist

Total attendance (Thousands)

10,000
5,000
1,000
0

Registration District Boundaries 1851

Kms   0   5   10
Miles 0   5   10

Reproduced from Ordnance Survey material on behalf of The Controller of Her Majesty's Stationery Office © Crown copyright MC100038389 2003

7.12 THE RELIGIOUS CENSUS OF 1851
WILLIAM SHEILS AND RICHARD LAWTON

The religious census of 1851, which recorded church attendance on Sunday the 30th March 1851 and whose results formed part of the Registrar General's statistical report for that year, provides us with the most detailed insight into religious affiliation in mid-Victorian England. It was, however, a census of worship and, at a time when various denominations were competing in a religious market place and attendance at services on a Sunday provided both social and communal recreation for large numbers of people, interpretation of the statistics, which survive at the parochial level, is fraught with difficulty.

Many denominations, the various branches of Methodism in particular, held more than one service on a Sunday, each with a distinctive purpose, so that members of such churches often attended both. Equally, services in Methodist chapels often took place in the afternoon and evenings, and it was possible that some individuals attended different Methodist services, or even the parish church in the morning and Methodist worship in the evening.

The best approach to turning the raw data — which, for the larger congregations at least, are often estimates — into satisfactory measures of religious affiliation, remains controversial. For the purposes of this section it has been decided to use the best-attended service for each denomination as the indicator.

Almost certainly this underestimates Methodist figures somewhat but, tested against other evidence for places like York which have been subject to detailed study, the effect on the overall picture is likely to be marginal. It has also been decided to exclude all Sunday school scholars from the calculations for, although Sunday schools were important elements in sustaining church and chapel membership, they were neither universal nor continuous. Their existence in a parish is testimony to the vigour of the denomination, or its leadership, in that place, but these schools often filled a wider educational purpose and inclusion of the numbers of pupils attending would distort the overall picture unduly. Despite these methodological difficulties and the shortcomings of the source itself, since some parishes failed to return figures, the census remains an essential source for the historian of religion and the historical geographer.

In the twenty-one registration districts with parishes within the present county, overall figures show that one-third of the population attended church on census Sunday, the proportion attending being significantly higher in the Vale of Mowbray, around Thirsk, Northallerton, Bedale and Richmond, where figures for attendance ranged between 38 and 42 per cent (**fig 7.21**). In this area, characterised by modest-sized market towns situated in a prosperous arable farming region, the hold of the Established Church remained strong and there were also significant numbers of Wesleyan Methodists.

This pattern was not repeated in similar circumstances in the southern Vale where, in Selby registration district, the proportion attending church was 28.7 per cent, the lowest figure for the county except for that in large and sparsely populated parishes of Wharfedale around Settle.

Although these two areas shared a low level of attendance, the character of that attendance was almost diametrically opposite: at Settle, the Anglicans remained by far the largest denomination, recording three-fifths of those attending; whilst at Selby, Anglicans numbered less than one quarter and Methodists represented over half of all attendances, with the Wesleyans forming over forty-four per cent of the total. There was also a significant congregation of Roman Catholics at Selby, clustered around the estates of the Stapleton family at Carlton by Snaith and accounting for 13.9 per cent of the attenders in the district.

The strength of the Established Church in Wharfedale was not repeated in Reeth registration district, covering the upper reaches of Swaledale, where Anglicans accounted for just over one-sixth and the Wesleyan Methodists comprised almost two-thirds of the churchgoing population, figures reflected in the surviving chapels at Arkengarthdale and Muker.

The figures, therefore, do not indicate a close relationship between settlement patterns, agrarian practice and religion, though no doubt these played their part, as they did at Bransdale on the North York Moors, whose remoteness from the parish church at Kirkbymoorside no doubt contributed to the large congregation of Wesleyan Methodists, numbering 330, who met there on Sunday evening.

Other factors related to religious affiliation included land ownership, as has been suggested in the case of Catholicism at Carlton, but perhaps the most important consideration of all was urbanisation, for the towns of the county were market places not only for the things of this world but also for those of the next. Recent work on the city of York has shown four denominations with substantial support in the city: the Church of England dominated with almost half of attendances; the Methodists, and chiefly the Wesleyans, accounted for almost thirty percent of attenders; old dissent was represented by Congregationalism which commanded just under ten per cent of churchgoers; and the long-established Catholic tradition of the city had recently been augmented by Irish immigration following the famine, so that these too represented over ten per cent of the city's churchgoers. Many migrants had come to York at the invitation of the Quakers, whose modest congregation of about 400 exercised influence in the city far in excess of its numbers.

This range of practice was also characteristic of other towns in the county: on the coast at Whitby, the 500 worshippers at the evening service in the parish church were dwarfed by 830 attending the Wesleyan chapel and 800 at the Primitive Methodists, whilst a further 250 met in the New Connexion chapel. In addition, a congregation of Presbyterians numbering 200 also met that evening, while small groups of Quakers and Unitarians met earlier in the day. At Scarborough, the Methodists almost matched the Anglicans in numbers, though here the Primitive Methodists were the stronger, with 560 attending the evening service, and in addition there were large congregations of Baptists (300) and Roman Catholics (250). Even at Settle and Knaresborough, where the Established Church remained strong, three varieties of Methodism could be savoured, whilst the former also contained a Quaker Meeting, and the latter congregations of both Baptists and Latter Day Saints.

If the chief numerical strength of all denominations was in the towns, in the countryside one or other branch of Methodism was to be found almost everywhere, and sometimes more

Registration District	C of E	Wes	Methodists Prim	Other	R C	Other	Total No of Worshippers
Askrigg (Aysgarth)	27.7	34.5	8.4	—	—	29.4	2,380
Bedale	50.7	35.3	6.6	—	1.0	6.3	3,787
Easingwold	52.3	36.4	6.7	1.3	3.2	—	4,279
Helmsley	39.7	46	8.4	2.4	3.1	0.3	4,184
Knaresborough	45.1	34.2	7.7	8.6	3.0	0.9	9,179
Leyburn	46.0	40.1	6.0	—	2.6	5.3	3,827
Malton	38.1	34.9	15.4	5.1	2.8	3.8	7,222
Northallerton	51.7	20.4	18.2	—	0.4	9.1	4,944
Pateley Bridge	22.6	43.1	33.8	—	—	0.7	2,907
Pickering	35.3	32.6	26.4	5.3	—	0.3	3,767
Reeth	17.6	64.7	6.2	—	—	11.6	2,402
Richmond	67.2	18.7	3.2	1.0	10.5	1.2	5,683
Ripon	45.7	28.5	7.9	7.5	3.8	6.5	6,111
Scarborough	38.7	34.2	15.7	1.2	2.8	7.4	8,960
Selby	23.4	44.5	10.8	4.5	13.9	2.9	4,425
Settle	60.1	24.2	6.1	3.8	0.8	5.0	3,724
Skipton	33.2	35.3	7.3	11.6	1.9	10.7	9,075
Stokesley	43.8	25.6	21.1	4.4	0.8	4.3	2,464
Thirsk	45.7	37.7	6.8	6.7	1.5	1.5	5,234
Whitby	31.3	28.9	12.9	11	10.7	5.1	7,980
York, outside city	61.4	33.6	4.1	0.9	0	0	6,140
City of York	41.7	29.5	4.4	1.9	11.3	11.1	11,322

Religious Census — Further Reading:

The most recent study of the religious census, comparing fifteen counties (not including North Yorkshire), is K D M Snell and P S Ell, *Rival Jerusalems: The geography of Victorian religion* (Cambridge: Cambridge University Press, 2000).

J R Wolffe, *Yorkshire returns of the religious census of 1851, I: The East Riding* (York 2000), contains returns for those parishes in North Yorkshire formerly in that riding; two volumes are forthcoming which will cover all parishes in the present county.

E Royle, The Church of England and Methodism 1770-1851, *Northern History* 33 (1997), looks at the city of York in some detail.

than one. Collectively the Methodists had made serious inroads to the earlier dominance of the Church of England: indeed their combined strength was greater than that of the Established Church in more than half of the registration districts of the county (see table above), although it must be said that the Anglicans remained strongest in the most populous districts (the coastal towns excepted, with Whitby having 31.3 per cent and Scarborough 38.7 per cent), and the Methodists were particularly strong in areas like Pickering, Skipton and Reeth, which contained scattered upland settlements. In this respect, the data from 1851 underlines significant changes in the religious geography of the county since 1750. There were some continuities also, especially in regard to the Quakers, who continued to have adherents throughout North Yorkshire even though their numbers were relatively small.

7.13 NATIONAL SCHOOLS 1846-7
JOHN ADDY AND ROGER WOLFE

Fig 7.22 has been drawn up using the Church-School Inquiry 1846-7, conducted by the National Society for Promoting the Education of the Poor in the Principles of the Established Church. This survey, covering the whole of Yorkshire, included 943 parishes with a population of 1,591,480, of which 82 made no return.

It is estimated that there were, in total, 1,809 schools of which 519 were in union with the National Society. This gives a total of 129,489 pupils taught at Sunday school, week-day school (or both), by 1,891 paid teachers (908 masters, 864 mistresses, 59 assistant masters and 60 assistant mistresses) and 7,873 gratuitous teachers (3,967 males and 3,906 females). For the North Riding the figures were 10,141 pupils taught at 89 schools by 83 masters, 57 mistresses and 2 assistant masters.

The chief aim of the National Society, founded in 1811, was to establish National Schools in every parish throughout the country, conducted on the Madras or monitorial system with education based on the catechism. The idea behind this was not to equip the children of the 'labouring classes' for social mobility, rather to enable them to be content with their station in life, or in other words, 'calculated to render them useful and respectable members of society' (Lawson & Silver, 1937, 241-3). The society was to be a check on the teaching of the British and Foreign Society founded in 1808, which was non-denominational.

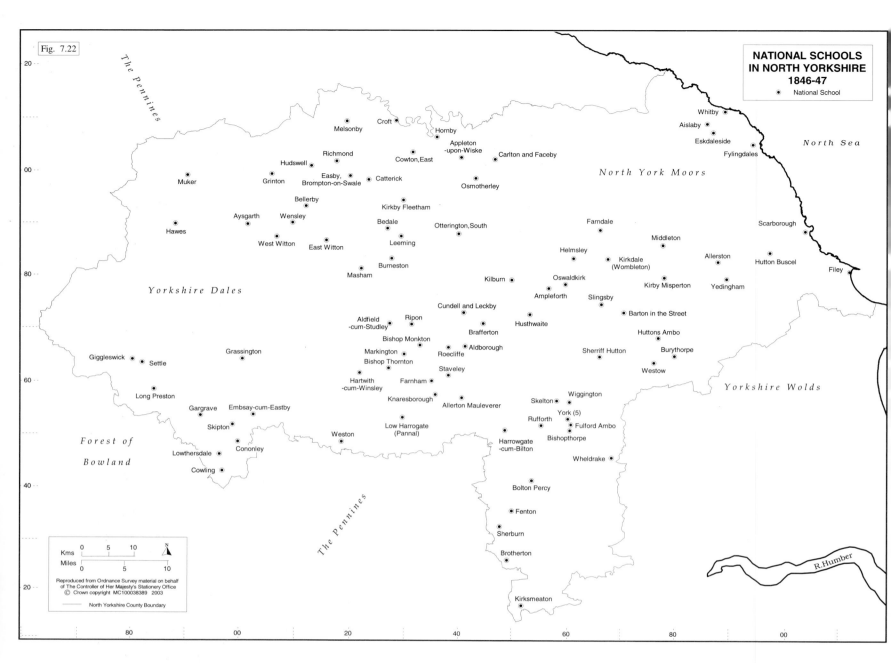

Fig. 7.22

NATIONAL SCHOOLS IN NORTH YORKSHIRE 1846-47

● National School

The Pennines

North Sea

North York Moors

Whitby
Aislaby
Eskdaleside
Fylingdales

Melsonby
Croft
Hornby
Appleton-upon-Wiske
Carlton and Faceby
Richmond
Cowton, East
Hudswell
Easby, Brompton-on-Swale
Catterick
Osmotherley
Muker
Grinton
Bellerby
Kirkby Fleetham
Farndale
Scarborough
Aysgarth
Wensley
Bedale
Otterington, South
Middleton
Allerston
Hutton Buscel
Hawes
Helmsley
Kirkdale (Wombleton)
Kirby Misperton
Yedingham
Filey
West Witton
East Witton
Leeming
Kilburn
Oswaldkirk
Ampleforth
Slingsby
Burneston
Masham

Cundell and Leckby
Barton in the Street
Aldfield-cum-Studley
Ripon
Husthwaite
Huttons Ambo
Grassington
Bishop Monkton
Brafferton
Sherriff Hutton
Burythorpe
Gigleswick
Settle
Markington
Aldborough
Roecliffe
Bishop Thornton
Staveley
Westow
Hartwith-cum-Winsley
Farnham
Long Preston
Knaresborough
Allerton Mauleverer
Wiggington
Gargrave
Embsay-cum-Eastby
Skelton
York (5)
Rufforth
Fulford Ambo
Skipton
Low Harrogate (Pannal)
Bishopthorpe
Weston
Harrowgate-cum-Bilton
Wheldrake
Lowthersdale
Cononley
Cowling

Yorkshire Dales

Yorkshire Wolds

Forest of Bowland

The Pennines

Bolton Percy

Fenton

Sherburn

Brotherton

R. Humber

Kirksmeaton

Kms 0 5 10
Miles 0 5 10

N

Reproduced from Ordnance Survey material on behalf of The Controller of Her Majesty's Stationery Office © Crown copyright MC100038389 2003

—— North Yorkshire County Boundary

Within a year of the founding of the National Society, the diocese of York decided to establish a diocesan society to supervise the building and running of National Schools in the parishes of the diocese. This society, known as the York Diocesan Society for the Education of the Poor in the Principles of the Established Church, would further the work of the National Society in the northern provinces. In 1812 the diocese of York was one of the largest in England, including the entire county of York — the rural deaneries of Richmond, Catterick and Boroughbridge, part of the unwieldy diocese of Chester excepted, and the entire county of Nottingham. Within three years of the creation of Ripon Diocese in 1836, York and Ripon decided to join forces to continue the expansionist educational policy of the York Diocesan Society.

The early archives of what later became the College of Ripon and York St John reveal that those involved were honest men who tried to fulfill their voluntary obligation to educate the poor children of York diocese. Viewed from the present situation, where every child has a right to free education, it is easy to criticise the limitations placed upon the diocesan society which was entirely dependent upon voluntary contributions to carry out its work, with a tendency to be always short of funds. On the occasions when money seemed plentiful, funds were used to found another National School. It was very much a 'hand-to-mouth' type of existence but, taking into consideration the limitations of the monitorial system, the rate of expansion between 1813 and 1844 is an impressive one.

The York Diocesan Society, like many others, was presented with the shortcomings of the monitorial system that had been adopted because it was most economical to run. Coming

Page 141

Bailey Street Council School, Stockton, c1890.
© College of York St John.

The Commercial College, Cambridge Street, York, 1904.
© College of York St John.

into existence at a time of war and distress when raising money for the purposes of education was most difficult, it was believed that the use of monitors who understood their subject would be more competent in explaining it to other children than an adult, who would be unlikely to adapt himself to their level of comprehension; further, monitors, by teaching, would improve themselves. In reality it appears that, once a child was selected as a monitor, its own education virtually stopped. Repeating the same lesson day after day became in due course mere rote learning.

The monitorial system did provide some basic education for the working classes at a minimal cost, but the high pupil:teacher ratio made it impossible, in large schools, for the teacher to give much attention to individual pupils. Monitors were often unable to explain explicitly to those in their charge what they were attempting to teach and quite frequently neglected to do this at all. One defect in this system of teaching was that all pupils were in one large room at the same time, so much of the teacher's time was spent in keeping order.

There was little continuity in attendance at school by the pupils. In rural areas, children were kept at home for the hay and corn harvest and for fruit-picking in September, often only attending school in the winter months. In the industrial areas, attendance varied with the demand for labour.

In 1844 it was estimated that one-quarter of the pupils left school at the age of twelve years, half completed their education at ten and the remainder terminated their education at nine. Those children who tended to remain at school the longest were children of small shopkeepers, foremen and skilled artisans who were destined for an apprenticeship or a clerk's job.

The conditions in National Schools were spartan and rigid with few instances of flexibility. In small rural schools, where boys were often employed in agriculture, it was allowed that boys under the age of eight should be taught in the same room as the girls. Taking into consideration the monotonous methods of teaching and the strict religious discipline, life in a National School must have been tedious indeed.

Apart from the state holidays, the only breaks children could look forward to were Ascension Day, Good Friday to Easter Tuesday, Whit Monday and Tuesday, Saturday, and Shrove Tuesday, with four weeks at harvest and two at Christmas. So occasional breaks were welcome, as when in 1832 York schools were closed for two weeks due to an outbreak of cholera in the city.

When comparison is made with other contemporary educational movements in the country, although many had high ideals, they offered little or no more than the National Society offered. Moreover, the York Diocesan Society was, by 1835, beginning to expand its curriculum. The society would cater for the children of those few parents who desired and could afford instruction for their children in English grammar, history, geography, mensuration (a type of calculus) and algebra at a charge of three shillings per quarter. Although a great deal of time and money had been spent on establishing National Schools in York Diocese, there was a pressing need for education of the poor and the quality of education in many of the existing schools left much scope for improvement.

Wolviston School, c1910 (in Co. Durham).
© College of York St John.

National Schools — Further Reading:

John Addy, *The York Diocesan Society — the provision & staffing of National Schools 1812-1840* (research monograph of the College of Ripon & York St John, no 1, 1986).

John Addy, *Introduction to Catalogue of the Archives of the Ripon & York College* (1998).

Church-School Inquiry (National Society Office, Westminster, 1846-7).

J Lawson & H Silver, *A Social History of Education in England* (London: Methuen, 1937).

8

AGRICULTURE

8.1   INTRODUCTION   ROBIN A BUTLIN

Historically, the agricultural character of North Yorkshire has reflected both the constraints and opportunities presented by its physiographic and climatic variations, and by changing processes of human influence, through time, at local, regional, national and even global scales.

The major physiographic sub-regional components here are: the Vale of York; the North York Moors; the Tabular Hills; the Howardian Hills and the Yorkshire Wolds; the coastal fringe and lowland; and the Pennine uplands and dales.

By the late seventeenth century, the structures of the agrarian systems of North Yorkshire contain clear evidence of a transition from medieval communal management systems towards a system of individual land ownership and management. This is particularly evident in the stages reached in the process of enclosure of common land, particularly open and common arable fields. A review of the evidence of glebe terriers (surveys of church land) for the seventeenth and eighteenth centuries suggests the continuing presence of between two and four open arable fields in settlements in North Yorkshire, but with the terriers for many parishes recording only closes (**fig 8.1**).[1]

The late eighteenth and nineteenth centuries witnessed widely differing trends in agriculture, nationally and regionally. Generally seen as a period of agricultural improvement, evidenced in the enclosures of common wastes, pastures and arable fields by act of parliament, and in the changes in agricultural technology and management, there were also in this period times of agricultural distress and depression, especially in marginal areas.

8.2   AGRICULTURE c1600-1780   ROBIN A BUTLIN

THE VALE OF YORK

In the sixteenth and seventeenth centuries, the varied pattern of fields, holdings and land use in the Vale of York reflected a long and slow process of evolution.[2] Studies of the southern part of the Vale between York and Selby suggest that the general pattern was of combinations of three, four or more open arable fields, located on higher, better-drained sites around the villages that formed the main settlement form, and with arable land comprising less than half the total area of the individual township (**fig 8.2**).

The holdings of individuals, which in total area varied greatly in size, were scattered throughout a patchwork quilt of lands and furlongs. The remainder of a township's land would be meadow (though this was not a widespread phenomenon) and pasture, often to be found on poorly drained lower-lying land, and subject to gradual encroachment as population increased. Closes, at the edge of the open fields, which were used for arable and pasture, seem to be symptomatic of a process of gradual small-scale enclosure of small parts of the fields.[3]

At Green Hammerton, west of York, there were three open arable fields in 1608 — Prickoe Field, Low Field and Coney Garth Field — with the regularity of location within the component furlongs of the open fields of the strip holdings of individual farmers suggesting an earlier system of regulation.[4] At Wheldrake, east of York, there were four such fields — North Field, North West Field, West Field and East Field — in the early eighteenth century.[5]

In the northern part of the Vale of York, piecemeal enclosure had removed most of the open-field arable systems by the mid-seventeenth century, but those that survived or had formerly existed seem to have done so as two- three- or four-field systems, in a complex also comprising significant numbers of closes, meadow and pasture. Open arable fields also survived in the Howardian Hills until the seventeenth and eighteenth centuries.[6]

Livestock on individual farms generally comprised a mixture of cows, oxen, fat cattle, sheep and pigs, with greater concentration on cattle-rearing and dairying in the west of the Vale and horse-breeding in the east. Land-use combinations in the late seventeenth century

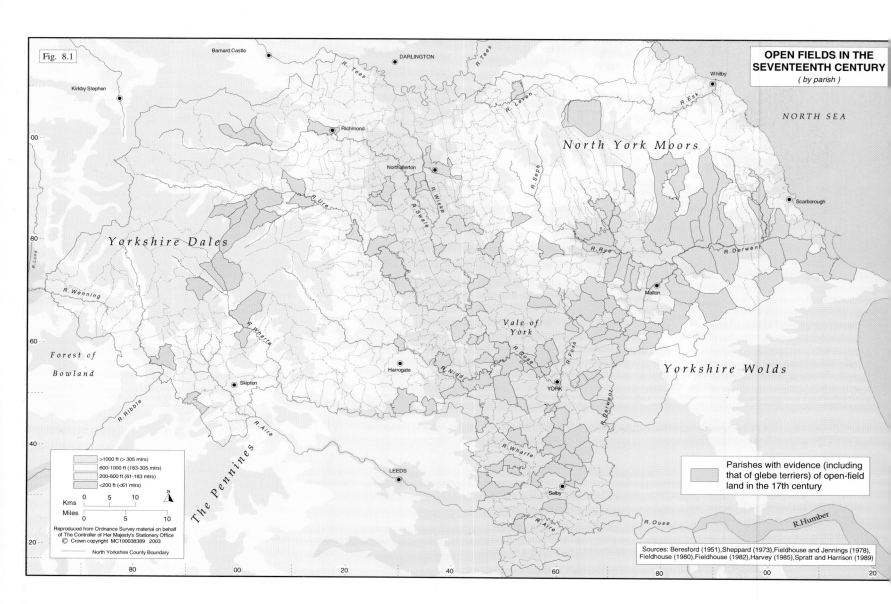

Fig. 8.1

NORTH SEA

North York Moors

Yorkshire Dales

*Forest of
Bowland*

*Vale of
York*

Yorkshire Wolds

Parishes with evidence (including
that of glebe terriers) of open-field
land in the 17th century

>1000 ft (> 305 mtrs)
600-1000 ft (183-305 mtrs)
200-600 ft (61-183 mtrs)
<200 ft (<61 mtrs)

Kms   0   5   10
Miles 0   5   10

Reproduced from Ordnance Survey material on behalf
of The Controller of Her Majesty's Stationery Office
© Crown copyright MC100038389 2003
_____ North Yorkshire County Boundary

Sources: Beresford (1951), Sheppard (1973), Fieldhouse and Jennings (1978),
Fieldhouse (1980), Fieldhouse (1982), Harvey (1985), Spratt and Harrison (1989)

The Pennines

were: corn-growing, cattle-rearing, and a mixture of the two.[7] In part of the central Vale was
Galtres Forest, with extensive common pastures, grazing and wood-use rights, a survivor of
the once-extensive forests (Galtres, Ouse, Derwent, and Ainsty) that surrounded York in the
early Middle Ages.[8]

THE VALE OF PICKERING.

This region had a variety of land-use arrangements. Open-field systems were characteristic
features of the better-drained lowland parts of the largely linear townships extending into the
poorly drained lower sections of the Vale, and also of the coastal settlements.

A pre-enclosure map of Speeton, a coastal township, dated 1772, shows four open fields —
Beacon Field, Mill Field, Cross Field and East Field — subdivided into long narrow strips
running with the slope of the land. At Hunmanby in 1700 there were four common arable
fields; and at Filey in 1791 there were three open fields, two large ones to the north and west
of the settlement, and a smaller 'Little Field' to the south.[9]

There were open-field townships in the west of the vale beyond Malton, though fewer on
its northern side, where enclosure had eaten away at the open fields before the beginning of
the eighteenth century. Pickering itself had two groups of three fields in 1700, and Thornton
and Farmaby each had three such fields, those at Farmaby being enclosed in 1678.[10] Further
east, there were three- and four-field arrangements, and other areas of open field whose
precise system of operation has not yet been determined. On the south of the Vale, the scarp-
foot villages all had open fields at the beginning of the eighteenth century. The actual
numbers and patterns varied from regular two- and three-field systems to more irregular
arrangements. There were three large open arable fields at Sherburn; West Heslerton had two
open fields, East Heslerton three.[11]

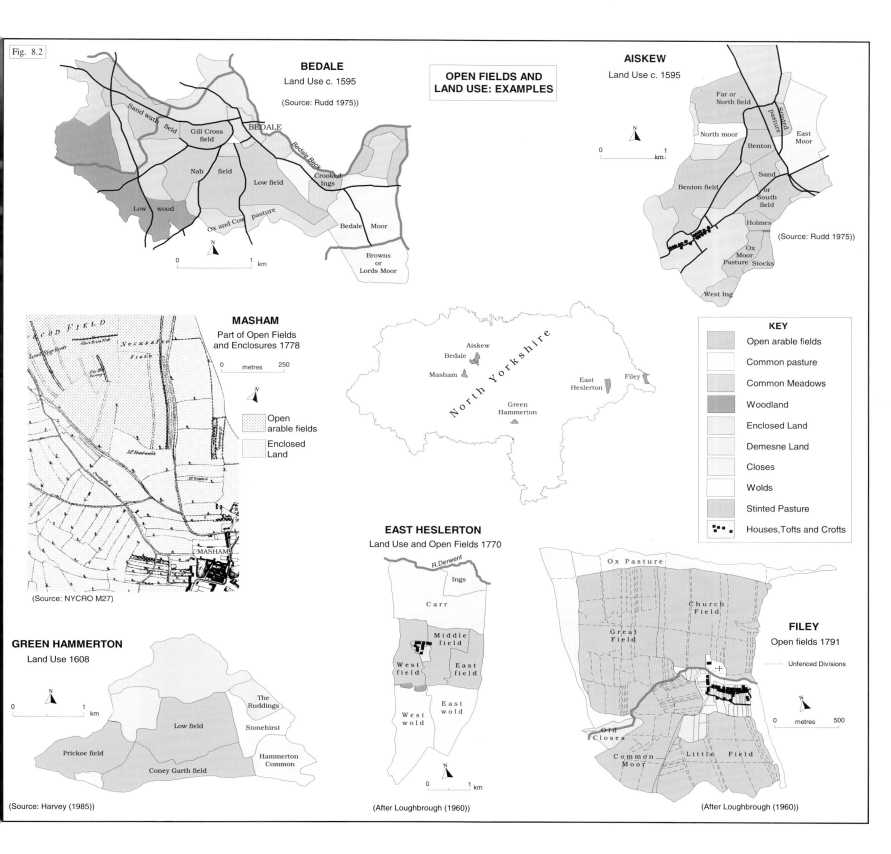

Fig. 8.2

OPEN FIELDS AND LAND USE: EXAMPLES

BEDALE
Land Use c. 1595
(Source: Rudd 1975))

AISKEW
Land Use c. 1595
(Source: Rudd 1975))

MASHAM
Part of Open Fields and Enclosures 1778
(Source: NYCRO M27)

Open arable fields
Enclosed Land

GREEN HAMMERTON
Land Use 1608
(Source: Harvey (1985))

EAST HESLERTON
Land Use and Open Fields 1770
(After Loughbrough (1960))

FILEY
Open fields 1791
Unfenced Divisions
(After Loughbrough (1960))

KEY

Open arable fields
Common pasture
Common Meadows
Woodland
Enclosed Land
Demesne Land
Closes
Wolds
Stinted Pasture
Houses, Tofts and Crofts

Pastureland for grazing was found in the higher parts of the coastal townships, and even higher and rougher moorland above the cultivated land of the northern townships. Another important land-use feature was the 'ings' land of the Vale itself: occasionally flooded land, which provided good grassland for grazing.

In the Tabular Hills region (so called because of the flat tops to the hills) at the northern edge of the Vale of Pickering, the field systems reflected the location of individual town-ships, and notably whether they comprised solely higher land or a linear combination of higher with lower land in the Vale. Three-field systems had been common in this region, with two sets of three fields in Brompton, Hutton Buscel, Middleton and Pickering; and arrangements more akin to Wolds 'outfields', combined with core arable, in some of the higher townships.[12]

THE YORKSHIRE WOLDS

The northern part of the Yorkshire Wolds, which abuts the Vale of Pickering on its south side and is part of North Yorkshire, showed early evidence of open arable fields not dissimilar from those of the northern side of the Vale, but with the addition of sheep-walk land, on the chalk plateau, which was also periodically ploughed up for supplementary arable. The arable fields were mainly located on the better-quality soils at the foot of the chalk scarp.[13] An analysis of an 1803 account of an enclosure at Staxton in 1803 describes the importance of the wold land: 'The chalkland, which rises to about 550 feet [170m] above sea-level on Staxton Wold, once presented a much more open appearance than it does today. The steep dry valleys, separated by smooth curving wolds, were covered with a close sward derived from continuous sheep grazing … There was a certain amount of cultivation on the wold because of the lack of available field land within the Vale [of Pickering] itself, so that the wold formed a type of "outfield", which was cultivated not more often than once in six years. After harvest the sward was allowed to regenerate naturally.'[14] Sheep-farming was clearly an important feature of the wolds system of land-use, reflected in a high percentage of farm capital being invested in sheep (about fourteen per cent),[15] making maximum use of the good-quality limestone pastures. Water supply, though, was a major problem.

THE NORTH YORK MOORS

The North York Moors are a very distinctive upland region of north-east Yorkshire, bounded to the east by the North Sea, to the north by the Tees basin, to the west by the Hambleton Hills and the northern Vale of York, and to the south by the Vale of Pickering. Their northern and western edges are steep scarps, while the southern transition to the Vale of Pickering is less dramatic. The high moors watershed reaches 1,500 feet (450m), and a series of river valleys penetrate the moors from south and north. These are Ryedale, Rosedale, Farndale, Bransdale and and Bilsdale in the south; Glaisdale, Danby Dale, Westerdale and Fryupdale in the north; and Eskdale running west-east to the sea at Whitby.

The agricultural potential varies within this region as a whole, between the barren high moors, the more fertile low moors and the dales themselves. The dales have an important history as the bases for medieval colonisation of dale and moor by monastic communities. Medieval cultivation systems included open arable fields in the dale villages, and scattered sites of arable in the woodland regions of the dales. In the low moors there was extensive village settlement with arable cultivation and extensive granges.[16]

Seventeenth-century surveys show the persistence of arable open fields in a number of places. At Thornton Dale in 1685 the system comprised two groups of three open fields, subdivided into furlongs and possibly reflecting, in this two-fold division, an attempt to regulate and rationalise the use of arable.[17]

By the time of the parliamentary enclosures, which profoundly affected communal cultivation and tenure of land in Midland England in the eighteenth century, and poorer land there and elsewhere in the nineteenth, there was very little arable and other land left to enclose in the North York Moors, apart from the south-east and parts of the coast. The experience of the North York Moors in largely missing out on Midland-pattern enclosure has been explained in terms of the absence of common arable from many areas, together with piecemeal enclosure. Thus:

'Some [parishes], like Danby and Bilsdale, had developed an agricultural pattern which included little or no common arable, though with a good deal of open common pasture on the surrounding moors. Others had experienced piecemeal enclosure from the late medieval period onwards. The manor of Whitby, for example, was entirely parcelled up before the abbey was dissolved in 1539, and Coxwold had lost most of its common fields by 1605.'[18]

At Snainton, on the northern edge of the Vale of Pickering, there had been three open arable fields in the thirteenth century — West Field, Middle Field and Heydon Field — but there were also other fields which, it has been suggested, were part of an irregularly cropped area of 'Outfield', the main open fields making up an intensively cultivated 'Infield' area. The explanation for this dual arrangement appears to lie in the value of the limestone soil, where the 'outfield' open arable fields lay, as sheep pastures.[19]

To the west of the Vale of York, the higher land of the Pennines and their foothills, penetrated by the dales formed by the rivers draining east and south-east to the Ouse, had a different balance of land-use and farming tradition. The altitudinal sequence was generally: open fields and meadows at or near the valley bottoms, with stinted pastures above, and unstinted commons and wastes above these. Open fields which had been extensive in the lower Dales in medieval times[20] remained in some areas, but they were generally smaller than those in the Vale of York and on the Wolds.

Fieldhouse[21] has analysed a survey of Grassington in Wharfedale, where in 1603 there were 412 acres (167ha) of open-field arable divided between three fields, with a total of 864 selions (strips of land) held by thirty tenants. The average size of the individual selions was half an acre (0.2ha). As elsewhere, the holdings of individuals were scattered throughout the fields, and closes existed both within and beside the open fields. There were three common fields at Kettlewell in upper Wharfedale, containing some closes. In Wensleydale at West Witton there were three small common fields — High, Low and East — totalling 120 acres (50ha). In Bishopdale there were four open arable fields at West Burton, two such fields at Thoralby which included meadow land, and four fields at Newbiggin. Thus, Fieldhouse concludes:

'... there was quite clearly a residue of common open-field farming in some of the townships of Coverdale, Wensleydale and Bishopdale ... Almost all the arable farming still practised in Wensleydale and its tributary dales at this time was in fact to be found in these surviving open fields.'[22]

In Swaledale the greater part of the open fields had disappeared by the sixteenth century, though there were remnants, at Healough for example.[23] Communal sharing of enclosed meadow and pasture continued, exemplified in Arkengarthdale in the seventeenth century.[24] Fieldhouse and Jennings assert that:

'... there is overwhelming evidence that most of the good meadow and pasture land in Swaledale had been divided up into enclosed fields by the end of the sixteenth century, and that there was a constant sub-dividing of large fields and intaking from the fellsides, to form more of the small closes which now typify the agrarian landscape of the dale ...'[25]

Of the small areas of surviving arable, the main crops were wheat, rye, oats and hard corn,[26] but the economy of Swaledale was predominantly pastoral.

The process of enclosure in this region was piecemeal but steady, intensifying in the sixteenth and seventeenth centuries, with the result that there had been much enclosure — certainly of Crown land — by the beginning of the seventeenth century, and by the end of the seventeenth century there were few vestiges of open fields. The parallel process of gradual intaking and enclosure of sections of the common pastures was also active from the sixteenth century, for example in Swaledale and Arkengarthdale. Fieldhouse has indicated, however, that enclosure did not put an end to co-operative land management, as enclosed areas of meadow and pasture continued to be co-farmed by two or more tenants, and indicated a long phase of transition from communal to individual farming.[27]

Above the arable and meadow land of the valley bottoms were the extensive areas of poor-quality common and waste land, used for grazing of animals and as sources of provision for wood, stone, peat, ling and bracken.[28] These formed the largest land-use areas — about 70 per cent — of manors in the region. There was a long tradition in the dales and moorland of sheep-farming, associated in the medieval period with the flocks of the large monasteries such as Fountains Abbey grazing the moorlands, including Malham Moor. The dissolution of the monasteries led to a change to smaller-scale freehold estates, but the tradition of sheep and cattle farming continued, with large fairs for livestock being held at Malham Moor, Middleham and Masham.[29] The moorland pastures were stinted — that is, the number of livestock allowed to graze on them was restricted.

The upland pastures were gradually affected by intake encroachment, but their major transformation came with the parliamentary enclosure acts of the eighteenth and nineteenth centuries (cf Chapman, section 8.4), by which time much of the open arable land had already been enclosed.

8.3   AGRICULTURE c1780–1900   ROBIN A BUTLIN

The agricultural geography of North Yorkshire in the period 1780–1900 varied regionally, and awareness of these regional variations is well documented by contemporary agricultural commentators (**fig 8.3**).

Agriculture c1600–1780 — Acknowledgements:
Permission for the insets in Figure 8.2 has been given by the following: Green Hammerton (Harvey, *Geografisker Annaler,* 67B (1985)-I, p36), with permission of Blackwell Publishing; Bedale, Masham and Aiskew, by North Yorkshire County Record Office; Filey and East Heslerton by Mr Brian Loughbrough.

Agriculture c1600–1780 — Further Reading:
M W Beresford, Glebe Terriers and Open Field, Yorkshire, *Yorkshire Archaeological Journal* XXXVI (1951), 325-68.

J E Kaner, Historic woodland in the Vale of York, in M A Atherden and R A Butlin (eds), *Woodland in the Landscape: Past and Future Perspectives* (Leeds: Leeds University Press, 1999), 120-39.

W Harwood Long, *A survey of the Agriculture of Yorkshire* (London: Royal Agricultural Society of England, 1969), 29.

B J D Harrison, The Medieval Landscape, in D A Spratt and B J D Harrison (eds), *The North York Moors* (Newton Abbot: David and Charles, 1989), 88-9.

B Loughbrough, 'Aspects of Enclosure of the vale of Pickering in the Eighteenth and Nineteenth Centuries' (unpublished MA thesis, University of Hull, 1960).

J McDonnell, After the Middle Ages: Agriculture and Settlement, in D A Spratt and B J D Harrison (eds), *The North York Moors* (Newton Abbot: David and Charles, 1989), 115.

J A Sheppard, Field Systems of Yorkshire, in A R H Baker and R A Butlin (eds), *Studies of Field Systems in the British Isles* (Cambridge: Cambridge University Press, 1973), 145-87.

J Thirsk, The farming regions of England, in J Thirsk (ed.), *The Agrarian History of England and Wales IV, 1500-1640* (Cambridge: Cambridge University Press, 1967), 32-3.

B Waites, *Moorland and Vale-Land Farming in North-East Yorkshire. The monastic contribution in the thirteenth and fourteenth centuries,* University of York, Borthwick Institute, Borthwick Papers no.32 (York: Borthwick Institute, 1967), 6-9.

Helmsley: ridge and furrow patterns of the former open fields, now under grass.
© North York Moors National Park Authority, NYM 71.

Harton village (in the Vale of York, on the River Derwent, nine miles (14km) north-east of York): manorial earthworks and ridge and furrow (relics of the former open-field system).
NMR 12330/19 © Crown copyright. NMR.

Flaxton Village (eight miles (13km) north-east of York): field patterns, showing contrasts between curvilinear tofts with former cultivation ridges and the square fields resulting from formal enclosure.
NMR 17063/07 © Crown copyright. NMR.

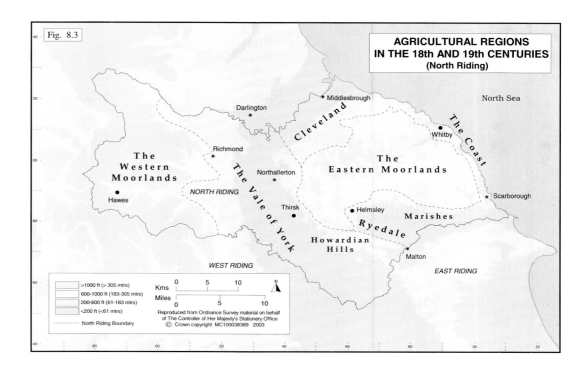

Fig. 8.3

**AGRICULTURAL REGIONS
IN THE 18th AND 19th CENTURIES
(North Riding)**

Reproduced from Ordnance Survey material on behalf
of The Controller of Her Majesty's Stationery Office
© Crown copyright MC100038389 2003

>1000 ft (> 305 mtrs)
600-1000 ft (183-305 mtrs)
200-600 ft (61-183 mtrs)
<200 ft (<61 mtrs)
North Riding Boundary

THE VALE OF YORK

J. Tuke, in his *General View of the Agriculture of the North Riding of Yorkshire* (1794), described the climate of the Vale as mild and temperate in its lower parts, but cold in the more elevated parts near the moors of the 'eastern moorlands' (the North York Moors).[1] He wrote that:

'In the Vale of York, one-third of the ground is in tillage, and two-thirds in grass. This is the common proportion; but where there are extensive open fields, and in some places where the soil is light, the proportion of tillage is larger, and may amount to about one-half.'[2]

Isaac Leatham, in his *General View of the Agriculture of the East Riding of Yorkshire* (1794), described the area around York (the Ainsty) in the following terms:

'The country is in general flat, with some general swells. The quantity of woodland is considerable; chiefly scattered, or in hedgerows … A few open townships only remain in the Ainsty; a considerable part is ancient inclosure, and several recent inclosures have been made. The farms are in general small, few exceed two hundred acres [80ha]; they contain an equal proportion of arable and grassland. The same modes of husbandry according to the difference and quality of the soil, are practiced here as in the East Riding. They breed some good horses, but not many cattle, and very few sheep; the breed of the latter is in general ordinary.'[3]

Agricultural commentators found the agriculture of the Vale of mixed quality at the end of the eighteenth century. Arthur Young in his tour of 1776 found that part of the Vale which had not been enclosed and improved relatively unproductive, characterized by small farms and low rents, though a distinction was made between the better farms on sand and gravel-based soils, and the poorer ones on clay. New four-course rotations were in evidence on the lighter soils, but on the clay soils the rotation was of two crops followed by a fallow year.[4] Common land was extensive, especially in the eastern part of the Vale (the former East Riding), and large areas, notably along the course of the Derwent, badly in need of better drainage (a condition that restricted corn-growing to drier parts), a process that started in the southern part of the Vale from the mid-eighteenth century.

Enclosure of common land on sandy soil land was largely completed in the Vale by the end of the eighteenth century, providing further opportunity for improvement in agricultural methods. Hastings has suggested that the Vale was the best-cultivated part of North Yorkshire at this time, but that conditions varied, with the main crops in the late eighteenth century being rye, maslin and oats, yet by the mid-nineteenth century the main crop was wheat. In addition:

'The northern Vale was also noted for its cattle breeding and the southern vale for the preparation of butter and old milk cheese. Produce travelled normally via Northallerton to York, which … acted as a clearing house for many of its products. The vessels of York trading companies plied a regular trade with London.'[5]

The railways, of course, changed the speed of movement of farm produce to the industrial districts of the north and to London in the later part of the nineteenth century. The predominantly arable areas of these lowlands suffered acutely from the agricultural depression of the late nineteenth century, notably on the stiffer clay lands around Thirsk.

Horses: a wood engraving from the 1930s.
© Marie Hartley.

Improved drainage, the practice of marling, and the influence of a growing number of agricultural societies, promoted the adoption of new farming techniques in the Vale and elsewhere from the end of the eighteenth century. Long cites the account, given in the *Transactions of the Yorkshire Agricultural Society* for 1839-40, of the improvement of an estate on sand land near Pocklington by drainage, marling and re-liming.[6]

A significant area of lowland in what was formerly North Yorkshire is now in Cleveland, which was during this period famed for the quality of its arable farming and for its degree of agricultural improvement. In the eighteenth century it had produced wheat, beans, corn, butter, store-cattle and horses, but by the end of the nineteenth century grassland predominated.[7]

An interesting feature of the Vale and areas adjacent to it was the development of thoroughbred horse-breeding in the nineteenth century. As Huggins has shown, in the nineteenth century Yorkshire as a whole became one of the important horse-breeding counties, with particular focus on the activity in north and east Yorkshire.[8] The principal dynamic was the change from breeding as a part-time activity by farmers, major landed gentry, racehorse trainers, and innkeepers, to a specialist industry centred on large stud farms and stud companies. The geography of thoroughbred breeding focused increasingly on the area around York itself:

'It was centrally situated, with excellent transport links, and excess stabling capacity. Breeding was also linked to training areas, such as Malton, Richmond or Middleham.'[9]

Haymaking in Wensleydale in the 1930s.
© Marie Hartley.

THE VALE OF PICKERING

The general impression given of this region in the eighteenth and nineteenth centuries is one of a predominance of grassland (about one-third arable) and whose potential would not be realised until extensive drainage work had been undertaken. Tuke writes of Ryedale and the 'East and West Marishes' which 'Form one vale, Pickering-Beck, dividing Ryedale from the Marishes; the surface of the lower parts of Ryedale is very flat, and a large proportion of it is liable to be flooded, the waters being much retarded and kept up by a mill of little value at Newsham, and by the extreme curvature of the river...'.[10]

One consequence of various means of agricultural improvement, including enclosure and improvement of water supply to the land at the southern edge of the North York Moors, notably by the engineering feats of Joseph Foord from 1773, was, as Spratt and Harrison have indicated, to change the land-use zoning in the townships on the northern edge and in the centre of the Vale of Pickering:

'... the old pattern of husbandry in the parishes lining the north edge of the Vale of Pickering had followed the medieval practice of hay-meadow and winter grazing on the carrs of the Vale bottom, arable fields and sheep folding on the south-facing limestone slopes, and rough summer grazing, especially for sheep, on the moor above. Improved drainage on the carrs, and the ability to graze more beasts on the higher and drier land, brought some reversal of roles. In several parishes, as Marshall commented, carr land was ploughed, and proved to yield heavier crops than the limestone soils above, while the latter were enclosed and put down to grass to feed the growing herds of beef and dairy cattle now being grazed on the Tabular Hills.'[11]

A specialist product of the rural economy of the Vale of Pickering was the rearing of coach-horses, noted by the commentators of the late eighteenth century, and still prominent in the early twentieth century, as noted by the author of the agriculture section of the *Victoria County History*:

'In the Vale of Pickering and adjoining districts a great many valuable coach horses are bred, which when four or five years old find a very ready sale, both at the home and Continental markets, commanding very high prices'. The writer of this article saw in the autumn of 1906 twelve fine specimens of this breed in a dealer's stables at Pickering, which 'he has just sold to the King of Italy, who seems to have a great liking for Yorkshire horses.'[12]

THE YORKSHIRE WOLDS

Arthur Young's account of the Wolds in his *Tour* of 1771 gives an idea of them in their pre-improved state:

'I remarked the whole way from York to Beverley that they used many oxen in their husbandry work, all the wagons I met had two oxen and two horses in them ... The adjoining moors are common to the houses around them, would let enclosed at 3s 6d or 4s an acre [0.4ha] without improvement and might be made with nothing but good husbandry worth 10s an acre.'[13]

Wensleydale sheep: an engraving from the 1930s.
© Marie Hartley.

Grouse shooting from butts, North York Moors.
© North York Moors National Park Authority, RO 0024.

Young's impressions were of a region ripe for improvement through enclosure of open fields and commons, a process already underway. By about 1812, enclosure by both Private Act and General Act had begun to change the basis of farming and the face of the countryside of the Wolds, of which about seventy per cent was enclosed by parliamentary enclosure act.[14] Open fields and commons largely disappeared, and were replaced by the geometrically laid-out patterns of fields and farms determined by the enclosure commissioners.

Enclosure was encouraged by the owners of the larger estates, whose energies were also behind the application of new farming machine technologies and crop rotations. Sheep and corn remained important, and were largely responsible for the severe effect of the agricultural depression on this region at the end of the nineteenth century.

THE NORTH YORK MOORS

In 1794 Tuke described the 'Eastern Moorlands' of North Yorkshire:

'This wild and extensive tract of mountains occupies a space of about 30 miles [50km] by 15 or upwards, [and] is penetrated by a number of fertile cultivated dales. The great altitude of these moors, renders the climate extremely cold and bleak, which will always be a bar to their improvement.'[15] He continued:

'The cultivated dales situated amongst these moors, are pretty extensive, some of them containing from five to 10,000 acres [2,000-4,000ha]; and Eskdale, and Bilsdale much more; the bottoms of the vales are mostly narrow, seldom more than 200 yards [180m], but the land is generally cultivated from half a mile to a mile [0.8-1.6km] up the hills, though the surface is in many places irregular. The climate is colder than in the country surrounding the district, yet corn will ripen very well, when sown in pretty good aspect.'[16]

This contrast between the moors of the high plateau and the dales incised therein is echoed by other contemporary commentators such as Arthur Young and William Marshall, and reflected in contrasting agrarian practices of the eighteenth and nineteenth centuries.

The unit of farming was on the whole quite small, with a strong subsistence element. In the dales in the eighteenth century, although there was some growing of rye, wheat and oats, the emphasis was predominantly pastoral, with beef cattle and sheep the main elements. Markets for cattle were at Malton, Egton and Stokesley, and sheep (proto-Blackface breeds) were valued as much for wool as for mutton.[17] Sheep were grazed on the moors, which also afforded rights for the cutting of peat and turf. There were extensive rabbit warrens on the moors, and by the late nineteenth century other uses such as grouse shooting and private afforestation were in evidence.[18]

Improvement in moorland farming in the late eighteenth and the nineteenth centuries followed enclosure of open fields and open moorland, and usually involved the paring and burning of land, the bringing of lime and of machines for improvement being consistently difficult. Parliamentary enclosure in the moors was restricted largely to the south-east, and to the coastal townships between Pickering and Scarborough (part of the old Forest of

Sheep on the North York Moors.
© North York Moors National Park Authority, BD0036.

Pickering), many of the Dales open fields having been enclosed by a process of attrition and by agreement over a long period of time.[19] The moors did not benefit, as did other parts of rural North Yorkshire, from the high farming period from the 1850s to the 1870s because of difficulties of access, but they suffered in common with others during the depression at the end of the nineteenth century.[20]

The Yorkshire Moors experienced agricultural improvement by major landowners in the eighteenth and nineteenth centuries, paying particular attention to the limited possibilities afforded by what was essentially marginal land. One of the major attempts at reclamation of moorland was undertaken in 1773 at Kempswithen, between Commondale and Baysdale, by Sir Charles Turner of Kildale. Kempswithen had better, loamy soil than the rest of the high moors, and by means of paring, burning and drainage, the application of lime and the building of stone walls, the land was laid to grass and to some corn cultivation.[21]

This enclosure had been abandoned from its original purpose by 1794, but Turner's other improvements on lower land in Kildale, and by other landowners in Middleton and Lockton Moor, were positively noted by contemporaries, indicating a continuation from earlier improvements by yeoman farmers.[22] Other changes in the rural economy, especially during the nineteenth century, included an increase in dairy farming to meet the demands of industrial populations for butter, cheese and milk.[23] More 'recreational' land-uses included fox-hunting and grouse-shooting.

THE PENNINE MOORLANDS AND DALES

Agriculture in the Yorkshire Dales in the eighteenth and nineteenth centuries essentially experienced the completion of the process of change from the older communal systems to systems based on individual ownership and use of land.

The pattern of land ownership varied. Hallas has shown that although in 1873 there were ten landowners with over 1,000 acres (400ha) in Wensleydale, comprising 34 per cent of the dale's land, with 11 per cent of Swaledale over 1,000 acres and owned by four landowners, both dales were well below the national average for the amount of land in estates of over 1,000 acres, and also below the average for the North Riding. Hence 'The two dales were, therefore, neither under aristocratic influence nor dominated by large estates'.[24] Of the areas of land not subject to common rights, in 1873 yeomen and small peasant proprietors in total held 59 and 73 per cent respectively of the land in Wensleydale and Swaledale, some of the very small plots of land reflecting the continuing practice of primogeniture (inheritance by the eldest — usually male — child), especially in Swaledale.[25] Lead mining and textiles remained important ingredients of the regional rural economies of the Dales until well into the nineteenth century.

One feature of the agriculture of this area was the diminution in the amount of corn grown: some was still being grown in Wensleydale, as recorded by Arthur Young in 1770, but by the middle of the nineteenth century 'it was reliably stated in government reports and

Haymaking, Gunnerside Bottoms, Swaledale: distinct landscape with stone walls and field barns.
© R White/Yorkshire Dales National Park Authority, YDP/125/2.

right Pinfold, Goathland.
© North York Moors National Park Authority, HG0001.

below right Drystone wall, North York Moors.
© North York Moors National Park Authority, CI 0016.

Further Reading:
J Tuke, *General View of the Agriculture of the North
    Riding of Yorkshire* (London, 1794).
I Latham, *General View of the Agriculture of the East
    Riding of Yorkshire* (London, 1794).
W Harwood Long, *A Survey of the Agriculture of
    Yorkshire* (London: Royal Agricultural Society,
    1969).
R P Hastings, Agriculture, in *Essays in North Riding
    History 1780-1850*, North Yorkshire County
    Record Office Publications no.28 (Northallerton:
    North Yorkshire County Record Office, 1981).
Arthur Young, *A Six Months' Tour Through the North of
    England* (London, 1771).
D A Spratt and B J D Harrison, After the Middle
    Ages: Agriculture and Settlement, in: D A Spratt
    and B J D Harrison (eds), *The North York Moors*
    (Newton Abbot : David and Charles, 1989),
    113-140.
C Hallas, *Rural Responses to Industrialisation. The North
    Yorkshire Pennines 1790-1914* (Lang: Bern, 1999).
R T Fieldhouse, Agriculture in Wensleydale from
    1600 to the Present Day, *Northern History* XVI
    (1980), 169-195
C Hallas, The Social and Economic Impact of a
    Rural Railway: the Wensleydale Line, *Agricultural
    History Review*, 34 (1986) 29-44.

learned agricultural journals that there was little or no tillage in the Yorkshire dales and that corn had to be brought from a distance, making Leyburn one of the dearest markets in the North Riding'.[26] This proved not to be entirely true, as the evidence of tithe records reveal that corn was grown in Wensleydale in the mid-nineteenth century, at places such as West Witton and Coverdale, though there was very little arable left in the dale by the beginning of the Second World War.[27]

The strength of the rural economy in the Dales derived from pastoral farming, with the balance between cattle and sheep having been in favour of cattle since the seventeenth century, and beginning to move back towards sheep by the late eighteenth century.[28]

Sheep were a significant part of agriculture in the region, initially for wool and meat, and also for their milk, which was turned into local cheese. Specialist breeding began in Wensleydale and Swaledale in the eighteenth century, leading to the development of the Wensleydale breed (from Leicester/Teeswater stock) for the lower slopes and valley floors, and the smaller Swaledale sheep which were kept on the higher moors.[29]

Dairy farming was important in the Dales, and enhanced by the coming of the railway in the middle of the nineteenth century. The construction of the North Eastern Railway line from Leyburn to Hawes, started in 1873 and finished in 1876, facilitated the movement of large numbers of sheep, cattle and other animals to the markets of the industrial regions, and from about 1894 of the movement of fresh milk, via Northallerton, initially to Newcastle-upon-Tyne, Sunderland, Darlington, Hull, York and Leeds, and then from the end of the century to London, Lancashire and a larger area of the West Riding.[30]

Grouse-shooting was a significant contributor to the landscape, culture and economy of the Yorkshire Dales region, facilitated in part by the coming of the railways. Done and Muir have shown how the coming of the railways 'allowed the southern shooters to reach the moorland estates without placing great demands upon their qualities of stamina and perseverance. It was easier to board a "grouse shooting special", complete with horse boxes and carriage flats, than it was to travel north in a convoy of family carriages, hiring relays of horses on the way. Branch lines gradually linked the small towns on the fringes of grouse shooting [eg Richmond, Pateley Bridge, Masham, Hawes, Grassington] to the national network.'[31]

8.4 PARLIAMENTARY ENCLOSURE   JOHN CHAPMAN

In so far as any county was 'typical' of the parliamentary enclosure movement, North Yorkshire has a strong claim to be the most representative. In total, parliamentary enclosure seems to have accounted for just under 450,000 acres (180,000ha) in North Yorkshire, or about 21.74 per cent of the county area (**fig 8.4**). This is a very close match to the figure for the whole of England, closer than any of the historic counties except Westmorland. Similarly, the breakdown into different types of land gives almost identical figures to those for the whole movement in England and Wales.[1]

The temporal pattern of acts in the county shows a close resemblance to the national one, with three periods of increased activity in the 1770s, the 1800s, and between 1845 and 1860, separated by relative troughs, though, as the graph (**fig 8.5**) shows, there was no decade without some acts from 1740 to 1890. The actual acreage involved follows a very similar pattern. In some parts of England the later enclosures tended to involve smaller areas, but in North Yorkshire, in common with other parts of northern England, the General Act of 1845 was often used to enclose large areas of moorland of low agricultural value, so the average acreage was high. By far the highest mean acreage for any decade was for enclosures in the 1880s.

The accompanying map shows the distribution of enclosures divided into five major time-periods, according to some of the major events believed to have influenced the process. The large blank in the North York Moors is misleading, since much of the moorland formed part of long narrow townships which ran up into the moor from the surrounding richer agricultural land, and the whole township tended to be enclosed by a single act. There is thus only one symbol, normally outside the moors themselves.

left and opposite page   Weaverthorpe Fields, enclosed in 1801: typical Wolds parliamentary enclosure landscape.
© J Chapman.

As can be seen, the earliest phase, prior to the outbreak of the Napoleonic Wars, shows a complex pattern, but with a strong tendency to avoid the high moorlands of the Pennines. The same was not true of the North York Moors, since the open fields of the Corallian Limestone, which fell within the same townships, were an early target. The Napoleonic phase, contrary to general theory, shows a concentration in the lowland open-field areas, as does most of the limited activity during the succeeding phase. As might be expected, the General Acts of 1836 and 1840 had little impact here, leaving much of the Pennine moorland and some scraps of lowland common to be dealt with under the Act of 1845.

The distinction between the types of land must be approached with care. In North Yorkshire, as in other parts of northern England, 'field' was often used for any land which was fenced off from the open moor, and did not necessarily imply that it was, or ever had been, arable. Thus the enclosure award for Raw Pasture in Fylingdales, in 1810, described the land concerned as 'the said open field or stinted pasture'; it was, in fact, a common pasture, and not an open field as the term would now normally be understood.[2] The 'old enclosures' frequently redistributed were not necessarily of any great antiquity. They often consisted of land which had been recently removed by various means from the fields or waste, though some were genuine ancient crofts, or other land which had never been legally open.

Very few acts or awards give detailed figures for the different types of land, and the only way of gaining accurate information is by totalling the individual allotments, which usually specify the former field or common in which they lay. This is a monumental task, and a ten per cent random sample, drawn originally from each of the historic Ridings, but reassembled to fit the modern boundaries, has been used instead. This suggests that approximately 36 per cent was open-field land, some 57 per cent common and waste, and that common meadow and 'old enclosures' each contributed 3.5 per cent. In other words, the parliamentary enclosure movement in North Yorkshire, as in the country as a whole, was primarily concerned with the reclamation and upgrading of pasture and waste, rather than the reorganisation of common arable.

This reclaimed land was very variable in quality and agricultural potential. Space prevents any detailed discussion of its subsequent history, but in many cases the 'improvement' consisted of little more than dividing off the land so that individual flocks or herds could be kept separate from their neighbours. Such land was often later abandoned during periods of agricultural depression. Conversely, some of the former commons on the southern fringes of the North York Moors allowed profitable intensive agriculture, and remain in such use to the present day.

This variability produced an unusual local response. In several North York Moors awards, enclosure of land judged to be of poor quality was made permissive, allowing the owner to concentrate on the better land, and enclose the rest when conditions and personal finances were right. In the Pennines this idea seems not to have been adopted, further differentiating the enclosure history of the two upland areas.

Parliamentary Enclosure — Further Reading:

B A English, *Yorkshire Enclosure Awards* (Hull: Hull University Studies in Regional and Local History no. 5, 1985).

J Chapman, Parliamentary Enclosure in the Uplands: the case of the North York Moors, *Agricultural History Review* 24 (1976), 1-17.

M E Turner, *English Parliamentary Enclosures* (Folkestone: Dawson, 1980).

M E Turner (ed.), *A Domesday of English enclosure acts and awards by W E Tate* (Reading: University of Reading, 1978)

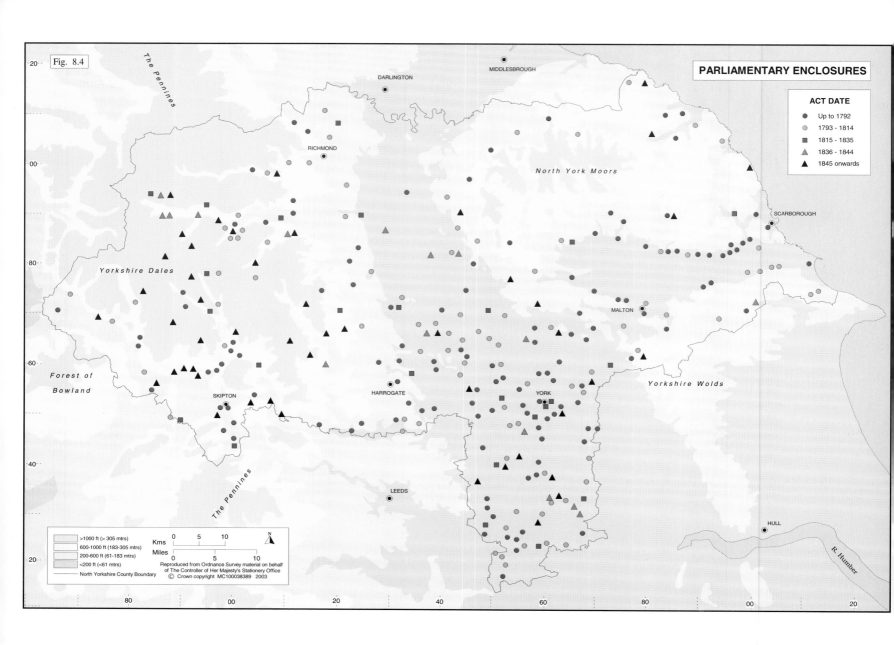

Fig. 8.4

PARLIAMENTARY ENCLOSURES

Reproduced from Ordnance Survey material on behalf of The Controller of Her Majesty's Stationery Office © Crown copyright MC100038389 2003

ACT DATE

Up to 1792
1793 - 1814
1815 - 1835
1836 - 1844
1845 onwards

>1000 ft (> 305 mtrs)
600-1000 ft (183-305 mtrs)
200-600 ft (61-183 mtrs)
<200 ft (<61 mtrs)
North Yorkshire County Boundary

The Pennines

Yorkshire Dales

Forest of Bowland

The Pennines

North York Moors

Yorkshire Wolds

R. Humber

DARLINGTON
MIDDLESBROUGH
RICHMOND
SCARBOROUGH
MALTON
SKIPTON
HARROGATE
YORK
LEEDS
HULL

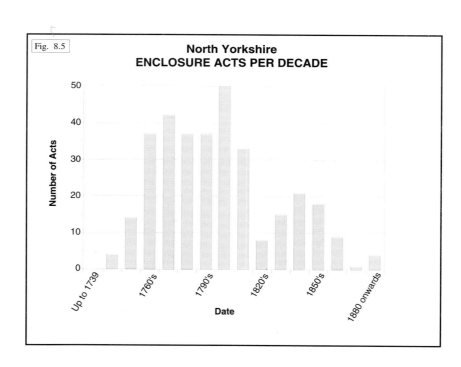

Fig. 8.5

North Yorkshire
ENCLOSURE ACTS PER DECADE

Number of Acts

Date

Up to 1739   1760's   1790's   1820's   1850's   1880 onwards

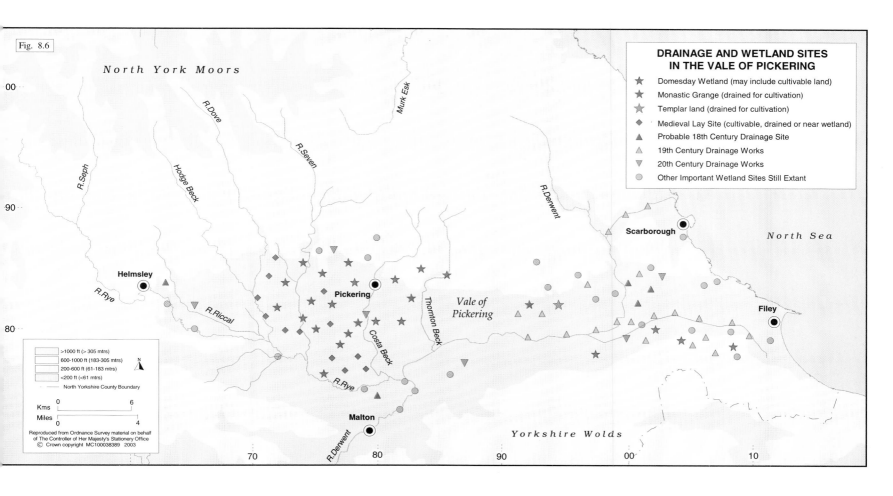

Fig. 8.6

**DRAINAGE AND WETLAND SITES
IN THE VALE OF PICKERING**

★ Domesday Wetland (may include cultivable land)
★ Monastic Grange (drained for cultivation)
★ Templar land (drained for cultivation)
◆ Medieval Lay Site (cultivable, drained or near wetland)
▲ Probable 18th Century Drainage Site
△ 19th Century Drainage Works
▽ 20th Century Drainage Works
● Other Important Wetland Sites Still Extant

>1000 ft (> 305 mtrs)
600-1000 ft (183-305 mtrs)
200-600 ft (61-183 mtrs)
<200 ft (<61 mtrs)
North Yorkshire County Boundary

Kms 0 ─────── 6
Miles 0 ─────── 4

Reproduced from Ordnance Survey material on behalf
of The Controller of Her Majesty's Stationery Office
© Crown copyright MC100038389 2003

8.5 DRAINAGE AND WETLAND SITES IN THE VALE OF PICKERING
NOËL JAMES MENUGE

The low-lying flat or gently undulating Vale of Pickering has an underlying solid geology of Kimmeridge Clay, and is overlain by glacial boulder clay, sands and gravels as well as post-glacial peat and alluvium. Part of the Vale contained a pro-glacial lake in the Pleistocene era, and many open water and marshy areas survived into historic times. Land use is mainly agricultural, with arable farming predominating in the east, and pastoral in the west.[1]

The Vale is an historical site of great importance for both drainage and wetland histories (**fig 8.6**), both in a sense as strong and as controversial as each other. Now one of the most fertile farming areas in the country, for which the Vale has to thank its wetland past, the Vale is increasingly a site of interest for those wishing to retain or study remaining wetlands within an area that is now more drained than wet.

This study is based upon a wide range of documentary sources. Although the map itself does not display sites of either wetland or drainage history before Domesday, it is pertinent to note that they existed. Prehistoric evidence exists for settlements around and within wetland areas, while we know that Roman roads and tracks within the area had ditches along each side for surface drainage.[2] The current study, however, begins with documentary evidence, and necessarily this must begin with the Domesday evidence for the Vale.

In this instance, place-name evidence provides us with many clues to the nature of the landscape. The Yorkshire Domesday identifies Odulfsmere, Chilusmares, Aschilemares and Maxudesmares all in Marishes, within the central vale. It also mentions Loft Marishes and Ghigomersc in Thornton Dale, in the upper northern part of the vale. All derivations of 'marishes', 'mersc' and 'mares' obviously identify marshy land.

Much land within the Vale is identified as waste; Waites suggests that, in some cases (as in the central Vale), this would have been because the land was wet and difficult to cultivate.[4] Some areas described as 'waste' do, however, contain cultivable land (mainly pasture), and the 'waste' in these cases is more likely to equate with 'wet' rather than 'unused'. For example, Amotherby (central to south-western) has 'Land for one plough', while Flixton, Folkton, Muston, Staxton (all eastern Vale) and Normanby (central Vale) include land for five, four, one, three and four ploughs respectively. Kirby Misperton, while described as partly waste, also contains twelve acres (5ha) of meadow, a well-known use for land that was often wet as a result of poor drainage or frequent flooding.

During the high and late Middle Ages, monasteries were largely in control of the drainage and cultivation of wetland areas within the vale. As will be seen, some of these areas reflect the earlier sites mentioned in Domesday. A subsidy of 1301 shows that there were eleven monastic marshland granges in the central vale alone. These were Loftmarsh (Rievaulx), Kekmarsh (Rievaulx), Lund (Rievaulx), Newhouse, South Marton, Edston (Malton Priory), Ryton (Malton Priory), Selleybrig, Kirby Misperton (Malton Priory), Rook Barugh and Normanby.[5] The same subsidy shows thirteen gravel/limestone granges in the peripheral vale (not shown on the map), and these were worth more by comparison to marshland granges due to their greater suitability for arable cultivation.

Although arable was introduced to reclaimed marshland, pastoral farming was easier. Nevertheless, by 1274 Kekmarsh was farming 300 acres (120ha) of arable as well as 300 acres of pasture.[6] Rievaulx's Loftmarsh and Kekmarsh (central vale) were the largest marshland arable holdings, while Lund was probably more important for sheep farming. While Rievaulx Abbey dominated the central vale, Yedingham Abbey dominated the eastern, an area consisting largely of carrs, marsh and lake.[7] Most of this land remained too wet to cultivate, however. The Templars managed to cultivate land east of Yedingham, in Foulbridge; part of their land was sown with wheat.[8]

Medieval lay farming was more usual in the western end of the Vale, owing to clay islands which stood as much as 100 feet (30m) above the wetter lands. Among these sites are Edston, Marton, Thornton Riseborough, Normanby, Salton, Great Barugh, Little Barugh, Kirby Misperton, North Holme and South Holme.[9]

There is also evidence for arable cultivation near the Rye; fields were at Brawby, Great Habton, Little Habton, Ryton Grange and the Manor House, over an area of nearly four miles (6.5km).[10] In spite of this intensive cultivation, though, most of the western vale was marsh or meadow and would have been used for pastoral farming.

There is little documentary evidence for drainage or wetland sites between the end of the medieval period and the eighteenth century, and this is reflected on the map. This does not mean that such sites were not extant, though, just rarely mentioned. The work of the Court of Sewers (established under Henry VIII) continued in this area, and there were brief mentions of wetland areas by such travellers as Leland at Seamer (c1508) and Young (Yorkshire wetlands generally, 1771), and by agriculturalists such as Marshall (the eastern vale described as in 'a state of *fenn*', 1788) and Tuke (1800).[11]

Marshall thought that the River Derwent should be banked out, and that various drains and ditches should be laid in the area, as did Tuke, in 1800. Effectively, this is what happened with the major drainage works of the nineteenth century, when the Derwent was straightened, the Hertford engineered, and the Scalby sea-cut dug to allow excess water to release itself quickly into the sea. These works began with the Parliamentary Act of 1800, which centred around the triangle of Muston, Yedingham and Wykeham in the eastern vale. This ensured systematic drainage in the area on a scale not seen previously, and affected townships included Staxton, Flixton, Folkton, Seamer, Willerby and Ebberston. The straightening of the Derwent and resulting main drains cannot be underestimated — much land on either side of the Derwent towards the eastern end of the vale was thus made cultivable, and largely dry, altering the farming patterns of the previous centuries within the space of only fifty years. The drainage patterns continue today.

Wetland heritage is still important within the vale, though, and is notably still extant, if diminishing. Important wetland sites today include the Sites of Special Scientific Interest (SSSIs) of Amotherby Ings (south-western) and the southern Wintringham Marsh (just below the specified Vale boundary).

SINC sites (Sites of Importance for Nature Conservation) include the five River Rye SINCs (western), Keld Held Springs (north-western), the Kelds and Holbeck Ings (western), the River Derwent Corridor (Hertford confluence to West Ayton), Brompton Beck (central-eastern), Brompton Mill and Fish Pond (north-eastern), Seamer Mere, the Mere (Seamer Valley), Cayton Meadow, Burton Riggs Gravel Pits, Filey Dams, Muston Buttoms, Well Springs, the River Hertford, Wykeham pits and woodland, and Fox Covert Ponds, Flixton Carr Plantation (all eastern). Also of importance are the proposed SINC site at Norton Ings (south-western), and the peat sites at Pickering Carrs (north-western), Wykeham Carr and Hutton Buscel Carr (eastern) and Hertford Carrs (eastern).

Other wetland areas co-exist among the drained and cultivated areas, and continue to provide a habitat for the remnants of the rich wetland flora and fauna that once pervaded the vale.

Drainage in Vale of Pickering — Sources and Further Reading:

W Chapman, *Report of William Chapman, Engineer, on the Means of Draining the Low Grounds in the Vales of the Derwent and Hertford, in the North and East Ridings of the County of York* (Newcastle: E Walker, 1800). Also held at Northallerton County Record Office, on mic film BD14.

M Atherden and R Missin, The Vale of Pickering Wetlands Project, in M Atherden (ed.), *Wetlands in the Landscape: Archaeology, Conservation, Heritage* (York: Place Research Centre, 2001), 108-137.

W Dugdale, *The History of Imbanking and Draining Divers Fens and Marshes, both in Foreign Parts and in this Kingdom, and of the Improvements thereby* (London: W Bowyer and J Nichols, 2nd ed., 1772).

D Hall, & J Coles, *Fenland Survey: an essay in landscape and persistence* (English Heritage, 1993).

B Loughborough, 'Some Geographical Aspects of Enclosure in the Vale of Pickering in the Eighteenth and Nineteenth Centuries' (unpublished MA thesis, University of Hull, 1960).

Noël Menuge, *A Guide to the Wetland Heritage of the Vale of Pickering* (York: Place Research Centre, York St John College, 2001).

D Powlesland, Excavations at Heslerton, North Yorkshire 1978-82, *Archaeological Journal* 143 (1986).

J Sheppard, 'The Drainage of the Marshlands of East Yorkshire' (unpublished PhD thesis, University of London, 1964).

W R Wightman, 'Some Aspects of the Historical Geography of the Vale of Pickering AD 1086-1350' (unpublished PhD thesis, University of Durham, 1964).

Unpublished sources held at the North Yorkshire County Record Office, Northallerton.

Rye Internal Drainage Board BD13.

Muston and Yedingham Drainage Board BD14.

Ouse and Derwent Drainage Board BD15

EARLY HISTORY

The succession of glacial periods in the Pleistocene left the European rabbit (*Oryctolagus cuniculus*) extinct throughout most of the Continent, persisting only in the milder region of the Iberian peninsula.[1] Its reappearance in western and central Europe was a very gradual process, largely aided by man.

The Romans, recognising the value of its fur and meat, and its sporting potential, introduced it from Spain into Italy, where they were already keeping and coursing the hare in *leporaria*[2] or hare-warrens on some villa estates. They placed the rabbit alongside the hare within these warrens, establishing a pattern of its breeding and nurture in managed enclosures. By the Middle Ages, rabbit warrens or coneygarths derived from this model were to be found in Spain, France and Germany.

ARRIVAL IN BRITAIN

Soon after the Conquest, the Normans brought the rabbit into Britain, prizing it for the table and clothing, and as a source of profit in home and overseas commerce.

Earliest records of the animal in Britain come from islands off southern England: for instance, a deed of 1135[3] transferring the ownership of Drake's Island with its rabbits to Plympton Priory on the mainland, and a grant in 1176[4] of tithes on rabbits captured in the Scillies. By the thirteenth century, warrens were spreading through England (eg Guildford and the Wirral),[5] into Scotland (eg Cramond in Lothian and Crail in Fife)[6] and into Ireland (eg Rosslare in Wexford);[7] there were royal coneygarths in Holderness,[8] and by the next century rabbit warrens feature across the Yorkshire landscape.

INDICATION OF WARREN SITES

Evidence for the existence of rabbit warrens (**fig 8.7**) comes from numerous sources: from cartographic names with rabbit-related elements (*coney, clapper, warren, rabbit, burrow* or *bury*, for example); from county and local maps, terriers, grants, leases and rentals, tithe maps and awards, and other local documentation; and from archaeological fieldwork. Various artefacts have left visible remains: warren lodges or houses, boundary or internal embankments or walls, pillow mounds, rabbit-types or pit-traps, muce-holes and vermin-traps.

Yorkshire is fortunate in having a variety of warren forms and features. The *warren lodge* or *house* in England ranges from such a mannered structure as Tresham's Triangular Lodge in Northamptonshire[9] or the flint tower of Thetford Lodge in the Breckland, to mere gutting-houses and lowly warreners' dwellings. In Yorkshire the ruins of Norton Tower[10] (SD976570), perched on a high escarpment, exemplify the fortified warren lodge, defensive against poachers and other miscreants, while Warren House at Woodhall, Carperby[11] (SD990895), is a farm cottage.

Embankments, ditches or *walls* may form outer or inner warren boundaries. At Cockmoor Dykes, Snainton[12] (SE9186), a set of parallel earthen embankments and ditches results from warrening activity re-using and adapting ancient territorial boundaries. Fine stone-wall boundaries are visible at Woodhall and at Gouthwaite[13] (SE1368).

Pillow mounds may be entirely earthen or incorporate stone consolidation. Douthwaite Dale, Hutton-le-hole[14] (SE7090), holds an extensive array; lesser numbers occur at Sutton-in-Craven (SD9943),[15] Copt Hewick (SE3471) and other sites.

Rabbit-types were pits up to one three feet (1m) wide and deep, revetted to prevent earthfall. Rabbits were trapped by being led into a tunnel above the pit with a trapdoor mechanism. Types were a labour-intensive method of taking rabbits, much used on the later large-scale commercial warrens. Examples are to be seen at Dalby[16] (SE8687), at Woodhall and at Bolton Abbey (SE0656).

Muce-holes were small apertures in the base of stone walls, allowing rabbit passage, encouraging entry into traps and type-tunnels, or controlling rabbit movements for the benefit of shooting parties.

Vermin traps on Dartmoor[17] were stone constructions into which vermin was led by a system of funnelled walls. In North Yorkshire, Woodhall Warren has unique vermin traps in the form of alcoves high on the inner face of a boundary wall where metal spring-traps were hidden to catch marauding vermin seeking exit.

SITING OF WARRENS

Warrens were most often on marginally economic land, with preference for well-drained, sandy or gravelly soils. So, sites occur on or near ancient trackways, battlefields, sheep rakes,

Rabbits & Rabbit Warrens — Acknowledgements:
No map of the managed rabbit warrens of North Yorkshire could claim to be comprehensive. Many manors, parks, ecclesiastical establishments and farms would at some time have a warren. This map (**fig 8.7**) shows sites known to the author at which documentation and/or fieldwork provides evidence and particulars of warrening. It amalgamates data from diverse sources, notably English Heritage (the National Monuments Record), the Yorkshire Dales National Park, the North Yorkshire Moors National Park Authority, Forest Enterprise, and many local archaeologists, historians, librarians and others who willingly provided information, helping to guide my own work and enquiries and to make this map a possibility. I owe an especial debt to Steve Moorhouse for his informed comments on the draft map and manuscript, without which the finished version would have been much the poorer.

Rabbits & Rabbit Warrens — Further Reading:
G E H Barrett-Hamilton and M A C Hinton, *A History of British Mammals* (London: Gurney and Jackson, 1910-22).

A Harris and D A Spratt, The rabbit warrens of the Tabular Hills, North Yorkshire, *Yorkshire Archaeological Journal* LXIII (1991), 177-206.

J E Harting, *The Rabbit* (*Fur, Feather and Fin* series) (London: Longmans Green & Co., 1898).

S A Moorhouse, Dovecotes and rabbit warrens, in M I Faull and S A Moorhouse (eds), *West Yorkshire: an Archaeological Survey to AD 1500* (Wakefield: West Yorkshire Metropolitan County Council, 1981), 752-7.

J Sheail, *Rabbits and their History* (Newton Abbot: David and Charles, 1971).

H V Thompson, The Rabbit in Britain, in H V Thompson and C M King (eds), *The European Rabbit* (Oxford: Oxford University Press, 1994), 64-107.

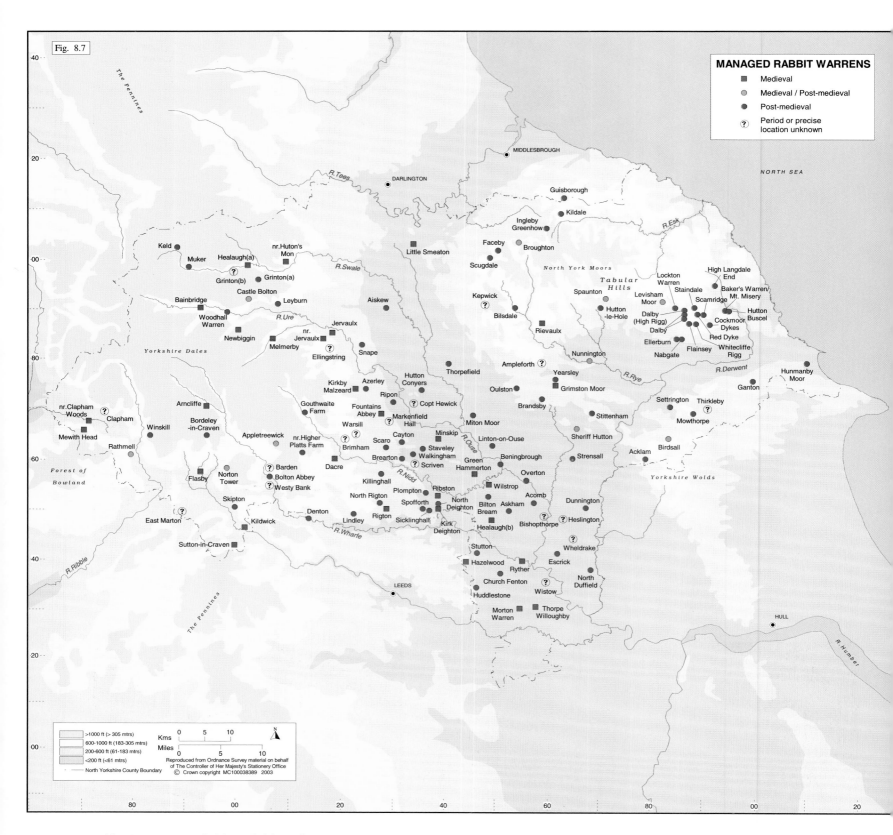

Fig. 8.7

MANAGED RABBIT WARRENS

■ Medieval
● Medieval / Post-medieval
● Post-medieval
? Period or precise location unknown

NORTH SEA

The Pennines

R.Tees

MIDDLESBROUGH

DARLINGTON

Guisborough

Kildale

Ingleby
Greenhow

R.Esk

Keld

nr.Huton's
Mon

Little Smeaton

Faceby

Broughton

North York Moors

Lockton
Warren

High Langdale
End

Muker
Healaugh(a)

Scugdale

Tabular
Hills

Baker's Warren
Mt. Misery

Grinton(b) Grinton(a)

Kepwick

Spaunton

Levisham
Moor

Staindale
Scamridge

Hutton
Buscel

R.Swale

Bainbridge
Castle Bolton Leyburn

Aiskew

Bilsdale

Hutton
-le-Hole

Dalby
(High Rigg)

Cockmoor
Dykes

Woodhall
Warren

R.Ure

Jervaulx

Rievaulx

Dalby

Red Dyke

Ellerburn

Whitecliffe
Rigg

Newbiggin
nr.
Jervaulx

Nunnington

Nabgate Flainsey

Melmerby

Ellingstring Snape

Ampleforth

R.Rye

R.Derwent

Hunmanby
Moor

Yorkshire Dales

Thorpefield

Yearsley

Ganton

Kirkby
Malzeard Azerley

Hutton
Conyers

Oulston

Grimston Moor

Settrington

Thirkleby

Ripon

Copt Hewick

Brandsby

Stittenham

Mowthorpe

Arncliffe

Gouthwaite
Farm

Fountains
Abbey

Miton Moor

Sheriff Hutton

Birdsall

nr.Clapham
Woods Clapham

Warsill

Markenfield
Hall

Acklam

Winskill

Bordeley
-in-Craven

Appletreewick

nr.Higher
Platts Farm

Brimham

Scaro

Cayton

Minskip

Linton-on-Ouse

Strensall

Yorkshire Wolds

Mewith Head

Rathmell

R.Ouse

Brearton

Staveley
Walkingham

Beningbrough

Forest of
Bowland

Flasby

Norton
Tower

Barden

Dacre

Scriven

Green
Hammerton

Overton

Dunnington

Bolton Abbey

Killinghall

Westy Bank

Ribston

Wilstrop

Heslington

Skipton

North Rigton

Plompton

Acomb

East Marton

Kildwick

Denton

Lindley

Spofforth

Rigton

North
Deighton

Bilton
Bream

Askham

Bishopthorpe

R.Ribble

R.Wharfe

Sicklinghall

Kirk
Deighton

Healaugh(b)

Wheldrake

Sutton-in-Craven

Stutton

Escrick

North
Duffield

LEEDS

Hazelwood

Ryther

Church Fenton

Wistow

The Pennines

Huddlestone

Morton
Warren

Thorpe
Willoughby

HULL

R.Humber

>1000 ft (> 305 mtrs)
600-1000 ft (183-305 mtrs)
200-600 ft (61-183 mtrs)
<200 ft (<61 mtrs)
North Yorkshire County Boundary

Kms 0 5 10
Miles 0 5 10

N

Reproduced from Ordnance Survey material on behalf
of The Controller of Her Majesty's Stationery Office
© Crown copyright MC100038389 2003

golf courses, sports fields, airfields, military camps and ranges, quarries and railway tracks. However, where nearness to monastery, manor or village dictated, or a situation in park or forest was needed, warrens might be situated on almost any sort of land.

Sloping land was frequently chosen to assist the rabbit's burrowing and scraping propensities, as did the softer earth used in constructing pillow mounds. A sunny aspect, too, would favour the animal's well-being. As can be seen from the map, access to lines of communication (roads, waterways and, later, railways) was a priority in siting, whether the intent was local or long-distance provision or marketing.

This, with the rabbit's climatic preferences, meant that highest terrains were in general low in order of preference for warren sites, even in post-medieval times when the rabbit had

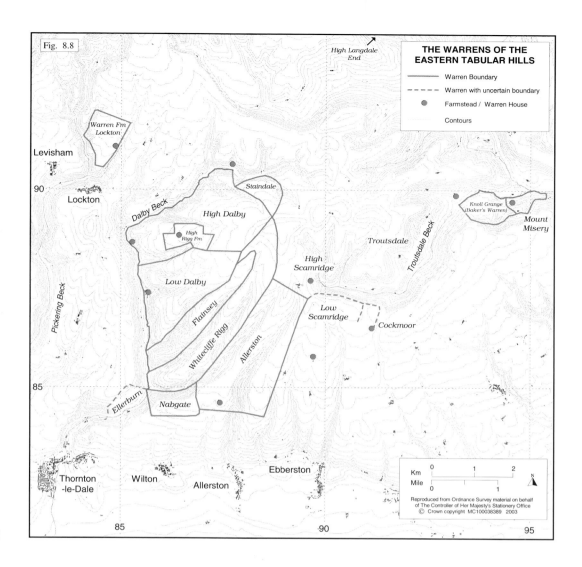

Fig. 8.8

THE WARRENS OF THE EASTERN TABULAR HILLS

——— Warren Boundary

- - - - Warren with uncertain boundary

● Farmstead / Warren House

Contours

High Langdale End

Warren Fm Lockton

Levisham

Lockton

90

Dalby Beck

Staindale

High Dalby

High Rigg Fm

Low Dalby

Flainsey

Whitecliffe Rigg

Allerston

Ellerburn

Nabgate

85

Pickering Beck

Troutsdale

Troutsdale Beck

Knoll Grange (Baker's Warren)

Mount Misery

High Scamridge

Low Scamridge

Cockmoor

Thornton -le-Dale

Wilton

Allerston

Ebberston

Km 0 1 2

Mile 0 1

Reproduced from Ordnance Survey material on behalf of The Controller of Her Majesty's Stationery Office © Crown copyright MC100038389 2003

85   90   95

below Pillow mounds (with prehistoric round barrows and also water races), Hutton Nab, North York Moors.

NMR 12381/12 © Crown copyright NMR.

bottom right Diagram of a rabbit type. Based on an illustration by T P Horner.

By permission of The Dalesman.

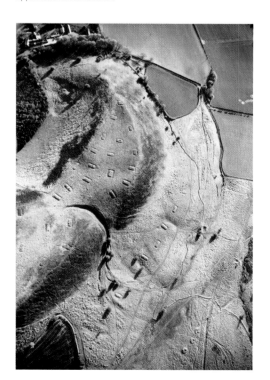

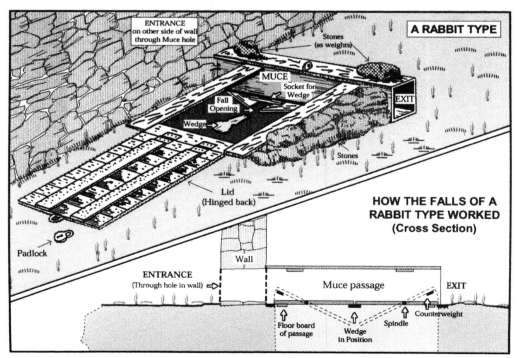

A RABBIT TYPE

ENTRANCE on other side of wall through Muce hole

Stones (as weights)

MUCE

Socket for Wedge

EXIT

Fall Opening

Wedge

Lid (Hinged back)

Stones

Padlock

HOW THE FALLS OF A RABBIT TYPE WORKED (Cross Section)

Wall

ENTRANCE (Through hole in wall) ⇨

Muce passage

EXIT

Floor board of passage

Wedge In Position

Spindle

Counterweight

acclimatised to the exigencies of British winters. Only 3 per cent of the 132 sites shown are at heights over 1,000 feet (330m); 27 per cent are between 600 feet and 1,000 feet high (180–330m); 35 per cent between 200 feet and 600 feet (60–180m); and 36 per cent (almost all within the Ouse–Wharfe river valleys and plain) are below 200 feet.

Silver-grey rabbit. Source: *Cunilicus, The Practical Rabbit Keeper* (1880). Fur of the silver-greys, bred at Woodhall warren from the eighteenth century, was exported as far abroad as Russia and China. Extremely vulnerable to myxomatosis, the silver-greys at Woodhall were entirely wiped out on the advent of the disease there in 1955.
Courtesy of Professor John Sheail.

WARRENS OF THE TABULAR HILLS

The conglomeration of large, commercially oriented warrens which arose and held sway on the Tabular Hills (**fig 8.8.**) during the eighteenth and nineteenth centuries was, at over 6,000 acres (2,400ha), the largest warren complex in North Yorkshire. The limestone and grit geology of the hills was immensely suitable; although a few smaller warrens were on clay and sandstone. In the heyday of these warrens, many thousands of rabbits were slaughtered yearly, and skins were transported as far as Manchester and shipped from Scarborough to London.

CONCLUSION

The rabbit's history is that of an ecologically restless entity, because of its opportunism, its ecological plasticity and its fecundity. Many of the vicissitudes it has encountered have been connected with man.

Both the Black Death and the Civil War favoured the success of feral colonies because of diminished custody and husbandry in warren and field. With the Agricultural Revolution of the eighteenth century and new methods of land fertilisation and winter fodder, more land became arable and stock could be overwintered, so demand for farmed rabbits as food decreased. At the same time, changes in the game laws favoured the feral rabbit which soon assumed pest proportions.

By mid-Victorian times the great commercial warren complexes of Devon, East Anglia and Yorkshire were in decline. The few warrens active after World War II were dealt a final blow by myxomatosis in the early 1950s. Today's feral rabbit has apparently weathered that threat and, despite the recent dangers of haemorrhagial virus, rabbit numbers are increasing apace in many parts.

9

INDUSTRY

9.1   INTRODUCTION   GRAHAM LEE AND ROBERT WHITE

North Yorkshire is generally thought of as a rural agricultural county, but its pastoral landscapes disguise a significant history of industrial activity.

Exploitation of its geological resources in particular has left distinct scars and patterns in the landscape. Some extraction, for iron and jet for example, dates back to prehistoric times, while Magnesian Limestone from the Tadcaster area was quarried for use in York in the Roman period.

Until the medieval period, most extractive industries were fairly small in scale but since then they have expanded considerably, both in size and landscape impact, particularly as innovations in transport infrastructure, especially canals and railways, and developing capital markets stimulated greater economic activity.

Even before this, however, some products had had more than a local market: lead from the Dales was transported by road, river and sea to London and the south-east in the twelfth century; while Scarborough pottery had a much wider distribution, as befits a seaport.

Industrial activity, especially before the expansion of urban centres in the nineteenth century, was frequently a part-time activity — many coal and lead miners, for example, also had smallholdings which provided a valuable stimulus to the family income, and has left a distinct settlement and enclosure pattern.

Mining for metals has included lead, iron, copper and zinc; there are also extensive areas of coal mining (generally from shallow shafts rather than deep mines); quarries for building stone, sand, gravel and other aggregates; and alum shales for the early chemical industry.

In addition to the Magnesian Limestone, the Carboniferous age rocks of the Pennines, the Yoredale Series limestones and sandstones, and the Millstone Grits have been extensively exploited for building stone, roofing stone and flags, as well as for more specialist products such as bakestones, grindstones and millstones.

Brickmaking, too, has been locally important, especially in areas devoid of good building stone, while other clays have been used for pottery manufacture — Scarborough in the east and Burton in Lonsdale in the west being but two examples. Glass was made in Hutton and Rosedale in the North York Moors in the sixteenth century.

Other industries developed around the county's agricultural products: nearly every town and village in the medieval period had a tannery, while candle-making made use of another animal by-product — tallow. Malting and brewing was widespread, especially in the agriculturally rich Vale of York and the market towns on the edge of the Vale of Pickering, and still flourishes in Tadcaster and Masham.

In the medieval period, water power was extensively harnessed for corn milling and fulling (the process of removal of grease from and compacting of woollen cloth): as transport infrastructure improved in the eighteenth century, numerous water-mill sites in the Pennines were converted to cotton, woollen, flax and even silk manufacturing. Many of these conversions were short-lived as the increasing scale of mechanisation placed too heavy a demand on the water resources of small upland streams, especially in summer, and transport costs limited the opportunities for the use of steam power. In the early twentieth century, however, many mill sites found a new lease of life generating hydroelectricity. Other streams were dammed to provide water resources for the larger industrial centres of the West Riding, most dramatically in Nidderdale.

The county's maritime resources generated their own industries, particularly fishing but also shipbuilding. The timber vessels used by Captain Cook in his voyages of exploration in the eighteenth century were built at Whitby. Selby and York were important river ports in the medieval period, while other settlements such as Cawood, Tadcaster and Boroughbridge also had a shipping trade.

The Leeds–Liverpool Canal, built between 1770 and 1816, stimulated a wide range of industrial activity in the Craven area, but the canal system was overshadowed by the development of the railway network from the 1840s. This established York as a major nodal point and manufacturing town, and greatly strengthened the position of other towns well connected to the railway network, such as Northallerton.

The railway industry stifled the development of the road network and the coaching industry which had been stimulated by the development of turnpike roads from the eighteenth century; but this in turn declined in favour of the internal combustion engine and road transport in the second half of the twentieth century. These stimulated the development of new industrial patterns, particularly small-scale manufacturing, warehousing and retail activity on the outskirts of towns well connected to the road network.

The lack of heavy industry within the present county boundary is partly due to the loss of centres such as Middlesbrough, Eston and Skinningrove by the 1974 local government re-organisation. In the mid-nineteenth century these villages were transformed by the iron and steel industry, initially based on locally mined ironstone, and helped by easy access to the rail system and the development of Middlesbrough as a seaport.

The topics covered in this section are just a sample of the wide range of industrial activity recorded in North Yorkshire.

Important sources for the study of the county's industry, especially in the nineteenth century, are the first- and second-edition 6" and 25" to the Mile Ordnance Survey maps, and the numerous directories which list the activities and occupations practiced by the principal inhabitants of the county.

9.2   CORN MILLING IN NORTH-EAST YORKSHIRE
JOHN K HARRISON

MEDIEVAL MILL STEADINGS

Most water corn mill sites in north-east Yorkshire (**fig 9.1**) are medieval in origin and, therefore, considerably older than is generally assumed.

While it is true to say that, except in Richmondshire and the Vale of Pickering, claims that such-and-such a mill existed at the time of the Domesday Survey are generally unfounded, it is certainly true that mills appeared in very large numbers in Norman times. This was as a result of population expansion and the enforcement of milling soke (feudal rights and customs). Archaeological and documentary evidence of open fields, planned villages, churches and mills provide ample proof of expansion of ploughing in early medieval times. In terms of research, the most neglected of this evidence has been that concerning corn mills.

Feudal custom (soke) that all grain should be ground at the 'lord's mill', and not in querns or hand mills, ensured that almost every village settlement had its water mill. Exceptions will always be of interest. Indeed, in most of the larger townships of the rich margins around the moorland and dales (for instance Guisborough, Great Ayton, Helmsley and Pickering) there were two mills on separate sites. Even within some of the moorland dales (Farndale and Bilsdale) the spread of ploughing can be traced in the evolution of secondary 'nether mills' or 'low mills'.

Lastingham Mill (SE 729905). This tiny mill, beyond the green porch of the house, illustrates the type which existed in the North York Moors before the agricultural improvements of the late eighteenth and early nineteenth centuries.
© J K Harrison, 1987.

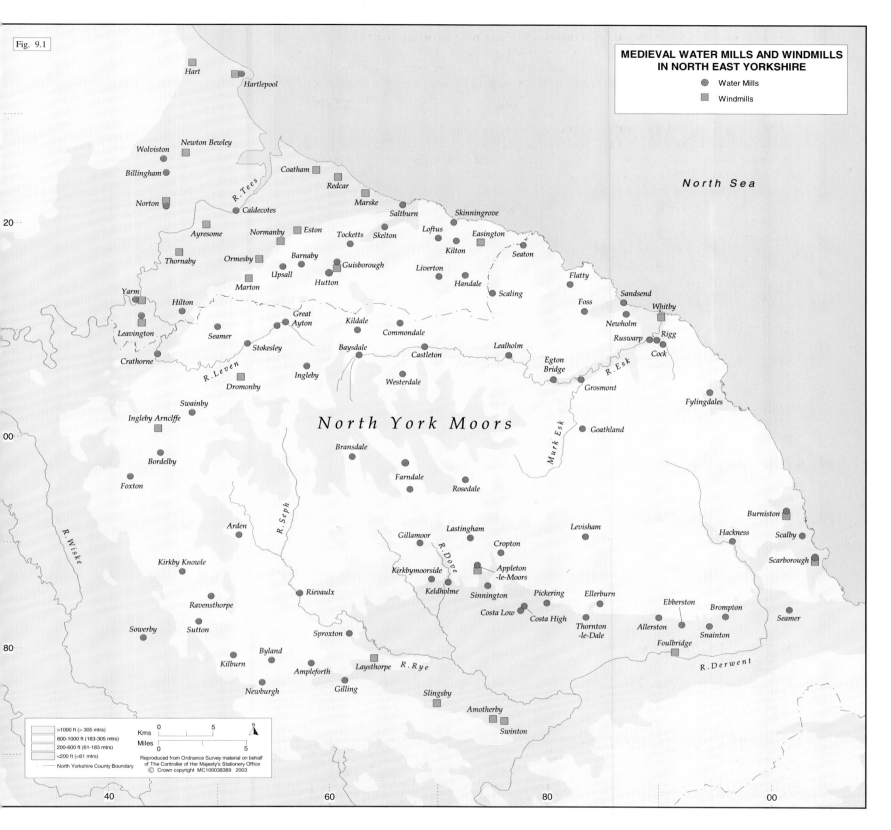

Fig. 9.1

MEDIEVAL WATER MILLS AND WINDMILLS IN NORTH EAST YORKSHIRE

● Water Mills
■ Windmills

North Sea

North York Moors

R. Tees
R. Leven
R. Wiske
R. Seph
R. Dove
R. Rye
R. Derwent
R. Esk
Murk Esk

Hart
Hartlepool
Wolviston
Newton Bewley
Billingham
Norton
Coatham
Redcar
Caldecotes
Marske
Saltburn
Skinningrove
Ayresome
Normanby
Eston
Tocketts
Skelton
Loftus
Easington
Kilton
Seaton
Thornaby
Ormesby
Barnaby
Guisborough
Liverton
Flatty
Sandsend
Upsall
Hutton
Handale
Scaling
Foss
Newholm
Whitby
Marton
Ruswarp
Rigg
Yarm
Hilton
Great Ayton
Kildale
Commondale
Lealholm
Cock
Leavington
Seamer
Egton Bridge
Crathorne
Stokesley
Baysdale
Castleton
Grosmont
Ingleby
Westerdale
Dromonby
Swainby
Fylingdales
Ingleby Arncliffe
Goathland
Bordelby
Bransdale
Foxton
Farndale
Rosedale
Arden
Burniston
Gillamoor
Lastingham
Levisham
Hackness
Scalby
Kirkby Knowle
Cropton
Scarborough
Kirkbymoorside
Appleton-le-Moors
Ravensthorpe
Rievaulx
Keldholme
Sinnington
Pickering
Ellerburn
Ebberston
Brompton
Sowerby
Sutton
Sproxton
Costa Low
Costa High
Thornton-le-Dale
Allerston
Snainton
Seamer
Byland
Foulbridge
Kilburn
Laysthorpe
Ampleforth
Slingsby
Newburgh
Gilling
Amotherby
Swinton

>1000 ft (> 305 mtrs)
600-1000 ft (183-305 mtrs)
200-600 ft (61-183 mtrs)
<200 ft (<61 mtrs)
North Yorkshire County Boundary

Kms 0 — 5
Miles 0 — 5

N

Reproduced from Ordnance Survey material on behalf of The Controller of Her Majesty's Stationery Office © Crown copyright MC100038389 2003

Beginning in the early twelfth century, the monasteries not only acquired many former manorial mills (for example, Whitby Abbey and Guisborough Priory), but in the case of Cistercians at Rievaulx and Byland, and at a number of nunneries (Handale, Rosedale and Arden), mills were built within the precincts themselves. These precinct mills served closed communities within the monasteries and did not operate under the manorial system.

References to windmills in north-east Yorkshire appear at the end of the twelfth century, and become more common during the thirteenth and fourteenth. Most were sited near settlements on the margins of the former marshlands of the Tees estuary where there was no suitable waterpower for milling, but there was also a scatter along the coast and in Ryedale. The precise sites are generally not known since they were built almost entirely of wood.

Ravenscar windmill (NZ 976006). Built in 1857 by William Hammond, owner of the Raven Hall estate, this was a very late attempt to provide milling capacity to the high grain growing fields of the north-east Yorkshire coast.
© J K Harrison.

The feudal underpinning of the manorial water and wind mills faltered with the poor climatic conditions and agricultural problems of the early fourteenth century, and ceased more or less completely with the Black Death of 1349. From this time, most corn mills were rented out or 'farmed'.

Also at this period, water-driven stocks for fulling (to finish by scouring and beating) woollen cloth were introduced. The earliest may have used surplus waterpower made redundant by the reduction in corn milling, and in some cases fulling stocks were set up on the same foundation as the older corn mills, particularly where there was ample water power.

LATER MILLS

The main distribution pattern of water-mill steadings was already well established by the end of the thirteenth century. Later centuries saw new layers of distribution overlaying the original medieval framework.

References to 'double mills', ie mills with two waterwheels each driving its own set of millstones with both sets being under a single roof, are found in sixteenth- and seventeenth-century records. As might be expected, these bigger mills were associated with prosperous settlements around the moorland margins. There were double mills, for example, at Hinderwell, Marske, Stokesley, Osmotherley, Thornton-le-Street, Newburgh and Pickering, but they were unknown within the dales of the North York Moors. Double mills were also found in the plains extending westward to the Pennines.

The fabric of almost all of these early mills was swept away as a result of industrialisation, urbanisation and agricultural development in the late eighteenth and early nineteenth centuries. Increased demand for wheat flour to feed the new urban populations of the coalmining towns of Sunderland and Newcastle, of London and even of Rotterdam, led to the coastwise shipping of flour, in place of grain.

Likewise, wheat flour was also carted to Leeds and the textile towns of the West Riding, where oats had formerly been the traditional fare. Further, the continued need for flour and meal for local consumption meant that mills in even the remotest dales were rebuilt and re-equipped during this period.

But, more importantly, new large water mills were built along the coast, for instance at Robin Hood's Bay, and along the navigable lower courses of the Tees at Leven Bridge and the Esk at Ruswarp. The working floors of these rebuilt and new-built mills were made taller and extra granary space was installed above the stone floors. There were more windows. Mills were equipped with at least one pair of French burr-stones which were specifically for milling good-quality flour. They were also equipped with silk reels for sifting the flour.

This same period saw the building of tower windmills. An early, small, stone-built tower survives at Ugthorpe, but most of these new towers, built around the estuary of the Tees, near Whitby and Scarborough, and around the southern and western margins of the moors, were very large, brick-built, and equipped with French burr millstones and flour screens. Indeed, they were equal in size and quality to the best Lincolnshire and East Riding windmills of the period. The survival rate of these tower mills has been very poor, and there are now remains only at Hawsker, Ravenscar, Kirkbymoorside and Brompton.

The survival rate among the steam mills which supplanted the older rural mills is also poor. These mills varied from modest ventures (Normanby, Whitby, Thirsk, etc) to the enormous mills at Yarm and Thornaby where foreign grain was imported, and the flour distributed by ship and later by railway.

From the early 1880s, roller milling began to replace milling with millstones, and the product, a white flour with no bran content, became increasingly popular. Under pressure from the railway transport of roller-milled white flour, most of the traditional rural mills of the region ceased flour milling by the end of the nineteenth century, and were either dismantled or kept only for grist milling for local farmers.

Though the survival rate for windmills and steam mills has been very poor, north-east Yorkshire possesses a fine heritage of well-crafted estate water-mills dating from, say, 1790 to 1855. These include the sensitively converted buildings at Easby, Ingleby Greenhow, Rosedale, Farndale Low and Stonegate; others which retain some machinery include Loftus, Kilton, Liverton, Troutsdale, Levisham, Costa High, Appleton, Lastingham, Farndale High, Raisdale, Rievaulx, Oldstead and Kepwick. There are splendid complete mills in Bransdale, Arden, Bilsdale Low, Thornton-le-Street and Hackness; and restored and operational mills at Danby and — most complete of all — Tocketts near Guisborough.

Corn Milling — Further Reading:
J K Harrison, *Eight Centuries of Milling in North East Yorkshire* (Helmsley: North York Moors National Park Authority, 2001).

9.3   THE WATER RACES OF THE NORTH YORK MOORS
ISABEL ANNE MCLEAN

Joseph Foord of Kirkbymoorside (1714-88) built some seventy miles (115km) of gravity-fed water races on the moors and limestone pastures of northern Ryedale. Engineered between the 1740s and 1760s, seven major races supplied the townships of Fadmoor, Gillamoor, Kirkbymoorside, Carlton, Nawton, Beadlam, Welburn, Skiplam, Pockley, Rievaulx and Old Byland (**fig 9.2**). Some functioned into the middle of the twentieth century, providing farms and villages with running water for agricultural and domestic use. Foord also built the longest mill leat (artificial water-channel) in North Yorkshire, serving Lastingham Mill. His sources were powerful springs and becks on the moors.

The water races were an early response to the need for agricultural reform in an area where farming practice was very backward. Delivering dependable water to livestock, the first water race reached Gillamoor, with a branch to Fadmoor, about 1747; ten years later this experimental race was extended to Kirkbymoorside. The enclosure of the common fields at Fadmoor and Gillamoor followed soon after, with Foord as surveyor.

In *The Rural Economy of Yorkshire* (1788), William Marshall recommended Foord's 'artificial rills' as both simple and effective.[1] John Tuke, writing for the National Board of Agriculture in 1800, said they formed a water-supply system which 'affords a wonderful accommodation to the occupier' and 'increases greatly the value of the property'.[2]

The table below gives the names of the main races, their dates of building and their lengths.

Between Helmsley and Kirkbymoorside, the rich soils of the Tabular Hills, lying to the south of the North York Moors, entirely lacked streams and wells. People and farmstock lived some 250 feet (75m) above the deeply cut valleys of the rivers Dove, Hodge, Riccal and Rye. The water was in the wrong place for these farming communities on the Duncombe Park estate.

Six of Foord's races, covering sixty-five square miles (170km²), brought them moorland water. In 1760, when Foord completed the Nawton race, the manor court recorded that farmers had 'contributed great sums of money to have water brought within ye manor (being in great scarcity in dry seasons) for themselves and cattle'.[3]

Gillamoor	c1747	5.5 miles (8.8km)
Kirkbymoorside (cont from Gillamoor)	c1757	3 miles (4.8km)
Carlton	1759	7 miles (11.5km)
Nawton	1760	9.4 miles (15.2km)
Pockley	1762	5.3 miles (8.5km)
Old Byland	1763	3.4 miles (5.4km)
Rievaulx	1768	12.7 miles (20.4km)
Starfits	nd	8.8 miles (14km)
Lastingham	nd	1.7 miles (2.7km)

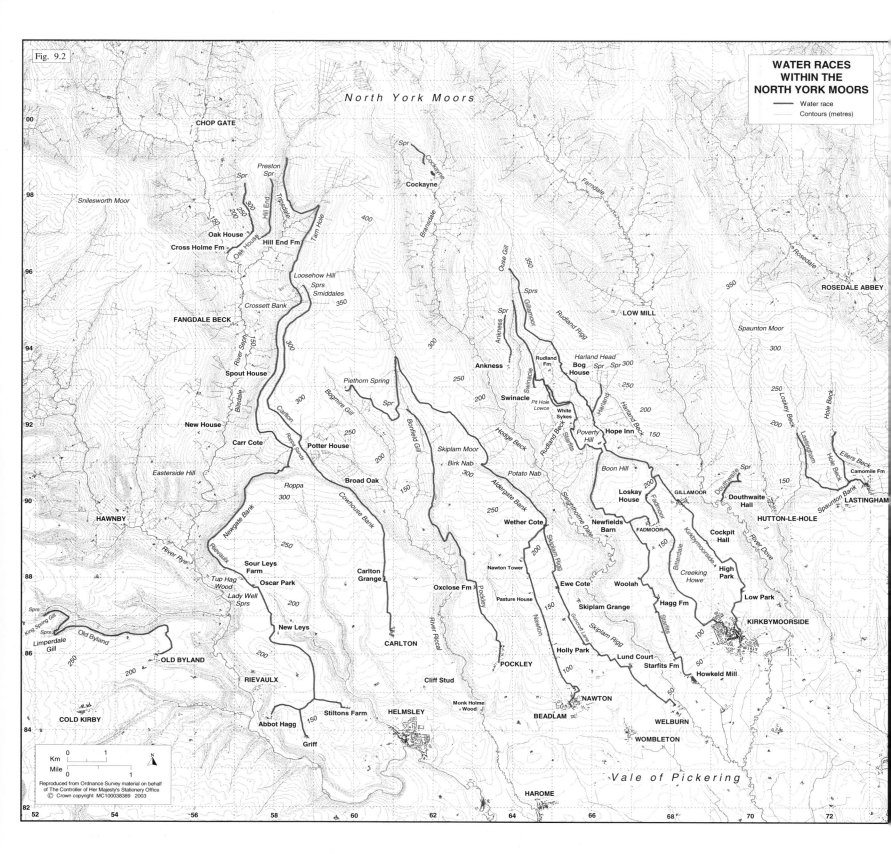

Fig. 9.2

WATER RACES WITHIN THE NORTH YORK MOORS

— Water race
— Contours (metres)

North York Moors

Vale of Pickering

Reproduced from Ordnance Survey material on behalf of The Controller of Her Majesty's Stationery Office
© Crown copyright MC100038389 2003

Old Byland's race, on Newburgh Priory land, ran entirely on pervious limestone. Here in 1760 a consortium of farmers begged Lord Fauconberg for a Foordian water race because 'the people begin to cry out for water in their springs and ponds'.[4]

Each race was financed by the landlord joining with his tenants to pay Foord's fee. Foord charged[5] £42 for Old Byland (three miles/5km), and somewhat under £100 for Kirkbymoorside (eight and a half miles/13.5km).[6] His main expense was paying men to dig and embank the cuts. He was his own surveyor and engineer.

The map (**9.2**) illustrates how the Duncombe estate races served three blocks of limestone uplands and every village on them. The system was obviously a direct consequence of the

top   The stone troughs which carried the Nawton race onto Bonfield Gill aqueduct. The gap was bridged by a wood trough.
© I A McLean.

above   A stone-flagged section of the Rievaulx race in Tarn Hole.
© I A McLean.

top right   The Nawton race curving round the head of a re-entrant on East Moors.
© I A McLean.

middle right   The Rievaulx race below Carr Cote, its degraded cut invaded by reeds.
© I A McLean.

bottom right   Bonfield Gill aqueduct. The Nawton race crossed the gap in a wooden trough and was then supplemented by a feeder race from the north before turning south (ie towards the camera).
© I A McLean.

geology and landforms of the area. Crucially, these enabled the races to contour south-east over many miles as continuous flow systems.

The moors tilt in a south-south-easterly direction from the main Cleveland watershed, as do the Tabular Hills and their north-facing escarpments. Having gained the foot of the escarpment, the races turned east or west to avoid the steep nabs and run across the scarp face. When they reached the scarp edge, they turned south to begin their function of watering farms *en route* to the villages at the bottom of the dip-slope. Foord's eye for the topography of this area was the key to his entire project.

To walkers on the moors today, the dry cuts of the old races afford the optical illusion of running uphill, so fine are the gradients. On the escarpment sections of the Starfits, Carlton, Nawton and Pockley races, the gradient is 1 in 317; on the first eight miles (13km) of the Rievaulx race, 1 in 400. The instrument Foord used (spirit level with telescope) is at Ryedale Folk Museum. It has been adapted for use with fixed elevations.

The races were vernacular works, brilliantly engineered. The cuts were made directly into the ground (no clay lining), and were generally two to three feet (0.6–0.9m) wide. They travelled through walls, under bridge-stones, and over becks and gullies (in wooden troughs termed 'aqueducts' on the six-inch Ordnance Survey maps of the 1850s). On the Nawton race a stone aqueduct still stands over Bonfield Gill Beck. Feeder races fed the main races; branches went to farms; large embankments carried races over hollows in the terrain. Off-lets and terminal spillways secured farms and streets against surges of storm water. Troughs and lift pumps served the villages.

As Foord said in 1760, for each race 'a proper person must be appointed … to look it over about once a month or when the water stops by stones or sods be tumbling in to throw them out'.[7] Manor courts appointed water surveyors to maintain the races against burrowing moles, cattle, carts, landslips, invasive reeds, silt and freeze-ups. Court verdicts attested to pollution caused by people keeping ducks, softening sheep skins and steeping thatching straw in the races.

In 1793 the Kirkbymoorside parliamentary enclosure award stipulated that the race should 'be preserved and kept in good condition' because 'it is of great consequence to the inhabitants'.[8]

For two centuries, villagers and farmers were entirely dependent on these races for water in their streets, houses, pubs, troughs, sheepwashes and steam engines (for threshing days). Old Byland race ran until 1938, Starfits until 1950, Carlton until 1959.

As Marshall said in 1788, Joseph Foord was 'a self-taught engineer of great ingenuity … to whom the country *owes* much.'

The Carlton water race on Cowhouse Bank c1950. Note the optical illusion that it runs uphill as it crosses the escarpment.
© Ryedale Folk Museum. Photo by R Hayes.

Water Races — Further Reading:
Isabel A McLean, *Water from the Moors: The Life and Work of Joseph Foord* (North York Moors National Park Authority, forthcoming).
J McDonnell (ed.), *A History of Helmsley, Rievaulx and District* (1963), 211-19.

9.4   COAL MINING   ROBERT F WHITE AND JOHN K HARRISON

Little is known about the early coal industry in North Yorkshire. There is archaeological evidence for coal being used in Roman York and it was burnt on military sites elsewhere in the county. There is no mention of coal in Yorkshire in the Domesday survey of 1086.

It is not until the thirteenth century that coal begins to be mentioned in contemporary documents, although the main coal mining areas in the region were in West Yorkshire and County Durham. The North Yorkshire industry, at least until the 1980s, was smaller in scale and did not trigger steam-based industrialisation. Locally, however, it was still very significant (**fig 9.3**).

The coal seams of the Pennines were the first to be exploited. Most were thin and variable in quality, but coal from the Tan Hill area was supplied to Richmond Castle in 1384 and was still being worked as late as 1934. Scores of grassed-over bell pits survive but, by the nineteenth century, mining was mainly from deeper shafts, with horse-power used to assist in pumping and winding operations. Open shafts are still a hazard to unwary walkers.

During the eighteenth and nineteenth centuries, much coal from this area was converted in primitive beehive ovens into coke, locally known as 'cinders', for use in lead smelting. Coke was lighter, cheaper to transport and had fewer impurities to affect the quality of the lead. An account book as early as 1682 shows a mining agent buying 'cinders' from Tan Hill for use at Old Gang. Most coal was carried by packhorse, but the coal mines at Tan Hill were one reason for the creation of the turnpike road between Reeth and what is now the A66 in 1770.

The coal mines on Preston, Grinton and Redmire Moors were more extensive, with spoil heaps from shallow bell pits scattered over some two and half square miles (6.5km²). Coal mining flourished as chimneys replaced firehoods in domestic buildings from the sixteenth century. Lead was also worked here, but the lead spoil heaps follow the line of the veins, and contain more limestone and traces of minerals than the scattered, grassed-over, shaley coal tips. Winding was normally with a jack-roller, a winch similar to those used in wells. There were few buildings so there are few other above-ground remains.

As with other minerals, the large monastic institutions were early exploiters of coal. The canons of Bolton were working coal in 1311, probably on Burnsall and Thorpe Moor. Jervaulx Abbey paid twenty quarters (1 quarter = 28lb) of coal a year for right of way through Mashamshire, and eight marks (roughly 66p in modern currency) for mining rights in Colsterdale. Byland Abbey mined coal in Nidderdale.

The topography of the Yorkshire Dales means that many coal seams outcrop at the surface. Even when the coal was of poor quality and unsuitable for domestic use, it was often worked for burning in limekilns. Several of the smaller mines were reopened in 1926 during the National Strike.

Some of the more visible remains of coal mining in the Yorkshire Dales can be found near Threshfield. These include the base for a steam winding-engine and, unusually for the Dales, a washery built in the late nineteenth century to improve the quality of the coal. This was still a small-scale enterprise compared with the main coal mining areas of the county — the 1871 census for example only records eight colliers at Threshfield. The route of a narrow-gauge tramway which linked the mine with limekilns at Skyrethorns quarry can still be traced.

To the west of the Craven Faults, which mark the western edge of the Yorkshire Dales, the coal seams of the Bentham Grit Group were worked around Bentham and Ingleton by shallow shafts about 100-200 feet (30-60m) deep from the early seventeenth century. Production here effectively stopped at the beginning of the twentieth century, but in 1913 the deep New Ingleton Pit was sunk. This worked four thick seams until 1936, although the mine site is now very difficult to identify.

The moorland coal mines of north-east Yorkshire, on the other hand, were modest ventures with shallow pits and little mechanisation. J W Ord described the moor coal as of '… slatey, inferior description … unconnected with any important coal band'. Very thin seams were dug, possibly on a seasonal basis. For example, the seam at Wethercote, on the west side of Bilsdale, was only forty to fifty inches (102-127cm) thick and that on Rudland Rigg was no more than fifty-eight inches (148cm).

The earliest surviving agreement (1715) for coal mining within the North York Moors allowed three new shafts to open at Ankness to the west of Farndale, in return for an annual rental of £100 to the Feversham estate. The estate could collect forty chaldrons (100 tons) of coal from the pithead for its own use. The description as 'new' pits shows that this was not the earliest mining at Ankness.

In 1780 an agreement was signed for rights to take coal on Rudland Rigg, and this would become the most extensively and destructively mined district in the region. By the mid-eighteenth century there was a scatter of shafts and drifts across a wide belt of moorland extending from Wethercote in the south-west to Rosedale Head in the north-east.

However, the working lives of these pits, most of them on the Feversham estate around Bransdale, Farndale and Bilsdale, were already coming to an end. In 1790 the Rudland field was extended into a new area called Upper Rudland where, however, the seam turned out to be uneven and less satisfactory. Coal supply was finite. It was reported in 1791 that at Blakey the seam was 'very near done', while at Carr Cote 'Widow Holmes has given up'. A year later a miner was given a lease to sink pits to look for coal left behind in earlier workings, and also that coal taken from the Sled Shoe colliery was of 'soft, mucky quality'.

The peak working period at a second and more compact colliery around Eskdale, particularly around Danby, Clitherbeck and extending to Fryup Dale Head, was roughly contemporary with that of the Feversham estate mines but working lasted longer. Though the seam was up to 112 inches (285cm) thick, the disadvantage was that it lay at the much greater depths of up to 150 feet (46m) and extraction was correspondingly more expensive.

In 1749 the Danby estate made a mining agreement for coals in the Clitherbeck Valley, and in 1753 a survey valued the Fryup Head colliery, for instance, at £20. In 1808 the Danby coals were noted as '… sufficient for the general use of the inhabitants'. In 1817 Young stated that '… the Danby pits employ about 40 to 50 people who may furnish daily an average from 200 to 300 bushels or upwards, sold at the pit for 4d per bushel' (a bushel was a measurement of volume equivalent to 2,219.6 modern cubic inches), but by 1840 there was evidence of decline when employment was down to about thirty-five men. In 1846, Ord reported that the use of Castleton coals had resulted in heavy losses at the Loftus alum works. As late as

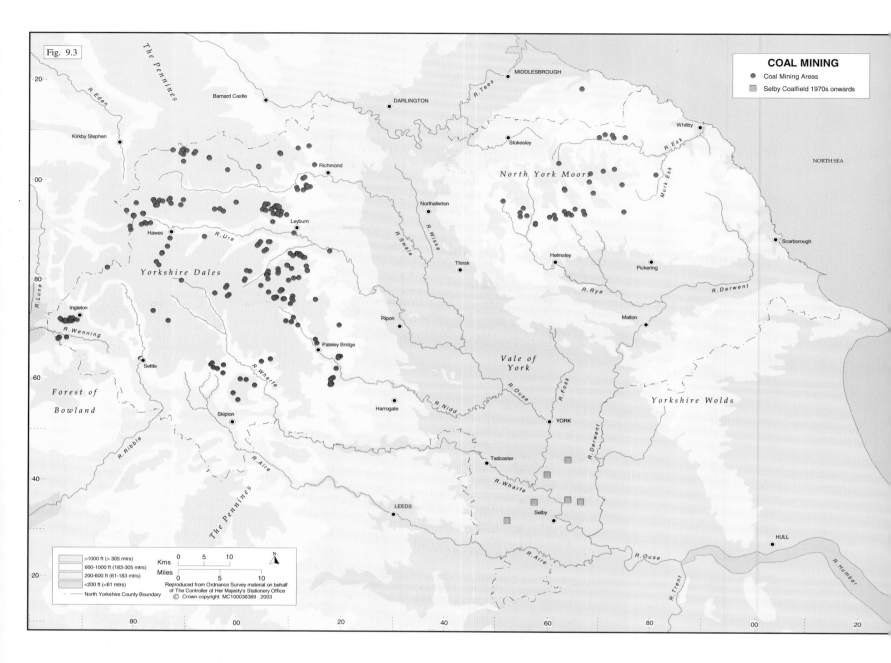

Fig. 9.3

COAL MINING
● Coal Mining Areas
▪ Selby Coalfield 1970s onwards

>1000 ft (> 305 mtrs)
600-1000 ft (183-305 mtrs)
200-600 ft (61-183 mtrs)
<200 ft (<61 mtrs)
North Yorkshire County Boundary

Kms
Miles

Reproduced from Ordnance Survey material on behalf
of The Controller of Her Majesty's Stationery Office
© Crown copyright MC100038389 2003

1890 queues of carts were still reported at Poverty Hill but, conversely, in 1893 Kelly reported that the pit had '... not been worked for a number of years'.

In both coalfields, drainage was by gravity; there is no evidence that pumping engines were used. In the Feversham estate pits, the coal was raised to the surface by hand using 'rowlers' (jack rolls) or 'turn gear' (windlass), while the much deeper (and larger, ten feet by six feet/ 3m x 2m) shafts in the Danby colliery were wound by horse gin.

The largest concentration of pits was on Rudland Rigg (over 600 pits, although not all worked at the same time), working at up to forty feet (12m) from the surface. These were not bell pits, but were spaced at 130-200 feet (40-60m) apart, and each shaft was linked to its neighbours by twin passages providing access to the pillar-and-bord workings. Pillar-and-bord was a method of working coal seams which involved the driving of access roads through the seams and leaving supporting pillars of coal. The amount of waste surrounding each shaft head indicates that, once in the seam, the bulk of the waste from the 230 inch (575cm) high workings was back-stowed. When raised to the surface, the coal was carried away from the workings in carts on tracks, some known by name (eg 'Coal Road' at Harland Colliery and 'Colliers Road' at Carr Cote in Bilsdale). The coal was used for lime-burning in the Tabular Hills and for domestic use in the townships.

The evidence of the former industry is clear, each abandoned shaft visible in the form of a hollow surrounded by a ring of waste, although the extracted sandstone from the thick bed through which the shafts were sunk is normally missing. The bulk of the waste has collapsed inwards and into the shaft; whether this was a result of deliberate back-filling is not clear,

Piethorne, Tripsdale (SE 605923). The collapsed shafts of this small, eighteenth-century colliery have provided protection which has allowed trees to grow in many.
© J K Harrison, 1994.

Rudland Rigg coal pits: shallow early coal pits on the North York Moors between Farndale and Bransdale.
© B E Vyner, 94/1.

Coal Mining — Further Reading:

S Gould and I Ayris, *Colliery landscapes: an aerial survey of the deep mined coal industry in England* (London: English Heritage, 1995).

A Harris, The Ingleton Coalfield, *Industrial Archaeology* 5 (4) (1968), 313-26.

J S Owen, The Moor Coals of North Yorkshire: The Danby area, *Cleveland and Teesside Local History Society* 6 (1969).

J S Owen, The Moor Coals of North Yorkshire: The Farndale and Bransdale area, *Cleveland and Teesside Local History Society* 10 (1970).

A H Whitaker, Coal mining in Bransdale and Farndale in the 18th century, *Ryedale Historian* 4 (1969), 55-62.

although in 1821 and 1854 individuals were fined for leaving pits open. Elsewhere, just one or two shafts in the Danby colliery were capped with sandstone blocks.

Also evident are the tracks leading away from the pits and still readily traced on aerial photographs. Ruins of dwellings remain in Clitherbeck dale and some at Danby End are still in use. There are sites of mine lodgings at Baysdale Head, Blakey Rigg and High Hamer. The last operation was in 1926 at Harland (due to the coal miners' strike).

There is also documentary evidence for slightly later coal-workings at Coxwold (1804) and Birdforth (1796-98). In 1796 'coals for the engine fire' were included in the production figures, and references to both the 'little gin' and the 'great gin' show that at Birdforth there was a greater degree of capitalisation, but working was, nevertheless, short-lived.

THE SELBY COALFIELD

In the late 1970s and 1980s the Selby Coalfield was developed, to work the up to eleven feet (3.3m) thick Barnsley seam in a 100 square mile (259km^2) area between York and Selby. Coal handling was concentrated at Gascoigne Wood drift mine. Five satellite mines were mainly for the transport of men and materials to the coal face. This was the largest capital project ever undertaken in the British coal industry.

North Yorkshire has a rich heritage of iron-working, particularly north-east Yorkshire where ironstone was still being mined as late as 1965 (**fig 9.4**). The ores derive from a series of ironstone seams of varying thicknesses. In addition, there are bog ores, ie iron minerals taken into solution by ground water and redeposited in boggy or slow-flowing waters. The latter were probably the main source of iron in the Iron Age (600 BC–AD 70).

There were two methods of production. The 'direct' or bloomery process was the technology used from the Iron Age to the medieval period. In this process, iron ore was smelted (reduced) directly to a malleable iron bloom. This had to be subsequently forged to a billet, and ultimately smithed into artefacts. The product of the bloomery process could either be ferritic iron (no alloying elements), phosphoric iron (iron containing up to about one per cent phosphorus) and steels (iron alloyed with up to about 0.8 per cent carbon).

In the second production method, the ore was smelted to cast iron (iron containing about four per cent carbon), which had to be refined to a malleable iron. This 'indirect' process normally utilised a blast furnace.

Evidence for Iron Age ironworking is present at Levisham Moor, where smelting slag was recovered from ditches dated to the late Iron Age or first century AD.[1] The furnace found near this location was assumed to be of Iron Age date, but some doubt must be placed on this interpretation and it is more likely to be medieval. The evidence from Roxby Moor[2] was interpreted as iron smelting but analysis did not confirm this, and smithing is more likely.[3] Spratt published a series of analyses of slags recovered from cairnfields and assumed to be Iron Age.[4] These show manganese contents ranging from 0.5–2.1 per cent, indicating that some of the slags (those with higher MnO values) derived from iron smelting.

There is no evidence for iron smelting in the Roman period. Smelting slags have recently been found close to Beadlam Villa, but they are unstratified.[5] Evidence for Anglian/Viking iron smelting is evidenced by place-names, eg Smiddales in Bilsdale. It should be noted that excavations at Fishergate[6] and Coppergate[7] in York demonstrate extensive and sophisticated use of iron and steel. However, metallurgical and elemental analyses were unable to identify the sources of the raw stock iron used.[8]

Hayes published a list of slag-heap sites for the North York Moors, but the vast majority lack any dating evidence.[9] Within the moors the fieldname 'Cinderfield(s)' is strongly indicative of iron-smelting sites. Other names such as 'Black' (eg Black Intake) may also be associated with slag heaps.

It is probable that the majority of slag heaps date from the medieval period when ironworking was widespread, but this remains to be proven. The earliest documentary references to ironstone mining and smelting after Domesday relate to various religious houses, including Fountains Abbey (Nidderdale) and Bylands Abbey (Vale of Pickering), Jervaulx (Wensleydale), Easby (Garsdale) and Guisborough Priory (Eskdale/Glaisdale).

By 1284, Knaresborough was the centre of an active iron industry, although it appears to have been relatively short-lived — by the fourteenth century there are references to trade in ironstone but not smelting. Other documented mining or processing locations include Pickering Forest (Levisham), Scarborough (Forge Valley), Richmondshire (with forges recorded at Catterick) and Skipton Chase. Foreign competition, in the form of imports from Spain and Sweden, are known from the early to mid-fourteenth century.

Research on the iron industry of Rievaulx Abbey has led to the excavation of one furnace dated to the late fourteenth century.[10] This was a slag-tapping shaft furnace built of clay.

Iron smelting has been identified at two monastic grange sites in Bilsdale, the Grange and Laskill.[11] The latter is of major significance since geophysics shows the furnace to be stone-built, square in plan (*circa* thirteen feet (4m) by thirteen feet) and probably water-powered. This furnace was recorded in the dissolution documents of Rievaulx Abbey, which also had a forge at Rievaulx.[12] Subsequently, in about 1570, the earl of Rutland had the Rievaulx furnace rebuilt, probably utilising the refectory building as the charcoal store and constructing more forges. The Rievaulx furnace ceased operation in the mid to late seventeenth century. Another early blast furnace was built in Rosedale.

There was a resurgence of ironworking activity in the nineteenth century in north-east Yorkshire and Cleveland when, in all, some eighty mines were sunk to exploit the ironstone seams across an area of some fifty-five square miles ($140 km^2$). Production from mining lasted from 1851 to 1965 (Skelton), at times producing forty per cent of the British total. In 1883, the year of maximum production, 6,756,000 tons of ironstone were dug.

The mines were mainly in three groups, with the largest exploiting the Cleveland Main Seam to the north of the moors. The second group, in the Esk and Murk Esk dales, exploited the Pecten and Avicula seams; with a third, smaller, group around Rosedale. The latter exploited the low-grade Top Seam but also two high-grade localised deposits of magnetite (forty-five per cent iron).

The Main Seam mines extended along the coast from Kettleness to Huntcliff and under the northern moors as far as Battersby, and it was this seam which mainly determined the extent of the mining field by the end of the nineteenth century. At its deepest point, near Skelton, it is some 270 feet (82m) below sea-level. At the Eston outlier, the Main Seam was eleven feet (3.35m) thick (in a few pockets up to eighteen feet/5.5m) and was mined along with the Pecten Seam below. Over a wide area, however, field thickness was eight feet (2.45m). The quality was low (approximately thirty-three per cent) but this disadvantage was offset by its availability in very large quantities.

In the early years, some ironstone was transported by boat from Whitby, Port Mulgrave, Staithes and Skinningrove to blast furnaces on the Tyne. Later, the bulk was transported by standard-gauge railways to major groups of ironworks located along the banks of the Tees — blast furnaces at Grangetown, South Bank and in the Ironmasters' District in Middlesbrough.

The bulk of the ironstone was transported away from the mine sites in the raw state to be processed at blast furnace plants. However, in a few cases the stone was calcined (burned at low temperature using approximately 1 ton of coal to 25 tons of ironstone) at the mine site. This converted low-iron carbonates into richer oxides, removed some of the sulphur and reduced moisture content. The enriched ore was cheaper to transport, an important consideration at the Rosedale mines where the railway included the lengthy Ingleby Incline. At Warren Moor and one or two exploratory sites, the stone was calcined in clamps. At Rosedale, Swainby and Wreckhills the stone was calcined in stone-built kilns, and in cylindrical kilns encased in riveted iron plates at Liverton.

In the early, heady days of the industry it was common for ironstone mining leases to include a clause that blast furnaces be built near the mines. Most such plans were aborted but blast furnaces were built within the moors at Wreckhills (blown in in 1858), Beck Hole (1860), Grosmont (1863), Glaisdale (1865) and Skinningrove (1872). The cost of transporting metallurgical coke from the Durham coalfield precluded large-scale development on these isolated rural sites and, except at Skinningrove, the plants remained small and did not expand into the production of wrought iron or steel.

The major growth of the 1860s and 1870s was concentrated on former marshland sites along the banks of the Tees, utilising the railways which converged from south-west Durham and North Yorkshire.[13] These were very large plants, specifically designed to smelt the low-grade Cleveland ironstone by using the biggest blast furnaces yet seen, equipped with heavy handling equipment. For a short period in the 1870s this concentration of ironworks on the banks of the Tees became the biggest iron-producing district in the world, the main products

Margrove Park, Skelton (NZ 655158). A terrace settlement built by the Stanghow Iron Company to serve ironstone mines in the early 1870s disrupted the former rural setting.
© J K Harrison, 1995.

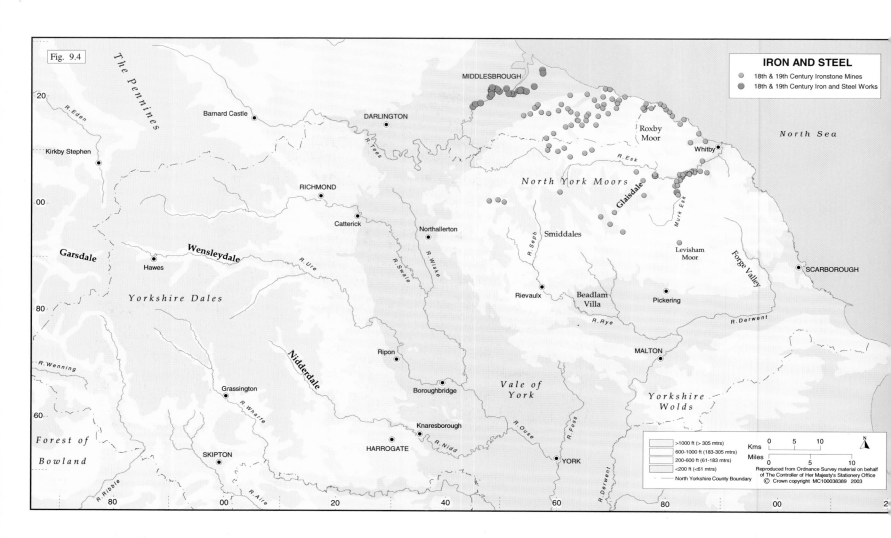

IRON AND STEEL

○ 18th & 19th Century Ironstone Mines
● 18th & 19th Century Iron and Steel Works

>1000 ft (> 305 mtrs)
600-1000 ft (183-305 mtrs)
200-600 ft (61-183 mtrs)
<200 ft (<61 mtrs)
North Yorkshire County Boundary

Reproduced from Ordnance Survey material on behalf
of The Controller of Her Majesty's Stationery Office
© Crown copyright MC100038389 2003

This view from the top of the shale tip at Kilton ironstone mine, which worked from 1875 to 1963, shows the surviving winding engine house to the left of the picture and the agricultural landscape beyond.
© J K Harrison, 1995.

being pig iron (unrefined cast iron as first produced from the furnace), and wrought iron rails and plates. Puddling furnaces, which converted cast iron to wrought iron, were located in Stockton and Middlesbrough.

Relics of heavy industry do not readily lend themselves to conservation and today there is little enough to remind us of the former scale of modern ironstone-working and ironmaking.

right   Huntcliff fan house, Brotton (NZ 697215). The purpose of this Guibal fan was to pull foul air out of the extensive ironstone workings under the Warsett Hill in the background of the picture.
© J K Harriwon, 1989.

bottom right   South Gare, Redcar (NZ 556271). This totally man-made landscape resulted from dumping slag from the innumerable blast furnaces of the Cleveland iron-making district into the mouth of the River Tees during the second half of the nineteenth century. The coke-making plant of the Redcar blast furnace can be seen in the background.
© J K Harrison, 1998.

Iron and Steel — Further Reading:

S K Chapman, *Gazetteer of Cleveland Ironstone Mines*, Langbaurgh Museums Service, research report no 1, 1975.

P Crew, The experimental production of prehistoric bar iron, *Journal Historical Metallurgy Society* 25 (1) (1991), 21-36.

J K Harrison, A Medieval Bloomery at Tarn Hole in Bilsdale in the North York Moors; a re-assessment of an excavation of the 1970s, *Cleveland Industrial Archaeologist* 26 (2000), 19-24.

C A Hempstead (ed), *Cleveland Iron and Steel, Background and Nineteenth Century History* (London: British Steel, 1979).

G S Lamplugh, *Special Reports on the Mineral Resources of Great Britain, XII: Bedded ores of the Lias, Oolites and later formations in England.* Memoirs of the Geological Society of Great Britain (London: HMSO, 1920).

J G McDonnell, Ore to Artefact — A study of early Ironworking Technology, *Science and Archaeology* (Glasgow: BAR British Series 196, 1987), 193-207.

J S Owen, *Cleveland Ironstone* (The Cleveland Industrial Archaeology Society and the North York Moors National Park Authority, 1998).

D H Rayner and J E Hemingway, *The Geology and Mineral Resources of Yorkshire* (Yorkshire Geological Society, 1974), 161-223.

T E Rounthwaite, Cleveland Ironstone Mining Branches, *The Railway Observer*, 1957, 1960, 1962.

R F Tylecote, *The Prehistory of Metallurgy in the British Isles* (London: Institute of Metals, 1986).

Quarrying and mining operations have left fascinating relics (including waggonways, rutways, drift entrances and exposed workings) in the foreshore and cliffs between Staithes and the ruined harbour walls at Port Mulgrave.

Ventilation fan houses survive at Skelton Shaft, Huntcliff and Lazenby Bank. The most interesting pit heads survive at Skelton Park, Kilton, Loftus (now the Tom Leonard Museum), Warren Moor and Lounsdale. Relics of calcining kilns survive at Swainby, Wreckhills and, most importantly, at both East and West Side workings in Rosedale.

Foundations remain of the blast furnace plants at Grosmont, Glaisdale and Wreckhills. Along the Tees, all sites are cleared, but there are two furnace 'bears' (a mass of cinder which forms on a blastfurnace hearth) at the Newport Ironworks site in the Ironmasters' District in Middlesbrough.

Sections of railway track-bed remain around Rosedale and Eston Nab, in Skinningrove and the Murk Esk valleys, and along the line of the Cleveland Extension Mineral (Paddy Waddell's) Railway from Kilton to Glaisdale which was never completed.

Mineral-working has had a major effect on the landscape of the Yorkshire Pennines (**fig 9.5**). The area forms part of the Northern Pennine Orefield described by Dunham and Wilson. This survey gives a detailed description of the geology, describes the principal veins and gives brief details of the main workings.[1]

The veins where lead ore is found were formed millions of years ago when hot saline liquids forced their way up through faults and fissures in the Carboniferous rocks. As these liquids cooled they formed mineral veins.

Lead was the most important mineral but, for a brief period in the mid-eighteenth century, copper ores were worked around Middleton Tyas (NZ230055) and calamine (zinc) ore was mined above Malham (SD880645).

The principal lead ore (galena — lead sulphide) is associated with other minerals known as gangue minerals, particularly barytes (barium sulphate, although rarely in workable quantities), witherite (barium carbonate), calcite (calcium carbonate) and fluorspar (calcium fluoride). Most galena has been found either as distinct 'ribs' running through a vein or mixed with the gangue minerals. Mineralisation could vary considerably over short distances, which made lead mining a highly speculative venture.

It is not known when these minerals were first exploited. A pre-Roman origin is likely as traces of copper ores have been found on some excavated sites, but the first firm evidence for organised metal production relates to a Roman industry with three, possibly five, lead ingots with Roman inscriptions being recorded. However, no field evidence for Roman or pre-Roman workings has been found.

Mining flourished during the medieval period, with large quantities of lead being needed for roofing, plumbing and glazing. Except for brief depressions, for example that caused by lead from monastery roofs entering the market after the Dissolution of the Monasteries, mining grew fairly steadily until the eighteenth century. It then expanded rapidly as new capital was invested in what had been an industry dominated by small-scale producers.

The recorded output of lead concentrates in Yorkshire between 1845 and 1938 was 330,118 tons, which suggests that the total output may have been in the order of 750,000 tons.[2] Output from the Yorkshire lead mines peaked at 12,406 tons of ore in 1857, which was then nearly thirteen per cent of national output.[3] It then fell steadily due to rising costs, the exhaustion of easily worked, high-grade deposits and a rise in cheaper imports, particularly from Spain and North America. Many mines closed in the 1870s and 1880s, although some larger mines struggled on into the twentieth century. Closure resulted in massive unemployment and migration from the mining areas. Some lead has since been produced during the working of barytes and fluorspar, but neither of these minerals is worked today.

MINING TECHNIQUES

Apart from collection of redeposited material from streams, most early mining would have concentrated on veins outcropping at or near the surface which were either visible in rock exposures or identified by the presence of metal-tolerant plants known as metallophytes.

Once a vein had been discovered, it could be worked by digging small pits, open-cast trenches and shallow shafts sunk along its line. Shallow shafts, which were rarely more than 100 feet (30m) deep, are often visible as lines of discrete circular mounds of spoil, with central depressions where the shaft has collapsed, sometimes at regular intervals along the vein. Shaft mounds are the most commonly recorded archaeological feature in the Yorkshire Dales.

As pumping and lifting technology developed in the post-medieval period, deep shafts were also used for extraction. These can be recognised by their much larger spoil heaps, and the remains of pumping and winding structures. Some of the best examples can be found on Grassington Moor.

Two other extraction techniques were widely used in the post-medieval period where the local topography permitted.

Hushing was a form of open-cast working, mainly used where the veins were cut by valleys. Water was collected in reservoirs above the area to be worked. These were then breached to release a torrent of water which would erode the soil and vegetation to expose the underlying rock and any veins. It is likely that veins found by hushing were mainly worked by open-cast methods, with hushing being used to flush away debris. Hushing resulted in huge quantities of material being transferred into the river systems. Very extensive hushes can be seen in Arkengarthdale and Gunnerside Gill.

As mines increased in depth, so did drainage and haulage problems which, from the late seventeenth century onwards, were largely solved by investment. The fortuitous position of many veins in relation to the valleys meant that large areas could be drained by driving adits, commonly known as levels, into the hillside below mining grounds. Adits were also dug beneath known veins and through dead ground to intersect with veins which were too deep to be easily worked from the surface.

Early levels, especially drainage levels, tend to be of small section. Most levels, however, were horse levels, normally some six feet (2m) high and four and half feet (1.4m) wide, large enough for a horse to draw a train of waggons along a tramway. This provided efficient haulage and resulted in the development of large dressing floors at the mouths of principal levels. Vast quantities of spoil were brought out through some levels, perhaps best seen in the extensive spoil heaps below Old Moulds Level (NY996026), the 1,600 feet (500m) long spoil heap from Hard Level in Old Gang Gill (NY971007), and the last lead mines to work in the area — Stang level (NZ009058) and Faggergill (NY989069).

Water was an important resource as well as a problem for the industry. The hillsides above the main mining areas are scored with leats (artificial water-channels) and dams. Water provided motive power for winding, pumping, dressing and smelting, for ventilation and a medium for dressing ore. The most complex water-management system is on Grassington Moor (SE030667) where the total length of the principal leats is over seven miles (11km), with falls as little as 1 in 680.

DRESSING

The material which left the mine was a mixture of ore, rock, clay and other vein minerals. This had to be 'dressed' or refined to separate out the ore before it could be smelted.

In early mines, breaking was done by hand and ore-rich material was washed in a controlled flow of water. The heavy lead ore was less mobile than other rock and could easily be collected. Dressing was very labour-intensive and was usually done close to the mine.

From c1800, larger mines began to mechanise their dressing operations using waterwheel-powered roller crushers to break the ore-rich material into a uniform size, and then washing the graded material through sieves in banks of dolly tubs and hotching tubs, and buddles (simple machines used to separate ore from rock). The waste water from these was channelled to settling tanks to maximise the retrieval of ore.

All dressing floors left spreads of finely crushed material on which little or nothing will grow. Mechanised dressing floors typically have a row of storage pits known as bouse teams, a wheel pit and a series of terraces on which the washing machinery stood.

SMELTING

The dressed ore was converted into metal by smelting. During the medieval period, lead ore was smelted in 'bales', simple bonfire-like furnaces. These were sited in relatively exposed hillside positions. They used large quantities of wood for fuel and were probably responsible for much deforestation. Over eighty bale sites have been recognised by the discovery of small quantities of slag or occasionally as place-names.

Ore-hearth smelting was introduced in the late sixteenth century. The ore-hearth, a small blast furnace with waterwheel-driven bellows, initially used mainly chop-wood (kiln-dried wood, also known as white coal) for fuel but later, probably due to increasing scarcity and rising cost of chop-wood, peat and coke. The largest peat store, at Old Gang, is 400 feet (120m) long. Vast quantities of peat must have been cut for use in the smelting industry, but the landscape and ecological implications of this have not yet been examined.

Early mills just had one hearth, but by the late nineteenth century many mills had four hearths. Molten lead flowed from the ore hearths into separate containers known as sumpter pots, from where it could be ladled or tapped into moulds or pigs. The ore hearths also produced large quantities of slag. This still contained metal and could be re-smelted on a slag hearth, often using coke as the principal fuel. More than eighty smelt mills are known from documents but only thirteen still have extensive above-ground remains.

In early smelt mills the gases produced during smelting escaped through vertical chimneys but, in the late eighteenth century, ground-level flues were introduced. Particles of lead oxides and sulphates settled on the sides of these flues, and could be collected and resmelted.

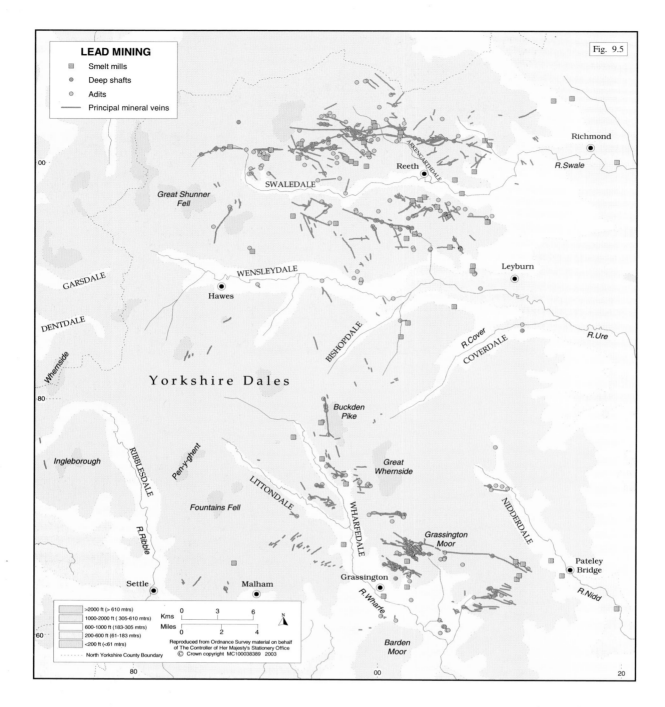

LEAD MINING
- ▫ Smelt mills
- ● Deep shafts
- ● Adits
- — Principal mineral veins

Fig. 9.5

Richmond

R.Swale

Reeth

SWALEDALE

*Great Shunner
Fell*

ARKENGARTHDALE

Leyburn

WENSLEYDALE

GARSDALE

Hawes

DENTDALE

BISHOPDALE

R.Cover

R.Ure

COVERDALE

Whernside

Yorkshire Dales

*Buckden
Pike*

Ingleborough

RIBBLESDALE

Pen-y-ghent

*Great
Whernside*

LITTONDALE

NIDDERDALE

Fountains Fell

WHARFEDALE

*Grassington
Moor*

Pateley
Bridge

R.Ribble

Grassington

R.Wharfe

R.Nidd

Settle

Malham

*Barden
Moor*

- ▨ >2000 ft (> 610 mtrs)
- ▨ 1000-2000 ft (305-610 mtrs)
- ▨ 600-1000 ft (183-305 mtrs)
- ▨ 200-600 ft (61-183 mtrs)
- ▨ <200 ft (<61 mtrs)
- --- North Yorkshire County Boundary

Kms 0 3 6
Miles 0 2 4

N

Reproduced from Ordnance Survey material on behalf
of The Controller of Her Majesty's Stationery Office
© Crown copyright MC100038389 2003

THE LANDSCAPE

The most obvious features of the industry are the large gorge-like hushes and the numerous spoil heaps at the entrances to the mines, many yet to be colonised by vegetation. Less obviously industrial are the remains of the dense network of footpaths, bridleways and roads which provided access to the mines, smelt mills and watercourses, and enabled lead to be taken to market.

Mining was a man's occupation, but some women and children worked on the dressing floors. They rarely lived close to the mines, but instead lived in the villages and hamlets in the main valleys, or in isolated cottages on the moorland fringe. Contemporary reports often say that miners boosted their incomes by having a few acres of land. Here they would keep a couple of cows and grow hay for the winter. Many also had vegetable gardens where they grew potatoes and cabbages, and kept a few hens and perhaps a pig.

After a century of decay and reclamation of building materials, the remains of the industry are now of economic benefit to the local community through heritage tourism. Since 1985 the Yorkshire Dales National Park Authority has carried out programmes of consolidation and interpretation at several leadmining sites, and laid out a leadmining trail on Grassington Moor.

Lead — Further Reading:

R Burt, P Waite, M Atkinson and R Burnley, *The Yorkshire Mineral Statistics 1845-1913* (Exeter: Department of Economic History, University of Exeter, 1982).

R T Clough, *The Lead Smelting Mills of the Yorkshire Dales* (privately published, Keighley, 1962).

K C Dunham, Epigenetic Minerals, in D H Rayner and J E Hemingway (eds), *The Geology and Mineral Resources of Yorkshire* (Leeds: Yorkshire Geological Society, 1974), 293-308.

K C Dunham and A A Wilson, *Geology of the Northern Pennine Orefield: Volume 2 Stainmore to Craven* (London: HMSO, Economic Memoirs of the British Geological Survey, 1985).

M C Gill, *Swaledale, its Mines and Smelt mills* (Ashbourne: Landmark Publishing, 2001).

R F White, Protecting the Remains of the lead smelting industry in the Yorkshire Dales National Park, in L Willies and D Cranstone (eds), *Boles and Smeltmills* (Matlock Bath: Historical Metallurgy Society, 1992), 65-6.

Old Gang lead smelt mill, Swaledale.
© R White/Yorkshire Dales National Park Authority, OG 426.

Leadmining at Hurst in Swaledale: levels, spoilheaps
and shallow shafts.
© R White/Yorkshire Dales National Park Authority, ANY 249/7.

9.7   ALUM AND CEMENT   DAVID PYBUS

HISTORY

Alum is a double salt of aluminium sulphate and either ammonium or potassium sulphate
(other alums exist but these were the main alums in the Yorkshire works). It was produced by
a lengthy and complex process, whereby the internal components of clay minerals in shales
were roasted in order to react with oxygen from the air. The sulphur in the shale produced
acid gases that further broke down the clay structures, while the oil content of the shale acted
as a fuel to raise the temperature and increase the reaction rate. The soluble aluminium
sulphate from the burnt shales was then dissolved in water, to which an alkali (stale urine in
the early history) was added to form the double sulphate.

Following the Dissolution of the Monasteries, there was a general search for indigenous
mineral resources. Alum was important as a mordant in the textile industry — England's
main export at the time — where it was used for 'sticking' vegetable dyes to fibres, as well as
a curing agent in the tanning of leather.

Cringle Moor: site of former jet and alum workings.
NMR 12370/18 © Crown copyright. NMR.

The alum industry ranged in various locations from around 1604 to 1871 (**fig 9.6**), and most of the alum production was concentrated on the edges of the Cleveland Hills/North York Moors where the outcrop seems more vertical. Some works were opened in relatively inaccessible sites, such as at Littlebeck.

Many of the practical aspects and problems of alum manufacture were associated with the sheer ignorance of the chemistry and processes involved. Experiments proved disastrous, and it was only in the early nineteenth century that an understanding of the process was developed. This understanding allowed alternative and cheaper methods of alum manufacture to be developed.

Technical problems were mainly to do with the selection of materials — early learning experiences soon identified the most appropriate materials and they seem to have been used with little modification until the end of the industry.

In the early seventeenth century, imported workers, variously described as Dutch and German, brought experience of the Continental process to the inexperienced Yorkshire works. Various trade secrets existed, but it is not known precisely how secret they were. Densities of liquors were measured by floating an egg in the solution, higher-density solutions (ready for making alum with) causing the egg to float, while lower-density (or weaker) solutions allowed the egg to sink. 'Say' dishes were used in the early seventeenth century — it is thought that this means assay dishes where the density was checked. Other problems included the corrosive nature of the process and its products.

In the early stages the investment was provided by the Crown, but it was soon seen by various entrepreneurs as an opportunity to generate income. Around the time that the Crown relinquished control (variously around 1679) to the private entrepreneurs, the processes were streamlined and became more profitable. The politics of alum manufacture were very complex, involving the Court of King James, one of his courtiers Sir Arthur Ingram, and many other prominent and notable persons of the seventeenth and eighteenth centuries.

As a result of the increase in demand for coals and urine imports, and alum exports, there was a considerable increase in shipping requirements. Initially the existing fleets of small ships (both native and captured Dutch ships) met this, but there was sufficient impetus to start the shipbuilding industry in Whitby in order to meet the increasing demand.

Economic pressures forced the early works to make what appeared to be good logistical decisions in designing the layout of later works and ensuring transport was co-ordinated.

A relatively naïve business sense caused many problems due to fluctuating supplies and prices. The latter rose and attracted more quarries into production, only to depress the prices and cause hardship to the owners and workers — what is known today as a 'boom and bust' cycle. The infrastructure was a source of problems until a more rational system developed in the mid-eighteenth century when a central refinery was developed to process the output of several quarries.

The alum works were probably at their most active when the nascent science of geology was developing. The fresh rockface exposures in the various quarries were useful for the early geologists to develop accurate and meaningful stratigraphies essential to the development of the modern science that we know. The quarrying operations were the equivalent of centuries of coastal erosion and the discarded nodules contained a very rich supply of fossil ammonites for the geologists to discover. Whitby Museum, with its premier collection of type ammonites and other fossils, would be seriously depleted had it not been for the supply of dogger stones.

It was found that, by roasting and crushing a particular type of dogger stone (a waste product of the alum mining process which decreased alum yield if included), cement was produced. This was the result of experimentation with the roasting of many types of stone. Although Parker is credited with the process, he was not systematic in his search, and the finding that impure limestone stones, when roasted, produced a perfect hydraulic cement was definitely chance.

Cement mining was common following the demise of alum quarrying, and production was known to have operated at Sandsend from around 1813 to 1933. Mining was confined to the top ten feet (3m) of shales — the dogger stones in this zone were called 'cement doggers' and had the best natural mix. The indicators of cement-stone mines can be seen in the back of alum quarry faces and take the characteristic form of fantail spoil dumps. Cement was mined at Rockhole/Asholme, Trucky Rock Hole, Sandsend, Kettleness and Runswick Bay (the Albert Iron and Cement Works).

UNDERSTANDING

Although there are many aspects of the alum and cement industries that warrant further study, it is likely that the generalities of both are understood — from contemporary documents, various retrospectives and more studious reports. Materials listed in the bibliography (and in their respective bibliographies) all contribute to a greater understanding of the industry.

Most of the remains at most of the works can be put into context and readily understood, although insufficient detailed survey has been undertaken in order to be able to assess the totality of the remains. Some structures require further investigation — there are two large walled structures at Boulby which defy rational explanation for the time being. There is a need for a study and close comparison of original sources to provide further insight into site operations and processes, together with a detailed examination of the questions for future research.

The collection of a comprehensive archive — to include, for example, Durham University's Baker-Baker Collection, and Mulgrave and other estate records, such as the Sheffield papers — would be of tremendous use. The Crown also hold large quantities of alum-related documents in their collections housed in the Public Record Office.

Many sites are suitable for interpretation to promote understanding. However, there is a need to ensure that their archaeological and historical value is not compromised — particular sites have suffered from mountain biking and scrambling. The national importance of many sites has now been recognised by their protection through ancient monument legislation.

The industry was clearly important to the development of Whitby as a port, but not its decline, together with the number of jobs created and the support industries required. Owing to a lack of banking system in the early days, the financial impact was distinct from the wider economic impact.

The social implications of moving villages on the workforce must have been tremendous and, coupled with the other infrastructure changes taking place in the area during the late eighteenth century (enclosure and rebuilding), there is scope to investigate the detailed stresses that existed. The complex local, regional and national political and economic background that enabled alum manufacture to continue for such a long time requires study and interpretation to improve accessibility.

The role of alum in the countrywide search for, and exploitation of, minerals needs to be established — this was one of a series of mining ventures that happened in the post-Reformation period and it may be useful to analyse the import of foreign workers as part of a trend.

Little or no work has been undertaken on the environmental effects of disposing of millions of tonnes of acidic red shales. Conflicting evidence is provided about the workers' clothes being in tatters owing to the acidic nature of the fumes; yet at the same time children were being held in the fumes to cure whooping cough. The longevity of people in the area was a continuing feature of contemporary reports.

The by-products of the industry included Epsom salts (magnesium sulphate) and copperas (ferrous sulphate). Copperas was another mordant chemical which could also be used for darker colours and for making black dyes, but the role the Yorkshire works played in its production remains to be explained.

Alum & Cement — Further Reading:

I Miller (ed.), *Steeped in History* (North York Moors National Park Authority and Oxford Archaeology (North), forthcoming).

D Pybus, and J Rushton, Alum and the Yorkshire Coast, in D B Lewis (ed.), *The Yorkshire Coast* (Normandy Press, 1991).

C Singer, *The Earliest Chemical Industry* (London: Folio Society, 1948).

The *Cleveland Industrial Archaeologist* 2 (1975).

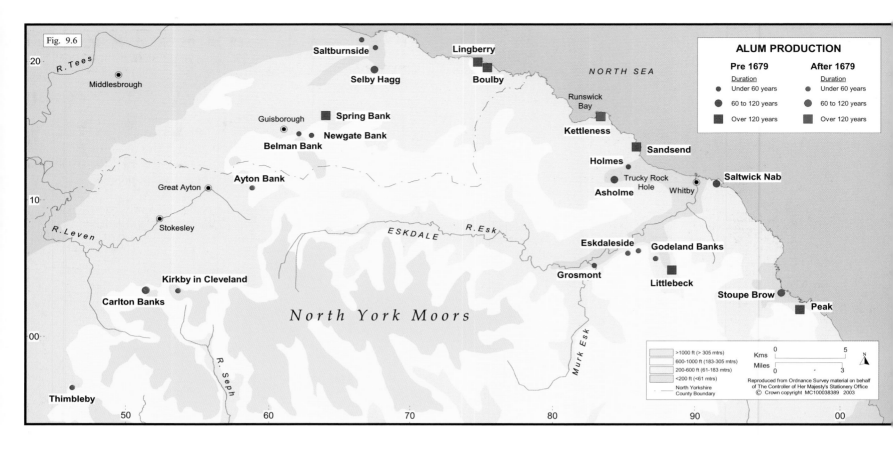

Fig. 9.6

ALUM PRODUCTION

	Pre 1679	After 1679
Duration		
Under 60 years	•	•
60 to 120 years	●	●
Over 120 years	■	■

R. Tees

Middlesbrough

20

Saltburnside

Selby Hagg

Lingberry

Boulby

NORTH SEA

Runswick Bay

Guisborough

Spring Bank

Newgate Bank

Belman Bank

Kettleness

Sandsend

Holmes

Trucky Rock Hole

Asholme

Whitby

Saltwick Nab

Ayton Bank

Great Ayton

10

R. Leven

Stokesley

ESKDALE

R. Esk

Eskdaleside

Godeland Banks

Grosmont

Littlebeck

Kirkby in Cleveland

Carlton Banks

00

North York Moors

R. Seph

Murk Esk

Stoupe Brow

Peak

Thimbleby

50   60   70   80   90   00

>1000 ft (> 305 mtrs)
600-1000 ft (183-305 mtrs)
200-600 ft (61-183 mtrs)
<200 ft (<61 mtrs)
North Yorkshire County Boundary

Kms 0 — 5
Miles 0 — 3

Reproduced from Ordnance Survey material on behalf of The Controller of Her Majesty's Stationery Office © Crown copyright MC100038389 2003

9.8   LIME PRODUCTION   ROBERT F WHITE

Limestone, of a variety of forms and ages, is one of the major rocks of North Yorkshire. Carboniferous limestones dominate much of the landscape of the Yorkshire Dales, especially the karst areas of Craven; a band of Permian Magnesian Limestone outcrops along the western edge of the vales of York and Mowbray; Jurassic limestones form the Tabular Hills of the North York Moors; and chalk from the Cretaceous period the landscape of the Wolds (**fig 9.7**).

Today limestone is mainly quarried for crushing as aggregate for the construction industry. It was extensively used as a flux in the iron and steel industry and for use in the chemical industry.

Historically, limestones have been extensively used as a building and walling material. The high cost of transporting stone overland meant that this was generally for the immediate locality, although Magnesian Limestone from the Tadcaster area was shipped downstream for use in York in the Roman period. Many higher-status medieval and post-medieval buildings close to navigable sections of the River Ure and Swale also benefit from Magnesian Limestone details. From the seventeenth century, many small quarries in the Dent area produced a polished limestone, known as Dent Marble, which was widely used in chimney-pieces and monuments.

Limekilns, of various forms and in various states of repair, are a common landscape feature of the limestone areas of North Yorkshire. The Yorkshire Dales Project identified over 880 mapped by the Ordnance Survey in the area of the national park in the 1850s. The majority of these would have been field kilns: small, isolated drystone structures, sometimes free-standing but more often partly built into a hillside with a deep bowl at the top and a large, arched opening at the front.

Within these kilns, limestone or calcium carbonate ($CaCO_3$) was burnt at about $900°C$ to make quicklime, using locally mined coal, or sometimes wood or peat, as a fuel. Quicklime or calcium oxide (CaO) is unstable and reacts violently with water. It did, however, have specific uses: dead animals were often buried with quicklime to prevent the spread of diseases; while the violent reaction could be harnessed to split rock in mining and quarrying. More often it was mixed with water, under controlled conditions, to form slaked lime, calcium hydroxide (CaOH).

Slaked lime was widely used in buildings and agriculture. Until the twentieth century it was the main ingredient of mortars, plasters, and limewashes or renders. Agriculturally its

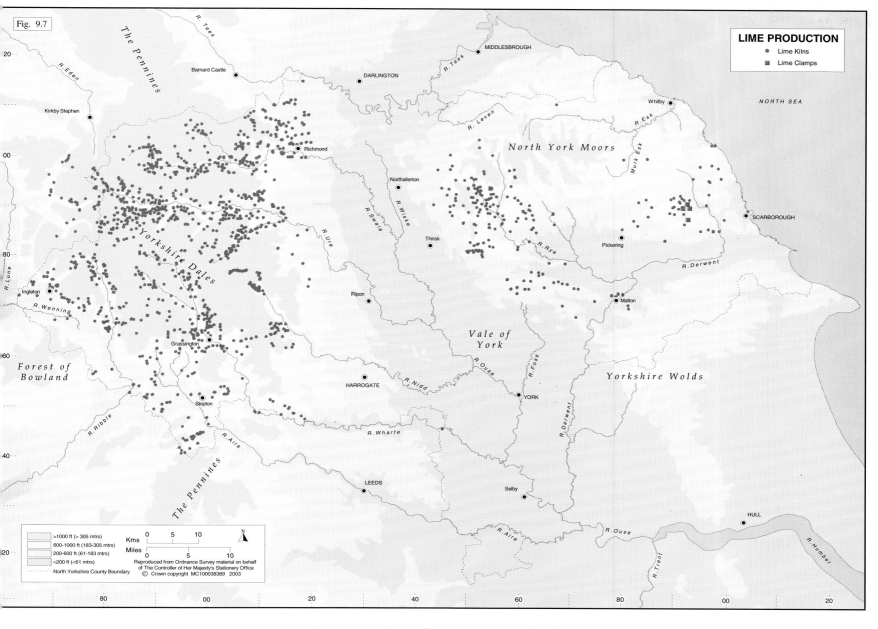

Reproduced from Ordnance Survey material on behalf of The Controller of Her Majesty's Stationery Office © Crown copyright MC100038389 2003

main use was to 'sweeten' or improve grassland by reducing the acidity of pastures, especially of intake land or reclaimed moorland during the enclosures of the eighteenth or nineteenth centuries. Lime was also used in local industries, particularly as a flux in lead and iron smelting and in tanning.

Most limekilns are found closely associated with small limestone quarries or areas of limestone pavement, but occasionally they can be found adjacent to transport routes. A few were built alongside the Leeds–Liverpool Canal to take advantage of the access to markets the canal provided and cheap coal brought by the canal.

The introduction of rail transport encouraged the construction of large industrial kilns such as the now-ruined Hoffmann kilns at Meal Bank Quarry, Ingleton, and Craven Lime Works, and thus stimulated the expansion of a few large limestone quarries in the Yorkshire Dales.

Economies of scale led to the abandonment of most of the small field limekilns though some, especially in the more isolated areas, continued in use until the early twentieth century.

Lime-burning was a labour- and fuel-intensive process, but the field kilns themselves represented a technology little changed from that of Roman times.

The earliest kilns were essentially bonfire clamps: a piled-up mixture of layers of limestone and fuel. Such kilns are known as pye or sow kilns, depending on their design, but were destroyed after every firing to retrieve the lime and have thus left very little in the way of remains, other than a slight circular or rectangular hollow surrounded by a low mound of unburnt or partially burnt stone and waste. Few such kilns have so far been identified in contrast to the large number of field kilns.

Field limekilns represented a larger capital investment, as it was necessary to build the kiln superstructure, but they had the advantages of being reusable and of being more fuel efficient. Most field kilns were about ten feet (3m) high and built of limestone, although the circular bowl was usually lined with sandstone or firebricks which would not react with the limestone fill during the burning process.

Kindling was laid in the bottom of the kiln and covered with layers of limestone, broken up into fist-sized lumps, and coal. Much of the skill in lime-burning lay in the careful filling of the bowl with the tipped layers of fuel and stone. After about forty-eight hours, as the fire burnt through the fill in the bowl, burnt lime could be shovelled out through the draw arch at the bottom of the kiln, while more unburnt limestone and coal could be tipped in at the top. Such kilns could work continuously, but it is more likely that burning was intermittent.

There are several variations in the detailed appearance of field limekilns. The most common forms are square or circular in plan, but intermediate types are also found. Most have only one bowl and one draw arch. The draw arches are normally semi-circular but some are pointed or have a series of stepped, recessed arches, while on some smaller kilns, flat lintels were used instead of the arch. The dimensions also vary, larger kilns generally being later or indicating a more commercial function.

Nineteenth-century commentators give some idea of the scale of the lime-burning industry and how it operated. Young said that the whole range of the limestone hills abounded with kilns. In many parts the farmers had kilns for use on their own farms. The lime was generally inferior to that imported from Sunderland, and that which was made in kilns along the coast from the Flamborough limestone was reckoned superior to both and sold at Upgang at 26s per chaldron [36 bushels]. He added that 4,000 chaldrons were brought from Sunderland to Whitby annually by sea.[1]

Sewell gives an instance of the trading of moor coal for lime about 1830. John Atkinson of Castle Howe Farm, Danby, brought forty waggon-loads of lime (1¼ tons each waggon) from Hutton to Castleton, working three waggons per day. Early morning he drove an empty waggon to Rosedale Head coal-pits near Ralph Cross and left it there, collecting a full one left the previous day which he exchanged (with some cash) for lime at Hutton-le-Hole.[2]

The rapid technological change of the lime industry with the development of the railway network is well represented at Craven Lime Works near Settle, close to the Settle-Carlisle Railway. Here the remains of three different types of industrial kilns survive and are currently being conserved by the Yorkshire Dales National Park Authority.

The oldest is a group of three massive draw kilns, essentially operating the same gravity-based technology as the field kilns; and a 420 feet (128m) long, twenty-two chamber horizontal Hoffmann kiln, where the fire circulated round a 795 feet (242m) long tunnel. These were both built, by different companies, in c1873. The Hoffmann kiln was very fuel efficient as waste heat from the burning chambers was used to preheat the next chambers to be burnt. The third group of kilns on the site, built some time before 1909 and now only represented by their stone support structures, were a pair of vertical steel Spenser kilns. In these kilns the fire was kept separate to the limestone charge and produced a purer product, for use as a flux in steelmaking and in the chemical industry.

The information presented on the accompanying map relates to the data currently available in the archaeological record systems for the county. Only that for the Yorkshire Dales National Park is likely to be anywhere near complete.

Lime Production — Further Reading:
M R G Trueman, The Langcliffe Quarry and Limeworks, *Industrial Archaeology Review* 14.2 (1992), 126-44.
D Johnson, *The Lime and Limestone Industries of the Yorkshire Dales, A History* (Tempus, forthcoming).
R Williams, *Limekilns and Limeburning,* Shire Album 236 (1989).

9.9   TEXTILES   RICHARD LAWTON

North Yorkshire's textile industries (**fig 9.8**) never achieved the significance of the worsted industry of the Bradford and Keighley area, the Leeds clothing and woollen district, or the cotton industries of Lancashire, but they did play a significant role in the rural economy of the Dales and towns such as Skipton, Settle, Bentham and Knaresborough.

In the fifteenth century, woollen cloth was made in York and Selby, and was emerging as a domestic industry in the Skipton area. By 1700 the urban centres had declined but, in the Pennine Dales, handicraft woollen and worsted spinning and weaving was flourishing, and card-making (a toothed implement used for raising the nap on cloth or for disentangling fibres before spinning) was a cottage industry employing women and children. Flax-spinning and linen-weaving was active in Knaresborough, Nidderdale and Tadcaster, and was widespread in Cleveland and parts of the North Yorkshire Moors.

By the mid-eighteenth century, Skipton, with some eighty weavers, Wharfedale and upper Ribblesdale had become North Yorkshire's main textile area. Thereafter, water-power sites in the Dales and the Leeds–Liverpool Canal, linking to east Lancashire cotton manufacturers, and the West Riding woollen and worsted areas (opened to Leeds by 1777 and to Burnley by 1796, though not completed until 1816), helped to promote both cotton and worsted factories in Craven.

Power spinning of cotton came to Skipton in 1784-5 and machine-made worsted thread soon followed. In 1828, the best-known Skipton factory, Belle Vue Mill, was built by John Dewhurst for worsted spinning and weaving.[1] Burnt down in 1831, it was rebuilt as a cotton mill.

The Settle area's cotton-spinning mills, dating from 1783, were promoted by local entrepreneurs (eg, Birkbecks, who also had mills at Linton). Many small spinning mills flourished in the area from the late eighteenth century; one, at Addingham, for silk-spinning and a few in and around Knaresborough for linen thread.

Despite the depression in linen manufacture in the 1770s, flax-spinning and linen mills were significant around 1800 for a number of townships in north-east Yorkshire (eg Helmsley, Castleton, Whitby, Great Ayton, Osmotherley and Ampleforth) and adjacent areas of the Vale of York (eg Appleton Wiske and Bishop Monkton).[2] Occupations listed in parish registers and in the 1803 militia muster list for the wapentake of Staincliff and Ewcross show how significant textiles had become in the economy of Craven.[3] Of 98 townships, 78 listed textile workers and 23 employed over 20, with most in and around Skipton and in the Settle area.

Despite the decline of handloom weaving from the 1830s, which affected many of the smaller parishes, textiles were still widespread. In 1835 the Craven area had forty-four cotton mills, mainly water-powered (an aggregate 459 horsepower as against 196 in steam), but the bigger cotton and worsted mills in Airedale were going over to steam.[4] In Skipton and adjacent townships, textiles employed forty-two per cent of adult male workers in 1851, and proportionately more of the female and child labour force. In upper Ribblesdale, though the cotton mills of the Settle area still employed one sixth of the male workforce, the census enumerators noted the stoppage of some mills in recent recession. Upper Wharfedale's cotton industry was collapsing: mills at Arncliffe and Litton closed in the 1860s; and that at Linton, which employed over 100 in 1851, was in decline.

The linen industry was also adversely affected both by depression in the late 1820s and early 1830s, and by competition from factory production outside the region which ousted handspinning and a dispersed handweaving industry from the 1830s. Mills were still active in 1851, however, at Rudby, Brompton, Osmotherley, Cote Gill and at Bentham where flax-processing occupied one sixth of its working population. Small-scale manufacture of high-quality goods continued in a few areas, notably focused on Knaresborough and adjacent townships, but by mid-century the handicraft linen trade was largely gone.

Despite the contraction in North Yorkshire's textile industries since 1800, they still employed over 5,600 adult workers in 1851, nearly half in cotton manufacture, two-fifths in woollen and worsted, and less than one-tenth in linen. The major mills were in the Skipton Registration District (with 73 per cent of textile workers), and upper Ribblesdale and Wharfedale (a further 13 per cent), with only 8 per cent in the linen districts.

By the 1890s most of Craven's rural mills had closed. The industry focused largely on the Skipton area's cotton and thread mills which, by the time of the 1911 census, employed nearly 5,300 (88 per cent) of North Yorkshire's textile workers, with a few in hemp and linen in Selby, York and Knaresborough.

Handicraft spinners, weavers and knitters, so important to the proto-industrial economy of the Dales, had largely gone by mid-century, and the last branch of the industry to be mechanised — wool-combing — collapsed in the late 1840s and was extinct by the mid-1850s.[5] A detailed analysis of census enumerators' books for 1851-91 for upper Wharfedale and upper Ribblesdale tells the same story. Nothing was left of the thriving rural handicraft and rural textiles industry of the early nineteenth century and, apart from Settle's 151 cotton operatives and 15 cotton and worsted workers in Linton, employment in the small mills was gone.

Textiles — Further Reading:

C Giles and I H Goodall, *Yorkshire Textile Mills 1770-1930* (London: HMSO, 1992).

R P Hastings, *Essays in North Riding History, 1750-1850* (Northallerton: North Yorkshire County Record Office Publications, no. 28, 1981).

R Lawton, The Economic Geography of Craven in the Early Nineteenth Century, in D R Mills (ed.), *English Rural Communities* (London: MacMillan, 1973), 155-181.

E Baines, *History of the Cotton Manufacture in Great Britain* (Manchester, 1835).

D Bythell, *The Sweated Trades. Outwork in Nineteenth-century Britain* (London: Batsford, 1978).

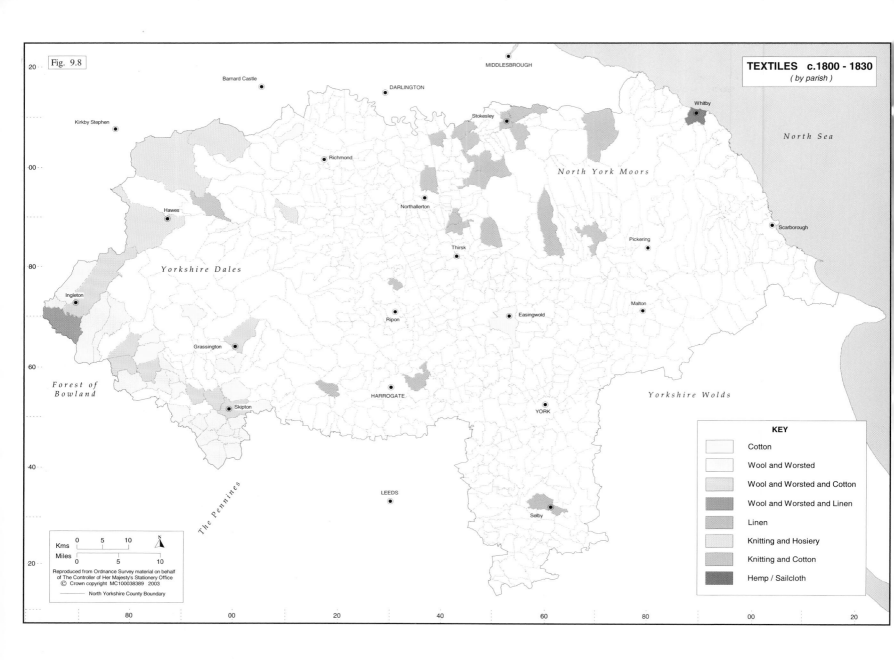

Fig. 9.8

TEXTILES c.1800 - 1830
(by parish)

MIDDLESBROUGH

Barnard Castle

DARLINGTON

Kirkby Stephen

Stokesley

Whitby

North Sea

Richmond

North York Moors

Northallerton

Scarborough

Hawes

Thirsk

Pickering

Yorkshire Dales

Ingleton

Malton

Ripon

Easingwold

Grassington

Forest of Bowland

HARROGATE

Yorkshire Wolds

Skipton

YORK

KEY

	Cotton
	Wool and Worsted
	Wool and Worsted and Cotton
	Wool and Worsted and Linen
	Linen
	Knitting and Hosiery
	Knitting and Cotton
	Hemp / Sailcloth

The Pennines

LEEDS

Selby

Kms 0 5 10

Miles 0 5 10

Reproduced from Ordnance Survey material on behalf
of The Controller of Her Majesty's Stationery Office
© Crown copyright MC100038389 2003

——— North Yorkshire County Boundary

20 00 20 40 60 80 00 20

Gayle Mill, Wensleydale. Built as a cotton mill in 1784,
with internal waterwheel, it had become a woollen
mill by 1804 and a saw mill before 1872.
© R White/Yorkshire Dales National Park Authority, GM12.

Bishop Monkton Mill. This famous flax mill is a
survivor of an earlier textile industry, now converted
into dwellings.
© J K Harrison, 1995.

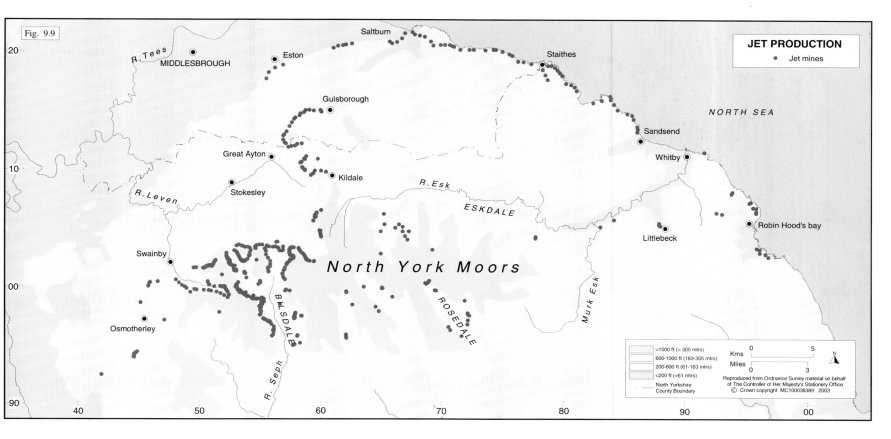

Fig. 9.9

JET PRODUCTION
• Jet mines

NORTH SEA

North York Moors

>1000 ft (> 305 mtrs)
600-1000 ft (183-305 mtrs)
200-600 ft (61-183 mtrs)
<200 ft (<61 mtrs)
North Yorkshire
County Boundary

Kms
Miles

Reproduced from Ordnance Survey material on behalf
of The Controller of Her Majesty's Stationery Office
© Crown copyright MC100038389 2003

9.10 JET   CAROL B COOK

Jet consists of fossilised timber (a variety of *Araucaria*, similar to but much larger than today's 'monkey puzzle' trees), deposited in marine sediments during the Jurassic period and then compressed for over 170 million years. It is similar to amber in texture and to coal in appearance. Within the United Kingdom, jet is found in north-east Yorkshire and Cleveland (**fig 9.9**). This is mostly 'hard' jet, which is tough and durable, capable of being carved and polished into fine ornaments. 'Soft' jet is brittle and thus less suitable but has still been worked within the region.

There is no regular seam of jet; it appears randomly throughout finely laminated Upper Lias shales known as the jet rock series which may be up to thirty feet (10m) in vertical thickness. This made mining a most speculative undertaking. These shales lie above the ironstone strata and beneath a freestone known as the 'top jet dogger'. Once free of the overlying pressures they may be opened like leaves in a book, often revealing paper-thin impressions of marine life and occasionally ammonites.

On the coast from Ravenscar to Saltburn, on the northern escarpment or in the valleys, shale was worked for jet in the nineteenth century. Where exposed to weathering, the shale is easily worked with a pick. A series of adits, or parallel drifts, was then driven into the hillside at the base of the jet shale. The working penetrated into the hillside until the shale became tougher, to the point known as the 'face', this seldom being further than 330 feet (100m). Finds range from wafer thin to five inches (12cm) thickness and up to six feet (2m) in length.

A team consisting of not more than six men worked each drift, usually in groups of three — ie one with a pick, one to barrow the shale and one to sort the material on the shale heap. By forming a platform of shale, it was possible to work through the full thickness of the shale to the overlying top jet dogger, which made a fairly stable roof. Wooden roof-supports were used as little as possible to save effort and cost.

A special pick was the jet miner's chief tool, well drawn out into two sharp points for better penetration of the shale. Because the drifts were not extensive and explosives were not used on account of breaking the jet, it was sufficient for ventilation to be left to natural air circulation. Lighting was most frequently by candle, often attached to the wall with a lump of clay, or mounted in a cut-away treacle tin. The first jet miners' lamps were made in Stockton and held a candle, with a spout on top to allow an air flow.

Wages for the charge-hand in 1873 were 18 shillings (90p) for six days, whilst other miners took home 16 shillings (80p). In summer they made good use of long days and fine weather; in the winter they could often work only on a limited basis. As an example, Swainby village,

Jet mining: Urra, Bilsdale.
© B E Vyner.

on the western extremity of the area, has thirty-eight recorded miners in 1871. These included local men who hoped to find a fortune on their own land holdings, and redundant ironstone miners following the collapse of the price of iron in the early 1870s.

Most of the carving and finishing work was completed in Whitby, which has given us the name 'Whitby Jet'. Agents acted on behalf of jet ornament manufacturers in purchasing rough jet from source, and at the height of the industry's prosperity had great difficulty in meeting demand.

The cleaned jet was first sawn into various thicknesses and shapes. The smallest pieces were made into beads so that none would be wasted. Foot-treadle grindstones were used to roughly shape the pieces into ovals and geometric shapes, before skilled carvers and turners engraved beautiful designs on to the surface using knives, chisels and gouges. A polish was finally put on the work with polishing boards, lubricated with oil, and finished by 'rougeing' over a revolving wheel covered with walrus hide. Intricate bits could be finished on a brush wheel.

Early artefacts made from jet have been recovered from burial mounds from Derbyshire to the north of Scotland. Much of this was probably collected from the beaches, although the jet shales in the base of the cliffs around Goldsborough (NZ 836 147) are accessible from the beach at low tide and may have been exploited.

Jet has been prized for some 4,000 years as an ornament, as a medical cure and in superstitious ritual, but it was not until the mid-nineteenth century that its popularity created a flourishing industry based on the customs of mourning and boosted by a developing tourist trade. Whitby merchants exhibited some items at the Great Exhibition held at the Crystal Palace in 1851. This was attended by Queen Victoria, who gave jet jewellery her approval. Following the death of Prince Albert in 1861, the trade expanded beyond all expectations to give an annual turnover in excess of £90,000. By 1871 Whitby recorded over 1,500 employees in almost 200 jet workshops, the most skilful carvers earning up to £4 each week.

This flourishing period of manufacture lasted from 1868 to the mid-1880s before a change in fashion had a devastating effect on the local economy. Cheap imports of black glass known as 'French Jet' and the use of 'soft' jet from Spain, and the development of bakelite, vulcanite and other alternative materials, gradually undermined the value of the original mineral.

Evidence of jet mining is visible in many valleys within the North York Moors National Park, and along the escarpment between Guisborough and Osmotherley. Collapsed drifts with sink holes and associated shale tips, devoid of vegetation, occur at regular intervals along the hillsides, together with the occasional remains of a jet miner's hut.

Some of the shale is a rich red colour as a result of spontaneous combustion, or deliberately setting fire to the heaps for subsequent use as a road material. The shale contains between 12 and 20 gallons of oil per ton (approx 80 litres/tonne, or eight per cent) and was often burned for months, emitting an unpleasant smell complained of, for example, by the inhabitants of Stokesley. Since 1980, jet jewellery has undergone something of a revival. The popularity of dark colours has encouraged the wearing of antique pieces, and the demand for new items of jet has created a renewed interest in carving.

Jet — Further Reading:

M McMillan, *Whitby Jet Through the Years* (Hull: L B Print Co, 1992).

H Muller, *Jet* (London: Butterworth & Co., Shire Series, 1987).

H Muller, Whitby Jet, in D B Lewis (ed.), *The Yorkshire Coast* (Normandy Press, 1991).

J S Owen, Jet Mining in North East Yorkshire, *Cleveland Industrial Archaeologist* 3 (1975).

10

URBAN HISTORY

10.1   URBAN RENAISSANCE, 1700–1830   ADAM MENUGE

Eighteenth-century England was predominantly a country of small towns, and North Yorkshire was no exception. But in the nineteenth century, when rising industrial towns experienced massive population growth, North Yorkshire's towns grew slowly, and some scarcely at all, preserving much of their earlier character.

Nevertheless, throughout the period they developed in ways that expressed both the material wealth, and the increasing cultural aspirations, of their residents, whether permanent or seasonal. Comparison of **fig 10.1** with that accompanying Richard Britnell's account of medieval boroughs, markets and fairs (**fig 6.22**) reveals a mixture of continuity and change.[1]

The definition of towns, however, remains problematic. Many smaller urban centres did not enjoy characteristically urban institutions of self-government but derived their identity from the aggregation of professional, educational, commercial and leisure services.

At one end of the spectrum, some towns clung to the mere tatters of an urban past. Boroughbridge and Aldborough formed a single parish but each returned two MPs. The former was described as 'a poor, mean town without trade or manufacture, except the accidental branch of electioneering';[2] while the latter, with no market and a population of less than 500, was stripped of its representation in 1832 when the so-called 'rotten boroughs' were abolished.

Towns which were disregarded by the promoters of turnpikes, canals and railways often suffered a slow ebbing-away of trade and prosperity. Hunmanby's market was 'partly declined' in the 1790s, when its remoteness from post-roads was remarked, and had ceased by the 1820s. Hovingham and Coxwold suffered a similar fate before the end of the eighteenth century. Easingwold, straddling a major thoroughfare, was more fortunate, but its growth was curtailed by distance from navigable water.

Bentham in the extreme west, and Catterick in the north, remained minor commercial centres despite the absence of a market. The prestige of both was bolstered by a grammar school, while in Catterick local incomes were supplemented by the Easter race-meeting.

The breeding, training and racing of horses underpinned the economies of several towns, including Middleham, which saw its market functions increasingly aggrandised by nearby Leyburn.

At the other end of the spectrum, York, with 22,529 inhabitants in 1821, was far from being the most populous centre in Yorkshire, but remained socially pre-eminent. It was more than twice the size of Whitby (10,615 including the neighbouring village of Ruswarp), a runaway mercantile success of the eighteenth century.

Whitby was followed by Scarborough (8,188) and Knaresborough (6,656), both profiting from nearby spas. Then came (in descending order) Ripon, Selby, Malton, Richmond and Skipton, all with populations between 3,400 and 4,600. Northallerton (2,626) and Thirsk (2,533) were smaller but possessed a range of institutions, services and amenities that raised them above the level of the remaining market and thoroughfare towns which, with the exception of Pickering (2,746) and Tadcaster (2,426), all had fewer than 2,000 inhabitants.[3]

Towns expressed their status in a variety of ways. For the city of York and the incorporated boroughs, the dignities and symbols of office called for suitable accommodation. York possessed its medieval guildhall, but much of its civic pride was invested in the architecturally refined Mansion House of 1726. York's prestige was massively reinforced by its legal institutions, manifested in the courts and gaol of York Castle, and by its archiepiscopal status, symbolised by the Minster, though the archbishop's palace was at Bishopthorpe.

By contrast, the smaller towns were frugal; most public buildings, such as courthouses and houses of correction, were funded by the county. Whitby and Ripon acquired new town halls only through private generosity.[4] One notable corporation scheme was York's New Walk, an elegant promenade beside the Ouse, laid out in 1733-4 and extended in 1768.

Much civic aspiration was channelled through private initiatives. Charitable institutions — hospitals, asylums, almshouses, dispensaries and schools — originated in private benefactions, but gestured at a wider spirit of enlightenment.

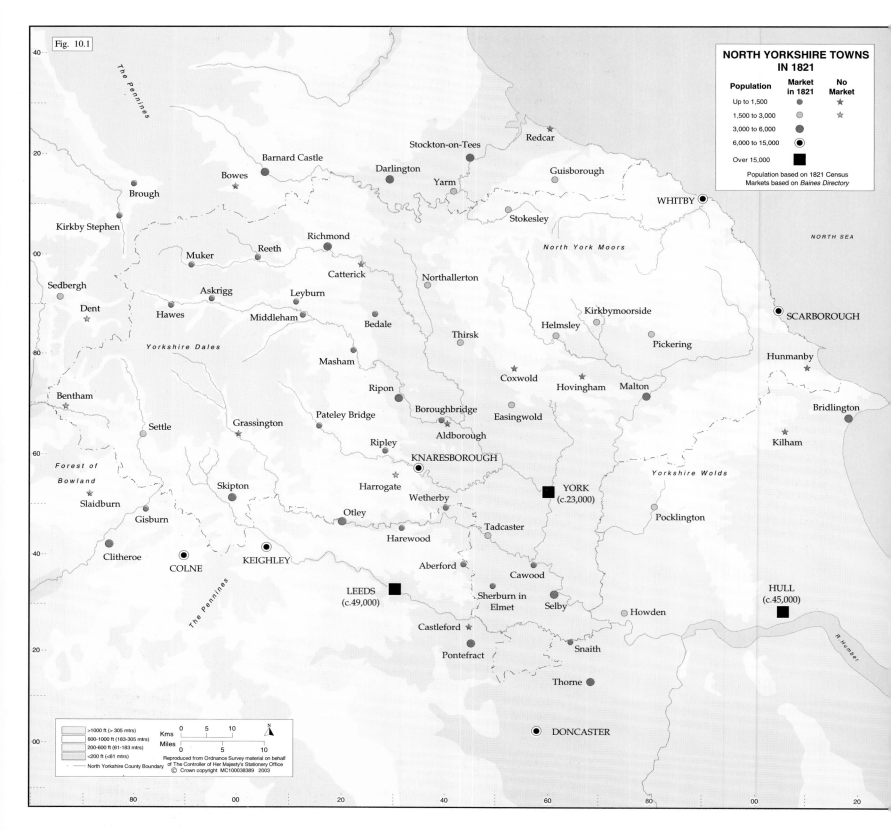

Fig. 10.1

NORTH YORKSHIRE TOWNS IN 1821

Population	Market in 1821	No Market
Up to 1,500	●	★
1,500 to 3,000	●	☆
3,000 to 6,000	●	
6,000 to 15,000	◉	
Over 15,000	■	

Population based on 1821 Census
Markets based on *Baines Directory*

The Pennines

Barnard Castle
Bowes
Brough
Kirkby Stephen
Sedbergh
Dent
Bentham
Muker
Reeth
Askrigg
Hawes
Middleham
Leyburn
Settle
Grassington
Skipton
Gisburn
Clitheroe
COLNE
KEIGHLEY

Stockton-on-Tees
Redcar
Darlington
Yarm
Guisborough
Stokesley
Richmond
Catterick
Northallerton
Bedale
Thirsk
Kirkbymoorside
Helmsley
Pickering
Masham
Coxwold
Hovingham
Malton
Ripon
Boroughbridge
Easingwold
Pateley Bridge
Aldborough
Ripley
KNARESBOROUGH
Harrogate
Wetherby
Otley
Tadcaster
Harewood
Aberford
Cawood
LEEDS (c.49,000)
Sherburn in Elmet
Selby
Howden
Castleford
Pontefract
Snaith
Thorne
DONCASTER

YORK (c.23,000)
Pocklington

WHITBY
NORTH SEA
North York Moors
SCARBOROUGH
Hunmanby
Bridlington
Kilham
Yorkshire Wolds
HULL (c.45,000)

North York Moors
Yorkshire Dales
Forest of Bowland
The Pennines

R. Humber

>1000 ft (> 305 mtrs)	
600-1000 ft (183-305 mtrs)	
200-600 ft (61-183 mtrs)	
<200 ft (<61 mtrs)	
— — North Yorkshire County Boundary	

Kms 0 5 10
Miles 0 5 10

N

Reproduced from Ordnance Survey material on behalf of The Controller of Her Majesty's Stationery Office
© Crown copyright MC100038389 2003

   More pervasive (if less altruistic) were those testaments of culture, prosperity and solidity that genteel, professional and mercantile inhabitants sought to present through the architecture of their own houses. All but the most impoverished towns have a handful or more of substantial houses built or rebuilt during this period in the cultivated *lingua franca* of the Classical style. Often disfigured by later commercial use of the ground floors, they congregate around market places and along the principal thoroughfares, but also (in ports such as York and Whitby) close to the commercial activity of the staithes. Only late in the period do suburban or out-of-town villas appear in any numbers, signalling a dissatisfaction with deteriorating town-centre environments sufficient to over-ride a merchant's desire to live close to his stock-in-trade.

Citizens frequently combined to remedy the shortcomings — or absence — of municipal enterprise. In leisure facilities, as in most matters of fashion, York led the way as the regional metropolis for the gentry of Yorkshire and the North, who gathered during the period of the assizes and races. Lord Burlington's Assembly Rooms in Blake Street, opened in 1730, were financed by subscriptions from the surrounding aristocracy and gentry, as was the grandstand on the Knavesmire racecourse.

Elsewhere, private enterprise achieved similar results: in Scarborough and Harrogate, assembly rooms ('long rooms'), coffee houses, billiard halls and luxury shops catered for leisured spa visitors; Malton boasted a suite of public rooms in Yorkersgate; and in Ripon the assembly rooms were in the new town hall (1801). But for many smaller towns the upper rooms of inns sufficed. Purpose-built theatres emerged in York (1763), Whitby (1784), Richmond (1788; still surviving), Ripon (1792), Malton (1814), Scarborough and Harrogate.

The proliferation of libraries reflected not only a thirst for knowledge and religious instruction, but also the rise of the novel as a form of polite entertainment. Subscription libraries or commercial circulating libraries sprang up in most North Yorkshire towns in the late eighteenth and early nineteenth centuries. Subscription newsrooms alleviated the draconian tax on newsprint and placed readers in touch with metropolitan opinion.

Slower to emerge were learned societies, mixing scientific and antiquarian research with the facilities of a library and museum. The Yorkshire Philosophical Society was formed in 1822 and acquired what became the Museum Gardens in 1827. Members of the Whitby Literary and Philosophical Society (1823) made distinguished contributions to palaeontology, archaeology and polar science. Scarborough's Philosophical Society followed in 1827.

Dramatic transformations of urban topography, encompassing open spaces as much as building projects, were largely confined to Harrogate and Scarborough. Elsewhere the new continued to jostle with the old, which attracted growing interest.

Seventeenth-century accounts of the spas at Scarborough and Knaresborough included William Simpson's *History of Scarborough Spaw* (1679), but the York printer Thomas Gent's homespun histories of York (1730) and Ripon (1733) inaugurated a new era, and Francis Drake's monumental *Eboracum* (1736) was a landmark. Hargrove's slim history of Knaresborough (1775) was followed by Charlton's *Whitby* (1779; superseded in 1817 by Young's compendious account), and histories of Northallerton (1791), Selby (1800), Richmond (1814) and Kirkbymoorside (1824).

Mirroring the larger European Renaissance, the future of the county's towns would never again be free of the past.

Urban Renaissance — Further Reading:

Peter Borsay, *The English Urban Renaissance* (Oxford: Clarendon Press, 1989).

Christopher Chalklin, *English Counties and Public Building* (London: Hambledon Press, 1998).

Kevin Grady, *The Georgian Public Buildings of Leeds and the West Riding*, for Knaresborough and Ripon (Leeds: Thoresby Society, 1989).

K L McCutcheon, *Yorkshire Fairs and Markets to the end of the Eighteenth Century* (Leeds: Thoresby Society, 1940).

10.2   YORK   CHRISTOPHER DANIELL

York lies in the Vale of York, which is itself an extension of the Trent–Humber basin. At the end of the last glacial period the watery landscape was littered with lakes, ponds and rivers.

York Minster, west front.
© R A Butlin.

Two rivers, the Ouse and the Foss, met at the point which later became York. Occasionally Neolithic material is found in the York area, left over from when Neolithic people fashioned flints besides the lakesides and streams.

The local river systems had a key influence upon York's development. The River Ouse (**figs 10.2, 10.3**) cut steep-sided banks at the point where it joined the Foss, and these banks (still visible as steep lanes running down towards the river from Coney Street) offered a good defensive position which the Romans used for their legionary fortress. Two sides of the legionary fortress walls have remained as part of the later city walls and moat, and there is speculation that the medieval city walls across the Ouse, on the civilian or *colonia* side, follow the line of the Roman walls as well, but no evidence has been found. The size of the Roman city, the second largest in England after London, was a natural destination for traders, settlers and invaders.

For centuries after the Romans, it was the River Ouse which provided the means for invaders to attack the city, as the river drains into the Humber which leads to the North Sea. This link with the North Sea meant that attacks could be made far inland by sea-going or migrating peoples. Anglo-Saxons, migrating from their north Germanic homelands, first attacked and then later settled in and around York.

The importance of the Roman city in terms of size and prestige attracted the Anglo-Saxon kings of Northumbria to the city, and their presence was a magnet for Christian missionaries. Following the conversion to Christianity of King Edwin, the king of Northumbria, by Paulinus, the first church was built in York. From that date, York has been the seat of the archbishop, whose archdiocese covers the North of England.

In the ninth century the Vikings followed the Anglo-Saxon routes across the North Sea and up the Humber. York became the heart of the Viking kingdom in the North of England, as the rich Viking archaeological deposits excavated at the Coppergate excavations testify (now on show at the Jorvik Centre).

The last successful military invasion was by the Normans, and William the Conqueror first arrived in York in 1068. The Normans had a huge impact on the topography of the city. They dammed the River Foss near its junction with the Ouse, thereby creating a lake and marsh known as the King's Fishpool, which was considered impassable. Its existence is the reason why the walls do not follow a complete circuit around the city and finish at the Red Tower. Slowly over the centuries, the Fishpool was filled in by silt or rubbish and Foss Islands Road is a reminder of its location.

The threat of attack along the Ouse also resulted in the Normans building two castles, one either side of the river to allow a chain to be put across it. Both castle mounds, or mottes, can still be seen — on one stands Clifford's Tower, and the other, today planted with trees, is across the Ouse in Bishophill.

Other Norman building campaigns included the rebuilding of the York Minster on a new site (there is still debate as to where the Anglo-Saxon minsters were located) and a host of churches around the city. Newly built churches included the Benedictine monasteries of St Mary's Abbey and Holy Trinity Priory, Micklegate, and many smaller parish churches. In some of the parish churches, such as St Denis's, Walmgate, and St Margaret's Walmgate, eroded Romanesque doorways can still be seen.

In the thirteenth century York became the base for the four main orders of friars — the Dominicans, Franciscans, Augustinians and Carmelites — each with a substantial presence in the city.

York's geographical position, roughly halfway between London and Edinburgh, ensured the city a key role in any plans to expand political power northwards. The Romans used York as an important garrison to supply the troops serving on Hadrian's Wall. York was also a natural point for the kings of England and Scotland to meet when signing peace treaties. In Edward I's reign, York's role became heightened when the king used the city as his base in his Scottish campaigns, situating both Court and Parliament in the city.

Between the thirteenth and fifteenth centuries, York flourished as part of an international trade network. The city had its own shipbuilding industry in the thirteenth century and was ranked seventh among the ports of the south and east coasts in 1203-4.

The wealth of the city was based on trade, much of it based upon the wool trade of North Yorkshire. Merchants and tradesmen grew rich, and built fine houses and spectacular guildhalls, notably the guildhalls of the Merchant Adventurers and Merchant Tailors, which still survive.

The rich were also patrons of churches, paying for building works and sumptuous stained-glass windows. The medieval glass still survives in large quantities, and particularly fine examples can be seen in the minster, All Saint's North Street, St Michael Spurriergate, and Holy Trinity Goodramgate.

The fourteenth and fifteenth centuries were the zenith of York's prosperity and thereafter it slowly declined in national importance, although it remained an influential regional market and a successful centre for local trade and commerce.

During the Tudor period, the Dissolution of the Monasteries (1536-7) had a profound impact on the topography of York, for the monasteries and friaries were closed down, and the sites were bought by speculators or the rich, either to sell on or to use as lodgings. The suppression of the larger monasteries included the Benedictine monastery of St Mary's Abbey, the four friaries and St Leonard's Hospital.

Despite the further closure of religious institutions, such as the chantries and the religious guilds, a small group of Catholics remained in the city. By the end of the sixteenth century about fifty people remained openly Catholic in their belief. One such was Margaret Clitherow, who was put to death by the York authorities. Today she is a Catholic saint and martyr, with her shrine in the Shambles.

York came to the forefront of national politics during the Civil Wars of the seventeenth century. The city allied itself to Charles I and the Royalist cause, whereas the towns of West Yorkshire and Hull were Parliamentarian in sympathy.

Initially the Royalists prospered, capturing various towns in West Yorkshire and briefly besieging the Parliamentarian forces of Lord Fairfax in Hull. However, the situation was reversed in spring 1643 when Fairfax laid siege to York. During the siege, particular damage was inflicted upon the districts of Walmgate and Bootham. Outside Walmgate the Parliamentarians used St Nicholas's Church tower as a gun battery, whilst the Royalists defending the city built cannon placements around the Walmgate stretch of the city walls. The resulting exchanges destroyed St Nicholas's Church (only the rebuilt tower remains) and damaged buildings inside the city walls. In Bootham the Parliamentarian attackers blew up St Mary's Tower (which held the records of St Mary's Abbey) and fought their way into King's Manor before being repelled by the Royalists.

The siege was lifted by the arrival of a Royalist relieving force and the two armies met at Marston Moor on the 30th June 1644. The Parliamentarian army led by Lord Fairfax won a decisive victory and he rode into York in triumph. From this time the Royalist cause in the North was effectively lost.

Sixteen years later Fairfax once again brought Yorkshire to the forefront of national politics, allying it to the restoration of the monarchy and thereby allowing Charles II to gain the throne. York thereafter passes out of national military history, though there were calls to arms during the Jacobite Rebellion and the Napoleonic Wars. In the Second World War a German bombing raid on the 29th April 1942 targeted the railway station, causing extensive damage in the surrounding area, although York Minster remained unscathed.

After the Civil Wars of the seventeenth century, the citizens concentrated on local issues and politics. During the Civil Wars a royalist printing press had been set up in St William's College and afterwards the tradition of printing continued. In 1719 the *York Mercury* was started, with a rival newspaper, *York Courant*, starting in 1725. Prominent merchants and intellectuals formed informal groups to discuss issues of the day, which led to the creation of the Yorkshire Philosophical Society in 1822. The society bought the grounds of St Mary's Abbey (now Museum Gardens), and built a museum there in 1827 and an observatory in 1833.

In the eighteenth century, building work transformed the look of the city. Whole streets took on the classical elegance associated with Georgian architecture, most notably Micklegate, St Saviourgate and Bootham. The Mansion House was built for the Lord Mayor and it became the official residence in 1730. In front of the Mansion House, the overflowing churchyard of St Helen's, Stonegate, was cleared away to allow coaches access to the newly built assembly rooms of 1731, which were designed by Lord Burlington. New Walk was also built by 1731, which gave the citizens a chance to promenade beside the River Ouse.

Some planned alterations to the city met public opposition, especially the council's attempts to demolish the city walls. Some sections of the defences were demolished, such as Skeldergate Postern and the barbican in front of Micklegate Bar, but the walls survived substantially intact.

Entertainment thrived in the city. A theatre was built in 1744 and today the current Theatre Royal stands on the same site. The fortunes of the theatre rose and fell, though in the eighteenth century the most profitable plays were those with elaborate mechanical machinery for the audience to marvel at, however bad the play. The races were, and are still, a great social occasion.

As well as being the seat of the Anglican Archbishop of York, York became a centre for Nonconformity. The Quakers became an important religious group, and influenced both the city's industry and social provision. In response to the appalling conditions in York's first

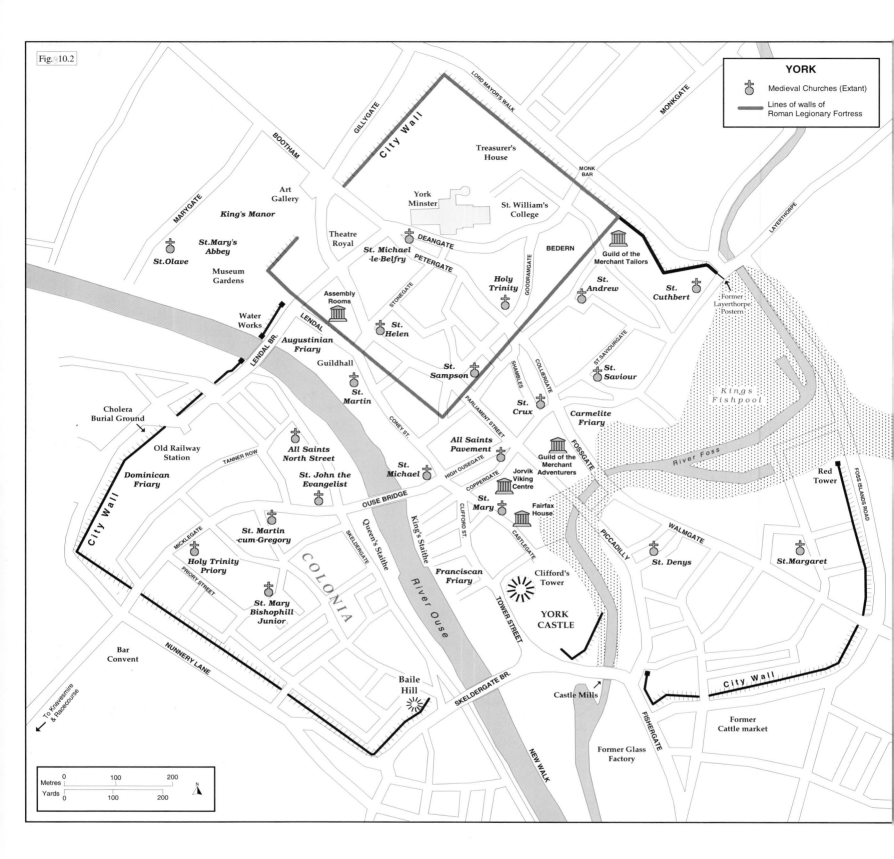

Fig. 10.2

YORK

✠ Medieval Churches (Extant)

━━ Lines of walls of
Roman Legionary Fortress

LORD MAYOR'S WALK

GILLYGATE

MONKGATE

BOOTHAM

City Wall

Treasurer's House

MONK BAR

LAYERTHORPE

MARYGATE

Art Gallery

York Minster

St. William's College

BEDERN

King's Manor

Theatre Royal

DEANGATE

Guild of the Merchant Tailors

St.Mary's Abbey

St. Michael -le-Belfry

PETERGATE

St. Olave

Museum Gardens

STONEGATE

Holy Trinity

GOODRAMGATE

St. Andrew

St. Cuthbert

Former Layerthorpe Postern

Water Works

Assembly Rooms

LENDAL

St. Helen

Augustinian Friary

LENDAL BR.

Guildhall

St. Martin

St. Sampson

SHAMBLES

COLLIERGATE

ST SAVIOURGATE

St. Saviour

Kings Fishpool

Cholera Burial Ground

Old Railway Station

TANNER ROW

All Saints North Street

CONEY ST.

St. Crux

Carmelite Friary

FOSSGATE

River Foss

Dominican Friary

City Wall

St. John the Evangelist

St. Michael

All Saints Pavement

HIGH OUSEGATE

Guild of the Merchant Adventurers

Red Tower

FOSS ISLANDS ROAD

OUSE BRIDGE

COPPERGATE

Jorvik Viking Centre

MICKLEGATE

SKELDERGATE

Queen's Staithe

King's Staithe

St. Mary

Fairfax House

CLIFFORD ST.

PICCADILLY

WALMGATE

St. Denys

St. Martin -cum-Gregory

COLONIA

St.Margaret

PRIORY STREET

Holy Trinity Priory

River Ouse

Franciscan Friary

CASTLEGATE

Clifford's Tower

St. Mary Bishophill Junior

TOWER STREET

YORK CASTLE

Castle Mills

Bar Convent

NUNNERY LANE

Baile Hill

SKELDERGATE BR.

Former Glass Factory

FISHERGATE

City Wall

Former Cattle market

To Knavesmire & Racecourse

NEW WALK

Metres 0 100 200

Yards 0 100 200

N

psychiatric hospital in Bootham, the Quakers opened the Retreat in 1796 where new and humane treatments were tried. Quakers were also active in prison reform and education, with Bootham and the Mount being Quaker schools. Other Nonconformist groups were prominent in the city, especially the Baptists, Methodists and Wesleyans.

A small Catholic community survived in York from the Reformation. In 1686 a convent on Blossom Street was founded, but the real expansion in numbers came in the nineteenth century with the influx of many Catholics from Ireland at the time of the Irish Famine.

In 1735 the York historian Francis Drake gave a pessimistic account of York trade, stating that, apart from four wine merchants, some export of butter and the making of a few 'trifles',

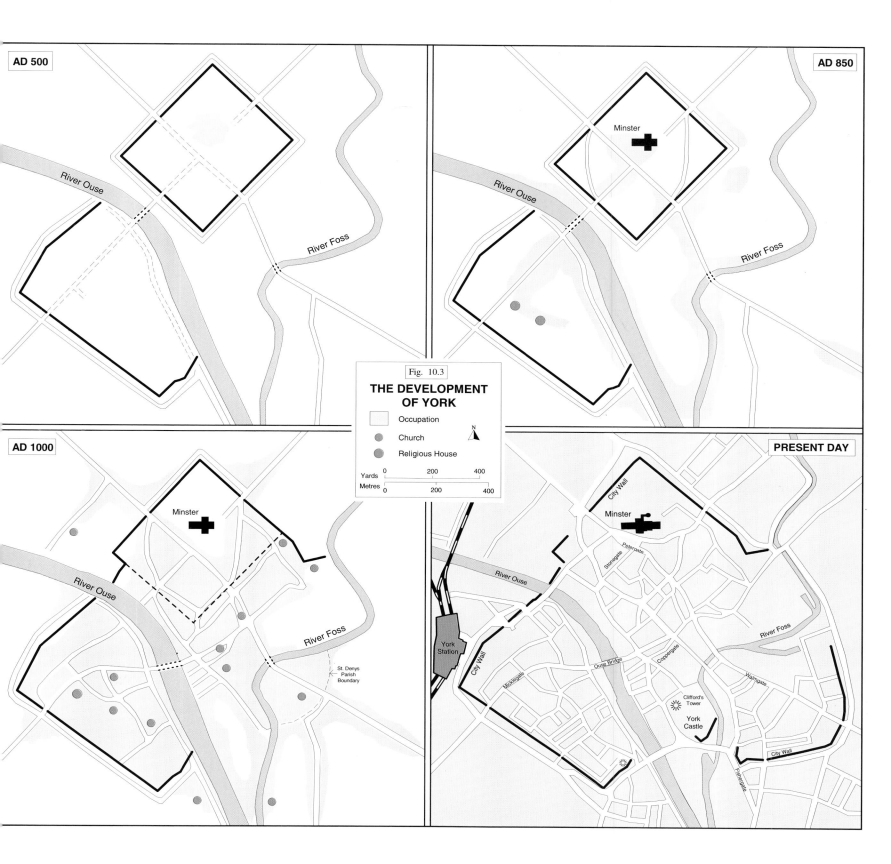

AD 500

AD 850

Minster ✚

Fig. 10.3

THE DEVELOPMENT
OF YORK

☐ Occupation

● Church

● Religious House

Yards |0   200   400|
Metres |0   200   400|

AD 1000

Minster ✚

River Ouse

River Foss

St. Denys
Parish
Boundary

PRESENT DAY

City Wall

Minster ✚

Peterpate

Stonegate

River Ouse

Coppergate

York
Station

Ouse Bridge

River Foss

City Wall

Micklegate

Clifford's
Tower

Walmgate

York
Castle

Fishergate

City Wall

no other trade took place in the city. This description is probably too harsh, but compared to
100 years later, trade in Drake's day was indeed minimal. York had none of the advantages of
the West Yorkshire manufacturing towns as the city had no water power or cheap coal, the
transportation of heavy goods was not easy and there were no large urban centres nearby to
fuel demand for products.

   A major impetus to York's industrial growth was the coming of the railways in the 1830s by
the agency of George Hudson, the self–styled 'Railway King'. At the height of his career in
1849 he controlled nearly a quarter of the total English railway network, with the heart of his
empire at York. Even after his dramatic downfall for financial irregularities, York remained an

Statue of the Roman Emperor Constantine, York Minster.
© R A Butlin.

The Ouse in flood, King's Staithe, York, 3rd November, 2000.
© R A Butlin.

Clifford's Tower, York.
© R A Butlin.

important railway centre with manufacturing workshops for engines and coaches. A new station was built outside the city walls, which when completed was the largest station in the world. Today the National Railway Museum is situated in York, a further reminder of the links between the railway industry and York.

The railway network meant easy transportation of goods such as glass, chemicals and iron. Walker's iron foundry became known worldwide for its specialist production of railings, and the firm produced railings not only for the British Museum but also for the botanical gardens in Mauritius. However, the increase of trade following the arrival of the railways was slight, and it was not until the late nineteenth century that the manufacture of chocolate in the city flourished, with three firms dominating production — Rowntree's Terry's and Craven's.

The population of York was steadily growing from the early nineteenth century and the insanitary conditions resulted in outbreaks of disease. In 1832 the most serious cholera outbreak in York's history started in a notorious slum in Skeldergate, popularly known as 'Hagworm's Nest'. The final toll was 185 mortalities out of a total of 450 cases. The victims were buried outside the city walls opposite the present railway station.

The number of people rose dramatically from the middle of the nineteenth century as the city experienced an influx of Irish as a result of Ireland's famine. Their poverty led them to settle in the cheapest and most run-down areas such as the Bedern and Walmgate, and it was not uncommon for whole families to live in a single room.

By 1900 York was a city of extremes, with the wealth of the gentry at one end and the slums at the other. In a famous survey entitled *Poverty, a study of town life*, Seebohm Rowntree

York: St Mary's Abbey.
© R A Butlin.

Fairfax House, Castlegate, York. Built in the early 1740s.
© R A Butlin.

York — Further Reading:

C H Feinstein (ed), *York 1831-1981. 150 Years of Scientific Endeavour and Change* (York: Sessions, 1981).

Francis Drake, *Eboracum: or the History and Antiquities of the City of York* (London, 1736).

Frances Finnegan, *Poverty and Prejudice: A Study of Irish Immigrants in York 1840-1875* (Cork: Cork University Press, 1982).

D M Palliser, *Tudor York* (Oxford: Oxford University Press, 1979).

Nikolaus Pevsner & David Neave, *The Buildings of England: Yorkshire – York and the East Riding*, 2nd edition (London: Penguin Books, 1995).

Royal Commission on the Historical Monuments of England, *York*, 5 vols (London: HMSO, 1962-81).

analysed the state of York and described the terrible conditions he found in 1901. He concluded that nearly ten per cent of the population were living below the poverty line. The Rowntree family had been especially active in creating better working and living conditions for their employees, a result of which was the 'model village' of New Earswick started in 1901.

Between the wars, large areas of slums were cleared in the more notorious areas of Hungate, Walmgate and the Bedern, and the populations were housed in new developments outside the city.

Since the Second World War, industry has contracted with the closure of the railway-carriage works, and the local chocolate firms of Rowntree's and Terry's being taken over by larger international firms of Nestlé and Suchard.

York has, however, blossomed academically with such educational establishments as: York St John College, founded in 1843; and more recently the university, founded in 1963; the College of Law; York College; and many state and private schools.

The main income of the city is, however, from tourism. York has a large number of attractions, the two best known being the Minster and the Jorvik Centre. Tourism is crucial to York's prosperity, but even at its busiest the city still retains its charm and the power to impress.

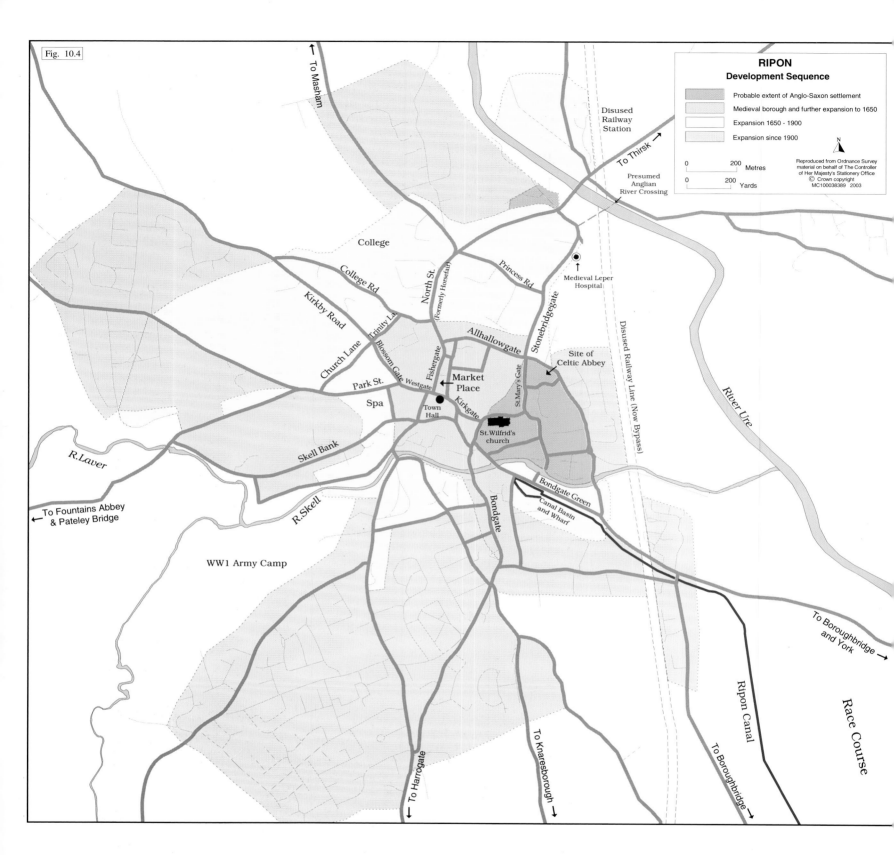

Fig. 10.4

RIPON
Development Sequence

Probable extent of Anglo-Saxon settlement

Medieval borough and further expansion to 1650

Expansion 1650 - 1900

Expansion since 1900

N

| 0 | 200 | Metres |
| 0 | 200 | Yards |

Reproduced from Ordnance Survey
material on behalf of The Controller
of Her Majesty's Stationery Office
© Crown copyright
MC100038389 2003

10.3   RIPON   MIKE YOUNGE

Situated on the western edge of the vale of York, the original settlement at Ripon lay to the
north of the River Skell near its confluence with the Ure (**fig 10.4**). A little upstream the
Skell was joined by the River Laver, leaving Ripon largely ringed by rivers. Retreating
glaciers had left extensive gravel deposits and several natural hills in the vicinity, yielding
cobble for builders in later times. Also available locally are outcrops of Permian magnesian
limestone and Triassic red sandstone.

Although there was much Prehistoric and Roman activity in the area, the founders of the Ripon settlement were an Anglian tribe who gave their farming community the name *rypum* (or *inhrypum*), possibly in the sixth century and certainly by the mid-seventh century.

At this point Ripon emerges clearly into the light of day through the works of contemporary chroniclers, who describe how a Celtic monastery (*c*AD 660), at one time housing St Cuthbert, was soon replaced by Abbot Wilfrid's well-endowed Benedictine monastery, probably shortly before the Roman Church tradition triumphed at the Synod of Whitby in 664. In 672 Wilfrid's prestigious new church in Ripon was consecrated.

Wilfrid's turbulent career put Ripon on the map, and appropriately he was buried there on his death in 709. His monastery continued, but suffered at the hands of an invading Saxon force from Wessex in 948.

Even so, in 995 Ripon was seen as a safe temporary refuge for St Cuthbert's body when it was brought down from the North-East to avoid marauding Vikings, but more peaceful Scandinavian incomers had already created new farming settlements near Ripon. Violence, however, was to return — whatever the extent of the Harrying of the North in 1069, *Domesday Book* (1086) already showed that the Ripon estates were reduced to a quarter of their former worth in Edward the Confessor's reign.

By the time of the Norman Conquest the monastery had gone, replaced by a collegiate church of canons controlled by the archbishops of York, and it was the latter who periodically rebuilt the great church over the next 500 years as the centrepiece of their Liberty of Ripon (a liberty was an area free from royal jurisdiction, and often under the jurisdiction of an archbishop). Their creation, in the twelfth century, of a purpose-built Norman borough with market place and burgage (a unit of land tenure in a town) plots, some distance to the west of the original settlement, had a dramatic effect on Ripon's economy. The street pattern that emerged has survived largely unchanged to the present day.

For centuries the weekly corn market, and the regular sheep and cattle fairs, bore witness to the fact that Ripon lay in an area of mixed farming, predominantly arable to the east and pasture to the west. From the late Middle Ages the town was also noted for its horse fairs.

It is clear from surviving records that the archbishops' borough was flourishing by 1200, bringing them a substantial income from the markets, fairs, burgage rents and the usual manorial tolls. Traders and craftsmen in the town profited from supplying the needs of the nearby Cistercian abbey of Fountains (founded 1132) as well as those of the numerous pilgrims who flocked to the shrine of St Wilfrid.

After the Battle of Bannockburn (1314), however, the town suffered a severe setback at the hands of Scottish raiders; later that century the Black Death also took its toll.

In the fifteenth century Ripon was spared direct involvement in the Wars of the Roses, and the town prospered on the basis of its successful cloth industry, but by the 1530s contemporaries noted that the latter was in sorry decline.

The Reformation dealt Ripon further blows — the loss of the Fountains trade, the confiscation of much of the collegiate church's wealth, the destruction of St Wilfrid's shrine, and costly involvement in both the Pilgrimage of Grace (1536) and the Rising of the North (1569).

Ripon.
Photograph courtesy of *Ripon Gazette*.

Signs of revival appear in the granting of two charters by James I in 1604, one re-endowing the collegiate church, the other re-ordering the town government and replacing the ancient office of wakeman with that of mayor. The Civil War brought little disruption, and Ripon appears to have prospered during the seventeenth century. 'As true steel as Ripon rowels' was a seventeenth-century proverb, alluding to a profitable manufacture of buckles and rowel spurs. Records reveal a local economy tightly regulated by at least fourteen trade guilds.

In the eighteenth century, Ripon's communications improved markedly through the turnpiking of local roads, the development of long-distance coach services and the opening of a canal (1773), the latter giving access to the Ouse and Humber waterways, and facilitating the supply of coal to the town.

The building trade boomed as 'Georgian' brickwork replaced or concealed timber framing, while the market place was enhanced by the obelisk (1702; restored 1781) and town hall (1801, incorporating the assembly rooms).

During the nineteenth century the population grew steadily, from about 3,000 to about 8,000. Crowded courts proliferated in the town centre but, on the outskirts, imposing Victorian terraces and villas sprang up, especially towards the railway station.

The advent of the railway in 1848, if fatal to the canal, brought immediate benefit to passengers, merchants and manufacturers; new industries were established, in particular the manufacture of paint and varnish, and agricultural machinery. New public buildings abounded — including churches, chapels, schools, a college, hospital, workhouse, prison, clock tower and sewage works.

In Edwardian times Ripon sought briefly to re-invent itself as a spa, despite having to pipe in the medicinal waters over several miles. However, its new up-market visitor trade was swiftly interrupted by the First World War which instead brought thousands of soldiers to the vast new Ripon Army Camp.

Continuing population growth in the twentieth century brought new housing, schools, supermarkets and light industry. The railway was lost (1969) but the canal re-opened as heritage tourism grew to be a key element in the local economy. Economic progress was mirrored by administrative changes: in 1836 the church became a diocesan cathedral, and in 1974 Ripon was given city status.

Ripon — Further Reading:
Edna Ellis *et al, A Ripon Record 1887-1986* (Chichester: Phillimore, 1986).
Thomas Gent, *The Ancient and Modern History of the Loyal Town of Rippon* (York, 1733).
The Ripon Millenary 1886 (Ripon, 1892).
Ripon: Some Aspects of its History (Clapham: Dalesman, 1972).
Celia Thomson, *The Book of Ripon* (Buckingham: Barracuda Books, 1978).

10.4 HARROGATE AND KNARESBOROUGH
PADDIE MORRISON

At the time of the Domesday Survey, Harrogate did not exist as a distinct entity, while the scanty returns for the Knaresborough area reflect the devastation inflicted by William the Conqueror on the Northumbrian rebels in 1069.

To consolidate their hold, the Normans created the Honour of Knaresborough, an administrative area divided by the River Nidd into the thinly populated Forest (containing modern Harrogate) and the Liberty, containing the borough and manor of Knaresborough and numerous villages.

The first lord of the honour was Serlo de Burgh, who probably built the first castle in Knaresborough. Later lords included Hugh de Moreville, one of Thomas Becket's murderers, and Edward II's favourite, Piers Gaveston. On the latter's death in 1312 it reverted to the Crown, whence it passed to John of Gaunt, Duke of Lancaster. It remains part of the Duchy to this day.

Situated between the fertile Vale of York and the Pennine uplands on which cattle and sheep were grazed, the town enjoyed a thriving market in the later medieval period (**fig 10.5**). Under a royal charter of 1310 a Wednesday market was held north of the castle, and burgage tenements occupied High Street, Finkle Street, Gracious Street and Briggate, the last leading to one of the town's two bridges. Further out of town, on smaller plots, lived the bondmen who worked for the landowners; the area is still called Bond End. In 1318, two years after Bannockburn, the town was burnt by the Scots, but its fortunes revived and in 1553 the burgesses won the right to elect two MPs.

The castle was increasingly neglected, however: a survey of 1538 refers to the ruinous state of the inner ward, though the walls and keep remained in good order. In the Civil War the town sided with the Royalists, but in 1644 surrendered to Fairfax's Parliamentary forces. Sir Henry Slingsby, one of the town's MPs under Charles I, was beheaded on Tower Hill and his estates were sequestered. The slighting of the castle in 1648 was compounded by the plundering of stone by local people.

The principal industry within the honour was textile production. In the thirteenth century a fulling (cloth-finishing) mill is documented near Tentergate, where material was stretched to dry on frames ('tenters'). Eventually linen production predominated, and water-powered mills were built alongside the Nidd. Flax was imported from Hull, but Knaresborough suffered from its distance from navigable water.

The difficulties of building a canal proving insurmountable, so in 1819 a railway was proposed which, had it been built, would have been the first public railway in the world.

Knaresborough's population grew rapidly from 4,202 in 1801 to 6,656 in 1821, making it North Yorkshire's fourth-largest town, while Harrogate boasted fewer than 2,000 permanent residents.[1] But poor communications stifled Knaresborough's industrial growth, and in the 1830s it entered a period of decline.

While Knaresborough's fortunes fell, Harrogate's continued to rise from its humble beginnings. Early settlement was scattered, with some hamlets. Harrogate Hall Farm, Knox House Farm and Hill Top Farm formed one such hamlet, surviving until the 1950s. Another was around a green at the junction of Bilton Lane, Crab Lane, King's Road and Skipton Road. Settlement probably also developed around the common, spreading down King's Road and along Skipton Road.

An attempt to enclose the common in the late seventeenth century was resisted by Sir Thomas Slingsby, fearing further erosion of his family's fortunes, and not finally accomplished until the Forest of Knaresborough Enclosure Act of 1770. By then Harrogate was a well-established spa, and the act accordingly made provision for public access to the 200 acres (80ha) of common known as the Stray, so that visitors could 'take the air'.

The medicinal properties of the springs were first recognised in the late sixteenth century by William Slingsby, who had tasted the waters at Spa in Belgium, and who realised that the Tewit Well was similar. Dr Edmund Deane, in his *Spadacrene Anglica* (1626), recommended the chalybeate Tewit Well and three sulphur springs, or wells. Chalybeate water, he claimed, was good for ailments ranging from catarrh to migraine, from worms to infertility. The sulphur waters, described by Defoe in the 1720s as 'foetid and nauseous', were said to be effective against rheumatism and gout if bathed in. Celia Fiennes drank two quarts (2.3l) of the water on two successive days in 1697, and noted that it was 'a good purge if you can hold your breath so as to drink them down'.

Like most seventeenth-century visitors, Celia Fiennes found accommodation in Knaresborough, but in time inns (and later hotels) opened close to the springs.

Initially Harrogate developed in two distinct parts. Low Harrogate grew next to the Sulphur Wells, where the Crown Inn was followed by the White Hart, the Swan and the Crescent. High Harrogate grew along the northern edge of the common, on Park Parade, Regent Parade and Granby Road, where the principal inns were the Queen's Head (1687), the Granby and the Dragon. High Harrogate became the more fashionable area, with shops and other amenities, a theatre (1788) and a racecourse on the Stray. By 1838 there were 51 hotels and lodging houses in High Harrogate, 79 in Low Harrogate and 21 in central Harrogate, a slightly later development.

Rail links with Leeds, Thirsk and York arrived in 1848, though services were promptly disrupted by the collapse of the Nidd Viaduct. The North Eastern Railway opened a new central station in Harrogate in 1862, offering direct journeys to London. This became the nucleus of the main shopping area in Parliament, James and Oxford (formerly Chapel) streets.

New spa developments were concentrated in Low Harrogate: the Royal Pump Room was erected over the Old Sulphur Wells, hydropathic hotels opened, and more hotels were built on the north side of the valley. Meanwhile fewer visitors drank the chalybeate waters of High Harrogate, where hotel numbers fell (the Dragon became a school). Spa treatments continued until 1969, when the Royal Baths closed.

Today Harrogate's extensive hotel facilities host a thriving conference trade, supplemented by a showground and exhibition centre. Knaresborough enjoys a large tourist trade, capitalising on its beautiful setting on a cliff overlooking the Nidd, and the old-fashioned charm of its streets.

Harrogate & Knaresborough — Further Reading:

Edmund Deane, *Spadacrene Anglica; or, the English Spaw-Fountain: being a brief treatise of the acid or tart fountaine in the Forest of Knaresborow* (London, 1626).

W Grainge, *The History and Topography of Harrogate and the Forest of Knaresborough* (London, 1871).

E Hargrove, *The History of the Castle, Town, and Forest of Knaresborough, with Harrogate and its Medicinal Waters* (York, 1775).

Bernard Jennings (ed), *A History of Harrogate and Knaresborough* (Harrogate: Harrogate WEA, 1970).

Arnold Kellett, *Historic Knaresborough* (Otley: Smith Settle, 1991).

Report of the Knaresborough Railway Committee (Knaresborough, 1819).

Thorpe's Illustrated Guide to Harrogate (1886; reprinted, Dewsbury: Chantry Press, 1986).

10.5   SCARBOROUGH   MICHAEL F HOPKINSON

The first recorded settlement, 'Skarthi's burgh', dates from before AD 965 (*Skarthi* is a Norse nickname meaning 'hare-lipped'), but the castle promontory has been occupied for much longer, with evidence of an Iron-Age hill fort and a Roman signal station (**fig 10.6**). It was both a Viking and a Saxon stronghold; under the Normans its merchants acquired the liberties (freedoms and rights) of burgesses by a charter of 1155. The present church of St Mary dates from the thirteenth century, and the settlement is one of only a handful of northern towns shown on Mathew Paris's map of England of 1250.

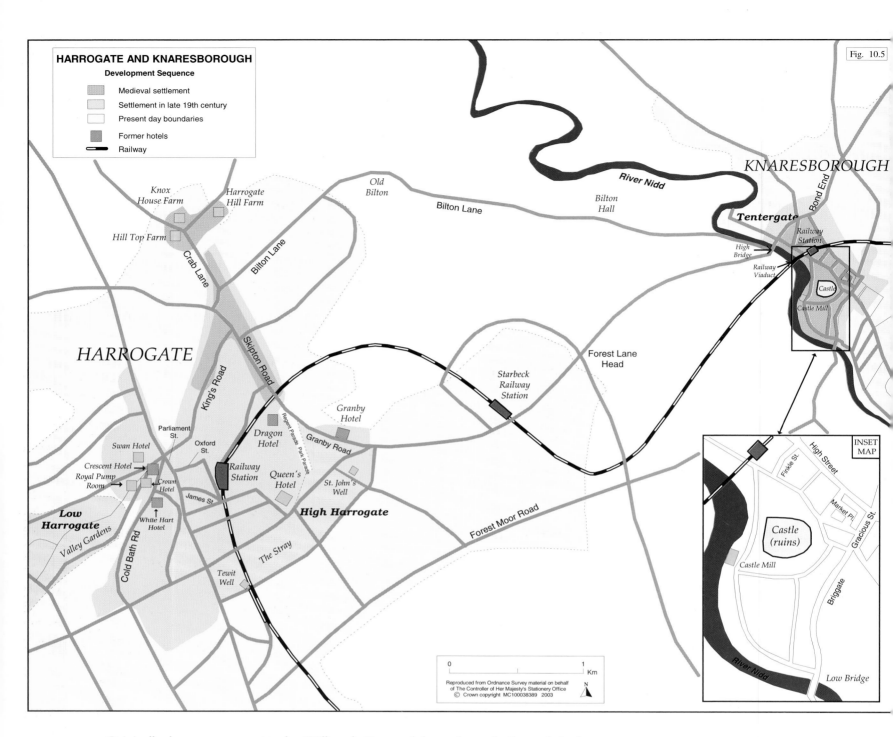

Fig. 10.5

HARROGATE AND KNARESBOROUGH
Development Sequence

Medieval settlement
Settlement in late 19th century
Present day boundaries
Former hotels
Railway

KNARESBOROUGH

River Nidd

Old Bilton

Bilton Lane

Bilton Hall

Tentergate

Bond End

Railway Station

High Bridge

Railway Viaduct

Castle

Castle Mill

Knox House Farm

Harrogate Hill Farm

Hill Top Farm

Crab Lane

Bilton Lane

HARROGATE

Skipton Road

King's Road

Forest Lane Head

Starbeck Railway Station

Parliament St.

Swan Hotel

Oxford St.

Dragon Hotel

Regent Parade Park Parade

Granby Hotel

Granby Road

Crescent Hotel
Royal Pump Room

Crown Hotel

Railway Station

Queen's Hotel

St. John's Well

James St.

High Harrogate

Low Harrogate

White Hart Hotel

Cold Bath Rd

Valley Gardens

The Stray

Tewit Well

Forest Moor Road

INSET MAP

Finkle St.

High Street

Market Pl.

Gracious St.

Castle (ruins)

Castle Mill

Briggate

River Nidd

Low Bridge

0   1 Km

Reproduced from Ordnance Survey material on behalf
of The Controller of Her Majesty's Stationery Office
© Crown copyright MC100038389 2003

N

Originally the manor was granted to William le Gros, and the castle was built as a defensive outpost against Danish attack in the years after the Norman Conquest. A small town grew up in the cove south of the castle, but both borough and castle were reclaimed by the Crown in 1265.

By this stage the town had outgrown its early ditch and ramparts, which ran in a semi-circle from the western edge of the castle to the sea, terminating at a small pier or harbour wall. The Crown responded by giving the residents the adjacent village of Falsgrave, so that expansion could take place. A major siege in 1312 showed that the sea gave only partial protection to the site.

Despite its strategic importance, the town experienced fluctuating fortunes: attacks by the Scots, French and Dutch — as well as the constant struggle and expense of maintaining the harbour as a safe anchorage on this exposed stretch of coast — meant that the town remained small and relatively poor. A sixteenth-century map shows perhaps 150 houses and two churches, and despite its coastal position Scarborough was rated for only a £30 contribution to 'ship money' in 1635, less than a quarter of the assessment for Hull.

The Royalist defender of the castle, Sir Hugh Cholmley, surrendered to the Parliamentarians after a lengthy siege in 1645, during which part of the great tower was destroyed. The castle was re-fortified in anticipation of Scottish attack in 1745, and remained garrisoned into

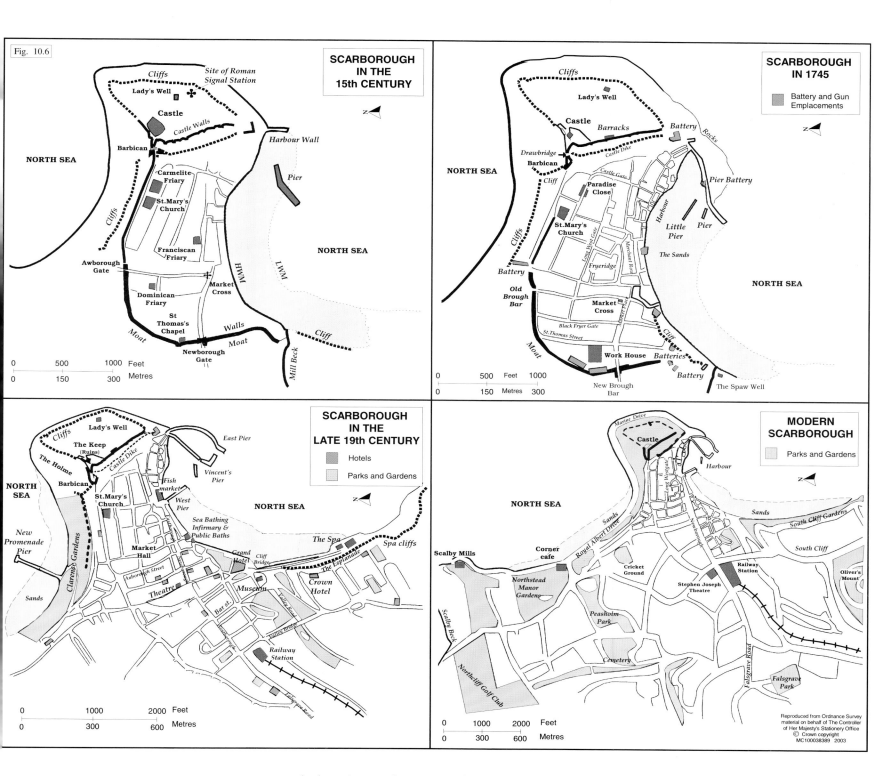

Fig. 10.6

SCARBOROUGH IN THE 15th CENTURY

SCARBOROUGH IN 1745

Battery and Gun Emplacements

SCARBOROUGH IN THE LATE 19th CENTURY

Hotels

Parks and Gardens

MODERN SCARBOROUGH

Parks and Gardens

Reproduced from Ordnance Survey material on behalf of The Controller of Her Majesty's Stationery Office © Crown copyright
MC100038389 2003

the late nineteenth century: it last saw action when the town was shelled by a German gun-boat during the First World War.

The discovery in the early seventeenth century of mineral springs on the southern outskirts of the town, near the present Valley Road, inaugurated a long period of development and prosperity as a resort. Developed by the enthusiastic Dr Wittie in the 1660s, the water was considered good for 'epilepsie, catalepsie, vertigo, leprosie, jaundice, and hypochondriak melancholie and windiness' (one can only hope that sufferers of all these diverse complaints did not congregate together at the same time).

By the early eighteenth century, spa buildings had been constructed near the beach, only to fall victim to a landslip in 1737. They were immediately rebuilt; sea-bathing was introduced, a 'long room' for social gatherings was erected in the upper part of town; and by 1798 the town was expanding through Westborough to Newborough on the northern side of the valley. Although the spa facilities were described by London visitors as 'very naked and scurvy' in appearance and furnishings, the food was good and accommodation cheaper than in the southern resorts of Bristol (Clifton) and Bath.

Scarborough: Roman signal station, medieval castle and walls, and the harbour.
NMR 12324/07 © *Crown copyright. NMR.*

Scarborough: beach and Grand Hotel.
© R A Butlin.

The construction of Cliff Bridge over Valley Road in 1826 connected the new districts to the old, and thereafter housing and hotels spread along the cliffs and Filey Road. The census of 1821 recorded a population of just over 8,000, making it a little smaller than Whitby and about a third of the size of York.

The old port was now neglected and impoverished: visitors commented on the unhygienic and wretched nature of both property and people. From now on, the future of Scarborough would lie mainly in the expansion of the tourist trade.

Population rose from 10,000 in 1841 to 17,000 in 1861, as the coming of the railway (1845), with a terminus in Westborough, opened up the town to mass tourism. By 1900 some 300,000 passengers per year were passing through the station. The new Spa Building (1856) by Joseph Paxton (designer of the Crystal Palace), the Esplanade (1850), Cuthbert Brodrick's towering Grand Hotel (1863–7), the Cliff Tramway (1875) and Clarence Gardens (1890) all helped transform the coastline into that of a fashionable and popular holiday resort.

The development of North Bay for the popular holiday market followed the construction of Marine Drive around the headland on which the castle stands. This was a difficult and costly undertaking: the coast here is very exposed and the road is still frequently closed during the winter months. By the 1930s, however, new amusement areas connected by an inland road bridge had been constructed around Peasholme Park, extending the resort area out to Scalby Mills. Today this area retains rather more of the traditional resort character than the more raucous South Bay promenade.

Scarborough — Acknowledgements:
The author wishes to acknowledge the help given in connection with this article by Chris Hall of the Scarborough District Planning Department.

Scarborough — Further Reading:
M Edwards (ed), *Scarborough: the story of 1,000 years* (Scarborough: Scarborough Archaeological Society, 1979).

T Hinderwell, *The History and Antiquities of Scarborough*, 2nd edition (York, 1811).

North Yorkshire Local Studies Unit, *Scarborough History Through Maps* (Northallerton: North Yorkshire County Council, 1972).

A Rowntree, *The History of Scarborough* (London: Dent, 1931).

T Whellan, *History and Topography of the City of York and the North Riding of Yorkshire* (2 vols, Beverley, 1857), I, 672–767.

M Whittaker, *The Book of Scarborough Spaw* (Buckingham: Barracuda Books, 1984).

Selby Abbey.
© R A Butlin.

Between the two, the old harbour has enjoyed a revival for pleasure boats and small fresh-fish shops, with a rather tatty funfair. The construction of Marine Drive put an end to shipbuilding at Scarborough but the harbour remained important for fishing boats until the 1950s, and still carries on a small trade.

Today Scarborough still retains some of the character and prestige of a major spa town, and rather more of the ambience of a popular seaside resort. Most of the former department stores have gone, though the local firm of William Boyes now has branches throughout North Yorkshire.

Many of the outdoor attractions in South Bay have also closed, some have been vandalised and neglected, and, at the southern end of the Sands, recent cliff collapses threaten property and have necessitated considerable reconstruction of sea defences.

As tourist preferences shift, Scarborough is increasingly vulnerable, but the town remains a lively commercial centre, with new regional attractions such as the Stephen Joseph Theatre.

10.6   SELBY   MICHAEL F HOPKINSON

Selby (**fig 10.7**) may have been established as early as AD 780 as a village on the eastern edge of the Saxon Kingdom of Elmet, one of a line of settlements on the west bank of the Ouse. The first post-Conquest abbey was founded here in 1069 by a French Benedictine monk, Benedict of Auxerre, close to where the Viking fleet had disembarked before their ill-fated battle at Stamford Bridge three years earlier.

The abbey and its staithes were built at a sharp bend in the river, on the undercut edge of the meander where the water is deeper. Subsequently the town's staithes and warehouses were almost all built along this right bank; Selby's port function concentrated here and inland around the broad Micklegate, which is still the town's market place.

As conflict between Normans and Vikings gave way in the twelfth century to trade, the 'sallow marshes' to the west of the nucleus, from which the settlement takes its name, were drained by the abbey to make farmland; the watercourse of Selby Dam was also cut, resulting in the drying out of the large common which now borders the north side of Gowthorpe.

Despite opposition from local people, drainage engineers from the Netherlands continued to expand the acreage of the abbey granges until the middle of the fifteenth century, and this part of the Ouse Valley became increasingly prosperous. There was another area of common land to the south of the market place, and a remnant of this survives today as Barlow Common, three miles (5km) south of the town centre.

The abbey, implicated when the uprising known as the Pilgrimage of Grace (1536) was raised in the area, was dissolved in 1539, and Selby declined during the later Tudor period. The town was unwilling to be sacrificed in the Civil War, and became the winter base for the Parliamentarians in 1642, but was the scene of fierce fighting in 1644. After the war, the town seems to have stagnated; the local Royalist castles were demolished and in 1690 part of the abbey collapsed.

Heavy floods also took their toll. They were recorded in 1315, 1564, 1625 and 1686, and recurred in 1794, 1857, 1947 and 2000. The underlying cause is an impervious clay layer, about five feet (1.5m) below the ground surface, which maintains a high water-table and makes building hazardous, especially close to the river.

The only solution was to build further from the Ouse and, once a bridge was finally constructed in 1792, residential districts spread both east of the river, and along the new turnpike road towards Monk Fryston and the Great North Road. Selby's swing bridge drew the admiration of contemporary visitors. Outwardly a robust and unsophisticated timber structure, it seems out of place in a county boasting so many graceful stone arches, but its seventy tons could be rotated in less than a minute by a mechanism no less elegant.

Assisted by the bridge, Selby's coaching trade grew, and the continued importance of the river port led to the demolition of the remaining conventual buildings of the abbey and their replacement by the fashionable houses of the Crescent and Park Street. The docks became increasingly important and warehouses expanded along Ousegate.

Growth southwards was stimulated by better roads, and most importantly by the region's first railway (1834). The Leeds & Selby Railway was constructed to export coal and woollen cloth from the West Riding. At Selby, goods were briefly transhipped to river boats for onward carriage to Hull, but by 1840 the line had been extended to the coast. Selby remained an important bridging point, however, as well as a waterway junction on the Aire & Calder

Selby — Further Reading:

R B Dobson, *Selby Abbey and Town* (Leeds: Elsworth Press, 1969; revised edition, Selby: Selby Abbey Trust, 1993).

H Farrar, *Selby* (York: Maxiprint, 1987).

W W Morrell, *The History and Antiquities of Selby* (Selby: Whittaker & Co, 1867).

J H Tillotson, *Monastery and Society in the Late Middle Ages* (Woodbridge: Boydell & Brewer, 1988).

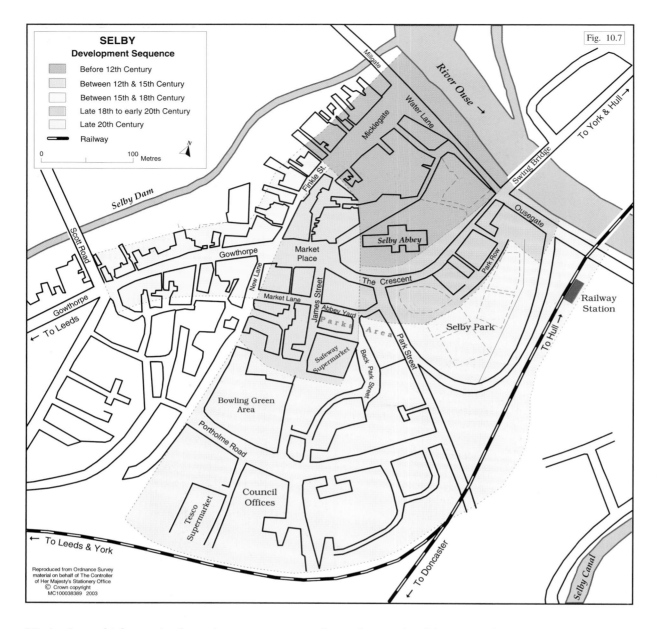

Reproduced from Ordnance Survey
material on behalf of The Controller
of Her Majesty's Stationery Office
© Crown copyright
MC100038389 2003

Navigation, which remained a major transport artery long after much of the national canal network had declined into insignificance.

The economic core of the town spread south and west, and the processing of new crops such as sugar beet added an industrial dimension to its functions. On the east bank of the river, new feed mills and associated low-cost housing extended the built-up area towards Barlby and Ricall — a move accelerated by the decision in the 1960s to develop the Selby Coalfield and build power stations at nearby Eggborough, Ferrybridge and Drax. The last alone consumed 50,000 tons of coal per day.

In the 1970s a major building scheme south of the Parks saw the location of a new supermarket, school, fire station and council offices around Bowling Green. This has reduced local traffic on the main route of Gowthorpe, but the narrow river crossing is still a major bottleneck, even though the bridge is now toll-free.

The river is today of little commercial significance, although shipbuilding was an important local industry until recently: the Sealink ferry *St Cecilia* was built here in 1986. Nowadays road traffic dominates as the town continues to be the major service centre for the communities of the Lower Aire, Derwent and Ouse valleys.

10.7 SKIPTON-IN-CRAVEN MICHAEL F HOPKINSON

Thomas Gray's 1762 description of Skipton as 'a pretty, large market town in a valley with one very broad street gently sloping downwards from the castle' is a fair summary of the centre of the town at any period in the last 800 years. In fact the castle is slightly offset to the

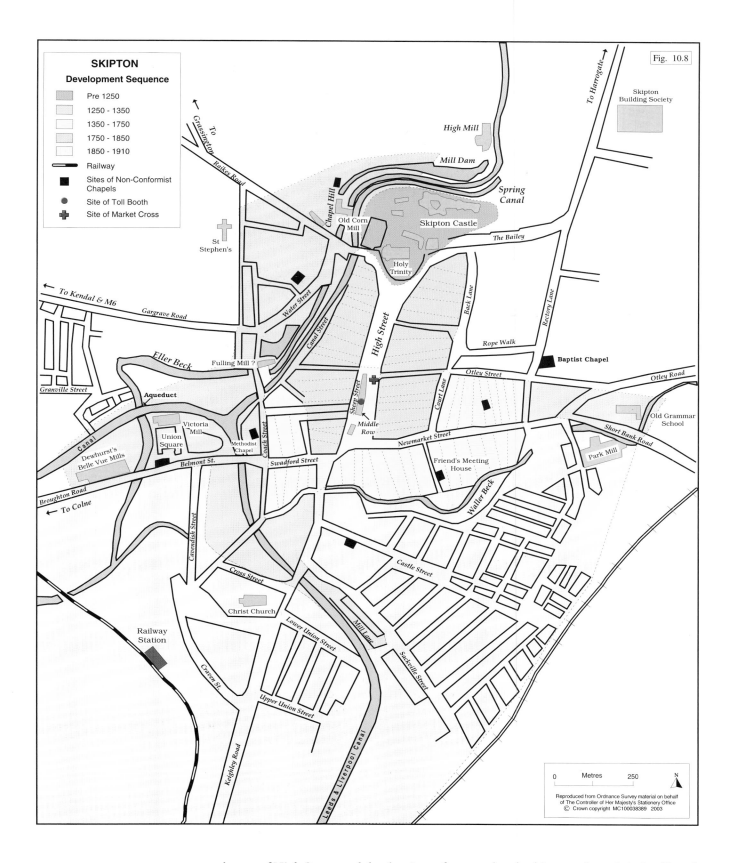

SKIPTON
Development Sequence

- Pre 1250
- 1250 - 1350
- 1350 - 1750
- 1750 - 1850
- 1850 - 1910
- ⌒ Railway
- ■ Sites of Non-Conformist Chapels
- ● Site of Toll Booth
- ✚ Site of Market Cross

Fig. 10.8

Skipton Building Society

High Mill

Mill Dam

Spring Canal

To Harrogate→

To Grassington

To Raikes Road

St Stephen's

Chapel Hill

Old Corn Mill

Skipton Castle

The Bailey

Rectory Lane

Holy Trinity

Water Street

← To Kendal & M6

Gargrave Road

Canal Street

High Street

Back Lane

Rope Walk

Baptist Chapel

Otley Road

Eller Beck

Fulling Mill ?

Otley Street

Granville Street

Aqueduct

Sheep Street

Court Lane

Old Grammar School

Victoria Mill

Middle Row

Newmarket Street

Short Bank Road

Canal

Union Square

Methodist Chapel

Coach Street

Swadford Street

Friend's Meeting House

Park Mill

Dewhurst's Belle Vue Mills

Belmont St.

Waller Beck

Broughton Road

← To Colne

Cavendish Street

Castle Street

Cross Street

Christ Church

Lower Union Street

Mill Lane

Railway Station

Craven St.

Sackville Street

Keighley Road

Upper Union Street

Leeds & Liverpool Canal

0   Metres   250   N

Reproduced from Ordnance Survey material on behalf of The Controller of Her Majesty's Stationery Office © Crown copyright MC100038389 2003

north-east of High Street, and the dominant feature when looking northwards is the Church of Holy Trinity which dates from about 1120.

The castle is built on higher ground, protected by a loop of Eller Beck. Commanding the strategically important Aire Gap, a natural routeway between Yorkshire and Lancashire, the defensive properties of the site were probably first exploited before AD 700. Of early fortifications nothing remains, but Robert de Romille erected a Norman castle, only for the Scots to destroy this in turn in 1152. De Romille's heirs, the earls of Albermarle, held the rebuilt castle until 1221, when the last earl rebelled against Henry III and the castle and manor were confiscated by the Crown.

Skipton.
© R White/Yorkshire Dales National Park Authority, 4007.

Briefly bestowed by Edward II on his favourite, Piers Gaveston, they were granted to the Clifford family in 1310. The Cliffords and their descendants the Sackvilles, earls of Cumberland, held Skipton until 1675, most notably under Lady Anne Clifford. Her daughter married the earl of Thanet and the family continued in possession until 1848. Thus the town remained an essentially intact estate for over 500 years, providing an almost perfect example of the evolution of a market town dominated by church and castle.

The main axis of the town (**fig 10.8**) was already established before the Cliffords took possession, comprising perhaps as few as a dozen or so habitations on either side of the church, beneath the castle walls. Borough status was achieved by 1266, and by 1350 about eighteen or twenty tofts (sites of houses) had been added on either side of the broad High Street, with a fully developed back lane on the east side (see map). The western boundary of the house plots was formed by Eller Beck as far south as the medieval fulling or cloth-finishing mill. The beck powered at least one other mill (for corn) just below the castle. To the south the town extended as far as Newmarket and Swadford Streets.

Between 1350 and 1550 the town flourished on the profits of sheep trading. Southward expansion being curtailed by Waller Beck, new plots were added at right-angles to the High Street plots, almost doubling the number of tofts. At least two dozen significant tradesmen were recorded in the lay subsidy rolls of 1379, only a generation after the Black Death.

The need to regulate market trade led to the erection of a substantial market cross, and later a tollbooth and associated buildings about two-thirds of the way down High Street. These formed the nucleus of what became Middle Row, dividing the market place from Sheep Street. Middle Row housed the old town hall from 1650 until 1862, when the present building was provided in High Street. The constriction of High Street was exacerbated by the encroachment of several other buildings in the seventeenth century, and new cross-streets were cut through to provide easier access to the back lanes.

Although the Cliffords supported the unsuccessful Lancastrian cause in the Wars of the Roses, and remained determinedly Catholic at the Reformation, the town continued to prosper, perhaps because during the Pilgrimage of Grace the Cliffords stood firm for the Crown — for which they were rewarded with the title of earls of Cumberland.

After 1650, Skipton's military role ceased: Cromwell allowed Lady Anne Clifford to re-occupy the castle only on condition that it was 'slighted', and subsequent rebuilding had to be of thinner walls which could not withstand cannon fire. In her diaries she resembles a medieval potentate, bountiful but autocratic, but by the time of her death in 1675 the whole urban climate was changing rapidly.

The Quakers had established a meeting place in the 1650s, followed by the Congrega-tionalists in 1700 and the Methodists in the 1750s. Nonconformist places of worship tended to be confined to the outskirts of the town, and provide an indication of seventeenth- and eighteenth-century urban expansion. Landmark buildings include the Friends' meeting house off Newmarket Street, the 1835 Methodist chapel (later fire station) in Coach Street and the Baptist chapel in Otley Street, dating from 1840.

Skipton — Further Reading:

W H Dawson, *History of Skipton* (Hailstone Collection, York Minster, 1882).

J K Ellwood, *Skipton: a pictorial revelation* (Clapham: Dalesman, 1975).

A M Gibbon, *The Ancient Free Grammar School of Skipton* (Liverpool: Liverpool University Press, 1947).

R Spence, *Skipton Castle in the Great Civil War* (York: University of York, 1991).

D J Williams, *Medieval Skipton* (Skipton: Craven Museum, 1977).

Skipton-in-Craven in the 1930s.
© Marie Hartley.

Renewed growth was stimulated by the introduction of mechanised cotton and worsted spinning in the late eighteenth and early nineteenth centuries, and the attendant development of transport infrastructure, especially on the south side of the town. Most notably, the Leeds–Liverpool Canal connected Skipton with Leeds in 1777, though the Yorkshire and Lancashire sections were not finally linked until 1816.

Dewhursts established a worsted spinning and weaving mill close to the canal to the west of the old town in 1828, together with workers' housing in Union Square. Burnt down in 1831, the mill was rebuilt the following year as a cotton mill and was known latterly for the manufacture of Sylko thread.

A railway linked Skipton with Bradford in 1847, and further lines opened in 1848, 1849 and 1888. The station was built on the south-west side of the town, near the canal and new factories.

This concentration of new industry and transport infrastructure relieved congestion in the older parts of town, allowing livestock markets to be held in High Street until 1906, and a horse fair until the 1920s; a general market survives today. During the Victorian era the textile industry enabled population to grow from 5,000 to 12,000, and by the end of the Second World War it stood at 14,000.

Tertiary-sector activities have now taken over, notably retailing and the office employment generated by the Skipton Building Society, whose new offices are located to the north-east of the town. In future the tourist industry — encouraged by proximity to the Dales — will probably assume even greater significance.

10.8   WHITBY   ROSALIN BARKER

Whitby stands astride the estuary of the Yorkshire Esk, a fast-flowing twenty-four mile (38km) river rising in Westerdale. The navigable estuary flows north for a mile (1.6km) through a narrow valley into the North Sea, between two headlands, each rising to about 200 feet (60m). The maximum width of the present harbour is about 120 yards (110m).

A monastic foundation was established on the headland on the east side of the Esk in the seventh century, but Whitby's economic hinterland made it an unpromising location for a town. Inland lie some 772 square miles (2,000km²) of inhospitable moorland, with largely pastoral farming. There are few mineral resources: alum lay undiscovered till the seventeenth century, while brown coal on the moor and iron in the Esk Valley were little exploited till the nineteenth century. It was, however, the only natural harbour offering shelter from all winds between the Tees and the Humber.

The burgage area (the area of boroughs subject to a legally-defined type of tenure) of medieval Whitby, established by an abbey charter of c1128, covers about forty-eight acres (19ha); approximately half is inter-tidal mud, leaving some twenty-four habitable acres. Much of that is precipitous: many of the lanes leading up from the harbour are long flights of steps. However, unlike other ports such as Bristol, Liverpool, Ipswich and Hull, the town was built on both sides of the river so that twice as many of the burgage tenements faced onto the prised harbourside.

During the Middle Ages, Whitby benefited from the influence and acumen of the Benedictine abbey, and the surviving Yorkshire lay subsidy returns of 1301 record that the town paid more tax than any except York. The port is sporadically recorded in national records, and in the only extant abbey *compoti* (accounts) of 1394-6, as having trade in fish, coal and wool.

There is some evidence of a trade in specie (coinage), and the harbour was sufficiently attractive to entice the Scots to raid in 1327, and commodious enough to contain the captured French fleet in 1451. Whitby was one of thirty ports in England expected to provide a ship-of-war to fight the French or the Scots during the medieval period.

The dissolution of the abbey in 1539 brought to an abrupt end the urban vitality of Whitby. The loss of the abbey's revenue and commercial skills, as well as probable depopulation, left a vacuum. The town remained, apparently, a fishing station, its pier, which Leland records as under construction just *before* the dissolution, in ruins, and its fleet reduced to a few small balingers.[1] By 1600, only two merchant vessels belonging to the port can be traced. The town was so bereft and remote that not even a conscience-appeasing endowed grammar school was founded.

The exploitation of newly discovered alum at the start of the seventeenth century changed the Whitby shipping industry for the next three centuries. Initially the necessary additional raw materials were imported to the Whitby storehouses in Scots and Dutch vessels, but slowly the opportunistic inhabitants of Whitby rose to the challenge.

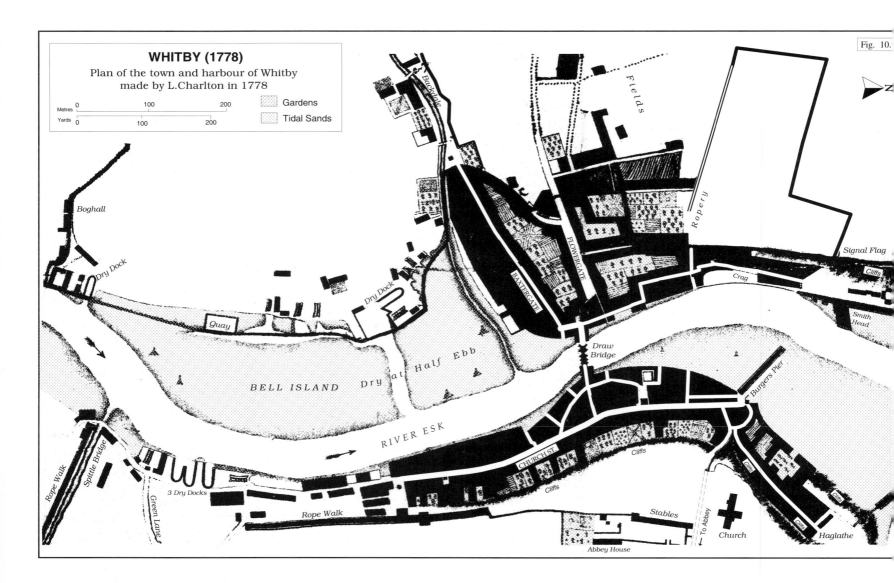

Fig. 10.

WHITBY (1778)

Plan of the town and harbour of Whitby
made by L. Charlton in 1778

Metres 0   100   200
Yards 0   100   200

Gardens
Tidal Sands

By 1612 there were at least twelve ketches (small two-masted vessels) belonging to Whitby; by 1625 the town was capable of building the *Great Neptune*, then the largest merchant ship in England, for the New England Company; Phineas Pett, the king's master shipbuilder, visited the port to inspect its yards in 1637, staying with the ailing Luke Foxe, one of the explorers of Hudson Bay, who had first come to Whitby to join the alum trade and remained to share its growing prosperity. General Fairfax himself took possession of the port for Parliament during the Civil War, because of its importance.

The declining fortunes of the ruling Cholmley family[2] loosened the manorial bonds in the town, and deeds and probate evidence for the turn of the seventeenth and eighteenth centuries show a widespread prosperity. Indeed, the known excusal rate of the 1673 Hearth Tax is lower, at under four per cent, than that of most other towns in England. Travel writers of the late seventeenth century unite in their admiration of the prosperity of the town.[3]

The main import for the alum works was coal, and this took Whitby's growing fleet to the Tyne and the Wear, where the potential of the London coal trade was also recognised. By the middle of the eighteenth century, a fleet of some 250 vessels, many of them well above the national average for tonnage, carried some thirty per cent of the coal export from the north-east, as well as half the timber imported from Norway; and, by the end of the century, twenty per cent of the Britain's immense trade with the Baltic.

Whitby provided the navy with transports in time of war, and though her whaling fleet was small, it was very successful. With its coveted status as a harbour-of-refuge, Whitby was able to finance piers and dry docks, while the shipbuilding output of the late eighteenth century was large (**fig 10.9**).

Recurring wars brought problems: blockade, losses of shipping to the enemy and of manpower to the press-gangs. But they also brought high wages, and high profits — as much as forty per cent on a year's trading. The end of each war brought inevitable collapse, as captured prizes joined the national fleet and returning seamen flooded the labour market.

Whitby — Further Reading:

Rev J C Atkinson, *Memorials of Old Whitby; or, Historical Gleanings from Ancient Whitby Records* (London, 1894).

Rosalin Barker, *The Book of Whitby* (Buckingham: Barracuda Books, 1990), and *Prisoners of the Tsar* (Beverley: Highgate Publications, 1992).

L Charlton, *The History of Whitby and of Whitby Abbey* (York, 1779).

R Gaskin, *The Old Seaport of Whitby* (Whitby, 1906).

R Weatherill, *The Ancient Port of Whitby and its Shipping* (Whitby, 1908).

Whitby harbour.
NMR 17065/26 © Crown copyright. NMR.

At the start of the nineteenth century some of the wealthiest ship-owners, gentrified and politicised, moved their headquarters to London or the Tyne, and much of the entrepreneurial skill was lost. Steam began to supersede sail, and the limitations of the narrow harbour became clear. Whitby continued as a commercial port, but her position as sixth in the table of ship-owning ports in England gradually slipped away.

The railway came in 1836, and brought early tourism, leading to the development of the West Cliff; iron was exploited, and jet; but the valuable alum industry, effectively a cartel producing enough to employ just a few sloops, declined in the face of the new chemical industries of Middlesbrough.

Despite success in the fishing industry, Whitby slowly became the quiet backwater she had been before the alum-driven boom.

11

HISTORIC LANDSCAPES

11.1   INTRODUCTION   ADAM MENUGE & NOËL JAMES MENUGE

North Yorkshire encompasses some of the most striking landscapes in England, from the rugged limestone topography of Craven to the smooth northern flank of the Wolds, from the deeply dissected mountain chain of the Pennines to the dead-level of the Vale of Pickering.

Geology provides the armature for these landscapes, and insofar as it influences climate, soil and vegetation it continues to shape their development. It is also responsible, as Alison Armstrong's contribution (section 11.3) demonstrates, for imparting much of the distinctive character of the county's towns and villages, through the different stones, bricks and tiles used in their construction.

Apart from the underlying morphology, however, little of what we see in the landscape is truly natural. The whole county has been denuded of forests, and lowlands in particular have been drained and enclosed, with massive consequences, both economic and ecological. Except in the most precipitous and inaccessible spots, these landscapes have been subject to human intervention and management, at varying levels of intensity, for thousands of years. Relics of ancient landscape, all but untouched by man, are correspondingly rare.

Ian Dormor's summary of the English Nature *Inventory of Ancient Woodland* (section 11.2) demonstrates that no 'primary' ancient woodland — that is, woodland preserving the character of the immediate post-glacial period 8-10,000 years ago — survives in areas exceeding five acres (2ha). The woodland we see today is thus either the product of a management regime at some period, or natural regeneration of areas formerly subject to human intervention.

Our use of the word 'landscape' derives from the art of painting. Adam Menuge's piece on the 'discovery' of North Yorkshire (section 11.5) examines some of the landscapes that drew visitors to the county in the eighteenth and early nineteenth centuries, and some of the antiquities and other curiosities that coloured their perceptions of physical forms.

The aesthetic principles which these early travellers imbibed and expounded found expression in many other ways. The builders of country houses (the subject of Edward Waterson's contribution — section 11.6) were often constrained in their choice of location by hereditary landholdings. Their houses nevertheless show a growing concern for landscape setting — the position of the house within the landscape and the prospects that could be had from it.

Valerie Hepworth and Deborah Turnbull discuss (in section 11.7) the landscapes-in-miniature which country-house owners created around their houses, and also remind us of their imitation, for wider enjoyment, in the form of public and institutional gardens.

The intimate landscapes created in the vicinity of smaller settlements are explored in Richard Muir's study of the routeways of Ripley[1] (section 11.8), and in Heather Beaumont's research into the township of Hebden (section 11.9).

Adam Menuge's contribution on field houses (section 11.4) looks at a particular type of landscape, recurring (with some variations) across the whole of the Yorkshire Dales, a combination of particular agricultural practices and vernacular building traditions.

Understanding whole landscapes calls, ideally, on a range of field, documentary and scientific skills for which the labels 'landscape history' or 'landscape archaeology' scarcely seem adequate. The objective has generally been to understand the signs on the ground, using primary documentary research to guide, interpret and extend the findings of field study. The greatest value of such work has perhaps been to open the eyes of a generation to the fact that landscapes are complex historical artefacts, which not only environ but shape our lives.

A number of the studies in this section draw on programmes for identifying and quantifying what in nature- and heritage-conservation circles is often termed 'the resource'. Once this is accomplished, change can be monitored against a known datum, priorities can be established, and the painstaking process of fleshing out the history and archaeology of individual landscapes and sites can proceed, informed by the wider picture.

The challenge for these detailed studies, as always, is to look beyond the 'what?' and the 'where?' to the 'why?'. This involves vexed questions of causation, and examination of the springs of both individual and social action. Here historians who have attempted the recreation of whole urban communities (for which the source material is typically much more extensive) may have much to offer.[2]

All specialisms run the risk of introspection. To avoid these the study of landscapes must exploit fully the intricacy and integrity of local evidence to pose questions about the nature of the historical process — how and why do landscapes change at the local level, what did they mean to contemporaries, how does a landscape condition its community and how does a community mould its landscape?

11.2 ANCIENT WOODLAND   IAN DORMOR

Ancient woodlands occupy sites that have been continuously covered by trees since at least AD 1600. In England, all woods over five acres (2ha) that meet both this criterion and that of being depicted on the Ordnance Survey First Edition 1-inch and 6-inch maps are listed in the English Nature *Inventory of Ancient Woodland*.

The *Inventory* identifies three categories of ancient woodland: 'primary', where the woodland is considered to be a relict of the post-glacial woodland of 8,000–10,000 years ago; 'ancient secondary', where the woodland has become naturally re-established on formerly wooded sites that were cleared of trees before AD 1600; and 'ancient replanted', where stands of planted trees, often in the form of plantations, now occupy sites identified as ancient woodland on the nineteenth-century Ordnance Survey First Edition maps.

Most of the ancient woodland of North Yorkshire (**fig 11.1**) falls into this last category, with the area of ancient replanted woodland extending to 20,042 acres (8,114ha), but in comparison with the rest of England, North Yorkshire's woodland cover is significantly less than many other counties.

Because the county covers such a large area, the North Yorkshire *Inventory of Ancient Woodland* is divided into three sections: (I) Craven and Richmondshire; (II) Harrogate, Hambleton, Selby and York; (III) Ryedale and Scarborough. The total extent of ancient woodland in North Yorkshire as percentage of land area is 1.67 per cent (34,360 acres/ 13,906ha). This is made up as follows:

Ancient semi-natural woodland:
Craven and Richmondshire	4,062 acres (1,644ha)
Harrogate, Hambleton, Selby and York	4,052 acres (1,640ha)
Ryedale and Scarborough	6,197 acres (2,508ha)

Ancient replanted woodland:
Craven and Richmondshire	1,910 acres (773ha)
Harrogate, Hambleton, Selby and York	7,327 acres (2,965ha)
Ryedale and Scarborough	10,813 acres (4,376ha)

The Craven and Richmondshire section includes the Yorkshire Dales National Park.

There are extensive tracts of moorland where the woodland is comparable with that which existed there 1,000 years ago. However, reclamation for agriculture has resulted in clearance of much of the damp lowland oak and oak-birch woodland from the valleys, and today the remaining ancient woodland is largely confined to steep slopes, inaccessible gills and along rocky scars in river valleys.

The lowland woods on acid soils derived from the Millstone Grit are a mixture of oak, wych elm, alder, ash and willow. In contrast, the Carboniferous Limestone country is relatively thinly wooded, with ash and hazel as the dominant species.

The Harrogate, Hambleton, Selby and York section covers the central part of the county, to include the Vale of York — an area of very diverse character that contains much intensively farmed land, the western flank of the North York Moors and the gritstone landscape of Nidderdale. Apart from two large concentrations near Selby and Knaresborough, the flat land is generally devoid of ancient woodland, whereas the upland areas carry more trees, particularly along the valley sides, but even here, many ancient woodland sites have been felled and replanted.

The largest concentration of ancient woodland exists in the Ryedale and Scarborough section, with most sites occupying positions on steep valley sides, and representing three per cent of the area. The loss of ancient woodland due to agricultural clearance has been less in this section than elsewhere in North Yorkshire. Of the surviving ancient woodland, seventy-five per cent (12,899 acres/5,220ha) occurs in the North York Moors National Park, but only thirty-six per cent of this is classified as ancient semi-natural woodland.

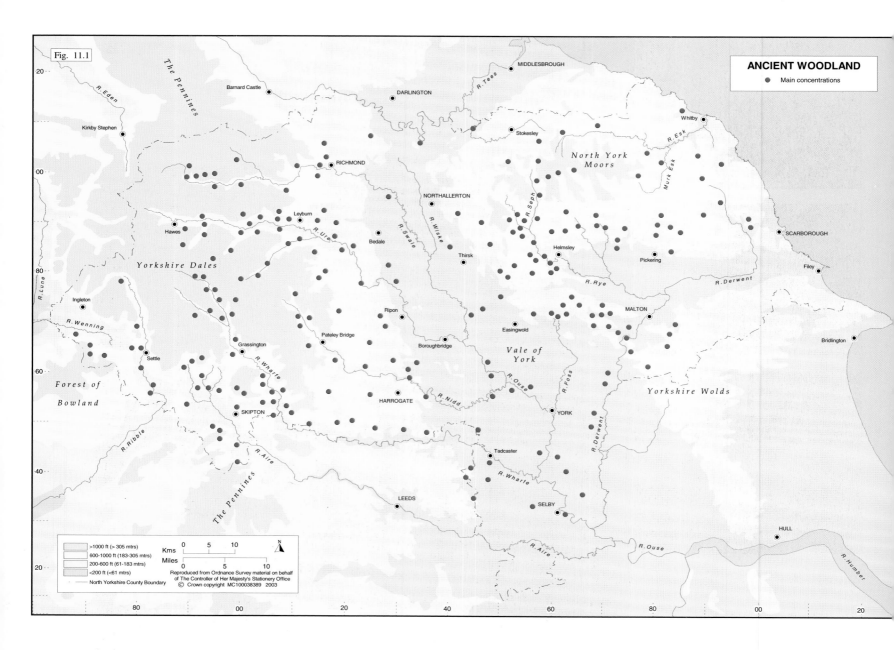

Fig. 11.1

ANCIENT WOODLAND
● Main concentrations

>1000 ft (> 305 mtrs)
600-1000 ft (183-305 mtrs)
200-600 ft (61-183 mtrs)
<200 ft (<61 mtrs)
North Yorkshire County Boundary

Kms
Miles

Reproduced from Ordnance Survey material on behalf
of The Controller of Her Majesty's Stationery Office
© Crown copyright MC100038389 2003

The Ryedale and Scarborough section also has the largest area of replanted ancient woodland in the county, resulting from the Forestry Commission dedication schemes of the 1950s and '60s, which encouraged landowners to fell ancient semi-natural woodland and replant with conifers.

Much of the ancient woodland occurs within the two national parks and the Nidderdale Area Of Outstanding Natural Beauty (AONB). In both national parks, woodlands and individual trees form a conspicuous component of the landscape, although ancient semi-natural woodland represents just 0.7 per cent of the Yorkshire Dales National Park.

Despite this paucity of ancient woodland, 18 of the 25 National Vegetation Classification (NVC) woodland communities are represented there, a factor that makes the Dales wood-land as a whole of national significance. Of particular importance are the oak woodlands on the Millstone Grit. Although ash has long been regarded as the characteristic species of the Carboniferous Limestone, its supremacy has become challenged by sycamore, a species particularly well-adapted to the climatic and soil conditions of this locality. In many ancient woods, sycamore has become widespread at the expense of ash, particularly in the absence of natural regeneration.

Many ancient semi-natural woods contain visible indications of their former management, with the archaeology of old woodland industries barely concealed beneath the woodland floor. These often reveal the sites of charcoal clamps, sawpits and chopwood kilns. They bear witness to the past role of woodland as a vital resource of fuel and raw materials.

However, many woods formerly managed as coppices are now neglected and overgrown, with the large stools of ash, hazel, sycamore, oak and alder reminders of their former

above top Old Spring Wood, Summerbridge.
© I Dormor

above middle Coppiced trees, Hutton Conyers.
© I Dormor

above Wood anemones.
© I Dormor

top right Braisty Woods, Nidderdale.
© I Dormor

middle right Coppiced hazel, Freeholders Wood, Aysgarth.
© I Dormor

bottom right Modern plantations and ancient woods near Burnsall, Wharfedale.
© I Dormor

importance. A few precious fragments of wood pasture with their characteristic ancient pollarded trees still remain, particularly in Wharfedale and Nidderdale, a tangible link with one of the earliest forms of woodland management.

Sadly, in many parts of the county, the woodlands have become derelict, having entered a period of decline coincident with the collapse of the leadmining industry in the mid-nineteenth century.

In order for woodland to survive in the landscape it must have a purpose, and it is the absence of a role that has resulted in the loss of much of the county's ancient woodland. The demise of traditional woodland management, with a consequent neglect of boundary fences and walls, and uncontrolled grazing, has resulted in many ancient woods becoming barely recognisable as such. Happily, this situation is being addressed through new initiatives funded by Lottery and European money with the aim of restoring indigenous woodland back to the countryside of North Yorkshire.

Ancient woodland is an immensely important part of our natural and cultural heritage, and hopefully it will continue to beautify the landscape in more enlightened times.

11.3 VERNACULAR BUILDING MATERIALS
ALISON C ARMSTRONG

Vernacular buildings are generally defined as the houses and other buildings of ordinary people, built largely from local materials, without professional assistance, prior to the nineteenth-century industrialisation of building processes.

North Yorkshire's vernacular buildings mostly date from the late seventeenth and the eighteenth century, when many thousands of houses and barns were built or rebuilt using stone, brick and tile in preference to the timber framing, crucks and thatch of earlier centuries.[1] For economic reasons, stone was usually obtained nearby, and bricks were made from local deposits, varying in colour and texture according to the properties of the clay.

The outward appearance of buildings is thus intimately related to local geology and soils. The uplands of the stone-rich Pennines and North York Moors are characterised by sturdy stone-walled structures, while in the lowland vales the Ice-Age deposits yield only stone cobbles, and clays suitable for soft-hued brick and tile. Similarly sandstone 'grey slates' predominate in the Pennines while, to the east, red-pantiled roofs are conspicuous.

The impact of vernacular buildings on the landscape, both as a visible presence and through changes wrought by the winning of building materials, is considerable (**fig 11.2**; for a complete map of solid geology see **fig 2.2**).

STONE

Geology does not translate straightforwardly into building materials, but is complicated by practical and economic considerations. Stones have differing properties of strength, tractability and durability.

On the North York Moors, for example, the Jurassic sandstone does not yield fissile stone suitable for roofing, and stone walls are topped instead by pantiled roofs. Soft stones (like chalk) or intractable stones (such as the limestones of Craven and the Dales) are seldom used far from their origin, whereas good freestone justified higher transport costs.[2]

In Conistone, Wharfedale, a substantial yeoman house and barns, built *c* 1686, had rubble walls of limestone, probably extracted from surrounding pastures. Sandstone, required for dressed work such as mullions and quoins, came from the township quarry high on the hill behind; roofing flags were brought from hilltop quarries seven miles (11km) away, while roof timber was chosen from woods twelve miles (19km) distant.

Yorkshire's oldest rocks include green Ingleton slates and dark grey Horton-in-Ribblesdale flags used for roofs, floors and 'boskins' (partitions in cow shippons) in the west of the county.

In the upper Pennine Dales, pale grey Carboniferous limestone forms poorly coursed rubble walls, often with projecting through-stones and brown sandstone dressings, which may be elaborately moulded. Exceptionally, around Langcliffe, the limestone breaks square enough for lintels. Traces of whitewash and 'slobbered' render clinging to rubble walls in Ribblesdale and Wensleydale suggest that this was once a typical finish. Fossil limestone 'marbles' were used for fireplaces in Dentdale and Nidderdale (both dark grey), and in Swaledale (buff-coloured).

Thin sandstones occur at the top of the limestone, especially north of Wensleydale where Castle Bolton (fourteenth century) stands below a ledge of quarried sandstone. West of Grinton in Swaledale, houses of *c* 1800 are entirely made of regular blocks of hard, golden gannister

Ancient Woodland — Further Reading:

A G Barber and R Cooke, *Woodland surveys in North-East England using the National Vegetation Classification* (Peterborough: Nature Conservancy Council, CSD Report 1238, 1990).

A Drewitt, *The Vegetation of the Yorkshire Dales National Park* (Grassington: Yorkshire Dales National Park Committee, 1991).

T Gledhill, Medieval Woodland in North Yorkshire, in M Atherden and R Butlin (eds), *Woodland in the Landscape: Past and Future Perspectives* (Leeds: Leeds University Press, 1998), 103-119.

K Graham and A Dalton, *Broadleaved Woodland in the Yorkshire Dales National Park* (Grassington: Yorkshire Dales National Park, 1993).

Nature Conservancy Council, *Inventory of Ancient Woodland — North Yorkshire*, Part I: Craven and Richmondshire Districts (Peterborough: Nature Conservancy Council, 1987).

Nature Conservancy Council, *Inventory of Ancient Woodland — North Yorkshire,* Part II: Harrogate, Hambleton, Selby and York Districts (Peterborough: Nature Conservancy Council, 1987).

Nature Conservancy Council, *Inventory of Ancient Woodland — North Yorkshire*, Part III: Ryedale and Scarborough Districts (Peterborough: Nature Conservancy Council, 1987).

O Rackham, *Ancient Woodland, its history, vegetation and uses in England* (London: Edward Arnold, 1980).

O Rackham, *Trees and Woodland in the British Landscape* (London: Dent, 1976; revised 1990).

sandstone. Further south, at High Bradley, near Skipton, structures before the late seventeenth century are of gritstone blocks worked from crag outcrops on the moorland common.

By the eighteenth century, flagstones which required less dressing, quarried under the old arable lands and above a worked-out coal seam, were being exploited for split quoins and thin wall-stones, making later buildings distinct. Bradley flags provided a rare source of roofing sandstone in an area of Craven where thatch predominated, and even Barden Tower (c1483), a manor house, had a turf roof.

The use of roofing flags spread rapidly, however, as quarrying expanded in the later eighteenth century. On the eastern flank of the Pennines, the Upper Carboniferous Millstone Grit includes beds of hard sandstone varying from thin, flaggy, fine-textured stone to pebbly 'millstone grit', which around Harrogate is red-stained. These hard sandstones were not sawn until the mid-nineteenth century; those which could be dressed on all surfaces to form squared blocks were known for centuries as ashlar.

On the North York Moors, yellow Middle Jurassic sandstones are widely used. Around Whitby, cut-ashlar blocks and quoins with margin-dressing or herringbone pick-tooling are typical. By contrast, villages on the north side of the vale of Pickering, and around Malton to the south, have houses of mixed rubble and quoins with pale Upper Jurassic calcareous gritstones, oolitic or shelly limestones and hard, grey gritstones.

The low Permian ridge east of the Pennines yields variable pale limestones. These were used for local houses, but Tadcaster freestone was also used for important medieval buildings in York. Northward the ridge is buried by glacial deposits but the creamy limestone, mixed with dressed glacial sandstone boulders, occurs in village houses around Bedale and Snape. Gypsum may have been worked near Ripon, as Norton Conyers Hall has plastered attic floors, unusual in the county.

On the Wolds the chalk is durable enough for eighteenth-century houses and barns, their white walls contrasting with red-brick quoins and footings. The black basalt lava of the Cleveland dyke also has some vernacular uses.

Boulders and cobbles, derived from glacial clays and moraines, are widely used in the vales and in some river valleys, and also on the high Ribblehead watershed in the Pennines. Boulders are usually roughly face-dressed and often inter-coursed with thin sandstone or brick. In the far west, around Burton in Lonsdale, boulder walls include a distinctive mixture of dark and pale limestones, dark Silurian sandstone and Lake District granites.

BRICK AND TILE

Brick and tile, first imported from the Low Countries, were being manufactured in York by the mid-fourteenth century.

Vernacular use begins in the seventeenth century, and increases with eighteenth-century exploitation of boulder clays and Jurassic shales in the vales of York and Pickering, and on the coast, where brick quickly supplanted earlier building traditions. 'Tumbled' brickwork protected the cut-bricks of gable-tops from the weather, while 'cogged' and 'dentilled' courses gave a decorative finish to the eaves. Even where stone was abundant, the small unit-size of brick made it attractive for features such as chimneys.

Plain tiles were used in York from the fifteenth century but it is pantiles, with their distinctive wavy profile, that dominate the county east of the Permian ridge, where during the eighteenth and nineteenth centuries they virtually eliminated thatch.

TIMBER

Structural timber is rarely visible in the North Yorkshire countryside today, though there are many timber-framed buildings dating from before the mid-seventeenth century in York, and small numbers in most of the county's towns.

Oak was the usual constructional timber, but elm was sometimes favoured over fireplaces because of its fire-resistant qualities. Ash, which flourishes on the Carboniferous Limestone, was used for some Pennine crucks, and for spine beams in upper Swaledale farmhouses, where birch logs form hayloft floors in field barns.

Native timbers were the product of managed woodland, wood pasture or coppices, but imported Baltic softwoods gradually became the norm for floor, and later roof timbers.[3]

THATCH

Thatch made from heather, or straw 'reeds', is now rare,[4] but many more buildings in the county preserve evidence in their gables for the steeply pitched thatched roofs that preceded flags or pantiles. Compacted layers of old thatch, to which the new was regularly added, are a rich potential source of botanical archaeology.[5]

Building Materials — Further Reading:

Alison C Armstrong, Stone, stone-working and vernacular buildings, *Yorkshire Vernacular Buildings Study Group Newsletter* 18 (1990).

Barbara Hutton & Barry Harrison, *Vernacular Houses in North Yorkshire and Cleveland* (Edinburgh: John Donald, 1984).

Marie Hartley & Joan Ingilby, *Life and Tradition in the Yorkshire Dales* (Otley: Smith Settle, 1997).

Marie Hartley & Joan Ingilby, *Life and Tradition in the Moorlands of North-East Yorkshire* (Otley: Smith Settle, 1990).

Arthur Raistrick, *Buildings of the Yorkshire Dales* (Clapham: Dalesman, 1989).

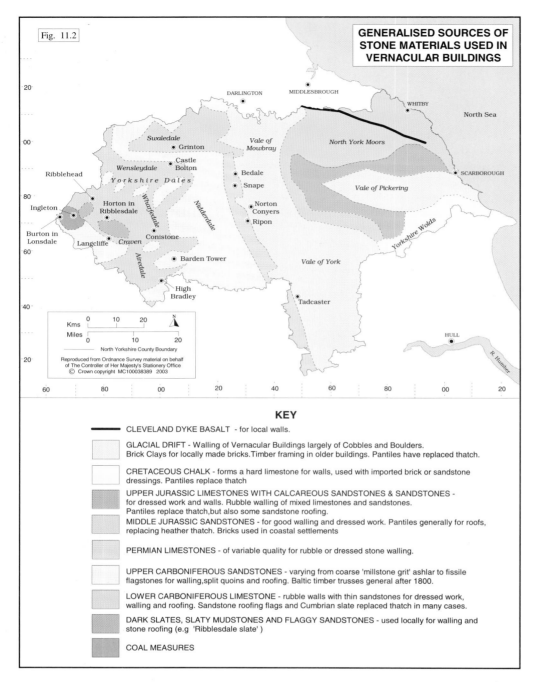

Fig. 11.2

GENERALISED SOURCES OF STONE MATERIALS USED IN VERNACULAR BUILDINGS

North Sea

DARLINGTON
MIDDLESBROUGH
WHITBY

Swaledale
Grinton
Vale of Mowbray
North York Moors

SCARBOROUGH

Castle Bolton
Wensleydale
Ribblehead
Yorkshire Dales
Bedale
Snape
Vale of Pickering

Ingleton
Horton in Ribblesdale
Wharfedale
Nidderdale
Norton Conyers
Ripon

Burton in Lonsdale
Langcliffe
Craven
Conistone
Yorkshire Wolds

Airedale
Barden Tower
Vale of York

High Bradley
Tadcaster

Kms 0 10 20
Miles 0 10 20
N

HULL

North Yorkshire County Boundary

Reproduced from Ordnance Survey material on behalf
of The Controller of Her Majesty's Stationery Office
© Crown copyright MC100038389 2003

R. Humber

KEY

──── CLEVELAND DYKE BASALT - for local walls.

GLACIAL DRIFT - Walling of Vernacular Buildings largely of Cobbles and Boulders.
Brick Clays for locally made bricks. Timber framing in older buildings. Pantiles have replaced thatch.

CRETACEOUS CHALK - forms a hard limestone for walls, used with imported brick or sandstone
dressings. Pantiles replace thatch

UPPER JURASSIC LIMESTONES WITH CALCAREOUS SANDSTONES & SANDSTONES -
for dressed work and walls. Rubble walling of mixed limestones and sandstones.
Pantiles replace thatch, but also some sandstone roofing.

MIDDLE JURASSIC SANDSTONES - for good walling and dressed work. Pantiles generally for roofs,
replacing heather thatch. Bricks used in coastal settlements

PERMIAN LIMESTONES - of variable quality for rubble or dressed stone walling.

UPPER CARBONIFEROUS SANDSTONES - varying from coarse 'millstone grit' ashlar to fissile
flagstones for walling, split quoins and roofing. Baltic timber trusses general after 1800.

LOWER CARBONIFEROUS LIMESTONE - rubble walls with thin sandstones for dressed work,
walling and roofing. Sandstone roofing flags and Cumbrian slate replaced thatch in many cases.

DARK SLATES, SLATY MUDSTONES AND FLAGGY SANDSTONES - used locally for walling and
stone roofing (e.g 'Ribblesdale slate')

COAL MEASURES

11.4 FIELD HOUSES OF THE YORKSHIRE DALES
ADAM MENUGE

The quintessential Dales landscape of rugged-sided valleys, laced with drystone walls and studded with small isolated field barns, is internationally renowned (**fig 11.3**). Although natural forces have shaped the larger elements of this landscape, it is in most other respects the outcome of massive human endeavour spanning hundreds of years and, in places, millennia.

It is the dispersed, yet surprisingly dense, pattern of agricultural buildings that renders it unique in the British Isles — the product of a highly individual adaptation of agricultural practices to climate and terrain, best seen in Swaledale, Wensleydale, upper Wharfedale and their tributary valleys, but found more or less everywhere in the Dales.

The key to this landscape is the hay crop, since in the traditional economy only hay will keep cattle ('beasts') alive during the lean winter months, when the pastures yield insufficient 'bite'. Only the most favoured areas of the valley bottoms were devoted to arable crops in the historic past, and this use diminished as improved communications reduced the need for local self-sufficiency in produce.

Much of the remaining land, from valley bottom to moor edge, was progressively parcelled up for hay meadows. The earliest tend to be close to the valley bottom in the vicinity of farmsteads, but a level sward was not a precondition for hay-cropping as long as

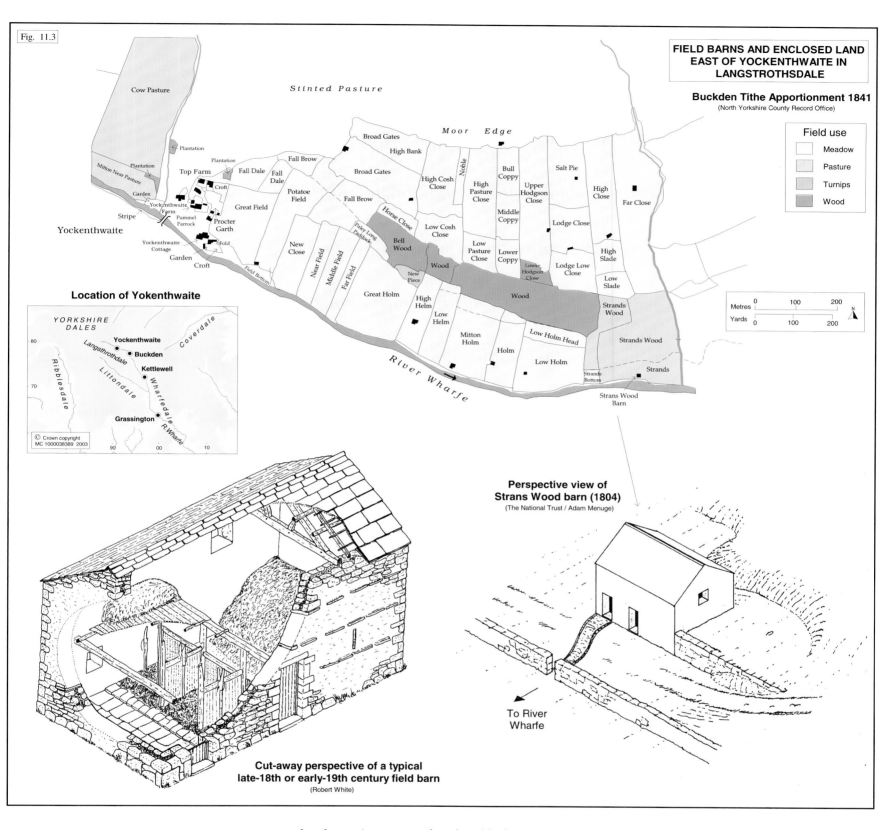

Fig. 11.3

FIELD BARNS AND ENCLOSED LAND EAST OF YOCKENTHWAITE IN LANGSTROTHSDALE

Buckden Tithe Apportionment 1841
(North Yorkshire County Record Office)

Field use

Meadow

Pasture

Turnips

Wood

Stinted Pasture

Cow Pasture

Moor Edge

Plantation

Mitton Near Pasture

Plantation

Plantation

Top Farm

Fall Brow

Broad Gates

High Bank

Fall Dale

Fall Dale

Broad Gates

Noble

Bull Coppy

Salt Pie

Garden

Croft

Potatoe Field

Fall Brow

High Cosh Close

High Pasture Close

Upper Hodgson Close

High Close

Far Close

Yockenthwaite Farm

Great Field

Horse Close

Middle Coppy

Lodge Close

Stripe

Pummel Parrock

Procter Garth

Fakey Long Paddock

Bell Wood

Low Cosh Close

Low Coppy

Lower Hodgson Close

High Slade

Yockenthwaite

Yockenthwaite Cottage

Fold

New Close

Wood

Low Pasture Close

Lodge Low Close

Low Slade

Garden

Croft

Fold

Field Bottom

Near Field

Middle Field

Far Field

Great Holm

High Helm

Wood

Lower Hodgson Close

Strands Wood

Low Helm

New Piece

Mitton Holm

Holm

Low Holm Head

Strands Wood

River Wharfe

Low Holm

Strands Bottom

Strands

Strans Wood Barn

Location of Yockenthwaite

YORKSHIRE DALES

Coverdale

Langstrothdale

Yockenthwaite

Buckden

Littondale

Kettlewell

Wharfedale

R. Wharfe

Grassington

© Crown copyright
MC 1000038389 2003

Metres 0 100 200

Yards 0 100 200

N

Perspective view of Strans Wood barn (1804)
(The National Trust / Adam Menuge)

To River Wharfe

Cut-away perspective of a typical late-18th or early-19th century field barn
(Robert White)

hand–mowing was employed, and before the end of the eighteenth century there were field barns above the 1,000 foot (330m) contour, many clinging to steep valley-sides.

Field barns or 'laithes' are not true barns, which were used to store and then thresh cereal crops. Neither are they found only out in the fields: a minority occur in or close to farmsteads. They are a combination of hay-barn and cowhouse (locally 'shippon'), forming an independent productive unit set apart from the farmstead.

The hay crop was mown in July or even as late as the beginning of August, dried in the fields, then stored in the 'mow' or 'mew' end of the building.

Every scrap of space was used, including a rough loft over the shippon. From November to May the cattle were stalled in the shippon, attended twice-daily by the farmer to fodder them

Field barns and field walls, Swaledale.
© R White/Yorkshire Dales National Park Authority, SW172.

with hay and let them out for water. Manure would accumulate in a gutter (or 'grewp') behind the stalls, to be mucked out and piled against the building prior to spreading on the hay meadows, where it supplemented the manure left by young sheep or 'hoggs' over-wintered on the lower ground. Perhaps the most important reason for the dispersed location of field barns was to minimise the labour of moving the heavy manure, in a landscape where wheeled carts were little used.

The cattle were then removed to higher pastures to ensure the maximum growth of flower-rich hay in time for the next harvest.

This virtuous cycle maximised the profit from rearing livestock on thin upland soils, which could be realised by sending beasts to market, or processing dairy products (such as Wensleydale cheese) for sale.

Owing to the heavy burden of labour implicit in both the annual and the daily cycle of use, field barns are located for convenience. Sometimes they are positioned beside a road or track; on other occasions they occur at the junction of two or more fields served by a single field barn. The steepness of the valley sides can be exploited, with forking-holes on the uphill side facilitating the loading of hay; frequently ground surfaces are artificially modified for the same reason. An adequate water supply is essential, and may be satisfied by proximity to a river or stream, by collecting spring water in a trough, or by the construction of a leat.

The buildings exhibit considerable variation in size and form. The oldest — probably dating from the seventeenth or early eighteenth century (though precise dating is seldom possible) — have roofs of cruck construction, designed for a covering of heather thatch. The evidence for this may survive as two steeply curving lines mirroring each other in a gable which has been raised for a later roof of 'grey slates'.

The simplest field barns are small structures, rectangular on plan, with a single entrance for both the shippon and the mew, which tend to divide the interior in proportions of roughly one third to two-thirds, or two-fifths to three-fifths. The majority, however, have separate entrances to the mew and shippon, the shippon entrance typically placed against one gable. Larger examples have shippons extending into outshots, or double shippons — one at each end of the mew. Some larger and later field barns incorporate conveniences such as a feeding passage or 'fothergang', or a porch.

Inside, the distinguishing features are confined to the shippon. Stall partitions, known as 'boskins', are made of flagstones, Horton 'slate' or timber — or a combination of timber and stone. The 'skellboose', dividing the shippon from the mew, is similar. The loft floor is usually a rough affair, sometimes using whole birch logs and a matting of hazel twigs rather than sawn joists and boards.

A less well-known Dales building type is the hogg house. Hoggs are yearling sheep: much of the future value of the flock is bound up in them and, with the onset of their first winter, special measures are taken to ensure their survival and to promote their growth. As in many upland areas of Britain, small scattered buildings provided shelter in the sharpest weather or during prolonged snow.

Dales Field Houses — Further Reading:

Marie Hartley & Joan Ingilby, *Life and Tradition in the Yorkshire Dales* (Otley: Smith Settle, 1997).

Marie Hartley & Joan Ingilby, *Dales Memories* (Clapham: Dalesman, 1986).

Kate Mason, Laithes: the barns of Craven, *Folk Life* 27 (1988-9), 85-94.

Adam Menuge & Jennifer Deadman, The hogg houses of upper Swaledale, in R White and P Wilson (eds), *Archaeology and Historic Landscapes in the Yorkshire Dales* (Leeds: Yorkshire Archaeological Society Occasional Series, forthcoming).

RCHME, *Houses of the North York Moors* (London: HMSO, 1987).

Yorkshire Vernacular Buildings Study Group, *Yorkshire Buildings* and *YVBSG Newsletter* (printed annually; summaries from the group's archives of buildings recorded; subscription details from the group secretary). e-mail: enquiries@yvbsg.org.uk. Publications available from: Lorraine Moor, 102 Queen Victoria Street, South Bank, York YO23 1HN.

These are typically simple structures, with low eaves, good ventilation, and few internal fixtures — a crib at ground-level, a hay-rack and a small loft for storing bedding such as bracken.

However, in the upper reaches of Swaledale, principally above Keld, some hogg houses take on a unique two-storeyed form which has as much to do with the wider ecology of the area as it does with the needs of sheep-husbandry. Upper Swaledale has an abundance of stone, which occurs in lengths suitable not only for lintels but capable of serving as joists up to ten feet (3m) long. It also suffers from a shortage of, and remoteness from, good sources of timber trees. Accordingly, a building type evolved which maximised the use of stone and minimised the need for timber, with narrow hogg houses on two storeys, the upper floor reached via an external ramp. The floor of the upper hogg house is sometimes constructed entirely of stone, while the roof may rely only on purlins (horizontal beams supporting roof rafters) alone, dispensing with the long timbers needed for trusses.

The preservation of the complex Dales ecology and of the landscape features to which it gave rise represents a considerable challenge to the various authorities responsible for conservation and the wider management of the Yorkshire Dales, particularly in a period of rapid agricultural change.

11.5 THE DISCOVERY OF THE LANDSCAPE
ADAM MENUGE

North Yorkshire's natural landscape is overlaid by innumerable archaeological traces and historical associations. A blend of all three forms the basis for most topographical writing, and informs countless artistic representations of the county. From journals and pictures we can distinguish something of what the landscape of North Yorkshire signified to earlier generations of travellers (**fig 11.4**).

Before the middle of the eighteenth century, appreciations of the county's diverse landscapes were rare. Celia Fiennes, who traversed the county in 1697 and 1698, confined herself almost exclusively to towns. She took in York, Knaresborough and Harrogate, Ripon and Newby Hall, Scarborough and Richmond, mixing her observations on minsters, spas and gardens with practical information on provisions and accommodation.

Daniel Defoe's *Tour through the Whole Island of Great Britain* (1724-6) was concerned above all to map the commercial life of the kingdom. It follows the towns on and near the Great North Road, and the ports between Humber and Tees, celebrating the 'rich, fruitful and populous' Vale of York, while avoiding 'black, ill looking, desolate moors' (a description of the country between Harewood and Ripley).[1]

In the later eighteenth century, among the cultivated classes, a richer imaginative engagement with landscape emerged.

Dr Richard Pococke, an Irish bishop who toured Yorkshire in 1750 and 1751, is an early instance. He retained an old-fashioned taste for 'curiosities', such as the petrifying springs at Knaresborough and Ingleborough, and the ebbing-and-flowing spring near Giggleswick.

He was also an energetic antiquary, conscientiously measuring and analysing archaeological remains. 'British' sites, notably the Devil's Arrows at Boroughbridge and the 'camp' at Nutwith Hill near Masham, together with such vestiges of Roman occupation as the excavated settlement at Aldborough and the fort at Bainbridge, interested him intensely. At Ripley he ignored the impressive seat of the Inglebys, dwelling instead on some inscribed pigs of Roman lead retrieved from near Greenhow Hill. The medieval period received more ample attention in architectural, historical and genealogical accounts of a series of castles, palaces, abbeys and churches.

In Northallerton, Pococke turned archaeologist again, trying to verify, through fieldwork, traditional accounts of the Anglo-Scottish Battle of the Standard (1138). Later historical periods are represented by brief notices of many country houses, and a detailed description of William Aislabie's gardens at Hackfall.

Pococke's travels exhibit a pronounced western bias, drawn by the limestone scenery of Craven, with its summits, caves and dramatic formations such as Malham Cove and Gordale Scar, and by the many waterfalls of Wensleydale. By contrast Swaledale, lacking major waterfalls, attracted few early visitors.

Other travellers varied their emphases, but itineraries were often similar. Forty years later, John Byng (later Viscount Torrington) took in Studley Royal and Fountains Abbey, extended his circuit northwards to include Richmond, Teesdale and (briefly) Swaledale, and in Wensleydale added Semerwater to his route, but only after seeing most of the same sites as

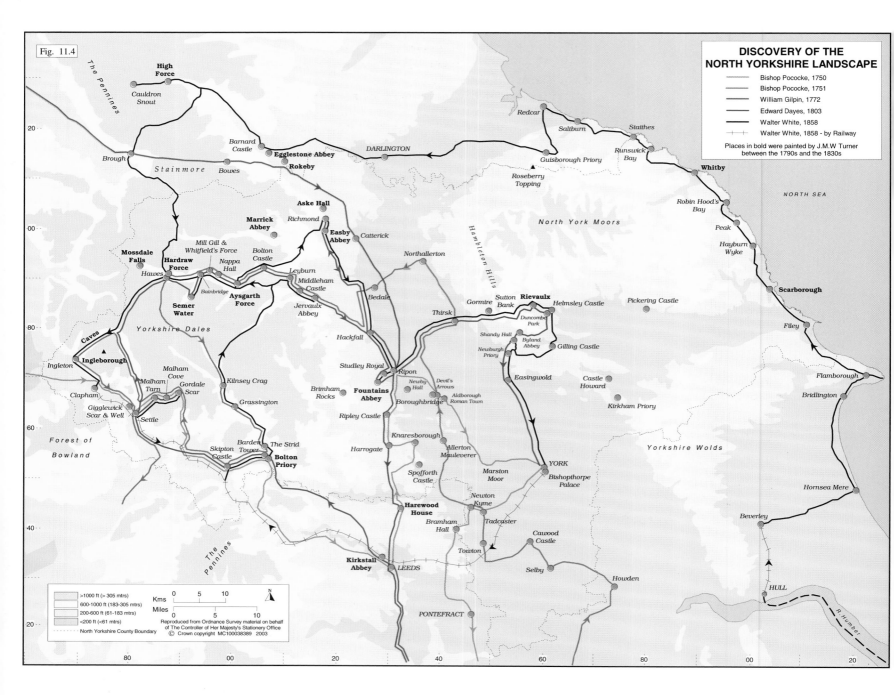

Fig. 11.4

DISCOVERY OF THE NORTH YORKSHIRE LANDSCAPE

Bishop Pococke, 1750
Bishop Pococke, 1751
William Gilpin, 1772
Edward Dayes, 1803
Walter White, 1858
Walter White, 1858 - by Railway

Places in bold were painted by J.M.W Turner between the 1790s and the 1830s

Reproduced from Ordnance Survey material on behalf of The Controller of Her Majesty's Stationery Office © Crown copyright MC100038389 2003

>1000 ft (> 305 mtrs)
600-1000 ft (183-305 mtrs)
200-600 ft (61-183 mtrs)
<200 ft (<61 mtrs)
North Yorkshire County Boundary

Pococke. Only Scarborough, a major spa since the seventeenth century, drew significant numbers of early visitors east of the vales of York and Mowbray.

In the second half of the eighteenth century, landscape appreciation became intensely fashionable; concepts and vocabulary grew increasingly sophisticated, liberating tourists from Pococke's over-use of the epithet 'romantic'. Burke's essay on the sublime, and the popularity of the seventeenth-century Italian artist Salvator Rosa, placed at the cultivated tourist's disposal a framework for appreciating towering cliffs and vertiginous chasms. In later decades the writings of William Gilpin and Richard Payne Knight elaborated the principles of the picturesque, which favoured unimproved landscapes and the textures of architectural decay.

A principal locus for the new landscape taste was the Lake District and, as Lakes tourism expanded, visitors to the western areas of North Yorkshire increased. Craven and the Dales lay on the easiest way from London and Cambridge (many early tourists, like the young William Wilberforce in 1779, were students), via the Great North Road and the principal trans-Pennine routes, and they came to be regarded as appetisers for the more substantial diet of Lakes scenery.

The second (1780) and subsequent editions of Thomas West's *Guide to the Lakes* included descriptions of the limestone caves around Ingleton; the poet Wordsworth, in his later *Guide*, gave detailed accounts of the three main approaches to the Lakes, via the Aire Gap, Wensleydale and Stainmore.

Discovery of the Landscape — Further Reading:

C Bruyn Andrews (ed.), *The Torrington Diaries*, 4 vols (London: Eyre & Spottiswoode, 1936-8).

James Joel Cartwright (ed.), *The Travels through England of Dr Richard Pococke*, 2 vols, Camden Society, N S, XLII (1888) & XLIII (1889).

Edward Dayes, *The Works of the Late Edward Dayes, containing an Excursion through the principal parts of Derbyshire and Yorkshire* (1805; rpt, London: Cornmarket, 1971).

Daniel Defoe, *A Tour through the whole Island of Great Britain*, 2 vols as 1 (London: Dent, 1974).

William Gilpin, *Observations, relative chiefly to Picturesque Beauty, made in the Year 1772, in several parts of England; particularly the Mountains, and Lakes of Cumberland, and Westmoreland* (London, 1786).

David Hill, *Turner in the North: A Tour through Derbyshire, Yorkshire, Durham, Northumberland, the Scottish Borders, the Lake District, Lancashire and Lincolnshire in the year 1797* (New Haven & London: Yale UP, 1996).

Christopher Morris (ed.), *The Journeys of Celia Fiennes* (London: Cresset Press, 1949).

Paul Romney (ed.), *The Diary of Charles Fothergill, 1805: An Itinerary to York, Flamborough and the North-Western Dales of Yorkshire*, Yorkshire Archaeological Society Record Series CXLII for 1982 (1984).

Walter White, *A Month in Yorkshire* (2nd edn, London: Chapman & Hall, 1858).

Arthur Young, *A Six Months Tour Through the North of England* (4 vols, 1771; rpt, New York: Augustus M Kelley, 1967).

Tourists who chose not to extend their tour to the Lakes were more likely to venture eastwards, but a lower quotient of landscape interest and, in many parts, a lower concentration of antiquarian sites, deterred many.

In 1803 the artist Edward Dayes struck north-eastwards from Ripon, to include Sutton Bank, Helmsley Castle, Duncombe Park and the abbeys of Rievaulx and Byland; but, turning south, he reached Easingwold where 'the face of nature losing its picturesque character, I proceeded, through thirteen miles of flat, uninteresting country, to York'. The artist Turner's chosen subjects confirm the point, their western emphasis countered only by views of a number of harbours. The vales of York, Mowbray and Pickering were seemingly beyond the reach of the picturesque taste.

It could narrow horizons in other ways, too: descriptions of industrial enterprises were once a staple of travellers' accounts, but when Byng visited Aysgarth Falls in 1792 he lamented that the erection of a cotton mill 'has completed the destruction of every rural thought'.

The North York Moors were also slow to win admirers. To agricultural improvers such as Arthur Young, their barren expanse was a standing reproach; to students of the picturesque, their topography was monotonous.

From the spa and sea-bathing resorts of Scarborough, Guisborough and Redcar, visitors explored the rugged coastline and its picturesque fishing villages. But increasingly the moors acquired a positive cultural energy of their own — romantic and uplifting.

The tourist potential of Whitby was released by the railway: a major seaport in the eighteenth and early nineteenth centuries, it developed a significant resort function through the efforts of the railway promoter, George Hudson, around 1850. Goathland emerged as a minor resort in later decades.

The lineaments of a distinctively modern tourism are apparent in Walter White's itinerary of 1857. White was a conscientious traveller, methodically quartering the county, doubling back on himself to avoid omissions, and taking advantage of railways where they accelerated a journey bereft of incident. He engaged, too, in a new form of literary tourism, notably in his visits to Greta Bridge (where the school inspired 'Dotheboys Hall' in Dickens's *Nicholas Nickleby*), Hart-leap Well (the subject of a poem by Wordsworth) and Shandy Hall, the eighteenth-century home of Laurence Sterne.

11.6 THE DEVELOPMENT OF THE COUNTRY HOUSE
EDWARD WATERSON

A country house (**fig 11.5**), in essence, is the principal house of a substantial landed estate, and the 'seat' of a family of gentry or aristocratic status. As such it is the expression of both the culture and the power of a political and economic élite — the successor, in more peaceable times, to the seigneurial castle or fortified manor house of the medieval period.

Birdsall House, northern Yorkshire Wolds. The house of the Lords Middleton in their estate village at Birdsall, which they owned from 1729. The house is older, and was modified from its original design from 1600 onwards, especially in the mid and late eighteenth century and in the early nineteenth century. The old church, abandoned in 1824, can be seen close to the house.
NMR 17047/33 © Crown copyright. NMR

Keldy Castle. A castellated house built in the early nineteenth century. Little of it now remains.
© Lord Grimthorpe.

Easthorpe Hall, north front, 1927. A late eighteenth-century house designed by John Carr of York.
© Lord Grimthorpe.

Country house owners ranged from potentates of national and regional significance to modest country squires. While many claimed long pedigrees, they were not always of ancient blood. Success in politics, the professions or commerce could also be translated into titles and landed property through marriage or purchase. But the distinctions of rank, coupled with the extent of landownership, set the country house apart from the merchants' villas which proliferated close to major urban centres in the eighteenth and nineteenth centuries.

At the wealthier end of the spectrum, North Yorkshire's country house owners might hold estates in more than one county, each with its own country house, as well as one or more town houses (typically in York or London).

Even among great magnates, however, building afresh could impose a crippling burden, and many houses evolved piecemeal, retaining elements from the medieval period onwards. Markenfield Hall changed little; its moat and its embattled tower bear the hallmarks of the need for defence from Scottish raiders.

Persisting almost to the end of the medieval period, Markenfield Hall, Nappa Hall, and the tower at Aske Hall form the southern extremity of a building type more often found in Northumberland, Cumbria and County Durham.

Arden Hall, western North York Moors, from Samuel Buck's *Yorkshire Sketchbook* c1719-20. The sketch shows the simplicity and 'no frills' approach to architectural fashion in North Yorkshire in the early eighteenth century. The core of the house at Arden is on the site of the former Arden Priory.

The disposal of monastic land following the Reformation offered new opportunities in the form of land, mineral wealth and building materials. Some houses were contrived in the shells of monastic buildings, as at Egglestone Abbey beside the Tees, and Newburgh Priory. Fountains Hall was built *c*1611 by Sir Stephen Proctor alongside the ruined abbey, and survives as a rare northern example of the prodigy-house style associated with the architect Robert Smythson.

Throughout the seventeenth century, many country house owners were content with simpler styles, often reflecting the architectural influence of the Low Countries, as in the mid-seventeenth-century remodelling of Norton Conyers Hall, with its shaped gables. This no-frills approach to the North Yorkshire country house is clearly seen in Samuel Buck's *Yorkshire Sketch-Book* of 1719-20, in which examples of high architectural fashion are conspicuous by their scarcity.

A notable exception was Castle Howard. Begun in 1701 to replace nearby Henderskelfe Castle, it was designed by Sir John Vanbrugh as a flamboyant baroque palace unparalleled in the county.

In contrast to the 'old wealth' of the Howards, Sir Edward Blackett applied the profits of the Tyneside coal industry to the construction of Newby Hall from 1705, while Duncombe Park was built *c*1710 with the fruits of a City career.

At Beningbrough the Elizabethan house was pulled down and a new brick house erected in its place, completed in 1716 to the designs of an enterprising York carpenter and joiner, William Thornton, for the Bourchiers, a long-established gentry family.

John Aislabie, Chancellor of the Exchequer and one of the few to profit from the South Sea Bubble (1720), retired to Studley Royal where — disgraced but wealthy — he rebuilt the house and transformed the park under the direction of Colen Campbell.

The consolidation of estates, and in some cases the injection of wealth by marriage from other parts of the county (especially the increasingly industrialised West Riding), provided the springboard for an increasing take-up of new architectural styles from the mid-eighteenth century onwards, capitalising in many cases on the abundant building stone of the county.

The quick-witted and talented York architect John Carr (1723-1807), who had worked with Robert Adam at Harewood House, provided the gentry and *nouveaux riches* with the houses they aspired to, such as Constable Burton Hall (1762-8) near Leyburn.

While the West Riding spent liberally and the East Riding frugally, the North Riding (mostly now in North Yorkshire) took a middle way with houses generally of a more manageable size — a factor in their long-term survival.

The higher ground of the Dales in the west, and the barren moorland of the North York Moors, did not lend themselves to landed estates capable of supporting country houses. On the moors, Mulgrave Castle near Whitby, with work by John Soane and gardens by Humphry

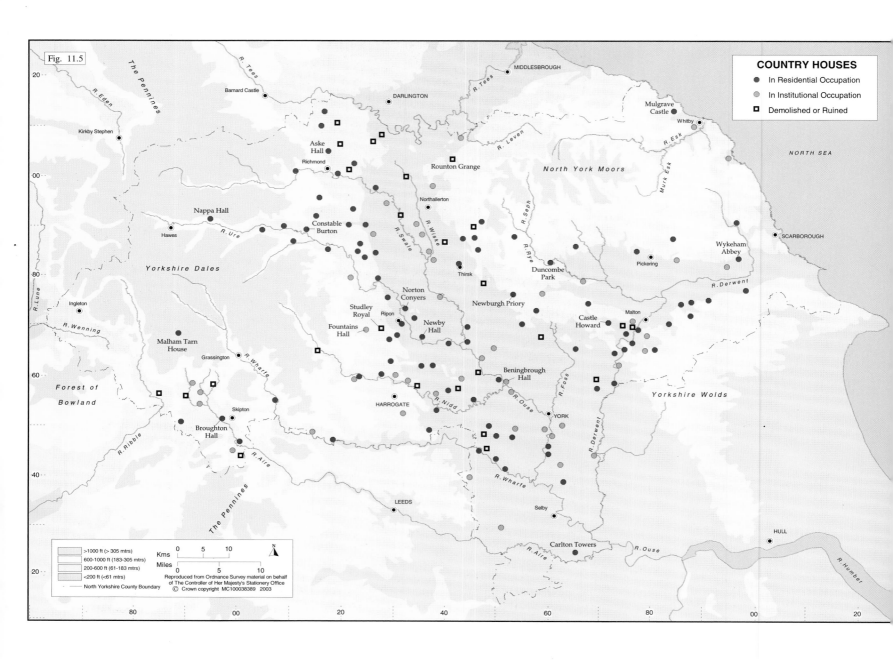

Fig. 11.5

COUNTRY HOUSES

- In Residential Occupation
- In Institutional Occupation
- □ Demolished or Ruined

The Pennines

R. Eden

R. Tees

MIDDLESBROUGH

Barnard Castle

DARLINGTON

R. Tees

R. Leven

Kirkby Stephen

Mulgrave Castle

Whitby

R. Esk

NORTH SEA

Aske Hall

Richmond

Rounton Grange

North York Moors

Murk Esk

Nappa Hall

Hawes

R. Ure

Constable Burton

Northallerton

R. Swale

R. Wiske

R. Seph

R. Rye

Wykeham Abbey

SCARBOROUGH

Yorkshire Dales

Thirsk

Duncombe Park

Pickering

R. Derwent

R. Lune

Ingleton

Norton Conyers

Newburgh Priory

R. Wenning

Studley Royal

Ripon

Newby Hall

Castle Howard

Malton

Fountains Hall

Malham Tarn House

Grassington

R. Wharfe

Beningbrough Hall

R. Foss

Yorkshire Wolds

Forest of Bowland

Skipton

R. Nidd

R. Ouse

R. Ribble

Broughton Hall

HARROGATE

YORK

R. Aire

R. Derwent

The Pennines

R. Wharfe

LEEDS

Selby

HULL

Carlton Towers

R. Aire

R. Ouse

R. Humber

>1000 ft (> 305 mtrs)
600-1000 ft (183-305 mtrs)
200-600 ft (61-183 mtrs)
<200 ft (<61 mtrs)
North Yorkshire County Boundary

Kms 0 5 10

Miles 0 10

N

Reproduced from Ordnance Survey material on behalf of The Controller of Her Majesty's Stationery Office
© Crown copyright MC100038389 2003

Duncombe House, Duncombe Park, Helmsley, built for Thomas Duncombe c1713 from designs by William Wakefield, a 'gentleman architect'. The wings and main block were rebuilt after a fire in 1879.
© North York Moors National Park Authority, NYM 62.

Castle Howard, south front. Castle Howard was designed for the third Earl of Carlisle by Sir John Vanbrugh, and built from 1691 to 1738.
© N Butlin.

Country Houses — Further Reading:

Ivan Hall (ed.), *Samuel Buck's Yorkshire Sketchbook* (Wakefield: Wakefield Historical Publications, 1979).

Jane Hatcher, *Richmondshire Architecture* (Richmond: C J Hatcher, 1990).

Patrick Nuttgens, *Brierley in Yorkshire: the Architecture of the Turn of the Century* (York: York Georgian Society, 1984).

Nikolaus Pevsner, *The Buildings of England: Yorkshire — The North Riding* (Harmondsworth: Penguin Books, 1966). Also volumes on the West Riding, and York and the East Riding.

Charles Saumarez Smith, *The Building of Castle Howard* (London: Pimlico, 1997).

Edward Waterson & Peter Meadows, *Lost Houses of York and the North Riding* (Thornton-le-Clay: Jill Raines, 1990). Also related volumes on the East and West Ridings.

Brian Wragg, *John Carr of York*, ed. Giles Worsley (Otley: Oblong, 2001).

Repton, is exceptional. Nineteenth-century industrial wealth from Middlesbrough and further afield paid for a number of houses, but these tended to be associated with sporting estates, and houses such as Keldy Castle (now ruinous) were country houses only in the loosest sense.

In the Dales, however, the landscape was more admired and Malham Tarn House, the mid-eighteenth-century shooting box of the Listers of Gisburn Park, was enlarged after 1852 to form the country house of the industrial millionaire, Walter Morrison.

Carlton Towers in the Aire Valley, remodelled in Gothic style in 1872 by Edward Welby Pugin, appears in hindsight to stand on the brink of an abyss.

From the 1880s to the 1940s, the country house and its way of life came under extreme pressure throughout the British Isles, as agricultural land and rental values fell in the face of New World competition, and fiscal pressures intensified. Country house owners found themselves lacking the means and, as political hostility to landed estates grew, the will to build extravagantly. Building continued, and to the highest standards, but rarely for traditional country house owners.

From the late nineteenth century come such innovative houses as Philip Webb's Rounton Grange (1872-6), for the Bells, ironfounders of Middlesbrough; while Crathorne Hall represents a more conservative Edwardian style. Walter Brierley, successor (after a long interval) to Carr's architectural practice, designed houses of lasting quality, including additions to Carr's Easthorpe Hall. In the west of the county, Sir Edwin Lutyens built the striking Gledstone Hall (1925-7) near Skipton.

It is notable that North Yorkshire enters the twenty-first century with one of the highest concentrations of country seats still occupied by landed gentry. The county's landowners rarely over-stretched themselves, kept their estates largely intact and made judicious marriages which once brought them land, but later industrial and commercial wealth.

Although several dozen important country houses were lost in the twentieth century, including Studley Royal and Halnaby Hall, it is a tribute to the tenacity of their owners that in percentage terms the losses in England's largest county are remarkably slight.

11.7 PARKS, GARDENS AND DESIGNED LANDSCAPES
VALERIE HEPWORTH AND DEBORAH TURNBULL

The English love of gardens, gardening and moulding the natural landscape is as deep-seated in North Yorkshire as in other parts of the country, and makes a major contribution to both the national and local heritage.

Designs range from the early seventeenth-century formal gardens of Sheriff Hutton Park to the great eighteenth-century landscape of Castle Howard; through the nineteenth-century

Broughton Hall: scrolled parterre and gazebo designed by Andrew Nesfield, 1855-7.
© V Hepworth.

Rievaulx Terrace: Ionic temple at northern end of terrace, c1758.
© D Turnbull.

formal gardens of Broughton Hall and Moreby Hall; the twentieth-century designs of St Nicholas and Gledstone Hall; to the public parks of York, Scarborough, Harrogate and Knaresborough.

Other sites of historical and aesthetic value in North Yorkshire include, for example, the landscape at the University of York, cemeteries, seaside gardens, hospital grounds and many smaller sites which do not feature on the national record established by English Heritage.

The forty sites shown on **fig 11.6** are specifically those in North Yorkshire which are on the English Heritage *Register of Parks and Gardens of Special Historic Interest in England*. The *Register*, dated 2000, is a highly selective list in which sites, not necessarily open to the public, are divided into three bands:

Sites of international importance	(Grade I)	5 sites in N Yorkshire
Sites of exceptional historic interest	(Grade II*)	10 sites in N Yorkshire
Sites with high level of historic interest	(Grade II)	26 sites in N Yorkshire

Sites over thirty years old are considered as historic, and include the grounds of private houses, public parks and other planned landscapes reflecting the landscaping fashions of their day.

Studley Royal: water garden and Temple of Piety.
© D Turnbull.

Castle Howard: Mausoleum designed by Nicholas
Hawksmoor, and New River Bridge.
© V Hepworth.

The main criteria used by English Heritage in assessing a landscape for listing include:
- the age of the main phase of development of the design
- the influence of the design in the development of taste
- the involvement of major designers
- the association of the site with significant persons or events
- the site as an early or representative example of a particular style
- the historic interest of the site in relation to other registered sites

Sites are judged not by ephemeral planting, but by longer-lived elements which they contain such as landforms, views, built structures, walled kitchen gardens, walks and rides, water features, trees, hedges and structural shrubberies.

North Yorkshire is particularly fortunate in possessing examples of sites pivotal in the development of garden and landscape design in Britain and abroad. Studley Royal, whose magnificent water gardens have been recognised as a World Heritage Site, Duncombe Park and Rievaulx Terrace, both Grade I listed and landmarks in the development of the English landscape style, with curving terrace walks culminating in classical temples, are all such. Castle Howard, also Grade I, was created between 1698 and 1738 on a vast scale, exhibiting a mix of geometric and less formal features, together with a large number of listed garden

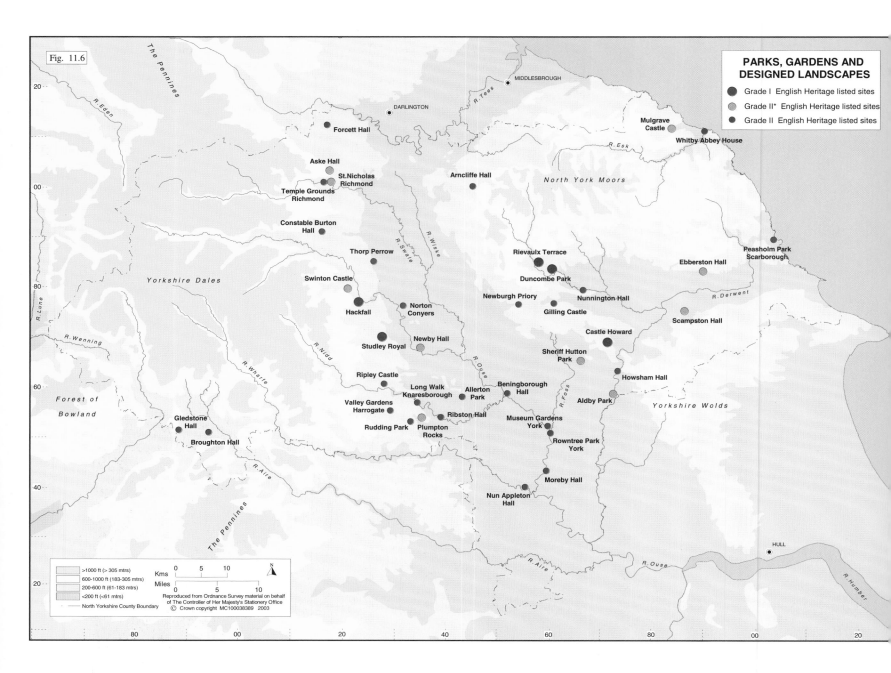

Fig. 11.6

PARKS, GARDENS AND DESIGNED LANDSCAPES

● Grade I   English Heritage listed sites
● Grade II* English Heritage listed sites
● Grade II English Heritage listed sites

The Pennines

R. Eden

R. Tees

MIDDLESBROUGH

DARLINGTON

R. Esk

Mulgrave Castle

Whitby Abbey House

Forcett Hall

Aske Hall

St.Nicholas Richmond

Temple Grounds Richmond

Arncliffe Hall

North York Moors

Constable Burton Hall

R. Swale

Thorp Perrow

Rievaulx Terrace

Peasholm Park Scarborough

Ebberston Hall

Swinton Castle

Duncombe Park

Yorkshire Dales

Newburgh Priory

Nunnington Hall

R. Derwent

Hackfall

Norton Conyers

Gilling Castle

Scampston Hall

R. Lune

R. Wenning

R. Nidd

Studley Royal

Newby Hall

Castle Howard

Sheriff Hutton Park

Forest of Bowland

Ripley Castle

Long Walk Knaresborough

Allerton Park

Beningborough Hall

R. Foss

Howsham Hall

Aldby Park

Yorkshire Wolds

Gledstone Hall

Valley Gardens Harrogate

R. Wharfe

Ribston Hall

Museum Gardens York

Broughton Hall

Rudding Park

Plumpton Rocks

Rowntree Park York

R. Ouse

R. Aire

Moreby Hall

Nun Appleton Hall

HULL

R. Ouse

R. Humber

>1000 ft (> 305 mtrs)
600-1000 ft (183-305 mtrs)
200-600 ft (61-183 mtrs)
<200 ft (<61 mtrs)
North Yorkshire County Boundary

Kms   0   5   10
Miles 0   5   10

Reproduced from Ordnance Survey material on behalf of The Controller of Her Majesty's Stationery Office
© Crown copyright MC100038389 2003

Castle Howard: Temple of the Four Winds (designed by Sir John Vanbrugh), and New River Bridge.
© V Hepworth.

buildings and often described as one of the foremost examples of 'the heroic age of English landscape architecture'.[1]

Several North Yorkshire parks and gardens on the *Register* are based on medieval deer parks, for example Allerton Park, Beningborough Hall, Sheriff Hutton Park, Ripley Castle and Constable Burton Hall. Newburgh Priory is on the site of an Augustinian priory founded in 1145 and granted a licence to enclose the park in 1383. The estate at Ribston Hall was owned by the Knights Templar in the thirteenth century, and later became well known as the home of the Ribston Pippin apple raised from seed *c*1707.

Many designers have been associated with North Yorkshire designed landscapes and, although a number spent a considerable length of time here, only the Mickle dynasty could be said to be from North Yorkshire. Adam Mickle II (1747–*c*1810) lived most of his working life in Bedale. A fine draughtsman who had worked for Lancelot 'Capability' Brown, he carried out commissions for sites from Wales to Durham, and supervised the development of the dramatic picturesque landscape at Swinton Castle and the lakes at Thorp Perrow.

above Duncombe Park: Doric temple at the south end of the terrace.
© D Turnbull.

right Birdsall house and gardens. The grounds were landscaped from a design by Thomas Knowleton from 1729, and included two small lakes in a valley to the west of the house. A third, larger lake was added in the 1750s.
NMR 17047/24. © *Crown copyright. NMR.*

William Kent (1685-1748), born in Bridlington (East Yorkshire) and acknowledged as without rival in landscape gardening during his lifetime, sketched the design for one of the most ambitious of all Gothick follies, the temple at Aske Hall and, through his principal heir in the Gothick tradition, Daniel Garrett, he may have influenced designs for Temple Grounds, Richmond.

Sir John Vanbrugh (1664-1726), assisted by Nicholas Hawksmoor (1661-1736), worked with Charles Howard, third Earl of Carlisle, laying out the monumental landscape at Castle Howard. Stephen Switzer (1682-1745) may have advised at Castle Howard and possibly also at nearby Duncombe Park. The water garden at Ebberston Hall attributed to Switzer is integral to the Colen Campbell designed hall of 1718.

Charles Bridgeman (d 1738) produced designs for Scampston Hall and possibly Duncombe Park. Thomas Knowlton (1691-1781), one of the most outstanding gardeners of his time, whose advice was constantly sought as horticulturist, garden designer and planter, laid out the gardens at Aldby Park.

The best-known English landscape designer, Lancelot 'Capability' Brown (1716-83), was consulted by Sir Lawrence Dundas at Aske Hall and Sir William St Quintin at Scampston Hall in the 1770s. Thomas White (1736-1811) who, like Adam Mickle II, had early in his career been in Brown's employ, worked at Newby Hall and was consulted at Mulgrave Castle. Humphry Repton (1752-1818), Brown's successor as the leading landscape designer of the day, produced proposals and his trade-mark 'red book' for Rudding Park in 1790 and for Mulgrave Castle in 1792-3.

Towards the end of his career William Sawrey Gilpin (1762-1843) lived for some time with a cousin at Sedbury in North Yorkshire. A great proponent of terraces, Gilpin drew up a scheme for a terrace wall, planting and extensions to the park at Beningborough Hall.

William Andrews Nesfield (1793-1881), who was at the forefront of reworking gardens in seventeenth-century styles, designed an elaborate scrolled parterre (flowerbed arrangement), fountain, gazebo and conservatory at Broughton Hall and, at Castle Howard, the south parterre, Atlas fountain and cascades.

In the twentieth century, Edwin Lutyens and Gertrude Jekyll collaborated at Gledstone Hall and James Russell created gardens at Rudding Park. Other landscapes are the result of collaboration between designers and owners or, as at St Nicholas, Richmond, the work of creative and talented individuals unrecognised as professional landscape designers.

The majority of North Yorkshire parks and gardens have developed over many centuries, with additions or alterations being made as needs and fashions changed. Because of English Heritage's thirty-year time rule, no recent designs are included; however, designed landscapes of quality and interest continue to be created. There are many more sites, not yet included on the English Heritage *Register*, of historical and aesthetic value whose history has yet to be fully unearthed and recorded.

The recording, conservation and restoration of North Yorkshire's designed landscapes is considered of the utmost importance in seeking to protect the parks and gardens which make such a rich and varied contribution to our landscape heritage.

Parks & Gardens — Further Reading:
English Heritage *Register of Parks and Gardens of Special Historic Interest in England,* North Yorkshire volume (held by planning authorities, main reference libraries, & available from English Heritage).

Christopher Hussey, *English Gardens and Landscapes 1700-1750* (London: Country Life, 1967).

Geoffrey Jellicoe, Susan Jellicoe, Patrick Goode, Michael Lancaster (eds), *The Oxford Companion to Gardens* (Oxford & New York: Oxford University Press, 1986).

11.8 THE ROUTEWAYS OF MEDIEVAL RIPLEY: A CASE STUDY
RICHARD MUIR

Transport networks are not all of one age. Rather, they are in a constant state of development, with some sections of the system decaying or being subsumed back into the countryside, while other sections are being upgraded and new connections are being forged.

Transport networks are not easy to reconstruct, but in any recreations of medieval settings the work should be attempted, for the networks provide the skeletons of cultural landscapes and will often condition other factors, like the development of settlements. Equally, they are conditioned by the presence of settlements and the patterns of commerce. **Fig 11.7** shows the fragility of the settlement in the region, while **fig 11.8** shows a reconstruction of these routeways in medieval Ripley,

Lanes of a prehistoric village are probably common, yet usually impossible to date. The oldest datable road is a section of the Roman road that ran from Ilkley to Aldborough. It was almost certainly intact and in use in Norman times, and may have remained so into the fourteenth century. Parts of it in the township fell into disuse and, in the seventeenth century, one abandoned section was recognised by villagers as the 'cam' of a lost road. In 1365 wagons loaded with lead and drawn by ten oxen each were hauled from Greenhow, above Pateley

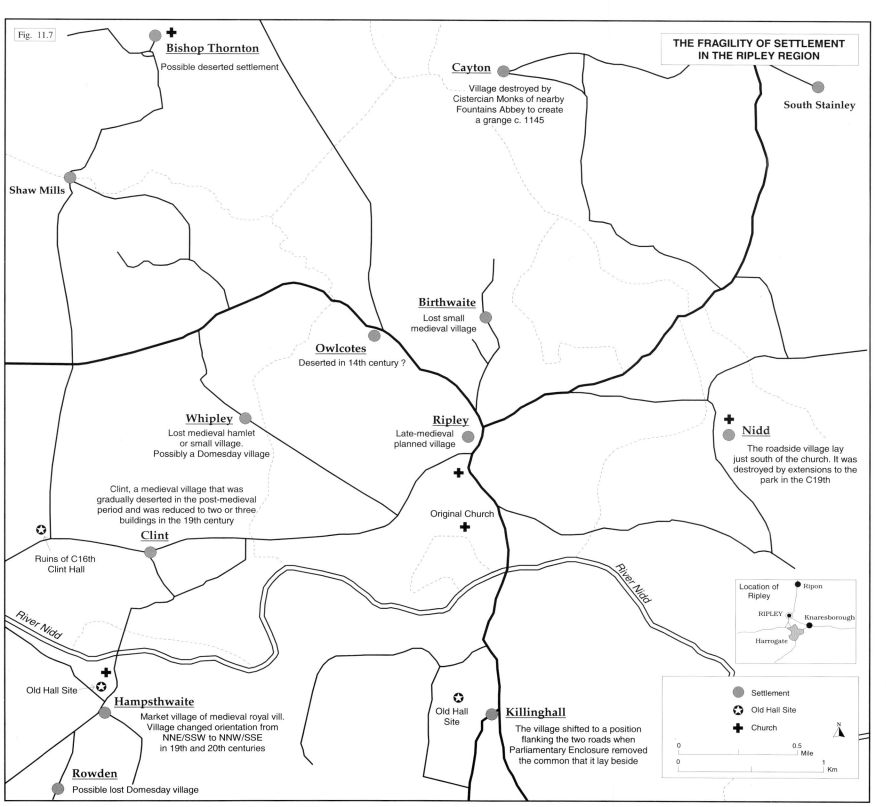

Fig. 11.7

THE FRAGILITY OF SETTLEMENT IN THE RIPLEY REGION

Bishop Thornton
Possible deserted settlement

Cayton
Village destroyed by Cistercian Monks of nearby Fountains Abbey to create a grange c. 1145

South Stainley

Shaw Mills

Birthwaite
Lost small medieval village

Owlcotes
Deserted in 14th century ?

Whipley
Lost medieval hamlet or small village. Possibly a Domesday village

Ripley
Late-medieval planned village

Nidd
The roadside village lay just south of the church. It was destroyed by extensions to the park in the C19th

Clint, a medieval village that was gradually deserted in the post-medieval period and was reduced to two or three buildings in the 19th century

Clint

Original Church

Ruins of C16th Clint Hall

River Nidd

River Nidd

Location of Ripley

Ripon

RIPLEY
Knaresborough

Harrogate

Old Hall Site

Hampsthwaite
Market village of medieval royal vill. Village changed orientation from NNE/SSW to NNW/SSE in 19th and 20th centuries

Old Hall Site

Killinghall
The village shifted to a position flanking the two roads when Parliamentary Enclosure removed the common that it lay beside

Settlement

Old Hall Site

Church

0   0.5
|————————————|
Mile
0   1
|————————————|
Km

N

Rowden
Possible lost Domesday village

Bridge, to Boroughbridge and may have passed through Ripley township.[1] The journey was plagued by the 'high mountains and muddy roads'.[2]

After the Roman routeway, the next datable routes were monastic rights of way. The township lay quite close to Fountains Abbey, and the adjacent township of Cayton was depopulated and the inhabitants replaced by lay brethren. The far-flung holdings of Fountains (and Byland) in Nidderdale demanded the use of efficient routeways.

Between 1157 and 1173, William son of Ketel de Scotton, probably the owner of the smaller of the two manors in Ripley township, granted Fountains a cart road through his estate from Hampsthwaite, via the middle of the (subsequently deserted) village of Owlcotes to a crossing on Cayton Beck close to the grange.[3] A little later in the century, Bernard the priest of Ripley, the owner of the larger manor, gave the monks a road that was

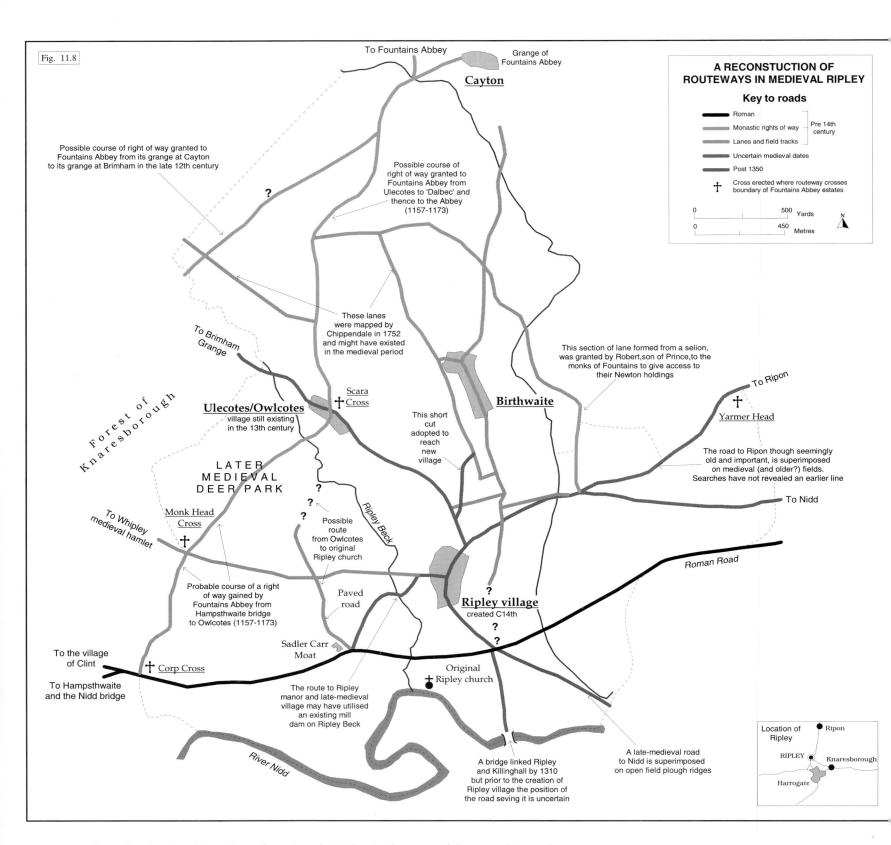

Fig. 11.8

A RECONSTUCTION OF ROUTEWAYS IN MEDIEVAL RIPLEY

Key to roads

Roman
Monastic rights of way — Pre 14th century
Lanes and field tracks
Uncertain medieval dates
Post 1350
† Cross erected where routeway crosses boundary of Fountains Abbey estates

To Fountains Abbey

Grange of Fountains Abbey

Cayton

Possible course of right of way granted to Fountains Abbey from its grange at Cayton to its grange at Brimham in the late 12th century

Possible course of right of way granted to Fountains Abbey from Ulecotes to 'Dalbec' and thence to the Abbey (1157-1173)

This section of lane formed from a selion, was granted by Robert, son of Prince, to the monks of Fountains to give access to their Newton holdings

To Brimham Grange

These lanes were mapped by Chippendale in 1752 and might have existed in the medieval period

Birthwaite

To Ripon

Forest of Knaresborough

† Scara Cross

Ulecotes/Owlcotes
village still existing in the 13th century

This short cut adopted to reach new village

† Yarmer Head

The road to Ripon though seemingly old and important, is superimposed on medieval (and older?) fields. Searches have not revealed an earlier line

LATER MEDIEVAL DEER PARK

To Nidd

To Whipley medieval hamlet

Monk Head Cross
†

Possible route from Owlcotes to original Ripley church

Ripley Beck

Probable course of a right of way gained by Fountains Abbey from Hampsthwaite bridge to Owlcotes (1157-1173)

Paved road

Roman Road

Ripley village
created C14th

To the village of Clint

† **Corp Cross**

Sadler Carr Moat

Original † Ripley church

To Hampsthwaite and the Nidd bridge

The route to Ripley manor and late-medieval village may have utilised an existing mill dam on Ripley Beck

A late-medieval road to Nidd is superimposed on open field plough ridges

River Nidd

A bridge linked Ripley and Killinghall by 1310 but prior to the creation of Ripley village the position of the road seving it is uncertain

0 — 500 Yards
0 — 450 Metres
N

Location of Ripley

Ripon
RIPLEY • Knaresborough
Harrogate

---

forty feet (12m) wide and ran from Scarah Bridge in the west of the township to the same causeway.[4]

Around 1200, Richard de Ripley granted the monks free transit through the township for cattle moving between their granges at Cayton and Brimham.[5] In the same century, Robert son of Prince granted the monks a strategically placed selion (strip of land) which could be converted into a track to give the monks access to their holdings in Newton.[6] Around 1250-80 some land called *Shandekefalde* ('Shand's cow fold') was mentioned as lying next to this 'way out to Newton'.[7]

Some medieval routeways in Ripley were abandoned but identified as earthworks using the techniques of landscape archaeology. A hollowed paved track which apparently linked

above   Ilkley to Aldborough Roman road passing through Ripley.
© R Muir.

top right   Ripley deer park.
© I Dormor.

bottom right   Ripley: left, holloway of paved medieval road; right, earthworks of medieval hunting tower.
© R Muir.

Ripley's Routeways — Further Reading:

D Austin, Medieval settlement in the North-East of England — retrospect, summary and prospect, in B E Vyner (ed.), *Medieval Rural Settlement in North-East England* (Durham: Architectural and Archaeological Society of Durham and Northumberland, 1990), 141-50.

M Chibnall, *The Ecclesiastical History of Orderic Vitalis* (Oxford: Oxford University Press, 1969).

W Grainge, *Harrogate and the Forest of Knaresborough* (London: John Russell Smith, 1871).

B Jennings (ed.), *A History of Nidderdale*, second edition (Huddersfield: Advertiser Press, 1983).

R Muir, Pollards in Nidderdale: a landscape history, *Rural History* 11 (2000), 95-11.

J Thorpe, *Ripley: Its History and Antiquities* (London: Whitaker, 1866).

the moated homestead at Sadler Carr to the former village of Owlcotes lies beneath a thin covering of turf in the deer park of Ripley Castle, sharing its alignment with a pre-Conquest co-axial field system that determines the alignments of the field systems in the region.

Various other trackways are recognised as narrow holloways running amongst the plough ridges on the furlong or culture boundaries. Often, these tracks are associated with abandoned settlement, the characteristic medieval hamlet of the locality being a few dwellings aligned along a roadside. The road linking Ripon and Nidderdale passes through the township. It is plainly superimposed on elements of an old field system, and in places it cuts older ridge and furrow, though the holloway of its original route cannot be identified.

The best results are obtained when the results of archaeological enquiry are complemented with evidence obtained from old maps and other documents.

The reconstruction of the course of the Roman road was achieved by linking, via causeways, holloways and sections of former lane indicated on a plan of 1752, the 'viable' section that now exists as a popular footpath through Hollybank Wood to a length of agger (a well-constructed embankment, giving an effectively drained base, for a Roman road) in the east of the township that carries the parish boundary between Ripley and Nidd.

The archaeological work identifying the spot where the 'lost' Roman road had crossed the Ripley Beck was confirmed by documentary research with the discovery in the manor court

Ripley: sheep graze the site of a former garden.
© R Muir.

rolls of Ripley for April 1631 of an account of an investigation by jurors into a parcel of land called 'Walkemill Inge' ('Walk Mill Meadow'). They went to the eastern part of a field called 'Little Chappell Flatt' ('Little [ancient] Chapel Furlong'), 'where it was shown to the foresaid jurors, that there is a way in the foresaid land, And clear evidence of a certain little raised way, of a large ditch, in English the cam [ridge] of an old ditche, lying between the orchard and the foresaid land, heading towards the little stream...'[8] (translated from the Latin).

11.9 HEBDEN TOWNSHIP, UPPER WHARFEDALE: A CASE STUDY HEATHER M BEAUMONT (*RESEARCH BY THE WEA HEBDEN HISTORY GROUP*)[1]

Features of the contemporary landscape and built environment reflect the organisation of Hebden at various phases of its history.[2] There is evidence of the course of the routeways, the layout of the medieval manorial settlement and its agricultural landscape, and developments dating from the seventeenth to nineteenth centuries. Many of these features appear on the labelled aerial photographs, taken during a balloon flight in June 1987[3] (pages 240 and 241).

GENERAL TOPOGRAPHY
Buildings in the nuclear village parallel Hebden Beck, lying above and to the west of its narrow gill (G) (p 240). The well-treed valley of the River Wharfe (W) appears towards the top of the photos; 'W' on the photo on page 241 also locates the confluence of beck and river. The township boundary runs centre stream along the Wharfe (*c* 500 feet/150m above sea-level), rising to the Nidderdale watershed (1,800feet/550m) and enclosing an area of *c* 3,600 acres (1,450ha), two-thirds of which is moorland overlying rocks of the Yoredale series and gritstone. Near the river the underlying rock is limestone, and the pattern of walls and field-markings identifies the common arable field (see photo on page 241). The location of the settlement site may have been influenced by proximity to crossing points of both beck and river, utilised by two intersecting routeways, one running east/west, the other north/south.

ROUTEWAYS
The road-bridge (RB), which crosses Hebden Beck and carries the Grassington to Pateley Bridge road (B6265), is the modern representative of a trans-Pennine route, possibly of prehistoric origin.

This route was heavily used during the monastic era. Around 1200 the lord of the manor, Simon de Hebden, granted Fountains Abbey the right of passage for their flocks and herds, passing to and from their grange at Kilnsey, and summer grazing around Malham and in the Lake District (**fig 11.9**). In 1631 the route through Hebden was described as providing the link between the Craven area and markets at Ripon, Knaresborough and York.

Hebden village in the 1930s.
© Marie Hartley.

Settlement at the northern end of the present nuclear village (see photo on page 240), at Town Hill (which includes Town Head farm, TH) and Brook Street (BS), relates to the crossing point of the beck and the course taken by the east-west route prior to the Grassington to Pateley Bridge turnpike being established (*c*1758–1822). The turnpike bridge was replaced by the road bridge (1827). An earlier, single-track bridge lies about 150 feet (50m) upstream from the road bridge, at the head of Brook Street (just discernible in shadow on page 240). Skeins of holloways (not illustrated) approach the beck from the east.

A second routeway passed along Back Lane (BL), southwards towards a forded crossing of the Wharfe. It featured in a Fountains Abbey charter of *c*1240, and provided access to Ilkley and lower Wharfedale, Skipton and Airedale (**fig 11.9**). The position of the ford (W on page 241) is marked by hippings (stepping stones) and a footbridge across the river, constructed in 1885 by the village blacksmith.

LAND AND BUILDINGS

The organisation of the southern part of Hebden reflects the layout of the medieval manor. Appearing in the Domesday survey, it subsequently was held by the de Hebdens and their descendants, the Tempests of Bracewell. The pattern of ownership changed in 1589, when possession passed to three trustee freeholders; by the time of the tithe survey (hereafter 'ts') of 1846-7, there were forty-seven property-owners in the township.

Hebden Hall (H) lies within an enclosure which also encompassed the manorial corn mill. The mill site was developed during the late eighteenth century, with the construction of a textile mill (now demolished) and mill cottages (MC). A stinted pasture (P) lay to the south-east: half the grazing rights were held by the lord of the manor and half by tenants. Part of this pasture, around Ranelands Farm (R), was converted to arable (East Field; EF), probably during the latter part of the thirteenth century in response to population pressure.

To the north of Hebden Hall, farms were laid out in a planned toft compartment (TC). Within each of the eight enclosures, house plots lay to the east, and crofts, gardens and barns to the west. The turnpike and its replacement (the B6265) cut across the toft compartment and common arable field.

Landholdings in that part of the arable field nearest to Back Lane (BL), known as West Field (WF on photo on page 241), relate to farms in the toft compartment (ts). Some walled field boundaries show the reverse-S (aratral curve) or bowed shape that reflects the line of medieval ploughing. Town Field (TF), an extension of West Field up to the township boundary, largely comprises long, narrow enclosures, also with curving walls that respect the marks of ridge and furrow, standing out boldly in the low evening sun. Field names (ts) include *Flatts* (FL) and Over*lands* (O), indicative of strip holdings. 'Corduroy' cultivation marks are comparatively recent (eg Napoleonic period).

Prior to the advent of the turnpike, the east-west route passed towards Grassington along a droving funnel (F), outside the arable field. While its perimeter boundary may date from the

Aerial photograph of Hebden village looking south-south-east.
© Heather Beaumont.

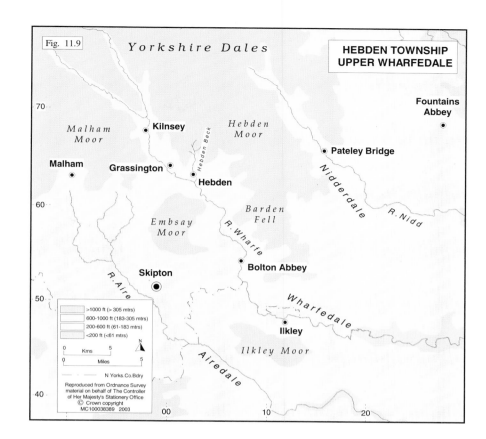

Fig. 11.9 — Yorkshire Dales — **HEBDEN TOWNSHIP UPPER WHARFEDALE**

Reproduced from Ordnance Survey material on behalf of The Controller of Her Majesty's Stationery Office © Crown copyright MC100038389 2003

below Aerial photograph of the common arable field looking south-east.
© Heather Beaumont.

Hebden Township — Further Reading:

Heather M Beaumont, Hebden Township Boundary Past and Present, in *Archaeology and Historic Landscapes in the Yorkshire Dales,* Yorkshire Archaeological Society Occasional Series, forthcoming.

Heather M Beaumont, The Historical Landscape of Hebden Township, Upper Wharfedale, forthcoming.

David Joy, with Hebden History Group, *Hebden: the History of a Dales Township* (Hebden: 2002).

Yorkshire Vernacular Buildings Study Group, Vernacular Buildings of Hebden, *Yorkshire Buildings* 27 (1991), 4–36.

medieval period, many internal divisions represent property boundaries (ts), and were probably walled between the late seventeenth and eighteenth centuries.

Houses within and outside the toft compartment (TC) show features characteristic of the seventeenth-century vernacular style. This was a time of agricultural prosperity in Craven, when yeomen farmers rebuilt thatched cruck-buildings in stone.

The late eighteenth- and nineteenth-century development of the lead industry in Grassington and Hebden brought an influx of population (Hebden census: 1801, *c*340; 1841, 480; 1861, 435). Houses were divided into cottages and there was infill building which tends to obscure toft boundaries. Public buildings date from this time, eg the Wesleyan chapel (1812), church (a chapel-of-ease of Linton parish, 1841) and school (1875). Today's population numbers around 250, of which thirty-six are children under seventeen years.[4]

12

HISTORICAL MAPS

12.1   INTRODUCTION   ROBIN A BUTLIN

From the mid-sixteenth century onwards, starting with Christopher Saxton's atlas of county maps of 1579, the mapping of England and Wales was a continuous process, accelerated with the foundation of the Ordnance Survey in the late eighteenth century and its progressive mapping at small and large scales in the nineteenth century.

Innovation was not continuous, however, and for much of the time from the early seventeenth to the late eighteenth centuries, 'new' maps were often just partly revised versions of old ones, without the benefit of new survey. Great improvement followed the foundation of the Ordnance Survey, and the earlier and then overlapping map production of medium-scale maps by commercial publishers of maps of individual counties.

Yorkshire exemplifies this trend, and has a rich cartographic history. This section examines five maps of Yorkshire, including North Yorkshire, which reflect mapping characteristics of the times in which they were produced.

The maps described and evaluated are Christopher Saxton's map of 1577, John Speed's map of 1611, Thomas Jefferys' map of 1777, Christopher Greenwood's map of 1817-18, and the first edition of the Ordnance Survey One-Inch map of 1859. They each afford glimpses of past landscapes, and also insights into the conditions and technicalities of their cartographic history.

12.2   CHRISTOPHER SAXTON'S MAP OF 1577

According to Whitaker, 'County Cartography really begins with the surveys of Christopher Saxton of Dunningley, near Leeds. We may justifiably be proud of him as a Yorkshireman, for he conducted the first definite survey of England and Wales, and produced an exceedingly creditable set of county maps. Although these were engraved by Dutch engravers, it is gratifying to note that the Yorkshire map (**Fig.12.1**) — which appeared on two sheets, in 1577 — was engraved by Augustine Ryther, a native of Leeds'.[1]

Christopher Saxton's year of birth was somewhere between 1542 and 1544: he described himself in 1596 as 'of Dunningley, in the parish of Westardslye in the county of Yorke, Gent., of age of fiftye twoo years or thereabouts'.[2] His initial training in the surveyor's and map-maker's art seems to have been at the hands of a local clergyman, John Rudd, vicar of Dewsbury (1554-70) and rector of Thornhill (1558-70), who was an experienced map-maker.

Rudd had in 1561 announced his intention of producing a map of England, though the project was not completed. Rudd was also chaplain to Henry VIII and a prebendary of Durham Cathedral, and it was through his contacts that Speed obtained introductions to court officials, including the man who became his patron, Thomas Seckford, a lawyer who was master of the Court of Requests to Queen Elizabeth from 1558 to 1585, and from 1581 Surveyor of the Court of Wards and Liveries.[3]

Another major contemporary influence was Sir William Cecil (Lord Burghley from 1571), Secretary of State and subsequently Lord High Treasurer, a great collector of maps, and advocate and practitioner of their use in government.[4] Ravenhill has suggested that 'the fact that proof copies of the maps when engraved were sent directly to Lord Burghley is further confirmation that this mapping exercise was an "official" survey promoted by the Crown on the advice of the Queen's ministers, as an act of deliberate policy designed to produce maps for the purposes of national administration, and, equally important, for the defence of the realm'.[5]

Saxton was rewarded for his work by grants of land from the Crown, including an estate in Suffolk in 1573, and appointment in 1574 as bailiff and collector of rents and profits of the manors of the priory and hospital of St John of Jerusalem in the city of London and county of Middlesex.[6] Curiously, he did not continue thereafter with producing county maps and atlases, but spent the rest of his life producing estate maps, many of them of estates in Yorkshire.

The maps were produced from actual survey data, probably using some form of triangulation based on high observation points and survey of local detail at lower altitudes, and also by use of information derived from existing published and cartographic sources.

Saxton's *An Atlas of England and Wales* was first published in 1579, the individual thirty-four maps of which it is made up having been engraved in groups in 1575, 1576, 1577 and 1578, all on single copper-plates with the exception of Yorkshire, which on account of its size had to be engraved on two.[7] The atlas itself included 'a frontispiece, showing [Queen] Elizabeth, the contents list (known in four different settings), and a plate showing the coats-of arms and tables of towns'.[8]

The map of Yorkshire covers two pages of the atlas, and comprises two sheets, joined at the centre (the join is slightly imperfect, as can be seen). It has a frame with the main orientations marked, a cartouche topped by the royal coat of arms and containing the name of the county in the north-east corner, and the coat-of-arms of Thomas Seckford, the sponsor and patron of the mapping project, in the south-west corner. In the south-east corner of the map is a scale, marked by a pair of dividers, within which appears the name of Christopher Saxton and under which appears the name of the engraver, 'Augustinus Ryther Anglus' ('Augustine Ryther, Englishman').The scale of the map was one inch to 3.3 miles (1:210,000).

The sea-area of the North Sea (German Ocean/*Oceanus Germanicus*) contains symbolic representations of galleons and fish/sea monsters, including a whale. The three Ridings of Yorkshire are marked, together with York and Ainsty, and topographic features shown as symbolic hills (with a 'molehill' type of symbol, very roughly proportional to the heights of the hills), rivers (crudely snake-like in depiction), and forests. The major forest names are given — Forest of Galtres and Swaledale Forest, for example — and other wooded areas shown by a high density of tree symbols.

Human settlement is shown by a six-fold sequence or hierarchy of symbols for settlements, churches and parks.[9] Major towns are shown as large collections of houses and churches, with crosses for cathedrals, the smallest settlements by a circle with a dot inside. Parks were symbolically marked as circular fenced areas.[10]

Although the plates were originally printed in black and white, they were subsequently hand-coloured according to different schemes. The colouring schemes on the map shown are fairly common: rivers and lakes in blue, woods green, hills in brown and green, settlements red, and county and Riding boundaries in varied colours.[11]

In a detailed examination of the topographic accuracy of some historical maps of Yorkshire, Jones has suggested that Saxton's map of 1577 is of varied quality.[12] Its record of settlement, compared with very much later maps, is good. The location of parks is thought to be less accurate, resulting from distant sketching and also errors at the engraving stage. The depiction of the main rivers compares favourably with that on nineteenth-century maps, the disposition of minor rivers less so.[13] Jones and others ascribe the accuracy of depiction of main rivers to the fact that they were both important means of, and obstacles to travel, and therefore significant contemporary features, though the evidence is that they were not fully surveyed by Saxton and his surveyors.[14]

This map thus affords both an important and innovative Elizabethan image of Yorkshire, including North Yorkshire, and also some ideas about the nature of Tudor map-making. It is an interesting testament to its impact that, for a variety of reasons, its main features remained unaltered in many later maps, thus perpetuating both its accuracy and inaccuracy.

12.3 JOHN SPEED'S MAP OF THE NORTH AND EAST RIDINGS OF YORKSHIRE, 1610

This map (**fig 12.2**) was printed in 1610, and was part of Speed's major atlas (*The Theatre of the Empire of Great Britaine*) published in 1611. The full title of the map is 'The North and East Ridins of Yorkshire'. At the bottom of the map, below the decorative scale, are the words: 'Performed by Iohn Speede. And are to be solde in Popes head Alley, against the Exchange by Iohn Sudbury and George Humbell. Cum Privilegio. 1610.'The scale of the original map is approximately four miles to one inch (1:250,000).

John Speed as a cartographer and map publisher had different origins and interests from Saxton. He was born around 1552 in Farndon in Cheshire. His father was a tailor, and John followed in his trade, moving to London by about 1582, where in addition to tailoring he showed a strong additional interest in history, antiquities and genealogies, which led to the production of illustrative historical maps, the first probably being a map of biblical Canaan, published in 1595. He had apparently shown talent as a map-drawer as a young man.[15]

Fig. 12.1

Copyright:
British Library C.7 c.1

He subsequently obtained the patronage of Sir Fulke Greville, later Lord Brooke, who obtained for him a post in the Customs and introductions to influential antiquary circles, including that of the Society of Antiquaries, whose members included William Camden and Robert Cotton.

He devoted his life after this to the writing of histories, including his *History of Great Britaine*, to which his atlas, the *Theatre of the Empire of Great Britaine,* was designed to be an introductory part.

In 1599 he formed a partnership with George Humble and John Sudbury, publishers and print-sellers, and they employed talented map-engravers, including Jodocus Hondius, a famous Flemish engraver, who was extensively involved in the production of the county maps which made up Speed's famous atlas.

The *Theatre* (thus–named following the example of the earlier world atlas by Abraham Ortelius, published in Antwerp in 1570 entitled *Theatrum Orbis Terrarum,* and in English as *The Theatre of the World* in 1606) was published in 1611 as a commercial enterprise, and included sixty-seven maps of England, Ireland, Scotland and Wales.

The individual county maps (continuing the earlier traditions of using the shire — the basis of regional government) were not based on original survey, as were (for the most part) Saxton's maps, but on the revision and modification of existing maps, including those of Saxton.

Fig. 12.2

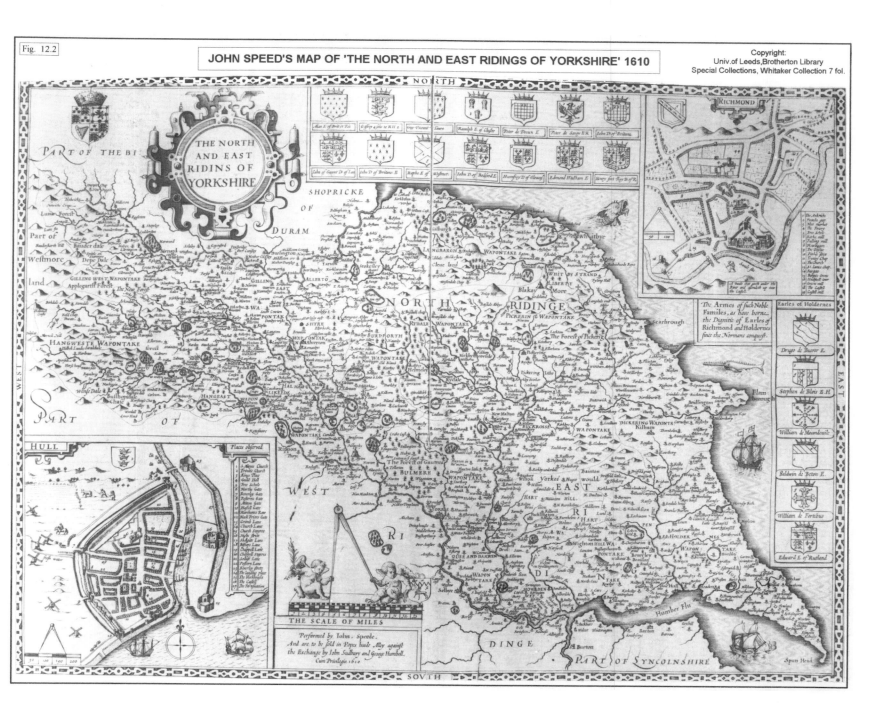

Copyright:
Univ. of Leeds, Brotherton Library
Special Collections, Whitaker Collection 7 fol.

JOHN SPEED'S MAP OF 'THE NORTH AND EAST RIDINGS OF YORKSHIRE' 1610

His much-quoted admission that 'I have put my sickle into other men's corn'[16] has been confirmed by his occasional direct acknowledgement of sources, and by scholarly analysis. Skelton has suggested that:

'… little of his cartographic work on the county maps seems to have been original; the phrase "Performed by John Speed", which occurs on most of the maps not explicitly ascribed to any cartographer, may be taken to mean that he copied, adapted or compiled from the work of others. On his base maps he inserted the boundaries and names of the hundreds and added plans of the "Cities and shire towns", the arms of the county nobility, the royal arms, and numerous historical illustrations such as battle scenes, antiquities or royal portraits. These materials were compiled from a variety of sources; Speed was a diligent reader and searcher in the libraries and collections of his antiquarian friends, such as Camden and Cotton.'[17]

His main sources were the county maps of Saxton and of the cartographer John Norden (1548–1628), together with those of William Smith, William White, Thomas Burrell and others, but his own travels and extensive research on published material were important contributions to the revisions that he made of the maps produced by others.

Speed published three separate maps of Yorkshire in his atlas: one of the whole of the county; one of the North and East Ridings; and one of the West Riding.

The map of the North and East Ridings includes a title cartouche, a scale at the bottom of the map, two rows of the coats of arms of twelve of the earls of Richmond at the top of the map and one row of six of the earls of Holderness on the eastern side. The royal coat-of-arms is reproduced in the north-west corner, and inset maps of Hull and of Richmond in the south-east and north-east corners respectively. On the reverse of the map there is descriptive text (not shown here). In the North Sea there are two ships and two intriguing sea-monsters, one heading with apparent evil intent towards Filey, the other surfacing near Whitby.

The administrative divisions of the Ridings — wapentakes — are shown in pricked lines and named on the map. Roads are not shown, but human settlements are marked with symbols for churches, usually depicting a village, groups of buildings for towns, parks by ring-fences (there are more of these than on Saxton's map, perhaps indicating Speed's interest in attracting as purchasers the owners of emparked properties).

The marking of woods and forests is by tree symbols, the names following those of Saxton, and relief is shown by a similar kind of 'mole-hill', though with more attempt at proportional representation by size. The rivers are as shown in Saxton's maps, and it seems that Saxton's map of 1577 was the main source of information for the maps of Yorkshire.

The inset town plans — in this case of Hull and Richmond — are innovations, and indicate the principal buildings by means of a key to numbered references on the plans themselves.

The map reproduced here is uncoloured — its original form — though many of Speed's county maps were subsequently coloured by hand.

Although in some respects it might be argued that Speed adds little in a geographical sense to the detail of Saxton's maps, it is perhaps important to acknowledge the additional genealogical, urban and historical information that he adds, not least the historical descriptions of counties on the reverse side from the map (though much of this was taken from Camden's *Britannia*). His maps from the *Theatre*, including the one here reproduced and considered, do represent a new and highly commercial approach to the production and selling of maps.

Delano-Smith and Kain have claimed that, as he did not have official financial support as had Saxton, 'Speed was free to concentrate on corrections in place-name spelling or location, some new information, and on surveying a number of towns to supplement the plans he copied from Norden. Driven by his need to recoup his expenses, Speed's outstanding contribution was to render each map as visually attractive as possible …'.[18]

12.4   THOMAS JEFFERYS' 'THE COUNTY OF YORK SURVEY'D', 1771-2

The survey for Jefferys' maps of the county of Yorkshire was carried out between 1767 and 70, and the map was published in twenty sheets in 1771 and 1772. The particular imprint reproduced here (from map 10, 'The Environs of Aldborough') is from the reprint by W Faden in 1796. The scale is 1:64,000 or one inch to one mile, and the extract shows the region around Helmsley and the western Vale of Pickering.

Jefferys' map of Yorkshire is part of a new impetus for the publication of county maps by commercial publishers and map-makers, at about the one-inch scale, in the second half of the eighteenth century.

Thomas Jefferys' map has been described by Whitaker in the following terms;

'The first map of the county on such a large scale, beautifully engraved, giving minute details, and printed on 20 plates, each about 22¾ x 23ins. (including the border, on the outer sheets). Hitherto the maps of the county have been compiled chiefly from Saxton's survey (Ogilby and Warburton having only surveyed roads), but this is an entirely new survey, from which most succeeding maps, down to the Ordnance Survey in 1815-17, were compiled.'[19]

The broader context of Jefferys' work and that of other county map-makers was that of rapidly increasing practical interest in the changing rural, urban and industrial landscapes of late eighteenth-century England, at times of revolutionary economic and landscape change, not least by the landowners and industrialists themselves, whose names were engraved on the county maps, including those produced by Jefferys, thus encouraging (it has been suggested) an advance subscription.[20]

Thomas Jefferys (*c*1719–71) was based in London, and had started as an engraver and geographer in London's map trade, publishing and engraving new editions of existing maps, including revisions of Saxton and compilations of maps of the Americas, but by the late 1760s was looking elsewhere for new publishing opportunities. Encouraged by prospect of the premiums offered by the newly founded Society for the Encouragement of Arts, Manufactures and Commerce for the production of county maps, he set in train surveys of Yorkshire and of counties in the south and east Midlands as a basis for the production of county maps.

The county surveys and maps with which Jefferys was involved were major commercial investments, involving substantial outlays in capital for employment of surveyors, purchase of instruments, payments for advertisements, and for the actual engraving, printing and selling process, and involved considerable financial risk (he had been declared bankrupt in 1766).[21]

Jefferys began by securing the services of three surveyors (he probably never went to Yorkshire himself): John Ainslie, who had been born in Jedburgh, Scotland; Joseph Hodskinson, probably from the North of England; and Thomas Donald, born in Cumberland. Harley and Harvey describe the survey sequence:

'Hodskinson surveyed the East Riding, much of the North Riding (from the coast as far west as Thirsk) and part of the West Riding south of a line from York and through Castleford and Huddersfield. He was joined by a surveying party under the direction of Thomas Donald, who surveyed most of the remaining part of the West Riding, and in 1769 by John Ainslie who, having just completed a survey of Westmorland, moved into the neighbouring part of the North Riding and the country south of Ripon.'[22]

The survey methods used included triangulation by theodolite (from high points such as hills, church towers and windmills) as a basis, with detail filled by plane-table survey and chain measurement). Plane-table survey is a long-established mapping technique, involving the use of a flat table or board on a supporting stand, a spirit-level and sight-rule, and a chain or measuring tape.

Latitude and longitude were marked at the margins of the printed maps, and they were among the earliest to use the Greenwich meridian.[23] The detail includes towns, villages, hamlets, farms, country houses and manors (sometimes with the names of the owners given), water-mills and windmills, iron and lead mines, coal pits, alum works, bridges, parks, rivers, hills, moors, wastes, rivers, marshes, open and enclosed roads including turnpikes, and administrative subdivisions. The estimate of heights is far from accurate, especially of the higher hills of the west and north-west.

Secondary material used for North Yorkshire included Warburton's map of 1720, Dickinson's 1750 map of South Yorkshire, plans of proposed canals from Leeds to Selby and Stainforth to the Trent, and various engraved plans of manors, farms and parts of the courses of rivers, including the Swale and Ouse.[24]

Overall, Jones suggests that comparison of Jefferys' 1771-2 map with the seventh series Ordnance Survey map confirms its general accuracy, but points to improvements in its later reprints, including that of 1800, which both highlight 'the weakness of stream representation, especially in the north-east', and 'confirm suspicions about the 1771 map'.[25] Accuracy in depiction of main roads was high, but of minor roads less so, both improving in the 1775 and 1800 editions. Quite significant adjustments were also made to the depiction of the coastline between the 1771 and 1800 editions.[26]

Not all of these are shown on the extract reproduced here (**fig 12.3**), but it does show the location and names of villages such as Ampleforth and Oswaldkirk, the town of Helmsley, Gilling, Newborough and Duncombe parks, and Rievaulx Abbey. Hill-shading is used to show the outlines of upland moor and of valleys, and there are details of fenced and unfenced roads, rivers and wooded areas.

For the historical geographer and the historian, Jefferys' map, like other maps of the county, is an important historical document, and a valuable record of the Yorkshire landscape. This has been summarised by Harley and Harvey in the following terms:

'For c1770 it is a uniquely consistent picture of Yorkshire … The interest of the map is enhanced by its publication during an early stage of the agricultural and industrial revolution. Although parliamentary enclosure was gathering pace, the Pennine uplands were still largely common land, as were the fenny marshes of the Vale of York and the Humberhead Levels. Common field arable cultivation dominated the West Riding communities and, in the North Riding, the practice of the Vale of Pickering'.[27]

Jefferys' maps are also valuable data sources for information on wind and water power: P Laxton has mapped the watermills and windmills in Yorkshire c1770 using Jefferys' maps,[28] and large-scale historical county maps are generally valuable sources of information on industrialisation.[29]

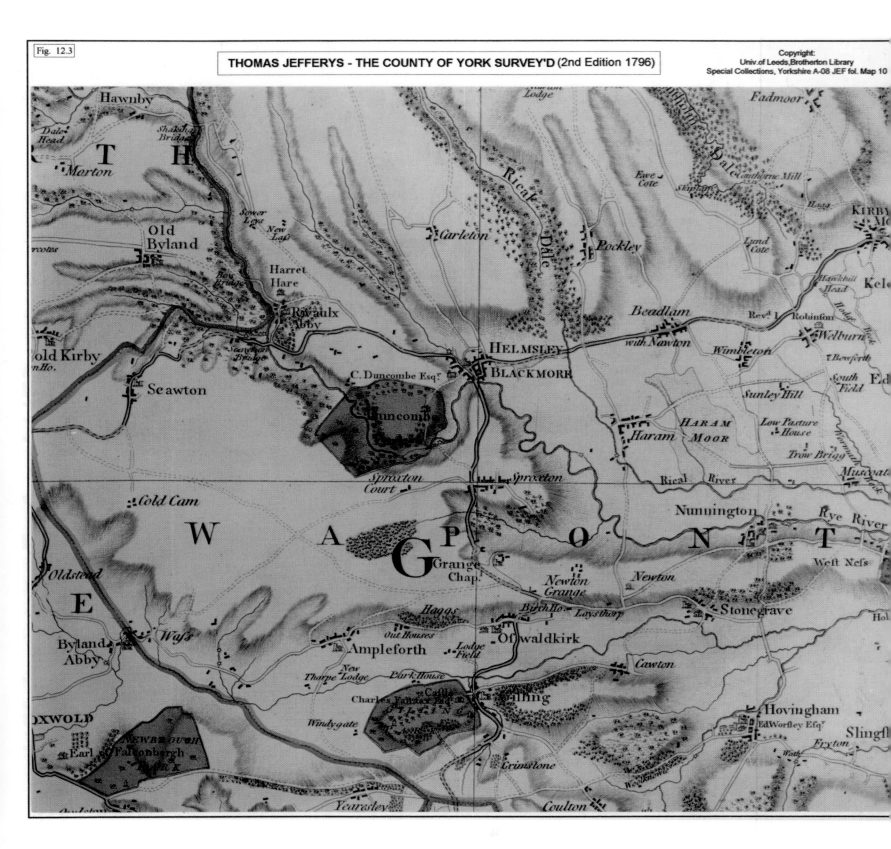

Fig. 12.3

Copyright:
Univ.of Leeds,Brotherton Library
Special Collections, Yorkshire A-08 JEF fol. Map 10

THOMAS JEFFERYS - THE COUNTY OF YORK SURVEY'D (2nd Edition 1796)

12.5 CHRISTOPHER GREENWOOD,
'MAP OF THE COUNTY OF YORK ...
SURVEYED IN THE YEARS 1815, 1816 & 1817'

We here focus on an extract from Christopher Greenwood's map, showing the district around the city of York. The scale of the map is 1:86,800 (1 inch to 1.37 miles).

Christopher Greenwood was a Yorkshireman: born in Gisburn in the West Riding in May 1786, he remained in that area into his twenties, possibly working, after leaving school, as a land surveyor in the Gisburn/Rimington area.[30]

Fig. 12.4

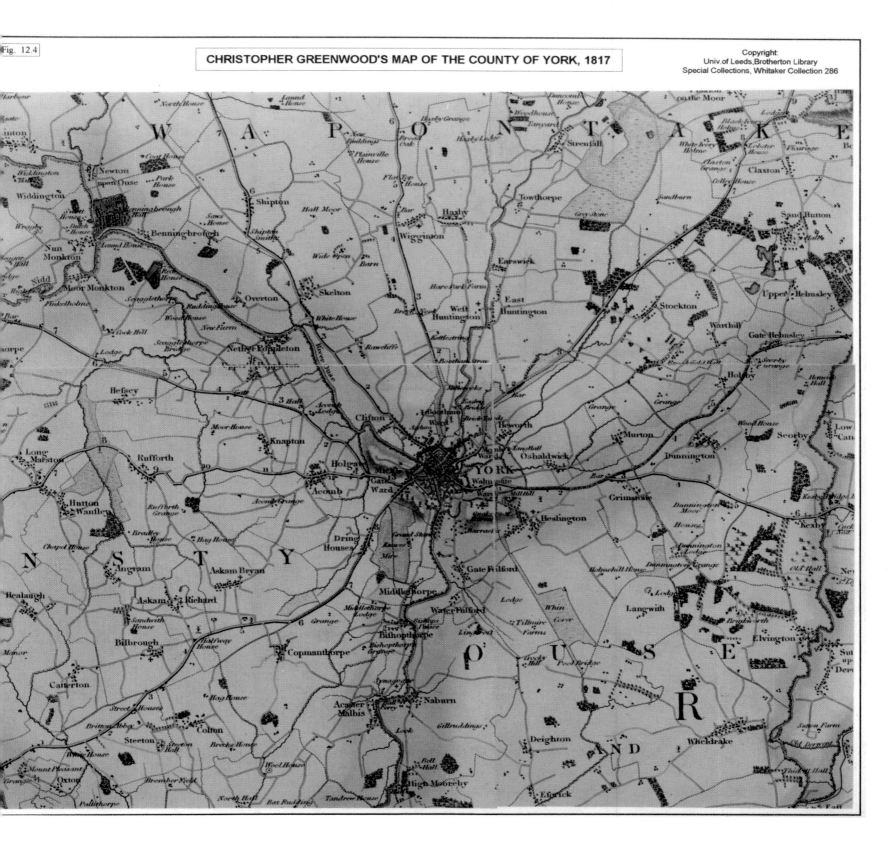

Copyright:
Univ. of Leeds, Brotherton Library
Special Collections, Whitaker Collection 286

In January 1816 he was advertising — from Wakefield, where he had become based — his intention to produce a county map of Yorkshire, though it is clear that he envisaged at this stage only a modest project, and not until later did he have the idea of producing a national survey on a county basis.

It appears that Greenwood needed additional technical expertise for his Yorkshire project, which he found in the form of Francis Giles, a surveyor and cartographer experienced in land and maritime survey, and in the production of town plans. Giles organised the trigonometrical survey for Greenwood's map of Yorkshire (based on Mudge's trigonometrical survey for the Board of Ordnance), and the production of the Yorkshire maps was mainly financed by Robinson, Son and Holdsworth, Leeds booksellers and stationers, and by a Wakefield stationer, John Hurst.[31]

The Mudge survey data for the Board of Ordnance, published between 1799 and 1811, provided the broad trigonometrical basis for the county maps, to which data was added from topographical survey in the field by surveyors using compass, chain and measuring wheel ('perambulator'). Further data was provided from scrutiny of secondary sources, including eighteenth-century topographical maps, the data from the early census of population, and local enquiries by surveyors about the spelling of place-names and the location of parish boundaries.[32]

The map of Yorkshire took about three years to produce, and it was published in 1817 in Wakefield and in Leeds in 1818 in nine sheets. The map is dedicated 'To the Nobility, Clergy and Gentry of Yorkshire'. It contains much detail, and is in some respects a forerunner of the Ordnance Survey maps, as Whitaker indicates:

'An exceedingly fine map, published considerably earlier than the One Inch Ordnance maps for Yorkshire, and except that it is drawn to a smaller scale, closely resembling them in style and execution. It shows towns, villages, hamlets, parishes, wapentakes, churches, chapels, castles, priories, houses, parks, woods, plantations, moors, commons, hills water mills, wind mills, coal pits, toll bars, main and cross roads, canals rivers and brooks.'[33]

The part of the map shown here (**fig 12.4**) depicts the district around the city of York. York itself, beginning to extend out along the major tributary roads, is a central feature. A firm impression is given of a region with a dense pattern of rural settlements in various forms, including emparked estates with their focal country houses, and a dense network of both major and minor roads. Villages and hamlets are named, and extensive areas of formally planted woodland shown.

This is a 'busy' rural landscape, evidencing the aftermath of major agrarian changes, especially after the enclosure of the remaining open fields and common lands in the late eighteenth and early nineteenth centuries. The recording of these changes was very much in Greenwood's mind when he envisioned the production of the map of Yorkshire, and Harley quotes the relevant arguments contained in his proposals:

'As no actual survey of the County has been taken since that by Jefferys in the Middle of the last Century, the Necessity of a new and actual Survey will be evident from a View of the Changes which have taken place within that Period, in the Manufacturing and Agricultural Parts of this extensive County, from the great increase of Population, and the consequent additional number of Villages, Hamlets, Gentleman's Seats, Manufactories and Mills, as well as from the vast Extent of Waste Ground that has since been inclosed, and brought into Cultivation; the various Changes that have taken place in the Roads in some Parts of the County, and the new Roads which have been cut in Others, and the Canals, which have within the last Sixty Years, been Cut to facilitate inland Navigation.'[34]

After the production of the Yorkshire map, Greenwood moved to London in 1818, from where his remaining county maps of other counties were published. He had, while engaged on the production of maps of Lancashire from 1816, conceived of a much bigger project: the production of an atlas of the counties of England and Wales, based on original survey. Christopher Greenwood and his younger brother, John, largely realised this goal, with the survey and publication of maps of thirty-three English counties and four Welsh counties at about the one-inch scale, and these were used and added to for the publication, between 1829 and 1834, of their *Atlas of the Counties of England*.[35]

These were among the last of the county surveys, at a time of growing influence of the Ordnance Survey, whose maps would eventually replace those published by the Greenwoods and their contemporaries. They afford extremely important historical evidence, with reasonable accuracy, for the understanding of the landscapes of the early nineteenth century.

12.6 THE FIRST EDITION OR OLD SERIES OF THE ORDNANCE SURVEY ONE-INCH MAP, 1859

The extract reproduced here (**fig 12.5**) is from the one-inch Old Series map sheet 92 NE Skipton, published in 1859, showing the region south and east of the small town of Pateley Bridge, including Nidderdale — the river valley in which it is located — and the dissected lower moorlands of the eastern Pennines, north of Knaresborough.

The immediate impression is of much detail, especially of human activity, together with strong representations of physiography, notably the hills and moors, by means of hachuring or

Fig. 12.5

FIRST EDITION ORDNANCE SURVEY MAP EXTRACT

hill-shading. Undoubtedly this represents a major advance in the accurate survey and representation of landscape at a scale of 1:63,360, the basis of much topographic mapping in Britain well into the twentieth century.

The origins of such maps lie in the work of William Roy, appointed in 1765 as surveyor general of coasts and engineer for making and directing military surveys in Great Britain. One of his works was the measurement of a base-line on Hounslow Heath, intended as the basis of a more general triangulation to connect with France, the latter being completed in 1790, and in 1791 the Trigonometrical Survey of the Board of Ordnance was founded, as its name suggests, to finish the complete triangulation of Britain.

The first Ordnance map — the one-inch map of Kent — was published privately in 1801, and the first official series of one-inch maps began in 1805. The map shown here is part of what is called the Old Series, which were published between 1805 and 1873, the extract shown here was part of sheet 92, published between 1857-9.

Prior to 1840, the one-inch maps were based on field surveys at two inches to the mile (1:31,680) and reduced to the one-inch scale, but thereafter, following the example of the survey of Ireland, field survey was on the six-inch scale with reduction to one-inch scale, and this was followed in the North of England.

After 1853, however, with the twenty-five inch to the mile survey of County Durham and its use for reduction to the one-inch scale, sheets 91-100 of the old series were reduced from surveys at the twenty-five inch scale,[36] including sheet 92, from the north-eastern part of which our extract is taken. This may explain in part the enormous wealth of detail on the map, though there are technical problems with the exact dating of individual printings, some of which may have been revised later but which still bear the date of the original printing.[37]

The first edition maps clearly contain much more detail than that on the county maps produced by publishers like the Greenwoods, with a greater number of minor roads and minor place-names. In addition to industrial features such as mills, residential and agricultural buildings are shown and named, and increased accuracy is evident in the depiction of buildings generally.[38] Although contouring was being experimented at the six-inch scale, the first edition one-inch maps contained hachuring (hill-shading), based on field-sketching, as the principal means of representation of relief.

In the extract, the valleys of the Nidd and the Washburn contain evidence of the changing industrial scene and its impact in rural areas. The Nidd Valley is the route of the Nidd Valley Railway, and its stations are clearly marked, as are a number of mills and a cotton factory. Contemporary settlements are shown in minute detail, and archaeological sites and antiquities marked using Gothic lettering. Quarries are marked across the region, and there is a wealth of place-names, the names of administrative units, physical features (including rivers, moors, hills, with heights given) and of historical regional features such as the Forest of Knaresborough. Plantations and areas of woodland are clearly marked and frequently named. Road detail is quite comprehensive.

The first edition of the Ordnance Survey map, together with its successors, is an extremely important tool for the investigation of the changing landscapes of Britain in the nineteenth century and thereafter.

Historical Maps — Acknowledgements:
I am most grateful to Paul Laxton of the Geography Department, University of Liverpool, for his expert comments on a first draft of this chapter. I wish also to acknowledge the following permissions to reproduce the maps described in this section: Christopher Saxton's map of Yorkshire dated 1577 (British Library C7 c1) reproduced, by permission of the British Library, from a version published by the British Museum in 1936; John Speed map: University of Leeds, Brotherton Library, Special Collections, Whitaker Collection 7 fol; Jefferys map: University of Leeds, Brotherton Library, Special Collections, Yorkshire A-08 JEF fol, map 10 *The Environs of Aldborough*; Christopher Greenwood: University of Leeds, Brotherton Library, Special Collections, Whitaker Collection 286 (the original map has been cut and bound on linen, hence the divisions).

Historical Maps — Further Reading:
H Whitaker, *A Descriptive List of the Printed Maps of Yorkshire and its Ridings, 1577-1900*, Yorkshire Archaeological Society Record Series, vol LXXXVI (Leeds, 1938).

A Raistrick, *Yorkshire Maps and Map-Makers* (Clapham: Dalesman Books, 1969).

J E Rawnsley, *Antique Maps of Yorkshire and Their Makers* (Guiseley: the author, 1970).

Sarah Tyacke and John Huddy, *Christopher Saxton and Tudor Map-Making* (London: British Library, 1980).

W Ravenhill, *Christopher Saxton's 16th Century Maps: The Counties of England and Wales* (Shrewsbury: Chatsworth House Library, 1993).

Ifor M Evans and Heather Lawrence, *Christopher Saxton: Elizabethan Map-maker* (Wakefield: Wakefield Historical Collections, 1979).

The Counties of Britain: A Tudor Atlas by John Speed (London: British Library, 1995).

C Delano Smith and R Kain, *English Maps: A History* (London: British Library, 1999).

R A Skelton, *County Atlases of the British Isles 1579-1850: A bibliography* (London: Carta Press, 1970).

J B Harley and J C Harvey, introduction, *The County of York Survey'd*, facsimile of 1775 edition (Margary: Lympne Castle, Kent, 1973).

J B Harley, *Christopher Greenwood, County Map-Maker, and his Worcestershire map of 1822* (Worcester and London: Worcestershire Historical Society, 1962).

J B Harley, *The Historian's Guide to Ordnance Survey Maps* (London: Standing Conference for Local History, 1964).

13

THE TWENTIETH CENTURY

13.1 INTRODUCTION   JOHN STILLWELL

Throughout the twentieth century, the county of North Yorkshire has been the largest geographical component of the Yorkshire region, characterised by the rural environments and landscapes that contrast so distinctly with the great conurbations covering much of West and South Yorkshire.

Whilst the spatial definition of the county has been changed to reflect new administrative regimes, the essential differences in place characteristics within North Yorkshire are represented by 'countryside character' areas (**fig 13.1**) defined in 1998 by the Countryside Commission[1] on the basis of physical, cultural and historical variables. These areas create identity and a sense of place.

In the west, they include the Yorkshire Dales and its fringe areas but also those parts of the Bowland Fells, the Bowland fringe and the Lancashire valleys that extend into Craven District. In the north, they include the Vale of Mowbray and the North Yorkshire Moors, and also parts of the Tees lowlands and the Cleveland Hills. Further to the south, the Vale of Pickering and the Yorkshire Wolds make up the eastern part of the county, with Vale of York having a central location and a large part of the Selby District being part of the extensive Humberhead Levels.

The character areas are complemented by 'natural areas', drawn up to reflect similar types of wildlife habitat, which provide a starting point for the identification of protected or conservation areas.

This section of the *Atlas* contains a series of maps and commentaries that provide some insights into a selection of themes that convey something about the people who live in North Yorkshire and their activities with respect to the physical environment in the last 100 years.

Section 13.2 begins with a definition of the North Riding in 1901, a synopsis of population change and an outline of some demographic indicators for the constituent local authority areas at the end of the century.

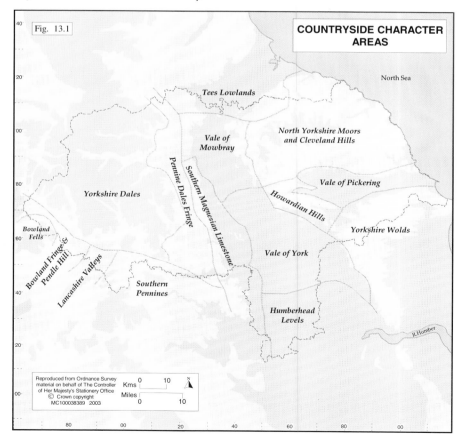

Fig. 13.1

COUNTRYSIDE CHARACTER AREAS

New communications: the A1 (Great North Road)–
M1 motorway link.
© Robert White/Yorkshire Dales National Park Authority, YDP 195/01

Changes in the North Yorkshire's key land-based economic activity, agriculture, are discussed in section 13.3, and the contrasting features of lowland and upland farming that have characterised the twentieth century are illustrated by the distribution of farm types by parish.

The pressures of agricultural development and urbanisation have led to a growth in public concern over the countryside and to a whole series of statutory measures to protect the natural environment, including the designation of a variety of types of area under either national or European legislation. Designated protected areas in North Yorkshire are reviewed and mapped in section 13.4, and the role of one particular agency, the Forestry Commission, is considered in section 13.5 in relation to the changes in woodland.

On the basis of a comparison of economic growth and unemployment with other regions in the European Union (EU) at the end of the twentieth century, North Yorkshire came out favourably with an index of GDP per capita in 1998 — equivalent to that of the European Union of 15 member states (EU15) and a total unemployment rate of 3.9 per cent in 1999, well below the EU15 average of 9.4 per cent.[2] At the national scale, North Yorkshire and York local education authorities both have educational performance levels well above the average for all local education authorities.

Moreover, the county also has a wealth of physical and cultural resources, many of which have been traditional tourist attractions for many years, attracting visitors from the rest of the country and from abroad. The locations of major tourist spots, and sites of sporting and recreational activity, are illustrated in section 13.6.

However, whilst North Yorkshire clearly has an abundance of positive features, GDP in the upland and coastal areas is less than two-thirds of the EU norm, average wages are less than two-thirds of the UK mean and the economy is overly dependent on an agricultural industry which is under severe pressure.

A census-based index of multiple deprivation is therefore used to give an indication of how social deprivation varies within the county in section 13.7, and an index of geographical access to services is mapped to draw attention to the problems of local service provision in rural areas. Some consideration is given to unemployment disparities, to the employment structure of the county as a whole at the end of the century, and to current housing issues, particularly in rural areas.

The final section of the chapter considers different aspects of the development of North Yorkshire in the future.

Initial attention is directed to the proposals and priorities associated with the acquisition of European Objective 2 funding over the period 2000-2006. Subsequently, development strategies proposed in the formulation of the county's structure plan are identified. The structure plan is the key spatial planning document that will guide local authorities and other stakeholders in their own detailed plans through to 2016; it is informed by the population and household projections for the county over the next two decades, and by the debate on alternative strategies for future development.

The boundaries of the area that we associate with North Yorkshire at the beginning of the twenty-first century are very different from those that demarcated the North Riding a century earlier and which remained relatively stable throughout the first seventy years of the twentieth century.

In 1901, the North Riding contained a county borough (Middlesbrough), three municipal boroughs (Thornaby-on-Tees, Richmond and Scarborough), a number of urban districts and the remaining rural districts. The definition of the 'registration county' was not consistent with that of the 'administrative county' insofar as the registration sub-districts of Sherburn and Norton were located in the East Riding registration jurisdiction but in the administrative county of North Riding; whilst Flaxton and Wath in the south, together with Startforth and Croft in the north, were included in the North Riding registration county but excluded for administration purposes.

The resident population of the registration county numbered 376,503 according to the 1901 census of population. Population increased by about 21 per cent between 1901 and 1921, and a further 15 per cent between 1921 and 1951, the largest increases taking place in the urban areas.

By 1951, the population of the North Riding administration county (**fig 13.2**) had reached 525,481, with Middlesbrough County Borough accounting for 28 per cent of the total.[3] Scarborough Municipal Borough had a population of nearly 44,000 (8.4 per cent of the county total), whereas the other metropolitan boroughs of Thornaby-on-Tees and Richmond contained 4.5 per cent and 1.2 per cent of the county population respectively. Redcar had become a metropolitan borough and contained a population of 27,500 (5.2 per cent), whilst Eston Urban District's population had reached 33,300 (6.3 per cent) by the middle of the period.

FROM RIDING TO SHIRE

The map of administrative boundaries changed radically during the second half of the century. Stockton-on-Tees, south of the River Tees, remained part of the North Riding until 1968, but the first major change was the disappearance of the Ridings and the creation of North Yorkshire as a result of local government reorganisation in 1974.

The main implication of the reforms was a southward shift of the county's centre of gravity. Middlesbrough, Guisborough and Redcar were partitioned off to the county of Durham (although Middlesbrough remained part of North Yorkshire for geographical and ceremonial purposes), and areas of the West and East Riding including Skipton, Harrogate, York and Selby were transferred to the new county.

By the time of the 1991 census of population, the usually resident population of North Yorkshire had reached 702,161, including 98,745 inhabitants within the district of York. The distribution of the population across the county by census ward in 1991 is illustrated in **fig 13.3**, indicating that the large majority of wards had populations of less than 3,000, with only a relatively small proportion, mostly in Harrogate and York, having more than 7,000 residents.

The second major change took place twenty years later when further local government reform, set in motion by John Major in 1991, resulted in the creation of the York Unitary Authority (UA) in 1996, covering an area much greater than that of the previous administration.[4] The land area of North Yorkshire (including York UA) extends to 8,321 million square metres, making it the largest county in England, with the administrative centre of the county council based in Northallerton.

The inset in **fig 13.3** illustrates the mid-year population estimates for 1998, showing that the current population living in North Yorkshire numbers 565,048 and that a further 177,356 live in the new York UA.

SOME DEMOGRAPHIC CHARACTERISTICS

The changing local government boundaries provide a major obstacle to the easy analysis of population change over time. Thus, the table overleaf provides a selection of indicators that summarise the demographic characteristics of the populations of North Yorkshire and York UA at the end of the twentieth century.[5]

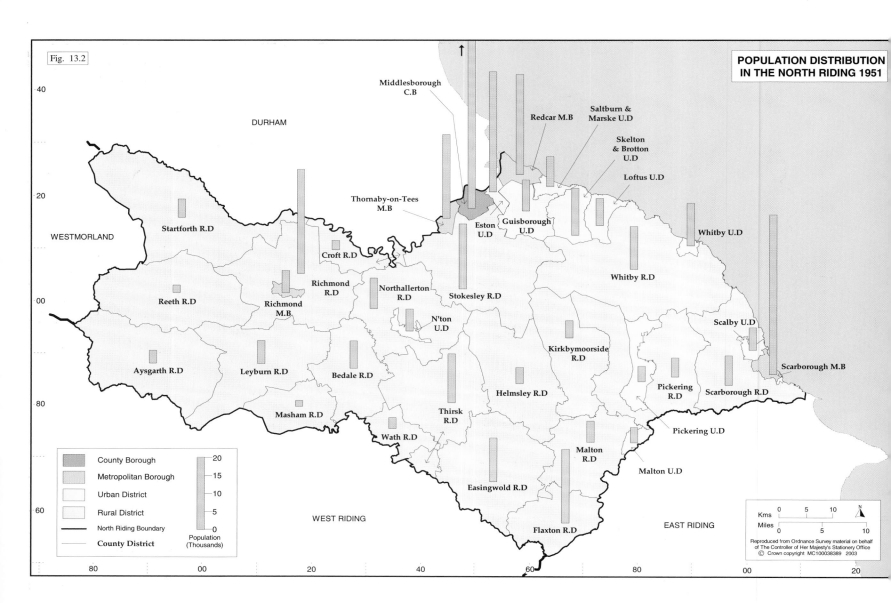

Fig. 13.2

**POPULATION DISTRIBUTION
IN THE NORTH RIDING 1951**

DURHAM

WESTMORLAND

Middlesborough
C.B

Redcar M.B

Saltburn &
Marske U.D

Skelton
& Brotton
U.D

Loftus U.D

Thornaby-on-Tees
M.B

Eston
U.D

Guisborough
U.D

Whitby U.D

Startforth R.D

Croft R.D

Richmond
R.D

Northallerton
R.D

Stokesley R.D

Whitby R.D

Reeth R.D

Richmond
M.B

N'ton
U.D

Scalby U.D

Aysgarth R.D

Leyburn R.D

Bedale R.D

Kirkbymoorside
R.D

Scarborough M.B

Helmsley R.D

Pickering
R.D

Scarborough R.D

Masham R.D

Thirsk
R.D

Pickering U.D

Wath R.D

Malton
R.D

Malton U.D

Easingwold R.D

WEST RIDING

Flaxton R.D

EAST RIDING

County Borough

Metropolitan Borough

Urban District

Rural District

North Riding Boundary

County District

20
15
10
5
0

Population
(Thousands)

Kms   0   5   10
Miles 0   5   10

Reproduced from Ordnance Survey material on behalf
of The Controller of Her Majesty's Stationery Office
© Crown copyright MC100038389 2003

DEMOGRAPHIC INDICATORS FOR NORTH YORKSHIRE DISTRICTS AND
YORK UA, 1997

	population increase 1981-97	total period fertility rate	standardised mortality rate	age under 5 (%)	age 5–15 (%)	age 16 to pensionable age (%)	over pensionable age (%)
Craven	8.5	1.76	95	5.5	13.9	57.1	23.4
Hambleton	13.2	1.73	89	5.8	13.6	61.3	19.3
Harrogate	8.6	1.56	100	5.8	13.3	61.2	19.7
Richmondshire	9.5	1.75	95	6.2	13.5	62.7	17.7
Ryedale	10.5	1.92	83	5.2	12.3	57.6	25.0
Scarborough	6.3	1.74	94	5.3	13.3	57.1	24.3
Selby	14.5	2.08	94	6.3	14.2	61.6	17.9
York UA	6.6	1.52	85	5.4	13.4	61.7	19.5
North Yorkshire	9.8	1.74	94	5.7	13.5	59.9	20.9
UK	4.7	1.73	100	6.3	14.2	61.4	18.1

Source: Office of National Statistics (1999: table 14.1)

The second column of the table emphasises the attractiveness of North Yorkshire as a place to live. The population increased by almost 10 per cent between 1981 and 1997, compared with a growth of 4.7 per cent in the UK as a whole. Much of North Yorkshire's expansion has been attributable to in-migration.

The third column shows the total period fertility rate (TPFR), the average number of children born to a woman if the current pattern of fertility persisted through the

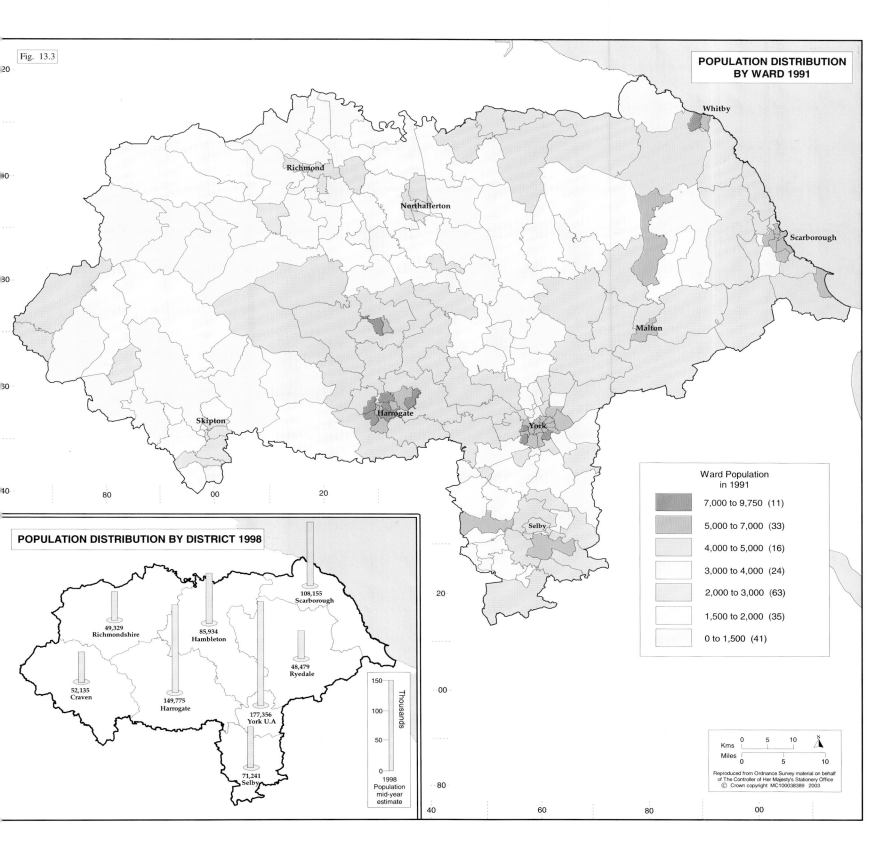

Fig. 13.3

POPULATION DISTRIBUTION BY WARD 1991

Whitby

Richmond

Northallerton

Scarborough

Malton

Harrogate

York

Skipton

Selby

Ward Population
in 1991

	7,000 to 9,750 (11)
	5,000 to 7,000 (33)
	4,000 to 5,000 (16)
	3,000 to 4,000 (24)
	2,000 to 3,000 (63)
	1,500 to 2,000 (35)
	0 to 1,500 (41)

POPULATION DISTRIBUTION BY DISTRICT 1998

108,155
Scarborough

49,329
Richmondshire

85,934
Hambleton

48,479
Ryedale

52,135
Craven

149,775
Harrogate

177,356
York U.A

71,241
Selby

Thousands

150

100

50

0

1998
Population
mid-year
estimate

Kms 0   5   10
Miles 0   5   10

Reproduced from Ordnance Survey material on behalf
of The Controller of Her Majesty's Stationery Office
© Crown copyright MC100038389 2003

childbearing years. Some geographical variations are evident. Selby has a TPFR in excess of two children and well above the national average of 1.7. This is consistent with Selby's population growth rate being three times the national average.

The values in column four refer to standardised mortality rates (SMR), ie the mortality rates adjusted for age structure. Apart from Harrogate, all other SMRs in North Yorkshire are below the UK average. York UA has a low SMR together with a low TPFR.

The last four columns show the percentage of the population aged below 5 years, between 5 and 15 years, between 16 and pensionable age, and over pensionable age.

The perception that North Yorkshire is a place where a relatively large number of older people live is born out by the comparison of the proportion of the population that is over pensionable age. In the county as a whole, 20.9 per cent are in this category compared to 18.1 per cent in the UK in 1997. Ryedale has the highest proportion of elderly, where one in four is over pensionable age.

At the other end of the age spectrum, the proportion aged under fifteen is 19.2 per cent, compared with a national average of 20.5 per cent.

Apart from Richmondshire, York and the remaining districts of North Yorkshire contain more older women than men. Excluding York, the proportions of men and women aged 60 and over were 21.1% and 26.3% in mid-1999 compared with the UK averages of 17.9% and 22.9% respectively. Of those people in North Yorkshire aged 60 and over, 14.5% of men and 24.2% of women were aged 80 and over. Harrogate and Scarborough have the highest proportions of very elderly and contain concentrations of residential care and nursing homes.

13.3   AGRICULTURE AND LAND-BASED INDUSTRY
CHRISTINE LEIGH

North Yorkshire's experience represents a microcosm of the trends taking place in English land-use change over the last 100 years. Although detailed local statistics are not always available, a broad pattern of rapid, accelerating and radical change in land use can be identified, in common with other rural areas.

The main traditional agricultural divisions of the county to a large extent follow the relief: the Pennine Dales to the west, predominantly concerned with cattle-rearing and sheep farming; the low-lying vales of York and Pickering characterised by intensive cash-crop production; and the North York Moors, largely moorland and rough grassland but with more arable land (and swathes of Forestry Commission planting) than the Dales because of lower rainfall and flatter summits.

Within these broad divisions, the pattern of agricultural and other rural land-uses has been established mainly by the outcome of changes in the economic circumstances of the UK, acting within the limits set by local physical environments and by the prevailing technology of the day.

KEY CHANGES

At the beginning of the twentieth century, agriculture was 'in convalescence after the buffeting of the last quarter of the nineteenth century'.[6] Prices for agricultural produce increased, although costs remained low and wages were a pittance. This situation did not improve for the next twenty-five years.

After the First World War, periodic severe depression hit the industry until the repeal of the Agriculture Act in 1920 saw prices 'come tumbling down like a pack of cards'.[7] During the 1920s and 1930s, capital improvements were virtually at a standstill, leading to the adoption of farming systems that were characterised by low expenditure rather than high output. This resulted in a considerable expansion of areas under rough grazing.

Throughout Yorkshire, as in most of Britain, the 1930s saw agriculture reach its nadir. Competition from overseas producers led to a decline in arable farming and a concentration on those commodities that had a degree of natural protection, such as milk and, to a lesser extent, vegetable and livestock production. Between 1902 and 1939, the movement of Yorkshire farmers into livestock is illustrated by the twenty per cent increase in cattle and the twelve per cent increase in sheep stocks that occurred.

The impact of improved transport and the advent of global competition had a pervasive effect upon the industry which continued throughout the century, always creating pressures towards those forms of land-use activity which conferred a competitive advantage.

A major impact of the Second World War was that half a million acres (200,000ha) of permanent grassland in Yorkshire were ploughed out by 1944 and mostly put to wheat and barley, while the reaction of livestock farmers was to reduce their holding of stock, which required imported feedstuffs.

However, there was a strong recovery after the war and, by 1962, there was a third more cattle of all sorts on Yorkshire farms than in 1939. The industry became more prosperous with a greater stability in the acreage of crops and grass and, in the 1950s, the upgrading and improvement of poorer land as the industry moved into a less pressurised period.

Although there was a big wartime increase in the number of workers on farms, largely of a temporary nature, the numbers employed in the industry have declined sharply and continuously since 1944.

Other drivers of change on the land-based economy of North Yorkshire during the last 100 years have had varying impacts in duration and intensity.

Urban growth has probably been the most significant and pervasive influence.[8] In the early part of the century, this influence was seen in the migration of people from rural to urban areas seeking higher wages or, indeed, work. This was followed by the spread of urban areas into the countryside and the loss of agricultural land to urban uses.

In the second half of the twentieth century, concomitant with the increase in personal mobility, there have been massive demands made for accessibility to the countryside for tourism, amenity and recreational uses from the surrounding conurbations of the North East, Lancashire and West Yorkshire. In 1949, the National Parks and Access to the Countryside Act was a landmark in the recognition of the needs of the urban majority for access to the countryside.

As pressure on the land increased, the need for management control became a dominant theme. The Countryside Act of 1968 made provision for the imposition of management controls for conservation and recreation in rural areas.

By the early 1980s the conflict between agriculture and conservation was keen, with conservationists particularly concerned about the intensification of agriculture and its effects. Although the brunt of this conflict was borne by lowland farming areas, in North Yorkshire there was extensive and continuing loss of open moorland to agricultural reclamation and afforestation. In a moorland study undertaken by the University of Birmingham and quoted by Blunden and Curry,[9] the North York Moors was shown to have lost twenty-five per cent of its rough pasture between 1950 and 1980.

Major political influences in the last part of the twentieth century have been dominated by the legislation introduced by the European Commission, particularly the Common Agricultural Policy (CAP), so that subsidy regimes and other land-use measures have helped to direct and shape the pattern of land-use activity that we see today. The emphasis now is on reducing agricultural surpluses rather than increasing levels of production.

Other large-scale consumers of land in North Yorkshire have been the Forestry Commission and the Ministry of Defence. In 1919, when the Forestry Commission was set up, competition for use of land for forestry increased steadily. Similarly, throughout the twentieth century, North Yorkshire was important for the provision of military training areas, a demand that is now reinforced with the major emphasis on Catterick and the surrounding areas as the Ministry of Defence has concentrated its activities into fewer areas nationally.

The grouse moors are also of particular importance in North Yorkshire, and while there is little quantitative evidence of their importance to the rural economy, figures for Scotland suggest that grouse shooting may create hundreds of jobs and contribute several million pounds to the rural economy.

AGRICULTURAL LAND-USE AT THE END OF THE TWENTIETH CENTURY

Drawing on evidence from two major surveys[10] and the census of population for 1991, we can establish a picture of the current land-use pattern and agricultural economy of North Yorkshire, together with an appreciation of the proportion of the labour force employed in agriculture, fishing and forestry in 1991.

Wensleydale, near Gayle.
© R Muir.

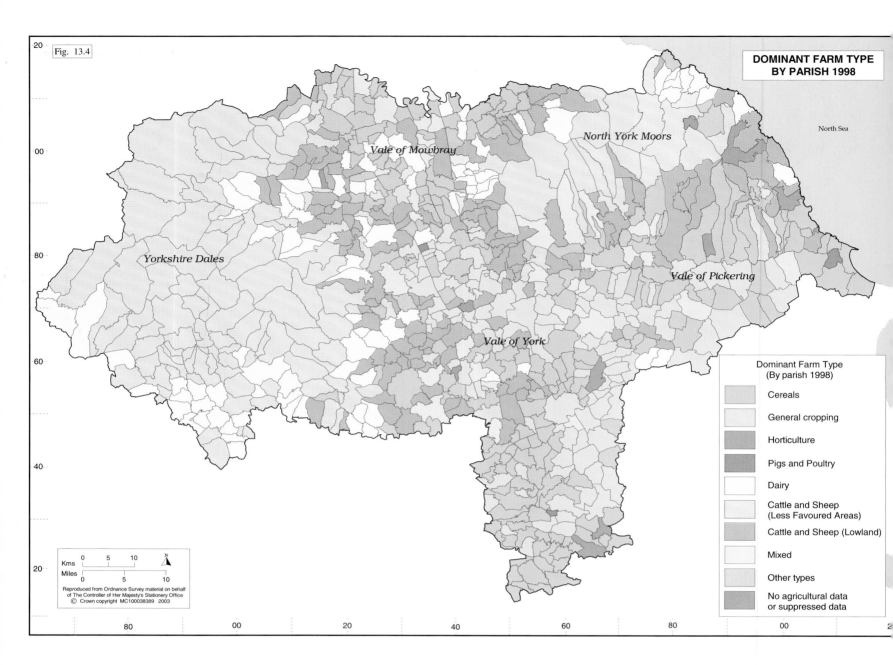

Fig. 13.4

**DOMINANT FARM TYPE
BY PARISH 1998**

North Sea

Vale of Mowbray

North York Moors

Yorkshire Dales

Vale of Pickering

Vale of York

Kms 0   5   10
Miles 0   5   10
Reproduced from Ordnance Survey material on behalf
of The Controller of Her Majesty's Stationery Office
© Crown copyright MC100038389 2003

Dominant Farm Type
(By parish 1998)

Cereals

General cropping

Horticulture

Pigs and Poultry

Dairy

Cattle and Sheep
(Less Favoured Areas)

Cattle and Sheep (Lowland)

Mixed

Other types

No agricultural data
or suppressed data

The pattern of farm activity, the size of farm holdings, the type of agricultural activity and the intensity of labour input are all interrelated, and strongly influenced by relief, soil characteristics and proximity to urban areas. But above all, they are now affected by competitive economic pressures with strong regulatory controls. **Fig 13.4** shows the pattern of farming activity at the end of the twentieth century, with a continuing clear distinction between the upland and lowland areas.

In the last decades, the shift in the balance of activity has seen big declines in dairying in favour of mixed farming (related to the European Community milk-quota system), whilst sheep farming has grown more than in the rest of England and Wales, especially so in the so-called 'less favoured areas' (the uplands). Cereal producers are concentrating more on quality and moving steadily into more industrial crops such as oilseed rape and sugar beet.

On average, farm sizes in North Yorkshire remain large: more than half are between 100 and 500 acres (40–200ha). The overall decrease in the acreage of agricultural land continues, as does the decline in the number of holdings, and the relative contribution of agriculture to GDP. The total number of agricultural holdings in the region in the period 1987-97 decreased by 8.2 per cent (faster than the rate for England as a whole).

In North Yorkshire, farms are overwhelmingly owned and managed by the farmer or through a family partnership. Most are long established (more than twenty years old) except along the coast and, because of the structure of the farming population, there is a strong tendency for farms to retrench into less intensive activity as they get older or decrease production.

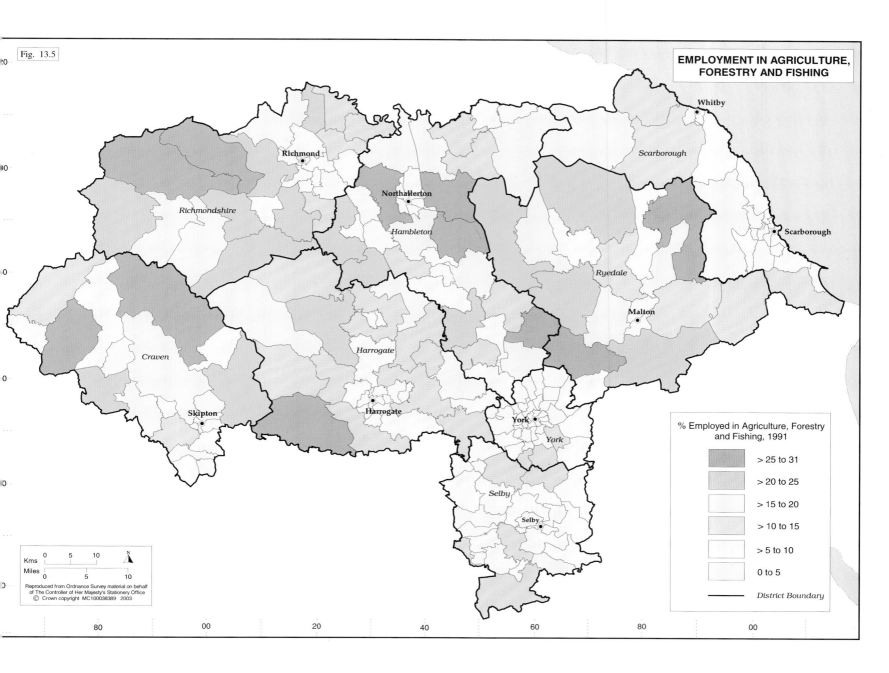

Fig. 13.5

EMPLOYMENT IN AGRICULTURE, FORESTRY AND FISHING

Whitby

Scarborough

Richmond

Northallerton

Scarborough

Richmondshire

Hambleton

Ryedale

Malton

Craven

Harrogate

Skipton

Harrogate

York

York

Selby

Selby

% Employed in Agriculture, Forestry and Fishing, 1991

	> 25 to 31
	> 20 to 25
	> 15 to 20
	> 10 to 15
	> 5 to 10
	0 to 5
——	*District Boundary*

Kms 0 5 10

Miles 0 5 10

N

Reproduced from Ordnance Survey material on behalf
of The Controller of Her Majesty's Stationery Office
© Crown copyright MC100038389 2003

80 00 20 40 60 80 00

Heather burning, Westerdale.
© B Vyner

Upper Nidderdale.
© R Muir.

The loss of jobs from the industry, which has been going on throughout the last century, amounted to a massive twenty-seven per cent in the period 1985 to 2000, with the decline especially severe for full-time workers, and seasonal and casual workers. The number of full-time workers declined by 18 per cent while part-time workers increased by 7 per cent, which was only half the national rate. However, the proportions of the labour force employed in agriculture, forestry and fishing still remain over twenty per cent in a large number of census wards across North Yorkshire (**fig 13.5**).

There has been a significant decline in average earnings for those in full-time employment. Objective 5b areas ('fragile rural areas' — see below) of North Yorkshire in 1988 showed average earnings of just £230 per week when compared with an average of £405 for England.

Thus, at the end of the century, the agricultural economy is in turmoil, with farm incomes in crisis. The trend of falling farm incomes, already marked in the 1980s, especially so for the hill lands, has become widespread. There is considerable variation across the region, with an average below £10,000 per annum for small, full-time farms, and net incomes of less than zero for many lowland cattle and sheep farms.[11]

The prices of beef cattle and sheep have fallen markedly in recent years, exacerbated by the disaster of BSE. Farm rental levels have been rising in recent decades and reached a level of £237 per acre (£96/ha) in 1995.

Farm subsidies are now all that keep many farmers on the land. Subsidy support contributes an average of fifteen per cent to farm receipts, but subsidies can be much higher (forty per cent) in some areas of upland cattle and sheep farming. The change in the balance of crops and livestock reflects these subsidy payments and quota systems.

Public opinion and the influence of the media in the reporting of health and ecological scares (eg genetically modified crops) have exacerbated the pressures on North Yorkshire farmers, as in the rest of the country.

FARM DIVERSIFICATION

Legislative emphasis on the maintenance of a healthy rural economy has stressed the need to diversify land-based activities, while at the same time encouraging the creation and promotion of access to landscapes and habitats of ecological value, moves that have been reinforced by changes in the CAP and GATT negotiations.

The impact of diversification in North Yorkshire is already well established. More than a third (35 per cent) of farms have engaged in some form of diversification such as contract farming, industrial crop production or outdoor activities, all of which are expected to expand; along with camping, caravanning and holiday letting businesses, the production of speciality foods, farm shops, and the growing of specialist organic foods, in which there has been a particularly rapid increase.

Most forms of diversification are temporary changes of normal farming patterns, mainly into cash or industrial crops; they are adopted mostly by large farms or adventurous small-scale farmers and, although widespread, they do not have a significant impact on farm incomes. Forestry schemes have not been popular because they sterilise agricultural land.

In the lowlands, and particularly in those more accessible to urban areas, some farmers are going into part-time, non-agricultural work. There are anxieties about planning, legal, tenancy and financial constraints on the farmer's freedom to diversify, especially so for tenant farmers. Service sector employment is growing as tourism has become an important part of the rural economy, but many farmers are of the view that saturation levels are now near in tourism and leisure-related activities, especially in the upland areas and in the national parks.

13.4   PROTECTED NATURAL LANDSCAPES
DEREK STATHAM

At the turn of the twentieth century, North Yorkshire had two main types of landscape: upland areas, characterized by large expanses of moorland vegetation interspersed by dales with pasture fields and stone walls; and lowland agricultural plains, with a good network of hedges and small copses.

Over the succeeding decades, substantial changes in agricultural techniques and demand for increased production led to an expansion of farmland, drainage of many wet areas, and intensification of cultivation and livestock-rearing (as indicated in the previous section).

There were, of course, many other changes in the scenic and ecological character of the land, including the abandonment of many mines and quarries, the creation of large sand- and gravel-workings, the building of reservoirs and the rapid expansion of commercial forestry, especially in the North York Moors.

The pressures for a whole host of developments to provide for modern living demands grew inexorably, including the erection of overhead lines for power supplies, numerous masts for communications, and a large expansion of housing and light industry in both town and country.

In the uplands, the moorland areas shrank in size, large parcels being reclaimed for farming and forestry, and most of the remaining moors were subject to drainage schemes to improve their capacity for grazing. In the past few decades, overgrazing has led to impoverishment of species and the expansion of grass and rushes at the expense of heather.

In the lowlands, the great changes in agricultural techniques have resulted in the widespread removal of hedges and copses to create larger fields, and the use of chemicals has severely depleted the populations of many species of plants, insects, birds and mammals. Only in recent years has this trend of decline in both natural habitat and loss of species abated.

On the positive side, the abandonment and removal of industrial remains in the Pennines and the North York Moors has created a wilder and unspoilt scene in some dales. Recent landscape enhancement schemes in the uplands, particularly in the national parks, have begun to reverse the decline in moorland habitat and to improve the upkeep of upland farms by renovating stone walls, for example.

GROWTH IN PUBLIC CONCERN

Early attempts to protect valued landscape in North Yorkshire stem from the activities of the National Trust, formed in 1895, and the Council for the Preservation (now Protection) of Rural England, one of the oldest branches of which was formed in the 1920s in Ryedale.

The study of the wildlife of Yorkshire has long held a special place in the minds of many Yorkshire folk, beginning with the West Riding Consolidated Naturalists Society in 1861. The society became Yorkshire Naturalists' Union (YNU) in 1877, a confederation of natural history societies and individual members with interests in Yorkshire's flora and fauna. The Yorkshire Naturalists' Trust (YNT) was formed as a limited company to buy Askham Bog, on the western outskirts of York, in 1946.

These local bodies set the scene for later action in three ways: they purchased land for conservation purposes; they persuaded owners, occupiers and local authorities to take action to conserve wildlife and scenic beauty; and, perhaps most importantly, they started an educational process of concern for the environment which was to bear fruit later in the twentieth century. In the early 1980s the YNT became the Yorkshire Wildlife Trust and today manages around seventy nature reserves.

On the official side, perhaps the most important development was the introduction of control by the community over changes in the landscape through the new system of town

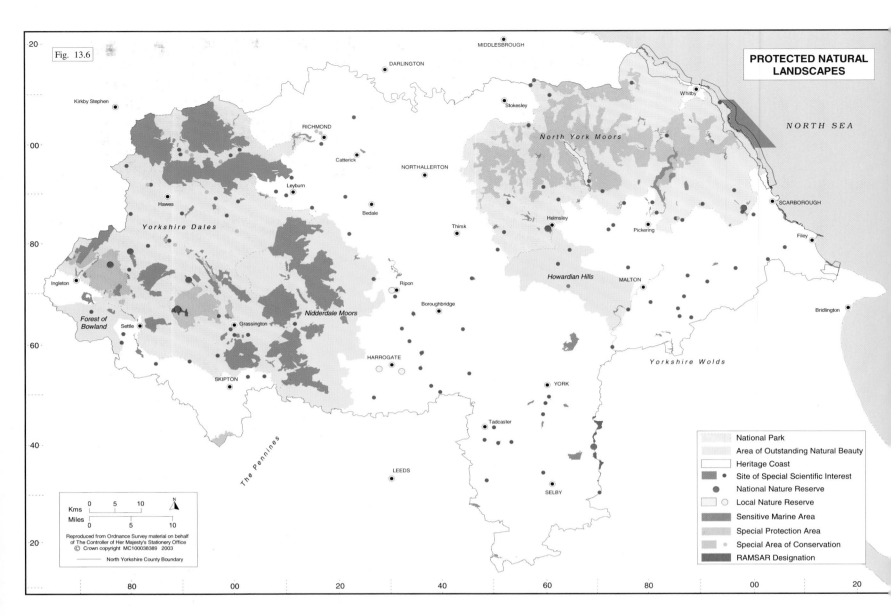

Fig. 13.6

PROTECTED NATURAL
LANDSCAPES

NORTH SEA

Legend:
- National Park
- Area of Outstanding Natural Beauty
- Heritage Coast
- Site of Special Scientific Interest
- National Nature Reserve
- Local Nature Reserve
- Sensitive Marine Area
- Special Protection Area
- Special Area of Conservation
- RAMSAR Designation

Kms 0 5 10
Miles 0 5 10
Reproduced from Ordnance Survey material on behalf
of The Controller of Her Majesty's Stationery Office
© Crown copyright MC100038389 2003
———— North Yorkshire County Boundary

and country planning. This was a response initially to the problems of crowded and insanitary housing conditions but was later to extend to building and land-use changes generally, and eventually to such matters as tree preservation, and protection of historic buildings and archaeological sites.

The earlier schemes were voluntary and patchy in their effect. The North Riding County Council was, however, one of the first authorities to establish planning schemes, with the county divided into areas such as 'moorland' and 'rural' where differing standards of controls over building and other developments were applied. These schemes were suspended during the Second World War when much damage was done to natural woodland and other natural habitats because of the need for timber and other natural resources.

STATUTORY INTERVENTION

In the wave of legislation that followed the end of the Second World War, two acts of Parliament in particular were to have a profound effect on the protection of wildlife and amenity.

The Town and Country Planning Act of 1947, and the National Parks and Access to the Countryside Act of 1949, established a system of controls over land use and management combined with positive planning measures that were to last with few changes until the end of the century. They were accompanied by an Agriculture Act that sought improvements in productivity.

No conflict was seen at the time between the purposes of these separate strands of legislative policy, but it was not long before the detrimental effects of intensifying agricultural production began to appear.

Apart from the introduction of controls over land-use changes, the concept of designating areas of land for their value as landscape, wildlife and archaeological resources was brought to fruition (**fig 13.6**).

Farndale Local Nature Reserve.
© North York Moors National Park Authority, NK 0073.

The designations concerned with the protection of landscape, such as the national parks and Areas of Outstanding Natural Beauty, with their background in the work of such bodies as the Council for the Preservation (now Protection) of Rural England and the Ramblers Association, were separated from the designations concerned with wildlife, such as the National Nature Reserves (NNR) and Sites of Special Scientific Interest (SSSI), with their background in the naturalist societies and university biology departments. These different cultural groups co-existed amicably but did not always co-ordinate their activities.

Perhaps the greatest single action to influence the protection of the natural landscape of North Yorkshire was the designation of the North York Moors National Park and the Yorkshire Dales National Park in 1952 and 1954 respectively. For the first time, it became statutory policy to preserve and enhance 'natural beauty' in these areas alongside the provision of public access and recreation. From small and humble beginnings, the park authorities were to grow in power and influence to become the dominant force in land use and management.

The protection of natural beauty was also the main objective of the Areas of Outstanding Natural Beauty, three of which were designated in the county: the Nidderdale Moors; the Howardian Hills; and a small part of the Forest of Bowland. These designations have had less impact in their areas than the national parks, partly because of the differences in the financial and administrative resources available but also because of the lack of status and public interest. Steps are at last being taken to improve both their status and performance.

Other designations introduced include the Heritage Coasts, brought in during the 1980s to put more emphasis on coastal protection.

Designations to protect wildlife include the National (NNRs) and local nature reserves (LNRs), SSSIs and a recent plethora of designations under various EU directives.

The aim of these designations varies from protection of small sites containing rare species to the sensitive management of habitats of special importance to wildlife over large areas. Apart from restrictions on farming practices and other forms of management within these areas, grants and advice are usually available to owners and occupiers of land.

The wildlife protective designations are paralleled by sites and areas designated to protect important archaeological remains, the most significant of which are the scheduled Ancient Monuments.

In recent years, more comprehensive attempts to control the actual day-to-day management of land for conservation purposes have been introduced. They include Environmentally Sensitive Areas, designated under EU legislation to encourage conservation-based farming practice; and green belts, which, although aimed primarily at preventing building around urban centres, also serve to protect the natural landscape.

Some of the most successful measures to protect important landscape have come about by the purchase and management of land for conservation by bodies such as the National Trust, the Woodland Trust and the Yorkshire Wildlife Trust. Often, the actions of these bodies have meant that land, wildlife and buildings of historic and ecological interest have been saved from destruction for all to enjoy.

All these designations, controls and protective ownerships, the most important of which are shown in **fig 13.6**, add up to a formidable panoply of protective measures for the natural landscape of North Yorkshire.

Sadly, though, it is only in recent years that there has been an attempt to relate them to the policies and grants governing agricultural and timber production. For much of the twentieth century, these policies pulled in the opposite direction, and were primarily responsible for the loss of natural habitat and environmental quality of much of the county.

13.5   THE IMPACT OF THE FORESTRY COMMISSION
JOHN MACKENZIE

The Forestry Commission is an organisation involved in the growing and harvesting of trees on both state and privately owned land. In order to assess the impacts of these activities in North Yorkshire, both positively and negatively, it is necessary to examine the commission's evolving policies during its relatively short existence.

HISTORICAL ASPECTS

The realisation of the amount of devastation to British woodlands as a result of the First World War brought home to the government of the day that there was an urgent need for a coherent national forest policy where previously none had been deemed necessary. The 1919 Forestry Act provided for the establishment of the Forestry Commission for the main purpose of building up a national reserve of timber to lessen the dependence on imported supplies, with the provision of rural employment as an important social objective. This was to remain successive governments' main policy for several decades.

Much was achieved in the early days, given the start from scratch with little forestry tradition at a time of post-war financial stringency and political uncertainty. North Yorkshire was quick off the mark with its first acquisition of Allerston estate in 1921 which spawned the modern Dalby Forest, soon to follow with the start of Wykeham Forest in the late twenties. The manpower requirement for this expansion had a positive social impact during the recession of the early thirties, especially through the establishment of a labour camp at Low Dalby at that time.

The Second World War fully justified the initial policies, and post-war policy plans (published in 1943) involved the Forestry Commission being entrusted with the afforestation of new land, and private owners being encouraged to carry out the replanting of felled and devastated woodland which had provided the bulk of the war effort.

The 1947 census of British woodlands was to confirm that some thirty-five per cent of North Riding woodlands needed restocking. The census also confirmed that, since the previous census in 1924, the total in the North Riding in private hands had fallen from some 59,300 acres to 55,350 acres (24,000ha to 22,400ha). But the Forestry Commission's impact on the woodland resource had been significant, increasing its holding from virtually nil to some 17,300 acres (7,000ha).

The 1945 Forestry Act introduced the dedication scheme under which private woodlands were to be 'dedicated' permanently to the growing of timber and, in return for grant aid,

The Newtondale section of Cropton Forest showing the evolving age structure of the forest.
© J Mackenzie.

Young seedlings for replanting, grown at Wykeham Forest nursery.
© J Mackenzie

approved management would be required. Although there was some early reluctance from owners to participate, this marked the start of a period of major expansion in British forestry, and North Yorkshire was significantly involved, mainly in the east of the county. As time passed, grant schemes would be modified and new ones introduced to meet changing circumstances.

In the 1950s — the boom years — the Forestry Commission played its part directly through mainly leasehold acquisition of smaller blocks in the west and north of the North York Moors, and more modestly further west. Under the 1951 Forestry Act, felling licence controls were introduced to indicate that it was contrary to the public interest that woodland could be cleared and left derelict.

By 1980, North Yorkshire's Forestry Commission woodland total had risen to some 58.000 acres (23,500ha) at its peak, which was forty-two per cent of the county's woodland resource (some seven per cent of the land area).

FOREST INDUSTRY AND PROFESSIONAL ASPECTS

Thus, through the Commission, a substantial positive impact was being made to maintain and increase the nation's woodland resource — albeit much with exotic conifers — to support the timber industry, and to ensure its renewability and sustainability.

Timber production was gathering momentum as the earlier plantings moved through the production phase. Mining timber was in high demand from North Yorkshire forests, by way of local sawmills, for the coalfields of Yorkshire and Nottinghamshire. The managed woodland sites in North Yorkshire in 1976 are illustrated in **fig 13.7**.

The 1970s heralded yet another governmental review, this time including a cost-benefit study, which limited the earlier rate of expansion, and focused attention on target rates of return and other financial priorities.

The 1980s, too, were difficult years due to the recession affecting British industry. Inflation was reducing timber revenues and, to reduce the call on public funds, the 1981 Forestry Act allowed for a proportion of the Forestry Commission's estate to be sold. Some fifteen per cent of its woodlands in North Yorkshire, including most of its holdings in the west and south, were identified for potential sale as part of a rationalisation policy.

The Forestry Commission has always made a significant professional impact on the timber industry and private growers, eg the provision of regular supplies to support investment in the manufacture of timber products; the provision of knowledge, advice and financial help through research and grant-aid to growers and harvesters to enable the most appropriate practices to be employed; and the protection of forest health through the monitoring of the major fungal and insect risks, and the implementation of controls where necessary.

ENVIRONMENTAL ASPECTS

Although some concerns had been raised in the 1930s about the negative impacts of afforestation, including the need for public access, which led to the creation of the first forest park in 1936 in Argyll, it was not until the 1960s that government paid heed to social factors other than employment in its 1963 policy review.

The provision for consideration of public access and recreation, as well as paying more attention to increasing the beauty of the landscape, paved the way for multi-purpose forestry

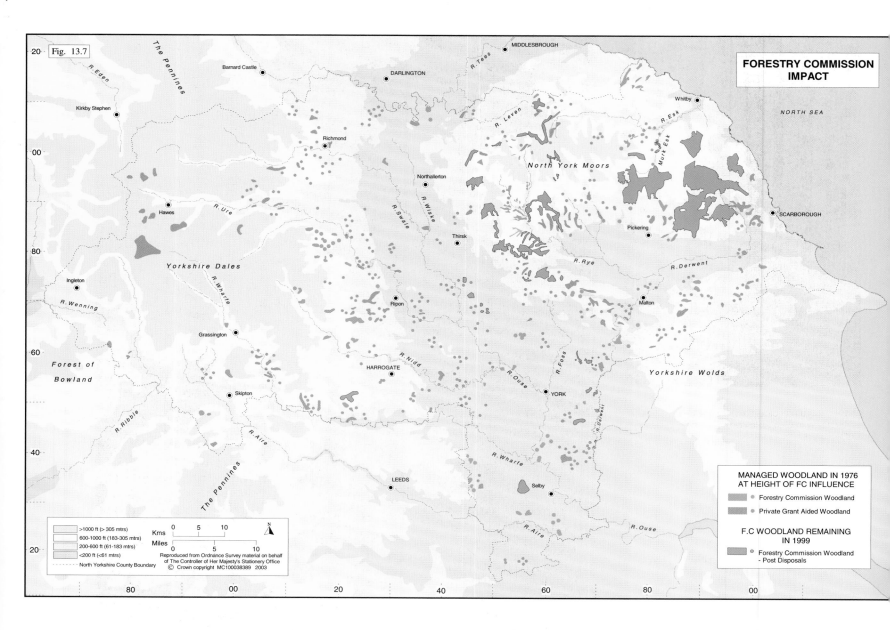

Fig. 13.7

MANAGED WOODLAND IN 1976
AT HEIGHT OF FC INFLUENCE

● Forestry Commission Woodland

● Private Grant Aided Woodland

F.C WOODLAND REMAINING
IN 1999

● Forestry Commission Woodland
- Post Disposals

>1000 ft (> 305 mtrs)
600-1000 ft (183-305 mtrs)
200-600 ft (61-183 mtrs)
<200 ft (<61 mtrs)
----- North Yorkshire County Boundary

Kms   0   5   10
Miles 0   5   10

Reproduced from Ordnance Survey material on behalf
of The Controller of Her Majesty's Stationery Office
© Crown copyright MC100038389 2003

as it is recognised today. The 1970s saw a marked increase in the provision of recreation facilities for both day and overnight visitors.

In North Yorkshire, the former were catered for mainly at Dalby Forest with its visitor centre and a range of facilities along its forest drive. Other more modest facilities were provided elsewhere in areas popular with the public. Overnight visitors were encouraged to use the west of Cropton Forest, with the provision of camping and caravanning facilities at Spiers House, and the investment in a forest cabin site at Keldy.

The 1985 Wildlife and Countryside (Amendment) Act provided further consolidation by establishing a statutory duty for the Commission to achieve a 'reasonable balance' between forest management for timber production and the conservation of natural beauty along with flora, fauna and physiographic features. The forests' biological and archaeological resource was also recognised as being valuable and requiring special protection.

The 1980s saw the Forestry Commission demonstrating its commitment to such policies with the publication of a series of guidelines setting out the standards to be aimed at, and developing consensus, co-operation and understanding with outside bodies. In 1985, a major new initiative was introduced to encourage the maintenance and development of broad-leaved woodland. The 1980s, too, saw the development of an education service which has had a significant impact on the public's awareness and understanding of the forest environment and its increasing multi-purpose potential.

With the increasing maturity of the Forestry Commission's woodlands, a further management commitment to sound environmental practice was the concept of 'restructuring' by way of forest design plans. These took a long-term view of the changes which harvesting would bring and were the subject of wide consultation.

above Autumn colour: larch with a beech understorey in Deepdale Forest nature reserve, Dalby Forest.
© J Mackenzie.

top right Wykeham Forest from Highwood Brow.
© J Mackenzie.

bottom right Forest recreation: children's adventure playground at Dalby Forest..
© J Mackenzie.

North–East England, including North Yorkshire, was at the cutting edge of these developments that in the 1990s led to a significant positive impact on the appreciation of the increasingly useful multi-purpose role for the commission's woodlands, particularly within the North York Moors National Park.

The Forestry Commission has achieved a great deal in its relatively short life, given the normal forest management cycle (fifty years), and has had an enormous impact in many ways, certainly in the east of North Yorkshire.

In the early development stages, the negative aspects were more readily recognised and emphasised by critics. But as the results of policies and management have evolved and are to be seen on the ground in an increasingly positive way, the vision of the early commissioners perhaps can be appreciated.

More remains to be done, and no doubt policies will continue to evolve to meet people's changing expectations.

13.6 TOURISM, SPORT AND RECREATION DEREK STATHAM

North Yorkshire is richly endowed with natural resources for outdoor recreation and tourism. Two national parks, three Areas of Outstanding Natural Beauty, heritage coasts with cliffs, coves and sandy beaches, large forest areas, and many attractive towns, resorts and villages combine to make the county a magnet for visitors from far and near.

Today, tourism is a chief employer and the tourist industry is a vital part of the economy. Many North Yorkshire residents also take part in outdoor recreation and the county has a strong sporting tradition in several activities, being particularly well known for its love of cricket and horse racing. **Fig 13.8** shows many of the sites of sporting activities as well as coastal and countryside sites and features popular with the tourist.

Tourism has a long pedigree, beginning with the popularity of the spa towns of Harrogate and Scarborough in the eighteenth century. The twentieth century witnessed an explosion of leisure activities, both outdoor and indoor, formal and informal. Early in the century, the railways played a key role in bringing urban visitors from the nearby conurbations to the seaside resorts of Scarborough, Whitby and Filey. This trend continued in the inter-war years but was accompanied by a great increase in visits to the countryside, particularly the Yorkshire Dales and the North York Moors, for rambling, potholing, climbing and sight-seeing.

COUNTRYSIDE RECREATION

After a lull during the Second World War, countryside recreation again became popular but, increasingly, based on the motor car rather than the railways which went into a period of decline from the 1950s onwards. Both the range of activities and the volume of participation increased rapidly, particularly during the 1960s and the 1970s with rising disposable incomes. Hitherto, minority activities such as sailing and angling became popular, and a whole host of new sports like hang-gliding, orienteering and sub-aqua diving appeared.

The rapid growth in outdoor recreation has posed some problems for local residents in popular areas, and for the planning and highway authorities who have had to cope with the seasonal and daily influx of many thousands of visitors. In the North York Moors National Park, for instance, over eight million day-visits are made for recreational purposes and the numbers are similar for the Yorkshire Dales National Park.

Inevitably, there has been some erosion along well-used footpaths, and congestion in popular villages and other tourist sites but, by and large, the county has adapted remarkably well to the transformation of the countryside during the century from an agricultural economy to one dominated by leisure and tourism. One reason for this has been the growth and development of increasingly sophisticated techniques of countryside management. These were pioneered in the national parks, and are now widely used to resolve problems of congestion and the over-use of sensitive sites.

ACCESS AND DIVERSIFICATION

The question of public access to the countryside, particularly the open fells and moorlands, was a contentious issue throughout the twentieth century.

Farmers and landowners were, on the whole, implacably opposed to public access in the countryside though the rights of way network, based on locally used paths, developed slowly for more public use during the century, with the National Parks, again, taking the lead in opening up the paths.

Only in the twenty-first century has the campaigning for open access to the fells and moors begun in the nineteenth century borne fruit with legislation finally in place to secure the right to roam in these areas.

Mountain biking in the North York Moors National Park.
© North Yotk Moors National Park Authority, RI 0010.

Steam train, North York Moors Railway.
© North York Moors National Park Authority, TG 0027.

Recreation at Sandsend (north of Whitby).
© North York Moors National Park Authority, RG0027

In the last years of the twentieth century, many farmers recognised, with support from government, the great potential of tourism and diversified their businesses to provide facilities such as bed and breakfast, farm trails, farm animal parks, caravan and camping sites.

Specialist provision for visitors outside the farms has been limited. A number of country parks, strategically sited to draw off visitors from the more sensitive areas of countryside, were developed in the 1970s and 1980s. Other facilities include visitor centres, study centres, and the forest drives, trails and other facilities provided by the Forestry Commission.

In the early twenty-first century, farmers are facing an increasingly difficult problem in making a living out of food production and the trend towards a more diversified use of the countryside, dominated by leisure use and conservation, seems set to continue.

SPORTING FACILITIES

Many North Yorkshire residents take part in countryside and outdoor pursuits but are no less interested in the more formal sports. Indeed, Yorkshire is famous for sporting excellence especially in the activities of cricket and horse racing.

Local cricket leagues still abound amid tense local rivalries, and county cricket is still played at Scarborough. Other team sports like soccer, rugby and hockey are popular but inevitably concentrated in the towns and larger villages.

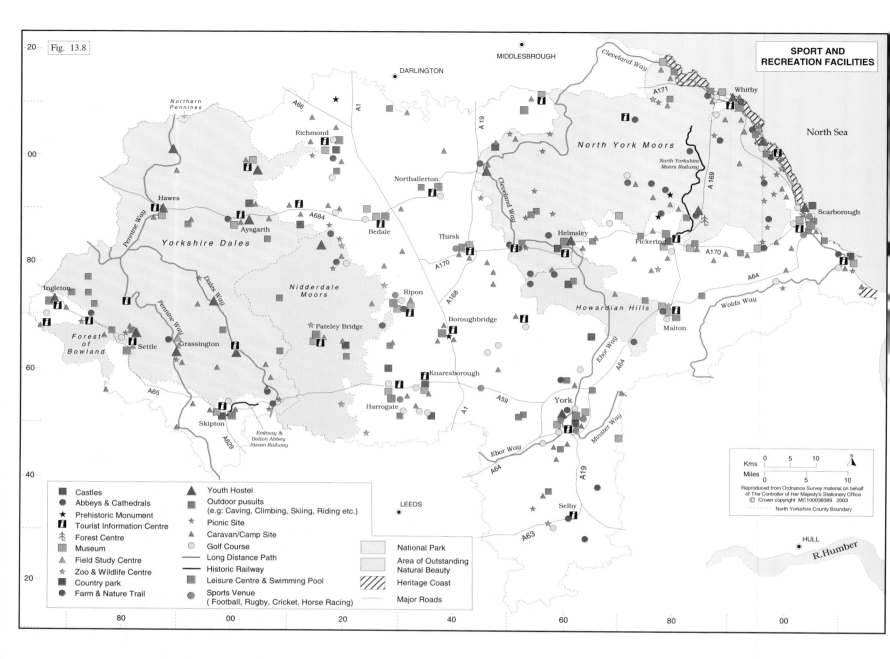

Fig. 13.8

SPORT AND RECREATION FACILITIES

DARLINGTON

MIDDLESBROUGH

Cleveland Way

North Sea

Richmond

Northern Pennines

North York Moors

Whitby

North Yorkshire Moors Railway

Hawes

A684

Yorkshire Dales

Aysgarth

Bedale

Northallerton

Cleveland Way

Thirsk

Helmsley

Pickering

Scarborough

Ingleton

Nidderdale Moors

Ripon

A168

Howardian Hills

Wolds Way

Forest of Bowland

Pennine Way

Dales Way

Settle

Grassington

Pateley Bridge

Boroughbridge

Malton

A64

A65

Knaresborough

York

Ebor Way

Munster Way

Harrogate

A1

A59

Skipton

A629

Embsay & Bolton Abbey Steam Railway

Ebor Way

A64

LEEDS

Selby

A19

A63

HULL

R. Humber

Kms 0 5 10

Miles 0 5 10

Reproduced from Ordnance Survey material on behalf of The Controller of Her Majesty's Stationery Office
© Crown copyright MC100038389 2003

North Yorkshire County Boundary

■ Castles	▲ Youth Hostel
● Abbeys & Cathedrals	■ Outdoor pusuits
★ Prehistoric Monument	(e.g: Caving, Climbing, Skiing, Riding etc.)
🛈 Tourist Information Centre	★ Picnic Site
⚕ Forest Centre	▲ Caravan/Camp Site
■ Museum	○ Golf Course
▲ Field Study Centre	— Long Distance Path
★ Zoo & Wildlife Centre	— Historic Railway
■ Country park	■ Leisure Centre & Swimming Pool
● Farm & Nature Trail	● Sports Venue
	(Football, Rugby, Cricket, Horse Racing)

National Park

Area of Outstanding Natural Beauty

Heritage Coast

Major Roads

Lilla Cross (waymark), Lyke Wake Walk. The Lyke Wake Walk, created in the 1950s, runs for forty-two miles (67km) from Osmotherley to Ravenscar, across the North York Moors.

© North York Moors National Park Authority.

Robin Hood's Bay: fishing and recreation.
© North York Moors National Park Authority, PT 0011.

During the latter half of the twentieth century, facilities for sport were provided on a more lavish scale. Most towns now have indoor leisure centres (23) catering for a wide variety of sports, squash courts, swimming pools (30), outdoor tennis courts and now increasingly indoor courts (2), with more specialist facilities such as synthetic turf pitches (9), synthetic athletics tracks (2) and an artificial ski-slope provided in suitable locations.[12]

Specialist sports using countryside sites such as motor-racing circuits and gliding were established from the 1930s onwards and, in more recent years, sites suitable for contemporary sports like hang-gliding and parascending have been established, particularly in the upland areas. Furthermore, according to data on funding provided by Sport England, North Yorkshire has benefited to the tune of almost £11 million in awards from the Lottery.

The county's racecourses have a much longer history. One of the oldest racecourses in the country was on the Hambleton Hills at Sutton Bank where racing dates back to the seventeenth century, although the only vestiges today are horse gallops and racehorse training facilities. Racing and training are an important part of both the county's economy and its social life. Many rural folk now keep ponies and horses, and pony trekking and gymkhanas, as well as the traditional point-to-point races, remain popular.

Field sports were particularly well developed in the early years of the twentieth century, and have become more commercialised in recent years with increasing emphasis on syndicates and lettings to clubs. Some of the finest grouse moors in the UK can be found on the eastern slopes of the Pennines and in the North York Moors. Although their heyday was in the late nineteenth and early twentieth century, many still thrive today under commercial management.

13.7 SOCIAL DEPRIVATION, EMPLOYMENT STRUCTURE AND HOUSING ISSUES   JOHN STILLWELL

In contrast to the richness of the physical environment that characterises much of North Yorkshire, and the fact that the majority of inhabitants are affluent and mobile, there are parts of the county experiencing a range of social problems including low incomes, unemployment, the loss of services such as village shops or pubs and the lack of public transport provision or affordable housing.

There is a minority of people suffering social exclusion and isolation. In a study for the Department of the Environment in the mid-1980s, McLaughlin[13] found that 8.2 per cent of the population in fourteen remote parishes in Wensleydale and Swaledale were living in poverty, compared with a national figure of 4.1 per cent. McLaughlin also noted a high level of poverty amongst the elderly, with over thirty per cent of his North Yorkshire sample living on or near the margins of poverty. These figures bear out the notion of hidden poverty in rural areas, and have been documented more comprehensively in a recent regional report for Yorkshire and the Humber by the Countryside Agency.[14]

Heavy dependence on agriculture creates a series of problems that have been more prominent in the remoter upland areas. A farm management survey[15] showed upland farmers were receiving very low incomes and were heavily dependent on EU subsidies. The sharp decline in the market price for lamb has been accentuated most recently by the foot and mouth crisis. Poor-quality land tends to prevent conversion to agricultural use other than rough grazing, which currently constitutes eighty per cent of the agricultural land-use in the North York Moors National Park, for example.

Although unemployment in most rural areas is not high by national or European standards, family members employed on many farms are often under-employed and poorly paid rather than being registered as unemployed.

The lack of education and limited formal qualifications can be seen as both an indicator of and a contributor towards social disadvantage. In McLaughlin's sample, 56.7 per cent of the population left school with no qualifications in the mid-1980s, compared with 52 per cent nationally, and this in a county with one of the best educational performance records in the country.[16]

DEPRIVATION INDICES
Deprivation in terms of educational achievement in rural areas is sustained by a number of access-related factors, including the physical distance people may have to travel to appropriate facilities and also the lack of suitable public transport.

Much of North Yorkshire is very sparsely populated: its overall population density is 27 persons per square mile (70/km^2) compared with 400 persons per square mile (1,037/km^2) in West Yorkshire, for example. In Ryedale District, the density falls to 12 persons per square mile (32/km^2).[17]

Access is one of six 'domains' included in a new census ward-level index of multiple deprivation (IMD2000) produced by the Department of the Environment, Transport and the Regions (DETR) that reflect different dimensions of deprivation, each of which is assembled from a number of indicators.[18]

The index of geographical access to services for all the wards in North Yorkshire is shown in **fig 13.9.** The access domain includes access to a post office and food shops in 1998, access to a GP in October 1997, and access to a primary school for all 5–8 year-olds in 1999. The first three variables are measured for recipients of Income Support, Income-Based Job Seeker's Allowance, Family Credit and Disability Working Allowance. In other words, the index focuses on people with low incomes (on benefits) since they are more likely to be experiencing disadvantage through lack of access when compared with those on higher incomes who are more able to afford public or private transport.

The least deprived out of 8,414 census wards in the country has an index value of -2.78 whereas the most deprived ward has an index of 2.95. North Yorkshire contains a large number of wards where the index of access to services is relatively high, with Ebberston (2.30) in Ryedale, and the Richmondshire wards of Aysgarth (2.38) and Grinton and Upper Swaledale (2.35) being ranked twelfth, thirteenth and fourteenth most deprived in the country.

The index of multiple deprivation (IMD) itself provides a powerful indicator of many key aspects of social exclusion, including the following domains, weighted accordingly: income (25 per cent); employment (25 per cent); health deprivation and disability (15 per cent); education, skills and training (15 per cent); housing (10 per cent); as well as the domain of geographical access to services (10 per cent). The IMD combines the domain indices for every ward to give an overall score that varies from 83.7 (most deprived) to 1.16 (least deprived).

The picture of multiple deprivation within North Yorkshire (**fig 13.10**) looks rather different from that identified by the access index, since the areas with the highest scores are mostly found in the county's urban centres. Scarborough's Castle and Eastfield wards, and Selby North and South, all have scores over forty and are ranked 590th, 722nd, 899th and 1,082nd respectively. At the other end of the social spectrum, Pannal has an IMD of 2.2 and is ranked 8,393rd out of 8,414 wards in England.

UNEMPLOYMENT AND JOBS

Unemployment levels in North Yorkshire are generally lower than in Great Britain as a whole but it is not surprising that the unemployment black-spots coincide with those areas in Scarborough and Selby that have high IMD scores.

In January 2000, the worst unemployment rate in the county (18 per cent) was to be found in Scarborough's Castle ward, with Weaponess in Scarborough (10.7 per cent), Selby Central (10.5 per cent) and Selby South (10.1 per cent) being the other wards with rates in excess of 10 per cent. Long-term unemployment rates involving those unemployed for more than six months vary across the county, from 27 per cent of claimants in Richmondshire to 33 per cent in Ryedale. The proportion of those unemployed for more than one year reaches levels over 20 per cent in both Scarborough and Selby.

The structure of employment in North Yorkshire in 1996 by broad sectoral division (**fig 13.11**) indicates the importance of service-sector jobs, many of which are found in the urban centres of York, Harrogate and Scarborough. Out of a total of 866,990 jobs in 1997, 27.9 per cent were in distribution, hotels and restaurants, and a further 25.8 per cent in public administration, education and health.

Agriculture and tourism employ a significantly larger proportion of the workforce than the average for Great Britain, whereas jobs in manufacturing, and the financial and business sectors are under-represented. Localised concentrations of jobs in coal mining and power generation are found in Selby, and in the defence industry in Richmondshire, associated with Catterick Garrison. Research and development, and financial services are well represented in Harrogate and Craven, whereas Harrogate and Skipton have developed new industries such as business tourism, financial services and new technology based on manufacturing firms.

One particularly interesting phenomenon has been the development of a cluster of high-technology firms in Ryedale.[19] These businesses had developed from two original companies founded by men who had lived and worked in the area.

Four of the firms originated from the Slingsby company founded in 1939 at Kirkbymoorside to build gliders. In the 1960s, the firm diversified into marine engineering, stimulated by the North Sea oil and gas explorations, and in 1983, split into two separate companies focusing on gliders and marine communications vehicles respectively. Two further companies emerged from the marine company in 1982 and 1983.

An even greater proliferation of firms can be traced back to another company, Micrometalsmith, founded in 1964 in Kirkbymoorside. Micrometalsmith spawned a separate company, Spectra Tek, in 1971, from which a further five firms were created during the 1980s. The Ryedale firms have generated substantial numbers of jobs, employing 716 people in 1993.

RURAL HOUSING

There is evidence that, because of the low-income nature of much of the work undertaken in remote rural areas, local people can find problems in entering the owner-occupied sector

Fig. 13.9

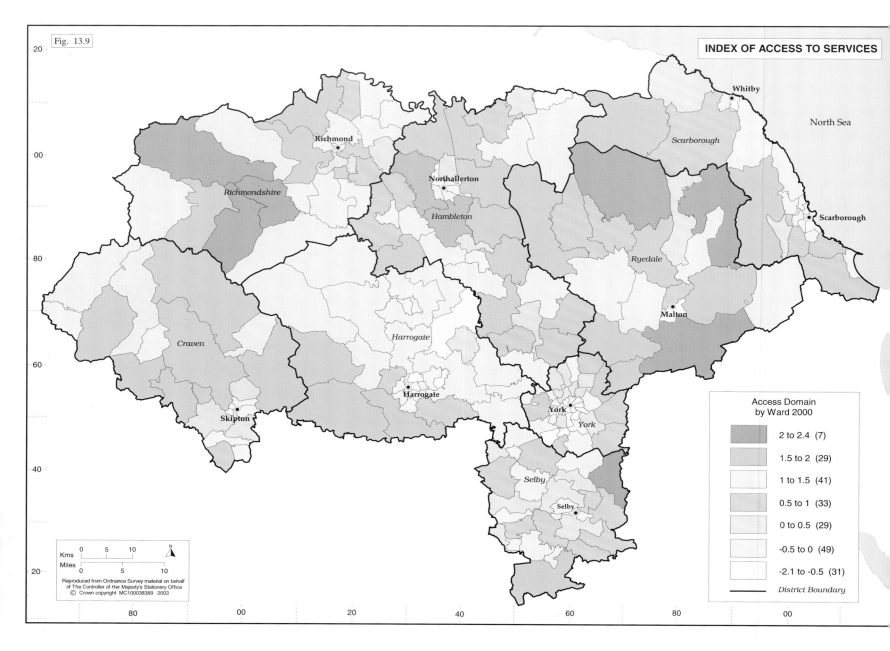

INDEX OF ACCESS TO SERVICES

North Sea

Whitby

Richmond

Scarborough

Richmondshire

Northallerton

Hambleton

Scarborough

Ryedale

Craven

Harrogate

Malton

Harrogate

York

York

Skipton

Selby

Selby

Access Domain
by Ward 2000

	2 to 2.4 (7)
	1.5 to 2 (29)
	1 to 1.5 (41)
	0.5 to 1 (33)
	0 to 0.5 (29)
	-0.5 to 0 (49)
	-2.1 to -0.5 (31)
	District Boundary

Kms 0 5 10
Miles 0 5 10

Reproduced from Ordnance Survey material on behalf
of The Controller of Her Majesty's Stationery Office
© Crown copyright MC100038389 2003

Staithes: a small fishing port, with a variety of housing
types.
© B E Vyner.

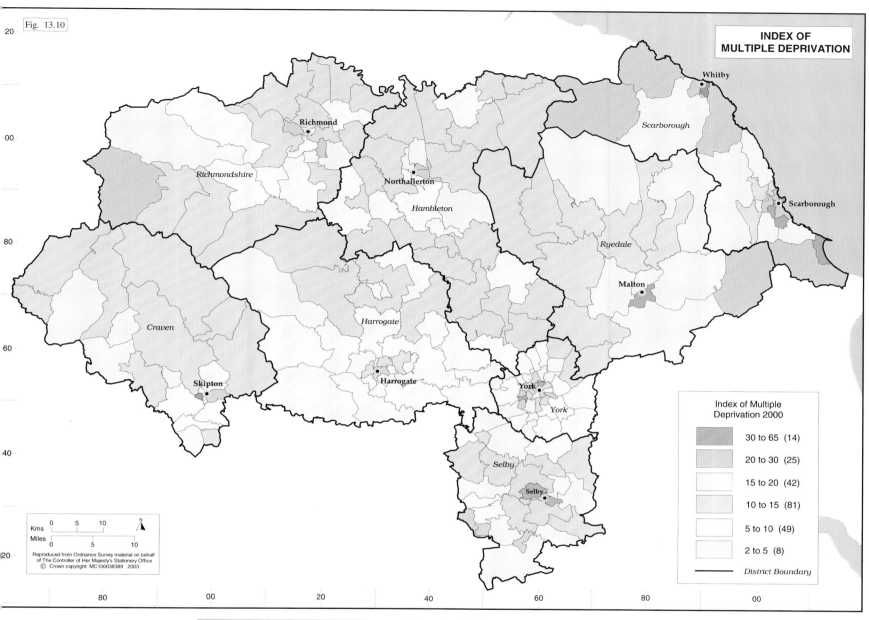

Fig. 13.10

**INDEX OF
MULTIPLE DEPRIVATION**

Whitby

Scarborough

Richmond

Richmondshire

Northallerton

Hambleton

Scarborough

Ryedale

Malton

Craven

Harrogate

Skipton

Harrogate

York

York

Selby

Selby

Kms 0 5 10
Miles 0 5 10

Reproduced from Ordnance Survey material on behalf
of The Controller of Her Majesty's Stationery Office
© Crown copyright MC100038389 2003

Index of Multiple
Deprivation 2000

30 to 65 (14)

20 to 30 (25)

15 to 20 (42)

10 to 15 (81)

5 to 10 (49)

2 to 5 (8)

District Boundary

80   00   20   40   60   80   00

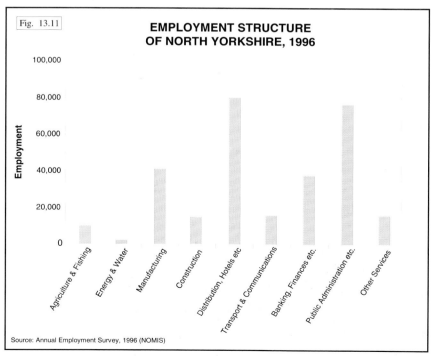

Fig. 13.11

**EMPLOYMENT STRUCTURE
OF NORTH YORKSHIRE, 1996**

100,000

80,000

Employment

60,000

40,000

20,000

0

Agriculture & Fishing
Energy & Water
Manufacturing
Construction
Distribution, Hotels etc
Transport & Communications
Banking, Finances etc.
Public Administration etc.
Other Services

Source: Annual Employment Survey, 1996 (NOMIS)

of the housing market in parts of environmentally attractive areas. North Yorkshire is typical of such areas and, as indicated previously, its appeal to in-migrants is reflected in the price of houses.

According to the Land Registry, the average price of residential property of all types in the last quarter of 1999 was £87,892 in North Yorkshire as a whole, compared with £65,994 in East Yorkshire, £64,651 in West Yorkshire and £56,592 in South Yorkshire.[20] The presence of second homes is particularly marked in parts of North Yorkshire, with over half the housing stock of some parishes falling in this category.[21]

The 1991 census indicated around 13,000 vacant dwellings in the county, and a further 9,000 were identified as second homes or holiday accommodation, about three-quarters of which were concentrated in and around the national parks and along the coast.

In addition to the problem of house purchase, there is also a lack of rented accommodation. At the time of the population census in 1991, over 72 per cent of the homes in North Yorkshire were owner-occupied in comparison with 66 per cent in Great Britain as a whole.[22]

The Government's Right to Buy housing policy, introduced originally in 1980, has had a major impact on the supply of affordable housing for rent. The impact of Right to Buy has been investigated in the Ripon area by McFarlane and Kettle[23] who report a sixteen per cent reduction in the amount of council housing available for rent to local families between 1989 and 1999. They also present evidence suggesting that a significant proportion of those who buy their council houses tend to return to the social rented sector having sold or transferred the property to a relative.

Findings such as these indicate that the shortage of affordable housing, particularly for young people, remains one of the most important problems confronting North Yorkshire in the future.

13.8 MAPPING THE FUTURE   JOHN STILLWELL

Planning and policy measures are fundamental driving forces that influence the development processes which in turn create the landscapes of the future. Whilst our domestic planning system requires the preparation of structure plans that set out guidelines for the future location of land to be used to accommodate new homes, shops, services and infrastructure, land use is increasingly influenced by policy-makers in Brussels with substantial funds at their disposal.

SUPPORT FROM EUROPE

The economic problems associated with the agricultural industry and the related social problems that have afflicted those living in more remote rural areas were formally recognised by the government through the designation of Rural Development Areas in 1984. Much of North Yorkshire was covered and all RDAs were reviewed by the Rural Development Commission in 1994.[24]

However, support for rural development has been increasingly shaped by funding programmes and procedures originating at the European level. In particular, there has been recognition by the European Commission that parts of North Yorkshire have been eligible for Objective 5b Structural Funds which aim to stimulate growth in 'fragile rural areas'. The Northern Uplands, containing much of the Yorkshire Dales and North York Moors, has been designated as the largest British Objective 5b area.

As part of the European Commission's quest to create a more integrated rural policy since the mid-1990s,[25] the Objective 5b programmes are being phased out, and new Objective 2 programmes for both urban and rural localities suffering structural economic problems (effectively combining Objective 2 and 5b programmes) are being introduced with some 'transitional' support for the poorer rural regions. The Objective 2 and transitional areas for North Yorkshire for 2000-2006 are indicated on **fig 13.12**.

The North Yorkshire Partnership Unit has been busy producing a delivery plan[26] for Objective 2 that aims to create sustainable wealth for the county by investing in new technologies that build upon the strengths and opportunities of upland and coastal Yorkshire.

The delivery plan has several key priorities. Firstly, there is a new entrepreneurship agenda that is designed to support the creation and survival of more high potential businesses by promoting the development of new businesses and business growth. Funding will support start-up and micro-businesses, and provide specialist advice for start-ups.

The second of the priorities is to improve competitiveness of existing companies throughout North Yorkshire by helping them to adapt to and anticipate changing customer demands.

The third priority involves re-connecting communities to economic growth and is more geographically targeted. The aim is to attempt to unlock the ability of communities to share in and contribute to economic and social revival. Based on the Index of Multiple Deprivation discussed previously, funding for an integrated package of community support will be targeted more closely at the most deprived wards, particularly those eight in Scarborough borough that are ranked in the top thirty per cent most deprived wards in England (**fig 13.10**). Similarly, in the upland areas, wards have been designated that will be targeted for a number of capacity-building and community based activities.

The fourth priority seeks to exploit the employment impact within the Objective 2 area's key locational assets. Market towns and their hinterlands hit by decline of services and agricultural activity will be identified for locally focused action based on so-called community investment prospectus areas, and coordinating activities will be undertaken in five clusters targeted for assistance (Craven, Harrogate, Scarborough, Richmondshire and Ryedale). In addition, a coastal development plan will be developed under this priority that will be prepared for Scarborough and Filey, and will focus on developing sites and infrastructure, business parks, offices, managed workspace and on re-investment in derelict sites and properties.

These initiatives demonstrate part of the policy response in North Yorkshire to the economic and related social problems that characterise different parts of the county, and EU funds will only be allocated if matched funds are available from other private and public sector sources.

POSSIBLE DEVELOPMENT STRATEGIES

In terms of physical planning, North Yorkshire County Council, the City of York Council and the North York Moors and Yorkshire Dales National Park Authorities are currently working together to prepare a new joint structure plan. This will replace the adopted structure plan[27] that was adopted in 1995 and covers the period up to 2006. The joint plan will provide strategic long-term guidance for development, conservation and regeneration throughout the whole of North Yorkshire, the city of York and the two National Parks for the period to 2016. The plan will deal with such issues as the use of land for housing, economic development, the protection of the environment, and the integration of land use and transportation.

One of the major considerations for the structure planners in North Yorkshire is the need to accommodate an increasing population. The Office of National Statistics' 1996-based population projections[28] suggest that North Yorkshire's population will increase by 10 per cent from 558,800 in 1996 to 616,500 in 2021 and, according to the DETR's 1996-based projections,[29] a 21.5 per cent increase in households is forecast.

The framework for the structure plan is provided by regional planning guidance (RPG12) for Yorkshire and the Humber, now approved,[30] which proposes that North Yorkshire and the city of York should provide 42,700 new dwellings between 1998 and 2016. RPG12 emphasizes urban renaissance and gives priority to the development of previously used urban land (brownfield sites), reinforcing a shift away from a policy of dispersing housing into the more rural areas. The brownfield target is 53 per cent. North Yorkshire is already committed to the provision of over 22,000 additional houses, and over 1,500 acres (600ha) of land has planning permission for employment use or is allocated in local plans.

One possible approach is therefore a continuation of the existing strategy which involves the concentration of the majority of housing and employment on the main urban areas of York, Harrogate and Scarborough, the market towns (**fig 13.12**) and some larger villages with growth potential because they have a good employment and service base, and good public transport links.

A number of other possible spatial strategies have been elaborated for consideration by the planning authorities.[31] These include the:
- concentration on existing settlements adjacent to West Yorkshire, recognising the importance of the links between Harrogate, York, South Craven and Selby with Leeds in particular;
- concentration on the main urban areas of York, Harrogate and Scarborough, making maximum use of the advantages of the largest towns for sustainable development;
- concentration on the market towns, building on their role as centres for services, facilities and employment for the surrounding rural areas;
- promotion of growth in larger villages with a range of facilities;

Further Reading:

M Hartley and J Ingilby, *Life and Tradition in the Yorkshire Dales* (Otley: Smith Settle, 1997). Illustrated with over 250 photographs, this work gives fascinating insights into farming activities and domestic practices in the Yorkshire Dales in the twentieth century.

M Hartley and J Ingilby, *Life and Tradition in the Moorlands of North-East Yorkshire* (Otley: Smith Settle, 1990). Text and illustrations that fix the shape and texture of twentieth-century life in the North York Moors.

M Hartley, and J Ingilby, *Yorkshire Album of Photographs of Everyday Life, 1900-1950* (London: J M Dent and Sons, 1988). Another interesting collection of photographs of life in Yorkshire in the first half of the twentieth century.

J Herriot, *James Herriot's Yorkshire* (London: Michael Joseph, 1979). Herriot's text illustrated with wonderful photographs by Derry Brabbs.

W H Long, *A Survey of the Agriculture of Yorkshire* (London: Royal Agricultural Society of England, County Agricultural Surveys, 1969). An excellent survey of farming in Yorkshire in the first half of the twentieth century.

A Mee, *Yorkshire: North Riding*, edition revised and edited by Frank Beckwith (London: Hodder and Stoughton – the Kings England series, 1970). One of forty county books by Arthur Mee providing archaeological, ecclesiastical and topographical information about every town and village in the North Riding.

North Yorkshire Federation of Women's Institutes, *North Yorkshire Within Living Memory* (Newbury: Countryside Books, 1995). Personal recollections and memories of life in North Yorkshire between 1900 and 1960.

N Pevsner, *Yorkshire: The North Riding* (London: Penguin – the Buildings of England Series, 1966). Provides a description of every building of architectural importance from cathedral to pumping station.

C Speakman, *Portrait of North Yorkshire* (London: Robert Hale, 1986). One of the famous series of 'Portrait' guides describing the landscape, culture, towns, agriculture and industry of North Yorkshire.

J Stillwell and C Leigh (eds), *Yorkshire and Humberside Monitoring the Past, Mapping the Future* (Leeds: Yorkshire and Humberside Regional Research Observatory, 1995). Assessment of the region in the last decade of the twentieth century and the characteristics and role of North Yorkshire within this context.

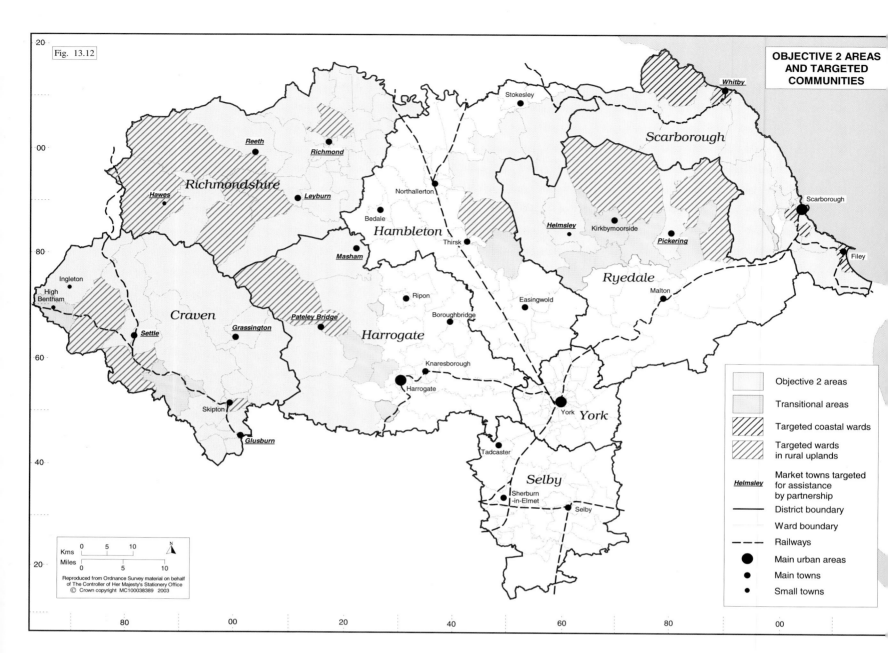

Fig. 13.12

OBJECTIVE 2 AREAS AND TARGETED COMMUNITIES

Whitby

Stokesley

Scarborough

Richmondshire

Reeth

Richmond

Hawes

Leyburn

Northallerton

Scarborough

Bedale

Hambleton

Helmsley Kirkbymoorside

Thirsk

Pickering

Filey

Masham

Ryedale

Malton

Ingleton

High Bentham

Craven

Ripon

Easingwold

Settle

Pateley Bridge

Grassington

Boroughbridge

Harrogate

Knaresborough

Skipton

Harrogate

York *York*

Glusburn

Tadcaster

Selby

Sherburn -in-Elmet

Selby

Kms 0 5 10

Miles 0 5 10

N

Reproduced from Ordnance Survey material on behalf of The Controller of Her Majesty's Stationery Office © Crown copyright MC100038389 2003

Legend:
- Objective 2 areas
- Transitional areas
- Targeted coastal wards
- Targeted wards in rural uplands
- *Helmsley* Market towns targeted for assistance by partnership
- District boundary
- Ward boundary
- Railways
- ● Main urban areas
- • Main towns
- · Small towns

- creation of one large new settlement or several smaller new settlements, providing the opportunity to build mixed communities to high design standards and service provision;
- concentration of development on the main rail corridors (**fig 13.12**), producing a more sustainable pattern of development in transport terms and a more effective integration of transportation and land use; and
- dispersal of development to upland, coastal and coalfield regeneration areas, attempting to contribute to the economic imbalances that exist in North Yorkshire.

In envisioning where future housing and economic developments should take place in North Yorkshire, it is necessary to recognise and preserve both the physical and cultural legacies that have given appeal to so many constituent parts of the county throughout the twentieth century.

In future years, we must also seek to achieve sustainable development and attempt to reduce dependence on the car, whilst conforming to the government's priority of using land previously developed or undeveloped within existing settlements. Furthermore, the special needs of the upland rural areas and of the pockets of multiple deprivation must be addressed.

The possible spatial strategies summarised above are not mutually exclusive, and a solution for new development that draws on a mix of elements taken from a number of the alternatives may well be the best option. It is a certainty that the debate on alternative futures will be revisited many times as North Yorkshire's development progresses through the twenty-first century.

14

CONCLUSION

ROBIN A BUTLIN

The maps and text of this *Atlas* have introduced many new ideas and much new information, combined with authoritative summaries of existing knowledge of the history and historical geography of North Yorkshire. There remain, however, gaps in our detailed knowledge, and further broad aspects of this history that need to be covered and included in future representations of the history of this large and significant area.

Our knowledge of the changing physical environs of North Yorkshire, as described in section 2, continues to improve, not least on grounds of increasing number of field sites examined and new technologies for the analysis of palaeo-ecological evidence. Important clusters of pollen-rich sites are found on the North York Moors and Millstone Grit areas of the Pennines but, owing to the scarcity of surviving peat deposits, coverage is poorer in the lowlands and calcareous uplands. Radiocarbon dating provides a chronology for pollen diagrams produced from evidence for sites such as those shown on **fig 2.10**, and others may be dated approximately by comparison with them.

One interesting feature that emerges from work of this kind is the dynamic of biodiversity and its lessons not only for understanding the past but also thinking about the future. It has been suggested,[1] for example, that the degree of biodiversity in Yorkshire as a whole increased during the Holocene (post-glacial) period to a maximum, probably in the eighteenth or early nineteenth century, but then experienced a steady decline thereafter through intensification of agriculture, the clearance of woodland and the burning of moorland heather. This trend to a more limited biodiversity, currently involving a reduction in the flora and fauna of Yorkshire, needs to be further researched and debated.

Much more also needs to be done to extend our understanding of the prehistoric, early historical and early medieval periods. We summarize much of the existing knowledge of prehistory in section 3. Excavation of important Early Mesolithic sites, such as that at Star Carr in the Vale of Pickering, continues to produce new material, and to effect revision of important aspects of culture and of chronology.

Although North Yorkshire has experienced human settlement for over 10,000 years, and holds much prehistoric evidence of great interest, our knowledge remains limited in comparison to areas of southern England or Scotland, partly a reflection of the limited number of fieldworkers working in the area. Outside the urban areas, fewer sites seem to be under threat from recent development, and there has thus been a limited amount of rescue archaeology.

The large number and contextual varieties of prehistoric sites in the county, identified by evidence such as earthworks and cropmarks, are impressive by their number and extent rather than by the findings from detailed excavations; these and major up-dated syntheses of the broader developments in prehistory, including contrasting regional variations of human and environmental experience, are required.

One interesting feature of North Yorkshire's prehistory is the ways in which contrasting sites and locations have been favoured in the past. Mesolithic activity appears to have been focused in places which are marginal today, such as the low-lying lands of the Vale of Pickering or the upland Pennines. The location of earlier Neolithic mortuary monuments on the uplands of eastern Yorkshire contrasts with the lowland river valley locations favoured later in the period, while there was much Bronze Age activity in eastern Yorkshire, and also on the Pennines.

The pre-Roman Iron Age experienced a developing intensity of settlement across the lowlands, the sites of which are frequently revealed by the evidence of air photography, and through the construction of roads and pipelines.

The locations chosen for sites of settlement and other activity in prehistoric times show the care taken in their choice, frequently involving a site at the junction of topographical, soil, drainage and vegetation zones. Boundaries of various forms associated with such sites were often long-lasting, and further work is needed on such continuity of occupance and function in prehistory, as well as the discontinuity between contrasting phases of settlement and land use.

We now have a fairly good idea of the outlines of Roman, Anglo-Saxon, and Scandinavian settlement in North Yorkshire (sections 4 and 5), but more detailed investigation is needed, through excavation of, for example: large cemeteries away from York; early levels underlying villa complexes; and evidence from non-villa rural sites. In addition, we require more extensive environmental evidence for that part of the region outside York.

More generally the question of the transition from the Roman to Anglian periods needs further illumination through large-scale exploration of sites by means of modern techniques focusing on later Roman and post-Roman levels.

There is very limited knowledge of the west of the county for the period prior to AD 850, and research on that region must be a priority, including examination of the character of settlement, nature of burial/funerary practices, and paucity of evidence of the British population.

For the whole of North Yorkshire, excavation of rural sites that might test the validity of the 'Heslerton model' would be helpful, as would also an increased understanding of the character and related activities of sites of Roman towns and *vici*, including York, in the fifth and sixth centuries. We need to know more about the origins of towns without apparent Roman antecedents, and further detailed excavation of monastic sites, following on from the important work at Kirkdale. The excavation of the post-AD 650 West Heslerton cemetery could afford comparison with the earlier excavated cemetery and with contemporary settlement evidence.

For the period after AD 850, further archaeological work is needed in York to test the 'Coppergate model' and, more broadly, to give clearer identities to the location and character of rural settlement through recognition and excavation of rural sites across the county, and by excavation of a large post-AD 850 cemetery. Of special importance to all of these questions and objectives would be further work designed to elucidate the environmental conditions and economies of the early medieval period.

For the period from the eleventh to the late sixteenth century (section 6), substantial existing material enables reconstructions to be made of the life, livelihoods, settlements and institutions of North Yorkshire, at least in outline.

Much work has been carried out on the nature of religious communities: major communities such as Fountains Abbey have been studied in great detail, and we know a lot about their buildings, spiritual and economic life, including that of their granges, and their regional and European links.

Castles and fortifications, and some aspects of urban life have also been researched in detail. We also have a fairly clear idea of the extent and nature of woodland and royal forests, but less of other aspects of environment and environmental change.

However, we lack detailed knowledge of the economic activities of the villages and smaller towns, gaps which can be repaired only by further detailed investigations of the documentary and field evidence. The agrarian arrangements of individual settlements can be reconstructed by reference to contemporary land ownership and management documents, and by painstaking investigation of the evidence provided by modern air photographs and site excavations. This frequently requires interdisciplinary teamwork and the sharing of insights from a wide range of perspectives.

We still know relatively little about the details of daily life of smaller medieval towns in North Yorkshire; the evidence and opportunities for research on these exist in various forms and the challenge needs taking up.

The city of York has received much attention from archaeologists and historians, and should continue to do so, but we need more detailed studies of such towns as Richmond and Ripon, Scarborough and Whitby, each of whose roots extend deep into the past.

Medieval population numbers and composition are very difficult to calculate, even in general approximation, lacking anything like census material, and the best prospect here is in detailed local studies. As with many other aspects of historical research, there is a growing interest for this period in gender perspectives on life in the past, and more is to be expected from this kind of research in the future.

Beyond the middle of the sixteenth century (section 7) we have somewhat better statistical bases for population reconstructions, initially through church and taxation records, and, from 1801, through census figures. The social and cultural compositions of county and local populations become rather more easily accessible, and we can outline the population demographic change of local communities.

Apart from York, however, there are very few detailed reconstructions of the demographic characteristics of North Yorkshire until the nineteenth century, a gap that needs to be filled. This is a subject on which the traditions of local population and genealogical studies, strongly supported by local history, WEA and extension studies groups could be built upon and co-ordinated to build up a better picture of the demography of North Yorkshire.

The history of the religious communities and traditions in North Yorkshire is an area that has also attracted much scholarly interest over the last twenty years: we now have a good idea of the evolution of these traditions from the sixteenth to the twenty-first century through the use of church registers, visitation documents, and the like.

The social, political and economic history of York has been extensively studied from the sixteenth century onwards, but parallel studies are needed for other towns in the region. The distribution of wealth, poverty, and various types of welfare provision through this period are covered in the relevant sections of this *Atlas*, as are the main features of North Yorkshire's electoral and political history, though there is doubtless more to be done.

A great deal is known of the transport history of the county, and its railway history will continue to attract interest.

Section 8 provides insights into the changes in agriculture from the seventeenth to the late nineteenth century. Much more work is needed, however, on the agrarian and rural history of North Yorkshire, especially on the detailed reconstruction of the economic life of rural communities, including their field systems, agricultural practices, and the processes of change from medieval to modern agricultural systems.

We know much about the formal processes of enclosure of open land by parliamentary act from the eighteenth to the mid-nineteenth century, but less about preceding processes of enclosure. The relevant data are available in large quantities, in both county and national record repositories.

It is remarkable how relatively little is known about the overall picture of the dynamics of estate management and ownership in North Yorkshire in comparison, for example, with the many important studies of estates in East Yorkshire and of the evolution of the rural landscapes of East Yorkshire.

Land drainage, of which a regional example is given in section 8 of the *Atlas*, is another area of agrarian history deserving of further attention, as are the effects of various periods of agricultural depression on rural life and landscape.

The study of the evolution of landscapes associated with industry, towns and aspects of rural activity is moving ahead, as shown in the examples provided in sections 9, 10 and 11 of the *Atlas*. Industrial landscapes, in the sense of landscape associated with manufacturing and extractive industries, are not a major feature of North Yorkshire but there are examples, many in rural areas.

The architectural history of major houses and vernacular buildings in both town and country is covered in outline in the *Atlas*, but here is a very rich harvest still awaiting future historians of landscape and taste: some interesting projects are already underway, including those dealing with garden history, and the prospects for detailed local analyses are evidenced in the two case studies included in section 11.

Section 10, which includes studies of seven smaller towns plus aspects of the history of the city of York, serves both to inform and to indicate opportunities for future research on the urban history of North Yorkshire. Such studies should avail of material not only on the built environment, but also on aspects of social, economic and political life of these urban areas in the nineteenth and twentieth centuries.

The cartographic history of North Yorkshire is discussed in Section 12 through a detailed analysis of five maps from the sixteenth to the nineteenth century. Representations of the county in these maps provide much more than basic geographical information: they symbolize a whole range of topographic and other perceptions, and they epitomise differing scholarly, political and commercial purposes in the production of such maps. There is a great wealth of cartographic information for the county as a whole; more work is needed not just on county maps but also on the larger-scale maps that were produced, for example for estate administration, the enclosure of common land, and the abolition of tithes.

The penultimate section in the *Atlas* (13) deals with important aspects of the twentieth century, including population, economic development, recreation, and conservation. The most recent data provide perspectives on still-prominent aspects of life, such as accessibility, economic and social deprivation, and the effects on the county of European Union development policies.

This points to the future, and a twenty-first century that has already produced a major catastrophe for North Yorkshire in the form of the devastating outbreaks of foot-and-mouth disease. When full and accurate data eventually become available, these could form the basis of an important map in any future edition of this *Atlas*.

Birstwith, Nidderdale.
© R Muir.

Positive aspects of the future, addressed by section 13, include those for enhancing the conservation of the environment and the very attractive historic heritage and landscapes of the county, and the outline of possible development strategies. Many institutions, not least English Heritage, the National Trust, the two national park authorities (Yorkshire Dales and North York Moors), together with the universities and various institutions of further and higher education in or adjacent to North Yorkshire, are already active in this kind of research.

We think that the *Atlas* itself reveals and highlights many hitherto unknown features of North Yorkshire's life and landscapes of the past, and anticipate that it will also help in the re-interpretation of those features which seem more familiar, thereby raising further questions and encouraging more investigation at a range of different levels. It will act we hope, as a useful basis for courses and debates in local and regional history, and to facilitate discussion of significant historical issues at larger geographical scales.

We are confident that it will serve to illustrate the extraordinary variety and richness of the historical heritage of North Yorkshire, and will be used to indicate priorities for fuller understanding and preservation of that heritage in the future.

REFERENCE NOTES

2.2 GEOLOGY

[1] P. R. Rodgers, *Geology of the Yorkshire Dales* (Nelson: Dalesman, 1978).

[2] C. Scrutton (ed.), *Yorkshire Rocks and Landscape* (Maryport: Ellenbank Press, 1994).

[3] P. Kent *et al., British Regional Geology, Eastern England from the Tees to The Wash*, second edition (London: HMSO, 1980).

[4] P.F. Rawson and J.K. Wright, *The Yorkshire Coast,* Geologists Association Guide no. 34 (London: The Geologists Association, 2000).

2.3 GLACIAL HISTORY

[1] The term Dimlington Stadial was proposed by J. Rose in 1985, in his paper: The Dimlington Stadial/Dimlington Chronozone: a proposal for naming the main glacial episode of the Late Devensian in Britain, *Boreas* 14, 225-230.

[2] There is considerable debate about the timing of pre-Devensian glaciations. Cold climatic phases are known to have occurred in oxygen isotope stages 12, 10, 8 and 6, but their expression on the ground in North Yorkshire is not yet clear.

[3] See, for instance, papers by: G.D. Gaunt, G.R. Coope, P.J. Osborne and J.W. Franks: An interglacial deposit near Austerfield, southern Yorkshire. *Institute of Geological Sciences Report* 72/4 (London: HMSO, 1972); G.D. Gaunt, D.D. Bartley and R. Harland, Two interglacial deposits proved in boreholes in the southern part of the Vale of York and their bearing on contemporaneous sea levels. *Bulletin of the Geological Survey of Great Britain* 48 (1974), 1-23.

[4] For a fuller discussion of probable ice-movements, see J.A. Catt, The Quaternary history and glacial deposits of East Yorkshire, in J. Ehlers, P.L. Gibbard and J. Rose (eds), *Glacial Deposits in Britain and Ireland* (Rotterdam: Balkema, 1991), 185-191.

[5] See, for example, W.A. Mitchell, *Western Pennines Field Guide.* (London: Quaternary Research Association, 1991); W.A. Mitchell, Drumlins in ice sheet reconstructions, with reference to the western Pennines, Northern England. *Sedimentary Geology* 91 (1994), 313-331; J. Rose, Landform development around Kisdon, Upper Swaledale, Yorkshire. *Proceedings of the Yorkshire Geological Society* 43 (1980), 201-219; E. Pounder, *Classic landforms of the Northern Dales.* Classic Landform Guides no. 10 (Sheffield: the Geographical Association, 1989).

[6] The age of the Basement Till at Dimlington has been the subject of recent debate, e.g. N. Eyles, A.M. McCabe and D.Q. Bowen, The stratigraphic and sedimentological significance of late-Devensian ice sheet surging in Holderness Yorkshire, UK. *Quaternary Science Reviews* 13 (1994), 727-759. See also D.J.A. Evans, S.A. Thomson and C.D. Clark, The glacial history of East Yorkshire. In M.D. Bateman, P.C. Buckland, C.D. Frederick and N.J. Whitehouse (eds), *The Quaternary of East Yorkshire and North Lincolnshire.* Quaternary Research Association Field Guide, 2001), 1-12.

[7] See G.D. Gaunt, The Devensian maximum ice limit in the Vale of York. *Proceedings of the Yorkshire Geological Society* 40 (4), no. 38 (2001), 631-637.

[8] Much early work on glacial retreat stages in the Dales was carried out by A. Raistrick, Periodicity of the glacial retreat in West Yorkshire, *Proceedings of the Yorkshire Geological Society* 21 (1927), 24-28. More recent summaries include: R.S. Arthurton, E.W. Johnson and D.J.C. Mundy, *Geology of the country around Settle.* Memoir for the 1:50,000 geological sheet 60 (England and Wales), (London: HMSO, 1988); A.H. Cooper and I.C. Burgess, *Geology of the country around Harrogate.* Memoir for 1:50,000 geological sheet 62 (England and Wales). (London: HMSO, 1993).

[9] Of the many classic studies of the glacio-karst of North Yorkshire, the following are noteworthy: K.M. Clayton, Explanatory description of the landforms of the Malham area, *Field Studies* 5 (1981), 389-423; M.M. Sweeting, Erosion cycles and limestone caverns in the Ingleborough district of Yorkshire, *Geographical Journal* 115 (1950), 63-78; A.C. Waltham, M.J. Simms, A.R. Farrant and H.S. Goldie, *Karst and Caves of Great Britain* (London: Chapman and Hall, 1997).

[10] See: A. Baker, P.L. Smart and R. Lawrence Edwards, Mass spectrometric dating of flowstones from Stump Cross Caverns and Lancaster Hole, Yorkshire: palaeoclimatic implications. *Journal of Quaternary Science* 11 (2), (1996), 107-114; M. Gascoyne, D.C. Ford and H.P. Schwarcz, Rates of cave and landform development in the Yorkshire Dales from speleothem age data. *Earth Surface Processes and Landforms* 8 (1983), 557-568; M. Gascoyne, H.P. Schwarcz and D.C. Ford, Uranium-Series ages of speleothem from Northwest England: correlation with Quaternary climate. *Phil. Trans. Royal Society of London* **B301** (1983), 143-164.

[11] A detailed account of Quaternary events in the southern part of the Vale of York is given by G.D. Gaunt, Quaternary history of the southern part of the Vale of York, in J. Neale and J. Flenley (eds), *The Quaternary in Britain* (Oxford: Pergamon, 1981), 82-97.

[12] Shorelines at 70metres and 45metres OD have been proposed: A. Straw, The Devensian glaciation, In A. Straw and K.M. Clayton (eds), *The Geomorphology of the British Isles: Eastern and Central England* (London: Methuen, 1979), 21-45.

[13] In 1902, P.F. Kendall postulated a series of 'glacier-lakes' on the North York Moors, which drained into one another via 'overflow channels': P.F. Kendall, A system of glacier-lakes in the Cleveland Hills, *Quarterly Journal of the Geological Society of London* 58 (1902), 471-571. Later work by K.J. Gregory has largely discredited this hypothesis: K.J. Gregory, Proglacial Lake Eskdale after sixty years, *Transactions of the Institute of British Geographers* 36 (1965), 149-162.

[14] See, for instance: R.L. Jones, Late Quaternary vegetation history of the North York Moors IV. Seamer Carrs. *Journal of Biogeography* 3 (1976), 397-406; R.L. Jones, Late-Devensian deposits from Kildale, north-east Yorkshire. *Proceedings of the Yorkshire Geological Society* 41 (1977), 185-188; R.L. Jones and G.D. Gaunt, A dated late Devensian organic deposit at Cawood, near Selby. *Naturalist* 101 (1976), 121-123; J.R.A. Giles, Late Devensian and early Flandrian environments at Dishforth Bog, North Yorkshire. *Proceedings of the Yorkshire Geological Society* 49 (1992), 1-9; D.D. Bartley, The stratigraphy and pollen analysis of lake deposits near Tadcaster, Yorkshire. *New Phytologist* 61 (1962), 277-287; D.H. Keen, R.L. Jones, R.A. Evans and J.E. Robinson, Faunal and floral assemblages from Bingley Bog, West Yorkshire, and their significance for Late Devensian and early Flandrian environmental changes. Proceedings of the Yorkshire Geological Society 47 (2), (1988), 125-138.

2.4 RIVERS

[1] K.A. Hudson-Edwards, M.G. Macklin and M.P. Taylor, 2000 years of sediment borne heavy metal storage in the Yorkshire Ouse basin, NE England, UK, *Hydrological Processes*, 13 (1999), 1087-1102; S.A. Longfield and M.G. Macklin, The influence of recent environmental change on flooding and sediment fluxes in the Yorkshire Ouse basin, north-east England, *Hydrological Processes*, 13 (1999), 1051-1066; M.G. Macklin, K.A. Hudson-Edwards and E.J. Dawson, The significance of pollution from historic mining in the Pennine orefields on river sediment contaminent fluxes to the North Sea, *Science of the Total Environment,* 194/195 (1997), 391-397; M.G. Macklin, M.P. Taylor, K.A. Hudson-Edwards and A.J. Howard, Holocene environmental change in the Yorkshire Ouse Basin and its influence on river dynamics and sediment fluxes to the coastal zone, in I. Shennan and J.E. Andrews (eds), *Holocene Land-Ocean Interaction and Environmental Change around the North Sea.* (London: Geological Society Special Publications 166, 2000), 87-96; M.P. Taylor, M.G. Macklin and K.A. Hudson Edwards, River sedimentation and fluvial response to Holocene environmental change in the Yorkshire Ouse Basin, northern England, *The Holocene,* 10 (2000), 201-212.

[2] A.J. Howard and M.G. Macklin (eds), *The Quaternary of the Eastern Yorkshire Dales. Field Guide* (London: Quaternary Research Association, 1998); A.J. Howard, D.H. Keen, T.M. Mighall, M.H. Field, G.R. Coope, H.I. Griffiths and M.G. Macklin, Early Holocene environments of the River Ure near Ripon, North Yorkshire, UK, *Proceedings of the Yorkshire Geological Society,* 53 (2000), 31-42. A.J. Howard, M.G. Macklin, S. Black and K.A. Hudson-Edwards, Holocene river development and environmental change in Upper Wharfedale, Yorkshire Dales, England, *Journal of Quaternary Science,* 15 (2000), 239-252.

[3] See A.J. Howard, M.G. Macklin *et al., op. cit.*; M.G. Macklin, M.P. Taylor *et al., op. cit.*; M.P. Taylor *et al., op. cit.*

[4] See M.G. Macklin, M.P. Taylor *et al., op. cit.*; M.P. Taylor *et al., op. cit.*

[5] See A.J. Howard, M.G. Macklin *et al.*, *op. cit.*; M.G. Macklin, M.P. Taylor *et al.*, *op. cit.*

[6] See M.G. Macklin, M.P. Taylor *et al.*, *op. cit.*; S.P. Merrett and M.G. Macklin, Historic river response to extreme flooding in the Yorkshire Dales, Northern England, in A.G. Brown and T.M. Quine (eds), *Fluvial Processes and Environmental Change* (Chichester: Wiley, 1999), 345-360. Note: radiocarbon dates which have been calibrated are quoted in years cal. BC or AD. Uncalibrated dates are quoted in radiocarbon years BP (before present).

[7] K.A. Hudson-Edwards, M.G. Macklin, R. Finlayson and D.G. Passmore, Medieval lead pollution in the River Ouse at York, England, *Journal of Archaeological Science*, **26** (1999), 809-19; M.G. Macklin, K.A. Hudson-Edwards and E.J. Dawson, *op. cit.*

[8] K.A. Hudson-Edwards, M.G. Macklin and M.P. Taylor., *op. cit.*

[9] S.P. Merrett and M.G. Macklin, *op. cit.*; S.A. Longfield and M.G. Macklin, *op. cit.*

[10] S.A. Longfield and M.G. Macklin, *op. cit.*

2.5 THE COAST

[1] R. Agar, Post glacial erosion of the North Yorkshire coast from the Tees Estuary to Ravenscar, *Proceedings of the Yorkshire Geological Society*, **32** (1960), 409-428.

[2] E.M. Lee, Coastal Planning and Management: the impact of the 1993 Holbeck Hall landslide, Scarborough, *East Midlands Geographer*, **21** (1999), 78-91.

[3] J. Schofield, *An historical and descriptive guide to Scarbrough and its environs* (York: W. Blanchard, 1787); E.M. Lee, A.R. Clark and S. Guest, An assessment of coastal landslide risk, Scarborough, UK, in D. Moore and O. Hungr (eds), *Engineering Geology: the View from the Pacific Rim* (1998), 1787-1794; E.M. Lee and A.R. Clark, The use of archive records in landslide risk assessment: historical landslide events on the Scarborough coast, UK, in E.N. Bromhead, N. Dixon and M.-L. Ibsen (eds), *Landslides: In Research, Theory and Practice* (London: Thomas Telford, 2000), 904-910.

[4] E.M. Lee and A.R. Clark, *op cit.*

[5] Revd. G. Young and J. Bird, A geological survey of the Yorkshire coast (Whitby: 1822).

[6] Hinderwell, quoted in Labistour, 1996.

[7] *The Gazeteer and New Daily Advertiser*, January 5th, 1788.

[8] D.K.C. Jones and E.M. Lee, *Landsliding in Great Britain* (London: HMSO, 1994); E.M. Lee and A.R. Clark, *op cit.*

2.6 THE CLIMATE

[1] D.R. Hindley, Importance of low sea-surface temperatures in inhibiting convection along the North Sea coast in summer, *Meteorological Magazine*, **101** (1972), 155-156.

[2] N. Pepin, D. Benham and K. Taylor, Modeling lapse rates in the maritime uplands of Northern England: implications for climate change, *Arctic, Antarctic and Alpine Research*, **31** (1999), 151-164.

[3] G. Manley, The climate at Malham Tarn, *Annual Report of the Council for the Promotion of Field Studies* (1955-56), 43-56.

[4] G. Manley, Temperature records on Fountains Fell, *Field Studies*, 5 (1979), 85-92.

[5] G.K. Chuan and J.G. Lockwood, Assessment of topographical controls on the distribution of rainfall in the central Pennines, *Meteorological Magazine*, **103** (1974), 275-287.

[6] D. Wheeler, North-east England and Yorkshire, in D. Wheeler and J. Mayes (eds), *Regional Climates of the British Isles* (London: Routledge, 1997), 158-80.

[7] N. Pepin *et al.*, *op. cit.*

2.7 CLIMATE CHANGE

[1] R.C. Chiverrell, A proxy record of late Holocene climate change from May Moss, Northeast England, *Journal of Quaternary Science*, **16** (2001), 9-29; J.J. Blackford and F.M. Chambers, Harold's Bog, East Bilsdale Moor, in D.R. Bridgland, B.P. Horton and J.B. Innes (eds), *Quaternary of Northeast England. Field Guide.* (Quaternary Research Association, 1999), 91-98.

[2] B. Smith, 'A palaeoecological study of raised mires in the Humberhead Levels' (Unpublished Ph.D. thesis, University of Wales, Cardiff, 1985).

[3] K.E. Barber, F.M. Chambers, D. Maddy, R. Stoneman and J.S. Brew, A sensitive high-resolution record of late Holocene climatic change from a raised bog in northern England. *The Holocene* 4 (1994), 198-205.

[4] M.A. Atherden, The vegetation History of Yorkshire: A Bog-Trotter's Guide to God's Own County, *Naturalist*, **124** (1999), 137-156; I.G. Simmons, M.A. Atherden, E.W. Cloutman, P.R. Cundill, J.B. Innes and R.L. Jones, Prehistoric Environments, in D.A. Spratt (ed.), *Prehistoric and Roman Archaeology of North-East Yorkshire.* CBA Research Report 87, revised edition (London: Council for British Archaeology, 1993).

[5] K.E. Barber, D. Maddy, N. Rose, A.C. Stevenson, R.E. Stoneman and R. Thompson, Replicated proxy-climate signals over the last 2000 years from two distant peat bogs: new evidence for regional palaeoclimate teleconnections. *Quaternary Science Reviews*, **19** (2000), 481-488.

[6] I.G. Simmons *et al.*, *op. cit.*

[7] M.E. Pigott and C.D. Pigott, Late-glacial and post-glacial deposits at Malham, Yorkshire, *New Phytologist*, **62** (1963), 317-334.

[8] J. Turner, V.P. Hewetson, F.A. Hibbert, K.H. Lowry and C. Chambers, The history of the vegetation and flora of Widdybank Fell and the Cow Green reservoir basin, Upper Teesdale, *Philosophical Transactions of the Royal Society of London, Series B*, **265** (1973), 327-408.

[9] R.C. Chiverrell, *op. cit.*

[10] This climate database was compiled in 1997 and is held at the PLACE Research Centre in York. It contains information gleaned from a wide range of historical and meteorological sources. For reasons of space these sources are not referenced here. The interested reader is directed to the database for more specific material.

[11] R.C. Chiverrell, 'Moorland vegetation change and climate change on the North York Moors during the last 2000 years' (Unpublished PhD thesis, University of Leeds, 1998); R.C. Chiverrell and M.A. Atherden, 'Climate Change and human impact — evidence from peat stratigraphy at sites in the eastern North York Moors', in D.R. Bridgland, B.P. Horton and J.B. Innes (eds), *op. cit.*, 113-130. M.A. Atherden, *op. cit.*; R.C. Chiverrell and M.A. Atherden, 'Post Iron Age vegetation history and climate change on the North York Moors: a preliminary report' in T.P. O'Connor and R.A. Nicholson (eds), *People as an agent of environmental change*. Symposia of the Association for Environmental Archaeology No.16 (Sheffield: Oxbow Books, 2000), 45-59; R.C. Chiverrell, *op. cit.*

[12] R.C. Chiverrell, *op. cit.*

[13] H.H. Lamb, *Climate, Past, Present and Future.* 2 vols. (London: Methuen, 1972, 1977).

[14] R.C. Chiverrell, *op. cit.*

2.8 VEGETATION HISTORY

[1] For a review of work in this field, see: M.A. Atherden, The vegetation History of Yorkshire: A Bog-Trotter's Guide to God's Own County, *Naturalist*, **124** (1999), 137-156.

[2] One such area lies just outside the county boundary, at Upper Teesdale, where numerous studies of vegetation history have been carried out. Many of them are summarised in: J. Turner, V.P. Hewetson, F.A. Hibbert, K.H. Lowry and C. Chambers, The history of the vegetation and flora of Widdybank Fell and the Cow Green reservoir basin, Upper Teesdale, *Philosophical Transactions of the Royal Society of London, Series B*, **265** (1973), 327-408.

[3] See, for example: I.G. Simmons and J.B. Innes, Prehistoric charcoal in peat profiles at North Gill, North Yorkshire Moors, England, *Journal of Archaeological Science*, **23** (1996), 193-197.

[4] G.W. Dimbleby, The Development of British Heathlands and their Soils (Oxford: Oxford Forest Memoirs no. 23, 1962).

[5] O. Rackham, *The History of the Countryside* (London: Dent, 1956).

2.9 SOILS

[1] The soils of parts of North Yorkshire have been mapped at detailed scales by soil surveyors. Areas which have not been surveyed have been examined by making observations of soil pits. Thus some parts of the county are known in great detail, with good accuracy; other parts are known only in a reconnaissance way. There is a very useful map in R.A. Jarvis, J.W. Alison, V.C. Bedelow, R.I. Bradley, D.M. Carroll, R.R. Furness, I.N.L. Kilgour and S.J. King, *Soils and their use in Northern England* (Harpenden: Soil Survey of England and Wales, 1984), which shows the areal extent of published soil surveys.

3.2 THE UPPER PALAEOLITHIC AND EARLIER MESOLITHIC

[1] I.G. Simmons, The history of the early human environment, in B.E. Vyner (ed.), *Moorland Monuments: studies in the archaeology of north-east Yorkshire, in honour of Raymond Hayes and Don Spratt* (York: CBA Research Report, 1995), 101, 7-10; D.A Spratt (ed.), *Prehistoric and Roman Archaeology of North East Yorkshire*, CBA Research Report (London: Council for British Archaeology, 1993), 87, 51-52; R. White 1997 *Yorkshire Dales: Landscapes Through Time* (London: Batsford/English Heritage, 1997); C. Smith, *Late Stone Age Hunters of the British Isles* (London: Routledge, 1992), 77-109.

[2] I.G. Simmons, *The Environmental Impact of Later Mesolithic Cultures* (Edinburgh: Edinburgh University Press, 1996), 8-27; I.G. Simmons, Prehistoric environments, in D.A. Spratt (ed.), *Prehistoric and Roman Archaeology of*

North East Yorkshire, CBA Research Report (London: Council for British Archaeology, 1993), 87, 17-33.

[3] J.G.D. Clark, *Excavations at Star Carr: an early Mesolithic site at Seamer near Scarborough, Yorkshire* (Cambridge: Cambridge University Press, 1954); T. Schadla-Hall, The early post-glacial in eastern Yorkshire, in T.G. Manby (ed.), *Archaeology in Eastern Yorkshire: essays in honour of T.C.M. Brewster* (Sheffield: Department of Archaeology and Prehistory, 1988), 25-34.

[4] A.J. Legge and P.A. Rowley-Conwy, *Star Carr Re-visited: a Re-analysis of the Large Mammals* (London: Birkbeck College, Centre for Extra-Mural Studies, 1998).

[5] D.A. Spratt (ed.), *Prehistoric and Roman Archaeology of North East Yorkshire*, CBA Research report (London: Council for British Archaeology, 1993), 87, 56-62.

3.3 THE LATER MESOLITHIC

[1] F. Elgee, *Early Man in North-East Yorkshire* (Gloucester, 1930).

[2] R.H. Hayes, *North-East Yorkshire Studies: Archaeological Papers* (Yorkshire Archaeological Society, 1988), 1-27.

[3] G.W. Dimbleby, The ancient forest of Blackamore, *Antiquity* 35 (1976), 123-8.

[4] D.A. Spratt and I.G. Simmons, Prehistoric activity and environment on the North York Moors, *Jnl Archaeol Sci*, 3 (1976), 193-210.

[5] I. Shennan, K. Lambeck, R. Flather, B. Horton, J. McArthur, J. Innes, J. Lloyd, M. Rutherford and R. Wingfield, Modelling western North Sea palaeogeographies and tidal changes during the Holocene, in I. Shennan and J. Andrews (eds), *Holocene Land-Ocean Interactions and Environmental Change around the North Sea* (London: The Geological Society, Special Publications 166, 2000), 299-319.

[6] I.G. Simmons, *The Environmental Impact of Later Mesolithic Cultures* (Edinburgh: Edinburgh University Press, 1996).

[7] Shennan *et al.*, *op. cit.*

3.4 THE NEOLITHIC

[1] I.G. Simmons, M. Atherden, E.W. Cloutman, P.R. Cundill, J.B. Innes and R.L. Jones, Prehistoric environments, in D.A. Spratt (ed.), *Prehistoric and Roman Archaeology of North-East Yorkshire* (London: CBA Research Report 87, 1993), 15-50.

[2] T. Darvill, Neolithic houses in England, Wales and the Isle of Man, in T. Darvill, and J. Thomas (eds), *Neolithic Houses in Northwest Europe and beyond* (Oxford: Oxbow, 1996), 77-111; T.G. Manby, Neolithic occupation sites on the Yorkshire Wolds, *Yorks. Archaeol Jnl.* 27 (1975), 23-60; T.G. Manby, 1974. *Grooved Ware Sites in the North of England* (Oxford: British Archaeological Reports 9, 1975); T.G. Manby, Grooved Ware sites in Yorkshire and northern England: 1974-1994, in R. Cleal and A. MacSween (eds), *Grooved Ware in Britain and Ireland*, Neolithic Studies Group Seminar Papers, 3 (Oxford: Oxbow, 1999), 57-75.

[3] P. Ashbee, *The Earthen Long Barrow in Britain* (London: Dent 1970); T.G. Manby, Long barrows of northern England: structural and dating evidence, *Scottish Archaeological Forum* 2 (1970), 1-28; B.E. Vyner, The excavation of a Neolithic cairn at Street House, Loftus, Cleveland, *Proc. Prehist. Soc.* 50 (1984), 151-95.

[4] T.G. Manby, 1988. The Neolithic in eastern Yorkshire, in T.G. Manby (ed.), *Archaeology in Eastern Yorkshire. Essays in Honour of T.C.M. Brewster FSA* (Sheffield: Department of Archaeology and Prehistory, University of Sheffield, 1988), 35-88; I. Kinnes, T. Schadla-Hall, P. Chadwick and P. Dean, Duggleby Howe reconsidered, *Archaeol. J.* 140 (1983), 83-108; T.C.M. Brewster, *The Excavation of Whitegrounds Barrow, Burythorpe* (Malton: East Riding Archaeological Research Committee, 1984).

[5] A.F. Harding, with G.E. Lee, *Henge Monuments and Related Sites of Great Britain. Air Photographic Evidence and Catalogue* (Oxford: British Archaeological Reports 175, 1987).

[6] A. Burl, The Devil's Arrows, Boroughbridge, North Yorkshire: the archaeology of a stone row, *Yorks Archaeol. Journ.* 63 (1991), 1-24.

[7] D.P. Dymond, Ritual monuments at Rudston, East Yorkshire, *Proc. Prehist. Soc.* 32 (1966), 86-95; D.N. Riley, Air survey of Neolithic sites on the Yorkshire Wolds, in T.G. Manby (ed.), *Archaeology in Eastern Yorkshire. Essays in Honour of T.C.M. Brewster FSA* (Sheffield: Department of Archaeology and Prehistory, University of Sheffield, 1988), 89-93.

3.5 THE BRONZE AGE

[1] G.W. Dimbleby, The Ancient Forest of Blackamore, *Antiquity* 35 (1976), 123-28; Smith, M.J.B., *Excavated Bronze Age Burial Mounds of Northeast Yorkshire* (Durham: Archit. & Archaeol. Soc. Durham & Northumb. Res. Rep., 3, 1961).

[2] C. Stoertz, *Ancient Landscapes of the Yorkshire Wolds* (London: RCHM England, 1997); D.A. Spratt (ed.), 1993. *Prehistoric and Roman Archaeology of*

North-East Yorkshire (London: CBA Research Rep. 87, 1993); T.G. Manby, Bronze Age Settlement in Eastern Yorkshire, in Barrett. J., & Bradley, R. (eds), *Settlement and Society in the British Later Bronze Age* (Oxford: British Archaeol. Rep., 83, 1980), 307-70.

[3] F. Elgee, *Early Man in North-east Yorkshire* (Gloucester, 1930); T.G. Manby, A. King, and B.E. Vyner, The Neolithic and Bronze Ages: a time of early agriculture, in P. Ottaway, T.G. Manby, and S. Moorhouse (eds), *The Archaeology of Yorkshire: an Assessment at the end of the Twentieth Century* (forthcoming).

[4] D. Coggins and K.L. Fairless, 1984. The Bronze Age Settlement of Bracken Rigg, Upper Teesdale, Co. Durham, *Durham Archaeol. Jnl.*, 1 (1984), 5-21; T. Laurie, T., 2001. Researching the prehistory of Wensleydale, Swaledale and Teesdale, in P. Ottaway *et al.* (forthcoming); T.G. Manby, The Bronze Age in Western Yorkshire, in T.G. Manby & P. Turnbull (eds), *Archaeology in the Pennines: Studies in Honour of Arthur Raistrick,* British Archaeol. Rep., 158 (Oxford: Oxbow, 1986), 55-126; Manby, 1980, *op. cit.*

[5] R. van de Noor and S. Ellis, 1999. *Wetland Heritage of the Vale of York: an Archaeological Survey* (Hull: University of Hull, 1999); E.V. Wright, *The Ferriby Boats: Seacraft of the Bronze Age* (London, 1990).

[6] I.M. Stead, An Iron Age hill-fort at Grimthorpe, Yorkshire, *Proc. Prehist. Soc.*, 34 (1968), 148-90; J. Radley, The prehistory of the Vale of York, *Yorks. Archaeol. J.*, 3 46 (1974), 10-22.

[7] T.C.M. Brewster, *The Excavation of Staple Howe* (Scarborough, 1963).

3.6 THE IRON AGE

[1] T.C.M. Brewster, *The Excavation of Staple Howe* (Scarborough, 1963); B.E. Vyner, The hillfort at Eston Nab, Eston, Cleveland, *Archaeol. Jnl.*, 145 (1988), 60-98; I.G. Simmons *et al.*, Prehistoric environments, in D.A. Spratt (ed.), *Prehistoric and Roman Archaeology of North East Yorkshire* (London: CBA Research report, 87, 1993), 43-44.

[2] C. Haselgrove, The later pre-Roman Iron Age between the Humber and the Tyne, in P.R. Wilson, R.F.J. Jones and D.M. Evans (eds), *Settlement and Society in the Roman North* (Bradford, 1984), 9-25; D.A. Spratt (ed.), *Prehistoric and Roman Archaeology of North East Yorkshire* (London: CBA Research Report, 87, 1993), 142-44; L. Still and B.E. Vyner, Air photographic evidence for later prehistoric settlement in the Tees Valley, *Durham Archaeol. Journ.*, 2 (1986), 11-23.

[3] L. Still *et al.*, A decade of air survey in Cleveland and the Tees Valley, *Durham Archaeol. Journal*, 5 (1989), 1-10.

[4] D.A. Spratt, The Cleave Dyke system, *Yorks. Archaeol. Journ.*, 54 (1982), 33-52; D.A. Spratt, *Linear Earthworks of the Tabular Hills* (Sheffield, 1989).

[5] H.G. Ramm, *The Parisi* (London: Duckworth, 1978); G.J. Wainwright and I.H. Longworth, The excavation of a group of round barrows on Ampleforth Moor, Yorkshire, *Yorks. Archaeol. Journ.*, 42 (1968), 283-94; B Hartley and L. Fitts, *The Brigantes* (Gloucester: Sutton, 1988).

4.1 ROMAN

[1] R.E.M. Wheeler, *The Stanwick Fortifications* (Oxford: Society of Antiquaries of London Research Report 17 (1954); C.C. Haselgrove *et al* Stanwick North Yorkshire Parts 1-3, *Archaeological Journal*, 147 (1990), 1-90.

[2] M. McCarthy, *Carlisle. History and Guide* (Stroud: Sutton, 1993), 3.

[3] D.C.A. Shotter, The Roman Conquest of the North-West, *Transactions of the Cumberland and Westmorland Antiquarian and Archaeological Society*, 100, 40 and 44 (figure 3).

[4] M.C. Bishop, A New Flavian Military Site at Roecliffe, North Yorkshire, *Britannia* (forthcoming).

[5] It is conventional to number Roman roads after the system devised by I.D. Margary in *Roman Roads in Britain*, 3rd edn (London: Baker, 1973), and it is his numbering that is used here.

[6] C. Moloney, Catterick Race Course, *Current Archaeology*, 148 (1996), 128-130.

[7] D. MacLeod, Cropmarks in the A1 Corridor between Catterick and Brompton-on-Swale, in P.R. Wilson, *Cataractonium: Roman Catterick and its hinterland. Excavations and research 1958-1997* (Council for British Archaeology Research Report 128, Part 1, 136-45 (2002)).

[8] R.G. Collingwood and R.P. Wright *The Roman Inscriptions of Britain Vol II Instrumentum Domesticum* Fascicule 1 (S.S. Frere, M. Roxan and R.S.O. Tomlin (eds), (Gloucester: Sutton, 1990), nos 2404.61-2404.64.

[9] A.L.F. Rivet and C. Smith, *The Placenames of Roman Britain* (London: Batsford, 1979).

[10] J. Creighton, The Place Names of East Yorkshire in the Roman Period, in J. Price and P.R. Wilson (eds), *Recent Research in Roman Yorkshire. Studies in Honour of Mary Kitson Clark* (Oxford: British Archaeological Reports, British Series 193, 1988), 387-406.

[11] T.C.M. Brewster, Excavations at Newham's Pit, Staxton, 1947-48, *Yorkshire Archaeological Journal*, 39 (1957), 193-223.

12 D.W. Harding, *Holme House, Piercebridge: Excavations 1969-70. A Summary Report* (Edinburgh: University of Edinburgh Department of Archaeology Project Paper 2, 1984).

13 M. Stephens, A Roman Site at Crab Lane, Crossgates, North Yorkshire, *Yorkshire Archaeological Society, Roman Antiquities Section Bulletin*, **17** (2000), 11-14.

14 P. Corder and J.L. Kirk, A Roman Villa at Langton, near Malton, East Yorkshire (Leeds: Roman Antiquities Committee, Yorkshire Archaeological Society, Roman Malton and District Report 4, 1932).

15 J. Evans, Later Iron Age and 'Native' pottery in the North-East, in B.E. Vyner (ed.), *Moorland Monuments. Studies in the archaeology of North-East Yorkshire in honour of Raymond Hayes and Don Spratt* (York: Council for British Archaeology Research Report **101**, 1995), 46-68.

16 See various examples from Brigantia in M. MacGregor, *Early Celtic Art in North Britain* (Leicester: Leicester University Press, 1976).

17 M. Henig, *The Art of Roman Britain* (London: Batsford, 1995).

18 R.H. Hayes, J.E. Hemingway, and D.A. Spratt, The Distribution and Litholity of Beehive Querns in Northeast Yorkshire, *Journal of Archaeological Science*, 7 (1980), 297-324; D. Heslop, *The North Yorkshire Beehive Quern Survey* (Yorkshire Archaeological Society Occasional Paper, forthcoming).

19 R. Inman, D.R. Brown, R.E. Goddard, and D.A. Spratt, Roxby Iron Age Settlement and the Iron Age in North-East Yorkshire, *Proceedings of the Prehistoric Society*, **51** (1985), 181-213.

20 R.H. Hayes, *Levisham Moor Archaeological Investigations. 1957-78* (Helmsley and Scarborough: North Yorkshire Moors National Park and Scarborough District Archaeological Society, 1983).

21 B.R. Hartley and R.L. Fitts, *The Brigantes* (Gloucester: Sutton, 1988), 69-70.

22 T.P. O'Connor, *Bones from the General Accident Site, Tanner Row* (London: Council for British Archaeology, The Archaeology of York: The Animal Bones 15/1, 1988), 117.

23 P.R. Wilson, *Cataractonium: Roman Catterick: A Roman town and its hinterland. Excavations and research 1958-1997* (Council for British Archaeology Research Report, 128 and 129, Parts 1 and 2 (2002).

24 P.R. Wilson, Aspects of the Yorkshire Signal Stations, in V.A. Maxfield and M.J. Dobson (eds), *Roman Frontier Studies 1989. Proceedings of the XVth International Congress of Roman Frontier Studies* (Exeter: University of Exeter Press, 1991), 142-147. See P. Ottaway, Excavations on the site of the Roman signal station at Carr Naze, Filey, 1993-4, *Archaeological Journal* (forthcoming), for a discussion of the case for the traditional view.

25 H.G. Ramm, Aspects of the Roman Countryside in East Yorkshire, in J. Price and P.R. Wilson (eds), *Recent Research in Roman Yorkshire. Studies in Honour of Mary Kitson Clark* (Oxford: British Archaeological Report, British Series 193, 1988), 81-88.

26 D.S. Neal, *Excavations on the Roman villa at Beadlam, Yorkshire* (Leeds: Yorkshire Archaeological Society, Yorkshire Archaeological Report **2**, 1996).

27 P. Rahtz, From Roman to Saxon at Wharram Percy, J. Price and P.R. Wilson (eds), *Recent Research in Roman Yorkshire. Studies in Honour of Mary Kitson Clark* (Oxford: British Archaeological Report, British Series **193**, 1988), 123-137.

28 E.J.W. Hildyard, A Roman and Saxon Site at Catterick, *Yorkshire Archaeological Journal* 38 (1955), 241-455; R.J. Cramp, Excavations at Catterick RAF Camp, in P.R. Wilson *Cataractonium: Roman Catterick: A Roman town and its hinterland. Excavations and research 1958-1997* (Council for British Archaeology Research Report, 2002). RAF Catterick is now known as Marne Barracks.

29 P. Rahtz and J. Bateman, Wharram Le Street Roman Villa 1978-1980, in P. Rahtz, C. Hayfield and J. Bateman, *Two Roman Villas at Wharram Le Street.* (York: York University Archaeological Publications **2**, 1986), 1-13.

30 R. Gilyard-Beer, *The Romano-British Baths at Well* (Leeds: Yorkshire Roman Antiquities Committee Research Report 1, 1951).

31 D. Powlesland and C. Haughton, *West Heslerton — the Anglian Settlement* (monograph in preparation).

32 See for example H.E.M. Cool, The parts left-over, in T. Wilmott and P. Wilson (eds), *The Late Roman Transition in the North* (Oxford: British Archaeological Reports, British Series **299**, 2000), 47-65.

33 For examples at Catterick see P.R. Wilson, P. Cardwell, R.J. Cramp, J. Evans, A. Thompson, R. Taylor-Wilson and J.S. Wacher, Early Anglo-Saxon Catterick and *Catraeth, Medieval Archaeology* 40 (1996), 29-50.

34 W. Hornsby, and S.D. Laverick, The Roman Signal Station at Goldsborough, near Whitby, *Archaeological Journal* 89 (1932), 202-219.

35 For a consideration of post-Roman Craven and a summary discussion of Elmet and Loidis with references see P.N. Wood, On the Little British Kingdom of Craven, *Northern History* 32 (1996), 1-20.

36 For a recent review of the archaeology of the Roman fortress and Roman York as a whole see P. Ottaway, *Roman York* (London: Batsford/English Heritage, 1993).

37 D. Phillips and B. Heywood, *Excavations at York Minster, volume 1: From Roman Fortress to Norman Cathedral* (HMSO: London, 1995).

38 See for example R.A. Hall, *Excavations in the Praetentura: 9 Blake Street* (York: Council for British Archaeology, The Archaeology of York: The Legionary Fortress 3/4, 1997)

39 For a recent discussion of the fortress defences see P. Ottaway, *Excavations and Observations on the Defences and Adjacent Sites 1971-90* (York: Council for British Archaeology, The Archaeology of York: The Legionary Fortress 3/3, 1996).

40 R.A. Hall, Roman warehouses and other riverside structures in Coney Street, in D. Brinklow, R. Hall, J. Magilton, and S. Donaghey, *Coney Street, Aldwark and Clementhorpe, Minor Sites and Roman Roads* (London: Council for British Archaeology, The Archaeology of York: Roman Extra-mural Settlement and Roads 6/1, 1986), 5-20.

41 Royal Commission on Historical Monuments (England), *An Inventory of the Historical Monuments in the City of York. 1:* Eburacum, *Roman York* (London: HMSO, 1962), 1-3; D. Brinklow, Main roads serving Roman York, in D. Brinklow, R. Hall, J. Magilton, and S. Donaghey, *Coney Street, Aldwark and Clementhorpe, Minor Sites and Roman Roads* (London: Council for British Archaeology, The Archaeology of York: Roman Extra-mural Settlement and Roads 6/1, 1986), 84-101.

42 For a recent review of the civilian settlements see P. Ottaway *Roman York* (London: Batsford/English Heritage,1993), and P. Ottaway, York: the study of a late Roman colonia, in H. Hurst (ed.), *The Coloniae of Roman Britain: New Studies and a Review*, Journal of Roman Archaeology, Supplementary Series 36 (1999), 136-151.

43 Royal Commission on Historical Monuments (England), *An Inventory of the Historical Monuments in the City of York. 1: Eburacum, Roman York* (London: HMSO, 1962), 119.

44 Royal Commission on Historical Monuments (England), *An Inventory of the Historical Monuments in the City of York. 1: Eburacum, Roman York* (London: HMSO, 1962), 54-57.

45 M. Carver, S. Donaghey, and A. Sumpter, *Riverside Structures and a Well in Skeldergate and Buildings in Bishophill* (London: Council for British Archaeology, The Archaeology of York: The Colonia 4/1, 1978).

46 Royal Commission on Historical Monuments (England), *An Inventory of the Historical Monuments in the City of York. 1: Eburacum, Roman York* (London: HMSO, 1962), 49.

47 D.W. Rollason, *Sources for York History to AD 1100*, The Archaeology of York 1 (York, Council for British Archaeology, The Archaeology of York: Sources for York History to AD 1100 1, 1998), 44.

48 P. Ottaway, *Excavations and Observations on the Defences and Adjacent Sites 1971-90* (York: Council for British Archaeology, The Archaeology of York: The Legionary Fortress 3/3, 1996), 287.

49 Royal Commission on Historical Monuments (England), *An Inventory of the Historical Monuments in the City of York. 1: Eburacum, Roman York* (London: HMSO, 1962), 53, 57; D. Brinklow, and S. Donaghey, A Roman building in Clementhorpe, in D. Brinklow, R. Hall, J. Magilton, and S. Donaghey, *Coney Street, Aldwark and Clementhorpe, Minor Sites and Roman Roads* (London: Council for British Archaeology, The Archaeology of York: Roman Extra-mural Settlement and Roads 6/1, 1986), 54-73; J. Magilton, A Roman building and Roman roads in Aldwark, in D. Brinklow *et al.* (1986), *op cit*, 32-47.

50 I.M. Stead, An Anglian cemetery on The Mount, York, *Yorkshire Archaeological Journal*, **39** (1958), 427-35; D. Tweddle, J. Moulden and E. Logan, *Anglian York: a Survey of the Evidence* (York: Council for British Archaeology, The Archaeology of York: Anglian York 7/2, 1999), 167-72.

51 For a summary of aerial reconnaissance up to 1982 see P. Chadwick and R. White, Aerial Photography in North Yorkshire, *Aerial Archaeology,* **12** (1991), 25-35. English Heritage currently fly anything up to twenty or thirty hours of reconnaissance over North Yorkshire each year, photographs are made available at the National Monuments Record (see below). Other archaeologists such as Robert White in the Yorkshire Dales National Park and Blaise Vyner over the North York Moors also continue to make a significant contribution.

52 The data is taken from the databases held by the National Monuments Record and shows all records of sites given a possible or likely Roman date and having remains visible either as cropmarks/soilmarks or earthworks. All records are marked on this map by a single point but many refer to extensive settlements and field systems often covering many hectares. Within the NMP project areas this information has been mapped to show the actual form of the remains, for other areas the records are usually only

of text form. Data and maps can be obtained from the National Monuments Record Centre, Kemble Drive, Swindon, SN2 2GZ.

[53] See C. Stoertz, *Ancient Landscapes of the Yorkshire Wolds* (London: RCHME, 1997).

[54] The brickwork field systems in South Yorkshire were surveyed from the air by Derrick Riley — D.N. Riley, *Early Landscape from the Air* (Sheffield: Department of Prehistory and Archaeology, University of Sheffield, 1980). Work by Tim Laurie and Andrew Fleming used field survey and limited excavation to explore some extensive field systems on the slopes and higher ground in Swaledale around Reeth — A. Fleming, *Swaledale valley of the Wild River* (Edinburgh: Edinburgh University Press, 1998).

[55] For the Roman villa at Whin Fields, Langton see the figures (29, 31, 32 and 35), in H. Ramm, *The Parisi* (London: Duckworth, 1978).

[56] R.F.J. Jones, The Hinterland of Roman York, in J. Price and P.R. Wilson (eds), *Recent Research in Roman Yorkshire* (Oxford: British Archaeological Reports, British Series 193, 1988), and R.F.J. Jones, *pers comm*.

[57] See C. Stoertz, *Ancient Landscapes of the Yorkshire Wolds* (London: RCHME, 1997), figure 26.

[58] Plans of the Wharram Grange and Settrington sites and some similar ones can be found in C. Stoertz, *Ancient Landscapes of the Yorkshire Wolds* (London: RCHME, 1997), figure 28. For Lilling Green see V.G. Swan, B.E.A. Jones, and D. Grady, Bolesford, North Riding of Yorkshire: a lost wapentake centre and its landscape, *Landscape History*, 15 (1993), 13-25.

[59] A. Kershaw, *Roman enclosure complex, Burythorpe, North Yorkshire. Air Photographic Transcription and Analysis* (unpublished report RCHME, 1994 — National Monuments Record HOB UID 1065923).

[60] See C. Stoertz, *Ancient Landscapes of the Yorkshire Wolds* (London: RCHME, 1997), and in particular the series of published maps.

[61] For a summary of the NMP project see P. Horne and D. MacLeod, The RCHME Yorkshire Dales Mapping Project in R. White and P.R. Wilson (eds), *Archaeology and Historic Landscapes in the Yorkshire Dales* (Yorkshire Archaeological Society Occasional Paper, forthcoming). All NMP maps are available through the National Monuments Record. A good summary of the evidence and further can be found in R. White, *Yorkshire Dales. Landscape through time* (London: Batsford/English Heritage, 1997).

[62] See A. Fleming, *Swaledale valley of the Wild River* (Edinburgh: Edinburgh University Press, 1998).

[63] K. Maude The Very Edge: Reappraising Romano-British Settlement in the Central Pennines; the Littondale Experience, in M. Nevell (ed.), *Living on the Edge of Empire: Models, Methodology and Marginality. Late-Prehistoric and Romano-British Rural Settlement in North-West England*, Archaeology North West Volume 3 (Issue 13 for 1998), 42-46.

[64] The mapping of air photo evidence for the Vale of York is currently underway by English Heritage.

[65] Evidence for intensive specialized sheep farming has been shown for an earlier period in the Fens by looking at the details of the field systems, the need for droveways, handling pens, and the subdivision of the landscape for pasture management. F. Pryor, Sheep, Stockyards and Field Systems: Bronze Age Livestock Populations in the Fenlands of Eastern England, *Antiquity*, 70 (1996), 313-324.

5. EARLY MEDIEVAL

[1] A detailed assessment of the evidence from Heslerton can be found on the Internet in D.J. Powlesland, West Heslerton — The Anglian Settlement: Assessment of Potential for Analysis and Updated Project Design, *Internet Archaeology* 5 (1998), (http://intarch.ac.uk/journal/issue5/westhes toc. html).

[2] E.T. Leeds, *Early Anglo-Saxon Art and Archaeology* (Oxford: Oxford University Press, 1936).

[3] P.R. Wilson, P. Cardwell, R.J. Cramp, J.Evans, R.H. Taylor-Wilson, A. Thompson, and J.S. Wacher, Early Anglian Catterick and *Catraeth*, *Medieval Archaeology*, 40, 29-50.

[4] Northern Archaeological Associates, Hollow Banks, Scorton, *Forum 2000, The Annual Newsletter of CBA Yorkshire* (2000), 8-11.

[5] I.M. Stead, An Anglian Cemetery on the Mount, York, *Yorkshire Archaeological Journal*, 39, 427-435; D. Tweddle, J. Moulden and E. Logan, *Anglian York: a Survey of the Evidence* (York: Council for British Archaeology, The Archaeology of York: Anglian York 7/2, 1999), 167-172.

[6] B.N. Eagles, *The Anglo-Saxon Settlement of Humberside* (Oxford: British Archaeological Reports, British Series, 68, 1979), 66-67, 200. Norton produced a Bugelknopffibeln Series 1 brooch in the nineteenth century (North Yorkshire County Sites and Monuments Record 0186239000).

[7] Although the excavation report covering the Early Anglo-Saxon or Anglian cemetery at West Heslerton has already been published (C. Haughton and D. Powlesland *West Heslerton: The Anglian Cemetery*

[col2]

(Yedingham: Landscape Research Centre, 1999), scientific analysis is continuing with particular reference to DNA and Trace Element analyses. These techniques promise to radically change our ability to interpret the evidence from cemeteries.

[8] D.J. Powlesland and C. Haughton *West Heslerton — The Anglian Settlement* (Yedingham: Landscape Research Centre, *forthcoming*).

[9] The 'Ladder Settlement' which follows the southern edge of the Vale of Pickering through East and West Heslerton parishes, has been shown through trial excavation to have been in use from the end of the Iron Age, or earlier, to the post-Roman period. D. Powlesland, Approaches to the excavation and interpretation of the Romano-British Landscape in the Vale of Pickering, in J. Price and P.R. Wilson (eds), *Recent Research in Roman Yorkshire. Studies in honour of Mary Kitson Clark (Mrs Derwas Chitty)* (Oxford: British Archaeological Report, British Series, 193, 1988), 139-150.

[10] *Ibid*

[11] *Ibid*.

[12] J.G. Rutter and G. Duke, *Excavations at Crossgates near Scarborough, 1947-56* (Scarborough: Scarborough and District Archaeological Society Research Report 1, 1958).

[13] A model of Early Anglo-Saxon settlement development based upon a pattern of shifting modest farmsteads was proposed following the remarkable and thorough excavations undertaken by Margaret Jones at Mucking in Essex during the 1970's; this model which contrasts with the evidence from West Heslerton was applied to Mucking by Helena Hamerow in her publication of the Mucking evidence — H. Hamerow *Excavations at Mucking. Volume 2: the Anglo-Saxon Settlement* (London: English Heritage, 1993). This model of shifting settlement owes most to the perception of the period, rather than to a full and detailed analysis of the evidence, indeed the rubbish disposal practices at West Heslerton reveal that in this period, when secure absolute dating is very difficult, we need be very careful when examining the evidence from *Grubenhäuser* in particular which appear only rarely to have contained primary rubbish.

[14] Buildings with an almost identical footprint and post-hole arrangement have been discovered as far apart as Thirlings in Northumbria (C. O'Brien and R. Miket, The Early Medieval settlement of Thirlings, Northumberland, *Durham Archaeological Journal*, 7, 57-91); Cowdery's Down in Hampshire (M. Millett, Excavations at Cowdery's Down, Basingstoke, Hampshire, 1978-81, *Archaeological Journal*, 140 (1983), 151-279); Mucking (H. Hamerow *Excavations at Mucking. Volume 2: the Anglo-Saxon Settlement* (London: English Heritage, 1993)); and West Stow (S.E. West, *West Stow: the Anglo-Saxon village* (Ipswich: Suffolk County Council, 1985), East Anglian Archaeology 24), as well as at Heslerton.

[15] The analysis of the huge animal bone assemblage from West Heslerton by Jane Richardson offers an unparalleled opportunity to examine aspects of animal husbandry, diet and agriculture in the Early Anglo-Saxon period; this is particularly important given the fact that at Mucking for instance almost no bone survived.

[16] K.H. Jackson *The Gododdin. The Oldest Scottish Poem* (Edinburgh: Edinburgh University Press, 1969).

[17] I. Williams, *Canu Aneirin* (Cardiff: University of Wales Press, 1938); O.G.S. Crawford Note on Catraeth and Catterick, in K. Jackson, The "Gododdin" of Aneririn, *Antiquity*, 13 (1939), 32-34.

[18] Bede, *A History of the English Church and People* (trans L. Sherley-Price), Book II, Chapter 14 (Harmondsworth: Penguin, revised edition 1968).

[19] M. Faull Settlement and Society in North-east England in the fifth century in P.R. Wilson, R.F.J. Jones and D.M. Evans (eds), *Settlement and Society in the Roman North* (Bradford: School of Archaeological Sciences, University of Bradford and Leeds: Roman Antiquities Section, Yorkshire Archaeological Society, 1984), 52.

[20] The ninth century *Historia Brittonum* suggests Elmet was incorporated in Deira in *circa* AD 616. M. Lapidge (ed.), *The Blackwell Encyclopaedia of Anglo-Saxon England* (Oxford: Blackwell, 1999), p. 165 for Elmet, pp. 239-240 for the date and origins of the *Historia Brittonum*.

[21] P. Ottaway, Excavations on the Site of the Roman Signal Station at Carr Naze, Filey, 1993-94, *Archaeological Journal*, 157, 105-108, 191-193.

[22] Dr R.A. Hall's comments have been invaluable in producing this part of the chapter, although mistakes and omissions are entirely the author's responsibility.

[23] *The Anglo-Saxon Chronicle* (ed. & trans D. Whitelock), entry for AD 787 or 789 (London: Eyre & Spottiswood, 1961). The Anglo-Saxon Chronicle in its various manuscripts is essentially a southern English document, however the D manuscript draws on earlier annals from York, as do parts of the E manuscript (P. Sawyer, Some sources for the history of Viking Northumbria, in R.A. Hall (ed.), *Viking Age York and the North* (London: Council for British Archaeology, Research Report 27, 1978), 3-4.

24 *The Anglo-Saxon Chronicle* (ed. & trans D. Whitelock), entry for AD 787 or 789 (London: Eyre & Spottiswood, 1961), entry for AD 875-6.

25 D.M. Hadley, *The Northern Danelaw its Social Structure* (London: Leicester University Press, 2000), 306.

26 For example Esbrid and Ælstan whose names are clearly Anglo-Saxon are found supporting the Hiberno-Norse King Ragnald in *circa* AD 918 — see D.M. Hadley, *The Northern Danelaw its Social Structure* (London: Leicester University Press, 2000), 12.

27 The material derives from evaluation excavations in 2001 on the north cliff of Abbey Plain undertaken by the English Heritage Centre for Archaeology. Information from S. Jennings and P. Busby (*pers comm*).

28 D.M. Wilson, The Scandinavians in England, in D.M. Wilson (ed.), *The Archaeology of Anglo-Saxon England* (Cambridge: Cambridge University Press, 1976), Figure 10.1; D.M. Hadley, *The Northern Danelaw its Social Structure* (London: Leicester University Press, 2000), Figure 6.

29 F. Elgee, *Early Man in North-East Yorkshire* (Gloucester: Bellows, 1930), 220-221.

30 R.A. Hall and M. Whyman, Settlement and Monasticism at Ripon, North Yorkshire, from the 7th to 11th centuries A.D., *Medieval Archaeology* **40** (1996), 140.

31 P. Abramson, Archaeology in the pipeline *North Craven Heritage Trust Journal 1999*, 4-5.

32 J. Graham-Campbell, A 'Vital' Yorkshire Viking Hoard Revisited, in M.O.H. Carver *et al* (eds), *In Search of Cult: Archaeological Investigations in Honour of Philip Rahtz* (Woodbridge: Boydell Press, 1993), 79-84.

33 W.P. Vaux, in *Archaeological Journal* **16**, 197; D.M. Wilson, An unpublished fragment from the Goldsborough hoard, *Antiquaries Journal* **37**, 72-73.

34 J. Graham-Campbell, A Viking Age harness-bow fragment from Cliffe, N. Yorkshire, *Medieval Archaeology* **42** (1998), 102-103.

35 M. Blackburn, A Viking-age silver ingot from near Easingwold, Yorks., *Medieval Archaeology* **34** (1990), 149-150.

36 M.J. Swanton, A rune-stone from Victoria Cave, Settle, Yorkshire, *Medieval Archaeology* **13** (1969), 211-214.

37 J. Watkin and F. Mann, Some Late Saxon finds from Lilla Howe, N. Yorks. and their context, *Medieval Archaeology* **25** (1981), 153-157.

38 D.M. Wilson, Some neglected Late Anglo-Saxon swords, *Medieval Archaeology* **9** (1965), 41-42.

39 H. Shetelig, Grave finds, in H. Shetelig and A. Bjørn (eds), *Viking Antiquities in Great Britain and Ireland, Part IV. Viking antiquities in England* (Oslo: Ascheloug, 1940), 15, 17.

40 See also G. Halsall, The Viking Presence in England? The Burial Evidence, in D.M. Hadley and J.D. Richards (eds), *Cultures in contact: Scandinavian Settlement in England in the Ninth and Tenth Centuries*. Studies in the Early Middle Ages 2 (Turnhout, Belgium: Brepols, 2000), 264-269.

41 J.R. Watkin, A Late Anglo-Saxon sword from Gilling West, N. Yorkshire, *Medieval Archaeology* **30** (1986), 93-99.

42 D.M. Metcalfe *An Atlas of Anglo-Saxon Coin Finds c.973-1086* (London: Royal Numismatic Society/The Ashmolean Museum Oxford, 1998).

43 A. King, Gauber High Pasture, Ribblehead — an interim report, in R. Hall (ed.), *Viking Age York and the North* (London: Council for British Archaeology Research Report **27**, 1978), 21-25.

44 R. White, *The Yorkshire Dales. Landscapes through time* (London; English Heritage/Batsford, 1997), 50-51. For Greenber Edge see M. Bowden and K. Blood, Reassessment of two late prehistoric sites: Maiden Castle and Greenber Edge, in R. White and P. Wilson (eds), *Archaeology and Historic Landscapes in the Yorkshire Dales* (Leeds: Yorkshire Archaeological Society, Occasional Paper 2, forthcoming).

45 A.R. Goodall and C. Paterson, Non-ferrous metal objects, in P.A. Stamper and R.A. Croft, *Wharram: A Study of Settlement in the Yorkshire Wolds VIII: The South Manor Area* (York: York University Archaeological Publications 10, 2000), 126, nos 22-23; H.M. Taylor and J. Taylor, *Anglo-Saxon Architecture*, vol. III (Cambridge: University Press, 1978), 1076-1077.

46 J.D. Richards, The Anglo-Saxon and Anglo-Scandinavian Evidence, in P.A. Stamper and R.A. Croft, *Wharram: A Study of Settlement in the Yorkshire Wolds VIII: The South Manor Area* (York: York University Archaeological Publications 10, 2000), 197-198.

47 J. Bayley, The Metalworking Evidence, in G. Milne and J.D. Richards, *Two Anglo-Saxon Buildings and Associated Finds* (York: York University Archaeological Publications 9, 1992), 199.

48 Cottam: an Anglo-Scandinavian Settlement on the Yorkshire Wolds, *Archaeological Journal* **156** (1999), 1-111.

49 M. Magnusson and H. Palsson (trans.), *King Harald's Saga* (London: Penguin, 1966), 141-142. For the validity of the source see T. Pearson, Early Medieval Settlement of the Yorkshire Coast, *Northern Archaeology* **17/18** (1999), 160 and M. Arnold, The Legendary Origins of Scarborough, in D. Crouch and T. Pearson (eds), *Medieval Scarborough* (Leeds: Yorkshire Archaeological Society Occasional Paper **1** (2001), 10.

50 T. Pearson, Early Medieval Settlement of the Yorkshire Coast, *Northern Archaeology* **17/18** (1999), 162.

51 G. Fellows Jensen, *Scandinavian Settlement Names in Yorkshire* (Copenhagen: I kommission hos Akademisk forlag, 1972), 5-41.

52 *Ibid.*, 42-71. In Yorkshire there is only a limited possibility of confusing names derived from the Old Norse -þorp with names derived from the Old English -þorp (ultimately derived from the same linguistic root), as these are not very common in the County (G. Fellows Jensen Scandinavian Settlement in Yorkshire — through the rear-view mirror, in B.E. Crawford (ed.), *Scandinavian Settlement in Northern Britain. Thirteen Studies of Place-Names in their Historical Context* (London: Leicester University Press, 1995), 183.

53 Including the so-called Grimston-hybrids. G. Fellows Jensen, *Scandinavian Settlement Names in Yorkshire* (Copenhagen: I kommission hos Akademisk forlag, 1972), 109-130; M. Gelling, *Signposts to the Past. Place-names and the history of England* (London: Dent, 1978), 228-229.

54 G. Fellows Jensen Scandinavian Settlement in Yorkshire — through the rear-view mirror, in B.E. Crawford (ed.), *Scandinavian Settlement in Northern Britain. Thirteen Studies of Place-Names in their Historical Context* (London: Leicester University Press, 1995), 171.

55 *Ibid.*, 172.

56 *Ibid.*, Figure 10.

57 *Ibid.*, 170.

58 R.N. Bailey, *Viking Age Sculpture in Northern England* (London: Collins, 1980), 38-39; G. Fellows Jensen Scandinavian Settlement in Yorkshire — through the rear-view mirror, in B.E. Crawford (ed.), *Scandinavian Settlement in Northern Britain. Thirteen Studies of Place-Names in their Historical Context* (London: Leicester University Press, 1995), 181.

59 *Ibid.*, 183.

60 A.P. Smyth The chronology of Northumbrian history in the ninth and tenth centuries, in R. Hall (ed.), *Viking Age York and the North* (London: Council for British Archaeology Research Report **27**, 1978), 10.

61 The distribution of churches shown on Maps 5.1 and 5.2 is largely based on information derived from H.M. Taylor and J. Taylor, *Anglo-Saxon Architecture* vols. I and II (Cambridge: Cambridge University Press, 1980), and vol. III (Cambridge: Cambridge University Press, 1978), with additions from J.T. Lang, Anglo-Saxons and Vikings, in D.A. Spratt and B.J.D. Harrison (eds), *The North York Moors Landscape Heritage* (Newton Abbot: David and Charles, 1989); N. Kerr and M. Kerr, *A Guide to Anglo-Saxon Sites* (London: BCA, 1982); and G. Sleight, St Owald's Church, Filey: A Late Saxon Minster? *Yorkshire Archaeological Journal* **70**, 67-71. The distribution of sculpture is based on J. Lang *Corpus of Anglo-Saxon Sculpture. Vol. III. York and Eastern Yorkshire* (Oxford: Oxford University Press, 1991); J. Lang, Lang *Corpus of Anglo-Saxon Sculpture. Vol. VI. Northern Yorkshire* (in preparation), and E. Coatsworth *Corpus of Anglo-Saxon Sculpture. Western Yorkshire* (in preparation). The author is grateful to Professor R.J. Cramp and Dr D.J. Craig of the Corpus of Anglo-Saxon Sculpture project for making map extracts and locational information for northern and western North Yorkshire available ahead of publication.

62 See D.M. Hadley, *The Northern Danelaw its Social Structure* (London: Leicester University Press, 2000), 241-272, for a summary of most of the sites referred to. For a discussion of the origins of early monasteries see R. Morris *Churches in the landscape* (London: Dent, 1989), 93-139. For recent work at Kirkdale, including discussion of a lead plate from a reliquary, ossuary or coffin see L. Watts, P. Rahtz, E. Okasha, S.A.J. Bradley and J. Higgitt, Kirkdale — The Inscriptions, *Medieval Archaeology* **41** (1997), 51-99; L. Watts, J. Grenville and P. Rahtz *Archaeology at Kirkdale* — supplement to *The Ryedale Historian* **18** (1996-1997); *Kirkdale Archaeology 1996-1997* — supplement to *The Ryedale Historian* **19** (1998-1999). For a recent consideration of Ripon see R.A. Hall and M. Whyman, Settlement and Monasticism at Ripon, North Yorkshire, from the 7th to 11th centuries A.D., *Medieval Archaeology* **40** (1996), 62-150. For Crayke see K.A. Adams, Monastery and village at Crayke, North Yorkshire, *Yorkshire Archaeological Journal* **62** (1990), 29-50.

63 P.S. Barnwell, L.A.S. Butler and C.J. Dunn *Streanæshalch*, Strensall and Whitby, in M.O.H. Carver (ed.), *The Age of Conversion in Northern Europe* (Woodbridge: Boydell and Brewer, forthcoming).

64 M.L. Faull, Late Anglo-Saxon Settlement Patterns in Yorkshire, in M.L. Faull (ed.), *Studies in Late Anglo-Saxon Settlement* (Oxford: Oxford University Department for External Studies, 1984), 130.

65 H.M. Taylor and J. Taylor, *Anglo-Saxon Architecture* vols. I and II (Cambridge: University Press, 1980).

66 J. Wall, Anglo-Saxon sundials in Ryedale, *Yorkshire Archaeological Journal* **69**, 93-117.

[67] See R. Morris *Churches in the Landscape* (London: Dent, 1989), 93-139 for a discussion on the origins of the parish system.

[68] M.L. Faull, Late Anglo-Saxon Settlement Patterns in Yorkshire, in M.L. Faull (ed.), *Studies in Late Anglo-Saxon Settlement* (Oxford: Oxford University Department for External Studies, 1984), 133.

[69] H.M. Taylor and J. Taylor, *Anglo-Saxon Architecture* vol. II (Cambridge: University Press, 1980), 716; see also J. Wall Anglo-Saxon sundials in Ryedale, *Yorkshire Archaeological Journal* 69, 105-108

[70] *Ibid.*, 718.

[71] J.T. Lang, Anglo-Saxons and Vikings, in D.A. Spratt and B.J.D. Harrison (eds), *The North York Moors Landscape Heritage* (Newton Abbot: David and Charles, 1989), 70.

[72] N. Kerr and M. Kerr, *A Guide to Anglo-Saxon Sites* (London: BCA, 1982), 49-51.

[73] R.N. Bailey, *Viking Age Sculpture in Northern England* (London: Collins, 1980), 82.

[74] J. Lang, *Corpus of Anglo-Saxon Sculpture. Vol. III. York and Eastern Yorkshire* (Oxford: Oxford University Press, 1991), 18-20, 146-148, 171-173, 187.

[75] *Ibid.*, 28-31.

[76] M.L. Faull, Late Anglo-Saxon Settlement Patterns in Yorkshire, in M.L. Faull (ed.), *Studies in Late Anglo-Saxon Settlement* (Oxford: Oxford University Department for External Studies, 1984), 137.

[77] C.R. Hart, The Early Charters of North England and the North Midlands (Leicester: Leicester University Press, 1975), numbers 122, 123, 125, 126, 129, 132 and 136.

[78] *Ibid.*, number 122.

[79] *Ibid.*, number 123.

[80] M.L. Faull, Late Anglo-Saxon Settlement Patterns in Yorkshire, in M.L. Faull (ed.), *Studies in Late Anglo-Saxon Settlement* (Oxford: Oxford University Department for External Studies, 1984), 135-136.

[81] M. Lapidge, J. Blair, S. Keynes and D. Scragg *The Blackwell Encyclopaedia of Anglo-Saxon England* (Oxford: Blackwell, 1999), 136.

[82] D. Hill, *An Atlas of Anglo-Saxon England* (Oxford: Blackwell, 1981), 97 and maps 175-177.

[83] M.O.H. Carver, Roman to Norman at York Minster, in D. Phillips and B. Heywood, *Excavations at York Minster I* (ed. M.O.H. Carver), (London: HMSO, 1995), 177-222.

[84] D.W. Rollason, *Sources for York History to AD1100.* (York: Council for British Archaeology, The Archaeology of York 1. E. James The post-Roman period to 1069, in D. Phillips and B. Heywood, *Excavations at York Minster I* (ed. M.O.H. Carver), (London: HMSO, 1995), 9-15

[85] C. Norton, The Anglo-Saxon cathedral at York and the topography of the Anglian city, *Journal of the British Archaeological Association* 151 (1998), 1-42.

[86] R. Morris, Alcuin, York and the *alma sophia*, in L.A.S. Butler and R.K. Morris (eds), *The Anglo-Saxon Church* (London: Council for British Archaeology, Research Report 60, 1986), 80-89.

[87] A.J. Mainman, *Pottery from 46-54 Fishergate* (London, Council for British Archaeology, The Archaeology of York: The Pottery 16/6, 1993). A.J. Mainman and N.S.H. Rogers, *Anglo-Scandinavian Finds* (York: Council for British Archaeology, The Archaeology of York: The Small Finds 17/14, 2000).

[88] R.L. Kemp, *Anglian Settlement at 46-54 Fishergate* (York: Council for British Archaeology, The Archaeology of York: Anglian York 7/1, 1996. D. Tweddle, The Anglian City, in D. Tweddle, E. Logan and J. Moulden *Anglian York: A Survey of the Evidence* (York: Council for British Archaeology, The Archaeology of York: Anglian York 7/2, 1999), 151-212. T.P. O'Connor, *Bones from 46-54 Fishergate* (London: Council for British Archaeology, The Archaeology of York: The Animal Bones 15/4, 1991). T.P. O'Connor, 8th-11th century economy and environment in York, in J. Rackham (ed.), *Environment & Economy in Anglo-Saxon England* (London: Council for British Archaeology, Research Report 89, 1994), 136-147.

[89] R.A. Hall, *Anglo-Scandinavian Structures* (York: Council for British Archaeology, The Archaeology of York: Anglo-Scandinavian York 8/4 (forthcoming). R.A. Hall, *et al: Anglo-Scandinavian Synthesis* (York: Council for British Archaeology, The Archaeology of York: Anglo-Scandinavian York 8/5 forthcoming). P. Walton, *Textiles, Cordage and Raw Fibre from 16-22 Coppergate* (London: Council for British Archaeology, The Archaeology of York: The Small Finds 17/5, 1989. P.J. Ottaway, *Anglo-Scandinavian Ironwork from 16-22 Coppergate* (London: Council for British Archaeology, The Archaeology of York: The Small Finds 17/6, 1992). J. Bayley, *1992: Non-ferrous Metalworking from 16-22 Coppergate* (London: Council for British Archaeology, The Archaeology of York: The Small finds 17/7, 1992). P. Walton Rogers, *Textile Production from 16-22 Coppergate* (York: Council for British Archaeology, The Archaeology of York: The Small Finds 17/1, 1997). A. McGregor, A.J. Mainman, and N.S.H. Rogers, *Bone, Antler, Ivory and Horn from Anglo-Scandinavian and Medieval York* (York: Council for British Archaeology, The Archaeology of York: The Small Finds 17/12, 1999). C.A. Morris, *Wood and Woodworking from Anglo-Scandinavian and Medieval York* (York: Council for British Archaeology, The Archaeology of York: The Small Finds 17/13, 2000). R.A. Hall, *Viking Age York* (London: English Heritage/Batsford, 1994).

[90] D.M. Palliser, York's West Bank: Medieval Suburb or Urban Nucleus?, in P.V. Addyman and V.E. Black (eds), *Archaeological Papers from York Presented to M.W. Barley* (York: York Archaeological Trust, 1984). D. Stocker, Monuments our Merchants: Irregularities in the Distribution of Stone Sculpture in Lincolnshire and Yorkshire in the Tenth Century, in D.M. Hadley and J.D. Richards (eds), *Cultures in Contact: Scandinavian Settlement in England in the Ninth and Tenth Centuries* (London: Leicester University Press, 2000), 203-205.

[91] R.A. Hall, *York* (London: Batsford/English Heritage, 1996)

6.2 MEDIEVAL WOODLAND

[1] T.D. Gledhill, 'Medieval Woodland in North Yorkshire', in M.A. Atherden and R.A. Butlin (eds), *Woodland in the Landscape: Past and Future Perspectives* (Leeds: Leeds University Press, 1997), 103-119.

[2] W.E. Wightman, 'The significance of waste in Yorkshire Domesday', *Northern History*, 5 (1970), 55-71.

6.4 MEDIEVAL ROYAL BUILDINGS

[1] R.A. Brown, *Castles from the Air* (Cambridge: Cambridge University Press, 1989); R.A. Brown, 'Castles: I. Medieval', in J. Turner (ed.), *The Dictionary of Art* (London: Macmillan, 1996), 6: 49-58; N.J.G. Pounds, *The Medieval Castle in England and Wales: A Social and Political History* (Cambridge: Cambridge University Press, 1990).

[2] Pounds, *The Medieval Castle in England and Wales*, 7.

[3] H.M. Colvin (ed.), with R.A. Brown and A.J. Taylor, *The History of the King's Works: Volumes I and II: The Middle Ages* (London: HMSO, 1963), 687, 779, 806, 829 (hereafter *HKW* I and II).

[4] *HKW* II, 687.

[5] *HKW* II, 780, 806, 925.

[6] *HKW* I, 235; *HKW* II, 671.

[7] *HKW* II, 687.

[8] *HKW* II, 780.

[9] *HKW* II, 688.

[10] *HKW* II, 688, 780.

[11] *HKW* II, 688, 832.

[12] *HKW* I, 241; *HKW* II, 832; H.M. Colvin (ed.), with D.R. Ransome and J. Summerson, *The History of the King's Works: Volume III: 1485-1660 (Part 1)*, (London: HMSO, 1975), 177, 226 (hereafter *HKW* III).

[13] *HKW* III, 177.

6.5 MEDIEVAL BATTLES

[1] P. Dalton, *Conquest, Anarchy and Lordship: Yorkshire 1066-1154* (Cambridge: Cambridge University Press, 1994), 211-27.

[2] Richard of Hexham, in *Chronicles of the Reigns of Stephen, Henry II and Richard I*, ed. R.J. Howlett (4 vols. Rolls Series 82, 1884-90), III, 159.

[3] K.J. Stringer, 'State-Building in Twelfth-Century Britain: David I, King of Scots, and Northern England, in John C. Appleby and Paul Dalton (eds), *Government, Religion and Society in Northern England 1000-1700* (Stroud: Sutton Publishing, 1997).

[4] *The Chronicle of Lanercost 1272-1346*, translated with notes by Sir Herbert Maxwell (Glasgow: James Maclehose and Sons, 1913), 226.

[5] A. Young and M. Stead, *In the Footsteps of Robert Bruce* (Stroud: Sutton Publishing, 1999), 162, *Chronicle of Lanercost*, 241.

[6] *Ibid.*, 239.

[7] J. Gillingham, *The Wars of the Roses: Peace and Conflict in Fifteenth Century England* (London: Weidenfeld and Nicolson), 76-83.

6.6 THE ANGLO-SCOTTISH WARS

[1] The Treaty of Edinburgh, later ratified at Northampton; see E.L.G. Stones (ed.), *Anglo-Scottish Relations 1174-1328* (Oxford: Clarendon Press, 1970), document number 41.

[2] For a more detailed analysis of the routes taken by the Scots in 1318, 1319 and 1322, see I. Kershaw, A Note on the Scots in the West Riding, 1318-1319, *Northern History*, XVII (1981), 231-239, and C. McNamee, *The Wars of the Bruces: Scotland, England and Ireland, 1306-1328* (East Linton: Tuckwell Press, 1997), 85-104.

[3] This battle became known as the 'Chapter of Myton', because of the large number of clergy in the English army.

[4] John of Brittany, earl of Richmond, had been sent to intercept the Scots on the orders of a somewhat panic-stricken Edward II, who at the time was staying nearby at Rievaulx Abbey.

[5] W. Stubbs (ed.), *Gesta Edwardi de Carnarvan Auctore Canonico Bridlingtoniensi*, Roll Series (London, 1883), 55.

[6] *Gesta Edwardi*, 57.

[7] E.A. Bond (ed.), *Chronica Monasterii de Melsa*, volume ii, Roll Series (1867), chapter 20.

[8] J. Stevenson (ed.), *Chronicon de Lanercost* (Edinburgh, 1839), 235.

[9] *Chronica Monasterii de Melsa*, chapter 16.

[10] McNamee, *Wars of the Bruces*, 101.

[11] In 1318, the Lanercost chronicle states that having plundered Knaresborough, the Scots 'searched the woods of the district to which men and their animals had fled'; *Chronicon de Lanercost*, 235. In 1319, the canons of Bolton Priory sought refuge in Skipton Castle; I. Kershaw, *Bolton Priory: The Economy of a Northern Monastery, 1286-1325* (Oxford: Oxford University Press, 1973), 16.

[12] Public Record Office E179/67/9/, m. 26; J. Topham (ed.), *Taxatio Ecclesiastica Angliae et Walliae auctoritate P. Nicholai IV, circa AD 1291* (Record Commission, 1802), pp 297-309. See also the maps drawn by Kershaw, 'Scots in the West Riding', 234-235, and McNamee, *Wars of the Bruces*, 86-87.

[13] *Calendar of Close Rolls 1318-23* (London, 1895), 166-167; Public Record Office E359/14, mm. 12d, 13d. See also the maps drawn by Kershaw, 'Scots in the West Riding', 234-235, and McNamee, *Wars of the Bruces*, 92-93.

[14] Public Record Office E179/67/9/, m.23. See also the maps drawn by D. Robinson in the back of *Beneficed Clergy in Cleveland and the East Riding, 1306-1340* (York: Borthwick Institute, Borthwick Papers 37, 1969), and McNamee, *Wars of the Bruces*, 102-103.

[15] In order to simplify the map, only those benefices where the valuation was reduced by 50% or more in 1318 and 1327, have been plotted.

[16] Kershaw, *Bolton Priory*, 67-68.

[17] J.A. Tuck, War and Society in the Medieval North, *Northern History*, II (1985), 42.

[18] Kershaw, Scots in the West Riding, p 232. This suggestion is supported by the fact that a large number of the exempt villages were held by the Percy family and the abbot of Fountains, who were undoubtedly among the more important landowners in Yorkshire.

[19] See I. Kershaw, 'The Great Famine and Agrarian Crises in England, 1315-1322', in R.H. Hilton (ed.), *Peasants, Knights and Heretics: Studies in Medieval English Social History* (Cambridge: Cambridge University Press, 1976), 85-132.

[20] The administrative offices of state first moved from Westminster to York in 1298, where they remained until 1305. This policy was repeated in 1319-1320, 1322-1323, 1327 and 1333-1338.

[21] Notably, when the abbot of Fountains sought permission in 1336 to demise the North Yorkshire granges of Baldersby, Marton-le-Moor and Kilnsey, he did so in order to alleviate the economic damage caused not by the Scottish raids, but by the 'general transit of nobles and common people during the war between the kingdoms of England and Scotland'; W.T. Lancaster (ed.), *Chartulary of Fountains Abbey* (Leeds, 1915), 111.

6.7 RELIGIOUS HOUSES
[1] Roberta Gilchrist, *Gender and Material Culture. The archaeology of religious women* (London and New York: Routledge, 1994), 66.
[2] Claire Cross and Noreen Vickers, *Monks, Friars and Nuns in Sixteenth Century Yorkshire* (Leeds: Yorkshire Archeological Society), Record Series 150 (1995 for 1991 and 1992), 2-3, 6-8.

6.8 CISTERCIAN GRANGES
[1] Colin Platt, *The Monastic Grange in Medieval England* (London: Macmillan, 1969), 196. 196.
[2] R.A. Donkin, *The Cistercians. Studies in the geography of medieval England and Wales*, Pontifical Institute of Medieval Studies, Texts and Studies 38 (Toronto: Pontifical Institute, 1978).
[3] Glyn Coppack, *Fountains Abbey* (London: English Heritage and Batsford, 1993), 82.
[4] Platt, *Monastic Grange*.
[5] James S. Donnelly, Changes in the Grange Economy of English and Welsh Cistercian Abbeys, 1399-1540, *Traditio* 10 (1954), 399-458.

6.9 POPULATION AND SETTLEMENT
[1] The 1377 poll tax population figures derive from P.R.O. E.179 various, were collected by Dr Carolyn Fenwick and supplied by Dr Richard Smith. They will be published in C.C. Fenwick (ed.), *The Poll Taxes of 1377, 1379,*

and 1381: Part 3, Records of Social and Economic History (Oxford: British Academy, forthcoming). See also J.I. Leggett (ed.), The 1377 Poll Tax Returns for the City of York, *Yorkshire Archaeological Journal*, XLIII (1971), 128-46; Assessment Roll for the Poll-Tax for Howdenshire ... 1379, *Yorkshire Archaeological Journal*, IX (1886), 129-62; Rolls of the Collectors in the West Riding of the Lay-Subsidy (Poll-Tax), 2 Richard I, *Yorkshire Archaeological Journal*, V 1-51, 241-66, 417-32; VI 1-44, 129-71, 287-342; VII 6-31, 145-86 (1879-84).

[2] Borthwick Institute of Historical Research (hereafter B.I.H.R.), C.P.F.59; J. McDonnell, Medieval assarting Hamlets in Bilsdale, North-East Yorkshire, *Northern History*, XXII (1986), 278-9.

[3] B.I.H.R., Prob. Reg. 3 fos. 417, 481; C.P.F.179.

[4] A. Pollard, The North-Eastern Economy and the Agrarian Crisis of 1438-1440, *Northern History*, XXV (1989), 88-105.

[5] B.I.H.R., C.P.F.79.

[6] V.H. Galbraith (ed.), *The Anonimalle Chronicle 1333-1381* (Manchester: Manchester University Press, 1927), 50, 58, 79, 124; E.A. Bond (ed.), *Chronica Monasterii de Melsa*, III, Rolls Series, XLIII (London: Longmans, Green, Reader, and Dyer, 1886); P.J.P. Goldberg, *Women in Late Medieval Society: Some Demographic Evidence from the York Region* (Unpublished M.A. dissertation, University of York 1982); A.H. Thompson, The Pestilences of the Fourteenth Century in the Diocese of York, *Archaeological Journal*, LXXI (1914), 97-154.

[7] D.M. Palliser, Epidemics in Tudor York, *Northern History*, VIII (1973), 45-63.

6.11 COMMUNICATIONS
[1] David Hey, *Yorkshire from AD 1000* (London: Longman, 1986), 84.
[2] Barrie Dobson, 'Mendicant Ideal and Practice in Late Medieval York', in P.V. Addyman and V.E. Black (eds), *Archaeological Papers from York Presented to M/W. Barley* (York: York Archaeological Trust, 1984), 117.
[3] Constance M. Frazer, The Pattern of Trade in the North-East of England, 1265-1350, *Northern History* IV (1969), 44-66

6.12 BOROUGHS, MARKETS AND FAIRS
[1] M.W. Beresford and H.P.R. Finberg, *English Medieval Boroughs: A Handlist* (Newton Abbott: David and Charles, 1973), 187-92; R.H. Britnell, Boroughs, Markets and Trade in Northern England, 1000-1216, in R.H. Britnell and J. Hatcher (eds), *Progress and Problems in Medieval England: Essays in Honour of Edward Miller* (Cambridge: Cambridge University Press, 1996), 67. For a market and fair in Selby, see W. Illingworth (ed.), *Placita de Quo Warranto* (London: Record Commission, 1818), 216.
[2] T.D. Hardy (ed.), *Rotuli Litterarum Clausarum*, 2 vols (London: Record Commission, 1833-4), I, 536; *Calendar of Charter Rolls*, 6 vols (London: H.M.S.O., 1903-27), I, 340, 361 bis, 379; II, 176; IV, 288; V, 155, 280, 310.
[3] *Calendar of Charter Rolls*, I, 22, 255.
[4] *Calendar of Charter Rolls*, I, 379; *Placita de Quo Warranto*, p. 219.
[5] *Calendar of Charter Rolls*, I, 415; II, 435; V, 178.
[6] *Rotuli Litterarum Clausarum*, I, 446; *Calendar of Charter Rolls*, I, 253; J. Parker (ed.), *Feet of Fines for the County of York, 1232 to 1246* (York: Yorkshire Archaeological Society, 1925), 102; *Calendar of Patent Rolls, Henry III*, 6 vols (London: H.M.S.O., 1901-13), IV, 477.
[7] *Calendar of Charter Rolls*, I, 290 (Barton le Street), 434 (Birdforth); II, 256 (Aldbrough), 457 (Hemingborough); III, 24 (Osgodby); V, 120 (Riccall), 243 (Sheriff Hutton); *Calendar of Patent Rolls, Edward III*, 16 vols (London: H.M.S.O., 1891-1916), VII, 527 (Kexby).
[8] I am greatly indebted to Dr Samantha Letters for information from her forthcoming *Gazetteer of Medieval Markets and Fairs*, the outcome of a recent research project funded by the Economic and Social Research Council.

7.2 DISSOLUTION OF THE MONASTERIES
[1] Claire Cross and Noreen Vickers, *Monks, Friars and Nuns in Sixteenth Century Yorkshire* (Leeds: Yorkshire Archeological Society), Record Series 150 (1995 for 1991 and 1992), 2.

7.4 POLITICAL LOYALTIES AND THE CIVIL WARS
[1] Quoted in J.T. Cliffe, *The Yorkshire Gentry from the Reformation to the Civil War* (London: Athlone Press, 1969), 336.
[2] Ibid., 337.

8.2 AGRICULTURE 1600-1780
[1] M.W. Beresford, Glebe Terriers and Open Field, Yorkshire, *Yorkshire Archaeological Journal*, XXXVI (1951), 325-368.
[2] M. Harvey, The Development of Open Fields in the Central Vale of York: a Reconsideration, *Geografiska Annaler*, 67B (1985), 35; T.A.M. Bishop,

Assarting and the growth of the open fields, *Economic History Review* (1935), 13-19; J.A. Sheppard, Field Systems of Yorkshire, in A.R.H. Baker and R.A. Butlin (eds), *Studies of Field Systems in the British Isles* (Cambridge: Cambridge University Press, 1973), 145-187.

[3] Sheppard, *op. cit.,* 165-6.

[4] Harvey, *op. cit.,* 37.

[5] Sheppard, *op. cit.,* 163.

[6] *Ibid.,* 166.

[7] J. Thirsk, The farming regions of England, in J. Thirsk (ed.), *The Agrarian History of England and Wales, IV 1500-1640* (Cambridge: Cambridge University Press, 1967), 32-3; W. Harwood Long, *A Survey of the Agriculture of Yorkshire* (London: Royal Agricultural Society, 1969), 36.

[8] J.E. Kaner, Historic woodland in the Vale of York, in M.A. Atherden and R.A. Butlin (eds), *Woodland in the Landscape: Past and Future Perspectives* (Leeds: Leeds University Press, 1999), 120-139.

[9] B. Loughbrough, 'Aspects of Enclosure of the Vale of Pickering in the Eighteenth and Nineteenth Centuries', M.A. thesis, University of Hull, 1960; Fig. 6 (Steeton), 18-19; Fig. 8 (Hunmanby), 20-21; Fig 9 (Filey), 20-22. Reproduced by kind permission of the author.

[10] *Ibid.* 24 *seq.*

[11] *Ibid.*

[12] Sheppard, *op. cit.,* 161-2.

[13] *Ibid.,* 160.

[14] B. Loughbrough, An Account of a Yorkshire Enclosure Staxton 1803, *Agricultural History Review,* **XIII** (2), (1965), 106.

[15] W. Harwood Long, *A Survey of the Agriculture of Yorkshire* (London: Royal Agricultural Society of England, 1969), 29.

[16] B. Waites, *Moorland and Vale-Land Farming in North-East Yorkshire. The monastic contribution in the thirteenth and fourteenth centuries,* University of York, Borthwick Institute, Borthwick Papers No.32 (York: Borthwick Institute, 1967), 6-9.

[17] B.J.D. Harrison, The Medieval Landscape, in D.A. Spratt and B.J.D. Harrison (eds), *The North York Moors* (Newton Abbot: David and Charles, 1989), 88-89.

[18] J. McDonnell, After the Middle Ages: Agriculture and Settlement, in D.A. Spratt and B.J.D. Harrison (eds), *The North York Moors* (Newton Abbot: David and Charles, 1989), 115.

[19] B.J.D. Harrison, The Medieval Landscape, in D.A. Spratt and B.J.D. Harrison (eds), *The North York Moors* (Newton Abbot: David and Charles, 1989), 88-91.

[20] A. Fleming, *Swaledale. Valley of the Wild River* (Edinburgh: Edinburgh University Press, 1998), 65-77.

[21] Fieldhouse, 'Some evidence of surviving open fields in the seventeenth-century Pennine Dales and the gradual elimination of communal agriculture', *Yorkshire Archaeological Journal,* 54 (1982), 111-118.

[22] Fieldhouse, *ibid.,* 112.

[23] R. Fieldhouse and B. Jennings, *A History of Richmond and Swaledale* (London and Chichester: Phillimore, 1978), 142-143.

[24] *Ibid.,* 143.

[25] *Ibid.,* 144.

[26] *Ibid.,* 149.

[27] Fieldhouse, *op. cit.,* 112.

[28] *Ibid.,* 117.

[29] W. Harwood Long, *A Survey of the Agriculture of Yorkshire* (London: Royal Agricultural Society, 1969), 51-52.

8.3 AGRICULTURE 1780-1900

[1] J. Tuke, *General View of the Agriculture of the North Riding of Yorkshire* (London, 1794), 12.

[2] *Ibid.,* 32.

[3] I. Latham, *General View of the Agriculture of the East Riding of Yorkshire* (London, 1794), 62.

[4] W. Harwood Long, *A Survey of the Agriculture of Yorkshire* (London: Royal Agricultural Society, 1969), 36.

[5] R.P. Hastings, Agriculture, in *Essays in North Riding History 1780-1850,* North Yorkshire County Record Office Publications No. 28 (Northallerton: North Yorkshire County Record Office, 1981), 14.

[6] W. Harwood Long, *op. cit.,* 37.

[7] *Ibid.,* 41.

[8] M.J. Huggins, 'Thoroughbred Breeding in the North and East Ridings of Yorkshire in the Nineteenth Century', *Agricultural History Review,* 42 (1994), 115-125.

[9] *Ibid.,* 120.

[10] Tuke, *op. cit.,* 15.

[11] D.A. Spratt and B.J.D. Harrison, After the Middle Ages: Agriculture and Settlement, in: D.A. Spratt and B.J.D. Harrison (eds), *The North York Moors* (Newton Abbot: David and Charles, 1989), 129.

[12] W. Page, 'Agriculture', *Victoria History of the County of York, II* (London: 1912), 465.

[13] Arthur Young, *A Six Months' Tour Through the North of England* (London, 1771), I, 146.

[14] J.E. Crowther, The incidence and chronology of Parliamentary Enclosure, in S. Neave and S. Ellis (eds), *An Historical Atlas of East Yorkshire* (Hull: Hull University Press, 1996), 66-67; A. Harris, *The Rural Landscape of the East Riding of Yorkshire, 1700-1850* (Oxford: Oxford University Press, 1961), 65-72.

[15] J. Tuke, *General View of the Agriculture of the North Riding of Yorkshire* (London, 1794), 16-17.

[16] *Ibid*

[17] W. Harwood Long, *op. cit.,* 44.

[18] *Ibid.,* 45.

[19] D.A. Spratt and B.J.D. Harrison, After the Middle Ages: Agriculture and Settlement, in: D.A. Spratt and B.J.D. Harrison (eds), *The North York Moors* (Newton Abbot: David and Charles, 1989), 114.

[20] *Ibid.*

[21] *Ibid.,* 121-2.

[22] *Ibid.,* 123.

[23] *Ibid.,* 133.

[24] C. Hallas, *Rural Responses to Industrialisation. The North Yorkshire Pennines 1790-1914* (Lang: Bern, 1999), 47-48.

[25] *Ibid.,* 49-52.

[26] R.T. Fieldhouse, 'Agriculture in Wensleydale from 1600 to the Present Day', *Northern History XVI* (1980), 179.

[27] *Ibid.,* 179-80.

[28] *Ibid.,* 182.

[29] *Ibid.,* 186-7.

[30] C. Hallas, 'The Social and Economic Impact of a Rural Railway: the Wensleydale Line', *Agricultural History Review,* 34 (1986), 29-44.

[31] A. Done and R. Muir, The Landscape History of Grouse Shooting in the Yorkshire Dales, *Rural History,* 12 (2), (2001), 200-201.

8.4 PARLIAMENTARY ENCLOSURE

[1] J. Chapman, The Extent and Nature of Parliamentary Enclosure, *Agricultural History Review,* 35 (1987), 25-35.

[2] N.Yorks CRO ZPA; Mic2078, J. Chapman, Parliamentary Enclosure in the Uplands: the case of the North York Moors, *Agricultural History Review,* 24 (1976), 337-341. Note that Staintondale is erroneously listed as Parliamentary in Table 1.

8.5 DRAINAGE AND WETLAND SITES IN THE VALE OF PICKERING

[1] M. Atherden and N. Menuge, *The Vale of Pickering Wetlands Project, Phase One Report* (York: PLACE Research Centre, 1998), 1.

[2] *Ibid.,* 10.

[3] Alecto Historical Editions, *The Yorkshire Domesday* (London, 1992).

[4] B. Waites, *Moorland and Vale Farming in North-East Yorkshire: The Monastic Contribution in the Thirteenth and Fourteenth Centuries.* Borthwick Paper no. 32 (York: Borthwick Institute of Historical Research, St. Anthony's Press, 1967), 4.

[5] *Ibid.,* 22-3.

[6] *Ibid.*

[7] *Ibid.,* 24-5.

[8] *Ibid.*

[9] *Ibid.,* 25.

[10] *Ibid.*

[11] L.T. Smith (ed.), *The Itinerary of John Leland in or about the years 1435-1543.* 5 vols., vol. 1 (Illinois: Southern Illinois University Press, 1964); A.Young, *A Six Month Tour Through the North of England Containing an Account of the present State of Agriculture, Manufactures and Population, in Several Counties of this Kingdom.* 4 vols (New York: Reprints of Economic Classics, Augustus M. Kelley, Publishers, 1967); W. Marshall, *The Rural Economy of Yorkshire.* 2 vols., vol. 1 (London: T. Cadell, in the Strand, 1788); J. Tuke, *General View of the Agriculture of the North Riding of Yorkshire* (London: B. Macmillan, 1800).

8.6 RABBITS AND RABBIT-WARRENS

[1] A.J. Stuart, *Pleistocene Vertebrates in the British Isles* (London: L 1982).

[2] Varro, *Rerum Rusticarum* III;12; 6-7.

[3] H.G. Hurrell, The little-known rabbit, *Countryside* **XY**

[4] H.P.R. Finberg, Some early Tavistock charters, *English Historical Review,* **LXII** (1947), 365.

[5] *Calendar of Close Rolls Henry III (1237-1242).*

[6] J.M. Gilbert, *Hunting and Hunting Reserves in Medieval Scotland* (Edinburgh: John Donald, 1979).

[7] R.J. Hayes, *Manuscript Sources for the History of the Irish Civilisation* (Boston: G.K. Hall, 1965).

[8] *Calendar of Patent Rolls Edward I (1301-1307),* 107.

[9] M.E. Finch, The wealth of five Northamptonshire families 1540-1640, *Northamptonshire Record Society,* **XIX** (1956), 1-246.

[10] S.A. Moorhouse, Norton Tower, Rylestone, North Yorkshire (*C.B.A. Forum 1991 Annual Newsletter of C.B.A. Yorkshire* IV, 1991), 29.

[11] A. Henderson, From coney to rabbit: the story of a managed coloniser. *The Naturalist* **CXXII** (1997), 101-121.

[12] D.A. Spratt, *Linear Earthworks of the Tabular Hills, North-east Yorkshire* [J.R. Collis Publications] (Sheffield: University of Sheffield, 1989).

[13] *Darlington and Stockton Times* (7 May 1999), 14.

[14] *Royal Commission on Historic Monuments,* NMR 12098/76.

[15] F. Villy, A preliminary note on certain earthworks at Sutton, near Keighley *Bradford Antiquarian,* **V** New Series (1912), 335-342.

[16] A. Harris and D.A. Spratt, The rabbit warrens of the Tabular Hills, North Yorkshire, *Yorkshire Archaeological Journal,* **LXIII** (1991), 177-206.

[17] R.G. Haynes, Vermin traps and rabbit warrens on Dartmoor, *Post Medieval Archaeology,* **IV** (1970), 147-164.

9.3 THE WATER RACES OF THE NORTH YORK MOORS

[1] W. Marshall, *The Rural Economy of Yorkshire,* (1788; Cadell reprint), I, 162-166.

[2] J. Tuke, 1800 *General View of the Agriculture of the North Riding of Yorkshire* (1800; Macmillan reprint), 242.

[3] Nawton manor court book, 11 Apr 1760, NYCRO, ZEW III, 9.

[4] Letter from Richard Chapman (estate steward), to Lord Fauconberg, 23 Mar 1760, Newburgh Priory estate papers, NYCRO, ZDV.

[5] Payment dated 26 Feb 1763, Newburgh Priory workmen's wages accounts, NYCRO, ZDV.

[6] W. Marshall, *ibid.,* 167.

[7] Chapman to Fauconberg, 23 Mar 1760.

[8] Kirkbymoorside enclosure award, 4 July 1793, NYCRO, I/Kirkbymoor-side.

9.5 IRON AND STEEL PRODUCTION

[1] R.H. Hayes, *Levisham Moor Archaeological Investigations 1957-78.* (Helmsley: North York Moors National Park, 1983), 3.

[2] R. Inman *et al.,* Roxby Iron Age Settlement and the Iron Age in North East Yorkshire, *Proceedings of the Prehistoric Society* 51 (1985), 181-214

[3] J.G. McDonnell, 'The Classification of Early Ironworking Slags', Unpublished PhD Thesis Aston University, 1986.

[4] N.H. Harbord and D.A. Spratt, Work in Progress — Examination of cinder from early iron working at Crown End, North Yorkshire Moors. *Journal of the Historical Metallurgy Society,* 9 Part 1 (1975), 32-33.

[5] S. Brown, 'An investigation into the potential of electromagnetic methods in the prospection of high temperature industries on Romano-British villa sites', Unpublished MSc Thesis, Bradford University, 2000.

[6] N.S. Rogers, N S 1993 *Anglian and other Finds from 46-54 Fishergate. The Archaeology of York* Volume 17/9 (York: York Archaeological Trust/Council for British Archaeology, 1993).

[7] P. Ottaway, *Anglo-Scandinavian Ironwork from Coppergate, York. Fasicule 17/6.* (York: York Archaeological Trust/Council for British Archaeology, 1993).

[8] J.G. McDonnell, 1993 The Metallurgical Analysis of the Ironworking Slags and Iron Artefacts in P. Ottaway, *Anglo-Scandinavian Ironwork from Coppergate, York. Fasicule 17/6* (York: York Archaeological Trust/Council for British Archaeology, 1993).

[9] R.H. Hayes, Early Iron-working Sites in North East Yorkshire. *Journal of the Historical Metallurgy Society,* 12 Part 1 (1978), 18-26.

[10] A. Powell, J.G. McDonnell, and C.M. Batt, What's the attraction? An assessment of the magnetic response of an iron smelting site. *Archaeometry,* 44 (4), (2002), 651-665.

[11] J.G. McDonnell, Monks and Miners: the iron industry of Bilsdale and Rievaulx Abbey. *Medieval Life* 11 (1999), 16-21; R.W. Vernon, J.G. McDonnell, and A. Schmidt, An Integrated Geophysical and Analytical Appraisal to the study of Early Iron-working: Three Case Studies, *Journal of the Historical Metallurgy Society* 32 (1998); R.W. Vernon, J.G. McDonnell, and A. Schmidt, The geophysical evaluation of an iron-working complex: Rievaulx and environs, North Yorkshire, *Archaeological Prospection,* 5 (4), (1998), 181-201.

[12] J.G. McDonnell, An Account of the Iron Industry in Upper Ryedale and Bilsdale, c. 1150-1650. *Ryedale Historian* 6 (1972), 23-49; H.R. Schubert, *History of the British Iron and Steel Industry* (London: Routledge and Kegan Paul, 1957).

[13] J.K. Harrison, Landscapes of Industry, Chapter 8 in D.A. Spratt and B.J.D. Harrison (eds), *The North York Moors Landscape Heritage* (Newton Abbot: David & Charles, 1989), fig 47.

9.6 LEAD

[1] K.C. Dunham and A.A. Wilson, *Geology of the Northern Pennine Orefield: Volume 2 Stainmore to Craven.* (London: HMSO, Economic Memoirs of the British Geological Survey, 1985).

[2] K.C. Dunham, Epigenetic Minerals, in D.H. Raynar and J.E. Hemingway (eds), *The Geology and Mineral Resources of Yorkshire,* Yorkshire Geological Society, Leeds (1974), 293-308.

[3] R. Burt, P. Waite, M. Atkinson and R. Burnley, *The Yorkshire Mineral Statistics 1845-1913* (Exeter: Department of Economic History, University of Exeter, 1982).

9.8 LIME

[1] G. Young, *A History of Whitby and Streoneshall Abbey with a Statistical Survey of the Vicinity* (Whitby: Clark and Medd, 1817), 802.

[2] J.T. Sewell, *An account of some Mediaeval roads Crossing the Moors South and South west of Whitby* (Whitby: Whitby Literary and Philosophical Society/ Horne and Son, 1923; reprinted 1971), 30.

9.9 TEXTILES

[1] C. Giles, and I.H. Goodall, 1992 *Yorkshire Textile Mills 1770-1930* (London: H.M.S.O, 1992).

[2] R.P. Hastings, *Essays in North Riding History, 1750-1850* (Northallerton: North Yorkshire County Record Office Publications, No. 28, 1981).

[3] R. Lawton, 1973 The Economic Geography of Craven in the Early Nineteenth Century, in D.R. Mills (ed.), *English Rural Communities* (London: MacMillan, 1973), 155-81. Ongoing unpublished work is extending this to the late-nineteenth century.

[4] E. Baines, *History of the cotton manufacture in Great Britain* (Manchester, 1835).

[5] D. Bythell, *The Sweated Trades. Outwork in Nineteenth-century Britain* (London: Batsford, 1978).

10.1 URBAN RENAISSANCE 1700-1830

[1] Middlesbrough, formerly in the North Riding, is conspicuous by its absence: a small village in 1821, its rapid expansion commenced in the 1830s.

[2] John G. Dunbar, ed., *Sir William Burrell's Northern Tour, 1758* (East Linton: Tuckwell Press, 1997), 129.

[3] By way of comparison, the following is a selection of populations today (mostly based on the 1991 Census): York 104,100; Harrogate 66,178; Scarborough 38,809; Selby 15,292; Ripon 13,806; Northallerton 13,774; Whitby 13,640; Skipton 13,583; Richmond 7,862. The rise of Harrogate and the stagnation of Whitby are particularly striking. Set against the figures for Leeds (424,294), Bradford (289,736), Hull (265,000), and Middlesbrough (145,800), they demonstrate just how far the county has remained dominated by small towns.

[4] In Whitby from the Colmondeley family; in Ripon (1801), from Mrs Allanson of nearby Studley Royal.

10.4 HARROGATE AND KNARESBOROUGH

[1] The figures for Knaresborough include Scriven and Tentergate.

10.8 WHITBY

[1] BL Add. MS 32, 656, *fo.* 54, Certificate of the bailiff of Whitby.

[2] Owing to inherited debt and Royalist compositions.

[3] D. Woodward, ed., *Descriptions of East Yorkshire, Leland to Defoe,* East Yorkshire Local History Series 39 (1985); Defoe (1720), remarked on the anomalous nature of the town's prosperity, seated as it was 'on a little nameless river, scarcely indeed worth a name, and yet…'.

11.1 INTRODUCTION

[1] A fuller account of Ripley appears in Richard Muir, *Landscape Detective: Discovering a Countryside,* Bollington, Cheshire: Windgather Press, 2001.

[2] For example, David Underdown's study of Dorchester, *Fire from Heaven: Life in an English Town in the Seventeenth Century,* London: Fontana, 1993.

11.3 VERNACULAR BUILDING MATERIALS

[1] The phrase 'Great Rebuilding' was coined by W.G. Hoskins to describe this phenomenon, which occurs at different times in different parts of England. See his The rebuilding of rural England, 1570-1640, *Past and Present*, **4** (1953), 44-89. The concept of a 'Great Rebuilding' has been much debated. For a local perspective, see Barbara Hutton, Rebuilding in Yorkshire: The Evidence of Inscribed Dates, *Vernacular Architecture*, **VIII** (1977), 819-24.

[2] For reasons of economy, materials were often recycled. A stone laithe dated 1735 at Burnsall, Wharfedale, has cruck timbers re-used as purlins, and documents tell of dismantling, re-using old stone and timber, and new mason's work.

[3] The Conistone house of c1686, mentioned earlier, had a floor of oak and 'firdeals'. Plans for a new field barn at Grinton, Swaledale, in 1820, specify Memel (i.e. Baltic), timber for the roof.

[4] Spout House, Bilsdale, is a surviving example maintained by the North York Moors National Park Authority.

[5] For example, cruck barns at Burnsall still have traces of heather thatch over steep, close-set rafters, though the sandstone flags which covered the eaves, and the sods which covered the gables and ridge, have gone.

11.5 THE DISCOVERY OF THE NORTH YORKSHIRE LANDSCAPE

[1] Daniel Defoe, *A Tour through the whole Island of Great Britain* (2 vols. as one, London: J.M. Dent, 1974), II, 227 & 211.

11.7 PARKS AND GARDENS

[1] Christopher Hussey, *English Gardens and Landscapes 1700-1750* (London: Country Life, 1967).

11.8 MEDIEVAL RIPLEY

[1] B. Jennings (ed.), *A History of Nidderdale*, second edn. (Huddersfield: Advertiser Press, 1983), p. 84.

[2] Leeds, Sheepscar Record Office, Ingilby MS 180.

[3] T.W. Lancaster, *Abstract of the charters and other documents contained in the Chartulary of the Cistercian Abbey of Fountains in the West Riding of the County of York*, Vol. I (Leeds: Whitehead of Leeds, 1915), f.105.

[4] *Chartulary of Fountains Abbey*, f.105.

[5] *Chartulary of Fountains Abbey*, f.105.

[6] *Chartulary of Fountains Abbey*, f.105.

[7] Leeds, Sheepscar Record Office, Ingilby MS 180.

[8] Leeds, Sheepscar Record Office, Ingilby MS 180.

11.9 HEBDEN TOWNSHIP

[1] WEA — Workers Educational Association. Research by: E.A. Bostock, H. Dye, T. Hannan-Witham, M. Hargraves, P. Hodge, M. Holmes, J. Joy, D. Newall, R. Smith, R.A. & J. Stockdale, M. & M. Vineall, L. Walker. Tutors: D. Joy & H.M. Beaumont. We are grateful to the WEA (North Yorkshire District), for development grants which helped to meet some of the expenses incurred in this study.

[2] Details of field observations, documentary sources and references appear in: Yorkshire Vernacular Buildings Study Group, Vernacular Buildings of Hebden, *Yorkshire Buildings* 27 (1991), 4-36; Heather M. Beaumont, Hebden Township Boundary, Past and Present, in *Archaeology and Historic Landscapes in the Yorkshire Dales* (Yorkshire Archaeological Society, Occasional Series, forthcoming); Heather M. Beaumont, The Historical Landscape of Hebden Township, Upper Wharfedale (forthcoming); David Joy, with the Hebden History Group, *Hebden: a History of a Dales Township* (Hebden: 2002).

[3] Copyright Mrs B. Bedford-Payne, whose kindness in allowing us to use these illustrations is gratefully acknowledged.

[4] Information supplied by P. Hodge from a survey of Hebden inhabitants in the year 2000.

12 HISTORICAL MAPS OF NORTH YORKSHIRE

[1] H. Whitaker, *A Descriptive List of the Printed Maps of Yorkshire and its Ridings, 1577-1900*, The Yorkshire Archaeological Society, Record Series, vol. LXXXVI (Leeds: Yorkshire Archaeological Society, 1938), ix.

[2] Sarah Tyacke and John Huddy, *Christopher Saxton and Tudor map-making* (London: The British Library), 1980, 24.

[3] W. Ravenhill, *Christopher Saxton's 16th Century Maps. The Counties of England and Wales* (Shrewsbury: Chatsworth House Library), 1993, 12; Ifor M. Evans and Heather Lawrence, *Christopher Saxton. Elizabethan Map-maker* (Wakefield: Wakefield Historical Collections), 1979, 6; Tyacke and Huddy, *op. cit.*, 24-25.

[4] P.D.A. Harvey, *Maps in Tudor England* (London: The Public Record Office and The British Library 1993), 47-58.

[5] Ravenhill, *op. cit.*, 13.

[6] Evans and Lawrence, *op. cit.*, 3.

[7] Tyacke and Huddy, *op. cit.*, 31.

[8] *Ibid.*, 36.

[9] Ravenhill, *op. cit.*, 18

[10] *Ibid.*

[11] *Ibid.*, 20.

[12] A.K. Jones, 'The Maps of Yorkshire, printed in the period 1577-1857, as sources of topographical information', unpublished PhD thesis, University of Leeds, 1981.

[13] *Ibid.*, 80-83.

[14] *Ibid.*, 83-6.

[15] N. Nicholson, Introduction to *The Counties of Britain: A Tudor Atlas by John Speed* (London: The British Library, 1995), 10.

[16] *Ibid.*, 13

[17] R.A. Skelton, *County Atlases of the British Isles 1579-1850. A bibliography* (London: Carta Press, 1970), 31-2.

[18] C. Delano-Smith and R. Kain, *English Maps. A History* (London: The British Library, 1999), 75.

[19] T. Whitaker, *A Descriptive List of the Printed Maps of Yorkshire and its Ridings, 1577-1900* (Leeds: Yorkshire Archaeological Society, Record Series **LXXXVI** 1933), 82.

[20] J.B. Harley and J.C. Harvey, *Introduction, The County of York Survey'd*, Facsimile of 1775 edition (Lympne Castle, Kent: Margary, 1973), 1.

[21] *Ibid.*, 1.

[22] *Ibid.*

[23] *Ibid.*, 2.

[24] Jones, A.K. *op. cit.*, 359-40.

[25] *Ibid.*, 369.

[26] *Ibid.*, 384.

[27] Harley and Harvey, *op. cit.*, 1.

[28] P. Laxton, Wind and water power, in J. Langton and R.J. Morris (eds), *Atlas of Industrializing Britain 1780-1914* (London: Methuen, 1986), 69-71.

[29] D. Smith, The representation of industry on large-scale county maps of England and Wales c. 1700-1840, *Industrial Archaeology Review*, 12 (1990), 153-177.

[30] J.B. Harley, *Christopher Greenwood County Map-Maker and his Worcestershire map of 1822* (Worcester and London: Worcestershire Historical Society, 1962), 2.

[31] *Ibid.*, 3-4.

[32] Harley, *op. cit.*, 28-37.

[33] Whitaker, *op. cit.*, 118.

[34] Harley, *op. cit.*, 5.

[35] Delano-Smith and Kain, *op. cit.*, 98.

[36] J.B. Harley, *The Historian's Guide to Ordnance Survey Maps* (London: Standing Conference for Local History, 1964), 9; J.B. Harley and Richard Oliver (eds), *The Old Series Ordnance Survey Maps of England and Wales, Volume 8* (Harry Margary: Lympne Castle, Kent, 1992).

[37] *Ibid.*, 10.

[38] Delano-Smith and Kain, *op. cit.*, 220.

13 THE TWENTIETH CENTURY

[1] Countryside Commission, *Countryside Character Volume 3: Yorkshire and the Humber* (Cheltenham: Countryside Commission, 1998).

[2] Table A50 in European Commission, *Unity, Solidarity, Diversity for Europe, its People and its Territory* Second Report on Economic and Social Cohesion Statistical Annex (Luxembourg: Office for the Publications of the European Communities, 2001).

[3] General Register Office, *Census 1951 England and Wales County Report Yorkshire East and North Ridings* (London: HMSO, 1954).

[4] R. Leach, New York?, *The Regional Review*, **6** (3), (1996), 11.

[5] Office of National Statistics, *Regional Trends* **34** (London: The Stationery Office, 1999).

[6] W.H. Long, *A Survey of the Agriculture of Yorkshire* County Agricultural Surveys No 6 (London: Royal Agricultural Society of England, 1969).

[7] *Ibid.*

[8] R.H. Best and J.T. Coppock, *The Changing Use of Land in Britain* (London: Faber and Faber, 1962).

[9] J. Blunden and N. Curry (eds), *The Changing Countryside* (Beckenham: The Open University and Croom Helm, 1985).

[10] C.M. Leigh, *Changes in the Land-Based Industries in Yorkshire and Humberside* (Leeds: The Yorkshire and Humberside Regional Research Observatory, 1992); Countryside Agency, *The State of the Countryside 2000: Yorkshire and The Humber* (Wetherby: Countryside Agency, 2000).

[11] M. Feist, Monitoring the State of the Countryside: the use of headline indicators, *The Regional Review,* 10 (3), (2000), 8–9.

[12] English Sports Council, *Sports Directory Yorkshire 1999* (London: English Sports Council, 2000)

[13] B. McLaughlin, *Deprivation in Rural Areas* (Research Report for the Department of the Environment and the Development Commission, 1986).

[14] Countryside Agency, *The State of the Countryside 2000 Yorkshire and the Humber* (Wetherby: Countryside Agency Publications, 2000).

[15] Askham Bryan College, *Farm Management Survey 1990/91* (York: Askham Bryan College, 1990).

[16] J.C.H. Stillwell and R. Langley, Information and planning in the education sector, Chapter 17 in J.C.H. Stillwell, S. Geertman and S. Openshaw (eds), *Geographical Information and Planning* (Heidelberg: Springer, 1999), 316–333.

[17] Office of National Statistics, *Regional Trends 34* (London: The Stationery Office, 1999).

[18] Department of Environment, Transport and the Regions, *DETR Indices of Deprivation 2000 Regeneration Research Summary Number 31* (London: DETR, 2000).

[19] C.M. Leigh and D.A. Harrison, *The Ryedale Phenomenon* (Leeds: University of Leeds, 1993).

[20] http://www.landreg.gov.uk/ppr/interactive/ppr ualbs.asp.

[21] Yorkshire Rural Community Council *Housing Needs in Wensleydale* (York: Yorkshire Rural Community Council, 1989).

[22] P. Lawless, Urban and rural problems and policies, Chapter 4 in J.C.H. Stillwell and C.M. Leigh (eds), *Yorkshire and Humberside: Monitoring the Past, Mapping the Future* (Leeds: Yorkshire and Humberside Regional Research Observatory, 1995), 61–75.

[23] N. McFarlane and J. Kettle, Homes like gold dust: the unintended impact of council house sales, *The Regional Review,* 10(2), (2000), 13–15.

[24] Rural Development Commission, *Rural Development Areas 1994* (London, RDC, 1994).

[25] N. Ward, European reforms and rural development, *The Regional Review,* 8 (3), (1998), 16–17.

[26] North Yorkshire Partnership Unit, *Executive Summary of the North Yorkshire Delivery Plan* (York: North Yorkshire Partnership Unit, 2000).

[27] North Yorkshire County Council, *North Yorkshire County Structure Plan* (Northallerton: NYCC, 1996).

[28] Office of National Statistics, *1996-based subnational population projections England, ONS Series PP3 No 19* (London: The Stationery Office, 1999).

[29] Department of Environment, Transport and the Regions, *Projections of Households in England to 2021* (London: DETR, 1999).

[30] Regional Assembly for Yorkshire and Humberside, *Advancing Together Towards a Spatial Strategy* (Wakefield: Regional Assembly, 1999). *RPG 12: Regional Planning Guidance for Yorkshire and the Humber to 2016* (Government Offices for Yorkshire and the Humber, October 2001).

[31] North Yorkshire County Council, City of York Council, North York Moors National Park Authority and Yorkshire Dales National Park Authority, *North Yorkshire Joint Structure Plan, Possible Development Strategies, Consultation Report* (Northallerton: NYCC, 2000).

14 CONCLUSION

[1] M. Atherden, The Vegetation History of Yorkshire: a Bog-Trotter's Guide to God's Own County, *Naturalist,* 124 (1999), 150.